DICTION
LAW

FOURTH EDITION

L B CURZON, BARRISTER

PITMAN
PUBLISHING

Pitman Publishing
128 Long Acre, London WC2E 9AN

A Division of Longman Group UK Limited

© Macdonald & Evans Ltd 1979, 1983
© Longman Group UK Ltd 1988, 1993

First published in Great Britain by Macdonald & Evans Ltd 1979
Second edition 1983
Third edition 1988
Fourth edition 1993

A CIP catalogue record for this book can be obtained from the British Library

ISBN 0 273 60101 6

Printed and bound in Great Britain

PREFACE TO THE FOURTH EDITION

This dictionary is presented as a guide to the highly-specialised vocabulary of English law – its background, principles and procedures – in a format which is intended to be of direct assistance to law students and others who may be interested in the terminology of the law and the legal system.

The items constituting the text are taken largely from the word stock of the subject areas which form the core of legal studies – jurisprudence, contract, torts, criminal law, constitutional law, land law, family law, and equity and trusts. Other areas such as legal history, evidence, civil and criminal procedure, and EC law, are also represented. Statutory definitions, judicial exegesis, and the occasional apothegm have been extracted from statutes, law reports and other branches of legal literature. References to statutes and cases are given so that readers may be guided to a deeper investigation of the words and phrases which form 'the currency of the law'.

During the five years which have passed since the publication of the third edition, developments in the law have been continuous, and often of a basic nature. Statutes, such as the Children Act 1989, the Courts and Legal Services Act 1990, the Environmental Protection Act 1990, the Criminal Justice Act 1991, and the Charities Act 1992, have produced changes and innovations in the language of our law; many examples are recorded in this edition. Parliament has created new statutory offences, such as *computer misuse, racialist chanting, prison mutiny*, and *aggravated vehicle-taking*. The *McKenzie man* is out; the *Gillick child* is in. *Reckless driving* has vanished; *traffic calming* has appeared. The *extended sentence* has gone; the *emergency protection order* has emerged. In a sense, a legal dictionary may be viewed as a record of aspects of the process of change which characterises English law.

Students should note that Parliament increasingly allows the use of delayed commencement provisions. As far as possible, therefore, this edition states the law as it would be if all the affected statutes were fully in force.

I wish to thank the lawyers, teachers and students who provided useful comments on the previous edition. I am grateful to Patrick Bond of Pitman Publishing for his assistance.

L B Curzon

L B Curzon is a barrister and author of many books and articles on legal topics. He has served as a law lecturer and college principal in this country and abroad and has been associated with several English examination boards in the subjects of Law and Economics.

HOW TO USE THE DICTIONARY

Order of entries

The entries in this dictionary are arranged in *strict alphabetical order*. This may be illustrated by the following example of a series of entries:

privilege
privilege, absolute
privilege, claim of
privileged communication
privileged nature of judicial statements
privileged will
privilege, legal professional
privilege of witness
privilege, parliamentary
privilege, public
privilege, qualified

Acts of Parliament

The titles of some Acts which are referred to repeatedly are abbreviated in accordance with the list below. In every case the abbreviation is followed by the appropriate date of the Act, thus: Th.A. 1968; T.C.G.A.1992. Abbreviations used for the titles of some Acts:

A.E.A.	Administration of Estates Act
A.J.A.	Administration of Justice Act
B.Ex.A.	Bills of Exchange Act
B.N.A.	British Nationality Act
C.C.A.	Consumer Credit Act
Ch.A.	Children Act
C.J.A.	Criminal Justice Act
C.J.J.A.	Civil Jurisdiction and Judgments Act
C.L.A.	Criminal Law Act
C.L.S.A.	Courts and Legal Services Act
Cos.A.	Companies Act
County C.A.	County Courts Act
C.P.A.	Consumer Protection Act
C. & Y.P.A.	Children and Young Persons Act
D.P.A.	Domestic Proceedings and Magistrates' Courts Act
E.P.A.	Employment Protection Act

E.P.(C.)A.	Employment Protection (Consolidation) Act
En.P.A.	Environmental Protection Act
F.L.R.A.	Family Law Reform Act
F.S.A.	Financial Services Act
H.A.	Housing Act
H.S.W.A.	Health and Safety at Work, etc., Act
H. & P.A.	Housing and Planning Act
I.A.	Interpretation Act
I.C.T.A.	Income and Corporation Taxes Act
Ins.A.	Insolvency Act
J.A.	Judicature Act
L.C.A.	Land Charges Act
L.G.A.	Local Government Act
L.G.H.A.	Local Government and Housing Act
L.G.P.L.A.	Local Government Planning and Land Act
Lim. A.	Limitation Act
L.P.A.	Law of Property Act
L.R.A.	Land Registration Act
Mat. C.A.	Matrimonial Causes Act
M.C.A.	Magistrates' Courts Act
M.H.A.	Mental Health Act
O.P.A.	Offences against the Person Act
P.C.C.A.	Powers of Criminal Courts Act
P.O.A.	Public Order Act
P. & A.A.	Perpetuities and Accumulations Act
P. & C.E.A.	Police and Criminal Evidence Act
S.C.A.	Supreme Court Act
S.G.A.	Sale of Goods Act
S.L.A.	Settled Land Act
S.O.A.	Sexual Offences Act
S.S.A.	Social Security Act
T.C.G.A.	Taxation of Chargeable Gains Act
T.C.P.A.	Town and Country Planning Act
Th.A.	Theft Act
Tr.A.	Trustee Act
T.U.L.R.A.	Trade Union and Labour Relations Act
T.U.L.R.(C.)A.	Trade Union and Labour Relations (Consolidation) Act
W.A.	Wills Act

Other abbreviations

The abbreviation 'O' stands for 'Order' and refers to grouping in the form of Orders of the Rules of the Supreme Court; 'r' refers to 'rule'; thus O. 88, r. 7.

Cross references

Cross-reference is achieved by the use of the abbreviation q.v., which appears in brackets following words that are further explained elsewhere, and by words in small capital letters which stand at the conclusion of the particular entry. Thus, consider the following entry:

life estate. An estate for the life of the tenant (e.g. by express limitation, such as a grant 'to X for life') or by operation of law (as in curtesy (q.v.)) or *autre vie* (q.v.). *See* ESTATE.

After studying the entry above, further reference ought to be made to *curtesy, autre vie* and, finally, *estate.*

Legal references

Many entries contain references to cases, statutes, orders, statutory instruments, Law Commission Reports, etc. They have been included for those who wish to make an intensive study of the subject-matter of those entries.

Abbreviated titles of selected principal law reports

Abbreviation	*Reports*	*Date*
Abr Ca Eq	Equity Cases Abridged	1667–1744
AC	Appeal Cases	1891 to present
Ad & E	Adolphus & Ellis	1834–40
A & E	Adolphus & Ellis	1834–40
ALJ	Australian Law Journal	1927 to present
All ER	All England Law Reports	1936 to present
App Cas	Appeal Cases	1875–90
Atk	Atkyns	1736–55
B	Beavan	1838–66
B & A	Barnewall & Alderson	1817–22
B & Ad	Barnewall & Adolphus	1830–4
Barn	Barnardiston	1726–34
Barn & Adol	Barnewall & Adolphus	1830–4
Barn & Ald	Barnewall & Alderson	1817–22
Barnard	Barnardiston	1726–34
Barn & Cress	Barnewall & Cresswell	1822–30
BC	British Columbia Law Reports	1867–1947
B & C	Barnewall & Cresswell	1822–30
BCC	Brown's Chancery Cases	1778–94
B & CR	Bankruptcy and Companies Cases	1918–41
Beav	Beavan	1838–66
Bell	Bell	1842–50
Benl	Benloe	1530–1627
Bing	Bingham	1822–34
Bing NC	Bingham, New Cases	1834–40
Blackst	Blackstone	1746–80
Bli	Bligh	1819–21
Bli NS	Bligh, New Series	1826–37
B NC	Bingham, New Cases	1834–40
BPC	Brown's Parliamentary Cases	1702–1801
Brac	Bracton's Note Book	1217–40
Brod & B	Broderip & Bingham	1819–22
B & S	Best & Smith	1861–70
BTR	British Tax Review	1956 to present
Bulstr	Bulstrode	1610–38

Burr	Burrow	1756–72
BWCC	Butterworth's Workmen's Compensation Cases	1908–50
Can LR	Canadian Law Review	1901–7
Car & P	Carrington & Payne	1823–41
Cas Eq Abr	Equity Cases Abridged	1667–1744
CB	Common Bench	1845–56
CB NS	Common Bench, New Series	1856–65
CCC	Cox's Criminal Cases	1844–1941
CC Chron	County Courts Chronicle	1848–59
CCC Sess Pap	Central Criminal Court Session Papers	1834–1913
CCR	Crown Cases Reserved	1865–75
C & F	Clark & Finnelly	1831–46
Ch	Chancery	1891 to present
Ch App	Chancery Appeal Cases	1865–75
Ch D	Chancery Division	1875–90
C & K	Carrington & Kirwan	1843–53
Cl & F	Clark & Finnelly	1831–46
CLJ	Cambridge Law Journal	1921 to present
CLR	Commonwealth Law Reports	1903 to present
CLYB	Current Law Year Book	1947 to present
C & M	Crompton & Meeson	1832–4
CMLR	Common Market Law Reports	1962 to present
Co	Coke	1572–1616
Com	Comyns	1695–1740
Com Cas	Commercial Cases	1895–1941
Com LR	Common Law Reports	1853–5
Conv NS	Conveyancer & Property Law, New Series	1936 to present
Co Rep	Coke	1572–1616
Cox CC	Cox's Criminal Cases	1843–1941
Cox Cty CC	Cox's County Court Cases	1860–1919
C & P	Carrington & Payne	1823–41
C & R	Clifford & Rickards	1873–84
Cr App R	Criminal Appeal Reports	1908 to present
Crim LR	Criminal Law Review	1954 to present
Cro Car	Croke	1625–41
Cro Eliz	Croke	1582–1603
Cro Jac	Croke	1603–25
Cromp & M	Crompton & Meeson	1832–4
Curt	Curteis	1834–44
D & B	Dearsly & Bell	1856–8
D & Ch	Deacon & Chitty	1832–5
D & E	Durnford & East's Reports	1785–1800
DLR	Dominion Law Reports	1912 to present
DM & J	De Gex, MacNaghten & Gordon	1851–7
Doug	Douglas	1778–85
Dunn	Dunning	1753–4
Durn & E	Durnford & East's Reports	1785–1800
E	East's Term Reports	1800–12
E & B	Ellis & Blackburn	1851–8

E & E	Ellis & Ellis	1858–61
EG	Estates Gazette	1858 to present
Eq	Equity Cases	1866–75
Eq Cas	Equity Modern Reports	1722–55
Esp	Espinasse	1793–1807
Ex	Exchequer Reports	1847–56
Ex	Exchequer Cases	1865–75
Exch Rep	Exchequer Reports	1847–56
Ex D	Exchequer Division	1875–80
Fam	Family Division	1972 to present
F & F	Foster & Finlayson	1856–67
For	Forrester's Chancery Reports	1735–8
Fost & Fin	Foster & Finlayson	1856–67
FSR	Fleet Street Patent Law Reports	1963 to present
Gal & Dav	Gale & Davison	1841–3
Giff	Gifford	1857–65
Gl & J	Glyn & Jameson	1819–28
Godb	Godbolt	1575–1638
H	Hare	1841–53
Hale Prec	Hale's Precedents	1475–1640
Hare	Hare	1841–53
H & C	Hurlstone & Coltman	1862–6
HL	House of Lords Appeals	1866–75
HL Cas	House of Lords Cases	1847–66
H & M	Hemming & Miller	1862–5
H & N	Hurlstone & Norman	1856–62
Hodg	Hodges	1835–7
Ho Lords C	House of Lords Cases	1847–66
Horn & H	Horn & Hurlstone	1838–9
Hurl and Nor	Hurlstone & Norman	1856–62
H & W	Harrison & Wollaston	1835–6
ICR	Industrial Cases Reports	1972 to present
IJ	Irish Jurist	1935 to present
ILJ	Industrial Law Journal	1972 to present
ILR	International Law Reports	1950 to present
IR	Irish Reports	1838 to present
IRLR	Industrial Relations Law Reports	1972 to present
Ir LT	Irish Law Times	1867 to present
ITR	Industrial Tribunal Reports	1966 to present
Jac & W	Jacob & Walker	1819–20
Jenk Cent	Jenkins' Reports	1220–1623
JP	Justice of the Peace & Local Government Review	1837 to present
JPL	Journal of Planning Law	1948 to present
Jur	Jurist Reports	1837–54
Jur NS	Jurist Reports, New Series	1855–66
K	Kenyon	1753–9
KB (or QB)	King's or Queen's Bench	1841 to present
Keb	Keble	1661–79
Keny	Kenyon	1753–9
K & J	Kay & Johnson	1854–8
Ld Ken	Kenyon	1753–9

Ld Ray	Raymond	1694–1732
Lew	Lewin	1822–38
LGR	Local Government Reports	1903 to present
LJ Adm	Law Journal Reports, Admiralty	1866–75
LJ Bk	Law Journal Reports, Bankruptcy	1832–80
LJ Ch	Law Journal Reports, Chancery	1822–1946
LJ CP	Law Journal Reports, Common Pleas	1822–80
LJ Ecc	Law Journal Reports, Ecclesiastical	1865–75
LJ KB (QB)	Law Journal Reports, King's (Queen's) Bench	1831–1946
LJ OS	Law Journal Reports, Old Series	1822–31
LJ PC	Law Journal Reports, Privy Council	1865–1946
LJ PD & A	Law Journal Reports, Probate, Divorce & Admiralty	1876–1946
LJ P & M	Law Journal Reports, Probate & Matrimonial	1858–75
Ll LR	Lloyd's List Law Reports	1919–50
Lloyd's Rep	Lloyd's List Law Reports	1951 to present
Lofft	Lofft's Reports	1772–4
LQR	Law Quarterly Review	1885 to present
LR	Law Reports	1865 to present
LR A & E	Law Reports, Admiralty & Ecclesiastical Cases	1865–75
LR CCR	Law Reports, Crown Cases Reserved	1865–75
LR Ch App	Law Reports, Chancery Appeal Cases	1865–75
LR CP	Law Reports, Common Pleas Cases	1865–75
LR Eq	Law Reports, Equity Cases	1865–75
LR Ex	Law Reports, Exchequer Cases	1865–75
LR HL	Law Reports, House of Lords	1865–75
LR PC	Law Reports, Privy Council Appeals	1865–75
LR P & D	Law Reports, Probate & Divorce Cases	1865–75
LR QB	Law Reports, Queen's Bench	1865–75
LR RP	Law Reports, Restrictive Practices Cases	1958 to present
LS Gaz	Law Society Gazette	1903 to present
LT	Law Times Reports	1859–1947
Lush	Lushington	1859–62
Madd	Maddock	1815–22
Mau & S	Maule & Selwyn	1813–17
M & C	Mylne & Craig	1835–41
M & G	Manning & Granger	1840–4
M & K	Mylne & Keen	1832–5
MLR	Modern Law Review	1937 to present
Mod Cas	Modern Cases	1702–45
Mod Rep	Modern Reports	1669–1755
Moo	Moody	1824–44
Moo	Moore	1817–27
Moo CC	Moody	1824–44
Moo & P	Moody & Payne	1827–31
Moo PC	Moore	1836–62
Morr	Morrell	1884–93

M & P	Moore & Payne	1827–31
M & S	Maule & Selwyn	1813–17
M & W	Meeson & Welsby	1836–47
Myl & Cr	Mylne & Craig	1835–41
Myl & K	Mylne & Keen	1832–5
Nev & M	Neville & Manning	1832–6
New Rep	New Reports	1862–5
NLJ	New Law Journal	1965 to present
N & McN	Neville & MacNamara	1855–1928
Not Cas	Thornton's Notes of Cases	1841–50
NR	New Reports	1862–5
NSWLR	New South Wales Law Reports	1880–1900
NSWSR	New South Wales State Reports	1901 to present
NZLR	New Zealand Law Reports	1883 to present
P	Probate	1891–1971
P & CR	Planning & Compensation Reports	1949 to present
PD	Probate Division	1875–90
P D & A	Probate, Divorce & Admiralty	1875–90
Pea	Peake	1790–4
Per & D	Perry & Davison	1838–41
Phil Ecc R	Phillimore's Reports	1809–21
Pl	Plowden's Commentaries	1550–80
Pr	Price	1814–24
QB (or KB)	Queen's or King's Bench	1841 to present
QBD	Queen's Bench Division	1875–90
Qd R	Queensland Law Reports	1958 to present
Rep	Coke	1572–1616
RHC	Road Haulage Cases	1950 to present
R & IT	Rating & Income Tax Reports	1924–60
Rom	Romilly's Notes on Cases	1767–87
RPC	Reports of Patents Cases	1884 to present
RTR	Road Traffic Reports	1970 to present
Russ	Russell	1823–9
Russ & M	Russell & Mylne	1829–31
Russ & R	Russell & Ryan	1799–1824
R & VR	Rating & Valuation Reports	1960 to present
Ry & M	Ryan & Moody	1823–6
Salk	Salkeld	1689–1712
SALR	South African Law Reports	1948 to present
SC	Sessions Cases	1906 to present
Sc	Scott	1834–40
SCC	Select Cases in Chancery	1724–33
Scot Jur	Scottish Jurist	1829–73
SCT	Scots Law Times	1893 to present
Sim	Simons	1826–52
SJ	Solicitor's Journal	1857 to present
Sol	The Solicitor	1934 to present
Sol J	Solicitors' Journal	1857 to present
S & S	Simons & Stuart	1822–6
St Tr	State Trials	1163–1820
St Tr NS	State Trials, New Series	1820–58
Swan	Swanston	1818–19

Tal	Talbot's Cases in Equity	1733–8
Taun	Taunton	1807–19
TC	Tax Cases	1875 to present
TLR	Times Law Reports	1884–1952
Tot	Tothill	1559–1646
TR	Taxation Reports	1939 to present
TR	Term Reports	1785–1800
Tyr	Tyrwhitt	1830–5
VATTR	Value Added Tax Tribunal Reports	1973 to present
Ves & B	Vesey & Beames	1812–14
Ves Jr	Vesey Junior	1789–1817
Ves Sen	Vesey Senior	1747–56
VLR	Victoria Law Reports	1875 to present
W Bl	Blackstone	1746–80
Wilm	Wilmot's Case Notes	1757–70
WLR	Weekly Law Reports	1953 to present
Wm Bl	Blackstone	1746–80
WN	Weekly Notes	1866–1952
WR	Weekly Reporter	1853–1906
W & W	Wyatt & Webb	1861–3
Y & C	Younge & Collyer	1834–43

A

abandonment. 1. Surrender or relinquishing of a chattel, right or claim, with the intention of not reclaiming it. 2. An action in the High Court is considered abandoned when a notice of discontinuance (q.v.) is served: see O. 21. 3. In the case of a constructive total loss (q.v.) in marine insurance, the assured may abandon the subject-matter to the insurer and treat the loss as if it were an actual total loss, after giving notice of abandonment. 4. Abandonment of a child means leaving it to its fate: *Watson* v *Nikolaisen* [1955] 2 QB 286. See C. & Y.P.A. 1963. 5. Abandonment of appeal is the withdrawal of appeal by leave of the court or on notice. See O. 59, r. 5. 6. Cessation of activities concerning use of land with no intention of their being resumed at any particular time: see *Pioneer Aggregates* v *Secretary of State for the Environment* [1984] 2 All ER 731.

abatement. 1. Abatement of action is the bringing to an end or the suspending of an action: see O. 15, r. 7; O. 28, r. 11; O. 34, r. 9. 2. Abatement of debts refers to proportionate reduction of payments where a fund cannot meet claims. 3. Abatement of legacies (q.v.) refers to receipt by legatees of only a fraction, or none, of their legacies when assets are insufficient to pay legacies in full. Pecuniary or general legacies abate proportionately before specific legacies. 4. Abatement of nuisances (q.v.) refers to their removal. Abatement notices may be served by a local authority in respect of a statutory nuisance: En. P.A. 1990, s. 80(1).

abdication. Voluntary renunciation of an office. See Declaration of Abdication Act 1936 (concerning Edward VIII).

abduction. Wrongful leading away of a person. It is an offence under S.O.A. 1956, s. 20, to abduct an unmarried girl under 16 from her parent or guardian. See *R* v *Tegerdine* (1982) 75 Cr App R 298.

abduction, child. It is an offence for a person "connected with a child under 16" (e.g., parent or guardian) to take or send the child out of the UK "without the appropriate consent": Child Abduction Act 1984, s. 1, as amended by Family Law Act 1986, s. 65. For the offence of abduction of a child by other persons, *see* s. 2. *See also* Child Abduction and Custody Act 1985, as amended by Family Law Act, s. 67 (providing a civil procedure for securing the return of children taken abroad without permission); Ch.A. 1989, s. 49 (abduction of child in care). See *In Re A.* (1992) The Times, 17 Feb (acquiescence in abduction).

abet. To assist in the commission of an offence when one is present actively or constructively. *See* ACCESSORY; ACCOMPLICE; AID OR ABET.

abeyance. Inactivity; state of suspension. An estate is in abeyance when there exists no person in whom it can vest. *See* SEISIN, ABEYANCE OF.

ab initio. From the beginning. 1. A trespasser *ab initio* is one who, being entitled by law to perform an act, abuses his authority, so that his act becomes wrongful from the very beginning. See *The Six Carpenters' Case* (1610) 8 Rep 146a; *Chic Fashions Ltd* v *Jones* [1968] 2 QB 299 (in which continuing existence of the doctrine was doubted). 2. A marriage is void *ab initio* if, e.g., either party was under 16 at the date of marriage.

ab intestato. From an intestate. "Succession *ab intestato*" refers to succession to the property of one who has not disposed of it by will. *See* INTESTACY.

abjuration. Renunciation by oath, e.g., as in an oath to leave the realm. See Promissory Oaths Act 1871.

abode. A place of residence (q.v.). Usually a question of fact rather than law: *Courtis* v *Blight* (1862) 31 LJCP 48.

"A man's residence, where he lives with his family and sleeps at night, is always his place of abode in the full sense of that expression": *R v Hammond* (1852) 17 QB 772. See *R* v *Barnet LBC, ex p Shah* [1983] 2 AC 309.

abode in UK, right of. A person has such a right if he is a British citizen or a Commonwealth citizen who immediately before the commencement of B.N.A 1981 was a Commonwealth citizen having the right of abode in the UK by virtue of the Immigration Act 1971, s. 2(1)(*d*) and has not ceased to be a Commonwealth citizen in the meanwhile: Immigration Act 1971, s. 2, as substituted by B.N.A. 1981, s. 39. See Immigration Act 1988, ss. 2, 3.

abominable crime. Phrase used in O.P.A. 1861, s. 61, to refer to sodomy (q.v.) and bestiality (q.v.).

abortion. Separation of a non-viable human foetus (q.v.) from its mother. Under the Abortion Act 1967, as amended by the Human Fertilisation and Embryology Act 1990, s. 37, there is no offence (see O.P.A. 1861, ss. 58, 59, Infant Life (Preservation) Act 1929, s. 5(1), substituted by 1990 Act, s. 37(4)) where a pregnancy is terminated by a registered medical practitioner if two practitioners are of the opinion that the pregnancy has not exceeded its 24th week and that its continuance would involve risk, greater than if the pregnancy were terminated, of injury to the physical or mental health of the pregnant woman or any existing children of the family; or the termination is necessary to prevent grave permanent injury to her physical or mental health; or that the continued pregnancy would involve risk to her life greater than if the pregnancy were terminated; or that there is a substantial risk that if the child were born it would suffer from such physical or mental abnormalities as to be seriously handicapped. See *Rance* v *Mid-Downs HA* [1991] 2 WLR 159.

abrogate. To repeal, annul, cancel abolish (generally by formal action).

abscond. To depart secretly or to hide oneself from the jurisdiction of the court so as to avoid legal process. See Ins. A. 1986, s. 358.

absconding by person released on bail. Failure, without reasonable cause, by one who has been released on bail in criminal proceedings, to surrender to custody. An offence under the Bail Act 1976, s. 6(1). A warrant (q.v.) for his arrest may be issued: s. 7(1). See *R* v *Reader* (1987) 84 Cr App R 294.

absence. 1. Non-appearance by a party to a writ or subpoena (q.v.). 2. Continuous absence of a spouse for seven years may be a defence to a charge of bigamy. See *R* v *Curgerwen* (1865) 29 JP 820. 3. Absence "beyond the seas" (q.v.) refers to absence from the UK and those adjacent islands belonging to the Sovereign.

absolute. Without conditions, complete, as in "decree absolute" (q.v.).

absolute assignment. Assignment of the entire interest of a chose in action (q.v.) so that it is transferred unconditionally to the assignee. It includes an assignment by way of mortgage: *Hughes* v *Pump House Hotel Co* [1902] 2 KB 190. See LPA 1925, s. 136.

absolute decree. *See* DECREE.

absolute and conditional discharge. Where a court by or before which a person is convicted of an offence (not being an offence the sentence for which is fixed by law) is of the opinion, having regard to the circumstances including the nature of the offence and the character of the offender, that it is inexpedient to inflict punishment, the court may make an order discharging him absolutely or, if it thinks fit, discharging him subject to the condition that he commits no offence during a specified period not exceeding 3 years: P.C.C.A. 1973, as amended by C.J.A. 1991, Sch. 1.

absolute duties. Duties to which there are no corresponding rights (e.g., according to Austin, a subject's duties to the Crown).

absolute liability. *See* STRICT LIABILITY IN CRIMINAL LAW.

absolute privilege. *See* PRIVILEGE, ABSOLUTE.

absolute title. In the case of a freehold (q.v.) registered with absolute title, the registered proprietor has a guaranteed title subject only to, e.g., entries on the register. In the case of a leasehold (q.v.) absolute title guarantees that the registered proprietor is the owner of the lease and that it was validly granted. *See* LAND REGISTRATION.

absolve. To release from some responsibility or obligation.

abstract and epitome of title. Narrative summary, which must be supplied by a landowner to a purchaser under contract of sale, of documents and events affecting title. The abstract states the history of title; the epitome is a schedule of documents going back to the root of title (q.v.). See L.P.A. 1925, s. 10.

abstracting electricity. See ELECTRICITY, DISHONEST ABSTRACTION OF.

abuse. Words of vituperation, insult, invective. It does not generally amount to defamation (q.v.); *Thorley* v *Kerry* (1812) 4 Taunt 355. See, however, *Lane* v *Holloway* [1968] 1 QB 379.

abuse of process. Tort based on damage caused by the improper use of a legal process for some purpose other than that for which it was designed. See O. 18, r.19; *R* v *Telford Justices ex p Badhan* [1991] 2 All ER 854; *R* v *J.A.K.* [1922] Crim LR 30. For abuse of process in relation to a murder trial, see *Hui Chi-ming* v *R* [1991] 3 WLR 495.

ABWOR. Assistance by way of representation. Refers to legal aid scheme (q.v.) as commonly used for, e.g., civil domestic proceedings in magistrates' courts, proceedings before Mental Health Review Tribunal. See Legal Aid Act 1988, ss. 2(4), 8(2).

ACAS. Advisory, Conciliation and Arbitration Service (q.v.).

acceleration clause. Provision in an agreement for repayment of a loan by instalments whereby if a stated number of instalments is not paid, all outstanding payments become due at once.

acceleration, doctrine of. Where interests in property have been conferred by a testator in succession, e.g., "to X for life, remainder to Y" and the gift to X is determined before the time envisaged by the testator, Y's interest is accelerated. If it is discovered that, e.g., X cannot take under the will (because he witnessed it), Y's interest becomes immediate. The doctrine does not apply to a contingent gift: *Re Scott* [1975] 2 All ER 1033. See *Re Davies* [1957] 1 WLR 922.

acceptance. 1. Acceptance of an offer to create a contract (i.e., an assent to all the terms of the offer) must be un-

qualified, and may be by words or conduct. It must generally be communicated to the offeror and must conform with the prescribed or indicated terms of the offer. See *Hyde* v *Wrench* (1840) 3 Beav 334; *Carlill* v *Carbolic Smoke Ball Co* [1983] 1 QB 256. Acceptance "subject to contract" means that the parties intend to be bound only when a formal contract is prepared and signed: *Chillingworth* v *Esche* [1924] 1 Ch 97. 2. Acceptance of goods under S.G.A. 1979, s. 35, is deemed to have taken place when a person indicates to the seller that he has accepted them, or when they have been delivered to him and he does an act in relation to them which is inconsistent with the seller's ownership, or when he retains them without informing the seller after a reasonable time that he has rejected them. 3. "Acceptance" in Th.A. 1968, s.20(2) is a term of art to be defined in the same way as in B.Ex.A. 1882: *R* v *Nanayakkara* [1987] 1 WLR 265. *See* OFFER.

acceptance, conditional. 1. Acceptance of offeror's offer by offeree, subject to a stipulation being met. 2. In relation to a bill of exchange (q.v.), where payment by the acceptor is made subject to a condition. See B.Ex.A. 1882, s. 19.

acceptance of a bill. Written signature by the drawee of a bill of exchange and the word "accepted" across the bill: B.Ex.A. 1882, ss. 17–19. He thereby undertakes to pay the bill when due. Acceptance *supra protest* (or "acceptance for honour") is acceptance of a bill when it has been dishonoured by one who has no interest in the bill so as to safeguard the drawee's good name: B.Ex.A. 1882, ss. 65–68. Acceptance may be general or qualified (q.v.). *See* BILL OF EXCHANGE.

acceptance of service. Statement by a solicitor, written on a form of acknowledgement, accepting service and undertaking to appear. Failure to appear may render the solicitor liable in negligence to his client. See O. 10, r.1.

acceptance, special. *See* SPECIAL ACCEPTANCE.

access. 1. The existence of opportunity of sexual intercourse between husband and wife. Evidence of impossibility of access may be given to rebut the presumption of legitimacy (q.v.). See

Mat.C.A. 1973, s. 48. 2. Access orders may be granted to enable persons who desire to carry out work to any land which is reasonably necessary for the preservation of that land to obtain access to neighbouring land to do so: Access to Neighbouring Land Act 1992, s. 1. 3. The owner of adjoining land has right of access to a highway: *Rowley* v *Tottenham UDC* [1914] AC 95. 4. An access order may be issued by a circuit judge under P. & C.E.A. 1984, s. 9, Sch. 1, allowing the police to obtain access to special procedure material (q.v.) which is of importance to an investigation. See *Barclays Bank* v *Taylor* [1989] 1 WLR 1066.

accession. 1. Succeeding to the throne. 2. Procedure whereby property belonging to X becomes property of Y because it has been affixed to or annexed with that which belongs to Y. *See* FIXTURES.

accessory. One who is concerned in the commission of an offence otherwise than as principal. An accessory *before the fact* was one who "being absent at the time of the felony committed doth yet procure, counsel, command or abet to commit [it]": 1 Hale PC 615. An accessory *after the fact* was one who, knowing that a felony had been committed, subsequently harboured or relieved the felon or in any way secured or attempted to secure his escape. See Accessories and Abettors Act 1861; *R* v *Fisher* [1969] 1 WLR 8. *See* PRINCIPAL.

accident. "Not a technical legal term with a clearly defined meaning. Speaking generally, but with reference to legal liabilities, an accident means any unintended and unexpected occurrence which produces hurt or loss": *per* Lord Linley in *Fenton* v *Thorley* [1903] AC 443. *See* INEVITABLE ACCIDENT.

accommodation bill. A bill of exchange (q.v.) to which a person who has not received value for it (the "accommodation party") has given his name, thus accepting liability and becoming, in effect, a surety for the person accommodated. See B.Ex.A. 1882, s. 28.

accommodation, priority need for. Category of persons requiring special consideration by a local authority and comprising: pregnant women; persons with whom dependent children reside; persons homeless as the result of an emergency; persons vulnerable as the result of old age, mental illness or physical disability: H.A. 1985, s. 59(1). See *R* v *Lambeth LBC, ex p Vagliviello* [1990] 22 HLR 393.

accomplice. One person associated with another, whether as principal or accessory (qq.v.), in the commission of an offence. Evidence of an accomplice may be admissible, but it is the judge's duty to warn the jury that it should be corroborated: *Davies* v *DPP* [1954] AC 378.

accord and satisfaction. This occurs where, following the conclusion of a contract, one party obtains his release from his obligation by promising or giving consideration (q.v.) other than that which the other party has to accept under the contract. The agreement is the accord; the consideration is the satisfaction. See *D. & C. Builders Ltd* v *Rees* [1966] 2 QB 617; *Budget Rent-A-Car* v *Goodman* [1991] 2 NZLR 715; *Deanplan* v *Mahmoud* [1992] EG 16.

accounting, false. An offence under Th.A. 1968, s. 17(1) "where a person dishonestly, with a view to gain for himself or another or with intent to cause loss to another, (*a*) destroys, defaces, conceals or falsifies any account or any record or document made or required for any accounting purpose; or (*b*) in furnishing information for any purpose produces or makes use of any account, or any such record or document as aforesaid, which to his knowledge is or may be misleading, false or deceptive in a material particular." See *R* v *Choraria* [1990] Crim LR 865; *Lee Cheung Wing* v *R* [1992] Crim LR 430.

accounting records. Records kept in accordance with Cos.A. 1985, s. 221, as amended by Cos.A. 1989, Part I, containing details of company's liabilities and assets and entries from day to day of receipts and expenditure and matters in respect of which the receipts and expenditure take place. See also s. 722. For "accounting standards", see Cos.A. 1989, s. 19.

accounting reference period. Company directors must prepare accounts by reference to an "accounting reference date", notice of which must be given to the Registrar of Companies. The reference date should be such that a company's first accounting reference period, ending on the reference date, will be at least six, but no more than eighteen, months in length, and, thereafter, twelve months: Cos.A. 1985, s. 224; Cos.A. 1989, s. 3. For alteration of period, see ss. 225, 226, and Cos.A. 1989, s. 3.

account, order for. Order made by the court so that sums due from one party to another resulting from transactions between parties may be investigated, e.g., as between principal and agent. See S.C.A. 1981, s. 61(1); O. 43, r. 2; *Codex Corp.* v *Racal-Milgo Ltd* [1984] FSR 87.

accounts, company. *See* COMPANY ACCOUNTS; COMPANY ACCOUNTS, PUBLICATION OF.

account, settled. Statement of accounts between parties, in writing, agreed and accepted by them as correct. A defence to a claim for an account. See *Re Webb* [1894] 1 Ch 83.

account stated. An admission of a sum of money due from one person to another where neither is under a duty to account to the other.

accretion. Growth of land resulting from gradual and imperceptible accumulation by natural causes. See *Southern Centre of Theosophy* v *State of S. Australia* [1982] AC 706. *See* AVULSION.

accrue. To increase, to fall due, to be added as an increase, to come into existence. A right "accrues" when it vests in some person.

accumulation. Process whereby interest is invested as it accrues. Under L.P.A. 1925, s. 164(1), no person may direct accumulation of income for any longer period than the grantor's or settlor's life, or a term of 21 years from the death of the grantor, settlor or testator, or duration of minority of a person living or *en ventre sa mère* (q.v.) at the death of the grantor, settlor or testator, or duration of minority of person(s) who under limitations of the instrument directing accumulation would, for the time being, if of full age, be entitled to income directed to be accumulated. Under P. & A.A. 1964, s. 13(1), additional periods are: 21 years from the date disposition was

made; duration of minority of any person in being at that date. The rule does not extend to accumulation of produce of timber or wood, provisions for payment of debts and raising of portions (q.v.).

accumulation and maintenance settlement. Settlement (q.v.) in which there is no interest in possession, but one or more beneficiaries will become entitled to an interest in possession on attaining a specified age not exceeding 25 years.

accusatorial procedure. *See* ADVERSARIAL PROCEDURE.

accused. One charged with an offence.

accused, non-appearance of. If the prosecutor appears, but the accused does not, the court may proceed in his absence: M.C.A. 1980, s. 11(1). Where a summons has been issued, the court must be satisfied that it was served on the accused a reasonable time before the trial: s. 11(2). A person may not be sentenced to imprisonment in his absence: s. 11(3). *See* POST, PLEA OF GUILTY BY; PROSECUTOR, NON-APPEARANCE OF.

accused, self-incrimination of. *See* SELF-INCRIMINATION.

acknowledgement. Avowal or assent to. 1. Acknowledgement of debt. Where right of action has accrued to recover a debt and the person liable acknowledges claim, the right is deemed to have accrued on and not before the date of acknowledgement: Lim.A. 1980, s. 29(5). 2. Acknowledgement of signature to will (q.v.). Testator's signature must be made or acknowledged in the presence of two witnesses. See W.A. 1837, s. 9 (as substituted by A.J.A. 1982, s. 17); *Re White* [1990] 3 WLR 187.

acquiescence. Consent which is expressed or implied from conduct, e.g., inactivity or silence. "Quiescence under such circumstances as that assent may be reasonably inferred from it": *De Bussche* v *Alt* (1880) 8 Ch D 314. See *In re A.* (1992) The Times, 17 Feb (acquiescence may require informed acceptance of infringement of rights). *See* LACHES.

acquittal. Discharge from prosecution following verdict of not guilty or successful plea in bar (q.v.), etc. There is generally no appeal against acquittal unless under the appropriate statutory authority. For deemed acquittals see also Prosecution of Offences Act 1985, s. 22(4).

acquittance. "A discharge in writing of a sum of money or other duty which ought to be paid or done": *Termes de la Ley.*

act. 1. Act of Parliament (q.v.). 2. That which is done by a person, generally consequent on volition. It may include a deliberate omission.

acte clair. Doctrine of EEC law whereby a national court which considers that a point of Community law raised before it is "sufficiently clear" may apply it without reference to the European Court (q.v.). See Treaty of Rome 1957, art. 177; *R* v *Sec. of State, ex p Schering* [1987] 1 CMLR 277.

action. Formal exercise of a right of suing for that which is due. Usually commences by writ (q.v.) or other mode as prescribed by the Rules of Court. See S.C.A. 1981, s. 151(1).

action, cause of. "A factual situation the existence of which entitles one person to obtain a remedy against another person": *Letang* v *Cooper* [1965] 1 QB 232.

action, circuity of. *See* CIRCUITY OF ACTION.

action, collusive. *See* COLLUSIVE ACTION.

action, derivative. *See* DERIVATIVE ACTION.

action, discontinuance of. *See* DISCONTINUANCE, NOTICE OF.

action, dismissal of. *See* DISMISSAL OF ACTION.

action on the case. Remedy for wrongs first given by the Statute of Westminster II 1285, whereby in a case in which a writ was found and in a similar case (*in consimili casu*) "falling under like law and requiring like remedy is found none", the clerks of Chancery could agree to make a new writ, or consult Parliament. *Assumpsit* (q.v.) is an example.

action, removal of. *See* REMOVAL OF ACTION.

actions, civil and penal. An action brought to enforce civil rights is a *civil action*. A *penal action* is aimed at the punishment of the party sued, e.g., by monetary penalty; the term is also used of an action for the recovery of a penalty given by statute.

actions, consolidation of. *See* CONSOLIDATION OF ACTIONS.

action, setting down of. *See* SETTING DOWN OF ACTION.

action, settlement of. *See* SETTLEMENT OF ACTION.

actions, real and personal. *Real* actions (*res* = thing) were brought at common law for the recovery of his land by a freeholder. See Real Property Limitation Act 1833 by which they were, in general, abolished. *Personal* actions, e.g., actions on contracts, derive from those relating to the enforcement of remedies against persons, in contrast to the recovery of things in real actions. *See* PROPERTY.

actio personalis moritur cum persona. A personal action dies with a party to the cause of the action. The rule was reversed by the Law Reform (Misc. Provs.) Act 1934: "On the death of any person . . . all causes of action . . . vested in him shall survive for the benefit of his estate." Thus, all causes of action in tort, save for defamation (q.v.) and the claim for damages for bereavement (q.v.), survive the deceased.

active trust. A trust (q.v.) which requires the trustee, known as an "active trustee", to perform active duties, e.g., to collect rent and profits and transfer proceeds to the beneficiary (q.v.). *See* BARE TRUST.

act, juristic. Act whereby legal persons create, alter or destroy rights and duties and, as a consequence, affect legal relationships between legal persons. A juristic act may be *unilateral* (e.g., disposing of property by will) or *bilateral* (e.g., agreement by contract). Elements of a juristic act are: actor (A) must direct his will to an end; A's will must be made manifest; A must have capacity in law to achieve desired result; A's aim must be legal.

Act of God. "An extraordinary circumstance which could not be foreseen, and which could not be guarded against": *Pandorf* v *Hamilton* (1886) 17 QBD 675. See *Nichols* v *Marsland* (1875) LR 10 Ex 255 – extraordinary rainfall; *Nugent* v *Smith* (1876) 1 CPD 423 – unusually bad weather at sea; *Southern Water Authority* v *Pegrum* [1989] Crim LR – overflow of water. *See* VIS MAJOR.

Act of indemnity. An Act legalising certain activities which were illegal at the time they were carried out, or exempting certain persons from particular penalties following on breaches of the law. See, e.g., 4 Hen VIII c. 8; Indemnity Act 1920.

act of law. An event, e.g., acquisition of title (q.v.), resulting other than from an act of the parties. *See* PURCHASER.

Act of Parliament. The will of the legislature, i.e., law made by the Queen in Parliament (i.e., Queen, Lords and Commons). Concurrence of the Lords may be dispensed with under certain circumstances: see Parliament Acts 1911 and 1949. An Act comes into force on the day it receives the Royal Assent (q.v.), unless otherwise stated. Acts may be public or private, local, general or personal. In construing an Act, the intention of the legislature predominates: *A.-G. for Canada* v *Hallett & Carey Ltd* [1952] AC 427. "An Act of Parliament is the exercise of the high-est authority that this kingdom acknowledges upon earth": Blackstone. *See* INTERPRETATION OF STATUTES.

Act of Parliament, citation of. *See* STATUTE, CITATION OF.

Act of Parliament, validity of. This cannot be questioned in court. "The court can only look at the Parliamentary roll": *per* Nourse J in *Martin* v *O'Sullivan* [1982] STC 416 (basis of the "enrolled Act rule"). See, e.g., *Pickin* v *British Railways Board* [1974] AC 765; *Manuel* v *A.-G.* [1983] Ch 77.

act of state. An act of the executive, i.e., the sovereign power of a country, that "cannot be challenged, controlled or interfered with by municipal courts. Its sanction is not that of Law, but that of Sovereign power and, whatever it may be, municipal courts must accept it as it is, without question": *Salaman* v *Sec of State for India* [1906] 1 KB 639. *See* PREROGATIVE, ROYAL.

Act, structure of. Constituent elements of a statute, including: long title; preamble; enacting words; short title; principal, subsidiary, administrative and transitional provisions; interpretation and definitions; repealing clause; date of coming into operation; area of operation clause (e.g., "This Act shall not extend to Scotland"); schedules.

actual military service. Phrase referring to a privileged will (q.v.) which allows, e.g., a soldier or airman "in actual military service" to make an informal will. It has been given a wide meaning so as to include, e.g., an airman undergoing training in Canada (*Re Wingham* [1943] P 187), a minor serving in the BAOR nine years after the end of the war (*Re Colman* [1958] 2 All ER 35).

actual notice. *See* NOTICE.

actus non facit reum nisi mens sit rea. An act does not itself constitute guilt unless the mind is guilty. The maxim embodies a cardinal doctrine of English criminal law. See *Fowler* v *Padget* (1798) 7 TR 509; *Younghusband* v *Luftig* [1949] 2 KB 354.

actus reus. A phrase referring to elements of the definition of an offence (save those which concern the condition of the mind of the accused) e.g., his conduct, its results and surrounding circumstances. Thus, the *actus reus* of false imprisonment (q.v.) is X's unlawful restraint of Y. Should any element of the *actus reus* not be present, the offence has not been committed. See, e.g., *R* v *Runting* (1989) 89 Cr App R 243. *See* CRIME.

ad colligenda bona. To collect the goods. Grant of administration made to preserve property when no next of kin, creditor or other person applies for administration and the property is in danger of perishing. See *Re Clore* [1982] Ch 456. *See* GRANT.

addiction. Compulsive psychological or physiological need for, e.g., a drug. *See* DRUG ADDICT.

address. In relation to an individual, his usual residential or business address. In relation to a firm, its registered or principal office in Great Britain; Cos. A. 1989, s. 53(1).

adduce. To present, or bring forward, e.g., evidence in support of some proposition or statement already made.

ademption. A specific legacy is said to be adeemed when, as result of implied revocation by testator, it is withheld or extinguished, wholly or in part. There is ademption in the following cases: 1. Testator makes a gift of "my gold watch" but sells it before his death: *Re Dowsett* [1901] 1 Ch 398. 2. Father or person *in loco parentis* (q.v.) may bequeath a legacy to a child and later make other provisions which, in effect, constitute a portion (q.v.): *Earl of Durham* v *Wharton* (1836) 10 Bli NS 526.

See *R* v *Sweeting* [1988] 1 All ER 1016. *See* LEGACY.

ad hoc. For this special purpose.

ad hoc settlements. *See* SETTLEMENTS, AD HOC.

ad hoc trust for sale. Where trustees for sale of land are either two or more persons approved or appointed by the Court, or their successors in office, or a trust corporation (q.v.), a sale overreaches certain prior interests: L.P.A. 1925, s. 2(2). The sale is known as an *ad hoc*, or special, trust for sale.

ad idem. Of the same mind; similar in essential matters. A binding contract, for example, requires *consensus ad idem* (agreement as to the same thing) by both parties. See *Raffles* v *Wichelhaus* (1864) 2 H & C 906.

adjacent. "Close to or nearby or lying by: its significance or application in point of distance depends on the circumstances in which the word is used": *English China Clays* v *Plymouth Corporation* [1974] 2 All ER 239.

adjective law. That portion of the law dealing with procedure and practice in the courts. *See* SUBSTANTIVE LAW.

adjoining. Touching. Includes "abutting on": Highways Act 1980, s. 329(1). See *Bucks CC* v *Trigg* [1963] 1 WLR 155.

adjourn. To postpone or suspend the hearing of a case until a further date. An adjournment *sine die* (without day) is for an indefinite time. "Adjournment of the House" refers to the suspension of a sitting of the Lords or Commons until the following or a later day.

adjournment of trial. The postponing of a trial of action by a judge who thinks it expedient "in the interest of justice" to adjourn "for such time, and to such place, and upon such terms, if any, as he thinks fit": O. 35, r. 3. See *Re Yates' ST* [1954] 1 WLR 564. For adjournment of a preliminary enquiry or a summary trial, see M.C.A. 1980, ss. 5, 10; *R* v *Walsall Justices, ex p W.* [1989] 3 All ER 460.

adjudication. Formal judgment or decision given by the court. In proceedings for bankruptcy an adjudication order declares the debtor bankrupt, so that he becomes subject to disabilities attaching to that status.

adjustment. Determining or settling of an amount entitled to be received by

the assured under a policy of marine insurance. *See* AVERAGE.

ad litem. For the suit. 1. A *guardian ad litem* may be appointed by the court to represent the interests of a child in certain proceedings: Ch. A. 1989, s. 41. See *R* v *Cornwall CC, ex p Cornwall Guardians* (1991) The Times, 20 Nov. 2. *A grant ad litem* may be made where representatives will not act and the estate must be represented in proceedings: *Re Simpson* [1936] P 40.

administer. Under the Medicines Act 1968, s. 130(9), to give to a person or animal, orally, by injection or by introduction into the body in any other way, or by external application, whether by direct contact with the body or not. See also O.P.A. 1861, s. 24; *R* v *Gillard* (1988) 87 Cr App R 64.

administration. 1. Process of managing affairs of a bankrupt by a trustee, or those of an absent person by an attorney or agent. 2. Process of collecting the assets of a deceased person, paying debts and distributing any surplus to those entitled. See A.E.A. 1925, s. 34 and Sch 1.

administration action. Action to obtain administration of the estate of a deceased person. Personal representative or any other person interested in the estate may bring proceedings by originating summons or writ. See S.C.A. 1981, s. 117.

administration bond. As a condition of granting administration to a person, the court may require one or two sureties to guarantee that they will make good any loss suffered by a person interested in the estate, following the breach of duties by administrator. See S.C.A. 1981, s. 120.

administration, limited. *See* LIMITED ADMINISTRATION.

administration of assets. *See* ESTATES, ADMINISTRATION OF.

administration of estates. *See* ADMINISTRATION; ESTATES, ADMINISTRATION OF.

administration order, county court. Order made by a county court where a debtor is unable to pay a debt, on application of the debtor, or creditor under a judgment obtained against the debtor or of the court's own motion during the course of any enforcement or other proceedings; C.L.S.A. 1990, s. 13, replacing County C.A. 1984, s. 112(1).

administration order relating to companies. An order directing that, while it is in force, the affairs, business and property of a company (q.v.) shall be managed by an administrator (q.v.) appointed by the court: Ins. A. 1986, s. 8(2). Its purposes include the survival of the company as a going concern, an advantageous realisation of assets, etc: s. 8(3). An application is by petition presented by the company, directors or creditors: s. 9(1), amended by C.J.A. 1988, s. 62. While in force, no resolution may be passed or order for a winding-up made: s. 11(3). See *Astor Chemicals Ltd* v *Synthetic Technology Ltd* [1990] BCLC 1. For discharge, see s. 18. *See* BANKRUPTCY.

administration, special. *See* LIMITED ADMINISTRATION.

administration suit. An action for the administration of the estate of a deceased person.

administration, summary. Where it appears to the court that, if a bankruptcy order (q.v.) were made, the aggregate amount of the bankruptcy debts so far as secured would be less than the prescribed small bankruptcies level, and that within the period of 5 years ending with the presentation of the petition the debtor has neither been adjudged bankrupt nor made a composition with his creditors or a scheme of arrangement, a certificate for summary administration of the bankrupt's estate may be issued: Ins. A. 1986, s. 275(1). *See* BANKRUPTCY.

administrative actions, remedies for control of. These are discretionary and comprise: prerogative orders (*certiorari, mandamus,* prohibition); *habeas corpus;* non-statutory remedies (e.g., injunctions, declarations); statutory remedies (e.g., rights of appeal); and collateral challenge (e.g., in actions for damages). Control of such actions does not involve an appeal in disguise; see *Healey* v *Minister of Health* [1955] 1 QB 221.

administrative tribunals. Tribunals outside the hierarchy of courts exercising jurisdiction conferred by Parliament, e.g., Rent Tribunals. Chairmen are generally selected from a panel and are appointed by the Lord Chancellor. The Council on Tribunals reviews their working. They are controlled generally by the issue of prerogative orders, i.e., certiorari, mandamus, prohibition (qq.v.).

administrator. (Fem: administratrix.) One appointed by the court to manage the property of a deceased person in the absence of an executor (q.v.). *See* GRANT.

administrator of a company. Appointed by the Court (see Ins. A. 1986, s. 8(2)) to "do all such things as may be necessary for the arrangement of the affairs, business and property" of the company: s. 14(1). He may summon a creditors' meeting if requested to do so by one-tenth in value of the company's creditors, or if so directed by the court: s. 17(3). See, e.g., *Re Atlantic Computer Systems plc* [1990] BCLC 859.

administrator of an estate, duties of. To collect, get in and administer real and personal estate of the deceased; to exhibit on oath a full inventory of the estate and render an account of its administration to the court; to deliver up to the High Court, when required to do so, the grant of probate or administration: A.E.A. 1925, s. 25, as substituted by A.E.A. 1971.

Admiralty Court. A part of QBD (q.v.) consisting of puisne judges (q.v.) of the High Court, assisted by nautical assessors (the Elder Brethren of Trinity House). See S.C.A 1981, ss. 6, 20–24; O. 75; and C.J.J.A. 1982, s. 26. It has instant jurisdiction (concerning civil cases arising, e.g., out of collisions) and prize jurisdiction (concerning seizure of enemy ships and cargoes). For the combined Admiralty and Commercial Court Registry, see SI 1987/1423; *Practice Direction* [1987] 1 WLR 1459; *Bain Clarkson* v *Owners of Sea Friends* [1991] 2 Lloyd's Rep 323.

admissibility, conditional. *See* CONDITIONAL ADMISSIBILITY.

admissibility, multiple. *See* MULTIPLE ADMISSIBILITY.

admissibility of evidence. Evidence is receivable by the court only if both relevant and admissible. In general, all evidence relevant to an issue is admissible; all that is irrelevant or insufficiently relevant ought to be excluded. See, e.g., *Hollington* v *Hewthorn & Co Ltd* [1943] KB 587. Must be distinguished from relevance (q.v.), which is based on that which is logically probative whereas admissibility refers to that which is legally receivable whether logically probative or not. "[The terms relevance and admissibility] are frequently, and in many circumstances legitimately, used interchangeably; but I think it makes for clarity if they are kept separate, since some relevant evidence is inadmissible and some admissible evidence is irrelevant . . .": *per* Lord Simon in *DPP* v *Kilbourne* [1973] AC 729. *See* EVIDENCE.

admission order and mental illness. Order made for admission to hospital by the Crown Court under the Criminal Procedure (Insanity) Act 1964, s. 5, or the Court of Appeal under the Criminal Appeal Act 1968, ss. 6, 14, 14A. See Criminal Procedure (Insanity and Unfitness to Plead) Act 1991, Sch. 1. *See* UNFITNESS TO PLEAD.

admissions. 1. In civil proceedings, those facts (or part of a case) admitted, or taken to be admitted by parties to an action. An admission may be made in answer to interrogatories (q.v.) or by the pleadings (q.v.); or on special application made during proceedings. See O. 27; SI 1989/2427; Civil Evidence Act 1968, s. 9. 2. In criminal proceedings, statements made voluntarily by the accused, which are adverse to his case, e.g., by admitting the offence, plea of guilty or confession. See C.J.A. 1967, s. 10 (provision for formal admission at or before trial); *R* v *Best* [1909] 1 KB 692. 3. "Admissions by conduct" may be implied from a party's conduct. See, e.g., *R* v *Cramp* (1880) 14 Cox CC 390. See P. & C.E.A. 1984, s. 82. *See* ADMISSIONS OF FACT, JUDGMENT ON; CONFESSION.

admissions by privies. Statements (informal) by persons who were, at the time of their making, in privity with a party (e.g., proprietor and predecessor in title, principal and agent). They may be used against that party as admissions. See, e.g., *Woolway* v *Rowe* (1834) 1 A & E 114.

admissions of fact, judgment on. Where, by his pleadings, a party makes admissions of facts, any other party may make an application to the court for judgment on those admissions: see O. 27, r. 3.

adopted children register. A register maintained by the Registrar-General at the General Register Office in which entries relating to adoption orders (q.v.) are made. Any person is entitled to search an index of the register: Adoption Act 1976, s. 50.

adoption. 1. Incorporation of international law into municipal law, e.g., by custom. 2. Process, effected by a court order, whereby parental responsibility (q.v.) for a child is given to the adopter(s). Recognised only after the Adoption of Children Act 1926. Regulated by Adoption Act 1976 and Ch. A. 1989. A person other than an adoption agency shall not make arrangements for the adoption of a child or place a child for adoption unless the proposed adopter is a relative of the child or he is acting in pursuance of a High Court order: 1976 Act, s. 11(1). For Adoption Contact Register, see Ch. A. 1989, Sch. 10, para 21. See also Adoption Rules 1984, amended by SI 1991/1880.

adoption, freeing child for. Where on the application by an adoption agency, an authorised court is satisfied in the case of each parent or guardian of the child that he freely and with full understanding of what is involved, agrees generally and unconditionally to the making of an adoption order, or his agreement to the making of the order can be dispensed with, the court may make an order declaring the child free for adoption: Adoption Act 1976, s. 18(1). See also 1976 Act, s. 18(2A); Ch. A. 1989, s. 88, Sch. 10.

adoption order. An order giving parental responsibility to the adopters, made on their application by an authorised court: Adoption Act 1976, s. 12(1), as amended by Ch. A. 1989, Sch. 10. It may be made by the Family Division, county court or magistrates' court. The court must give prime consideration to the child's long-term welfare before making an order: s. 6. An order is not generally made unless the child is free for adoption: s. 16(1). Notification to adopt cannot be made more than two years before the order: see Ch. A. 1989, Sch. 10.

adoption order, status conferred by. An adopted child is treated in law, where the adopters are a married couple, as if he had been born as a child of the marriage and, in any other case, as if he had been born to the adopter in wedlock, and as if he were not the child of any person other than the adopter(s): Adoption Act 1976, s. 39.

adoptive Acts. Acts which become effective in a local authority's area only after formal adoption by that authority. See, e.g., the provisions relating to licensing systems in the L.G. (Misc. Provs.) Act 1982, s. 1.

adoptive relationship. Relationship existing by virtue of the Adoption Act 1976, s. 39. An adoptive parent must be at least 18: Ch. A. 1989, Sch. 10. A male adopter is known as the adoptive father, a female adopter as the adoptive mother: 1976 Act, s. 41.

adult. Person of full age (18). See MAJORITY.

adulteration. An offence under, e.g., Food Act 1984, s. 38, resulting from the adding of a substance to food which renders it dangerous to health, if done with the intention that it should be sold in that state for human consumption. See FOOD, OFFENCES IN RELATION TO.

adultery. An act of voluntary sexual intercourse (which need not be completed) between two persons not married to each other, but one or both of whom are married at the time of the act to a third person. If the respondent has committed adultery and the petitioner finds it intolerable to live with the respondent, it may be evidence of irretrievable breakdown of a marriage, which is now the sole ground for the presentation of a divorce petition: Mat. C.A. 1973, s. 1. The onus of proof is on the petitioner. Damages for adultery cannot now be claimed: Law Reform (Misc. Provs.) Act 1970. For effect of cohabitation after discovery of adultery, see Mat. C.A. 1973, s. 2(1).

adultery, proof of. Modes of proof include: confessions; respondent's previous convictions (see Civil Evidence Act 1968, s. 11); finding of adultery and paternity in earlier civil proceedings; results of blood tests concerning paternity (see the F.L.R.A. 1969, s. 20(1), as amended by Ch. A. 1989, s. 89). The standard of proof for adultery seems to be the balance of probabilities.

ad valorem. In proportion to the value. In the case of an *ad valorem* tax, the amount paid is proportionate to the value of the article taxed.

advance freight. See FREIGHT.

advancement. 1. Power of advancement allows a trustee (q.v.) to apply capital for the advancement or benefit of any person entitled to capital of the trust property or any share in it: Tr.A. 1925, s. 32. 2. Presumption of advancement, i.e., that a gift was intended, arises where a voluntary conveyance has been made to the wife or child of the donor or to a person to whom he stands in *loco parentis* (q.v.). See *Calverley* v *Green* (1984) 56 ALR 483. See PORTION.

adversarial procedure. System in most common law countries whereby parties to a dispute and their representatives have the primary responsibility for finding and presenting evidence. The judge does not investigate the facts. See *Air Canada* v *Secretary of State for Trade (No. 2)* [1983] 1 All ER 910. See INQUISITORIAL PROCEDURE.

adverse occupation of residential premises. It is an offence for a person who is on premises as a trespasser, after having entered as such, to fail to leave on being required to do so by or on behalf of a displaced residential occupier of the premises or a protected intending occupier (i.e., one who has in those premises a freehold interest or leasehold interest with not less than 21 years still to run who acquired the interest for money or money's worth, who requires the premises for his own occupation as a residence and is excluded by the trespasser): C.L.A. 1977, s. 7(1),(2). For defences available to the accused, see s. 7(6)–(8).

adverse possession. Refers to one person's occupation of land which is inconsistent with the right of another who claims to be the true owner. Minor acts of trespass do not constitute adverse possession. There must be real possession, accompanied by intent to possess; possession must be adverse to the owner and must not have been given by permission. See *Bucks CC.* v *Moran* [1989] 3 WLR 152; *Browne* v *Perry* [1991] 1 WLR 1297; Limitation Act 1980, ss. 15(1), 32 (12 year period for action to recover land). See LIMITATION OF ACTIONS.

adverse witnesses. Witnesses who disappoint the party calling them, i.e., they are unfavourable and hostile witnesses (q.v.).

advertent and inadvertent negligence. *See* NEGLIGENCE, ADVERTENT.

advertisement. Public announcement or notice. Includes, under C.C.A. 1974, s. 189(1) "every form of advertising, whether in a publication, by television or radio, by display of notices, signs, labels, showcards or goods, by distribution of samples, circulars, catalogues, price lists or other material, by exhibition of pictures, models or films, or in any other way . . .". See T.C.P.A. 1990, ss. 220, 336(1); Broadcasting Act 1990, s. 9. Public advertisement of a reward for the return of stolen or lost goods "to the effect that no questions will be asked" is an offence under Th.A. 1968, s. 23. See *Denham v Scott* [1983] Crim LR 558; C.P.A. 1987, s. 24(6); SI 1988/915.

advertiser. In relation to an advertisement, this means any person indicated by the advertisement as willing to enter into transactions to which the advertisement relates: C.C.A. 1974, s. 189(1).

advice on evidence. Document prepared by counsel following the close of pleadings (q.v.), on instructions by a party's solicitor. It surveys the dispute, enumerates facts in issue and how they should be dealt with, and expresses an opinion concerning the possibility of success and the appropriateness of a settlement.

Advisory, Conciliation and Arbitration Service. A body set up under E.P.A. 1975, s. 1, charged with a general duty of promoting the improvement of industrial relations, and encouraging the extension, development and reform of collective bargaining. It is controlled by a council, comprising a chairman and six members, nominated by CBI, TUC, and three independent members. See T.U.L.R.(C.)A. 1992, s. 247.

advocacy and litigation services. Any services which it would be reasonable to expect a person who is exercising, or contemplating exercising, a right of audience, or a right to conduct litigation, in relation to proceedings, or contemplated proceedings, to provide; C.L.S.A. 1990, s. 119.

advocate. Any person exercising a right of audience (q.v.) as a representative of, or on behalf of, any party to legal proceedings: see C.L.S.A. 1990, s.

27(9). An "authorised advocate" is a person who has a right of audience granted by an authorised body, e.g., General Council of the Bar, Law Society: s. 119(1). For immunity from actions in negligence and for breach of contract, see s. 62. For legal professional privilege, see s. 63.

Advocate General. An assistant to a judge of the Court of Justice of the European Communities. He is not a member of the Court, but advises, rather like *amicus curiae* (q.v.), making reasoned submissions on matters referred to it. Submissions are given orally before judgment is given. See Treaty of Rome 1957, arts. 166, 167. *See* COURT OF JUSTICE OF THE EUROPEAN COMMUNITIES.

advowson. Incorporeal hereditaments (q.v.) to which the law of real property applies, consisting of the perpetual right to present to an ecclesiastical living. The owner of the right is known as the "patron". See Lim.A. 1980, s. 25; Patronage (Benefices) Measure 1986.

aedificatum solo, solo cedit. That which is built upon land becomes part of the land. *See* FIXTURES.

aequitas est quasi aequalitas. Equity is, as it were, equality. See *Jones v Maynard* [1951] Ch 572.

aerodromes, safety at. It is an offence for a person, by means of any device, substance or weapon intentionally to commit at an international aerodrome an act of violence which causes or is likely to cause death or serious personal injury, or endangers or is likely to endanger the safety of persons at the aerodrome: Aviation and Maritime Security Act 1990, s. 1(1). False statements relating to baggage, identity documents, are offences under the Aviation Security Act 1982, s. 21, as amended by the 1990 Act, s. 5.

affidavit. Written statement, sworn or affirmed (usually before a Commissioner for Oaths (q.v.)), in the name of the deponent. See O. 38, r. 2(3) (evidence given on affidavit). Statements on affidavit are not generally subjected to cross-examination (q.v.). Affidavits used in interlocutory matters may contain certain hearsay evidence: O. 41, r. 5(2). *See* EVIDENCE, HEARSAY.

affidavit of documents. When a party has received a list of documents (q.v.) he may give notice to the other party requiring verification by affidavit. See O. 24, r. 5.

affiliation order. An order of the magistrates' court adjudging, finding or declaring a person to be the father of a child and (usually) providing for the maintenance of the child. See Affiliation Proceedings Act 1957, which was superseded by F.L.R.A. 1987, Part II, abolishing affiliation proceedings.

affinity. Relationship resulting from marriage, e.g., between a wife and her husband's blood relations, as opposed to consanguinity, i.e., relationship by blood.

affirm. 1. To confirm a judgment, as where an appellate court confirms the judgment of a court below it. 2. To make a solemn declaration instead of taking an oath (if one has no religious belief, or the taking of an oath is contrary to a religious belief). The usual form is "I . . . do solemnly, sincerely and truly declare and affirm that the evidence which I shall give shall be the truth, the whole truth, and nothing but the truth." See Oaths Act 1978, s. 6. 3. To declare expressly or impliedly with full knowledge of the facts an intention to proceed with a contract. Lapse of time may be evidence of affirmation. See *Leaf* v *International Galleries* [1950] 2 KB 86.

affirmanti non neganti incumbit probatio. The burden of proof is on him who affirms, not on him who denies.

affirmative pregnant. An assertion in a pleading, implying, or not excluding, some negative. See NEGATIVE PREGNANT.

affray. A person is guilty of affray if he uses or threatens unlawful violence towards another and his conduct is such as would cause a person of reasonable firmness present at the scene to fear for his personal safety: P.O.A. 1986, s. 3(1). Where two or more persons use or threaten the unlawful violence, it is the conduct of them taken together that must be considered: s. 3(2). The offence may be committed in private as well as in public places: s. 3(5). See *R* v *Rogers-Hinks and Others* (1989) 11 Cr App R (S) 234; *R* v *Davison* [1992] Crim LR 31.

affreightment. A contract of affreightment, in the form of a bill of lading (q.v.) or charterparty (q.v.), is an undertaking by a ship owner to carry goods for a person, known as the *freighter,* in his ship for reward. See FREIGHT.

aforethought. Premeditated; deliberate. See MALICE AFORETHOUGHT.

a fortiori [ratione]. For a stronger reason.

after-acquired property. A husband was entitled at common law absolutely on his marriage to the property belonging to his wife, including that which she acquired after marriage. The separate treatment of a married woman's property was introduced by L.P.A. 1925, s. 170. For accountability concerning after-acquired assets, see *Schuller* v *Schuller* [1990] 2 FLR 193.

after care condition. Phrase used in relation to planning permission, referring to steps to be taken, after working of minerals, to bring land to the required standard for use in agriculture, forestry, or for amenity: see T.C.P.A. 1971, s. 30A (inserted by T.C.P. (Minerals) A. 1981, s. 5); T.C.P.A. 1990, Sch. 5. *See.* RESTORATION CONDITION.

A.-G. Attorney-General (q.v.).

age. "A person: is over or under a particular age if he has, or as the case may be has not, attained that age: is between two particular ages if he has attained the first but not the second": S.S.A. 1975, Sch. 20. See FULL AGE.

agency. "A consensual relationship in which one (the agent) holds in trust for and subject to the control of another (the principal) a power to effect certain legal relations of that other": Seavey.

agency by estoppel. Requirements are: a representation, a reliance on that representation, alteration of a party's position as a result of that reliance: *per* Slade J in *Rama Corporation* v *Proved Tin Ltd* [1952] 2 QB 147; *Armagas Ltd* v *Mundogas SA* [1985] 2 All ER 385.

agent. Generally one who is employed so as to bring his principal into contractual relationships with other persons. An agency can be created: by express agreement, verbally or in writing; by implication or conduct (see *Summers* v *Solomon* (1857) 7 E & B 879); by estoppel (q.v.); by necessity, as when a person has been entrusted with another's property, the preservation of which requires certain actions, e.g., feeding and stabling an animal (see *GN Rwy v Swaffield* (1874) LR 6 Ex 132). ("In considering what is reasonably necessary any material circumstances must be taken into account, e.g., danger, distance, accommodation, expense, time and so forth": *per* Lord Lindley in *Phelps & Co. v Hill* [1891] 1 QB 605.) An agency may be terminated by operation of law or action of parties. *See* RATIFICATION.

agent and principal, duties of. A principal's duties are generally: to pay the agent his agreed remuneration; to indemnify the agent against expenses, liabilities and claims incurred in discharging the agency. An agent's duties are: to respect his principal's title; to exercise his duties with appropriate care and skill (see *Chaudry v Prabhakar* [1988] 3 All ER 718); to perform those duties personally; to avoid conflict between his personal interests and those of the principal; to account for and hand over to the principal all money due.

agent and principal, remedies of. Agent's remedies include: action for breach of contract, set-off, lien on goods, stoppage in transitu, action for taking of an account. Principal's remedies include: dismissal, actions in conversion or breach of contract, prosecution under Prevention of Corruption Acts 1906 and 1916.

agent, mercantile. *See* FACTOR.

agent provocateur. "A person who entices another to commit an express breach of the law which he would not otherwise have committed and then proceeds to inform against him in respect of such an offence": *Royal Commission on Police Powers* 1928 (Cmd 3297), cited in *R v Mealey and Sheridan* (1975) 60 Cr App R 59. If a crime is procured by an *agent provocateur*, that is in itself no defence, but it may result in a lighter sentence. See *R v McEvilly* (1975) 60 Cr App R 150; *R v Edwards* [1991] Crim LR 414. *See* ENTRAPMENT.

agent, special. An agent employed to transact particular business only.

agent's signature. A *descriptive signature* shows that the agent has contracted personally, e.g., "as charterer"; see *Universal Steam Navigation Co v McKelvie*

& Co [1923] AC 492. A *representative signature* indicates the representative nature of the signatory and does not result in the agent's personal liability; e.g., "on account of my principal, P". See *Lester v Balfour Williamson Ltd.* [1953] 2 QB 168.

agent, universal. An agent appointed, usually by power of attorney (q.v.), with unlimited authority to act for his principal.

age of consent. *See* CONSENT, AGE OF.

age, pensionable. In the case of a man, 65; in the case of a woman, 60: S.S.A. 1975, s. 27(1); S.S.A. 1979, s. 4.

age, proof of. Procedure whereby a person's age is proved by: production of a birth certificate and evidence of identity; declaration of a deceased person against interest or in the course of duty; someone present at birth. In some cases, see, e.g., S.O.A. 1956, s. 28(3), there may be an "inference of age" from appearance.

aggravated assault. An assault (q.v.) such as that committed upon a woman, meriting a more severe punishment than that following a common assault. See O.P.A. 1861, ss. 38, 43; and Th.A. 1968, s. 8 (under which a person guilty of assault with intent to rob is liable to life imprisonment).

aggravated burglary. *See* BURGLARY.

aggravated vehicle-taking. *See* VEHICLE-TAKING, AGGRAVATED.

aggrieved person. "A man who has suffered a legal grievance, a man against whom a decision has been pronounced which has wrongfully deprived him of something, or wrongfully refused him something, or wrongfully affected his title to something": *per* James LJ in *Ex p Sidebotham* (1880) 14 Ch D 458. See *Cook v Southend BC* [1990] 2 WLR 61. *See.* LOCUS STANDI.

agistment. The taking of another's animals to graze on one's pastures for reward. See Agricultural Holdings Act 1986, s. 18(5).

agnates. Relations by the father's side, e.g., one's son, brother, sister. *See* COGNATES.

agreement. A consensus of minds, or evidence of such consensus, in spoken or written form relating to anything done or to be done. "A declared concurrence of will of two or more persons whereby a change in their legal spheres is intended": Gareis. *See* CON-TRACT.

agreement, conditional. An agreement, the operation of which is dependent on the occurrence of an uncertain event. See *Hargreaves Transport Ltd v Lynch* [1969] 1 WLR 215.

agreement, inferred. *See* INFERRED AGREE-MENT.

agreement, modifying. An agreement varying or supplementing an earlier agreement: C.C.A. 1974, s. 82(2).

agreement, multiple. A term used under C.C.A. 1974, s. 18, to refer to an agreement, the terms of which place a part of it within one category of agreement mentioned in the Act, and another part of it within a different category of agreement so mentioned, or within a category of agreement not so mentioned, or which place it or a part of it within two or more categories of agreement so mentioned.

agreement, non-commercial. A consumer credit agreement (q.v.) or a consumer hire agreement not made by the creditor or owner in the course of a business carried on by him: C.C.A. 1974, s. 189(1).

agreements, regulated. *See* REGULATED AGREEMENTS.

agricultural holding. "The aggregate of the land (whether agricultural land or not) comprised in a contract of tenancy which is a contract for an agricultural tenancy, not being a contract under which the land is let to the tenant during his continuance in any office, appointment or employment held under the landlord": Agricultural Holdings Act 1986, s. 1(1). "Agricultural land" is land used for agricultural purposes in relation to a trade or business. Security of tenure is conferred. Notice period is generally one year and is operative only if, e.g., consent is given by the Agricultural Land Tribunal and land is required for non-agricultural use. Rent may be fixed, in absence of agreement, by an arbitrator appointed under the 1986 Act, s. 6. See Agricultural Holdings (Am.) Act 1990; *Crawford v Elliott* [1991] 13 EG 163; *E.W.P. v Moore* [1992] 2 WLR 184.

agricultural occupancies, assured. Tenancies or licences granted to agricultural workers and governed by H.A.

1988, Part I, ch. III. An occupancy must fulfil "the occupation condition" (e.g., it must be under an assured, but not an assured shorthold, tenancy) and "the employment condition" (based on the Rent (Agriculture) Act 1976, Sch. 3, defining "qualifying worker").

agriculture. This includes horticulture, fruit growing, seed growing, dairy farming, livestock breeding and keeping, forestry, the use of land as grazing land, meadow land, osier land, market gardens and nursery grounds: Agricultural Holdings Act 1986, s. 96(1). See T.C.P.A. 1990, s. 336(1).

AID. Artificial insemination by donor (q.v.).

aid or abet. Knowingly assisting the perpetrator of a crime. "Aiding and abetting almost inevitably involves a situation in which the secondary party and the main offender are together at some stage discussing the plans which they may be making in respect of the alleged offence, and are in contact so that each knows what is passing through the mind of the other". *A.-G.'s Reference (No. 1 of 1975)* [1975] 2 All ER 684. "Whosoever shall aid, abet, counsel or procure the commission of any misdemeanour at common law or by virtue of any Act passed or to be passed, shall be liable to be tried, indicted and punished as a principal offender": Accessories and Abettors Act 1861, s. 8. See also the M.C.A. 1980, s. 44; *R v Coney* (1882) 8 QBD 534; *Wilcox v Jeffrey* [1951] 1 All ER 464; *R v Calhaem* [1985] QB 808; *Hui Chiming v R* [1991] 3 All ER 897. For "passive assistance" in the commission of an offence, see *R v Bland* [1988] Crim LR 41. *See* ABET; ACCESSORY; AC-COMPLICE; PROCURING AN OFFENCE.

AIDS. Acquired immune deficiency syndrome, characterised by a failure of function of the human body's immune system. *See* the AIDS (Control) Act 1987, requiring periodical reports on matters relating to AIDS to be made to the Secretary of State by Regional and District Health Authorities: see s. 1, as amended by NHS and Community Care Act 1990, Sch. 9. See *R v Malcolm* (1988) 9 Cr App R(S.)487; *Fountain v DPP* [1988] Crim LR 128. For HIV (human immune deficiency virus thought to cause AIDS) see *Re HIV Haemophiliac Litigation* (1990) The Guardian, 28 Sept; *R v More* [1991] Crim LR 140; *R v Stark* [1992] Crim LR 384.

aids. 1. Services due from a tenant to his lord, e.g., ransom for an imprisoned lord. Abolished under Tenures Abolition Act 1660, 2. A *grant in aid* may be made to a local authority by Parliament to support the revenue from rates. *See* BLOCK GRANT.

air pollution. A local authority may require the occupier of any premises (except private dwellings) in its area to furnish information concerning the emission of pollutants and other substances into the air from those premises: Control of Pollution Act 1974, s. 80(1), as amended by En. P.A. 1990, Sch. 15. See also the Clean Air Acts 1956–68, which imposed fines for the emission of dark smoke from buildings in certain areas. *See* ENVIRONMENTAL PROTECTION.

air, right to flow of. The right can subsist as an easement (q.v.) if claimed in respect of some defined channel, e.g., a ventilator. See *Cable v Bryant* [1908] 1 Ch 259.

airspace, interference with. A possible trespass created by an intrusion into another's airspace. See Civil Aviation Act 1982; *Woollerton & Wilson Ltd v Richard Costain Ltd* [1970] 1 WLR 411. "In none of [the cases] is there an authoritative pronouncement that [in the phrase 'trespass to land'] 'land' means the whole of space from the centre of the earth to the heavens": *Commissioner for Rwys v Valuer-General.* [1974] AC 328. See *Bernstein v Skyviews* [1977] 2 All ER 902 – no right of privacy in air-space. See Civil Aviation Act 1982, s. 77. *See* CUJUS EST SOLUM (ETC).

alcoholism. Addiction to excessive consumption of alcoholic liquor. An alcoholic state induced by voluntary drinking does not constitute a defence. It could be treated as a duress (q.v.) for purposes of defence of diminished responsibility (q.v.) if defendant's intellectual or emotional impairment was caused by damage resulting from the alcoholism or by drinking which had been rendered involuntary by the alcoholism. See *R v*

Tandy [1989] 1 All ER 267; *R v Inseal* [1992] Crim LR 35.

alcohol on coaches and trains. It is an offence to permit intoxicating liquor to be carried on a public service or railway passenger vehicle to or from a designated sporting event, or to have intoxicating liquor in one's possession during the period of such an event when in any area of a designated sports ground from which the event may be directly viewed: Sporting Events (Control of Alcohol etc.) Act 1985, ss. 1, 2, as amended.

alcohol, prescribed limits in driving. *See* PRESCRIBED LIMITS OF ALCOHOL IN BLOOD, ETC.

aleatory contract. (*Alea* = dice.) Contract in which a party's duty of performance depends upon some uncertain event, e.g., a wagering contract. See *Ellesmere v Wallace* [1929] 2 Ch 1. *See* BET.

alias. (*Alias dictus* = otherwise called.) Second, or assumed, name.

alibi. Elsewhere. An excuse. Argument by an accused person alleging that at the supposed time of the commission of the offence he was elsewhere. He may not bring evidence to support an alibi, except with leave of the court, unless he has given particulars to the prosecution within seven days of the end of committal proceedings. See C.J.A. 1967, s. 11 (as amended by C.J.A. 1987, Sch. 2, para. 2); *R v Cooper* (1979) 69 Cr App R 229; *R v Anderson* [1991] Crim LR 361.

alien. At common law, one who was "born out of the allegiance of our sovereign Lord the King": Littleton. Under B.N.A. 1981, s. 51(1), it means a person who is neither a Commonwealth citizen, nor a British protected person, nor a citizen of the Republic of Ireland. An *alien enemy* is a subject of a state with which this country is at war, or who resides voluntarily or carries on business in enemy, or enemy-occupied, territory. See *Sooracht's Case* [1943] AC 203; *Milltronics v Hycontrol* [1990] FSR 273. *See.* NATURALISATION.

alienable. Capable of being transferred.

alienate. To exercise the power of disposing of or transferring property.

alienation. Power of disposing of or transferring an interest in property; the exercise of that power by an *alienor* to an *alienee.*

alienation, restraint on. Conditions attempting to fetter the right to dispose of or transfer freely an interest in possession in property. Generally void. See, e.g., *Re Dugdale* (1888) 38 Ch D 176; *Caldy Manor Estate Ltd* v *Farrell* [1974] 3 All ER 753.

alieni juris. Of another's right. Term used to refer (in contrast to *sui juris* (q.v.)) to persons subject to the authority of another, e.g., minors.

alimentary trust. A protective trust (q.v.).

alimony. (*Alimonia* = nourishment.) "That allowance which a married woman sues for on separation from her husband": Cowel. Maintenance pending suit (q.v.) has replaced alimony pending suit; financial provision for a spouse has replaced an order for permanent alimony: see Mat.C.A. 1973, Part II, as amended.

aliquis non debet esse judex in propria causa quia non potest esse judex et pars. No man should be a judge in his own cause, since he cannot act at the same time as judge and party. The "rule against bias".

aliter. Otherwise.

aliunde. From elsewhere.

allegation. A statement of fact in proceedings made by a party who undertakes to prove it. *See* AVERMENT.

allegiance. "Such natural or legal obedience which every subject owes to his prince": *Termes de la Ley*. Allegiance may be due not only from subjects (wherever they may be), but also from aliens resident in British territory or elsewhere if they retain British passports: *Joyce* v *DPP* [1946] AC 347. Breach of allegiance may amount to treason (q.v.). *See* LOYALTY.

allegiance, oath of. *See* OATH OF ALLEGIANCE.

all fours. Cases or judgments alike in all material respects are said to "run on all fours".

allocatur. It is allowed. Term referring to certificate of allowance of costs issued by taxing office. See O. 62, r. 22.

allocutus. Demand by court of a convicted person, asking whether he has cause to show why judgment should not be pronounced against him.

allodial land. Land owned outright, i.e., owned absolutely and not held of any lord or superior. No subject of the Crown in England may hold land allodially; he can hold only an estate (q.v.) in land; see *Minister of State for the Army* v *Dalziel* (1943) 68 CLR 261.

allonge. Slip of paper securely attached to a negotiable instrument, e.g., a bill of exchange (q.v.), on which endorsements may be made. See B.Ex.A. 1882, s. 32.

allotment, letter of. Notification to an applicant that shares in a company have been appropriated to him, usually by a resolution of the board of directors. Generally, allotment signifies acceptance of an offer to take shares. There is no binding contract until an allotment is made and a letter has been posted, or has reached the allottee in another way. The allottee acquires an unconditional right to be included in the company's register of members: s. 738(1). See *Household Fire Insurance Co* v *Grant* (1879) 4 Ex D 216. *See* SHARE.

allow. Permit (q.v.). "A man cannot be said to allow that of which he is unaware, or that which he cannot prevent"; *per* Darling J in *Crabtree* v *Fern Spinning Co.* (1901) 85 LT 549.

all-risks policy. Insurance policy requiring the person insured to take all reasonable steps to prevent loss. "All the insured has to do is to prove that there was a loss due to a fortuitous happening of some sort": *per* Hodgson J in *Port-Rose* v *Phoenix Assurance plc* (1986) 136 NLJ 333.

alteration. A material alteration (e.g., of a date), which alters the sense or effect of an instrument, generally invalidates it. An alteration in a deed (q.v.) is presumed to have been made before or at the time of execution; an alteration in a will (q.v.) is presumed to have been made after the time of execution. See W.A. 1837, s. 21; *Cooper* v *Bockett* (1846) 4 Moo PC; *Re Adams* [1990] 2 WLR 924.

alteration of share capital. A company may alter its capital if authorised by its articles of association (q.v.): Cos.A. 1985, s. 121. A resolution in a general meeting is needed and notice must be given to the Registrar: s. 123. Shares may be *consolidated*, e.g., by the amalgamation of smaller into larger, and *subdivided*, or converted to stock. Nominal or authorised capital (q.v.) may be increased and unissued nominal capital cancelled. See ss. 135–141. *See* SHARE.

alternative counts. *See* COUNTS, ALTERNATIVE.

alternative danger, principle of. Common law principle relating to tort, arising where the plaintiff has not necessarily contributed by negligence (q.v.) to his injuries if, as the result of the defendant's negligence, the plaintiff was placed in a dilemma and, "in the agony of the moment," chose a wrong alternative. See, e.g., *Jones v Boyce* (1816) 1 Stark 493.

alternative, pleading in the. Inclusion in pleadings (q.v.) of two or more inconsistent sets of material facts and the claiming of relief in the alternative.

alternative verdict. *See* VERDICT, ALTERNATIVE.

amalgamation. The combination of two or more companies into one company or into a unit controlled by one company. See Cos.A. 1985, ss. 425, 427, as amended; and Ins.A. 1986, ss. 110, 111. See *Re Savoy Hotel* [1981] Ch 351.

ambiguity. Uncertain meaning or equivocation. 1. *Patent ambiguity* (e.g., a blank space in a deed) is one apparent on the face of the instrument. It cannot generally be resolved by parol evidence (q.v.). See *Watcham. v A.-G. for E. Africa.* [1919] AC 533. 2. *Latent ambiguity* (e.g., "my horse I leave to my nephew John", where the testator had two nephews of that name) is one not apparent on the face of the instrument. It may generally be resolved by parol evidence (q.v.). For the rectification, etc, of wills see the A.J.A. 1982. ss. 20–22. *See* EQUIVOCATION.

ambulatory. (Literally, able to walk.) Capable of being revoked. Thus, a man's will is ambulatory until the moment of his death. See *Vynior's Case* (1609) 8 Co Rep 81b.

ameliorating waste. Alterations which, in fact, improve land: *Doherty v Allman* (1877) 3 App Cas 709 – injunction refused where tenant was converting dilapidated store houses into dwellings. *See* WASTE.

amendment. Correction of a defect in a writ or pleadings, or in criminal proceedings. "I know of no kind of error or mistake which, if not fraudulent or intended to overreach, the court

ought not to correct, if it can be done without injustice to the other party": *Cropper v Smith* (1884) 26 Ch D 700. After service, a writ may be amended once without leave before the close of pleadings: O. 20, r. 3. Amendment at any stage on such terms as may be just is allowed under O. 20, r. 5. See *Tilcon Ltd v Land Investments Ltd* [1987] 1 WLR 46.

amends, tender of. An offer of money tendered in satisfaction of the alleged committing of a wrong. Where used as a defence, money tendered must be brought to court.

amenity. That which is conducive to comfort or convenience. "In relation to any place includes any view of or from that place": Petroleum (Consolidation) Act 1928, s. 23.

amenity, loss of. Also referred to as "loss of faculty" and "loss of enjoyment of life". Result of injuries depriving the plaintiff of some enjoyment. See *Povey v Governors of Rydal School* [1970] 1 All ER 841; *W. v W.* (1991) NLJ 15.

amenity, preservation of. Basis of provisions relating to buildings of special interest, trees, caravan sites, etc. See, e.g., T.C.P.A. 1971, s. 65 (substituted by H. & P.A. 1986, s. 46); En. P.A. 1990, s. 3. *See* PRESERVATION ORDER.

a mensa et thoro. From board and bed. A decree in the ecclesiastical courts (q.v.), prior to Mat.C.A. 1857, which had the effect of a judicial separation (q.v.).

amicus curiae. Friend of the court. A person who is not engaged in the case, but who brings to the court's attention a point which has apparently been overlooked. See *Morelle v Wakeling* [1955] 2 QB 379; *Sherdley v Sherdley* [1987] 2 WLR 1071; *Lord Chancellor's Practice Direction,* 7 Oct. 1991.

ammunition. Defined in the Firearms Act 1968, as ammunition for any firearm, and includes grenades, bombs and other like missiles, whether capable of use with a firearm or not, and "prohibited ammunition" (which includes any ammunition containing, or designed or adapted to contain, any noxious liquid, gas or other things: s. 5(1), (2)). See Firearms (Amendment) Act 1988; *R v Stubbings* [1990] Crim LR 811.

amnesty. An act of government by which certain past offences are pardoned.

analogy, use of. Use in legal argument of a principle based on two things resembling each other in one or more respects. ("A certain proposition is true of the one, therefore it is true of the other": J.S. Mill.)

anatomical examination. The examination by dissection of a body for purposes of teaching or studying, or researching into, morphology: Anatomy Act 1984, s. 1(1). The examination must be carried out on properly-licensed premises: ss. 2(1), 3. It is an offence to carry out such an examination in contravention of the Act: s. 11.

ancestor. 1. One from whom a person is descended. 2. Before L.P.A. 1925, a person from whom real property was inherited. See *Zetland* v *Lord Advocate* (1878) 3 App Cas 505; *Knowles* v *A.-G.* [1951] P 4.

ancient demesne. Tenure, abolished by L.P.A. 1922, s. 128, whereby the land of tenants was passed by common law conveyance. See *Iveagh* v *Martin* [1961] 1 QB 232.

ancient document. A document 20 years old or more. "Ancient documents coming out of proper custody and purporting on the face of them to show exercise of ownership . . . may be given in evidence without proof of possession or payment of rent as being in themselves acts of ownership and proof of possession": *Malcolmson* v *O'Dea* (1863) 10 HLC 593. See Evidence Act 1938, s. 4; *Bristow* v *Cormican* (1878) 3 App Cas 641. *See* DOCUMENT.

ancient lights. A right which arises "when the access and use of light . . . shall have been actually enjoyed . . . for the full period of 20 years without interruption . . . unless it shall appear that the same was enjoyed by some consent or agreement . . . by deed or writing": Prescription Act 1832, s. 3. See, e.g., *Pugh* v *Howells* (1984) 48 P & CR 298. See also Rights of Light Act 1959.

ancient monument. Any scheduled monument or other monument, which, in the opinion of the Secretary of State is of public interest by reason of the historic, architectural, tradi-

tional, artistic or archaeological interests attaching to it: Ancient Monuments and Archaeological Areas Act 1979, s. 61(12) as amended, Schs. 1, 2. See National Heritage Act 1983.

ancillary credit business. Business comprising or relating to: credit brokerage; debt adjusting; debt-counselling; debt-collecting; the operation of a credit reference agency: C.C.A. 1974, s. 145(1).

ancillary probate. *See* PROBATE, ANCILLARY.

ancillary relief. Phrase used, e.g., under Matrimonial Causes Rules 1977, and Family Proceedings Rules 1991, referring to an order for maintenance pending suit, financial provision order, property adjustment order, variation order, etc. See Mat.C.A. 1973, ss. 22–24, 26(1); s. 31(2) for orders that can be varied; *Re T.* [1990] 1 FLR 1. *See* PRODUCTION APPOINTMENT.

animal. Term which includes (*a*) any kind of mammal, except man, (*b*) any kind of four-footed beast, which is not a mammal, (*c*) fish, reptiles, crustaceans and other cold-blooded creatures not falling within (*a*) or (*b*) above: Animal Health Act 1981, s. 87. "Any creature other than a bird or fish": Food Safety Act 1990, s. 53. "Wild animals" are animals not normally domesticated in Britain: Zoo Licensing Act 1981, s. 21(1). See the Animal Health and Welfare Act 1984; Protection of Animals (Am.) Act 1988.

animals, classification of. Animals *domitae naturae* or *mansuetae naturae* (tame or domesticated, e.g., horses); animals *ferae naturae* (of a wild nature), e.g., monkeys. Under the Animals Act 1971, s. 2(2), liability arises, in the case of an animal of a non-dangerous species if: damage is of a kind which the animal, unless restrained, was likely to cause, or which if caused by the animal, was likely to be severe; likelihood of the danger or its severity is due to the animal's characteristics not likely to be found in animals of that species; those characteristics are known to its keeper, or his servant, or a member of the household under 16 years. See also Dangerous Wild Animals Act 1976; *Hunt* v *Wallis* (1991) The Times, 10 May. *See* DANGEROUS SPECIES; DANGEROUS WILD ANIMALS.

animals, dangerous. *See* DANGEROUS WILD ANIMALS.

animal, wild. "Any animal (other than a bird) which is or (before it was killed or taken) was living wild": Wildlife and Countryside Act 1981, s. 27(1). See *McQuaker* v *Goddard* [1940] 1 KB 687.

animus. Intention; disposition. 1. *animus deserendi.* Intention of deserting. 2. *animus furandi.* Intention of stealing. 3. *animus manendi.* Intention of remaining. 4. *animus non revertendi.* Intention of not returning. 5. *animus possidendi.* Intention of possessing (see e.g., *R* v *Secretary of State for the Environment, ex p Davies* (1990) 61 P & CR 487; *Marsden* v *Miller* (1992) The Times, 23 Jan); 6. *animus quo.* Intention with which. 7. *animus revocandi.* Intention of revoking. 8. *animus testandi.* Intention of making a will.

annexation. Joining or uniting one thing to another, e.g., the acquisition of territory by conquest or subjugation. For annexation of chattels to land, see, e.g., *Deen* v *Andrews* (1986) 52 P & CR 17. *See* FIXTURES.

annoyance. "The expression 'annoyance' is wider than 'nuisance', and a thing that reasonably troubles the mind and pleasure – not of a fanciful person or of a skilled person who knows the truth, but of the ordinary sensible English inhabitant of a house, seems to me to be an 'annoyance', although it may not appear to amount to physical detriment to comfort": *Tod-Heatley* v *Benham* (1888) 40 Ch D 80. See also *Wood* v *Cooper* [1894] 3 Ch 671.

Annual Practice, The. *See* RULES OF THE SUPREME COURT.

annual return. Document required under the Cos. A. 1985, s. 363, as amended by Cos. A. 1989, s. 139, which must be filed annually with the Registrar of Companies, made up to the company's return date (initially one year from incorporation) after the annual general meeting and must be accompanied by a copy of the auditors' report and balance sheet. It must contain particulars set out in Cos. A. 1989, s. 139.

annuity. An annual payment of a sum of money as a personal obligation of the grantor or charged on personalty or a mixed fund. See *Hill* v *Gregory* [1912] 2 KB 61. An annuity, which before 1 January 1926, was capable of being registered in the register of annuities, is void against a creditor or purchaser of any interest in the land charged with the annuity, unless it is registered in the register of annuities or register of land charges: L.C.A. 1972, Sch. 1, para. 4. The fact that an annuity is registered does not prevent it being overreached. See also I.C.T.A. 1988, s. 348.

annul. To declare judicial proceedings or their outcome to be no longer of legal effect.

annulment. 1. Annulment of adjudication. The court may annul (see Ins. A. 1986, s. 282, amended by H.A. 1988, s. 117) an adjudication in bankruptcy (q.v.) where, e.g.: in its opinion the debtor should not have been judged bankrupt, or it is proved that the debts have been paid in full, or it approves a composition (q.v.) or scheme. 2. Annulment of marriage. 3. Appeal for annulment. Under Treaty of Rome, arts. 173, 174, the European Court of Justice (q.v.) may, on appeal, annul an action of the EEC Council or Commission (q.v.) because of the lack of jurisdiction, or violation of an essential procedural matter, or infringement of the Treaty, or misuse of powers.

annus, dies et vastum. Year, day and waste (q.v.).

answer. 1. Statement of defence (q.v.) delivered in reply to statement of claim (q.v.). See O. 26, r. 1 (in connection with interrogatories (q.v.)). 2. In proceedings for divorce, the defence of a respondent or correspondent to a petition (q.v.).

antecedent negotiations. Defined in relation to credit agreements, as including, e.g., negotiations with a hirer or debtor conducted by the owner or creditor in relation to the making of a regulated agreement: C.C.A. 1974, s.1.

antecedent rights. Rights existing in their own sake, prior to the commission of a wrongful act, e.g., one's right not to have reputation attacked unjustifiably. Contrasted with *remedial rights* (which arise from the infringement of a primary right), e.g., rights to damages after events of this nature.

antecedents. Term used to refer, e.g., to an offender's record and other history.

Where, after the conviction of an offender, a police officer gives evidence of the offender's character and antecedents, he must confine himself to evidence of the previous convictions, home circumstances, etc, and matters in the offender's favour.

ante-date. Dating of a document before the date on which it was drawn up. See B.Ex.A. 1882, s. 13(2).

ante litem motam. Before litigation commenced.

ante-natal care, time off for. Right of a pregnant employee not to be unreasonably refused time off during her working hours to receive ante-natal care: Employment Act 1980, s. 13.

anticipation, restraint on. Settlements of property on women were at one time accompanied by restraints on their assigning income before it became due. Restraints of this nature were abolished by Law Reform (Married Women and Tortfeasors) Act 1935 and Married Women (Restraint upon Anticipation) Act 1949.

anticipatory breach. Term referring to the repudiation (q.v.) of a contract before the time for performance. The other party may immediately treat the contract as though it were discharged and sue for damages. See *Hochster v De La Tour* (1835) 2 E & B 678; *Woodar Investments v Wimpey Ltd* [1980] 1 All ER 571. *See* BREACH OF CONTRACT.

Anton Piller order. High Court order to defendant to permit plaintiff to enter defendant's premises to inspect, remove or make copies of documents. Plaintiff must show that there is a danger of property or vital evidence being removed. Generally applicable to copyright cases: see *Anton Piller KG v Manufacturing Processes Ltd* [1976] Ch 55; *Rank Film Distributors Ltd v Video Information Centre* [1982] AC 380 (order limited by possibility of self incrimination); *Columbia Picture Industries v Robinson* [1987] Ch 38. May be available in matrimonial disputes: *Emmanuel v Emmanuel* [1982] 1 WLR 669. See also S.C.A. 1981, ss 37, 72, as amended: *Booker McConnell plc v Plascow* [1985] RPC 425 (safeguards for defendant to be included in order); *Universal Thermosensors Ltd v Hibben* (1992) The Times, 22 Feb (review of safeguards).

apology. In an action for libel (q.v.), an apology accompanied by payment of money into the court may be pleaded as a defence or in mitigation of damages. In a case of unintentional defamation, an offer of amends, comprising the published correction of a statement complained of and an apology, may be tendered. See Libel Acts 1843 and 1845; Defamation Act 1952; O. 82, r. 7.

a posteriori. From effect to cause; from subsequent conclusions.

appeal. "The transference of a case from an inferior to a higher tribunal in the hope of reversing or modifying the decision of the former": *Edlesten v LCC* [1918] 1 KB 81. In general, the right of appeal must be given by statute.

Appeal Committee of House of Lords. *See* HOUSE OF LORDS, JURISDICTION OF.

Appeal, Court of. *See* COURT OF APPEAL.

appeal, frivolous. A court considering an appeal may dismiss it summarily if it is regarded as frivolous or vexatious. See C.J.A. 1988, s. 157; *R v Taylor* [1979] Crim LR 649 (an unarguable defence which was bound to fail).

appeal, interlocutory. Appeal from an order made by a master which lies as of right, in general, to a judge in chambers: O. 58, r. 1. An appeal lies from the judge to the Court of Appeal, usually only by leave of the judge or the Court of Appeal, save, e.g., where liberty of the subject is involved.

appeal, reopening of. Following the hearing and dismissal of an appeal by the Court of Appeal, or the abandonment of a notice of appeal, a re-opening is not allowed (save in the case of a procedural defect in the hearings). The applicant may petition the Home Secretary, who can refer the case to the Court.

appeals, civil. Appeal lies: from a district registrar to a judge in chambers (O. 58); from a registrar of the Fam D or a master in the QBD or the Ch D to a judge in chambers or the Court of Appeal (O. 58, rr. 1, 2); from the county court to the Court of Appeal; from the High Court to the Court of Appeal (O. 59); from the Court of Appeal to the House of Lords (Administration of Justice (Appeals) Act 1934, s. 1). See S.C.A. 1981, s. 54(6); *Carter Ltd. v*

Clarke [1990] 2 All ER 209; *Mallory* v *Butler* [1991] 1 WLR 459 (leave to appeal out of time).

appeals, criminal. Appeal lies: from courts of summary jurisdiction to Crown Court (M.C.A. 1980, s. 108); from justices by way of case stated to High Court (s. 111); in indictable cases, from Crown Court to Court of Appeal (Criminal Division) (Criminal Appeal Act 1968, s. 45), from Court of Appeal to House of Lords (q.v.). For right of prosecution to appeal on a point of law following acquittal on indictment, see C.J.A. 1972, s. 36(1). See also C.L.A. 1977, s. 44, as amended; *R* v *Shama* [1990] 2 All ER 602; C.J.A 1988, ss. 35. 36, allowing the A.-G. to refer certain sentences to Court of Appeal (Civil Division) if the sentences seem unduly lenient; *R* v *Berry* (No. 2) [1991] 2 All ER 789.

appearance, entering. Procedure, following service of a writ of summons, now abolished and replaced by acknowledgement of service and notice of intention to defend. See O. 12.

appeal, failure to. Failure of party to appear when an action is called. If neither party appears, the action can be struck off the list. If one party fails to appear, the judge may proceed with the trial. See O. 35, r. 1.

appellant. The person making an appeal.

appellate jurisdiction. Power of a court to hear an appeal.

appendant. Annexed to a hereditament (q.v.) by operation of law, e.g., a common of pasture. Can generally be claimed by prescription (q.v.). *See* APPURTENANT.

appointee. *See* APPOINTMENT, POWER OF.

appointment, excessive. Exercise of a power of appointment (q.v.) which is excessive in the circumstances, e.g., where the appointor grants an interest greater than that authorised by the power, or where he appoints to persons who are outside the class of objects of the power. See *Re Boulton's ST* [1928] Ch 703; *Re Hay's ST* [1981] 3 All ER 786.

appointment, power of. The power given to a person, usually by trust or settlement, enabling him to dispose of an interest in property which is not his. If A confers on B the right to exercise a power of appointment, and B exercises

it in favour of C, A is the *donor* of the power, B is the *donee* or *appointor,* C is the *appointee,* B's exercise of the power is the *appointment.* Powers may be: *public* (conferred by statute) and *private*; *general* (enabling the appointor to appoint in favour of any person) and *special* (enabling the appointment to be made only to members of a given class); *hybrid* (neither special nor general). See L.P.A. 1925, s. 1(7), under which the exercise of a power creates an equitable interest. See *Re Rank's ST* [1979] 1 WLR 1242. *See* POWER.

appointor. *See* APPOINTMENT, POWER OF.

apportionment. Division into parts which are proportionate to interests and rights of parties, See Apportionment Act 1870; and L.P.A. 1925, s. 140. Where a duty arises to convert assets of a hazardous and wasting nature in the interests of a remainderman, trustees must apportion between capital and income ("equitable apportionment"). See *Howe* v *Lord Dartmouth* (1802) 7 Ves 137. *See* REMAINDER.

apprehension or prosecution, impeding. *See* IMPEDING APPREHENSION OR PROSECUTION.

apprentice. A person bound by contract to serve and learn from a master who, in turn, undertakes to instruct him in a trade or profession. The contract must be in writing or by deed, and is usually signed also by the parent or guardian. It is binding on a minor if beneficial to him. See *Dunk* v *George Waller & Son* [1970] 2 QB 163.

approbate and reprobate. Phrase referring to a person who, taking a benefit under an instrument, must either accept or reject the instrument as a whole. *Qui approbat non reprobat* (q.v.). See *Codrington* v *Codrington* (1875) 45 LJ Ch 660; *Express Newspapers* v *News (UK) Ltd* [1990] 3 All ER 376.

appropriation. 1. Allocation of a sum of money for expenditure. An "appropriation in aid" refers to a transaction whereby a government department receives money from a source other than the Exchequer and is allowed to set it off against expenses. The annual Appropriation Act gives legal force to Parliament's decisions on the Government's estimates. 2. Exercise of control over property.

appropriation, dishonest. *See* DISHONEST.

appropriation of payments. *See* PAYMENTS, APPROPRIATION OF.

approval, sale on. Where goods are delivered to a buyer on approval, or sale or return, the property passes to the buyer when he adopts the transaction, e.g., by signifying approval. If he does not signify approval or acceptance to the seller, the property passes to him if he retains the goods on the expiration of a fixed time or, if no time has been fixed, on the expiration of a reasonable time: S.G.A. 1979, s. 18. See *Poole* v *Smith's Car Sales Ltd* [1962] 1 WLR 744.

approvement. Common-law right of a lord of the manor to enclose waste lands over which his tenants exercised pasture rights. Approvement of a common now requires consent of the Secretary of State for the Environment, after a local inquiry. See L.P.A. 1925, s. 194, as amended.

approximation of laws of EEC. Under the Treaty of Rome 1957, members of the EEC agree that the activities of the Community shall include "the approximation of laws of Member States to the extent required for the proper functioning of the Common Market": art. 3(*b*). *See* EEC.

appurtenant. Belonging to; necessary to the enjoyment of a thing. Annexed to a hereditament (q.v.) by an act of parties or statute, e.g., a right of way (which can generally be claimed by express grant or prescription (q.v.)). "An appurtenant right must be related to the needs or use of the dominant tenement. For this reason an exclusive right to grazing, or taking timber, or fishing without limit, cannot exist as appurtenant to another property": *Anderson* v *Bostock* [1976] Ch 312. See also *Hill* v *Cabras* (1987) 54 P & C R 42.

a priori. From cause to effect; from previous assumptions.

aqua cedit solo. Water passes with the soil. Ownership of water generally goes with that of the soil below.

arbitration. The settling of a dispute by an arbitrator. Where arbitrators cannot agree they may appoint an "umpire". The decision of an arbitrator is known as an "award". Procedure on arbitration is based on the ordinary rules of English law. An award may be enforced, with leave of the High Court, as an order of the court. Where so directed by the High Court, an arbitrator or umpire must state, in the form of a special case for the opinion of the High Court, an award or question of law arising. See the Arbitration Acts 1950, 1975, 1979; Consumer Arbitration Agreements Act 1988; O. 73; *Antaios Cia Naviera SA* v *Salen Rederierna AB* [1984] 3 All ER 229; *Aden Refinery* v *Ugland Management Co* [1987] QB 650; *Geogas SA* v *Trammogas Ltd* [1991] 1 WLR 776. A specialised form of county court procedure is also called arbitration but is outside the Arbitration Acts. *See* SMALL CLAIMS.

arbitration agreement. An agreement in writing, including an agreement contained in an exchange of letters or telegrams, to submit to arbitration present or future differences capable of settlement by arbitration: Arbitration Act 1975, s. 7(1).

arbitration agreement, domestic. An agreement that does not provide for arbitration in a foreign state, and to which the parties are neither nationals of nor habitually resident in a foreign state: Arbitration Act 1979, s. 3(7).

arbitration and interest. An arbitrator had no common law jurisdiction to award interest for late payment: *President of India.* v *La Pintada Compania* [1985] AC 104. See now power conferred by Arbitration Act 1950, s. 19 A (added by A.J.A. 1982, s. 15, Sch 1, Part IV).

arbitration award, judicial review of. The confirmation, variation, setting aside of the award, or its remission to the reconsideration of the arbitrator or umpire, by the High Court: Arbitration Act 1979, s. 1.

arbitration clause. "It embodies the agreement of both parties that, if any dispute arises with regard to the obligations which one party has undertaken to the other, such dispute shall be settled by a tribunal of their own constitution": *Heyman* v *Darwins Ltd* [1942] AC 356.

arbitration convention award. "An award made in pursuance of an arbitration agreement in the territory of a State, other than the UK, which is a party to the New York Convention [on the Recognition and Enforcement of Foreign Arbitral Awards 1958]": Arbitration Act 1975, s. 7(1). See *Govt of Kuwait* v *Snow and Partners* [1984] AC 426; *Hiscox* v *Outhwaite* [1991] 3 WLR 297.

arbitrator. A disinterested person selected by agreement of contesting parties (or by the court) to hear and settle some disputed question between them. See Arbitration Acts 1950–1979; C.L.S.A. 1990, s. 99 (arbitration by official referee).

arbitrator, quasi-. *See* QUASI-ARBITRATOR.

arbitrators, appointment of. Appointment may be by: mutual consent of the parties to an arbitration agreement; nomination by a third person, e.g., the president of a professional body; the court.

Archbishop. Head of the clergy in a province. His jurisdiction is within his diocese and throughout the province, in which he acts as superior ecclesiastical judge. The two Archbishops in England are Canterbury and York. See Ecclesiastical Jurisdiction Measure 1963; Patronage (Benefices) Measure 1986, s. 39(1).

Arches, Court of. *See* COURT OF ARCHES.

arguendo. In the course or by way of argument; by way of hypothetical illustration.

argumentative affidavit. An affidavit including an indirect argument on the relation of the alleged facts to the essence of the matter in question. See O. 41, r. 5. *See* AFFIDAVIT.

armchair principle. A rule of construction (q.v.) applied to wills. "You may place yourself, so to speak, in [the testator's] armchair, and consider the circumstances by which he was surrounded when he made his will to assist you in arriving at his intention": *Boyes* v *Cook* (1880) 14 Ch D 53.

armed. "An ordinary English word and, ordinarily it involves either physically carrying arms or it would involve proof that to a defendant's knowledge arms were immediately available. It is not necessary to prove an intent to use those arms if the situation should require it": *per* Tucker J in *R* v *Jones* [1987] 1 WLR 692. See Firearms Act 1968; *R* v *Kelt* [1977] 1 WLR 1365.

Armed Forces. Royal Navy, Royal Marines, regular army and regular air force, and any reserve or auxiliary force of those services called out on permanent service or called into actual service or embodied: Customs and Excise Management Act 1979 s. 1(1). See the Armed Forces Acts 1986, 1991.

arm's length, at. 1. Out of reach of personal influence. 2. Conduct of negotiations in a strict formal manner. See, e.g., *Stanton* v *Drayton Commercial Investment Co* [1983] 1 AC 501.

arraign. To bring the named accused to the bar of the court so that the indictment (q.v.) can be read to him and he can be asked to plead to it. Unless the defendant is mute, insane or refuses to plead, he must plead personally to the arraignment. "It is only after arraignment, which concludes with the plea of accused to the indictment, that it is known whether there will be a trial, and, if so, what manner of trial": *R* v *Vickers* [1975] 2 All ER 945. *See* PLEADINGS.

arrangement, deeds of. Under the Deeds of Arrangement Act 1914 (as amended by Ins.A. 1986), which refers to arrangements between the debtor and assenting creditors before bankruptcy proceedings are instituted, registration is necessary, e.g., where an assignment has been made for the benefit of creditors generally. A deed which is not registered within seven days of execution is generally rendered void as against the purchaser of any land relating to it or affected by it unless registered under L.C.A. 1972, s. 7(2).

arrangement, voluntary, company. Proposals made under Ins.A. 1986, Part I, by a company's directors to its creditors for a composition (q.v.) in satisfaction of its debts or a scheme of arrangement of its affairs: s. 1. Meetings summoned under s. 3 decide whether to approve the arrangement, with or without modifications: s. 4.

array. A body of jurors.

arrears. Money remaining unpaid, in relation to a debt, after the agreed time for payment.

arrest. To restrain and detain a person by lawful authority. "Whether or not a person has been arrested depends not on the legality of the arrest but on whether he has been deprived of his liberty to go where he pleases": *Spicer* v *Holt* [1977] AC 987. See *Hart* v *Chief Constable of Kent* [1983] RTR 484.

arrestable offence. An offence for which the sentence is fixed by law or for which a person may be sentenced to imprisonment for five years, and, specifically, an offence under enactments such as the Customs and Excise Management Act 1979, s. 1(1), Official Secrets Acts 1911 and 1920, S.O.A. 1956, ss. 14, 22, 23, Th. A. 1968, ss. 12(1), 25(1): see P. & C.E.A. 1984, s. 24(1), (2). Any person may arrest without a warrant anyone committing such an offence or anyone whom he reasonably suspects to be committing such an offence: s. 24(4).

arrestable offence, serious. An offence specified under P. & C.E.A. 1984, Sch. 5 Part I (e.g., treason, murder, manslaughter, rape) or under an enactment mentioned in Part II (e.g., hostage-taking, carrying firearms with criminal intent): s. 116(1). Any other arrestable offence is "serious" only if its commission leads, or is intended to lead, to e.g., serious harm to State security, serious injury, financial loss, interference with investigation of offences, death: s. 116(3), (6).

arrest and warrant. Arrest may be made *with* a warrant (q.v.), i.e., by order for arrest. Arrest *without* warrant ("summary arrest") is permissible in the exercise of the common law power of arrest (q.v.), in relation to arrestable offences (q.v.) or where otherwise authorised by statute (e.g., Town Police Clauses Act 1847, s. 28—see *Wills* v *Bowley* [1983] 1 AC 57). See P. & C.E.A. 1984, s. 17; *Abbassy* v *CPM* [1990] 1 All ER 123.

arrest, common law power of. Constables and private citizens have a power of arrest without warrant where: a breach of the peace (q.v.) was committed in front of the arresting person; the arrestor reasonably believed that a breach of the peace would be committed in the immediate future, although none had been committed; a breach of the peace had been committed and it was reasonably feared that it would be renewed: *R* v *Howell* [1982] QB 416. *See* ARREST; ARREST AND WARRANT.

arrest conditions, general, and non-arrestable offences. Under P. & C.E.A. 1984, s. 25, a constable may arrest a person for a "non-arrestable" offence if it appears that service of a summons is impracticable or inappropriate and at least one of the conditions under s. 25(3) applies, e.g., the person's name is unknown and cannot be readily ascertained or there are reasonable grounds for believing that arrest is necessary to prevent the person suffering or causing physical harm or causing loss or damage to property.

arrested development of mind. This may be classified as follows: 1. *Severe abnormality*, when the patient's state includes subnormality of intelligence and is of such a nature or degree that he is incapable of living an independent life or guarding himself against serious exploitation. 2. *Subnormality*, when the patient's state is one (not amounting to severe subnormality) including subnormality of intelligence and which requires or is susceptible to medical treatment or other special care. See M.H.A. 1983.

arrest for questioning by police. *See* QUESTIONING BY POLICE.

arrest, malicious. Arrest (in civil cases) effected maliciously and without reasonable cause.

arrest of judgment. The move by an accused person between conviction and sentence that judgment be not given because of defects in the indictment. It forms no bar to a new indictment. *See* INDICTMENT.

arrest of ship. Judicial process of securing maritime claims against a shipowner (see O. 75). It begins with the issue of a writ *in rem*, executed by the Admiralty Marshal, affixed to the ship's mast, following which the Marshal has custody of the arrested property. See, e.g., *The World Star* [1986] 2 Lloyd's Rep 274; *The Sea Friends* [1991] 2 Lloyd's Rep 1991.

arrest or prosecute, discretion to. *See* DISCRETION TO ARREST OR PROSECUTE.

arrest, powers of private persons to. Very limited powers are available under some statutes and in the case of arrestable offences (q.v.). Following such an arrest (colloquially called a "citizen's arrest"), the person arrested must be taken before a police officer or magistrate as soon as reasonably practicable: *John Lewis & Co* v *Tims* [1952] AC 676. See P. & C.E.A. 1984,

s. 24(4), (5); *R* v *Self* (1992) The Times, 10 Mar (precondition of citizen's arrest is an offence committed).

arrest, reasonable grounds for. "The circumstances of the case should be such that a reasonable man acting without passion or prejudice would fairly have suspected the person of having committed the offence": *per* Lord Devlin in *Shaaban Bin Hussein* v *Chang Fook Kam* [1964] 3 All ER 1626.

arrest, resisting. Refusal to submit to arrest. "It is the corollary of the right of every citizen to be free from arrest that he should be entitled to resist arrest unless the arrest is lawful": *Christie* v *Leachinsky* [1947] AC 573. See also *R* v *Spencer* (1863) 3 F & F 857.

arrest, search upon. Power to search a person to ascertain the property he has on him lies with the custody officer (q.v.) in a police station: see P. & C.E.A. 1984, s. 54(6).

arrived ship. "Before a ship can be said to have arrived at a port she must, if she cannot proceed immediately to a berth, have reached the position within the port where she is at the immediate and effective disposition of the charterer": *per* Lord Reid in *The Johanna Oldendorff* [1974] AC 479 (the so-called "Reid test"). See *Bulk Transport Ltd* v *Seacrystal Shipping Ltd* [1987] 1 WLR 1565.

arson. The common law offence of arson (maliciously and voluntarily burning the dwelling house of another) was abolished under the Criminal Damage Act 1971, s. 11(1). By s. 1(3), offences committed under s. 1 are charged as arson. See *R* v *Aylesbury Crown Court, ex p Simmons* [1972] 3 All ER 574; *R* v *Cooper* [1991] Crim LR 324.

articles. Clauses or rules in a document, e.g., articles of partnership or clerkship (binding a person to serve as an articled clerk).

articles of association. *See* ASSOCIATION, ARTICLES OF.

artificial insemination by donor. Known also as AID. Introduction of semen into the uterus by other than natural means. Where, as the result of the artificial insemination of a woman who at the time was a party to a marriage and was inseminated with the semen of some person other than the other party to the marriage, then, unless it is shown that the other party did not consent to the insemination, the child will be treated in law as the child of the parties to the marriage: F.L.R.A. 1987, s. 27(1). For the case of unmarried couples, see Human Fertilisaton and Embryology Act 1990, s. 28.

artificial person. A body, e.g., a corporation (q.v.) recognised by law as having rights and duties. Known also as a "juristic person". See I.A. 1978, s. 5, Sch. 1; *Lee* v *Lee's Air Farming Ltd* [1961] AC 12; *Bumper Development Corp.* v *CPM* [1991] 4 All ER 638. *See* NATURAL PERSON.

ascertained goods. Goods identified and agreed upon when a contract is made. See S.G.A. 1979, s. 16; *The Elafi* [1982] 1 All ER 208. *See* UNASCERTAINED GOODS.

asportation. Carrying away with a view to stealing. An essential feature of larceny (q.v.) in which the slightest removal sufficed: *R* v *Walsh* (1824) 1 Moo 14.

assault. A crime and a tort resulting from an act by which any person directly, negligently, intentionally, or possibly recklessly, causes another to apprehend reasonably the immediate application to himself of unlawful physical violence: *Fagan* v *Metropolitan Police Commissioner* [1969] 1 QB 439. Example: where X advances towards Y, shakes his fist, threatening to beat Y there and then, so that Y is put in fear of immediate violence. The term is often used to include battery, in which case it is an offence under O.P.A. 1861. Common assault (and battery) are summary offences: C.J.A. 1988, s. 39. Assault and battery are separate statutory offences: *DPP* v *Little* [1992] 1 All ER 299. For assault as a tort, see *Stephens* v *Myers* (1830) 4 C & P 349. See also *DPP* v *Majewski* [1977] AC 443; *R* v *Gladstone Williams* [1987] 3 All ER 411; *DPP* v *Taylor* [1992] 1 All ER 299. *See* BATTERY; BODILY HARM, GRIEVOUS.

assault, consent and. *See* CONSENT AND ASSAULT.

assault, indecent. *See* INDECENT ASSAULT.

Assembly. An institution of the EEC (q.v.), known as the European Parliament (q.v.).

assembly, public. *See* PUBLIC ASSEMBLY.

assent. Agreement. "The instrument or act whereby a personal representative effectuates a testamentary disposition by transferring the subject-matter of the disposition to the person entitled to it": *Re King's WT* [1964] Ch 542. Executors and administrators (qq.v.) may transfer interests in realty and leaseholds (qq.v.) by means of an assent in writing: A.E.A. 1925, s. 36.

Assent, Royal. *See* ROYAL ASSENT.

assent, vesting. *See* VESTING ASSENT.

assessment. The act of determining or apportioning. Used in relation to damages (q.v.), liability to tax, etc.

assessors. Persons with specialist knowledge appointed to assist the court, e.g., in Admiralty business. They generally take no part in making decisions. See S.C.A. 1981, s. 70; O. 33, r. 6; County C.A. 1984, s. 3, as amended by C.L.S.A. 1990, s. 14; *The Savina* [1976] 2 Lloyd's Rep 26.

assets. Physical property or rights which have a value in monetary terms. 1. The assets of a business include: *current assets*, e.g., stock, cash; *fixed assets*, e.g., machinery, goodwill. Under Cos.A 1985, Sch 4, para 77, fixed assets were defined as those intended for use on a continuing basis in the company's activities; current assets are those not intended for such use. (See I.C.T.A. 1988, s. 742(9); T.C.G.A. 1992, chap. II.) 2. The assets of a deceased person consist of the property available for the payment of his debts and liabilities, and include, e.g., his property, subject to the general power of appointment (q.v.) which he exercised by will; entailed property held by him: A.E.A. 1925, s. 32.

assets, administration of. *See* ESTATES, ADMINISTRATION OF.

assets, distribution of. *See* DISTRIBUTION OF COMPANY ASSETS.

assets, marshalling of. *See* MARSHALLING.

assets, wasting. *See* WASTING ASSETS.

assign. 1. To transfer property to another by assignment (q.v.). Used specifically in relation to the transfer of a reversion or lease (qq.v). 2. An assignee (q.v.). For covenants not to assign, see, e.g., *Field* v *Barkworth* [1986] 1 WLR 137; Landlord and Tenant Act 1988 (imposing a qualified duty on the landlord to consent to assignment); *Midland Bank* v *Chart Enterprises* [1990] 44 EG 68. See *Crago* v *Julian* [1992] 1 All ER 744.

assignee. A person to whom an assignment is made.

assignment. 1. *Legal.* Under the L.P.A. 1925, s. 136, as amended, debts and other legal choses in action (q.v.) may be assigned. The assignment must be absolute, in writing, followed by express notice in writing to the debtor or trustee. Assignment of contractual rights consists of the transfer from B to C of the benefit of one or more obligations that A owed to B. See *Linden Garden Trust Ltd* v *Lenesta Ltd* (1992) The Times, 27 Feb. 2. *Equitable.* An assignment which does not comply with requirements of a legal assignment. It need not be in writing if intention is clear. 3. *By operation of law.* A contract may be assigned automatically by operation of law, e.g., on bankruptcy and on death. *See* NOVATION.

assignment of lease. *See* LEASE, ASSIGNMENT OF.

assignor. A person who transfers property rights or powers (e.g., the freehold interest or freehold reversion) to another by assignment.

assistance, writ of. Obsolete writ used by Court of Chancery to enforce order for possession of land. Replaced by writ of possession (see O. 46, r. 3).

assisting offenders. "Where a person has committed an arrestable offence, any other person who, knowing or believing him to be guilty of the offence or of some other offence, does without lawful authority or reasonable excuse any act with intent to impede his apprehension or prosecution shall be guilty of an offence": C.L.A. 1967, s. 4(1).

assize. 1. A statute or ordinance, e.g., Assize of Clarendon 1166. (The term was derived from the *session* of King and Council.) 2. Assize Courts tried criminal cases under commissions of oyer and terminer (q.v.). They were abolished under the Courts Act 1971, s. 1.

assize, petty. Procedure introduced by Henry II, enabling justices in eyre to grant a remedy for loss of seisin (q.v.).

associated employers. Any two employers are treated as associated if one is a company of which the other (directly or indirectly) has control, or if both are companies of which a third person (directly or indirectly) has control: T.U.L.R. (C.)A. 1992, s. 297; *Umar* v *Pliastar* [1981] ICR 727.

association, articles of. A document which regulates a company's internal affairs, consisting of regulations governing the rights of members *inter se* and the conduct of the company's business, e.g., the appointment and powers of directors. Table A (q.v.) may be used as the articles of a company limited by shares. Articles are subject to the memorandum of association (q.v.) and cannot give any power not given by the memorandum. They can be altered by special resolution at a general meeting: Cos.A. 1985, ss. 7–9. See Cos.A. 1989, s. 128. Any alteration must benefit the company as a whole: *Greenhalgh* v *Arderne Cinemas Ltd* [1951] Ch 286. When registered, the articles and memorandum of association form a contract binding members to the company: see *Hickman* v *Kent Sheep-Breeders Association* [1951] 1 Ch 881. See *Cane* v *Jones* [1980] 1 WLR 1451. *See* COMPANY.

association clause. A clause in a company's memorandum of association (q.v.) in which the subscribers declare that they wish to be formed into a company and agree to take the number of shares opposite their names.

association, memorandum of. A document (see Cos.A. 1985, s. 2) which regulates a company's external activities and constitution, and which must be drawn up on the formation of a company. It states the company's name, objects, registered office, domicile, amount of company's nominal capital, number and amount of shares, etc. It can be varied by special resolution: Cos.A. 1985, s. 4, but the alteration must be confirmed by the court if a dissentient minority petitions: Cos.A. 1989, s. 110. See also Cos.A. 1989, s. 108 (company's capacity not limited by its memorandum), s. 110. *See* COMPANY NAME.

assumpsit. He has undertaken. 1. "A voluntary promise made by word": *Termes de la Ley*. 2. A common law action for damages abolished by virtue of the J.A. 1925, brought for breach of contract not under seal. *See* INDEBITATUS ASSUMPSIT.

assurance. 1. "That which operates as a transfer of property": *Re Ray* [1896] 1 Ch 468. 2. A contract which guarantees payment of a sum on the happening of a specified event which must happen sooner or later, e.g., death. *See* LIFE ASSURANCE.

assured shorthold tenancy. An assured tenancy (q.v.) which is a fixed-term tenancy granted for a term certain of not less than 6 months; and in respect of which there is no power for the landlord to determine the tenancy at any time earlier than 6 months from the beginning of the tenancy and in respect of which an appropriate notice has been served: H.A. 1988, s. 20. For assured agricultural occupancies, see 1988 Act, ch. III.

assured tenancy. Tenancy under which a dwelling-house is let as a separate dwelling, if the tenant (or each of the joint tenants) is an individual and occupies the dwelling-house as his only or principal home, and the tenancy is not excluded under s. 1(1)(c): H.A. 1988, s. 1. "Dwelling-house" may be a house or part of a house: s. 45. Security of tenure is conferred by s. 5: landlord must serve a notice seeking possession and obtain a county court order. "Old-style" assured tenancies created under H.A. 1980 are converted under H.A. 1988 into the "new-style" assured tenancies.

asylum. 1. A refuge, an inviolable place of retreat and relative security. 2. In international law may be *territorial* (granted by a state on its own territory), or *extra-territorial* (granted in respect of, e.g., consular premises, legations). 3. An establishment for the detention and care of sufferers from mental disease: Mental Treatment Act 1930, s. 20(1). Now referred to as "mental hospital": See the M.H.A. 1983, Part II.

asylum, political. *See* POLITICAL ASYLUM.

at sea. Phrase used, e.g., relating to privileged wills (q.v.), by which a mariner or seaman "being at sea" may make an informal will. "At sea" has been given an extended meaning so as to include, e.g., a Merchant Navy apprentice on leave between voyages and due to rejoin his ship – *In b Newland* [1952] P 71. See also *In b Rapley* [1983] 1 WLR 1069.

attachment. 1. Arrest under a writ of attachment, e.g., because of disobedience relating to a court order. Generally replaced by punishment for contempt. See O. 52. 2. Enforcement of direction to pay money, by attachment of earnings order. See Attachment of Earnings Act 1971 (amended by A.J.A. 1982, ss. 53–54 and F.L.R.A. 1987, Sch. 2); Maintenance Enforcement Act 1991, Sch. 2. A "consolidated attachment order" can be made under s. 17 for payment of two or more judgment debts. 3. Attachment of debts relates to procedure in garnishee proceedings (q.v.). See O. 49, r. 1.

attainder. "When a man hath committed a felony or treason and judgment is pronounced upon him": Cowel. The property of one who was attaint was forfeited, but this was abolished under the Forfeiture Act 1870.

attempt, common law offence of. Performance of an act which may be regarded as a movement to the commission of an offence and which cannot reasonably be interpreted as having any other objective than the commission of the offence: *R* v *Button* [1900] 2 QB 597. Abolished under Criminal Attempts Act 1981, s. 6(1).

attempt, intention and. "In any case where (a) apart from this subsection a person's intention would not be regarded as having amounted to an intent to commit an offence; but (b) if the facts of the case had been as he believed them to be, his intention would be so regarded, then [for the purposes of s. 1(1) of this Act] he shall be regarded as having had an intent to commit that offence": Criminal Attempts Act 1981, s. 1(3). See *R* v *Khan* [1990] 2 All ER 783.

attempt, statutory offence of. "If with intent to commit an offence to which this section applies, a person does an act which is more than merely preparatory to the commission of the offence, he is guilty of attempting to commit the offence": Criminal Attempts Act 1981, s. 1(1). Applies to any offence which, if completed, would be triable as an indictable offence (q.v.) except: conspiracy; aiding and abetting; assisting offenders or accepting consideration for not disclosing information about an arrestable offence: s. 1(4). A person may be guilty of attempting to commit an offence even though the facts are such that the commission of the offence is impossible: s. 1(2). See *R* v *Shivpuri* [1987] AC 1; *R* v *Gullefer* [1990] 3 All ER 882; *R* v *Ball* (1990) 90 Cr App R 378; *R* v *Jones* [1990] 1 WLR 1057 (old case law of no help in construing the 1981 Act).

attendance. In relation to a "letting with board or attendance", which does not constitute a protected tenancy (q.v.), means "service personal to the tenant provided by the landlord in accordance with his covenant for the benefit or convenience of the individual tenant for his use or enjoyment of the demised premises": *Palser* v *Grinling* [1948] AC 291.

attendance allowance. Non-contributory benefit payable (under S.S. Contributions and Benefits Act 1992, s. 64) to those so disabled that they require constant attendance (which must be certified by an Attendance Allowance Board). For attendance allowance for terminally ill, see s. 66.

attendance centre. A place at which offenders under 21 were required to attend and given, under supervision, appropriate occupation or instruction, in pursuance of an order made under the C. & Y.P.A. 1969, s. 15(2A), (4); or the C.J.A. 1982, s. 17: C.J.A. 1991, ss. 6, 67.

attestation. The signature of a document by one who is not a party to it, but who is the witness to the signature of another. The W.A. 1837 requires the attestation of two witnesses. See also L.P. (Misc. Provs.) A. 1989, s. 1(3). See *Re Colling* [1972] 1 WLR 1440; and A.J.A. 1982, s. 17. *See* WILL, VALIDITY OF.

attorney. One appointed by another to act in his place. *See* POWER OF ATTORNEY.

Attorney-General. The chief law officer of the Crown and head of the English Bar. His duties include representing the Crown in legal proceedings and conducting some Crown prosecutions. He is usually a member of the House of Commons and has ministerial responsibility for the DPP, Crown Prosecution Service, Serious Fraud Office, Treasury Solicitor's Department. He may stay proceedings by *nolle prosequi* (q.v.). He may be a member of the cabinet. His consent is necessary in some cases before prosecution: see, e.g., Official Secrets Act 1911, s. 8. "As the guardian of the public interest, the

Attorney-General has a special duty in regard to the enforcement of the law . . . it is his duty to represent the public interest with complete objectivity and detachment": *A.-G. (ex rel McWhirter)* v *IBA* [1973] QB 629.

Attorney-General and relator actions. Where the A.-G. has refused his consent to relator proceedings in the civil courts, a private citizen who asserts that the public interest is involved by threat of a breach of the criminal law has no right to go to the civil courts for a remedy either by way of injunction or a declaration: *Gouriet* v *Union of Post Office Workers* [1978] AC 435. "That it is the exclusive right of the Attorney-General to represent the public interest . . . is not technical, nor procedural, not fictional. It is constitutional": *per* Lord Wilberforce. *See* RELATOR.

Attorney-General's References. The A.-G. may refer to the Court of Appeal (Criminal Division) points of law, following an acquittal after trial in the Crown Court: see C.J.A. 1972, s. 36(1). (The Court of Appeal may refer the point to the House of Lords if it appears that the House should consider it: s. 36(3).) "We hope to see this procedure used extensively for short but important points which require a quick ruling of this court before a potentially false decision of law has too wide a circulation in the courts": *per* Lord Widgery CJ (see *Re A.-G.'s Ref (No 1 of 1975)* [1975] QB 773).

attorney, grants to. *See* GRANTS TO ATTORNEY.

attorney, power of. *See* POWER OF ATTORNEY.

attornment. 1. The acknowledgment of one person that he holds goods on behalf of another: S.G.A. 1979, s. 45(3). 2. Agreement of an estate owner to become the tenant of one who has acquired the estate next in reversion or remainder. See *Regent Oil Co* v *J. Gregory Ltd* [1966] Ch 402.

auction. Public sale of property by an auctioneer to the highest bidder. See, e.g., Sale of Land by Auction Act 1867; S.G.A. 1979, s. 57. An *auctioneer* is one who is licensed to conduct sales by auction. A contract comes into existence as the result of an auctioneer's acts, when a bid is accepted and his hammer falls (or in other customary manner) and a bidder may retract his bid until that event. See *British Car Auctions* v *Wright* [1972] 1 WLR 1519; *Moore* v *Khan-Ghauri* [1991] 32 EG 63; Unfair Contract Terms Act 1977, s. 12(3). *See* MOCK AUCTION.

auctioneer's obligations. Stated in *Benton* v *Campbell, Parker & Co* [1925] 2 KB 410, as: warranting his authority to sell; warranting that he knows of no defect in his principal's title; undertaking to give quiet possession against the price received by him; undertaking that possession will be undisturbed by the principal or himself. See *Derbyshire CC* v *Vincent* (1990) The Times, 19 June.

audi alteram partem. Hear the other side. It is a principle of natural justice (q.v.) that no man should be condemned unheard. See, e.g., *Local Government Board* v *Arlidge* [1915] AC 120; *Ridge* v *Baldwin* [1964] AC 40.

audience, right of. Right to appear and conduct proceedings in court. Under C.L.S.A. 1990, s. 27, it may be exercised by a person who has a right of audience granted by an appropriate authorised body (e.g., General Council of the Bar); or who has no such right but has a right of audience under statute (e.g., County C.A. 1984, ss. 60, 61) or granted by the court in question; or where he is employed to assist in the conduct of litigation and the proceedings are in chambers in the High Court or a county court (and are not reserved family proceedings).

audit. Detailed inspection of accounts, usually by a person not employed within the organisation.

Audit Commission. Body, consisting of officers of the Commission or private accountants, set up under Local Government Finance Act 1982, s. 11, to take an audit of local authority accounts. Public notice must be given of the annual audit; the accounts are open to public inspection. See *Lloyd* v *McMahon* [1987] AC 625; *Bookbinder* v *Tebbit (No. 2)* [1992] 1 WLR 217.

auditor. A member of a recognised body of accountants who examines accounts. See Cos.A. 1985, ss. 236, 237; Cos.A. 1989, ss. 9, 25; F.S.A. 1986, Part I, Chap. XI. An auditor's report must be attached to a company's balance sheet: Cos.A. 1985, s. 238(3). It must be read at the general meeting and must be available for inspection by any member: Cos.A. 1985, s. 241(2). Appointment and duties of auditors must be in accordance with Cos. A. 1985, ss. 384–394, and Cos.A. 1989, ss. 118–123, Sch. 11. An auditor's duties are to prepare reports for company members; to acquaint himself with his duties under statute; to exercise reasonable care. See *Secretary of State for Trade and Industry* v *Hart* [1982] 1 All ER 817; *Caparo Industries plc* v *Dickman* [1990] 1 All ER 568; SI 1991/1566.

Auditor General. *See* COMPTROLLER.

auditor's standards. "His vital task is to see that errors are not made, be they errors of computation, or errors of omission or commission, or downright untruths . . . To perform this task properly he must come to it with an inquiring mind – not suspicious of dishonesty . . . but suspecting that someone may have made a mistake somewhere and that a check must be made to ensure that there has been none": *per* Lord Denning in *Fomento Ltd* v *Selsdon Ltd* [1958] 1 WLR 45. See *Re Gerrard* [1968] Ch 455. For auditors' rights, see Cos.A. 1989, s. 120.

authenticate. To make valid and effective by proof or by appropriate formalities as required by law.

authorised capital. The total amount of capital which a company is authorised by its memorandum of association (q.v.) to issue. Known also as "nominal" or "registered" capital. *See* COMPANY; ISSUED CAPITAL.

authorised securities. Securities in which trustees may invest under Tr.A. 1925. *See* INVESTMENT, TRUSTEES' POWERS OF.

authority. 1. Judicial decision or opinion expressed by an author of repute used as grounds of a statement of law. 2. Rights bestowed by one person on another allowing full performance of an act. 3. A body exercising powers, e.g., a local authority (q.v.).

automatism. "An act done by the muscles without any control by the mind, such as a spasm, a reflex action or a convulsion, or an act done by a person who is not conscious of what he is doing, such as an act done whilst suffering from concussion or whilst sleepwalking" (q.v.): *Bratty* v *A.-G. for Northern Ireland* [1963] AC 386. Actions resulting from a state of automatism are involuntary and, as such, not generally punishable. Where automatism is due to mental disease, the defence is known as "insane automatism" (see *R* v *Burgess* [1991] 2 WLR 1206) and the M'Naghten Rules (q.v.) apply; in such a case the burden of proof is on the accused. See *Roberts* v *Ramsbottom* [1980] 1 All ER 7 (unsuccessful defence to negligence); *Broome* v *Perkins* [1987] Crim LR 271; *R* v *Hennessy* [1989] 1 WLR 287.

autonomic legislation. Legislation by a body which has independent power to legislate for its own members, e.g., The Law Society, General Medical Council.

autonomy. 1. Independence, 2. Power of self-government. 3. Power of an association which is not a State to make law for itself.

autopsy. *See* POST-MORTEM.

autrefois acquit. Formerly acquitted. A plea in bar that the accused has been acquitted previously of the same offence. "The test to establish the plea is (1) that defendant had been previously acquitted of the same offence, or (2) that he could have been convicted at the previous trial of the offence with which he is subsequently charged, or that the two offences are substantially the same . . .": *Re Wilson* [1948] 1 WLR 680. It is for the judge to decide the issue: C.J.A. 1988, s. 122. See *DPP* v *Porthouse.* [1989] RTR 177. *See* NEMO DEBET BIS VEXARI.

autrefois convict. Formerly convicted. A plea in bar that the accused has been previously tried and convicted by a court of competent jurisdiction for the same offence. The offence with which he is charged must be the same, or practically the same, offence as that with which he was previously charged. See *Connelly* v *DPP* [1964] AC 1254 (in which the plea was considered extensively by the House of Lords); *Iremonger* v *Vissenga* [1976] Crim LR 524; *R* v *Green* [1992], The Times, 14 July.

autre vie. The life of another. A tenant *pur autre vie* is a tenant for the life of another, as where A grants land to B "during the life of C". Exists only in equity. *See* CESTUI QUE VIE.

available market. Phrase used in S.G.A. 1979, s. 50(3), providing that where there is an available market for goods, the measure of damages for breach of contract is prima facie the difference between the contract price and the market price at the date of the breach. See *Lazenby Garages Ltd v Wright* [1976] 1 WLR 459; *Shearson Lehman Hutton Ltd v Maclaine Watson Ltd (No.2)* [1990] 3 All ER 723.

available on request. A reference in a written contract to its being subject to "the general conditions available on request", suffices to incorporate into that contract the terms contained in a current edition of those conditions. See *Smith v S Wales Switchgear* [1978] 1 All ER 18.

aval. Guarantee for payment. See *G & H Montage v Irvani.* [1989] FLR 390; *Banco Atlantico SA. v British Bank of the Middle East* [1990] 2 Lloyd's Rep 504.

average. Derived from *averia* (damage). Used in contracts for carriage of goods by sea to refer to apportionment of loss. 1. *General average loss* is caused by an act which occurs where an extraordinary sacrifice is voluntarily and rea-sonably made so as to preserve property, e.g., jettison of cargo. The loss is borne rateably by all those interested: Marine Insurance Act 1906, s. 66. 2. *Particular average* arises where the property is damaged by an accident not suffered for the general benefit, e.g., loss of a ship's boat. The loss remains where it falls.

averment. Allegation or affirmation made in pleadings (q.v.).

a vinculo matrimonii. From the bond of matrimony. A decree for the dissolution of a marriage, formerly pronounced by the ecclesiastical court. See DIVORCE.

avoidance. Setting aside; making null or void.

avoidance and evasion of tax. See TAX AVOIDANCE AND EVASION.

avulsion. Removal, by the sudden and perceptible action of water, of soil from one person's land and its deposit on another's. Ownership of such soil does not change, as is general in the case of accretion (q.v.).

award. See ARBITRATION.

B

B. Baron (judge of the Court of Exchequer (q.v.)).

backed for bail. A warrant issued by a magistrate can be endorsed with a direction that the person named shall, on arrest, be released on bail (q.v.) on specified terms. See M.C.A. 1980, s. 117; and C.L.A. 1977, s. 38, as amended. *See* WARRANT.

bad debt. A debt which, seemingly, cannot be recovered. See Value Added Tax Act 1989, s. 22; Finance Act 1990, s. 11.

bad faith. Characterised by dishonesty. See *Cannock Chase DC* v *Kelly* (1977) 36 P & CR 219.

bail. *Bailler* = to deliver. Release of a person arrested on his giving security or accepting specified conditions. A person arrested may be granted bail under a duty to surrender to custody (q.v.). He may be required to provide a surety to secure his surrender: ss. 3, 8. On withholding of bail he may apply to the Crown Court or High Court: s. 5(6). See also C.J.A. 1967; Courts Act 1971; P.C.C.A. 1973; and M.C.A. 1980; C.J.A. 1988, s. 153 (court must give reasons when granting bail in cases of murder, manslaughter, rape). Bail need not be granted if the court is satisfied that there are substantial grounds for believing that the defendant, if released, would fail to surrender to custody, or would commit an offence while on bail or interfere with witnesses: 1976 Act, Sch. 1, para. 2. See S.C.A. 1981, s. 81 (as amended by C.J.A. 1982, s. 29) for the High Court's powers to grant bail; C.J.A. 1988, s. 154; *Murphy* v *DPP* [1990] 2 All ER 390.

bail, continuous. Direction by the magistrates' court, where the accused is remanded on bail, with or without sureties, instructing him to appear at every time and place to which the proceedings may be adjourned from time to time: Bail Act 1976: M.C.A. 1980, s. 128.

bailee. *See* BAILMENT.

bailee, unconscious. Where a defendant becomes possessed of goods belonging to a plaintiff through a third party's mistake, and the defendant believes that the goods were his, or is not aware that they belonged to anyone but himself, he can be described properly as an "unconscious bailee", and before dealing with the goods he has a duty to use a sufficient standard of care in all the circumstances to ascertain that they were his own: *AUX Ltd* v *EGM Solders Ltd* (1982) The Times, 7 July.

bailiff. Originally "an officer that belongeth to a manor, to order the husbandry": *Termes de la Ley*. Now a person employed by a sheriff (q.v.) to serve and execute writs (q.v.) and processes. See Courts Act 1971, s. 22; SI 1992/729.

bail in criminal proceedings. "Bail grantable in or in connection with proceedings for an offence to a person who is accused or convicted of the offence, or bail grantable in connection with an offence to a person who is under arrest for the offence or for whose arrest for the offence a warrant (endorsed for bail) is being issued": Bail Act 1976, s. 1(1).

bailment. The delivery of goods by one person (the "bailor") to another (the "bailee") so that they might be used for some specified purpose, upon a condition that they shall be redelivered by the bailee to, or in accordance with the specified directions of, the bailor, or kept until he reclaims them. Examples: deposit of goods in a railway luggage office; pawning of goods. The bailee is under a duty to take reasonable care of the goods and to return them in accordance with the terms of the contract of bailment. See *Coggs* v *Barnard* (1703) 2 Ld Ray 909;

Clough Mill Ltd v *Martin* [1985] 1 WLR 111; *O'Sullivan* v *Williams* (1992) NLJ 717.

bailor. *See* BAILMENT.

bail with sureties. Granting of bail on condition that the person provides one or more sureties for the purpose of seeing that he surrenders to custody (q.v.): Bail Act 1976. In considering the suitability of a proposed surety, regard is had to his character, financial resources, proximity to the accused: s. 8(2).

balance. "What remains after something has been taken out of a fund": *Re Burke Irwin's Trusts* (1918) 1 IR 350.

balance of probabilities. Concept in the law of evidence relating to the standard of proof whereby the party upon whom the legal burden of proof rests is entitled to a verdict in his favour if he has established some preponderance of probability in his favour. See *Hornal* v *Neuberger Products* [1957] 1 QB 247. *See* STANDARDS OF PROOF.

balance sheet. A statement showing assets and liabilities of a business at a given date. A company's balance sheet must give a true and fair picture of the company at the end of the financial year. See Cos.A. 1985, s. 228(2). It must comply with requirements of Cos.A. 1985, Sch. 4, as amended. *See* COMPANY ACCOUNTS, PUBLICATION OF.

ballot. A system of voting involving secret votes. See, e.g., Representation of the People Act 1985; T.U.L.R.(C.)A. 1992 (right of union members to a ballot before industrial action); *Monsanto PLC* v *TGWU* [1987] 1 All ER 358; *Post Office* v *UCW* [1990] 3 All ER 199; *Code of Practice on Trade Union Ballots* 1990, 1991. *See* INDUSTRIAL ACTION; STRIKE.

banishment. Expulsion from the king's realm. See, e.g., 39 Eliz I c. 4, under which "dangerous rogues" could be banished.

bank. Financial institution engaged in the accepting of deposits of money, granting of credit (by loan, overdraft, etc) and other transactions such as the discounting of bills, dealing in foreign exchange, etc. See Banking Act 1987; *United Dominions Trust Ltd* v *Kirkwood* [1966] 2 QB 431. *See* BANK, AUTHORISED.

bank, authorised. Institution recognised by the Bank of England as satisfying certain criteria: see Banking Act 1987, ss. 8–18. Criteria (see Sch. 3) include: business directed by at least two individuals; directors to be fit and proper persons; business to be conducted in a prudent manner with integrity and appropriate skills; business possesses the prescribed minimum amount of net assets.

banker. One engaged in the business of banking. "The relation between a banker and a customer who pays money into the bank is the ordinary relation between debtor and creditor, with a super-added obligation, arising out of the custom of bankers to honour the customer's drafts": *Joachimson* v *Swiss Bank Corporation* [1921] 3 KB 110. For restrictions on use of banking names, see Banking Act 1987, Part III

bankers' books. Under Bankers' Books Evidence Act 1879, s. 3, a copy of an entry in a banker's book was received as prima facie evidence of such an entry and of the transactions and accounts recorded therein. By virtue of the Act of 1879, s. 9 (amended in 1979 and 1987), the expression includes ledgers, day books, cash books, account books and other records used in the ordinary business of the bank, whether in written form or kept on microfilm, magnetic tape, or other forms of retrieval mechanism. See *State of Norway's Application* [1987] QB 433; *Williams* v *Summerfield* [1972] 2 QB 513—permission granted to the police to inspect the bank accounts of an accused person. *See* BANKER'S DUTY OF SECRECY; EVIDENCE.

banker's customer. The term "signifies a relationship in which duration is not of the essence. A person whose money has been accepted by a bank on the footing that they undertake to honour cheques up to the amount standing to his credit is . . . a customer of the bank . . . irrespective of whether his connection is of short or long standing": *Commissioners of Taxation* v *English, Scottish and Australian Bank* [1920] AC 683. See *Redmond* v *Allied Irish Banks* [1987] FLR 307.

banker's customer's duty of care. A bank's customer owes no wider duty of care to the bank in the operation of a current account beyond a duty to refrain from drawing a cheque in a manner which facilitates fraud or forgery, and a duty to inform the bank of the forgery of a cheque drawn on his account as soon as he becomes aware of it. He is not under a duty to check his bank statements for unauthorised debit items. See *Tai Hing Cotton Mill Ltd v Liu Chong Hing Bank Ltd* [1986] AC 519; *Barclays Bank plc v Khaira* (1991) The Times, 19 Nov.

bankers' draft. *See* DRAFT.

banker's duty of secrecy. A bank has a legal obligation to keep a customer's affairs secret: see *Hardy v Veasey* (1868) LR 3 Exch 107; *Tournier v National Provincial and Union Bank of England* [1924] 1 KB 461. Disclosure may be compelled by process of law (see Bankers' Books Evidence Act 1879, s. 7); e.g., on application of any party to legal proceedings; service of a *subpoena duces tecum* (q.v.); where the bank's interests require disclosure. The customer may give express or implied consent to disclosure. *See* BANKERS' BOOKS.

banking instrument. Any cheque or other instrument to which the Cheques Act 1957, s. 4, applies; any document issued by a public officer intended to enable a person to obtain payment from a government department of a sum mentioned in the document; any bill of exchange or promissory note, postal order, money order, credit transfer, credit or debit advice.

Banking Supervision, Board of. Established under the Banking Act 1987, s. 2, to supervise aspects of the banking system. Consists of the Governor, Deputy Governor and an executive member, of the Bank of England and six independent members appointed by the Chancellor of the Exchequer: s. 2(2), Sch. 1.

bankrupt. "An individual who has been adjudged bankrupt and, in relation to a bankruptcy order it means the individual adjudged bankrupt by that order": Ins.A. 1986, s. 381(1). Essentially, an insolvent debtor whose estate will be administered and distributed under appropriate rules, following a direction of the court, for the benefit of his creditors.

bankrupt, creditor in relation to. A person to whom a bankruptcy debt (q.v.) is owed and, in relation to an individ-

ual to whom a bankruptcy petition relates, a person who would be a creditor in the bankruptcy if a bankruptcy order were made on that petition: Ins.A. 1986, s. 383(1).

bankruptcy. The legal processes related to insolvency. See Ins.A. 1986.

bankruptcy debt. Includes any debt or liability to which the bankrupt is subject at the commencement of the bankruptcy, any debt or liability to which he may become subject after the commencement of the bankruptcy by reason of any obligation incurred before the commencement of the bankruptcy, any amount specified in a criminal bankruptcy made against him: Ins.A. 1986, s. 382(1).

bankruptcy, discharge from. Discharge releases a bankrupt from all bankruptcy debts: Ins.A. 1986, s. 281, as amended by Ch. A. 1989, Sch. 11 and Child Support Act 1991, Sch. 5. A bankrupt is discharged automatically after 3 years from commencement of bankruptcy (2 years in the case of summary administration procedure). Where a person has previously been adjudicated bankrupt and was an undischarged bankrupt at any time in the period of 15 years ending with the commencement of bankruptcy, he must apply for discharge by order of the court (under s. 280): s. 279.

bankruptcy offences. A person guilty of any of these offences, which apply where the court has made a bankruptcy order on a bankruptcy petition, is liable to imprisonment or a fine or both: non-disclosure of all his property; concealment of any property or debt or books and papers; false statements; fraudulent disposal of property; absconding; fraudulent dealing with property obtained on credit; obtaining credit or engaging in business; failure to keep proper accounts; gambling or rash and hazardous speculation: see Ins.A. 1986.

bankruptcy order. "An order adjudicating an individual bankrupt": Ins.A. 1986, s. 381(2).

bankruptcy order, annulment of. The court may annul an order if it appears that it should not have been made, or, to the extent required by the rules, the expenses of bankruptcy have been paid or secured. The order may be annulled whether or not the bankrupt has been discharged. See Ins.A. 1986, s. 282, as amended.

bankruptcy petition. A request for a bankruptcy order (q.v.) to be made against an individual. It may be presented to the court by the individual himself, or a creditor, or the person bound by a voluntary arrangement approved under Ins.A. 1986, Part VIII. It may not be presented unless the debtor is domiciled in England or Wales, is personally present there on the day of presentation of the petition, or, at any time in the period of 3 years ending with that day he has been ordinarily resident, or has had a place of residence, in, or has carried on business in England or Wales. The petition may not be withdrawn without leave of the court. *See* CREDITOR'S PETITION; DEBTOR'S PETITION.

bankruptcy, priority of debts in distribution. Preferential debts (see Ins.A. 1986, s. 386) are paid in priority to other debts; they rank equally among themselves after bankruptcy expenses are paid in full, abating in equal proportions where the bankrupt's estate is insufficient to meet them. Debts which are neither preferential nor owed to a spouse rank equally between themselves and are paid, after preferential debts, in full, abating in equal proportions in the case of an estate insufficient to meet them. *See* INSOLVENCY, PREFERENTIAL DEBTS IN.

bankruptcy, statement of affairs in relation to. In the case of a bankruptcy order (q.v.) made otherwise than on a debtor's petition (see Ins.A. 1986, s. 272(2)), the bankrupt must submit to the official receiver (q.v.), within 21 days from the date of the order, particulars of creditors, debts, assets, other liabilities and such other information as may be prescribed. It is a contempt of court (q.v.) to fail to provide the statement: s. 288. For a company's statement of affairs, see s. 131.

bankruptcy, trustee in. Appointed by a general meeting of the bankrupt's creditors, or by the Secretary of State or the court: Ins.A. 1986 (see s. 292). The bankrupt's estate vests in the trustee immediately on his appointment taking effect: s. 306(1). Any property acquired by the bankrupt after the date of the bankruptcy order may be vested in the trustee: s. 307(1). For his powers, see s. 314, Sch 5.

bankrupt, official receiver and. Where a bankruptcy order has been made, the bankrupt is under a duty to deliver to the official receiver possession of his estate and all relevant books and papers. Failure to comply is a contempt of court (q.v.). See Ins.A. 1986, s. 291.

bankrupt, public examination of. Following a bankruptcy order, the official receiver may apply to the court for a public examination of the bankrupt in relation to his affairs, dealings, property and causes of his failure. Those who may participate include the official receiver, trustee, special manager of the bankrupt's estate and creditors who have tendered a proof in bankruptcy: Ins.A. 1986, s. 290.

bankrupt's estate. Comprises all property belonging to or vested in the bankrupt at the commencement of the bankruptcy. It does not include: tools, books, vehicles and other items of equipment necessary to him for personal use in employment, business or vocation; such clothing, bedding, furniture, household equipment necessary for his family's domestic needs; property held by the bankrupt on trust for any other person: Ins.A. 1986, s. 283, amended by H.A. 1988, s. 117. Any disposition of property made by a bankrupt during the period since the presentation of the petition is void, except when made with the consent of the court or subsequently ratified: s. 284.

bankrupt's property, seizure of. At any time after a bankruptcy order (q.v.) has been made, the court, on application of the official receiver or trustee, may issue a warrant for the seizure of property comprised in the bankrupt's estate, and to search for and seize property or documents: Ins.A. 1986, s. 365.

banns. Proclamation in church in the form of a public notice of an intended marriage. Banns must be published on three Sundays preceding the marriage. See Marriage Act 1949, ss. 5–14, amended by Marriage (Prohibited Degrees of Relationship) Act 1986; *Chard v Chard* [1956] P 259.

bar. 1. An impediment, as in bars to divorce (q.v.). 2. A place in court where a prisoner is stationed, or where barristers speak for their clients. 3. The English Bar is the professional body of barristers. 4. The profession of barrister.

Bar Council. The General Council of the Bar of England and Wales, created in 1894. Most of its functions were taken over in 1974 by the Senate of the Inns of Court and the Bar (q.v.). It is concerned with maintaining the standards of the Bar and with improvements in its services. It may make its own bye-laws and rules (for which judicial sanction is not required). See, e.g., C.L.S.A. 1991, s. 31 (rights of audience); *R v General Council of the Bar, ex p Percival* [1990] 3 WLR 323.

bare licensee. One who has been given permission to enter a place for his own purposes, so as not to be a trespasser. Example: X grants a gratuitous permission to Y to walk across X's field. Known also as a "mere licensee". See *Berg Homes v Grey* (1979) 253 EG 473. *See* LICENCE.

bare trust. A trust (q.v.) which requires the trustee to act as a mere repository of the trust property, with no active duties to perform, as where X devises property to Y in trust for Z. Y's only duty is to convey the legal estate (q.v.) to Z. Y is a "bare trustee". See *Christie v Ovington* (1875) 1 Ch D 279; Banking Act 1987, s. 106(1).

bargain. Agreement, contract (q.v.).

bargain and sale. A popular method of conveyancing in the sixteenth century, later abolished under L.P.A. 1925, s. 51. V, the vendor, contracted to sell land to P, the purchaser, and to receive the purchase price. V was said to have "bargained and sold" the fee simple (q.v.) to P, and V was considered seised to the use of P. Under the Statute of Uses 1535 P was considered to have the legal estate. This method was used to convey a legal estate without public formalities.

bargain, unconscionable. A catching bargain (q.v.).

bar, pleas in. when the indictment (q.v.) is put to the defendant, he can raise pleas alleging some reason why he should not be tried and maintaining that there should be an enquiry

forthwith into that reason. Examples: *autrefois acquit* (q.v.); *autrefois convict* (q.v.).

barratry. 1. Common law offence (common barratry) committed by one who frequently incited or maintained quarrels at law. Abolished under C.L.A. 1967. 2. Wrongs which prejudice a shipowner or charterer, committed wilfully by the master or crew of a ship. See *Shell International v Gibbs* [1983] 2 AC 375.

barring of entailed interest. Procedure whereby a tenant in tail puts an end to the fee tail (q.v.). A tenant in tail in possession, if of full age, may execute a deed which, in effect, converts the entail into a fee simple (q.v.): Fines and Recoveries Act 1833, s. 15. A tenant in tail whose interest is in remainder may, if of full age, convert the entail into a fee simple with the consent of protector of settlement (q.v.). A tenant in tail, of full age, whose interest is in remainder may, without the protector's consent, partially bar the entail (thus creating a base fee). L.P.A. 1925, s. 176, allows the devise or bequest of entails under specified conditions, so that, in effect, the beneficiary takes the fee simple absolute. See also Lim.A. 1980, s. 27. *See* BASE FEE.

barrister. A person called to the Bar by one of the Inns of Court (q.v.). His function is primarily that of an advocate and he has exclusive right of audience in certain types of judicial proceedings. He may not sue for fees, which are deemed to be in the nature of an honorarium: *Wells v Wells* [1914] P 157. See C.L.S.A. 1990, s. 61 (barrister's right to enter contract for provision of his services). He is immune from actions for negligence. "If a barrister is to be able to do his duty fearlessly and independently he must not be subject to the threat of an action for negligence": *Rondel v Worsley* [1969] 1 AC 191. See, for cases of claims in negligence in pre-trial work, *Saif Ali v Sydney Mitchell & Co* [1980] AC 198. For suspension in cases of misconduct, see *Re H.* [1981] 3 All ER 205. For discrimination by or in relation to barristers, see C.L.S.A. 1990, s. 64, modifying Sex Discrimination Act 1975, s. 35, and Race Relations Act 1976, s. 26.

barrister's cab-rank rule. A practising barrister is bound to accept any brief to appear before a court in the field in which he professes to practise at a proper professional fee, having regard to the length and difficulty of the case. Special circumstances such as a conflict of interest or the possession of relevant and confidential information may justify his refusal to accept a particular brief: see *Code of Conduct for the Bar*. For "double booking" (i.e., acceptance of briefs in different trials beginning on the same day), see *Re A Barrister* (1989) The Independent, 3 Mar.

barrister's duty to the court. "He has a duty to the court which is paramount. It is a mistake to suppose that he is the mouthpiece of his client to say what he wants: or his tool to do what he directs. He is none of these things. He owes allegiance to a higher cause . . . the cause of truth and justice . . . He must disregard the most specific instructions of his client if they conflict with his duty to the court": *per* Lord Denning in *Rondel* v *Worsley* [1969] 1 AC 191. See *Orchard* v *SE Electricity Board* [1987] 3 WLR 102.

barrister's fees. There is no contractual relationship between an instructing solicitor and a barrister, so that payment of fees is a "matter of honour", not a legal obligation. (The barrister, however, may refer a defaulting solicitor to The Law Society.) "A counsel can maintain no action for his fees, which are given not as a salary, but as a mere gratuity which a counsellor cannot demand without doing wrong to his reputation": Blackstone. See HONORARIUM.

barrister's professional obligation. "A barrister cannot pick or choose his clients. He is bound to accept a brief from any man who comes before the courts. No matter how great a rascal he may be. No matter how given to complaining. No matter how undeserving or unpopular his cause. The barrister must defend him to the end": *per* Lord Denning in *Rondel* v *Worsley* [1969] 1 AC 191.

barter. The practice of exchanging goods for goods or services: see *La Neuville* v *Nourse* (1913) 3 Camp 351. Excluded from S.G.A. 1979. For part-barter, see *Simpson* v *Connolly* [1953] 1 WLR 911.

base fee. "That estate in fee simple into which an estate in tail is converted where the issues in tail are barred, but persons claiming estates by way of remainder or otherwise are not barred": Fines and Recoveries Act 1833, s. 1. A base fee may be converted into fee simple absolute (q.v.) in the following ways: (1) Fresh disentailing deed. (2) Owner of base fee in possession may enlarge it into fee simple by will. (3) Union of base fee with remainder in fee. (4) Lapse of time: Lim.A. 1980, s. 27. *See* BARRING OF ENTAILED INTEREST.

basic norm. *See* LAW, PURE THEORY OF.

bastard. An illegitimate child, i.e., one born out of lawful wedlock. See now F.L.R.A. 1987, Part I.

battered wife. "A woman who has suffered serious or repeated physical injury from the man with whom she lives": from Minutes of Evidence of Select Committee on Violence in Marriage, 1974. *See* INJUNCTIONS, MATRIMONIAL.

battery. A crime and a tort involving the actual, intended (or negligent) and direct use of unlawful physical force on a person without his consent (and with hostility: *Wilson* v *Pringle* [1986] 2 All ER 440). It includes even the slightest force; no actual harm need result; it is actionable *per se*. A summary offence under C.J.A. 1988, s. 39. Consent, self-defence, lawful and reasonable chastisement may be defences. In common usage "assault" (q.v.) is often a synonym for battery; in law they are distinct. See *Kenlin* v *Gardiner* [1967] 2 QB 510; *Fagan* v *Metropolitan Police Commissioner* [1969] 1 QB 439; *Freeman* v *Home Office (No. 2)* [1984] QB 524.

battle, trial by. Norman procedure, in essence an appeal to the "God of battles" to bring victory to the rightful party. The plaintiff and defendant, or their "champions", fought, the outcome being considered as a divine judgment. Abolished in 1819 after an attempt to claim procedure was made in *Ashford* v *Thornton* (1818) 1 B Ald 405.

beach. The foreshore (q.v.). It includes land above the high-water mark which is in apparent continuity with the beach at high-water mark, or which possesses a character more akin to the foreshore than the hinterland: *Tito* v *Waddell (No 2)* [1977] Ch 106.

bearer. *See* BILL OF EXCHANGE.

bearer shares. Shares (q.v.) for which no register of ownership is kept by the issuing company. They must pass physically from seller to buyer and are usually lodged with a bank.

Beddoe order. Leave granted to trustees by the court so as to enable them to sue or defend and to be reimbursed out of the trust estate: *Re Beddoe* [1893] 1 Ch 547; *Midland Bank Trust Co* v *Green* [1980] Ch 590.

begin, right to. *See* RIGHT TO BEGIN.

behaviour, breakdown of marriage and. "Behaviour is something more than a mere state of affairs or a state of mind . . . [it is] action or conduct by the one which affects the other. Such conduct may take the form of an act or omission . . . and, in my view, it must have some reference to the marriage": *per* Baker J in *Katz* v *Katz* [1972] 3 All ER 219. See Mat C. A. 1973, s. 1(2)(b); *Bannister* v *Bannister* (1980) 10 Fam Law 240; *Richards* v *Richards* [1984] AC 174; *Buffery* v *Buffery* [1988] 2 FLR 365. *See* UNREASONABLE CONDUCT.

bench. Used in a collective sense to refer to the judges or magistrates in a court. A barrister who becomes a judge is said to be "raised to the bench".

Benchers. The governing body of each of the Inns of Court (q.v.). They are judges or senior members of the Bar (q.v.) and have control over the admission of students and calls to the Bar. Appeal from their decisions is to the Lord Chancellor and judges of the High Court who sit as "visitors" (q.v.).

bench warrant. Order for the immediate arrest of a person issued by a court, e.g., for failure to appear on breach of the condition of bail (q.v.). *See* WARRANT.

beneficial freehold owner. One who, holding the fee simple absolute (q.v.) in law and equity, is the "sole owner" of land.

beneficial interest. The equitable interest of a beneficiary (q.v.). Thus, if land is held by X in trust for Y, X has the legal estate, Y has the beneficial interest.

beneficiary. 1. One entitled for his own benefit, i.e., for whose benefit property is held (e.g., by a trustee). Known also as *cestui que trust.* (q.v.). 2. One who receives a gift under a will.

beneficiary, remedies of. Rights of a beneficiary arising where a trustee departs from the terms of a trust (q.v.) or where he is in breach of some duty imposed on him by statute or equity, including an order for an account; injunction; damages; tracing order. *See* TRACING TRUST PROPERTY.

benefit of clergy. Privilege formerly exempting clergymen from the criminal process. A "criminous cleric" was brought before the King's court, tried by a church court and handed back to the King's court for punishment: Constitutions of Clarendon 1164. In 1352 the privilege was allowed to secular clerks, the test being literacy (usually a test of ability to read the so-called "neck verse" – the first verse of Psalm 51 – "Have mercy upon me, O God"). Abolished by C.L.A. 1827 and Felony Act 1841.

benefits, contributory. Classified under S.S. Contributions and Benefits A. 1992, s. 20 as: unemployment benefit, sickness benefit, invalidity benefit, maternity allowance, widow's benefit, retirement pensions, and child's special allowance. See also S.S. Administration Act 1992. Non-contributory benefits include: attendance allowance, severe disablement allowance, invalid care allowance, disability living allowance, guardian's allowance, certain classes of retirement pensions (categories C and D) and age additions: s. 63.

benefits, false representations. If a person, for the purpose of obtaining benefits under S.S.A. 1973, or S.S. Contributions and Benefits Act 1992, or S.S. Administration Act 1992, makes a statement or representation which he knows to be false or produces documents which are false in a material particular, he shall be guilty of an offence: S.S.Administration Act 1992, s. 112.

benefits, overpayment. Where, as a result of a claimant's misrepresentation, fraudulent or otherwise, an overpayment has been made, the Secretary of State is entitled to recover: S.S.Administration Act 1992, s. 71.

benevolent society. A society established for a benevolent or charitable purpose under the Friendly Societies Act 1974.

Benjamin order. Where personal representatives (q.v.) may experience delay in winding up and distributing an estate because they are not sure whether a missing beneficiary (q.v.) is alive or not, the court may make an order authorising distribution on the assumption that, e.g., the beneficiary is dead: *Re Benjamin* [1902] 1 Ch 723. See *Re Green's WT* [1985] 3 All ER 455.

bequeath. To dispose of personal property by will.

bequest. A gift by will of personal property, known also as a "legacy" (q.v.).

bereavement, damages for. A claim for damages for bereavement, under the Fatal Accidents Act 1976, may be brought for the benefit of the wife or husband of the deceased: s. 1A (inserted by A.J.A. 1982, s. 3). The right of a person to claim under s. 1A does not survive for the benefit of his estate on his death: Law Reform (Misc. Provs.) Act 1934, s. 1A (inserted by A.J.A. 1982, s. 4). See *Hicks* v *S. Yorks Police* [1992] 1 All ER 690.

besetting. *See* WATCHING AND BESETTING.

best evidence rule. "The judges and sages of the law have laid it down that there is but one general rule of evidence, the best that the nature of the case will allow": *Omychund* v *Barker* (1745) 1 Atk 21. The rule required, in effect, that the best or most direct evidence of a fact should be adduced, or its absence accounted for. Example: the best evidence of the existence of the contents of a letter is its production in court. The rule no longer applies as the court admits all relevant evidence: *Kajala* v *Noble* (1982) 75 Cr App R 149. *See* EVIDENCE.

bestiality. The offence of buggery (q.v.) committed with a beast. See *R* v *Higson* (1984) 6 Cr App R (S) 20.

bet. Something staked on the outcome of a contingency. Often used as a synonym for wager. See, e.g., Betting, Gaming and Lotteries Acts 1963–1985; Lotteries and Amusements Act 1976; Betting and Gaming Duties Act 1981; Finance Act 1987. It did not include a stake hazarded in the course of gaming: Gaming Act 1968, s. 53. Sch. 2;

City Index v *Leslie* [1991] 3 All ER 180 (betting on stock market). *See* GAMING; LOTTERY; WAGERING CONTRACT.

betterment. 1. An increase in the value of real property because of beneficial public works nearby. 2. Prospective developmental value of land.

beyond reasonable doubt. *See* PROOF BEYOND REASONABLE DOUBT.

beyond the seas. Outside the UK, Channel Islands and the Isle of Man. See *Rover International Ltd* v *Cannon Film Sales Ltd* [1987] 1 WLR 1597. A defendant's absence "beyond the seas" no longer prevents time running for purposes of limitation of actions (q.v.).

bias. Lacking impartiality. "Its proper significance is to denote a departure from the standard of even-handed justice which the law requires from those who occupy judicial office": *Franklin* v *Minister of Town and Country Planning* [1948] AC 87. See *R* v *Mulvihill* [1990] 1 All ER (alleged bias of judge); *R* v *Gough* (1992) The Times, 3 June (bias of jury); *R* v *Romsey Justices ex p Gale* [1992] 156 JPN 202 (appearance of bias).

bias, rule against. An implied requirement of natural justice (q.v.), namely, that no man shall be a judge in his own cause. See, e.g., *Herring* v *Templeman* [1973] 3 All ER 569.

bid. To make an offer for some thing which is being sold by auction (q.v.). A bid may generally be retracted before acceptance: S.G.A. 1979, s. 57(2). Where a sale is subject to a reserve price and bids fail to reach that level, the highest bid can be treated as a "provisional bid" which may be accepted later if the seller agrees: *Willis & Son* v *British Car Auctions* [1978] 1 WLR 438.

bid, referential. *See* REFERENTIAL BID.

bigamy. The offence committed by a married person who "shall marry any other person during the life of the former husband or wife, whether the second marriage shall have taken place in England or Ireland or elsewhere": O.P.A. 1861, s. 57. It is triable either way (M.C.A. 1980, Sch. 1, para. 5(*i*)). To prove bigamy, the prosecution must show: proof of the first marriage of the accused; its validity; its subsistence at the date of the second marriage (q.v.); proof of a second marriage by the accused with some person other than the lawful spouse. See *R* v *Curgerwen* (1865) 1 LR 1 CCR 1; *R* v *Tolson* (1889) 23 QBD 168.

bilateral discharge. Applies to executory contracts. Discharge may take the form of: extinction of the contract; extinction and substitution of a new agreement; partial dissolution of the contract, e.g., by modification of terms. *See* CONTRACT.

bill. 1. Bill in Parliament. A draft Act which is discussed by Parliament and is known as an Act (q.v.) when it has received the Royal Assent (q.v.). It may be *private* (e.g., referring to a particular person or town) or *public* (relating to the whole country) or *hybrid* (q.v.). A *Private member's bill* is introduced by a MP not acting for the government. A *personal bill* (now rare) relates to the estates, property, status of an individual (see e.g., Marriage Enabling Bills). 2. An account delivered to a debtor by a creditor. 3. Formerly, a written petition complaining of a wrong, e.g., a bill in equity, seeking redress – the forerunner of the writ (q.v.). 4. A written instrument, e.g., bill of exchange (q.v.).

bill of costs. Statement of account furnished by a solicitor to his client, relating to work done on his client's behalf. See *Bartletts de Reya* v *Byrne* (1983) 127 SJ 69. *See* COSTS.

bill of exchange. An unconditional order in writing, addressed by one person to another, signed by the person giving it, requiring the person to whom it is addressed to pay on demand, or at a fixed or determinable future time, a sum certain in money to or to the order of a specified person or to bearer: B.Ex.A. 1882, s. 3(1). Person who gives the order to pay is the "drawer"; person to whom the order to pay is given is the "drawee"; person to whom the payment is to be made is the "payee".

bill of exchange, defect in title. The title of a person who negotiates a bill is defective when he obtained the bill, or the acceptance thereof, by fraud, duress, or force and fear, or other unlawful means, or for an illegal consideration, or when he negotiates it in breach of faith, or under such circumstances as amounted to a fraud: B.Ex.A. 1882, s. 29(2).

bill of exchange, discharge of. A bill of exchange is discharged when all the rights and liabilities attaching to it are nullified, in one of the following ways: by payment in due course; by renunciation; by cancellation; by material alteration; by delivery up. See B.Ex.A. 1882, ss. 59, 61–64.

bill of indictment. A bill which charges a person with an indictable offence and is signed by an officer of the court, can become an indictment (q.v.). It may be preferred by direction or with the consent of a High Court judge, or by direction of the Court of Appeal, or where a person is committed for trial by examining magistrates. See A.J. (Misc. Provs.) A. 1933, s. 2; Indictments (Procedure) Rules 1971, r. 4; *Practice Direction* [1990] 1 WLR 1633; *R* v *Raymond* [1981] 2 ER 246.

bill of lading. Document used in foreign trade, signed by the shipowner, master or other agent, stating that goods have been shipped on a named ship, and setting out the terms on which they have been delivered to and received by the shipowner. It acts as a document of title to the goods and is evidence of the contract for their carriage. It is not a fully negotiable instrument (q.v.). See Carriage of Goods by Sea Act 1992. For rights under shipping documents, see s. 2. For meaning of "contract of carriage," see s. 5(1).

Bill of Rights. An Act of 1688, providing that suspension of laws was illegal, that subjects had a right to petition the King, that parliamentary elections ought to be free, that debates in Parliament ought to be free, that excessive fines ought not to be imposed "nor cruel and unusual punishment inflicted", etc. See *R* v *Secretary of State for Home Affairs, ex p Herbage (No. 2)* [1987] QB 1077; *Rost* v *Edwards* [1990] 2 All ER 641.

Bill of Rights for UK. Suggested enactment of a "constitutional code of human rights" in UK based on the principle, *inter alia*, that it "would remove certain fundamental values out of the reach of temporary political majorities, governments and officials and into the realm of legal principles applied by the courts" (Cmnd 7009).

bill of sale. A document "given with respect to transfer of chattels used in cases where possession is not intended to be given": *Johnson* v *Diprose* [1893] 1 QB 512. It must be registered within seven days of making. An *absolute bill* is governed by Bills of Sale Act 1878; a *conditional bill* (e.g., by way of security) is governed by Bills of Sale Amendment Act 1882. See also Bills of Sale Acts 1890 and 1891; and *NV Slavenburg's Bank* v *Intercontinental Natural Resources* [1980] 1 All ER 955.

Bill, passage through Parliament. Stages are generally as follows: introduction into the Commons (unless Bill commences in the Lords); first reading (purely formal, not accompanied by debate); second reading (most important stage, calling for full debate); committee stage (in which Bill is considered in close detail); report stage (often purely formal); third reading (often without debate); consideration of Lords' amendments; Royal Assent (q.v.).

bill procedure, voluntary. Procedure whereby the prosecution applies to a High Court judge for leave to prefer a bill of indictment (q.v.) against an accused person, e.g., after refusal by the magistrates to commit. See A.J. (Misc. Provs.) A. 1933, s. 3(2)(b), and Indictments (Procedure) Rules 1971. Should be granted only where there is good reason to depart from normal procedure, and the interests of justice demand it: *Practice Direction (Court of Appeal)* (1991) 1 Jan. See *R* v *Manchester Crown Court, ex p Williams* (1990) 154 JP 589 (judge's decision to issue a voluntary bill may not be the subject of an application for judicial review (q.v.)).

bills in a set. Bills of exchange executed in duplicate, triplicate, etc. Payment of one part of a set discharges the other parts also: B.Ex.A. 1882, s. 71.

bind over. To require a person to enter into a bond or recognisance to perform or abstain from performing an act. See M.C.A. 1980, s. 115; *Howley* v *Oxford* (1985) 81 Cr App R 246; *R* v *Morpeth Ward Grand Justices ex p Joseland.* (1992) NLJ 312.

birth. Act of commencing existence separate from one's mother. *See* ABORTION; BORN ALIVE.

birth, attendance by persons at. A person other than a registered midwife or registered medical practitioner may not attend a woman in childbirth: Nurses, Midwives and Health Visitors Act 1979, s. 17(1).

birth certificate. A certified copy of an entry in the register. It is evidence of the birth stated therein: Births and Deaths Registration Act 1953, s. 34(6). *See* BIRTH, REGISTRATION OF.

birth, citizenship by. *See* CITIZENSHIP, BRITISH, ACQUISITION BY BIRTH OR ADOPTION.

birth, concealment of. "If any woman shall be delivered of a child, every person who shall by any secret disposition of the dead body of the said child, whether such child died before, at, or after its birth, endeavour to conceal the birth thereof, shall be guilty of a misdemeanour": O.P.A. 1861, s. 60. See *R* v *Opie* (1860) 8 Cox 332.

birth, proof of. Process of proving a person's birth by: production of the birth certificate; evidence of someone present at the birth; declaration of the deceased person against interest or in the course of duty. See Civil Evidence Act 1968; Births and Deaths Registration Act 1953; Ch. A. 1975, s. 93; P. & C.E.A. 1984, s. 68.

birth, registration of. Procedure, which must be completed within 42 days of birth, consisting of furnishing the following particulars: date, place of birth, name, surname and sex of child; name, surname, place of birth and occupation of father; name, surname, maiden surname, surname at marriage, place of birth of mother; mother's usual address; name, surname, qualification, address and signature of informant; registrar's signature. See Births and Deaths Registration Act 1953; National Health Service Act 1977, s. 124; F.L.R.A. 1987, Part V. For re-registration, see 1987 Act, s. 25; SI 1991/2275. *See* BIRTH CERTIFICATE.

blacking of goods. Refusal of employees, who are taking industrial action, to handle or work on materials supplied by the employer so as to evade the effects of that action.

blackleg. One who continues, or attempts to continue, his work while his colleagues are on strike (q.v.).

black-letter law. Colloquialism referring to statements of fundamental legal principles and details ("what the law is") as compared with discussions of "what the law ought to be".

blackmail. Originally payment for immunity from raids, levied by freebooters in the north of England. Now an offence under Th.A. 1968, s. 21(1): "A person is guilty of blackmail if, with a view to gain for himself or another or with intent to cause loss to another, he makes any unwarranted demand with menaces (q.v.) and for this purpose a demand with menaces is unwarranted unless the person making it does so in the belief (*a*) that he had reasonable grounds for making the demand *and* (*b*) that the use of menaces is a proper means of reinforcing the demand." See *R* v *Cutbill* (1982) 4 Cr App R (S.) 1; *R* v *Bevans* (1988) 87 Cr App R 64; *R* v *Hadjou* (1989) 11 Cr App R (S.) 29; *R* v *Christie* (1990) 12 Cr App R (S.) 540.

blank transfer. Transfer of shares executed without the transferee's name being filled in on the document of transfer. *See* SHARE.

blasphemy. The offence of denying, in a scandalous way, Christianity, the Bible, the Book of Common Prayer. The Blasphemy Act 1697 was repealed by C.L.A. 1967. It remains a common law offence. See *Bowman.* v *Secular Society Ltd.* [1917] AC 406; *R* v *Gott* (1922) 16 Cr App R 87. An intention to blaspheme is not required; the offence is committed by an insulting, immoderate, vilifying or offensive reference to God or Christianity: *R* v *Lemon* [1979] AC 617. See *R* v *Bow St. Magistrates ex p Choudhury* [1990] 3 WLR 986.

blight notice. Notice served on a prospective land-acquiring authority, in the case of a proposed land development plan, stating that the owner has genuinely and unsuccessfully attempted to sell the land for a reasonable price on the open market, and requiring the authority to purchase it. The authority must serve any counter-notice within two months. See T.C.P.A. 1990, s. 150.

block grant. Central government aid to local authorities, based on the difference between an authority's total expenditure and an assumed contribution from rates. See Local Government Finance Act 1988, s. 78.

blood relationship. The connection between persons descended from one or more common ancestors. Persons are said to be of the *whole blood* to one another if descended from the same pair of ancestors (e.g., X and Y, brothers, who have the same father and mother); of the *half blood* to one another if descended from only one common ancestor (e.g., X and Y, who have the same father but different mothers).

blood tests. 1. In some civil proceedings relating to paternity, the court may direct that a blood test be made to ascertain whether a party to the proceedings is or is not thereby excluded from being the father. See F.L.R.A. 1969, Part 3; F.L.R.A 1987, Sch. 2; *W* v *W.* (*No. 4*) [1964] P 67; *O* 112; P. & C.E.A. 1984, ss. 62, 63. 2. A person arrested under the Road Traffic Act 1972, ss. 6–12 (as substituted by Transport Act 1981, Sch. 8) could be obliged to provide a specimen of blood for a laboratory test. See, e.g., *Grix* v *Chief Constable of Kent* [1987] RTR 193; *Midland* v *DPP* [1990] RTR 201. See DNA PROFILING; PATERNITY, DECLARATION OF.

blue book. Government publication, e.g., a report of a Royal Commission. *See* PARLIAMENTARY PAPERS.

blue chip. A well-established company's shares which have a high status as investments. See *Re Kolb's Will Trusts* [1962] Ch 531.

blue pencil test. Phrase referring to severance (q.v.) of contract. "Severance can be effected when the part severed can be removed by running a blue pencil through it" without affecting the remaining part: *Attwood* v *Lamont* [1920] 3 KB 571.

board. As in "board and lodging". Within the Rent Act 1977, s. 7(1), it may be constituted by the provision of any quantity of food which is not *de minimis*, and which includes the ancillary services involved in preparation, and the provision of crockery and cutlery: *Otter* v *Norman* [1988] 3 WLR 32.

board meeting. Meeting of the directors of a company (q.v.) held for the despatch of business. Questions are decided by majority vote; the chairman has a casting vote. See Table A, art. 88.

bocland. Bookland. Land which, in pre-Norman Conquest times, was held by charter, handbook, or other written title.

bodily harm, grievous. Formerly interpreted to mean "some harm sufficiently serious to interfere with the victim's health or comfort": *R* v *Ashman* (1858) 1 F & F 88. See O.P.A. 1861, ss. 20, 47. In *DPP* v *Smith* [1961] AC 290 it was stated that there is "no warrant for giving the words 'grievous bodily harm' a meaning other than that which the words convey in their ordinary and natural meaning. 'Bodily harm' needs no explanation, and 'grievous' means no more and no less than 'really serious'." See also *R* v *Savage* [1991] 4 All ER 698. *See* MALICE; WOUNDING.

bodily harm, proof of. A verdict of assault occasioning actual bodily harm on a charge under O.P.A. 1861, s. 47, may be returned upon proof of an assault together with proof that actual bodily harm was occasioned by the assault. The prosecution must prove, for a charge of grievous bodily harm under s. 20, that defendant either intended or foresaw that his act would cause harm: *R* v *Savage* [1991] 4 All ER 698.

body corporate. "A succession or collection of persons having in the estimation of the law an existence and rights and duties distinct from those of the individual persons who form it from time to time": Co Litt 250a. Examples: a registered company; a local authority (q.v.); a body controlled by royal charter. See *Salomon* v *Salomon & Co Ltd* [1897] AC 22. *See* CORPORATION.

bomb hoax. It is an offence to place any article in any place or dispatch any article by post, rail or other means with the intention of inducing in some person a belief that it is likely to explode or ignite and cause personal injury or damage to property: C.L.A. 1977, s. 51(1). It is an offence to communicate information which is known to be false with the intention of inducing in a person a false belief that a bomb or other thing liable to explode or ignite is present in any place or location: s. 51(2). For penalties, see s. 51(4) as amended by C.J.A. 1991, s. 26; SI 1991/2208.

bona fide. In good faith; honestly.

***bona fide* holder for value.** *See* HOLDER IN DUE COURSE.

***bona fide* purchaser.** *See* PURCHASER FOR VALUE WITHOUT NOTICE.

bona vacantia. Ownerless goods. 1. Goods found with no apparent owner. In general they are deemed to belong to the first finder, except in the case of shipwrecks, treasure trove (q.v.) (which belongs to the Crown), etc. 2. Under A.E.A. 1925, the residuary estate of an intestate goes, in default of any person taking an absolute interest, to the Crown, Duchy of Lancaster or Cornwall, as *bona vacantia*. The Crown or Duchy may provide for the dependants of the intestate and for other persons for whom he might reasonably have been expected to make provision. See also Inheritance (Provision for Family Dependants) Act 1975, s. 24.

bond. 1. Agreement under seal whereby a person (the "obligor") binds himself to another (the "obligee") to perform or refrain from an action. It may be a "simple bond" – without condition, or a "common money bond" – given to secure payment of money. It binds the obligor's real and personal estate: L.P.A. 1925, s. 80. 2. An interest-bearing document based on a long-term debt, usually issued by corporations.

bond, performance. Bond usually given by a bank as a guarantee of satisfactory performance of a contract by a party. It is usually payable on demand without proof or condition. A "conditional bond" requires justification of the claim for payment. See *Tin's Industrial Co.* v *Kono Insurance* (1988) 4 Con LJ 157.

bondwashing. Practice whereby shares are sold with an accrued dividend and bought back as soon as the shares have gone ex dividend; hence payment of accrued dividend is treated as a capital gain, and not as income, so that tax advantages result. See I.C.T.A. 1988, s. 732; SI 1992/568.

bonus. That which is received over and above what is expected, e.g., a gratuity, an additional dividend.

bonus shares. A company deciding to finance expansion from reserves comprising undistributed profits may bring its issued capital (q.v.) into line with the capital it employs by issuing bonus shares to existing shareholders to the value of the additional capital. See the Cos.A. 1985, s. 88. *See* SCRIP.

book debt. A debt arising in due course of a business and due to its proprietor which would in the ordinary course of that business be entered in "well kept books relating to that business": *per* Buckley J in *Independent Automatic Sales* v *Knowles* [1962] 3 All ER 27. See *Northern Bank* v *Ross* [1990] BCC 883.

books of account. Documents and other records which must be prepared and kept by a company, including, e.g., a balance sheet (q.v.), profit and loss account, auditors' report, directors' report. See Cos.A. 1985, Sch. 4.

books, partnership. *See* PARTNERSHIP BOOKS, INSPECTION OF.

books, statutory. *See* STATUTORY BOOKS.

born alive. A child is considered to have been born alive (for purposes of the Infant Life (Preservation) Act 1929) when it exists as a live child, that is, breathing and living by reason of its breathing through its lungs alone, without deriving any of its living or power of living by or through any connection with its mother: see *R* v *Handley* (1874) Crim Law Cas 79. A foetus (q.v.) of 18–21 weeks *en ventre sa mère* (q.v.) which was incapable of breathing was not "a child capable of being born alive" within the 1929 Act, s. 1: *C. v S.* [1987] 1 All ER 1230; *Rance* v *Mid-Downes HA* [1991] 2 WLR 159.

borough. In early times a fortified town or castle. Later, a town or city incorporated by charter, with a corporation consisting of a mayor, aldermen and councillors. The title is no longer generally used. See L.G.A. 1972.

borough, English. Ancient mode of descent by which land in, e.g., Surrey, Sussex and localities of Nottingham, descended to the youngest son. Abolished under A.E.A. 1925.

borough quarter sessions. Court presided over by a Recorder (q.v.) and held four times a year. It had civil, criminal, original and appellate jurisdiction which passed to the Crown Court (q.v.) by virtue of the Courts Act 1971.

borrow. To obtain temporarily with the intention, or purpose, of returning to the lender. For borrowing and theft, see Th.A. 1968, s.6; *R* v *Bagshaw* [1988] Crim LR 321.

bote. 1. (Anglo-Saxon) graduated compensation for injury. 2. (Anglo-Saxon) contributions by landowners, e.g., brycg-bot – for repair of bridges, burhbot – for repair of fortresses. *See* ESTOVERS.

bottomry. Obsolescent term, meaning pledge of a ship and freight so as to secure a loan which allows a ship to continue its voyage. *Respondentia* is a pledge of the freight only. *See* HYPOTHECATION.

bought as seen. Phrase suggesting that the purchaser has bought what he had seen. When used in a sale which was not a sale by description, it confirms merely that the purchaser had seen the goods he had purchased, and does not exclude implied terms as to fitness or quality in respect of defects which could not be seen: *Cavendish-Woodhouse Ltd* v *Manley* (1984) 82 LGR 376.

boundaries, offences committed on. Where an offence is committed on the boundary between areas (e.g., of counties) or within five hundred yards of such a boundary, or in a harbour or river lying between such areas, the offence may be treated as having been committed in any of those areas: M.C.A. 1980, s. 3(1).

boundary. That which indicates or fixes some limit, e.g., a fence, wall. See *Lee* v *Barrey* [1957] 1 All ER 191. *See* HEDGE AND DITCH PRESUMPTION.

boundary commissions. Bodies set up under the House of Commons (Redistribution of Seats) Acts 1949 and 1958 (see Parliamentary Constituencies Act 1986, Sch. 1) one each for England, Scotland, N Ireland and Wales, each chaired by the Speaker (q.v.). They report to the Home Secretary on suggested electoral boundaries. See L.G.A. 1992, setting up the Local Government Commission, and abolishing the Local Government Boundary Commission.

boycott. To engage in an organised refusal to deal with a person or body, e.g., a manufacturer or supplier. See *Quinn* v *Leathem* [1901] AC 495.

breach. The infringing or violation of a right, duty or law.

breach, anticipatory. *See* ANTICIPATORY BREACH.

breach of close. Unlawful entry on another's land.

breach of confidence. See CONFIDENCE, BREACH OF.

breach of contract. The refusal or failure by a party to a contract to fulfil an obligation imposed on him under that contract, resulting from, e.g., repudiation of liability before completion, or conduct preventing proper performance. The contract is discharged where the breach results in the innocent party treating it as rescinded and where it has the effect of "depriving the party who has further undertakings still to perform of substantially the whole benefit which it was the intention of the parties as expressed in the contract as the consideration for performing those undertakings": *Hong Kong Fir Shipping Co v Kawasaki Kisen Kaisha* [1962] 2 QB 26. See *Photo Productions Ltd v Securicor Transport Ltd* [1980] AC 827 (discussion by the HL of the nature of fundamental breach).

breach of privilege. Actions which constitute a contempt of a parliamentary privilege (q.v.).

breach of promise of marriage. Failure to fulfil a promise to marry. Action for breach was abolished by the Law Reform (Misc. Provs.) Act 1970, s. 1(1). *See* ENGAGEMENT TO MARRY.

breach of statutory duty. See STATUTORY DUTY, BREACH OF.

breach of the peace. Offence (most commonly under P.O.A. 1936, s. 5 (now repealed)) committed whenever harm is actually done, or is likely to be done to a person, or in his presence to his property, or wherever a person is in fear of being so harmed through assault, affray, riot, unlawful assembly or other disturbance: *R v Howell* [1982] QB 416. "The possibility of a breach must be real to justify any preventive action": *per* Skinner LJ in *Moss v Maclachlan* (1985) 149 JP 167. See *Lamb v DPP* [1990] 154 JPN 172; P. & C.E.A. 1984, s. 17(6). *See* FEAR OR PROVOCATION OF VIOLENCE.

breach of trust. The result of some improper act or omission relating to the administration of a trust or the interests of the beneficiaries (q.v.) arising under it. It may arise from failure to carry out the trustee's general duties or some abuse of his powers. A trustee is generally liable for any loss caused directly or indirectly to the trust property and to the beneficiaries' interests as a result of the breach. For the court's power to relieve a trustee from the consequences of a breach of trust, see Tr.A. 1925, s. 61; see also Lim.A. 1980, s. 21. *See* TRUST.

break clause. An option to terminate a clause in a lease (q.v.) which may be exercised after a certain period, e.g., at the end of the tenth and twentieth years of a 30-year lease. Time is of the essence in serving notice to terminate.

breakdown of marriage. A court hearing a petition for divorce (q.v.) should not hold that the marriage has broken down irretrievably unless satisfied by the petitioner of one or more of the following facts: that the respondent has committed adultery (q.v.) and the petitioner finds it intolerable to live with the respondent; that the respondent has behaved in such a way that the petitioner cannot reasonably be expected to live with the respondent; that the respondent has deserted the petitioner for a continuous period of two years immediately prior to the presentation of the petition; that the parties to the marriage have lived apart for at least two years immediately preceding the presentation of petition and that the respondent consents to the grant of a decree; that the parties have lived apart for a continuous period of at least five years immediately preceding the petition: Mat.C.A. 1973, s. 1(2).

breaking and entering. Term referring to the felony of burglary committed by one who, in the night, broke and entered a dwelling-house with intent to commit any felony therein: Larceny Act 1916, s. 25, repealed by Th.A. 1968. *See* BURGLARY.

breathalyser. Device consisting of a measuring bag or some other device (e.g., Alcometer) used in the administration of a breath test to a motorist by a constable who has reasonable cause to suspect him of having alcohol in his body or having committed a road traffic offence while his vehicle was in motion. See Road Traffic Act 1988, s. 11(2). For prescribed limits, see s. 11(1). *See* PRESCRIBED LIMITS OF ALCOHOL.

breath test. A constable in uniform may require a person to provide a specimen of breath for a breath test if he has reasonable cause to suspect him of having alcohol in his body while driving or attempting to drive or in charge of a motor vehicle on a road or other public place, or if the person has been driving, attempting to drive or in charge of a motor vehicle, or if he is reasonably believed to have been involved in an accident: Road Traffic Act 1988, s. 6. See e.g., *DPP* v *Pearman* (1992) The Times, 27 Mar.

brewster sessions. Annual meeting of licensing justices to consider applications for licences, renewals, etc. relating to the sale of alcoholic liquor. Must be held within the first two weeks of February; Licensing Act 1964, Sch. 1, as amended. See Licensing Act 1988, s. 14. *See* LICENSING OF PREMISES.

bribery. The offence of taking, or bestowing, or promising, a price, reward or favour intended to influence the judgment or conduct of a public official. In its legal sense it implies corruption: *Gardner* v *Robertson*, 1921 SC 132. See e.g., Public Bodies Corrupt Practices Act 1889; Representation of the People Act 1983, s. 113. *See* CORRUPTION.

bridging loan. Generally a short-term advance made by a bank to a customer pending the receipt by the customer of funds from some other source. See C.C.A. 1974, s. 58(2)(*b*).

bridleway. Way over which the public have right of way on foot, on horseback or leading a horse, with or without a right to drive animals along the highway: Horses (Protective Headgear etc.) Act 1990, s. 3.

brief. Written instructions to a barrister (q.v.) from a solicitor (q.v.) relating to the representing of a client in legal proceedings. Usually includes a narrative of the facts, copies of documents, etc.

British Commonwealth. *See* COMMONWEALTH.

British dependent territories citizenship. *See* CITIZENSHIP, BRITISH, DEPENDENT TERRITORIES.

British overseas citizen. *See* CITIZEN, BRITISH OVERSEAS.

British possession. Any part of Her Majesty's dominions outside the UK; and where parts of such dominions are under both a central and a local legis-

lature, all parts under the central legislature are deemed, for the purposes of this definition, to be one British possession: I.A. 1978, Sch. 1.

British protected person. One who is a member of any class of persons declared to be British protected persons by an Order in Council or by virtue of the Solomon Islands Act 1978: B.N.A. 1981, s. 50(1). See also s. 32(1); *Motala* v *A.-G.* [1991] 3 WLR 903. Applies to former protectorates, protected states or UK trust territories. The status is not transmissible.

British protectorates. Territories which, although not colonies and not part of HM Dominions, were governed in internal and external affairs by Britain.

broadcasting. The act of making public by means of radio or television transmission. See Telecommunications Act 1984, s. 6(5); C.J.A. 1987, s. 11(15); Copyright, Designs and Patents Act 1988, s. 6(1). A broadcast programme is publication in permanent form for purposes of defamation (q.v.) under the Defamation Act 1952. For "cable programme service", see 1988 Act, s. 7.

Broadmoor. An institution, classified as a "special hospital" (q.v.), providing treatment for patients (formerly known as criminal lunatics) with dangerous, violent or criminal propensities, under conditions of special security. See M.H.A. 1983, Part III.

brokage, marriage. Contract by which one person undertakes, in consideration for a money payment, to procure a marriage for another. Generally illegal and void: *Hermann* v *Charlesworth* [1905] 2 KB 123.

broker. 1. "One who makes a bargain for another, and receives a commission for so doing": *per* Cleasby J in *Fairlie* v *Fenton* (1876) LR 5 Exch 169. 2. "In relation to securities, means a member of the Stock Exchange who carries on his business in the UK and is not a market maker (q.v.) in securities of the kind covered": Finance Act 1986, Sch. 18. Known also as "broker-dealer".

brokerage. Payment or commission earned by a broker. Sum paid to a person by a company (q.v.) under authority in the articles for placing shares (q.v.).

brothel. "A place resorted to by persons of both sexes for the purpose of prostitution": *Singleton* v *Ellison* [1895] 1 QB 607. Under the S.O.A. 1956, ss. 33, 36, it is an offence to keep or manage a brothel or knowingly to permit the whole or part of premises to be used for the purposes of habitual prostitution. See *Stevens* v *Christy* (1987) Cr App R 249; *Elliott* v *DPP* (1989) The Times, 19 Jan; *Jones* v *DPP* (1992) The Times, 4 June. See also S.O.A. 1967, s. 6. *See* DISORDERLY HOUSE

brutum fulmen. An empty threat.

budget. An estimate of government expenditure and revenue for the ensuing financial year presented to Parliament by the Chancellor of the Exchequer (q.v.), usually every April, Budget proposals are embodied in a Finance Bill.

budgeting loans. Interest-free loans intended to meet intermittent expenses (e.g., for household equipment) of those on income support (q.v.).

buggery. "It is an offence for a person to commit buggery with another person or animal": S.O.A. 1956, s. 12(1). The act consists of sexual intercourse *per anum* by a man with a man or woman, or sexual intercourse *per anum* or *per vaginam* by a man or a woman with an animal. (There is no such offence as "rape *per anum*": *R* v *Gaston* (1981) 73 Cr App R 164.) Under the S.O.A. 1967, s. 1, it is not an offence for a man to commit buggery with another man provided that the parties consent, that they have attained the age of 21 and that the act was done in private. See *R* v *Tierney* (1990) 12 Cr App R (S.) 216 (buggery of animal); *R* v *Wood* [1991] Crim LR 926.

bugging. Electronic surveillance (q.v.).

building. "Its ordinary and natural meaning is, a block of brick or stone work covered in by a roof": *Moir* v *Williams* [1892] 1 QB 264. For purposes of Building Act 1984, the word means any permanent or temporary building and, unless the context otherwise requires, it includes any other structure or erection of whatever kind or nature: s. 121(1). See T.C.P.A. 1990, s. 336. For "building operations", see Planning and Compensation Act 1991, s. 13. See *Denetower Ltd* v *Toop* [1991] 1 WLR 945. *See* MESSUAGE.

building lease. 1. Lease made partly in consideration of some person erecting new or additional buildings or improving or repairing buildings: S.L.A. 1925, s. 44. A building lease for 999 years may be made by a mortgagor or mortgagee in possession or tenant for life (q.v.): L.P.A. 1925, s. 99; S.L.A. 1925, s. 41. 2. Lease made by a landlord generally for 99 years, at a rent known as "ground rent", the lessee covenanting to erect buildings.

building scheme. Where land is developed, as in the case of a building scheme, e.g., for a housing estate, the developer can require the purchaser of a plot to enter into a restrictive covenant (q.v.) based upon a mutually-perceived common intention, so as to maintain the character of the estate. See *Gilbert* v *Spoor* [1983] Ch 27.

building society. A society incorporated under Building Societies Act 1986 (or repealed enactments, e.g., Building Societies Act 1962) whose "purpose or principal purpose is that of raising, primarily by the subscriptions of members, a stock or fund for making to them advances secured on land for their residential use": s. 5. See I.C.T.A. 1988, s. 476.

building society advances. Advances made to members secured by a mortgage (q.v.) of a legal estate, or an equitable interest in land in England, Wales or N. Ireland, or a heritable security over land in Scotland, and, for such purposes, the society may hold land with the right of foreclosure: Building Societies Act 1986, s. 10(1). Advances may be made secured on land overseas: s. 14.

Bullock order. Where the plaintiff joins two defendants in the alternative because he is unsure as to which one is liable, he may be able to obtain an order against the unsuccessful defendant to pay the costs (q.v.) of the successful defendant: *Bullock* v *London General Omnibus Co* [1907] 1 KB 264. The plaintiff is not entitled to such an order as of right. See O. 15, r. 4.

burden of adducing evidence. The onus on the plaintiff or prosecutor of adducing sufficient evidence (q.v.) to satisfy the court that a hearing ought to continue. Known also as "evidential burden".

burden of proof. The obligation of proving facts. Used in a number of senses, e.g.: *general burden* (proving a case); *specific burden* (proving an individual issue); *evidential burden* (adducing sufficient evidence in support of a disputed fact) (see *Jayasena* v *R* [1970] AC 618). In general the burden lies on the party who substantially asserts the affirmative of the issue (i.e., the plaintiff or prosecution). It may shift when the plaintiff or prosecution establishes a prima facie case. See Prevention of Corruption Act 1916, s. 2; *Woolmington* v *DPP* [1935] AC 462; *R* v *Edwards* [1975] QB 27; *Morris* v *London Iron and Steel Co* [1988] QB 439. *See* PROOF.

burden of proof, shifting of. Phrase used in the law of evidence to indicate the moving of the burden of proof (i.e., the obligation to prove facts) from one side to the other, as where, e.g., there exists a disputable presumption of law in favour of one party (so that his adversary must rebut it) or where the subject-matter of one party's allegation is peculiarly within the opponent's knowledge (so that the latter must rebut the allegation). See, e.g., *DPP* v *Williams* [1989] Crim LR 382; *R* v *Desai* (1992) The Times, 3 Feb. *See* EVIDENCE.

burglary. *Burge-breche* = breach of a borough. Under Th.A. 1968, s, 9(1), a person is guilty of burglary if "he enters any building or part of a building as a trespasser and with intent to commit any such offence as is mentioned in sub-s.(2) [stealing, inflicting grievous bodily harm, etc.]; or, having entered any building or part of a building as a trespasser he steals or attempts to steal anything in the building or part of it or inflicts or attempts to inflict on any person therein any grievous bodily harm." "Aggravated burglary" is committed by one who commits burglary and has with him any firearm or imitation firearm, weapon of offence or explosive: s. 10(1). See *R* v *Stones* [1989] 1 WLR 156. Burglary (but not aggravated burglary) is triable either way (M.C.A. 1980, Sch. 1, para. 28). For penalties, see Th.A. 1968, s. 7, amended by C.J.A. 1991, s. 26; *A.-G.'s Ref (Nos. 19, 20 of 1990)* [1991] Crim LR 306.

burial, prevention of. It is an offence against public order to prevent the proper burial (or cremation) of a human body without lawful excuse: *R* v *Hunter* [1974] QB 95; *R* v *Swindell* (1981) The Times, 9 October.

business. Includes any trade (q.v.), profession or vocation: Counter-Inflation Act 1973, s. 21(1). Under the Fair Trading Act 1973, s. 137(2), it included a professional practice and any other undertaking carried on for gain or reward or which is an undertaking in the course of which goods or services are supplied otherwise than free of charge. See Landlord and Tenant Act 1954, Part II, C.P.A. 1987, s. 45; *Re Ogilby* [1942] Ch 288.

business day. "Any day other than a Saturday, a Sunday, Christmas Day, Good Friday or a day which is a bank holiday in any part of Great Britain": Ins.A. 1986, s. 251.

business liability. Term used in Unfair Contract Terms Act 1977, s. 1(3) to refer to liability for breach of obligations or duties arising from things done or to be done by a person in the course of a business (whether his own business or another's) or from the occupation of premises used for the occupier's business purposes. See also Occupiers' Liability Act 1984.

business name. Under the Business Names Act 1985 the use of certain types of business name (suggesting, e.g., links with government departments) is prohibited in the case of a business which does not consist of the surname of a sole trader, the surnames or corporate names of all members of a partnership, or the name of a company, in the case of a corporate business: ss. 1, 2. Disclosure of persons using business names may be required on business letters, orders, invoices and receipts: s. 4. See SI 1992/1196. *See* COMPANY NAME.

business, special. *See* SPECIAL BUSINESS.

business tenancy. A tenancy comprising property occupied by a tenant for the purposes of a business carried on by him or for those and other purposes. See *Pittalis* v *Grant* [1989] 3 WLR 139.

business, trading. *See* TRADING BUSINESS.

business travel. "Travelling which a person is necessarily obliged to do in performance of the duties of his employment": I.C.T.A. 1988, s. 168(5).

buyer. Under the S.G.A. 1979, s. 61(1), is "a person who buys or agrees to buy goods". A buyer in good faith does not acquire title to an object stolen from its rightful owner: *National Employers Insurance Assn.* v *Jones* [1988] 2 WLR 952.

bye-law. Also "by-law". "An ordinance affecting the public or some portion of the public imposed by some authority clothed with statutory powers, ordering something to be done or not to be done and accompanied by some sanc-tion or penalty for its non-observance . . . it has the force of law within the sphere of its legitimate operation": *Kruse* v *Johnson* [1898] 2 QB 91. It is subject to confirmation by the appropriate minister and may be declared invalid by the courts if, e.g., not made in the manner prescribed by statute, or if repugnant to the law of the land, or unreasonable. See *DPP* v *Hutchinson* [1990] 2 All ER 836; *Bugg* v *DPP* (1992) The Independent, 8 Sep.

C

C. 1. Chancellor (q.v.). 2. Abbreviation for Command Papers. *See* COMMAND PAPERS, NUMBERING OF; PARLIAMENTARY PAPERS.

C.A. Court of Appeal (q.v.).

Cabinet. "A hyphen which joins, a buckle which fastens, the legislative part of the state to the executive part": Bagehot. A group of ministers selected by and presided over by the Prime Minister (q.v.), collectively responsible for the general character and policy of legislation, consisting of the political heads of government departments and others. Cabinet ministers are also members of the Privy Council (q.v.). *See* MINISTERIAL RESPONSIBILITY.

Cabinet documents, national security and. "No court will compel the production of cabinet papers . . . the Cabinet is at the very centre of national affairs, and must be in possession at all times of information which is secret or confidential. Secrets relating to national security may require to be preserved indefinitely": *per* Lord Widgery in *A.-G.* v *Times Newspapers* [1976] QB 752.

cadit quaestio. The matter ends; it admits of no further argument.

Calderbank letter. A procedural device allowing a party to an action to offer to settle on a "without prejudice as to costs" basis, while reserving the right to bring the offer to settle to the attention of the court when the question of costs is dealt with. Originally named after *Calderbank* v *Calderbank* [1976] Fam 83; see now O. 22, r. 14; O. 33, r. 4A; O. 62, r. 9; Matrimonial Causes (Costs) Rules 1988; *C. & H. Engineering* v *Klucznick* (1992) The Times, 26 Mar.

call. 1. As in "call to the Bar" – the ceremony in the Inns of Court during which students who have passed the appropriate examinations and kept terms are admitted as barristers (q.v.). 2. As in "call" made by a company

(q.v.) whereby directors are empowered to ask shareholders for instalments of payment for shares. Calls cannot be made until the minimum subscription has been allotted. 3. As in "call on contributories" whereby a company or its liquidator makes a demand on those liable to contribute to the payment of debts.

cancellation. The act of nullifying or invalidating an instrument, e.g., by striking out signatures. The act must be accompanied by the intention to cancel.

cancellation, delivery up of documents for. An equitable remedy whereby a void document is delivered up and cancelled, e.g., lest some person be deceived by it, as where a guarantee was procured by misrepresentation (see *Cooper* v *Joel* (1859) 1 De G F & J 240), or a conveyance had been forged (see *Peake* v *Highfield* (1826) 1 Russ 559).

cannabis. Hallucinogenic, controlled drug (q.v.) obtained from hemp (*cannabis sativa*). It is an offence under the Misuse of Drugs Act 1971 to import, export, have in one's possession, produce or supply (except by authorisation) the drug or to cultivate any plant of the genus *Cannabis*. See *R* v *Hedley* (1990) 90 Cr App R 70.

canon. 1. Generally, a rule of *canon law*, i.e., a Roman ecclesiastical law system, first codified in 1139. *Canon law* also refers to the law of the Church of England. (Canon law does not bind the laity: *Middleton* v *Croft* (1736) 2 Atk 690.) 2. A body of writings.

canonical disability. Impotence (q.v.).

canvassing. 1. Soliciting votes from, e.g., electors. 2. Where one individual visits another off trade premises in order to obtain the entry of another into a regulated agreement (q.v.): C.C.A. 1974, s. 48. Canvassing for debtor-creditor agreements (q.v.) off trade premises is illegal: s. 49(1).

capacity of child in criminal law. *See* DOLI CAPAX.

capacity to contract. The legal competency, power or fitness to enter and be bound by a contract. Thus, an infant (q.v.) generally lacks contractual capacity, save where he binds himself by contract for necessaries or for other matters relating to his benefit. See *Doyle* v *White City Stadium* [1935] 1 KB 110; and *Hart* v *O'Connor* [1985] AC 1000 (mental incapacity). *See* CONTRACT; MINORS' CONTRACTS.

capax doli. *See* DOLI CAPAX.

capias. That you take. Name of a group of writs, e.g., *capias ad respondendum* (issued for the arrest of a defendant against whom an indictment had been found); *capias in withernam* (*wither* = against: *nam* = seizure) (writ issued in case of replevin (q.v.) where goods had been removed to an unknown place, and the taking of other goods to the same value was authorised).

capital. 1. In commercial usage, the capital of a business is its net worth, i.e., the value of its assets less the amount owing to its creditors. 2. In company law, it refers to, e.g., authorised, issued or paid-up capital. For "capital distribution", see T.C.G.A. 1992, s. 122.

capital allowances. Allowances available to persons carrying on a trade, profession, vocation or employment who have incurred capital expenditure on certain types of asset (including machinery and plant) (q.v.) for the purpose of their business. See, e.g., Capital Allowances Act 1968; Finance Act 1989, Part II; T.C.G.A. 1992, s. 41(4).

capital, alteration of. *See* ALTERATION OF SHARE CAPITAL.

capital, called-up. In relation to a company (q.v.) equals the aggregate of the calls made on shares (whether or not paid) plus any share capital paid up without being called and any share capital to be paid on a specified future date: Cos.A. 1985, s. 737.

capital clause. Clause in memorandum of association (q.v.) setting out company's nominal, i.e., authorised capital (q.v.), number and denomination of shares. In the case of a public company (q.v.) the clause must state an amount not less than the authorised

minimum: Cos.A. 1985; ss. 11, 118. *See* TABLE B.

capital gains tax. Tax introduced by the Finance Act 1965, levied on "chargeable gains" made on the disposal of chargeable assets. See Capital Gains Tax Act 1979; Finance Act 1989, s. 122; T.C.G.A. 1992, Part I. See *Aberdeen Construction Group Ltd* v *IRC* [1978] 1 All ER 963; *Kirkham* v *Williams* [1991] 1 WLR 863.

capital interest, qualifying. Means, in relation to any body corporate, an interest in shares comprised in the equity share capital of that body corporate of a class carrying right to vote in all circumstances at general meetings of that body corporate. For "equity share capital", see Cos.A. 1985, s. 744.

capitalisation. In relation to profits of a company (q.v.), means applying profits in wholly or partly paying up unissued shares in the company to be allotted to members as fully or partly-paid bonus shares, or transferring profits to capital redemption reserve: Cos.A. 1985, s. 280; Table A. For reorganisation of capital, see *Dunstan* v *Young, Austen & Young* [1987] STC 709.

capital, loan. Any debenture stock or funded debt issued by a corporate body or other body formed or established in the UK or any capital raised by such a body, being capital which is borrowed, or has the character of borrowed money, whether in the form of stock or any other form and stock or marketable securities issued by the government of a Commonwealth country outside the UK: Finance Act 1986, s. 78(7).

capital money. 1. Money that is paid to trustees of a settlement in the exercise of a statutory power, e.g., money raised by mortgage of land for purposes authorised by S.L.A. 1925, sale of land or heirlooms under S.L.A. 1925, s. 67(2). 2. Money that should be treated as capital, e.g., that paid under a fire insurance policy which the tenant for life (q.v.) was obliged to maintain. See S.L.A. 1925, s. 81. *See* SETTLEMENT.

capital movements, free. A component of the EEC's internal market arrangements. Restrictions on movements of capital belonging to residents of member states are to be abolished: Treaty of Rome, art. 67; Directive 88/361. Relevant domestic rules must be liberalised: art. 68; Cases 203/80, 26/83. *See* EEC.

capital, paid-up. The sum of the payments for shares received by a company.

capital punishment. Death by hanging (q.v.). Now a punishment only for high treason (q.v.) and piracy (q.v.) with violence. Capital punishment for murder was abolished by the Murder (Abolition of Death Penalty) Act 1965, and a sentence of life imprisonment substituted.

capital redemption business. The business (not being life assurance business or industrial assurance business) of effecting and carrying out contracts of insurance, whether effected by the issue of policies, bonds or endowment certificates or otherwise, whereby, in return for one or more premiums payable to the insurer, a sum or series of sums is to become payable to the insured in the future: I.C.T.A. 1988, s. 458(3).

capital redemption reserve. Made up of amounts equal to nominal value of shares cancelled as a result of the company redeeming or purchasing its own shares out of distributable profits.

capital, reduction of. *See* REDUCTION OF CAPITAL.

capital reserve. Non-distributable funds retained in a business. "Statutory capital reserves" include share premium account and capital redemption reserve (q.v.) fund. See Cos.A. 1985, s. 130.

capital, reserve. *See* RESERVE CAPITAL.

capital, serious loss of. When the net assets of a public company (q.v.) fall to one half or less of called-up share capital, the directors, not later than 28 days from the day at which the loss became known to a director, must call an extraordinary general meeting (q.v.): Cos.A. 1985, s. 142.

capital, share. *See* SHARE CAPITAL.

capital transfer tax. Tax charged at progressive rates, cumulatively, on the value of property transferred by chargeable transfers and made by a person in his lifetime. Introduced under Finance Act 1975, Part III. See Capital Transfer Tax Act 1984 (now known (see 1986 Act, Part V, s. 100) as the In-

heritance Tax 1984). Abolished by Finance Act 1986. For "potentially exempt transfers", see 1986 Act, s. 101, Sch. 19. See INHERITANCE TAX.

caption. 1. Arrest. 2. Heading of a legal instrument.

car. *See* MOTOR CAR.

caravan. A structure capable of being moved by towing or being transported on a motor vehicle or a trailer and designed or adapted for human habitation. See Caravan Sites and Control of Development Act 1960, s. 1(4); Caravan Sites Act 1968, s. 13; L.G.P.L.A. 1980, ss. 70, 173; Mobile Homes Act 1983; I.C.T.A. 1988, s. 367; *Wye Forest DC* v *Secretary of State for the Environment* [1990] 1 All ER 780.

care. The degree of attention or diligence that may fairly and properly be expected in given circumstances.

care and supervision order. Order made by the court, placing a child under 17 in the care of a designated local authority or under the supervision of a designated local authority or probation officer: Ch.A. 1989, s. 31(1). The court must be satisfied that the child is suffering or is likely to suffer significant harm, attributed, e.g., to his being beyond parental control: s. 31(2). For effect of care order, see s. 33. For education supervision order, see s. 36. The welfare of the child must be the paramount consideration. A care order may last until the child is 18. "Significant harm" relates to ill treatment or the impairment of health or development: ss. 31, 105. See *Re O.* (1992) The Times, 6 Mar.

care, common duty towards visitors. "A duty to take such care as in all the circumstances of the case is reasonable, to see that the visitor will be reasonably safe in using the premises for the purposes for which he is invited or permitted by the occupier to be there": Occupiers' Liability Act 1957, s. 2(2).

care, duty of. *See* DUTY OF CARE.

care for safety, duty of. Duty of an occupier of premises ("the common duty of care") owed to all his visitors, except trespassers, under the Occupiers' Liability Act 1957, s. 2. Under the Defective Premises Act 1972, s. 7, a landlord has a duty of taking reasonable care to see that persons who might be affected by defects in the premises he has let are reasonably safe from danger or injury. For the duty of care owed to "non-visitors" see Occupiers' Liability Act 1984.

careless and inconsiderate driving. *See* DRIVING, CARELESS AND INCONSIDERATE.

carelessness. The quality of an act which deviates materially from the standard of care which would be expected in the circumstances from a reasonable person. *See* NEGLIGENCE.

care, servant's contractual duty of. "The servant owes a contractual duty of care to his master, and a breach of that duty founds an action for damages for breach of contract": *per* Ackner LJ in *Janata Bank* v *Ahmed* [1981] IRLR 457.

cargo. 1. Anything carried or to be carried in a ship or other vessel: Docks and Harbours Act 1966, s. 58(1), as amended. See *National Dock Labour Board* v *John Bland & Co* [1971] 2 All ER 779. 2. Goods which are, or are to be, or have been loaded in a ship, excluding a passenger's personal baggage carried on board by him, and including anything taken on board a ship from the sea or sea-bed with a view to its being discharged to shore: Dock Work Regulation Act 1976, Sch. 4, Part I.

carnal knowledge. Phrase used in early statutes to mean sexual intercourse. See now S.O.A. 1956, s. 44.

carriage of goods by air, liability relating to. In general, a carrier is liable without proof of breach of contract or negligence on his part. Only the actual consignor and consignee have claims in respect of damage to goods. See Carriage by Air Act 1961; Carriage by Air (Supplementary Provs.) Act 1962; Carriage by Air and Road Act 1979; and *Rustenberg Platinum Mines* v *S African Airways* [1977] 1 Lloyd's Rep 564.

carriageway. Way constituting or comprised in a highway (q.v.), being a way (other than a cycle track) over which the public have a right of way for the passage of vehicles: Highways Act 1980, s. 329(1).

carrier, common. One who, by profession, undertakes for money payment the carrying of goods for those who employ him. His duties include the receiving and carrying of goods of the type he professes to carry; the carrying of goods by a reasonable route; delivery without unreasonable delay. He may be sued for damages if he wrongfully refuses to carry goods. See Carriers Acts 1830 and 1865; *Belfast Ropework Co* v *Bushell* [1918] 1 KB 210; *Rosenthal* v *LCC* (1924) 131 LT 563.

carrier, common, liability for safety of goods. Generally, liability, as an insurer of goods, for loss or damage except where caused by Act of God (q.v.), act of Queen's enemies, consignor's fault, goods' inherent vice.

carrier, private. A carrier who is not a common carrier (q.v.), i.e., who is never bound to carry. He is liable for any loss caused by his negligence. See *James Buchanan & Co* v *Hay's Transport Services* [1972] 2 Lloyd's Rep 535.

carrier's lien. Common law lien under which a carrier is entitled to keep possession of goods until he is paid freight owing to him for their carriage: *Skinner* v *Upshaw* (1702) 2 Ld Raym 752.

case. 1. A legal action or trial. 2. Argument put forward in legal proceedings.

case stated. A statement of the facts in a case submitted, e.g., by magistrates for the opinion of a higher court (such as the Divisional Court). Application for statement can be made by the defendant, prosecutor or a "person aggrieved" (although not a party). Application must identify the point of law on which opinion is sought. See M.C.A. 1980, s. 111; S.C.A. 1981, s. 28; *Berry* v *Berry* [1987] Fam 1; *Loade* v *DPP* [1990] 1 All ER 36.

cash. Term applied to ready money of the current coin of the realm, including notes of the Bank of England. Under C.C.A. 1974, s. 189(1), it includes money in any form. "Cash price" is the price at which a person indicates that he is willing to sell goods to cash purchasers: *R* v *Baldwin's Garage* [1988] Crim LR 438.

casual ejector. The nominal defendant (known as "Richard Roe") in an action of ejectment (q.v.). (This type of action was abolished by the Common Law Procedure Act 1852.)

casus belli. Occasion of war. An event which is used to justify a war (q.v.).

casus omissus. A case not provided for by the law. See, e.g., *Gladstone* v *Bower* [1960] 2 QB 284; *R* v *Munks* [1964] 1 QB 304; *Fisher* v *Bell* [1961] 1 QB 394.

catching bargain. An entrapping or unconscionable bargain, e.g., a loan made on extortionate terms to one who has an expectancy (e.g., an expectant heir). See C.C.A. 1974, s. 137; *Cresswell* v *Potter* [1978] 1 WLR 255. *See* UNCONSCIONABLE TRANSACTION.

cattle. "Bulls, cows, steers, heifers and calves"; Animal Health Act 1981, s. 89(1).

cattle trespass. Damage done by cattle trespassing on land of their owner's neighbour. Was actionable *per se*, without proof of damage. See Animals Act 1971, s. 4. *See* STRAYING LIVESTOCK.

causa causans. The immediate cause. "The real effective cause of damage": *Pandorf* v *Hamilton* (1886) 17 QBD 675.

causa proxima et non remota spectatur. It is the immediate, not the remote, cause that should be considered. "It were infinite for the law to consider the causes of causes and their implications one of another; therefore it contenteth itself with the immediate cause": Bacon. The *causa proxima* "is the cause proximate in efficiency, not necessarily in time": *Leyland Shipping Co* v *Norwich Union* [1918] AC 350.

causa remota. Remote cause; one operating indirectly through intervention of other causes. *See* NOVUS ACTUS INTERVENIENS.

causation. The relation of cause and effect. Where an *actus reus* (q.v.) is so defined that the occurrence of stated consequences is required (e.g., that the *actus reus* of the accused caused a death), the conduct of the accused which is alleged to have been the cause of those consequences has to be proved. See, e.g., *R* v *Jordan* (1956) 40 Cr App 4 153; *R* v *Blaue* [1975] 1 WLR 1411; *R* v *Malcherek* [1981] 1 WLR 690; *R* v *Cheshire* [1991] 3 All ER 670. *See* NOVUS ACTUS INTERVENIENS.

cause. 1. A suit or action. 2. That which produces or contributes to some event. "If a man intending to secure a particular result does an act which brings that about, he causes that result": *Alphacell Ltd* v *Woodward* [1972] 2 All ER 475.

cause of action. "A factual situation, the existence of which entitles one person to obtain from the court a remedy against another person": *Letang* v *Cooper* [1960] 2 All ER 929.

causes, concurrent. *See* CONCURRENT CAUSES.

caution. 1. A warning. 2. A formal warning issued by the police to offenders who admit an offence, where the police have no intention of prosecuting. For warning before arrest, see *Groom* v *DPP* [1991] Crim LR 713. 3. Any person interested in registered land (q.v.) may lodge a caution with the Registrar against any dealing with that land. Entry of dealing with such land may not then be made on the register unless the cautioner has received notice. See L.R.A. 1925, ss. 53, 54; L.R.A. 1986; *Elias* v *Mitchell* [1972] Ch 652; *Woolf Project Management Ltd* v *Woodtrek Ltd* (1987) The Times, 22 October.

caution to detained persons. Administered on arrest: "You do not have to say anything unless you wish to do so, but what you say may be given in evidence." In the case of a written statement under caution, the maker must sign (or make his mark on) the following clause: "I have read the above statement and I have been able to correct, alter or add anything I wish. This statement is true. I have made it of my own free will." See *Code of Practice* issued under the P. & C.E.A. 1984.

caveat. Warning, usually in the form of an entry in a register intended to prevent some action being taken without notice being given to person issuing the warning (the *caveator*). See, e.g., the S.C.A. 1981, s. 108, which allowed a caveat against a grant of probate (q.v.) or administration to be entered in the principal registry or district probate registry; L.R.A. 1925, s. 30.

caveat emptor. Let the buyer beware. In general, the buyer is expected to look to his own interests. "The apotheosis of nineteenth-century individualism": Atiyah. See S.G.A 1979, ss. 13, 14. *See* CONDITION; WARRANTY.

caveat venditor. Let the seller beware.

C.B. Chief Baron of the Exchequer.

Cd. Abbreviation for Command Papers. *See* COMMAND PAPERS, NUMBERING OF; PARLIAMENTARY PAPERS.

Central Criminal Court. Established by the Central Criminal Court Act 1824 as an assize court, exercising criminal jurisdiction in the Greater London area. Popularly known as the "Old Bailey". Abolished by the Courts Act 1971, but it has been retained in name, so that when the Crown Court (q.v.) sits in London it is known as the Central Criminal Court: S.C.A. 1981, s. 8(3). The Lord Mayor of London and any City Alderman may sit as a judge with a High Court or circuit judge, or recorder. Appeal lies to Court of Appeal (Criminal Division).

Central Office of the Supreme Court. Departments which carry out the administrative business of the Supreme Court; they include those of the Masters' Secretary and Queen's Remembrancer, Action, Filing and Records, Crown Office and Associates, Supreme Court Taxing Office. See S.C.A. 1981, s. 96 and O. 63.

certainties, the three. The necessary conditions for the creation of a valid private trust, stated by Lord Eldon in *Wright* v *Atkyns* (1823) Turn & R 143 and by Lord Langdale in *Knight* v *Knight* (1840) 3 Beav 148 thus: ". . . the words must be imperative . . . the subject must be certain . . . the object or persons intended to have the benefit must be certain."

certificate, evidence by. *See* EVIDENCE BY CERTIFICATE.

certificate, land. A certificate under seal of the Land Registry given to the current registered proprietor (q.v.) as his document of title. See L.R.A. 1925, s. 63(1). It records details of the registered land (q.v.) e.g., charges, incumbrances, class of title. The certificate is retained by the Land Registry if a charge on the land is registered or protected by mortgage caution (q.v.): L.R.A. 1935, s. 65.

certificate of incorporation. *See* INCORPORATION, CERTIFICATE OF.

certificate of shares. Document enabling a shareholder to show a good prima facie title to his shares. See Cos.A. 1985, s. 186; Cos.A. 1989, s. 130. The shareholder has a right to a certificate which should be prepared and ready for delivery within two months of the allotment of shares or their transfer. See also Forgery and Counterfeiting Act 1981, s. 5(6).

certificate to commence business. A trading certificate (q.v.).

certification officer, union. Appointed under T.U.L.R.(C.)A. 1992, s. 2, with responsibilities for, e.g., maintaining lists of unions and employers' associations, determining independence of unions. There is a right of appeal from his decisions to the Employment Appeal Tribunal (q.v.). *See* TRADE UNION.

certiorari. To be fully informed of. Originally a writ from the High Court to an inferior court commanding proceedings to be removed to a superior court "that conscionable justice may be therein administered": *Termes de la Ley*. Abolished under A.J. (Misc. Provs) A. 1938, s. 7, which replaced it with an order of certiorari. Used, e.g., to review and to quash decisions of tribunals. See S.C.A. 1981, ss. 29, 31; *R* v *Central Criminal Court, ex p Raymond* [1986] 1 WLR 710.

certum est quod certum reddi potest. That which can be made certain is to be treated as certain. See, e.g., *Duncombe* v *Brighton Club and Norfolk Hotel Company* (1875) LR 10 QB 371.

cessante ratione legis, cessat ipsa lex. With the reason of the law ceasing, the law itself ceases. See *Miliangos* v *George Frank Ltd* [1976] AC 443.

cessate grant. When a grant limited as to time has been made and has ceased to have effect at the end of that time, a subsequent grant is known as a *cessate* or *supplemental* grant. It is, in effect, a renewal of the entire original grant. *See* GRANT.

cesser. 1. A ceasing (usually of liability), determination or (premature) end. Thus, a "cesser clause" in a charterparty (q.v.) states that the charterer's liability ceases when the cargo has been landed. 2. "Provision for cesser on redemption" is a clause in a mortgage (q.v.) providing for the ending of a term of years when the loan is repaid. See L.P.A. 1925, s. 116. 3. "Cesser of interest" refers to the determination of an interest which may then pass to another.

cestui que trust. Shortened form of *cestui à que trust* ("he for whom is the trust"). The beneficiary (q.v.). Plural: *cestuis que trust. See* TRUST.

cestui que use. Shortened form of *cestui à qui oes le feoffment fut fait.* One to whose use property was conveyed. Thus, X conveyed land to Y to the use of Z and his heirs. Z was known as *cestui que use. See* TRUST; USE.

cestui que vie. Shortened form of *cestui à que vie* (he for whose life . . .). He for whose life a grant of land is made. Thus, where X is a tenant "for the life of Y", Y is *cestui que vie*. *See* AUTRE VIE.

chain of representation. An executor of a sole or last surviving executor of a testator is the executor of that testator. So long as the chain is unbroken, the last executor in the chain is the executor of every preceding testator. The chain is broken by failure to obtain probate or to appoint an executor, or by an intestacy. See A.E.A. 1925, s. 7. *See* EXECUTOR.

chain of title. Successive conveyances from the original source to the present owner. *See* TITLE DEEDS.

challenge to jury. Procedure whereby, before a jury is sworn, the prosecution or defence may challenge the members "for cause" on statutory grounds (disqualification, ineligibility) or common law grounds (privilege of peerage, previous convictions, lack of qualifications, actual or presumed bias). See Juries Act 1974, s. 12; C.J.A. 1988, s. 118; *Practice Note* [1988] 3 All ER 1086; *R v Ford* [1989] 1 QB 868 (fact that juror is of a particular race cannot be the basis of a challenge for cause). The prosecution may require a person to "stand by", i.e., not to sit on the jury unless there are insufficient members of the panel to constitute a full jury.

chambers. Usually, the offices of a judge in which application by way of summons may be heard; or the offices of counsel. See *R v Agar* [1990] 2 All ER 442; *R v Pitman* [1991] 1 All ER 468.

champerty. (*Campi partitio* = dividing of land.) An offence and tort abolished under the C.L.A. 1967, ss. 13, 14, resulting from a person's maintenance (q.v.) of another in an action, on condition that the subject matter of the action was to be shared by them. Abolition of criminal and civil liability does not affect "any such rule of law as to the cases in which a contract is to be treated as contrary to public policy or otherwise illegal": s. 14(2). See *Brownton Ltd v Inbucon Ltd* [1985] 3 All ER 499.

Chancellor. 1. Lord High Chancellor (known as the Lord Chancellor). Appointed by the Crown on the Prime Minister's advice. He is the principal legal dignitary, a member of the Cabinet (q.v.), the government's legal adviser, and Speaker of the House of Lords, presiding at judicial proceedings on appeal. Under C.L.S.A. 1990 he has responsibilities for the appointment of the Legal Services Ombudsman (q.v.) and the Advisory Committee on Legal Education. 2. Chancellor of the Exchequer, political head of the Treasury (q.v.) and responsible for control of national revenue and expenditure. A member of the Cabinet (q.v.), who presents the annual budget (q.v.) to Parliament.

chance-medley. *Chance medlée* = mingled chance. The killing of an aggressor in self-defence upon some sudden affray. It was considered excusable homicide. "The doctrine has no longer any place in the law of homicide": *R v Semini* [1949] 1 KB 405.

Chancery, Court of. *See* COURT OF CHANCERY.

Chancery Division. A division of the High Court of Justice (q.v.) consisting of the Lord Chancellor (q.v.) a Vice-Chancellor, and other puisne judges (q.v.). Matters over which it has jurisdiction include companies, administration of estates, execution of trusts, contested probate. It sits in London and eight provincial centres. A single judge of the Division may hear appeals, e.g., from the Commissioner of Inland Revenue. See S.C.A. 1981, s. 5, Sch. 1.

Chancery Masters. Deputies of the judges of the Chancery Division. *See* MASTERS OF THE SUPREME COURT.

change of voyage. Takes place "where after the commencement of the risk, the destination of the ship is voluntarily changed from the destination contemplated by the policy": Marine Insurance Act 1906, s. 45(1). *See* DEVIATION OF SHIPS.

character, evidence as to. Evidence as to the character of a party (i.e., reputation, disposition) may be given in the following circumstances: 1. *In criminal cases.* Evidence of the good character of the accused can always be given in chief or cross-examination (q.v.). Evidence of bad character may be given with leave of the judge to rebut the evidence of the good character of the accused, or if he has attacked the character of any witness for the prosecution. Evidence of character may be given after conviction. See *Lowery* v *R* [1974] AC 85. See Criminal Evidence Act 1898, s. 1(f)(iii) (as amended by Criminal Evidence Act 1979, s. 1). 2. *In civil cases*. Evidence of good character may not be given (except in rebuttal) so as to aggravate damages. Evidence of the plaintiff's bad character is admissible, e.g., where his character is in issue (e.g., in defamation). *See* EVIDENCE.

charge. 1. A criminal accusation. 2. Judge's instruction to a jury. 3. Expenses. 4. An incumbrance, e.g., on land, which secures payment of money. Charges over land capable of subsisting at law are, under L.P.A. 1925, s. 1(2), e.g., charges by way of legal mortgage. Other charges take effect as equitable interests. See L.C.A. 1972. 5. A *fixed charge* is a charge on specific property. A *floating charge* may be created by a company to secure debentures. See *Re Yorks Woolcombers Assn Ltd* [1903] 2 Ch 284; Cos.A. 1985, s. 395; *Re Woodroffes Ltd* [1986] Ch 366; *Re Curtain Dream plc* [1990] BCLC 925. The floating charge "is ambulatory and hovers over the property until some event occurs which causes it to settle and crystallise into a specific charge": *Barker* v *Eynon* [1974] 1 All ER 900. See A.J.A. 1977, s. 7(1). *See* CHARGE, CRYSTALLISATION OF.

charge by way of legal mortgage. A mortgage may be created by a charge by deed expressed to be by way of legal mortgage: L.P.A. 1925, s. 85(1). The mortgagee has the same protection, powers and remedies as if he had taken a lease of a fee simple (q.v.). See *Regent Oil Co* v *J. A. Gregory Ltd* [1966] Ch 402. *See* MORTGAGE.

charge, crystallisation of. Conversion of a floating charge to a fixed charge, e.g., as on the winding-up of a company. See Cos.A. 1985, Part XII; Cos.A. 1989, s. 100.

charge, general equitable. *See* EQUITABLE CHARGE, GENERAL.

charges, joinder of. *See* JOINDER OF CHARGES.

Charges Register. *See* REGISTER AT LAND REGISTRY.

charging clause. Clause authorising a solicitor who is a trustee (q.v.) to charge for his professional services: see *Re Royce's WT* [1959] Ch. 626.

charging order. A judgment creditor (q.v.) can apply on affidavit (q.v.) for an order imposing a charge on the debtor's land, securities, or funds in court. See Charging Orders Act 1979, s. 1. He could also apply by summons for an order charging a partnership interest: Partnership Act 1890, s. 23. See O. 50; O. 81, r. 10; C.J.A. 1988, s. 78; *Harman* v *Glencross* [1986] 1 All ER 545 (ancillary relief in divorce); *Howell* v *Montey* (1991) 61 P & CR 18 (charge to be made absolute). *See* JUDGMENTS, ENFORCEMENT OF.

charitable trust. A trust by the terms of which the income is to be applied exclusively for purposes of a charitable nature. For disqualification of trustees, see Charities Act 1992, s. 48. Trusts of this kind were named in the preamble to the statute of Charitable Uses 1601 as trusts for the relief of poverty, the advancement of education, the advancement of religion, other purposes beneficial to the community. "Charity is necessarily altruistic and involves the idea of aid or benefit to others": *Re Delaney* [1902] 2 Ch 642. See *R* v *District Auditor ex p W. Yorks MCC* (1986) 26 RVR27; *Guild* v *IRC* [1992] 2 WLR 397. *See* CHARITY; TRUST; INVESTMENT, ETHICAL, BY CHARITIES.

Charities, Central Register of. Set up under Charities Act 1960, and amended by Charities Act 1992, s. 2, and kept by the Charity Commissioners: to provide a permanent central record of property devoted to charity; to provide information to the public concerning charities; to provide an authoritative means of determining whether an organisation is charitable in law or not. Registration is generally compulsory: s. 4(6), as amended by the 1992 Act. There are some exceptions in the case of, e.g., "exempt charities", "excepted charities", very small charities with no permanent endowment, places of religious worship registered under the Places of Worship Registration Act 1855. See SI 1992/1901.

charity. "Any institution, [i.e., trust or undertaking] corporate or not, which is established for charitable purposes and is subject to the control of the

High Court in the exercise of the court's jurisdiction with respect to charities": Charities Act 1960, s. 45(1). See Charities Act 1992, s. 19 (accounting records); T.C.G.A. 1992, s. 256; *Re Hummeltenberg* [1923] 1 Ch 237; *Re Koeppler's WT* [1985] 2 All ER 869; *Re Hetherington* [1989] 2 WLR 1094 (trusts for saying of masses). For exemption from taxes of trading profits used for charitable purposes, see I.C.T.A. 1988, s. 505. For mortgaging of charity land, see 1992 Act, s. 34.

Charity Commissioners. A statutory body (see Charities Acts 1960 and 1992) which administers charities, secures the effective use of charity property and investigates abuses, removing trustees from office where necessary. See, e.g., *Mills v Winchester Diocesan Board of Finance* [1989] 2 All ER 317.

charter. 1. Written instrument executed between parties, e.g., a deed (q.v.). 2. Instrument from the Crown granting rights and privileges. See *Crown Estate Commissioners v City of London* (1992) The Times, 11 May (construction of old Royal charters). 3. A constitution, e.g., the Charter of the United Nations Organisation.

charterparty. A document by which a shipowner lets his ship to a charterer for the purpose of carrying a cargo, or undertakes that his ship will carry a cargo. It must be in writing, with or without seal. A charterer has no proprietory interest in the ship: *Port Line Ltd v Ben Line Steamers Ltd* [1958] 2 QB 146. A *charterparty by way of demise* is one by which master and crew are the charterer's servants for the duration of the charterparty: *Baumwoll v Furness* [1893] AC 8. See *The Fantasy* [1991] 2 Lloyd's Rep 391 (meaning of "at charterer's risk").

chattels. Generally property other than freeholds (q.v.), i.e., personal property. 1. *Chattels real.* "Interests issuing out of or annexed to real estates, of which they have one quality, viz, immobility, which denotes them real, but want the other, viz, a sufficient, legal indeterminate duration, and this want it is that constitutes them chattels": Blackstone. Example: leaseholds (q.v.). 2. *Chattels personal.* Pure personalty, e.g., choses in possession (q.v.) choses

in action (q.v.). See A.E.A. 1925, s. 55(1); *Re Crispin's WT* [1975] Ch 245.

cheat. "A deceitful device for defrauding another of his known right contrary to the plain rules of common honesty": 1 Hawk PC. "To cheat and defraud is to act with deliberate dishonesty as to the prejudice of another person's proprietary right": *R v Sinclair* [1968] 3 All ER 241. The common law offence was abolished by Th.A. 1968, s. 32, except for offences relating to public revenue (see *R v Mavji* (1987) 84 Cr App R 34). Under Th.A. 1968, s. 25(5) "cheat" means an offence under s. 15, i.e., dishonestly obtaining property belonging to another with the intention of permanently depriving the other of it: *R v Rashid* [1977] 1 WLR 298; *R v Doukas* [1978] 1 WLR 372. See REVENUE, CHEATING.

check-off practice. Procedure whereby employers agree to deduct employees' union subscriptions directly from pay and transfer them to the union. Workers must agree to the procedure as a term of the employment contract: *Williams v Butlers Ltd* [1974] IRLR 253.

cheque. A bill of exchange (q.v.) drawn on a banker, payable on demand: B.Ex.A. 1882, s. 73. A *crossed cheque* is one crossed with two parallel lines between which is written, e.g., the name of a bank, or the words "and company" (often abbreviated), the purpose being to provide security against fraud by ensuring the cheque is paid only into a banking account. See also s. 76. See *R v Clugston* [1991] Crim LR 857 (sentencing policy in cheque frauds). For "cheque voucher", see Finance Act 1982, s. 44(5). See Cheques Act 1992 (non-transferable cheques; use of printed phrase "account payee" on cheques).

cheque card. Card issued by a bank and presented with a cheque to a supplier of goods or services who, as a result, is assured of payment by that bank. The drawer of the cheque represents that he has authority from the bank to use the card so as to oblige the bank to honour the cheque; where he has no such authority he may be guilty of obtaining a pecuniary advantage by deception, contrary to Th.A. 1968, s. 16(1): *R v Charles* [1977] AC 177. See *R* v *Navvabi* [1986] 1 WLR 1311; *R* v *Bevan* [1987] Crim LR 129.

cheque, countermand of payment. Revocation by drawer of the authority to pay a cheque. Must be written and unequivocal: see the B.Ex.A. 1882, s. 75; *Barclays Bank* v *W. J. Simms* [1979] 3 All ER 522 (there is no reason in principle why a bank cannot recover money paid under a stopped cheque).

cheque, issue of. A cheque is "issued" at the time of its first delivery, complete in form, to the person who takes it as a holder. B.Ex.A. 1882, s. 2.

cheque, overdue. Cheque which has been in circulation for an unreasonable time. Can only be negotiated subject to any defect of title; is not, therefore, a negotiable instrument. See B.Ex.A. 1882, s. 36(2), (3).

cheque, post-dated. Cheque dated subsequently to actual date on which drawn, and issued before the date it bears. See B.Ex.A. 1882, s. 13(2); *Royal Bank of Scotland* v *Tottenham* (1894) 71 LT 168.

cheque, stale. Cheque which is "out of date", i.e., one bearing a date six months or more prior to presentation. See *London County Banking Co* v *Groome* (1881) 8 QBD 288.

chief rent. A type of perpetual rentcharge (q.v.), known also as "fee farm rent", occurring where a vendor, on the sale of a fee simple (q.v.), in lieu of taking the purchase money in a lump sum, reserves to himself a rent payable to himself and his heirs in perpetuity.

child. Under C. & Y.P.A. 1933, s. 14, a person under 14. Under Marriage Act 1949, s. 78, Ch.A. 1989, s. 105(1) and Family Law Act 1986, s. 7, a person under 18. In Mat.C.A. 1973, s. 52(1), it included, in relation to one or both of the parties to a marriage, an illegitimate or adopted child of that party or of both parties. See also Inheritance (Provision for Family and Dependants) Act 1975, s. 25(1).

child abduction. *See* ABDUCTION, CHILD

child abuse. Colloquialism applied to cases involving a pattern of physical, often sexual, assaults on a young child. For guidelines, see *In re A. and Others* [1991] 1 WLR 1026.

child assessment order. Granted by the court to a local authority if an applicant has reasonable cause to believe that a child is suffering or is likely to suffer significant harm and an assessment is needed to determine whether the child is suffering or is likely to suffer such harm: Ch. A. 1989, s. 43. An "emergency protection order" is issued if the court has cause to believe that a child is likely to suffer significant harm if not removed: s. 44. For removal of children by police, see s. 46.

child benefit. Cash benefit payable (taxfree) to the person responsible for a child (and replacing family allowances), i.e., one under 16, or under 19 if receiving full-time education. See S.S. Contributions and Benefits Act 1992, Part IX.

child destruction. "Any person who with intent to destroy the life of a child capable of being born alive, by any wilful act causes a child to die before it has an existence independent of its mother, shall be guilty of" child destruction: Infant Life (Preservation) Act 1929, s. 1(1). The section does not apply where the act was done in good faith for the purpose of preserving the mother's life. See, also, Abortion Act 1967, s. 5. See *R* v *Virgo* (1988) 10 Cr App R (S.) 427; *R* v *Johnson* (1990) 12 Cr App R (S.) 219. *See* ABORTION; BORN ALIVE; UNBORN PERSONS, KILLING OF.

child minding and day care. Local authorities are obliged to register those who act as child minders and who provide day care for children under 8 on premises (other than domestic) within the authority's area: Ch. A. 1989, s. 71(1). For definition of "child minder", see s. 71(2). For cancellation of registration, see s. 74.

child of the family. In relation to the parties to a marriage, means, under Ch. A. 1989, s. 103(1), a child of both of those parties or any other child, not boarded out with those parties, who has been treated by them as a child of their family.

child, parental responsibility for. If a child's parents were married to each other at the time of his birth, they each have parental responsibility: Ch. A. 1989, s. 2; otherwise the mother only has it: s. 2(2). The father is not the natural guardian of his legitimate child: s. 2(4). Parental responsibility means all the rights and duties, powers, responsibilities and authority which by law a parent has in relation to the child and his property: s. 3(1). A person with parental responsibility may not act in any way which would be incompatible with any order made under the Act: s. 2(8).

children. Refers, in general, to descendants of the first degree. See *Re Coley* [1901] 1 Ch 40.

children, employment of. Under C. & Y.P.A. 1933–63, a child could not be employed if under 13, before 7 am or after 7 pm, or before the close of school on a school-day, or for more than two hours on any school-day or Sunday, or when he might have been required to carry, lift or move anything so heavy as to be likely to cause injury. See also Children (Performances) Regulations 1968, Employment of Children Act 1973 (under which local education authorities supervised details of proposed employment, etc: s. 2), and the Education (Work Experience) Act 1973, as amended.

children, indecency with. See GROSS INDECENCY.

children, indecent photographs of. It is an offence for a person to take, or permit to be taken, any indecent photograph of a person under the age of 16, or to distribute or show such a photograph, or to have such a photograph in his possession with a view to its being distributed or shown by himself or others, or to advertise that he distributes, shows or intends to show such a photograph: Protection of Children Act 1978, s. 1(1); C.J.A. 1988, s. 160. For defences, see s. 1(4). See *R v Owen* [1988] 1 WLR 134; *R v Graham-Kerr* [1988] 1 WLR 1098.

children in need, services and accommodation for. It is the general duty of every local authority to provide an appropriate range and level of services to safeguard the welfare of children in need and to promote the upbringing of such children by their families: Ch. A. 1989, s. 17. For provision of accommodation, see s. 20. A "child in need" is one who is disabled or whose health or development may be significantly impaired without the provision of services by a local authority: s. 17(10).

children's evidence. See EVIDENCE OF CHILD IN CIVIL AND CRIMINAL PROCEEDINGS.

children's homes. No child shall be cared for and provided with accommodation in an unregistered children's home: Ch. A. 1989, s. 63(1). For power of inspection, see s. 80.

child support officers. Appointed by the Secretary of State, under Child Support Act 1991, s. 13, with functions in relation to maintenance of "qualifying children" (see 1991 Act, s. 3(2)). See MAINTAIN, LIABILITY TO.

child's welfare. See WELFARE OF A CHILD.

Chiltern Hundreds. The voluntary retirement of an MP is not permitted; but he can retire, in effect, by accepting an office of profit under the Crown, i.e., the nominal office of "Steward or Bailiff of Her Majesty's three Chiltern Hundreds of Stoke, Desborough and Burnham" – a sinecure office with only nominal duties and fees. See House of Commons Disqualification Act 1975, s. 4. See HUNDRED; OFFICE OF PROFIT.

chirograph. A deed written on a sheet of paper which was then divided, with "chirographum" (i.e., "autograph") written in capital letters between the division. A part was given to each party. An indented cutting was known as an "indenture" (q.v.).

Chivalry, Court of. See COURT OF CHIVALRY.

chose. A thing. 1. A *chose in action* is "when any man hath cause, or may bring an action for some duty due to him": *Termes de la Ley*. "All personal rights of property which can only be claimed or enforced by action, and not by taking physical possession": *per* Channell J in *Torkington v Magee* [1902] 2 KB 427. Examples: debts, patents, trademarks, copyrights. See *Chan Man-sin v A.-G. of Hong Kong* [1988] 1 All ER 1 (theft of chose in action). 2. A *chose in possession* is a movable chattel, the right in which can be enforced by taking physical possession. Example: one's goods.

Church of England. The established church of which the Sovereign must always be a member (Act of Settlement 1700, s. 3). Organised into dioceses (43) grouped into two provinces (Canterbury and York). Dioceses are subdivided into 14,300 parishes. The central governing body is the General Synod. Doctrine is governed by the

Thirty-nine Articles (see 13 Eliz. 1 c. 12). Ecclesiastical law of the Church is a part of the law of the land: *Mackonochie* v *Lord Penzance* (1881) 16 App Cas 4. For "communicant member", see the Patronage (Benefices) Measure 1986, s. 39(1).

c.i.f. contract. Cost, insurance, freight. If a merchant agrees to sell goods "at £x per unit c.i.f. Liverpool Docks", the sum includes the price of the goods, insurance premium and freight payable to Liverpool Docks. Generally, property in the goods passes to the buyer on shipment. See *The Wise* [1989] 2 Lloyd's Rep 451.

circuit judges. Judges appointed by the Queen on recommendation of the Lord Chancellor from those who have a 10-year Crown Court or 10-year county court qualification (see C.L.S.A. 1990, s. 71) or hold the position of Recorder (q.v.) or who have held a full-time appointment for at least 3 years in one of the offices listed in the Courts Act 1971, Sch. 1, Part 1A, inserted by C.L.S.A. 1990, Sch. 10. See the S.C.A. 1981, s. 8. For each circuit there are at least two presiding judges appointed by the Lord Chancellor from among the puisne judges of the High Court: C.L.S.A. 1990, s. 72. For removal of a circuit judge from office, following a conviction, see The Times, 6 Dec. 1983.

circuit system. The country is divided into circuits for the purpose of hearing criminal and civil cases: S Eastern, Midland and Oxford, Northern, North-Eastern, Western, Wales and Chester. Circuit committees were set up in 1972, under the Courts Act 1971, s. 30, to advise the Lord Chancellor on such questions "as he may from time to time refer to them".

circuity of action. Course of proceedings longer than is necessary. May provide grounds for dismissal of an action: *Post Office* v *Hampshire CC* [1980] QB 124.

circulars, government. Communications published by government departments to local authorities, etc, relating e.g., to statements of government policy. They have been held to constitute delegated legislation: *Jackson, Stansfield & Sons* v *Butterworth* [1948] 2 All ER 558. Judicial review (q.v.) may extend to departmental "guidance circulars"

issued without specific authority: *Gillick* v *W. Norfolk HA* [1986] AC 112. See *R* v *Secretary of State for Home Department ex p Lancs Police Authority* (1991) The Times, 19 Nov. (circulars should be construed in the way in which an educated person, acquainted with the factual context, would construe them, by giving to them their commonsense meaning).

circumstantial evidence. *See* EVIDENCE, CIRCUMSTANTIAL.

citation. 1. Summons giving notice to a person to appear before the court. 2. Notice issued by an executor applying for probate (q.v.) in solemn form, calling upon persons to appear and show why probate should not be granted. 3. The referring to a decided case of legal authority in support of an argument. See *R* v *Sheffield Stipendiary Magistrate ex p Stephens* (1992) The Times, 16 Mar. (excessive citing of cases).

citation of Act. *See* STATUTE, CITATION OF.

citizen, British Overseas. A citizen of the UK and Colonies who did not become a British citizen or a British Dependent Territories citizen when B.N.A. 1981 came into operation, becomes a British Overseas citizen: s. 26.

citizen's arrest. *See* ARREST, POWERS OF PRIVATE PERSONS TO.

citizenship, British, acquisition by birth or adoption. After commencement of B.N.A. 1981, a person born in the UK is a British citizen if at the time of his birth his father or mother is a British citizen, or settled in Britain, or if he is a foundling, or if he is born in the UK and one of his parents subsequently becomes settled here or if he becomes settled here or if he becomes registered as a British citizen, or if he is adopted in the UK and the adopter is a British citizen: s. 1.

citizenship, British, acquisition by descent. A child born overseas is a British citizen if, at his birth, one of his parents is British (though not by descent) or is employed overseas in the service of the British Government or the EEC: B.N.A. 1981, s. 2. For classes of persons regarded as British citizens by descent, see s. 14.

citizenship, British, acquisition by registration. British Dependent Territories citizens, or British Overseas citizens, or British subjects or British protected persons may apply for registration as British citizens after satisfying certain residential period and other requirements (five years' presence in the UK, etc.). See B.N.A. 1981, ss. 4, 5, 7, 8 (registration by virtue of marriage), 9, 10.

citizenship, British, acquisition by registration of minor. The Secretary of State may register any minor as a British citizen on application. A minor born abroad may be registered as a British citizen, within 12 months of his birth, or, where he is stateless, and one of his parents is a British citizen by descent and a grandparent was a British citizen otherwise than by descent: B.N.A. 1981, s. 3. See also s. 32.

citizenship, British, automatic acquisition of. British citizenship is acquired automatically by all those citizens of the UK and Colonies who had the right of abode (see Immigration Act 1971, s. 2) in the UK at the commencement of B.N.A. 1981: s. 11. For exceptions, see s. 11(2).

citizenship, British, Dependent Territories. Status bestowed under B.N.A. 1981, Part II, in certain circumstances on those living in the dependent territories, e.g., Bermuda, Falkland Islands, Gibraltar, Hong Kong. See B.N.A. 1981, Sch. 6.

citizenship, British, renunciation and resumption of. Under B.N.A. 1981, s. 12, a person may renounce his citizenship if he has, or expects to acquire, another nationality or citizenship. Under s. 13, he may resume citizenship (on one occasion only) if he is of full capacity and the renunciation was necessary to enable him to retain or acquire some other citizenship or nationality.

citizenship, Commonwealth. Every person who, under B.N.A. 1981, is a British citizen, or British Overseas citizen, or a British subject or a citizen of a country listed in Sch. 3, has the status of Commonwealth citizen: s. 37 (as amended by B.N. (Falklands) A. 1983, s. 4).

citizenship, deprivation of. *See* DEPRIVATION OF CITIZENSHIP.

City of London. An area of London, of 670 acres with its own administrative government consisting of a Lord Mayor, Court of Aldermen, common councillors and the city companies.

civil. Opposite sense of, e.g., criminal (as in a civil action) or military.

civil commotion. A serious riot, falling short of attempted insurrection. "The disturbances must have sufficient cohesion to prevent them from being the work of a mindless mob": *per* Mustill J in *Spinney's Ltd v Royal Insurance Co* [1980] 1 Lloyd's Rep 406.

civil disobedience. "A public, non-violent, conscientious yet political act contrary to law, usually done with the aim of bringing about a change in the law or policies of the government": Rawls (*A Theory of Justice*, 1971).

civilian. 1. One who is versed in Roman, i.e., civil, law (q.v.). 2. One who is not a member of the military forces.

civil law. 1. "The law each people has settled for itself, peculiar to the State itself": Justinian's *Institutes*. 2. The entire *corpus* of Roman Law. 3. Non-military law. 4. Non-criminal law. 5. Legal systems based originally on Roman law.

Civil List. An annual appropriation charged on the Consolidated Fund (q.v.), received by the Crown for purposes of maintaining the royal household, etc.

civil marriage. *See* MARRIAGE, CIVIL.

civil remedy. A remedy available to a private individual as the outcome of civil proceedings, e.g., damages, compensation, order of specific performance, injunction, declarations as to rights, orders of mandamus, prohibition, certiorari (qq.v.).

Civil Service. The body of servants of the Crown, some 597,000 (other than, e.g., those holding political or judicial office or members of HM Forces) who serve in a civil capacity and are paid wholly and directly out of money voted by Parliament. See Fulton Report 1968. The Civil Service Appeal Board is a judicial, independent public law body, established under the prerogative powers of the Crown: *R v CSAB ex p Cunningham* [1991] IRLR 297.

civil wrong. A tort (q.v.).

C.J. Chief Justice.

claim. 1. The demand or assertion of a right. 2. A privilege (q.v.).

claim of privilege *See* PRIVILEGE, CLAIM OF.

claims, small. *See* SMALL CLAIMS.

claim, statement of. *See* STATEMENT OF CLAIM.

clameur de haro. An ancient form of outcry after felons or trespassers. Apparently survives in the Channel Islands. (For a report of its wording and use in Guernsey, see (1983) The Times, 5 August.)

class closing rules. Rules of construction based on *Andrews* v *Partington* (1791) 3 Bro CC 401, relating to gifts to a class (e.g., "the children of A and B who shall attain 21") and to perpetuities (q.v.). Thus, a class will be closed artificially when one member is entitled to be paid, having attained a vested interest. They will not be applied where there is evidence of a contrary intention: see *Re Tom's Settlement* [1987] 1 WLR 1021; *Re Drummond* [1988] 1 WLR 134.

class gift. A gift is said to be to a class of persons when it is "to all those who shall come within a certain category or description defined by a general or collective formula, and who, if they take at all, are to take one divisible subject in certain proportionate shares": *Pearkes* v *Moseley* (1880) 5 App Cas 714. Example: "to all my sons who shall live to the age of 30". It is contingent until the identity of every member is ascertained. See P. & A.A. 1964, s. 4; *Re Clifford's ST* [1980] 1 All ER 1013; and *Re Tom's Settlement* [1987] 1 WLR 1021.

class rights. Rights attached to different classes of share (q.v.), concerning, e.g., voting, dividends, as set out in a memorandum and articles of association (qq.v.) or terms of share issue. See Cos.A. 1985, ss. 129, 125 (variation of class rights).

clause. A subdivision of a document; an individual section of a Parliamentary Bill.

clausum fregit, quare. Wherefore he broke into the close. Term used with reference to trespass to land (q.v.). In its developed form it was a writ, *c.* 1245, giving a lessee an action for damages against a party who had ejected him.

clean break principle. Concept in family law of encouraging spouses to diminish the bitterness of family breakdown by making a clean break with the past: see *Minton* v *Minton* [1979] AC 503; *Clutton* v *Clutton* [1991] 1 All ER 340. See Mat. C.A. 1973, s. 25A(1).

clean hands. He who comes into equity must come with clean hands, i.e., the plaintiff must have a clear conscience as regards the past. See *Overton* v *Banister* (1844) 8 Jur 906; *Quadrant Communications Ltd* v *Hutchinson Telegraph Ltd* (1991) The Times, 4 Dec.

clearance area. Term used in H.A. 1985 to refer to an area made the subject of a declaration by the local authority (q.v.) if satisfied that, e.g., the houses in the area are unfit for human habitation and ought to be demolished and that alternative accommodation can be made available for those who will be displaced, and that the authority has sufficient resources for this purpose.

clear days. Generally, days reckoned exclusively of those on which anything is begun and terminated.

clerks, judges'. *See* JUDGES' CLERKS.

clerks, principal. *See* PRINCIPAL CLERKS.

clerk to the justices. *See* MAGISTRATES' CLERK.

client. In relation to contentious business (q.v.), any person who as principal or on behalf of another person retains or employs a solicitor, and any person who is liable to pay a solicitor's costs. In relation to non-contentious business, any person who as principal or on behalf of another has express or implied power to retain or employ, and does retain or employ, a solicitor, and any person liable to pay a solicitor's costs: Solicitors Act 1974, s. 87.

clogging the equity of redemption. No agreement which clogs the equity, i.e., which makes a mortgage irredeemable, will be recognised by the courts. See *Kreglinger* v *New Patagonia Meat Co* [1914] AC 25; *Lewis* v *Frank Love Ltd* [1961] 1 WLR 261. *See* MORTGAGE.

close. 1. Enclosed land. 2. Termination of proceedings, as in "close of pleadings" (q.v.).

close company. A company which, for purposes of corporation tax, is considered as under the control of five or fewer participators or by any number of participators who are directors or, if on a winding-up, the larger part of the assets will ultimately be distributed to five or fewer participators (disregarding the rights of any loan creditors): I.C.T.A. 1988, ss. 414–430, as amended; *Collins* v *Addies* [1991] BTC

244. The term does not apply to a company not resident in the UK. A "participator" is, e.g., one who owns share capital and has voting rights in the company, or a loan creditor of the company (except where the loan arises in the ordinary course of banking). *See* COMPANY.

closed-shop agreement. An agreement whereby employers agree to employ only union members. It is now unlawful to refuse a person employment on grounds related to union membership: T.U.L.R.(C.)A. 1992, s. 137.

closing order. An order prohibiting the use of the premises to which it relates for any purposes not approved by the local housing authority (q.v.): H.A. 1985, s. 267(2). Refers also to a local authority order relating to shops' closing hours (see Shops Act 1950).

closing speeches. Speeches by each side before the summing-up. Generally, the prosecuting counsel speaks first; the defence usually has the right to the final word to the jury: Criminal Procedure (Right of Reply) Act 1964.

club. A voluntary association of persons meeting together for recreational or social purposes. Members are generally liable only to the extent of their subscriptions to a common fund. The remedy for wrongful expulsion is a declaration or injunction (q.v.). See *Lee v Showmen's Guild of Great Britain* [1952] 2 QB 329.

Cm; Cmd; Cmnd. Abbreviations for Command Papers. *See* COMMAND PAPERS, NUMBERING OF; PARLIAMENTARY PAPERS.

co. Abbreviation of "company" (q.v.).

coastal waters. In relation to the UK, Channel Islands and Isle of Man, so much of the waters adjoining the countries respectively as is within the fishery limits of the British Isles and, in relation to any other country, so much of the waters adjoining that country as is within the distance, to which provisions of the law of that country corresponding to the provisions of the 1934 Act extend: Whaling Industry (Regulation) Act 1934, s. 17; Fishery Limits Act 1964, s. 3(3); Water Resources Act 1991, s. 104(1).

code. A systematical collection, in comprehensive form, of laws, e.g., the Code of Hammurabi (eighteenth century BC), the *Code Napoléon* (1804).

code of practice. Rules of practical guidance with respect to the requirements of some statute, or to professional standards of behaviour. See, e.g., the Highway Code (q.v.); the City Code on Takeovers and Mergers. Failure to observe a code does not generally render a person liable to proceedings, but it may be admissible in evidence. See *R v Spens* [1991] 1 WLR 625.

codicil. "An addition or supplement added into a will or testament after the finishing of it, for the supply of something which the testator had forgotten, or to help some defect in the will": *Termes de la Ley*. It must be executed with all the formalities appropriate to the execution of a will. *See* TESTAMENT; WILL.

codifying statute. An Act which codifies the whole of case and statute law on a particular matter, e.g., O.P.A. 1861 and B.Ex.A. 1882. For the interpretation of a codifying statute see *Bank of England v Vagliano Bros* [1891] AC 107. *See* CONSOLIDATION ACT.

coercion. The use of physical or moral force in an attempt to interfere with the exercise of free choice. See *R v Ditta* [1988] Crim LR 42 (marital coercion). *See* DURESS; UNDUE INFLUENCE.

cognates. Those related on the mother's side. *See* AGNATES.

cognisance, judicial. Judicial notice (q.v.).

cohabitation. Living together (q.v.) as or as if husband and wife. See, e.g., *Atkinson v Atkinson* (1987) 137 NLJ 847.

cold weather payments. Payments made to certain persons in receipt of income support (q.v.) out of the Social Fund, when the average mean daily temperature remains equal to or falls below 0°C. See SI 1988/1724.

collateral. 1. Belonging to the common ancestral stock, although not in direct line of descent. 2. Collateral security (in the case of a bank loan) means: security deposited by some person other than the customer himself; or impersonal security, e.g., life policies, as contrasted with personal security, e.g., a guarantee. 3. Collateral contracts exist where there is one contract, the consideration for which is the making of some other contract, e.g., "If you will make this contract we discussed, then I will give you £1,000."

collective bargaining. Negotiations relating to the conditions and terms of employment carried on between trade unions and employers or their associations. A "collective agreement" is one resulting from such bargaining. It may be written, oral, formal or informal. It is not intended to be legally enforceable unless in writing and containing a provision to that effect. See T.U.L.R.(C.)A. 1992, ss. 178, 179. *See* TRADE UNION.

collective resale price maintenance, prohibition of. *See* RESALE PRICE MAINTENANCE, COLLECTIVE, PROHIBITION OF.

collective responsibility. Doctrine at the basis of the constitutional convention that the Cabinet (q.v.) is collectively responsible to Parliament for the conduct of the Executive. It requires that Ministers shall be loyal to government policy and that the government as a whole shall resign if defeated on a vote of no confidence. *See* MINISTERIAL RESPONSIBILITY.

collision. The accidental striking together of two or more objects. For collision at sea, see, e.g., *The Sea Star* [1976] 2 Lloyd's Rep 477; *The Filitria Legacy* [1986] 2 Lloyd's Rep 257. For "agony of the moment" defence, see *The State of Himachal Pradesh* [1987] 2 Lloyd's Rep 97.

collusion. Agreement, usually secret, for some deceitful or unlawful purpose. Collusion in the presentation of a petition for divorce (q.v.) is no longer a bar to divorce. See Mat. C.A. 1973, s. 19.

collusive action. *See* COMMON RECOVERY.

colony. "Any part of Her Majesty's dominions outside the British Islands except: (a) countries having fully responsible status within the Commonwealth; (b) territories for whose external relations a country other than the UK is responsible; (c) associated states": I.A. 1978, Sch. 1.

colore officii. By virtue of one's office.

combination order. Measure under C.J.A. 1991, s. 11, consisting of community service of up to 100 hours combined with a probation order of 1–3 years.

comity. Willingness by the courts of one jurisdiction to give effect to the decisions of another jurisdiction, as a matter of mutual respect, and in the absence of any obligation. See *Fayed.* v *Al-Tajir* [1987] 2 All ER 396.

Command Papers. *See* PARLIAMENTARY PAPERS.

Command Papers, numbering of. The six series are as follows: 1833–69 (number, with no prefix, e.g., "3989"); 1870–99 (numbered with prefix "C", e.g., "C 3550"); 1900–18 (numbered with prefix "Cd", e.g., "Cd 9005"); 1919–56 (numbered with prefix "Cmd", e.g., "Cmd 8778"); 1957 to late 1986 (numbered, with prefix "Cmnd", e.g., "Cmnd 3456"); and the current series (numbered with the prefix "Cm", e.g., "Cm 145").

command theory of law. Concept, elaborated by Austin, in 1832, of law as existing when a population habitually obeys, as a duty, the general and continuing commands of a person or group enjoining acts and forbearances, within the context of sanctions for disobedience. "Thus, law is the command of the uncommanded commanders of society": Hart.

Commercial Court. Puisne judges (q.v.) of the High Court who hear actions in the Commercial list "arising out of the ordinary transactions of merchants and traders; amongst others, those relating to the construction of mercantile documents, export or import of merchandise, affreightment, insurance, banking and mercantile agency and mercantile usages". See O. 72. See S.C.A. 1981, s. 6; *L.C.J.'s Practice Direction* [1990] 1 All ER 528 (modified in 1992), concerning the Northern Circuit Commercial Court, established 1990, which does not form a part of the Commercial Court.

commission. 1. Remuneration paid to an agent. 2. Formal authority to exercise a power. 3. A body directed to perform a duty, the members of which are known as "commissioners". Thus, a Commission of the Peace was appointed by the Crown, consisting of persons who were to act as justices of the peace (q.v.) in certain districts. 4. A Royal Commission is set up by the government to investigate aspects of policy. See, e.g., the Commission set up in 1991 to consider the criminal justice system. 5. Examination on oath under terms of O. 39, e.g., where a witness is ill or likely to be abroad at the time of the hearing.

Commissioners for Oaths. Solicitors who administer oaths, e.g., to those making affidavits (q.v.). See Commissioners for Oaths Act 1889; and Solicitors Act 1974, s. 81, under which solicitors holding practising certificates have powers of a Commissioner for Oaths.

Commission for Racial Equality. See RACIAL EQUALITY, COMMISSION FOR.

Commission of EEC. Body consisting of nationals of member states appointed for 4 years by common accord of their governments with the task of ensuring the proper functioning and developing of the common market: Treaty of Rome 1972, art. 155. They are expected to be completely independent in the performance of their duties. The Commission watches over the application of EEC legislation (q.v.), formulates proposals and implements policies. See EEC.

Commission of Review. Ecclesiastical body consisting of three Lords of Appeal in Ordinary and two Lords Spiritual to whom appeal lies from a Commission of Convocation which has tried a non-doctrinal offence by a bishop or archbishop, or a matter tried by the Court of Ecclesiastical Causes Reserved (relating to ritual, doctrine and ceremonial of the church).

Commissions for local administration. See LOCAL ADMINISTRATION, COMMISSIONS FOR.

committal for sentence. Procedure whereby magistrates, who are of the opinion that a greater punishment should be inflicted on an offender than they are empowered to impose, commit the offender to the Crown Court (q.v.) for sentence. Matters relating to sentence must be left to the Crown Court. See M.C.A. 1980, ss. 37, 38, as amended by C.J.A. 1991, s. 25; and P.C.C.A. 1973; ss. 24(2), 42 (relating to probation, conditional discharge, community service orders, suspended sentences).

committal for trial. The sending of a person for trial following a preliminary investigation before magistrates. The court may exercise the option of committing without consideration of all the evidence before it if made up of written statements in the form required by M.C.A. 1980, s. 102 and if defendant is legally represented. See I.A. 1978, Sch. 1. See COMMITTAL, SHORT.

committal in civil proceedings. Method of enforcing a judgment by committal to prison, available e.g., in cases of disobedience of an order of the court. See A.J.A. 1970, s. 11; O. 45. The disobedience, which must amount to contempt of court, must be more than casual, accidental and unintentional. See CONTEMPT OF COURT.

committal proceedings. Proceedings involving the oral presentation of evidence before a magistrates' court acting as examining justices: M.C.A. 1980, s. 150(1). The function of these proceedings is to ensure that "no one shall stand his trial unless a *prima facie* case has been made out": *per* Lord Widgery in *R* v *Epping Justices, ex p Massaro* [1973] QB 433. See *R* v *Governor of Canterbury Prison, ex p Craig* [1990] 2 All ER 654.

committal proceedings, reporting of. Written reporting or broadcasting of committal proceedings is generally forbidden, except in relation to, e.g., names of parties, counsel, solicitors, witnesses, etc: see M.C.A. 1980, s. 8. The accused may apply for the restriction to be lifted: s. 2. If, in the case of two or more accused, one objects to the making of an order lifting the restriction, the court must hear representations and may make an order only if satisfied that it is in the interests of justice to do so: s. 2A (inserted by C.J. (Amendment) A. 1981, s. 1(2).

committal, short. A procedure whereby magistrates, at their option, may commit for trial without consideration of the evidence; known as "paper committal". It may not be used if the defendant has no solicitor acting for him: see M.C.A. 1980, ss. 6(2) *(a)*, *(b)*.

committee. A group of persons appointed or elected by a larger, parent body to carry out general or specific delegated duties. See *R* v *Secretary of State, ex p Hillingdon LBC* [1986] 1 WLR 192.

Committee of the whole House. Procedure used in the Lords or Commons whereby, following a resolution, the House resolves itself into a Committee of the Whole House under the chairmanship (in the Commons) of the Chairman of Ways and Means and (in the Lords) the Chairman of Committees. The procedure may be used, e.g., in the passage of a Bill of fundamental constitutional significance. No other business can be taken while the Committee is sitting.

committee, select. Committee appointed by a House of Parliament, to consider and take evidence on some subject and to report to the House. Committees include Committee of Privileges, Public Accounts, European Legislation. Civil servants and other persons may be called upon to give evidence. An action for slander cannot be brought for statements given in evidence before a Commons Committee: *Griffin* v *Donnelly* (1881) 6 QBD 307.

commit to custody. To commit to prison or, where any enactment authorises or requires committal to some other place of detention instead of committal to prison, to that other place.

common. Land subject to rights of common. "Includes any land subject to be enclosed under the Inclosure Acts 1845–82, and any town or village green": T.C.P.A. 1990, s. 336. See *Hampshire CC* v *Milburn* [1990] 2 WLR 1240. *See* COMMON, RIGHT OF.

common assault. An assault (q.v.) which is not of an aggravated nature. A summary offence under C.J.A. 1988, s. 39. Punishable under O.P.A. 1861, s. 42. See *R* v *Beasley* (1981) 73 Cr App R 44. *See* AGGRAVATED ASSAULT.

common carrier. *See* CARRIER, COMMON.

common employment. At common law a master was not liable for the negligent harm resulting from the action of one of his servants towards a fellow-servant engaged in a common employment at the time of the accident. See *Radcliffe* v *Ribble Motor Services Ltd* [1939] AC 215. The doctrine was abolished by Law Reform (Personal Injuries) Act 1948, s. 1(1).

commonhold. Suggested land ownership scheme (see Cm 1345 (1990)) as an alternative to the ownership of flats on a long leasehold basis, allowing the freehold ownership of each individual unit of a building with an incorporated management association, run by the unit owners, responsible for services and facilities.

common informer. *See* INFORMER.

common land. Land subject to rights of common and wasteland of a manor not subject to such rights. See Commons Registration Act 1965; Common Land (Rectification of Registers) Act 1989. For right to graze, see *Matthews* v *Wicks* (1987) The Times, 25 May. *See* COMMON, RIGHT OF.

common law. "The common sense of the community, crystallised and formulated by our forefathers." Blackstone speaks of "the chief cornerstone of the laws of England which is general and immemorial custom, or common law, from time to time declared in the decisions of the courts of justice; which decisions are preserved among our public records, explained in our reports, and digested for general use in the authoritative writings of the venerable sages of the law." The phrase apparently came into use at the end of the thirteenth century, when reference is found in the Year Books (q.v.) to "*la commune ley*".

common law, declaratory theory of. *See* DECLARATORY THEORY OF COMMON LAW.

common-law market. *See* MARKET.

common-law marriage. Colloquialism (". . . inaccurate but expressive": *per* Bridge LJ in *Dyson Holdings* v *Fox* [1975] 3 All ER 1030) referring to the extra-marital relationship arising out of cohabitation as man and wife, based on an informal agreement to form a marriage relationship, but without any religious or civil ceremony. The phrase has also been used to refer to a marriage celebrated under a common-law form where, e.g., a clergyman is unavailable. See *Taczanowska* v *Taczanowska* [1957] P 301. *See* MARRIAGE.

common-law wife. Colloquialism, and misnomer, referring to a woman living with a man to whom she is not married, as if she were his wife: see *Davis* v *Johnson* [1978] 2 WLR 182.

Common Market. Term formerly used as a synonym for the EEC (q.v.) which, under the Treaty of Rome 1957, art. 2, has as a task the promotion of a harmonious development of economic activities throughout the Community by establishing a common market and approximating the economic policies of member states.

common parts of a building. They include the structure and exterior, and common facilities provided, whether in the building or elsewhere, for persons who include the occupiers of one or more flats in the building: Local Government and Housing Act 1989, s. 138.

Common Pleas, Court of. *See* COURT OF COMMON PLEAS.

common recovery. Mode of barring estate tail (q.v.) by a collusive action, abolished by Fines and Recoveries Act 1833. Process comprised the following steps: (1) Friendly plaintiff, A, brings action against tenant in tail, B; (2) B conveys life estate to "tenant to the praecipe" (q.v.), C; (3) C vouches B to warranty; (4) B vouches the common vouchee (a court official), D, on fiction that D had conveyed land to B with warranty of title; (5) D admits fiction and leaves court; (6) Judgment is given against D, so that the land is held to belong to A, and D must give land of equal value to C; (7) No land is given by D, and B's land goes to A under the judgment, the land now being rid of the estate tail; (8) A conveys land back to B in fee simple. *See* FEE TAIL.

common, right of. A *profit à prendre* (q.v.), i.e., a right to take something off the land of another. Classified as: appendant, appurtenant, in gross, *pur cause de vicinage* (q.v.), or, according to the subject-matter, as a common of pasture, turbary, etc. Rights of common must be registered with a local authority. See Commons Registration Act 1965; *Re Yately Common* [1977] 1 All ER 505.

Common Serjeant. Formerly a judicial officer of the City of London, who sat in the Central Criminal Court (q.v.). Now a circuit judge *ex officio*. See Courts Act 1971, Sch. 2.

Commons, House of. *See* HOUSE OF COMMONS.

commons, registration of. Registration with county councils of persons claiming to be or established as owners of common land in England and Wales. See Commons Registration Act 1965; Common Land (Rectification of Registers) Act 1989; *New Windsor Corporation v Mellor* [1975] Ch 380.

common, tenancy in. A tenancy in which tenants held in undivided shares and there was no right of survivorship (q.v.); only unity of possession was required. Existed where, e.g., land was limited to two or more persons and words of severance (q.v.) were used, e.g., "to X and Y in equal moieties". After 1925 a legal estate may not be held under tenancy in common. Under L.P.A. 1925, s. 34, where a legal estate has been limited to tenants in common it vests in them as joint tenants upon the statutory trusts for sale. The tenancy in common continues in equity "for giving effect to the rights of persons interested in the land": L.P.A. 1925, s. 35. See L.P.A. 1925, s. 36(4); *City of London Building Society v Flegg* [1988] AC 54.

Commonwealth. 1. The period from the execution of Charles I (1649) to the restoration of the monarchy (1660). 2. The Commonwealth of Nations (or British Commonwealth), i.e., a group of independent nations (the UK and nations once part of the British Empire) recognising the British monarch as Head of the Commonwealth. See, e.g., Pakistan Act 1990.

Commonwealth citizen. A person who is a British citizen, British Dependent Territories citizen, British Overseas citizen, or British subject, or who is a citizen of a country listed in Sch. 3: B.N.A. 1981, s. 37(1). See Immigration Act 1988, s. 1, repealing Immigration Act 1971, s. 1(5).

commorientes. Persons dying together on the same occasion at the same time. Under L.P.A. 1925, s. 184, they are presumed, for purposes affecting title to property, to have died in order of seniority. The statutory presumption does not apply in the case of intestate spouses. See A.E.A. 1925, s. 46(3); Intestates' Estates Act 1952, s. 1(4), Sch. 1.

communication, privileged. *See* PRIVILEGED COMMUNICATION.

communications, interception of. It is an offence intentionally to intercept a communication in the course of its transmission by post or by means of a public telecommunication system: Interception of Communications Act 1985, s. 1. For warrants for interception, issued in the interests of national security or the prevention or detection of serious crime or the safeguarding of the national economic well-being, see ss. 2–4.

communis error facit jus. Common error may make law. See *Baker* v *Bolton* (1808) 1 Camp 493.

communities. Divisions of districts in Wales. Basically they resemble English parishes but community councils need not meet more than once a year.

Communities, European. See EUROPEAN COMMUNITIES.

community care grants. Grants payable from the Social Fund to those who experience "special difficulties arising from special circumstances", e.g., after hospital treatment, and who are in receipt of income support (q.v.).

community charge. Known colloquially as "poll tax", which replaced rates on domestic properties. Introduced under Local Government Finance Act 1988. Abolished by Local Government Finance Act 1992, ch. I. See COUNCIL TAX.

Community, European Economic. See EEC.

community homes. Homes for the accommodation and maintenance of children in the care of local authorities: Ch. A. 1989, s. 53. For "voluntary homes", managed by voluntary organisations, see s. 60.

Community law. The directly applicable law of the EEC treaty and instruments made by the institutions of EEC. It operates as a separate system side by side with English law but, in the event of a conflict, it takes precedence over domestic law. "No provisions of municipal law, of whatever nature they may be, prevail over Community law": *Internationale Handelgesellschaft* v *EVSt* [1972] CMLR 255. See *R* v *Secretary of State ex p Factortame Ltd* [1991] 3 All ER 769 (a national court must set aside any rule of national law which prevents directly effective Community law from being fully effective). In general, community law becomes part of the law of the UK if it is, in its nature, and under the EEC treaties, self-executing, or is the subject of a separate enactment by Act of Parliament, or is implemented, under the European Communities Act 1972, s. 2(2), by statutory instrument. Treaty articles have direct effect if clear, unambiguous, unconditional, and, in themselves, become effective without further action by EC or member states: *Van Gend en Loos* (case 26/62). See COMMUNITY LAW, SOURCES OF; COURT OF JUSTICE OF THE EUROPEAN COMMUNITIES.

Community law, sources of. Sources of EEC law are: the treaties (e.g., Treaty of Rome 1957) with their annexes and protocols; conventions between member states; administrative acts; judicial decisions of the Court of Justice of the European Communities (q.v.) and the Court of First Instance (q.v.).

Community law, state liability under. The principle of state liability for damage caused to an individual by infringement of Community law committed by that state is inherent in the scheme of the EEC Treaty: *Francovich* v *Italian Republic* (1991) The Times, 20 Nov.

Community legislation, forms of. The Council and Commission of the EEC (q.v.) may: (1) make *regulations*, which have a general application and are binding in their entirety and directly applicable in all member states without the need for further enactment; (2) issue *directives*, which are binding, only as to the result to be achieved, on member states; (an individual may rely on a precise, unconditional ("vertical") directive against a member state: *Van Duyn* v *Home Office (No. 2)* [1975] 3 All ER 190; there are no "horizontal" direct effects as between persons); *R* v *London Boroughs Transport Committee ex p Freight Transport Association* [1991] 1 WLR 828; (3) take *decisions* binding in their entirety upon those to whom they are addressed; (4) make *recommendations* or deliver *opinions*, which have no binding force. See Treaty of Rome 1957, art. 189; *R* v *Goldstein* [1983] 1 WLR 157. The European Court has decided that a member state may not base criminal proceedings against a person arising from the content of an unimplemented directive.

Community legislation, interpretation of. "Beyond doubt the English courts must follow the same principles as the European Court . . . No longer must [the English courts] examine the words in meticulous detail. No longer must they argue about the precise grammatical sense. They must look to the purpose or intent . . . They must divine the spirit of the Treaty and gain inspiration from it": *H. P. Bulmer Ltd* v *J. Bollinger SA.* [1974] Ch 401. See *Macarthy Ltd* v *Smith* [1981] 1 All ER 111; *Garland* v *BR Engineering Ltd* [1982] 2 All ER 402. "Any question as to the meaning and effect of any Community instrument shall be treated as a question of law and, if not referred to the European Court, be for determination as such in accordance with the principles laid down by a relevant decision of the European Court": European Communities Act 1972, s. 3(1). "The Treaty of Rome is the supreme law of the country, taking precedence over Acts of Parliament": *per* Hoffman J in *Stoke on Trent CC* v *B & Q* [1990] 3 CMLR 867. See *Costa* v *ENEL* (Case 6/64).

community service order.   Known also as "a community sentence": C.J.A. 1991, s. 6. In the case of a person who has attained the age of 16 and has been convicted of an offence punishable with imprisonment, a court may make an order requiring him to perform unpaid work, within 12 months, for a specified number of hours (40–120, and, in some cases, 240). Breach of the order may be punished by fine, revocation of order and punishment for original offence. See P.C.C.A. 1973, ss. 14–17, as amended by C.J.A. 1982, s. 68, Sch. 12 and C.J.A. 1991, ss. 6, 10, Sch. 2 (enforcement of orders); *R* v *Porter* (1991) The Times, 30 July; *R* v *Siha* (1992) The Times, 13 Feb.

commutative contract.   Contract (q.v.) based on each party giving and receiving an equivalent.

commutative justice.   *See* JUSTICE, COMMUTATIVE, DISTRIBUTIVE AND CORRECTIVE.

commute.   To substitute one punishment for another.

Companies Court.   Collective title given to those judges of the Chancery Division (q.v.) nominated by the Lord Chancellor, who have jurisdiction in relation to certain matters derived from the operation of companies. Thus, they have jurisdiction to wind up any company (q.v.) registered in England.

companies register.   Register based on Cos.A. 1985, Part XII, recording charges created by companies on or after January 1st 1970, other than floating charges (q.v.). Must be registered at the Land Charges Registry if they are to bind any purchaser. See L.C.A. 1972, s. 3; *Property Discount Corp* v *Lyon Group* [1981] 1 All ER 379.

company.   An association of persons formed for the purposes of an undertaking or business carried on in the name of the association. May be classified as *chartered companies* (formed by the grant of a charter from the Crown), *statutory companies* (formed under an Act of Parliament), *registered companies* (formed under Cos.A.), or as *public companies* limited by shares, or by guarantee, or unlimited. See Cos.A. 1985, Part I. *See* LIMITED LIABILITY.

company accounts.   Accounts prepared under the Cos.A. 1985, s. 227, as amended by Cos.A. 1989, Part I, which must be prepared in accordance with Sch. 4; they include a balance sheet, and profit and loss account ("individual company accounts"): Cos.A. 1989, s. 4. They should disclose with reasonable accuracy, at any time, the financial position of the company at that time: Cos.A. 1985, s. 221, as amended by Cos.A. 1989, s. 2. See SI 1990/515.

company accounts, publication of.   A company (q.v.) "shall be regarded as publishing any balance sheet or other account if it publishes, issues or circulates it or otherwise makes it available for public inspection in a manner calculated to invite members of the public generally, or any class of members of the public, to read it": Cos.A. 1985, s. 742(5). See Cos.A. 1989, s. 238.

company books.   *See* STATUTORY BOOKS.

company, British.   A company incorporated under the laws of Great Britain, over which a Commonwealth citizen has control, or two or more Commonwealth citizens are together in a position to exercise control, or over which such a company, or two or more such companies, or such a company and a Commonwealth citizen are together in a position to exercise control: National Film Finance Corporation Act 1981, s. 9(3). *See* COMPANY; COMPANY, CONTROL OF.

company charges, register of.   *See* REGISTER OF COMPANY CHARGES.

company contracts, form of.   Contracts on behalf of a company may be made in the forms stated in Cos.A. 1985, s.

36, corresponding generally to those prescribed for the contracts of private individuals.

company, control of. The power of a person to secure by means of the holding of shares or possession of voting power in or in relation to that company or any other body corporate, or by virtue of powers conferred by the articles of association (q.v.), or other document, that the affairs of the company are conducted in accordance with the wishes of that person: I.C.T.A. 1988, s. 840.

company, dormant. *See* DORMANT COMPANY.

company, family. *See* FAMILY COMPANY.

company, holding. *See* SUBSIDIARY COMPANY.

company identification. The duty of a company to ensure that its name appears outside its place of business, on its correspondence, etc. See Cos.A. 1985, ss. 348–351.

company, investigation of. The Department of Trade is empowered to investigate the affairs of a company (q.v.) (see Cos.A. 1985, s. 431); the ownership of a company (see Cos.A. 1985, s. 442); the share dealings of a company (see Cos.A. 1985, ss. 444, 446, 447, as amended by Cos.A. 1989, s. 63).

company investment. *See* INVESTMENT COMPANY.

company let. Colloquialism for the practice of a landlord letting residential property to a limited company, possibly with a view to avoiding the creation of an assured tenancy (q.v.) or the provisions of the Rent Acts. See, e.g., *Kaye* v *Massbetter Ltd* [1991] 39 EC 129.

company, limited. *See* LIMITED COMPANY.

company limited by guarantee. *See* GUARANTEE, COMPANY LIMITED BY.

company manager. "Any person who in the affairs of the company exercises a supervisory control which reflects the general policy of the company for the time being or which is related to the general administration of the company is in the sphere of management. He need not be a member of the board of directors": *per* Shaw LJ in *Re a Company* [1980] Ch 138.

company, medium-sized. Under Cos.A. 1985, s. 248(2), a company is treated as medium-sized if it satisfies any two

of the following criteria (see S.I. 1986/1865 for these values): the amount of its turnover does not exceed £8M; the balance sheet total does not exceed £3.9M; the average number of employees does not exceed 250. See COMPANY, SMALL.

company meetings. *See* MEETINGS, COMPANY.

company, members of a. *See* MEMBERS OF A COMPANY.

company name. The name of a public company (chosen by the promoter) must end with "public limited company" (plc) or the Welsh equivalent: Cos.A. 1985, s. 25(1). In the case of a private company, "limited" or "Ltd" will suffice. Certain names will not be registered, e.g., those suggesting a connection with the Government: s. 26(1). A company may by special resolution change its name: s. 28(1). It is an offence to trade under a misleading name: s. 33. *See* BUSINESS NAME.

company, officers of a. Term which includes directors, managers and secretary. See Cos.A. 1985, s. 744. Auditors and company solicitors may be included.

company, oversea. *See* OVERSEA COMPANY.

company, participator in. *See* CLOSE COMPANY.

company, partnership. *See* TABLE G.

company, private. *See* PRIVATE COMPANY.

company, public. *See* PUBLIC COMPANY.

company, quoted. A company (q.v.) which satisfies the conditions that its shares or some class thereof are listed in the Official List of the Exchange and are dealt in on the Stock Exchange regularly from time to time. For "unquoted company", see Cos.A. 1985, s. 389(2)(a).

company register of members. *See* REGISTER OF MEMBERS.

company, registration of. Procedure whereby a company is registered by the Registrar of Companies on delivery of documents including a memorandum of association, printed articles of association, a statement in prescribed form of names of intended first director(s) and first secretary, statement of capital and statutory declaration by the solicitor engaged in the formation of the company, or by a named director or secretary, of compliance with the requirements of the Acts relating to registration. See Cos.A. 1985. ss. 12, 13, 359 (rectification of register).

company, related. In relation to an institution or the holding company of an institution, means a body corporate (other than a subsidiary) in which the institution or holding company holds a qualifying capital interest, i.e., an interest in the relevant shares of the body corporate held on a long-term basis so as to secure a contribution to its own activities by the exercise of control or influence arising from that interest: Cos.A. 1989, Sch. 10, para 37.

company's common seal. Required in the case of deeds, share certificates and warrants, contracts which would necessitate a deed if entered into by a private person. See Cos.A. 1985, s. 39; Cos.A. 1989, s. 130(7), Sch. 17, para 3. A company's official seal is a facsimile of the common seal, with the addition on its face of the name of the territory in which it is to be used.

company secretary. Appointed, usually at a board meeting, by the directors of a company. He can act as agent for the company and is an officer of the company. A sole director may not be the secretary. See Table A, art. 99.

company, small. Under Cos.A. 1985, s. 248(1), a company is treated as small if it satisfies any two of the following criteria (see S.I. 1986/1865 for these values): the amount of turnover does not exceed £2M; the gross assets do not exceed £975,000; the average number of employees does not exceed 50. See COMPANY, MEDIUM-SIZED.

company's profits. See PROFITS, COMPANY'S.

company statutory. See STATUTORY COMPANY.

company, unlimited. See UNLIMITED COMPANY.

company, unregistered. See UNREGISTERED COMPANY.

compellability of witnesses. See WITNESSES, COMPELLABLE.

compensation. Payment for loss or injury sustained, e.g., as under Criminal Damage Act 1971, s. 8 (compensation for destruction or damaging property of another). See also P.C.C.A. 1973, s. 35 (as amended by C.J.A. 1982, s. 67) (under which a convicted person was required to pay compensation for injury, loss or damage resulting from the

offence or any other offence taken into consideration by the court in determining sentence); C.J.A. 1988, ss. 89, 104. See *Herbert* v *Lambeth LBC* (1991) The Times, 27 Nov; Planning and Compensation Act 1991.

Compensation Board, Criminal Injuries. *See* CRIMINAL INJURIES COMPENSATION BOARD.

compensation scheme, investors'. Established in 1987 under F.S.A. 1986, s. 54(1), allowing compensation to investors where a fully-authorised investment business is unable or likely to be unable to meet the due claims of its clients. Administered by Investors Compensation Scheme Ltd, under F.S. Rules 1990. Financed partly by self-regulating organisations recognised under F.S.A. 1986, and partly by insurance. See *Securities and Investment Board* v *Financial Intermediaries Ltd* [1991] 3 WLR 889.

competence of witnesses. *See* WITNESSES, COMPETENCE OF.

competition, distortion of. The Treaty of Rome 1957, art. 85, prohibits as incompatible with the Common Market (q.v.) all agreements and practices which have as their object or effect the prevention, restriction or distortion of competition within the Common Market. Art. 86 makes illegal the abuse of a dominant position by exploitative acts, e.g., unfair prices or anti-competitive acts, e.g., mergers. See, e.g., *London European Airways* v *Sabena* [1989] 4 CMLR 662; Case 6/72. For exemptions, see e.g., Regulations 1983/83 (exclusive distribution), 4078/88 (franchising).

competition for prizes. A competition where, e.g., the allocation of prizes depends on the outcome of sporting events and competitors have to forecast that outcome. Generally unlawful if conducted in or through any newspaper, or in connection with any trade or business or sale of articles: Lotteries and Amusements Act 1976, s. 14(1).

competition law. That part of the law dealing with matters such as those arising from monopolies and mergers, restrictive trading agreements, resale price maintenance, and agreements involving distortion of competition affected by EEC rules.

competitive practices, anti-. A person engages in an anti-competitive practice if, in the course of business, he pursues a course of conduct which, of itself or when taken together with a course of conduct pursued by persons associated with him, has or is intended to have or is likely to have the effect of restricting, distorting or preventing competition in connection with the production, supply or acquisition of goods in the UK, or the supply or securing of services in the UK: Competition Act 1980, s. 2(1). See F.S.A. 1986, s. 126. For exemptions, see 1980 Act, s. 2(2)–(5).

complainant. One who makes a complaint (q.v.). "In relation to a person accused of a rape offence or an accusation alleging a rape offence, means the woman against whom the offence is alleged to have been committed": S.O. (Amendment) A. 1976, s. 4(6). Anonymity of complainants in rape offence cases is assured by s. 4(1).

complaint. 1. The initiating step in civil proceedings in the magistrates' courts: see M.C.A. 1980, Part II. 2. Allegation against a person. A complaint in a sexual case—the fact that it was made and its particulars—may be corroborative of the complainant's credibility or absence of consent. The complaint in such a case must have been made at the first reasonable opportunity after the offence and must not have been made merely in answer to questions of a leading or threatening nature: *R v Osborne* [1905] 1 KB 551. See *R v Camelleri* [1922] 2 KB 122.

complaint, hearing of. Procedure before a magistrates' court (q.v.) in which the substance of a complaint is stated to the defendant, the court hears the evidence and the parties, and makes the order for which the complaint is made or dismisses the complaint: M.C.A 1980, s. 53. For the procedure in the event of non-appearance of the parties, see ss. 55–57.

completely constituted trust. A trust which has been perfectly created, in that the settlor has done everything in his power necessary to transfer his interest in the trust property to a trustee for the benefit of the intended beneficiaries, or has declared himself a trustee of that property. See *Letts v IRC* [1956] 3 All ER 588. *See* TRUST.

completion. Final stages in, e.g., a contract for the sale of land, effected by delivery up of the land with good title, acceptance of title and payment of agreed price.

composition. 1. Sum of money accepted by creditors in satisfaction, or adjustment, of debts. Can be registered under Deeds of Arrangement Act 1914. 2. The ingredients of which a product is made, the proportions and degrees of strength, purity, etc. See Medicines Act 1968, s. 132, as amended.

compos mentis. Of sound mind.

compound. 1. To settle or adjust by agreement, e.g., by accepting a composition (q.v.). See Customs and Excise Management Act 1979, s. 152. 2. Compounding a felony, i.e., the offence of agreeing for consideration not to prosecute or impede a prosecution, was abolished effectively by C.L.A. 1967. 3. Compounding an arrestable offence (q.v.), i.e., accepting or agreeing to accept consideration for not disclosing information which might be of material assistance in prosecuting an offender, was made an offence under C.L.A. 1967, s. 5(1).

compound settlement. The one settlement formed by a series of separate instruments. See S.L.A. 1925, s. 30(3). *See* SETTLEMENT.

compromise. Settlement out of court of claims in dispute. "The word implies some element of accommodation on each side. It is not apt to describe total surrender. A claimant who abandons his claim is not compromising it": *Re NFU Development Trust Ltd* [1973] 1 All ER 135.

comptroller. Controller. One who examines accounts relating to public money. The Comptroller and Auditor- General is the head of the National Audit Office (see National Audit Act 1983, s.3). He carries out an audit and certification of government departments and a large range of public sector bodies; audit of nationalised industries and other public authorities is excluded. A certification audit may be followed by a "value for money" examination: 1983 Act, s. 6(1). See I.A. 1978, Sch. 1.

compulsion. *See* DURESS.

compulsory purchase order. An order for the purchase of land made in accordance with the statutory procedure:

see, e.g., Compulsory Purchase Act 1965; Acquisition of Land Act 1981; H.A. 1985, Part XVII, Sch. 22; Planning and Compensation Act 1991. The acquiring authority makes an order in draft which is submitted to the confirming authority (usually the Minister), objections are heard by an inspector and the order is confirmed, modified or rejected. Disputes may be heard by the High Court. See L.G.P.L.A. 1980, s. 91, as amended; *Hughes v Doncaster MBC* [1991] 2 WLR 16. *See* MARKET VALUE.

compulsory winding-up by the court. Procedure whereby a company (q.v.) is wound up if, e.g., it has passed a special resolution to wind up, or it is unable to pay its debts or it has failed to commence operations within a year of incorporation or the court believes it equitable that it should be wound up. See Ins. A. 1986, ss. 117, 122.

compurgation. Procedure whereby an accused person made a sworn denial of the accusation and brought together 12 persons who swore on oath to the validity of his statement. Abolished by Civil Procedure Act 1833.

computer. Any device for storing and processing information: Civil Evidence Act 1968, s. 5. For the use of computers, etc. for certain company records, see Cos.A. 1985, s. 723. See Data Protection Act 1984; Computer Misuse Act 1990 (creating offence of unauthorised access to computer material); *Derby & Co. v Weldon* (No.9) [1991] 1 WLR 652 (computer data base as "document").

computer documents, statements in. Under Civil Evidence Act 1968, s. 5, statements contained in documents produced by computers became admissible of a fact stated therein of which direct oral evidence would have been admissible if, e.g., throughout the material time the computer had been operating properly and had been supplied with information of the kind contained in the statement. Under P. & C.E.A. 1984, s. 69, a statement in a computer record became admissible as evidence of the facts contained in it *only* if: there were no reasonable grounds for believing that the statement was inaccurate because of improper use of the computer; it could

be shown that the computer was operating properly; and the rules of the court had been complied with. See also Sch. 3, Part II, paras. 8–11; *R v Spivey* (1990) 91 Cr App R 186.

computer misuse. Under the Computer Misuse Act 1990, it is an offence: to secure unauthorised access to computer material (s. 1(1)); to commit conduct sufficient to establish the previous offence with intent to commit or facilitate more serious offences (s. 2); to cause an unauthorised modification of computer material (s. 3). See *A.-G.'s Reference (No. 1 of 1991)*.

concealed fraud. In the case of land, this means "designed fraud by which a party knowing to whom the right belongs, conceals the circumstances giving that right, and, by means of such concealment, enables himself to enter and hold": *Petre v Petre* (1853) 1 Drew 397. The deliberate destruction of another's title deeds is an example. In such a case time does not run until the plaintiff has discovered, or could with reasonable diligence have discovered, the fraud: Lim. A. 1980, s. 32(1).

concealment. 1. Suppression of, or neglect to communicate, a material fact. If fraudulent, it may provide grounds for rescission of contract. 2. Concealment of a valuable security, dishonestly and with a view to gain or with intent to cause loss to another, is an offence under Th.A. 1968, s. 20(1). See *R v Kanwar* [1982] 2 All ER 523 (concealing stolen goods).

concealment of birth. *See* BIRTH, CONCEALMENT OF.

concert parties. Groups of persons acting in concert to acquire a company's shares. See Cos.A. 1985, ss. 204–7. Members of such groups must keep one another informed of their existing interests, acquisitions and disposals of shares in the company: s. 206.

conciliation. Settlment of a dispute outside the courts by reference to a third party. In domestic proceedings it is the process of assisting parties to deal with the consequences of a marriage breakdown and to resolve differences by reaching agreement.

conclusive evidence. *See* EVIDENCE, CONCLUSIVE.

concubinage. The state of cohabitation of unmarried persons.

concurrent and consecutive sentences. Following the conviction of the defendant of several offences, the court may impose separate sentences to be served at the same time (concurrently) or to follow on another (consecutively). *See* SENTENCE.

concurrent causes. Two or more events which are causative in relation to a plaintiff's injury so that both are considered proximate. See *Baker v Willoughby* [1970] AC 467; *Rouse v Squires* [1973] QB 889.

concurrent interests. Interests in land held at one and the same time, by two or more persons, e.g., grant of land "to X and Y in fee simple". X and Y "hold concurrently" or "hold in co-ownership".

concurrent lease. A lease (q.v.) created out of a reversion on an existing lease and existing concurrently with another lease of the same property. See *Adelphi Estates v Christie* (1983) 47 P & CR 650.

concurrent tortfeasors. Persons who, having committed a tort (q.v.), are each answerable in full for the entire damage caused to the plaintiff.

concurrent writs. Writs in duplicate, or those issued, e.g., for service on two or more defendants in an action or for service on a person whose whereabouts are unknown. See O. 6, r. 6.

condition. The declaration of circumstances essential to the occurrence of an event, e.g., the exercise of a right. Some restriction, limitation, qualification. 1. "Conditions in deed" are those which are actual and expressed; "conditions in law" are implied. 2. A *condition precedent* is one which delays the vesting of a right until the occurrence of a particular event, e.g., "to X if he graduates in law"; a *condition subsequent* is one which provides for the defeat of an interest on the occurrence or non-occurrence of a particular event, e.g., "to X on condition that he shall never sell out of the family": *Re Macleay* (1875) LR 20 Eq 186; a *condition concurrent* is one under which performance by one party is rendered dependent on performance by the other at the same time. See, e.g., *Re Da Costa* [1912] 1 Ch 377. 3. A condition in a contract for the sale of goods is a vital stipulation, the breach of which may give rise to a right to treat the contract as repudiated: S.G.A. 1979, s. 11(3). See *Wickman Machine Tools Sales Ltd v Schuler AG* [1972] 2 All ER 1173; *Bunge Corpn. v Tradax* [1981] 1 WLR 715 ("The courts should not be too ready to interpret contractual clauses as conditions": *per* Lord Wilberforce); *Interfoto Picture Library v Stiletto Visual Programmes* [1989] QB 433 (need to draw attention to onerous and unusual conditions); S.G.A. 1979, s. 11(3). See WARRANTY.

conditional acceptance. *See* ACCEPTANCE, CONDITIONAL.

conditional acknowledgement. A procedure for acknowledging service of a writ whilst reserving the right to have it set aside for some irregularity, etc.: see O. 12, rr. 7–8. *See* SERVICE, ACKNOWLEDGEMENT OF.

conditional admissibility. Phrase referring to evidence, the relevance of which may be conditional on the giving of later evidence. Evidence so admitted is said to have been admitted *de bene esse* (q.v.).

conditional agreement. *See* AGREEMENT, CONDITIONAL.

conditional discharge. *See* ABSOLUTE AND CONDITIONAL DISCHARGE.

conditional fee. A fee simple with an attached condition which cuts it short, e.g., grant of land "to A in fee simple on condition that he shall not marry X, Y or Z". *See* DETERMINABLE FEE; FEE SIMPLE ABSOLUTE IN POSSESSION.

conditional fee agreement. Written agreement between person providing advocacy or litigation services (q.v.) and his client which does not relate to criminal proceedings and other proceedings listed in C.L.S.A. 1990, s. 58(10) or to a contentious business agreement (defined by Solicitors Act 1974, s. 59), and which provides for that person's fees and expenses, or any part of them, to be payable only in specified circumstances: C.L.S.A. 1990, s. 58. *See* CONTINGENCY FEE.

conditional interest. An interest on condition subsequent. *See* CONDITION.

conditional sale agreement. Agreement for the sale of goods or land under which the whole or part of the purchase price is payable in instalments, and the property in the goods or land is to remain in the seller until the conditions of the agreement are fulfilled.

See C.C.A. 1974, s. 189(1); and S.G.A. 1979, s. 25(2).

conditional will. A will executed with the intention that it shall be rendered operative only on the occurrence of a specified event. See *Re Govier* [1950] P 237.

condition concurrent. *See* CONDITION.

condition precedent. *See* CONDITION.

conditions of sale. Terms upon which land is to be sold. In the case of a contract by correspondence, L.P.A. 1925, s. 46, provides that it shall be governed, subject to contrary intention expressed, by the Statutory Form of Conditions of Sale.

condition subsequent. *See* CONDITION.

condonation. Pardon or forgiveness. Specifically, forgiveness of a matrimonial offence. No longer an absolute bar to divorce. *See* DIVORCE, BARS TO.

conduct, unreasonable. *See* UNREASONABLE CONDUCT.

confessing error. Agreement by a successful party to an action that a judgment should be reversed, following the allegation by the other party of an error in law or fact.

confession. Includes any statement wholly or partly adverse to the maker, whether made to a person in authority (q.v.) or not, and whether made in words or otherwise: P. & C.E.A. 1984, s. 82(1). The court may reject a confession unless it can be shown that it was not obtained by oppression (q.v.) of the maker or obtained in circumstances rendering it unreliable: s. 76(2). See Code of Practice for the Detention, Treatment and Questioning of Persons by Police Officers (Code C, April 1991). For confessions of mentally-handicapped persons, see 1984 Act, s. 77; *R v Moss* (1990) 91 Cr App R 371. See *R v Miller* [1986] 1 WLR 1191 (confession of paranoid schizophrenic); *R v Silcott and Others* (1991) The Times, 9 Dec (relevance to confession of mental condition of defendant). *See* OPPRESSION LEADING TO CONFESSION.

confession and avoidance. The admission by a party of the truth of an allegation ("confession") but, at the same time, an allegation of other facts which apparently alter or nullify the effects ("avoidance") e.g., where the defendant agrees that he struck the plaintiff, but did so only in self-defence. See, e.g., *Lush v Russell* (1850) 5 Ex 203; O. 18, r. 8(1).

confession of defence. Where the defendant alleges a ground of defence which has arisen after the commencement of the action and the plaintiff delivers confession of that defence.

confidence, breach of. Equitable doctrine whereby the donee of confidential information relating, e.g., to a business, and which requires protection, is under a duty not to use that information to the donor's detriment. See *Bullivant v Ellis* [1987] ICR 464; *In re British and Commonwealth Holdings plc* (1991) The Times, 8 Nov; *Mainmet Holdings v Austin* [1991] FSR 538.

confidential communication. A communication which is privileged as being protected from disclosure in evidence given in proceedings, e.g., a communication between a party and solicitor made during those proceedings.

confidential information. Information, generally relating to industry or trade, reasonably believed by the owner to be such that its unauthorised release would be injurious to him or advantageous to others, and to be not in the public domain: *Thomas Marshall (Exports) v Guinle* [1978] 3 WLR 116. *See* TRADE SECRET.

confinement. 1. Imprisonment. 2. Labour resulting in the issue of a living child, or labour after 24 weeks of pregnancy resulting in the issue of a child, alive or dead: see, e.g., Social Security Contributions and Benefits Act 1992, as amended by Still-Birth Act 1992, s. 2.

confiscate. To deprive of property by seizure. A confiscation order against one who has benefited from his offence may be imposed by the Crown Court or a magistrates' court: C.J.A. 1988, Part VI. See Drug Trafficking Offences Act 1986, s. 1; *R v Richards* (1991) The Times, 11 Dec.

conflict of laws. *See* PRIVATE INTERNATIONAL LAW.

confusion of goods. The inter-mixing of goods of the same type, belonging to two or more owners, so that identification of the separate parts cannot be made.

congenital disabilities, civil liability relating to. Under the Congenital Disabilities (Civil Liability) Act 1976 a child has a cause of action if born disabled as the result of a tortious act done to one of his parents before the child's birth or conception: s. 1. "Disabled" refers to the child being born with any deformity, disease or abnormality, including predisposition to physical or mental defect in the future: s. 4(1). See Human Fertilisation and Embryology Act 1990, ss. 35, 44; *McKay* v *Essex Area Health Authority* [1982] QB 1166.

conjugal rights, restitution of. Prior to 1971 a spouse could petition for a decree which, in effect, ordered a deserting spouse to return to cohabitation. Abolished under Matrimonial Proceedings and Property Act 1970, s. 20.

connected persons. Persons who are considered, under Cos.A. 1985, to be "connected with a director": s. 346. They include a director's spouse, child, company or partner with which he is associated, persons acting as trustees of a trust under which the beneficiaries include the director or other connected persons. See 1985 Act, Part I; I.C.T.A. 1988, s. 228. Sch. 13.

connivance. Passive consent or co-operation in relation to a wrong-doing. Specifically, permission for, or acquiescence in, a respondent's adultery. It was an absolute bar to divorce until it was abolished by Divorce Reform Act 1969. See *Mudge* v *Mudge* [1950] P 173.

consanguinity. *See* AFFINITY.

consensual. Expressing, or made as the result of, the mutual consent of parties to some course of action.

consensus ad idem. *See* AD IDEM.

consent. Compliance with or deliberate approval of a course of action. It is not generally binding if obtained by coercion, fraud or undue influence (q.v.).

consent, age of. Usually refers to the age at which a female is legally competent to consent to sexual intercourse. Raised from 12 to 13 in 1875, and to 16 in 1885.

consent and assault. Consent is generally a defence to a charge of assault (q.v.), but this is subject to considerations of public policy. In the absence of some good reason, e.g., properly conducted games, assault cannot be rendered lawful by consent if it caused, or was intended to cause, actual bodily harm. See *A.-G's Ref (No. 6 of 1980)*

[1981] QB 715; *R* v *Brown and Others* [1992] 2 WLR 441 (consent no defence to sado-masochistic assaults).

consent, informed. The doctrine of informed consent, i.e., the duty of completely disclosing information to a patient as to medical treatment before it is undertaken, is no part of English law; a doctor is bound merely to disclose such information as is reasonable to allow a patient to make a rational choice whether or not to accept treatment; *Sidaway* v *Bethlehem Royal Hospital Governors* [1984] 1 All ER 1018. See *Blyth* v *Bloomsbury Health Authority* (1987) The Times, 11 Feb.

consent judgment. O. 42, r. 5A, makes it possible for parties to an action in the Queen's Bench Division, who are legally represented, to consent to a judgment which will (*inter alia*) embody their settlement of the dispute.

consent order. In relation to an application for an order for financial provision or property adjustment, concerning matrimonial proceedings, means an order in terms to which the respondent agrees: Matrimonial and Family Proceedings Act 1984, s. 7. For variation, see s. 11.

conservation areas. Areas of special architectural or historic interest, the character or appearance of which it is desirable to preserve or enhance, and designated as conservation areas by a local planning authority: En.P.A. 1990. Demolition within the area is controlled: s. 74(1). See also Planning (Listed Buildings and Conservation Areas) Act 1990 s. 69; *Lakeland DC* v *Secretary of State for the Environment* [1992] 1 All ER 573.

consideration. That which is actually given or accepted in return for a promise. "Some right, interest, profit or benefit accruing to one party, or some forbearance, detriment, loss, or responsibility given, suffered or undertaken by the other": *Currie* v *Misa* (1875) LR 10 Ex 153. Example: X receives £50 for which he promises to deliver goods to Y, the £50 is the consideration for the promise to deliver the goods. Consideration is *executed* when the act constituting the consideration is performed; it is said to be *executory* when it is in the form of promises to be performed at a future date. Consideration is required for all simple contracts. It must be legal; it must not be past; it must move from the promisee. See, e.g., *Roscorla v Thomas* (1842) 3 QB 234; *Dunlop Tyre Co v Selfridge & Co* [1915] AC 847; *Lipkin Gorman v Karpnale* [1991] 3 WLR 10. For the consideration for a bill of exchange (q.v.), see B.Ex.A. 1882, s. 27.

consideration, good. *See* GOOD CONSIDERATION.

consideration, past. Consideration which is wholly executed and finished before a promise is made. Example: X does some service for Y and, subsequently, Y promises X that, in consideration of that service, he will pay X a sum of money. There is no consideration to support Y's promise and it cannot be sued on. See *Re McArdle* [1951] Ch 669.

consideration, valuable. Consideration (q.v.) must be something which is of some value in the eye of the law: *Thomas v Thomas* (1842) 2 QB 851. See A.E.A. s. 55(1) (xviii). *See* GOOD CONSIDERATION.

consistory court. A court held by a diocesan bishop and presided over by a chancellor for the trial of ecclesiastical causes arising within his diocese.

Consolidated Fund. The general account, established in 1786, into which government receipts are paid and out of which payments are made in the form of standing charges, known as Consolidated Fund services.

Consolidation Act. An Act which repeals or re-enacts or collects in a single statute previous enactments and amendments relating to a topic. Acts of this nature may be passed without customary debate in Parliament: Consolidation of Enactments (Procedure) Act 1949. Examples: Legal Aid Act 1974; Solicitors Act 1974. Differs from codification, which systematises statutes and case law. *See* CODIFYING STATUTE.

consolidation of actions. A number of pending actions relating to the same subject-matter tried together by order of the court. see O. 4, r. 9; *Healey v Waddington & Sons Ltd* [1954] 1 WLR 688.

consolidation of mortgages. Where one person creates at least two separate mortgages in favour of one mortgagee,

that mortgagee has a right to require that the mortgagor, on seeking to exercise his equitable right to redeem one of the properties, shall redeem both of the properties or neither of them: *Jennings v Jordan* (1880) 6 App Cas 698. It is allowed only where the legal date for redemption (q.v.) has passed (for both mortgages) and where the right to consolidate has been reserved by at least one of the mortgages and where the equities of redemption are vested in one person and the mortgages in another, or where that position has existed at some time in the past. See L.P.A. 1925, s. 93; *Pledge v White* [1986] AC 187. *See* MORTGAGE.

consortium. 1. A business combination. 2. Right of one spouse to companionship and affection of the other. See *Lawrence v Biddle* [1966] 2 QB 504; *Hodgson v Trapp* [1988] 18 Fam Law 60 (cause of action for impairment of consortium survives). See A.J.A. 1982, s. 2, for the abolition of certain claims for loss of services.

conspiracy. The statutory offence was created by C.L.A. 1977, s. 1(1) (for which a new text was substituted by Criminal Attempts Act 1981, s. 5(1)): "If a person agrees with any other person or persons that a course of conduct shall be pursued which, if the agreement is carried out in accordance with their intentions, either (a) will necessarily amount to or involve the commission of any offence or offences by one or more of the parties to the agreement, or (b) would do so but for the existence of facts which render any of the offences impossible, he is guilty of conspiracy to commit the offence or offences in question." See *R v Cooke* [1986] AC 909; *R v Levitz* (1990) Cr App R 33. *See* CONSPIRACY TO DEFRAUD.

conspiracy at common law. "The crime of conspiracy is the creation of the common law and peculiar to it": *DPP v Doot and Others* [1973] 1 All ER 940. The offence of conspiracy at common law was abolished under C.L.A. 1977, except in relation to conspiracy to defraud (q.v.) and in so far as it may be committed by entering into an agreement to engage in conduct which tends to corrupt public morals or outrages public decency but would not amount to or involve the commission of an offence if carried out by a single person otherwise than in pursuance of an agreement: s. 5. See now C.J.A. 1987, s. 12. *See* CONSPIRACY TO DEFRAUD.

conspiracy, exemptions from liability for. A person is not guilty of conspiracy to commit any offence if he is an intended victim of that offence: C.L.A. 1977, s. 2(1). A person is not guilty of conspiracy to commit any offence(s) if the only other person or persons with whom he agrees are (both initially and at all times during the currency of the agreement) persons of any one or more of the following descriptions: his spouse; a person under the age of criminal responsibility; and an intended victim of that offence or of each of those offences: C.L.A. 1977, s. 2. See *R v Longman* (1980) 72 Cr App R 121; *R v Chrastny (No. 1)* [1992] 1 All ER 189.

conspiracy, restrictions on institutions of proceedings for. Under C.L.A. 1977, s. 4(1), proceedings may not be instituted except by or with the consent of DPP (q.v.) if the offence or each of the offences in question is a summary offence. Consent of A.-G. (q.v.) may be required under s. 4(2).

conspiracy to defraud. If a person agrees with any other person(s) that a course of conduct shall be pursued and that course of conduct will necessarily amount to or involve the commission of any offence(s) by one or more of the parties to the agreement if it is carried out in accordance with their intentions, the fact that it will do so shall not preclude a charge of conspiracy to defraud being brought against any of them in respect of the agreement: C.J.A. 1987, s. 12(1). See, e.g., *Wai Yu Tsang v R* [1992] Crim LR 425 ("intention to defraud" means an intention to practise a fraud on another, or an intention to act to the prejudice of another's right). *See* DEFRAUD.

conspiracy, tort of. Combination of two or more persons, without lawful justification, so as to cause wilful damage to another, or the agreement to perform an unlawful act with resulting damage. See *Lonrho Ltd v Shell Petroleum Ltd* [1980] (No.2) AC 173.

constable. An officer of the law whose task it is to help in maintaining the peace and bringing to justice those who infringe it. The words "constabulary" and "police" are synonymous: *Rubin v DPP* [1989] 2 All ER 241. See Police Act 1964.

constat. It follows. It is clear beyond argument.

constituency. One of the basic, separate electoral units in the UK in which eligible persons elect a Member of Parliament. See Parliamentary Constituencies Act 1986, Sch. 2, para. 1.

constitution. 1. The manner in which a state or other body is organised. 2. The body of fundamental doctrines and rules of a nation from which stem the duties and powers of the government and the duties and rights of the people. "That assemblage of laws, institutions and customs . . . according to which the community hath agreed to be governed": Bolingbroke. The UK's constitution is based on statute, common law and convention. See Royal Commission on the Constitution 1973 (Cmnd 5460).

construction. The process of construing (i.e., discovering and applying the meaning of) written instruments, e.g., by resolving ambiguities and other uncertainties. Often used synonymously with "interpretation": *Chatenay v Brazilian Submarine Telegraph Co* [1891] 1 QB 79. See *Franklin v A.-G.* [1974] QB 185.

construction, rules of. Decisions of the courts relating to the interpretation of documents: e.g., the meaning of a document must be sought for in the document itself (*Simpson v Foxon* [1907] P 54); the intention may prevail over the words used (*Lloyd v Lloyd* (1837) 2 My & Cr 192); words are to be taken in their literal meaning (*Wallis v Smith* (1882) 21 Ch D 243); a deed is to be construed as a whole (*East Ham Corporation v Sunley* [1965] 1 WLR 30).

constructive. Not directly expressed; inferred.

constructive desertion. Conduct of a respondent equivalent to the expulsion of a petitioner from the matrimonial home with the intention of ending consortium (q.v.). It is conduct equivalent to "driving the other spouse away": *Boyd* v *Boyd* [1938] 4 All ER 181. Examples: husband's adultery; husband's accusing wife of immorality and telling her to go; treasonable activities of wife resulting in her conviction (*Ingram* v *Ingram* [1956] P 390). It may be an indication of irretrievable breakdown of marriage and grounds for proceedings leading to, e.g., separation and maintenance. *See* DESERTION; DIVORCE.

constructive dismissal. Indirect dismissal as where, e.g., employer unilaterally changes terms of relationship so that an employee has virtually no choice but to resign. See E.P. (C.)A. 1978, s. 55.

constructive fraud. Equity considers as fraud those transactions which lead the court to the belief "that it is unconscientious for a person to avail himself of the legal advantage which he has obtained": *Torrance* v *Bolton* (1872) 8 Ch App 118. Equity will set aside, e.g., inequitable dealings with the weak, poor and ignorant (see *Miller* v *Cook* (1870) 40 LJ Ch 11; L.P.A. 1925, s. 174); appointments made by the exercise of a special power (q.v.) for a corrupt or foreign purpose (see *Re Dick* [1953] Ch 343; and L.P.A. 1925, s. 157).

constructive knowledge. Knowledge which a person might reasonably have been expected to acquire from facts observable or ascertainable by him or from facts ascertainable by him with the help of appropriate expert advice which it is reasonable for him to seek: see Lim, A. 1980, s. 14A(10), as inserted by Latent Damage Act 1986, s. 1. *See* KNOWLEDGE.

constructive malice. Malice proved indirectly from attendant circumstances when the state of mind of the accused cannot be proved. Abolished with reference to homicide by Homicide Act 1957, s. 1(1), the marginal note to which reads "Abolition of constructive malice": "Where a person kills another in the course or furtherance of some other offence, the killing shall not amount to murder unless done with the same malice aforethought (express or implied) as is required for a killing to amount to murder when not done in the course or futherance of another offence . . . A killing done in the course or for the purpose

of resisting or avoiding or preventing a lawful arrest, or of effecting or assisting an escape or rescue from legal custody shall be treated as a killing in the course or furtherance of an offence." *See* MALICE AFORETHOUGHT.

constructive manslaughter. *See* MANSLAUGHTER, CONSTRUCTIVE.

constructive notice. Where a purchaser fails to make a reasonable investigation he will be deemed to have had notice of what would have been discovered had he made the normal and customary enquiries. See L.P.A. 1925, s. 199; L.P.A. 1969, ss. 24, 25; Cos.A. 1985, s. 711A, inserted by Cos.A. 1989, s. 142(1).

constructive total loss. Where the subject-matter insured is reasonably abandoned because the actual total loss appears unavoidable, or the expenditure to prevent actual total loss would exceed the value of the subject-matter if it were saved. Example: the sinking of a vessel, so that the cost of raising it will be greater than its value if recovered. See Marine Insurance Act 1906, s. 60(1); *Assicurazioni Generali* v *Bessie Morris SS Co* [1892] 1 QB 571.

constructive trust. A trust (q.v.) imposed by equity, irrespective of the express or presumed intentions of the parties, in the interest of conscience and justice where one person obtains an advantage by acting unconscionably, fraudulently or inequitably, as where X, an agent acting on behalf of his principal, Y, makes a profit directly out of his work and X is held to be a constructive trustee for that profit to Y. See *Keech* v *Sandford* (1726) Sel Cas Ch 261; *IDC Group* v *Clark* [1992] 8 EG 108.

construe. To discover and apply the meaning of a written instrument. *See* CONSTRUCTION.

consultation. The seeking of information from others. "The essence . . . is the communication of a genuine invitation to give advice and a genuine consideration of that advice": *per* Webster J in *R* v *Secretary of State for Social Services ex p Assn of Metropolitan Authorities* [1986] 1 WLR 1.

consumer. "In relation to goods, means any person who might wish to be supplied with the goods for his own private use or consumption": C.P.A. 1987, s. 20(6).

consumer credit agreement. A personal credit agreement (q.v.) under which the creditor provides the debtor with credit not exceeding a statutory amount: C.C.A. 1974, s. 8(2). It is a regulated agreement (q.v.) under the Act. The agreement may be of the following types: *restricted use* (credit facilities used for stipulated purposes only); *unrestricted use* (debtor is free to use the credit in any way he wishes); *debtor–creditor–supplier* (credit supplied by supplier himself or an independent creditor); *debtor–creditor* (credit provided with no agent between supplier and creditor).

consumer credit business. A business relating to the provision of credit under consumer credit agreements (q.v.) which are regulated agreements (q.v.): C.C.A. 1974, s. 189(1).

consumer, dealing as. A party to a contract "deals as consumer" in relation to another party if he neither makes the contract in the course of a business nor holds himself out as doing so, and the other party does make the contract in the course of a business and in the case of a contract governed by the law of sale of goods or hire-purchase, or by s. 7 [of this Act], the goods passing under or in pursuance of the contract are of a type ordinarily supplied for private use or consumption: Unfair Contract Terms Act 1977, s. 12(1).

consumer goods. Any goods which are ordinarily intended for private use or consumption: C.P.A. 1987, s. 10(7).

consumer goods, guarantee of. In the case of goods of a type ordinarily supplied for private use or consumption, where loss or damage arises from the goods proving defective while in consumer use (i.e., while a person is using them or has them in his possession for use, otherwise than exclusively for the purposes of a business) and results from the negligence of a person concerned in the manufacture or distribution of the goods, liability for the loss or damage cannot be excluded or restricted by reference to any contract term or notice contained in or operating by reference to a guarantee of the goods: Unfair Contract Terms Act 1977, s. 5. This section does not apply as between parties to a contract under which, or in pursuance of which, possession or ownership of the goods passed: s. 5(3).

consumer hire agreement. Agreement based on a bailment of goods for a period of not more than three months, requiring payment of not more than a statutory amount, which is not a hire purchase agreement: C.C.A. 1974, s. 15(1).

consumer hire business. A business relating to the bailment of goods under consumer hire agreements (q.v.) which are regulated agreements (q.v.): C.C.A. 1974, s. 189(1).

consumer protection. Legislation designed to protect the economic and other interests of consumers. Examples: Trade Descriptions Act 1968; Fair Trading Act 1973; C.C.A. 1974; C.P.A. 1987; Food Safety Act 1990. *See* CONSUMER SAFETY.

consumer safety. A person is guilty of an offence if he supplies any consumer goods (q.v.) which fail to comply with the general safety requirement, or offers or agrees to supply any such goods, or exposes or possesses any such goods for supply (q.v.): C.P.A. 1987, s. 10(1). The "general safety requirement" involves goods being reasonably safe (q.v.) having regard to all the circumstances, including, e.g., published standards of safety, instructions or warnings given with the goods: s. 10(2). For defences, see ss. 4 (the "state of the art" defence), 10(4), 39 (due diligence). The Secretary of State has power to make appropriate safety regulations, serve prohibition and suspension notices: ss. 11–14. For civil proceedings, see s. 41. *See* DUE CARE.

consumer sale. A sale of goods by a seller in the course of business where the goods are of a type ordinarily bought for consumption or private use and sold to a person who does not buy or hold himself out as buying them in the course of business. See Unfair Contract Terms Act 1977.

consumer trade practice. Phrase used in the Fair Trading Act 1973 to mean any practice carried on in connection with the supply of goods or services to consumers, relating, e.g., to terms and conditions of supply, promotion, methods of salesmanship, packing of goods, methods of demanding or securing payment.

consummation of a marriage. The completion of a marital union by ordinary and complete sexual intercourse. Incapacity (permanent and incurable) of either party, or wilful refusal, to consummate (q.v.) makes a marriage voidable. See Mat.C.A. 1973, s. 12 (*a*), (*b*); *W.* v *W.* [1967] 1 WLR 1554.

contact order. An order requiring the person with whom a child lives to allow the child to visit or stay with the person named in the order: Ch.A. 1989, s. 8. For restrictions, see s. 9.

contemnor. One who has committed contempt of court (q.v.). See *Wright* v *Jess* [1987] 1 WLR 1076 (committal of contemnor to prison in his absence); *Taylor* v *Pensico* (1992) The Times, 12 Feb (contemnor to be given chance to mitigate).

contemporanea expositio. Contemporaneous interpretation. The reading of a document as it would have been read at the time of making. "In the construction of ancient deeds and grants, there is no better way of construing them than by usage: *contemporanea expositio* is the best way to go by": *A.-G.* v *Parker* (1747) 3 Atk 576. See *Campbell College* v *Valuation Commissioners for N. Ireland* [1964] 2 All ER 705.

contempt of court and strict liability rule. The "strict liability rule" means the rule of law whereby conduct may be treated as a contempt of court as tending to interfere with the course of justice in legal proceedings, regardless of intent to do so: see Contempt of Court Act 1981, s. 1. It applies only to publications (e.g., by speech, writing, or broadcasts addressed to the public at large) if it creates a substantial risk that the course of justice will be seriously impeded or prejudiced, and if the proceedings in question are "active", e.g., when a warrant for arrest has been issued: s. 2, Sch. 1. See *Home Office* v *Harman* [1983] 1 AC 280; *A.-G.* v *Hislop* [1991] 2 WLR 219; *A.-G.* v *Sport Newspapers* [1991] 1 WLR 1194; *M* v *Home Office* [1992] 2 WLR 73 (contempt by minister). For principles of sentencing, see *R* v *Moran* (1985) 81 Cr App R 51.

contempt of court, defences. These include innocent publication or distribution, contemporary report published in good faith, part of discussion of public affairs: Contempt of Court Act 1981, ss. 3–5. See *A.-G.* v *David English* [1983] 1 AC 116; *R* v *McDaniel* (1990) 12 Cr App R (S.) 44.

contempt of statute. A mere rule of construction, and not a crime, whereby the courts may infer a Parliamentary intent to impose liability for breach of statutory duty: *R* v *Horseferry Road Magistrates' Court, ex p IBC* [1986] 2 All ER 666.

contempt of the House. An act or omission which brings into contempt the authority of a House of Parliament, or which directly obstructs its proceedings. In effect, a breach of parliamentary privilege (q.v.).

contentious business. Business before a court or arbitrator, not being business which falls within the definition of non-contentious or common form probate business in S.C.A. 1981, s. 128, i.e., in general, business of a lawyer where there is a contest between the parties: Solicitors Act 1974, s. 87(1). See also ss. 56–75; *Re Simpson Marshall* [1959] Ch 229.

contentious probate business. Comprises actions to revoke a grant previously made in solemn form, actions relating to applications for administration ("interest actions") and actions as to the validity of wills. These actions are usually brought in the Chancery Division and begin with issue of a writ of summons out of Chancery Chambers (see O. 76). *See* PROBATE.

context. Parts of, e.g., a document connected with a particular passage or sentence. "The real question which we have to decide is what does the word mean in the context in which we find it here, both in the immediate context of the subsection in which the word occurs and in the general context of the Act": *Re Bidie* [1948] 2 All ER 995. See also *Abrahams* v *Cavey* [1968] 1 QB 479.

contiguous. Touching, adjoining. See *Haynes* v *King* [1893] 3 Ch 439.

contingency. Something related to a possible future and uncertain event.

contingency fee. An arrangement between a client and his legal representative whereby the latter agrees to represent the former on the understanding that the fee to be paid will be an agreed percentage of the amount recovered and that, should the client's claim fail, the representative shall not be paid. Common in USA, but not in UK. *See* CONDITIONAL FEE AGREEMENT.

contingent legacy. A legacy (q.v.) bequeathed on an expressed contingency, e.g., that the legatee shall marry.

contingent remainder. A remainder is contingent if the grantee is unascertained or if the title depends on the occurrence of a designated event. Example, a grant "to X for life, remainder in tail to his first son who shall attain the age of 21". See *Chinn v Collins* [1981] AC 533. *See* REMAINDER.

continuous bail. *See* BAIL, CONTINUOUS.

continuous employment. In general, for the purposes of employees' statutory rights of employment, employment is presumed to be continuous unless the contrary is shown. For rules of computing, see E.P.(C.)A. 1978, Sch. 13. See, e.g., *Pearson v Kent CC* [1992] ICR 20.

contra. Against; opposite.

contraband. 1. Goods, the import or export of which is forbidden. 2. Specifically, goods which, in time of war, may not be supplied by a neutral to a belligerent without risk of seizure.

contra bonos mores. Against morals. "Contrary to a good way of life": *Hughes v Holley* [1987] Crim LR 253. "Whatever is *contra bonos mores et decorum*, the principles of our law prohibit, and the King's court as the general censor and guardian of the public manners, is bound to restrain and punish": *Jones v Randall* (1744) 1 Cowp 17. See also *Shaw v DPP* [1962] AC 220; *Knuller v DPP* [1973] AC 435.

contract. A legally binding agreement. "A promise or set of promises which the law will enforce": Pollock. "Contracts when entered into freely and voluntarily shall be held sacred and shall be enforced by courts of justice": *Printing and Numerical Registering Co v Sampson* (1875) LR 19 Eq 462. *Contracts under seal,* known also as *deeds or specialty contracts,* must be in writing. *Simple contracts* include oral contracts and contracts which require some writing. *Implied contracts* arise from the assumed intentions of the parties. *Contracts of record* arise from obligations imposed by a court of record (q.v.). Contract generally involves: (1) offer and unqualified acceptance; (2) *con-sensus ad idem* (q.v.); (3) intention to create legal relations; (4) genuineness of consent; (5) contractual capacity of the parties; (6) legality of object; (7) possibility of performance; (8) certainty of terms; (9) valuable consideration. For formation of contracts, see e.g., *Blackpool Aero Club Ltd v Blackpool BC* [1990] 3 All ER 25.

contract, appropriate currency of the. In relation to contract damages, unless an appropriate currency is expressly stated in the contract, the appropriate currency will be that which truly expresses the plaintiff's loss, or that in which the loss was felt. See *The Federal Huron* [1985] 3 All ER 378.

contract, bilateral. Contract in which the parties must fulfil reciprocal obligations. *See* UNILATERAL CONTRACT.

contract, breach of. *See* BREACH OF CONTRACT.

contract by correspondence. *See* CORRESPONDENCE, CONTRACT BY.

contract, custom and. "An alleged custom can be incorporated into a contract only if there is nothing in the express or necessarily implied terms of the contract to prevent such inclusion and, further, that a custom will only be imported into a contract where it can be so imported consistently with the tenor of the document as a whole": *per* Lord Jenkinson in *London Export Corp v Jubilee Coffee Roasting Co* [1958] 2 All ER 411.

contract, discharge of. *See* DISCHARGE.

contract, divisible. *See* DIVISIBLE CONTRACT.

contract, formal. *See* FORMAL CONTRACT.

contract for sale of land, formalities. A contract for the sale or other disposition of an interest in land can only be made in writing and only by incorporating all the terms which the parties have expressly agreed in one document, or, where contracts are exchanged, in each: L.P. (Misc. Provs.) A. 1989, s. 2. This does not apply to contracts to grant short leases (see L.P.A. 1925, s. 54(2)); contracts made in the course of a public auction; contracts regulated under F.S.A. 1986, or to matters involved in the creation or operation of resulting, implied or constructive trusts (q.v.): s. 2(5). See *Record v Bell* [1991] 1 WLR 853; *Tootal Clothing Ltd v Guinea Properties Management Ltd* (1992) The Times, 8 June.

contract, freedom of. "A basic principle of the common law of contract . . . is that the parties are free to determine for themselves what primary obligations they will accept": *per* Lord Diplock in *Photo Productions Ltd v Securicor Transport Ltd* [1980] AC 827. "There is the vigilance of the common law which, while allowing freedom of contract, watches to see that it is not abused": *per* Denning J (considering exemption clauses) in *John Lee & Sons Ltd v Railway Executive* [1949] 2 All ER 591. See *Lombard Tricity Finance Ltd v Paton* [1989] 1 All ER 918 (unilateral variation).

contract, incapacitation and. A party who incapacitates himself, by his own act or default, from performing his obligations under a contract, is regarded as having refused to perform them. "To say 'I would like to but cannot', negatives intent to perform as much as 'I will not'": *per* Devlin J in *Universal Carriers v Citati* [1957] 2 QB 401.

contracting out. Removing oneself from an obligation. For contracting out of a credit agreement, see C.C.A. 1974, s. 173(1).

contract, measure of damages in. *See* MEASURE OF DAMAGES IN CONTRACT.

contract, naked. *See* NUDUM PACTUM.

contract of employment. A contract of service (or apprenticeship) which may arise from an agreement expressed in writing, orally or from conduct. See T.U.L.R.(C.)A. 1992, s. 295(1); E.P.(C.) A. 1978, s. 153. Under E.P. (C.) A. 1978, s. 1, employers must give a written statement (usually within 13 weeks of the beginning of employment) to employees (who normally work for more than 16 hours a week) relating to, e.g., scale of remuneration, terms and conditions of work, hours of work, holiday pay, grievance procedures, length of notice (but this does not amount to a contract). See also Employment Act 1989, Sch. 6; *Johnstone v Bloomsbury HA* [1991] 2 WLR 1362.

contract of record. Judgments and recognisances (qq.v.) enrolled in the records of proceedings of a court of record.

contract of sale. Includes an agreement to sell as well as a sale: S.G.A. 1979, s. 61(1). Price is generally one of the essentials of sale so that there may be no contract of sale if it remains "to be agreed" by the parties.

contract of service. A contract, written or oral, express or implied, to execute personally any work. It usually implies a relationship of "master and servant". It has been held to exist where M (the master) has the power of selection of S (his servant), where M pays S wages, where M has the right to control S's method of work, where M has the right to suspend or dismiss S: *Short v Henderson* (1946) 62 TLR 427. Whether or not a contract is "of services" is to be judged by an objective test: *Davis v New England College of Arundel* [1977] ICR 6. *See* INTEGRATION TEST.

contract, open. *See* OPEN CONTRACT.

contractor. *See* INDEPENDENT CONTRACTOR.

contract, privity of. *See* PRIVITY OF CONTRACT.

contract, root of. *See* ROOT OF CONTRACT.

contracts, applicable law of. The Contracts (Applicable Law) Act 1990 incorporates into UK law the Rome Convention 1980 under which parties to a contract are free to choose which laws shall govern it and, where the choice is not made, the contract will be governed by the law of the country "with which the transaction has its closest and most real connection".

contracts, collateral. *See* COLLATERAL.

contract, severance of. *See* SEVERANCE.

contracts, illegal. *See* ILLEGAL CONTRACTS.

contracts, minors'. *See* MINORS' CONTRACTS.

contracts of adhesion. *See* STANDARD FORM CONTRACTS.

contract, spot. Contract for immediate delivery and payment. See *Thames Sack Co Ltd v Knowles* (1918) 88 LJ KB 583.

contracts required to be in writing. The group of contracts which are valid only if written, including bills of exchange, marine insurance, bills of sale, acknowledgement of statute-barred debts, certain contracts relating to hire-purchase, contracts for the sale or other disposition of certain interests in land (L.P. (Misc. Provs.) A. 1989, s. 2).

contracts, standard form. *See* STANDARD FORM CONTRACTS.

contract terms, unfair. *See* UNFAIR CONTRACT TERMS.

contractual liability, avoidance of. As between contracting parties (where one of them deals as consumer or on the other's written standard terms of business), then, as against that party, the other cannot by reference to any contract term, when himself in breach of contract, exclude or restrict any liability of his in respect of the breach, or claim to be entitled to render a contractual performance substantially different from that which was reasonably expected of him, or, in respect of the whole or any part of his contractual obligation, to render no performance at all except in so far as the contract term satisfies the requirement of reasonableness: Unfair Contract Terms Act 1977, s. 3.

contract under seal. A contract expressed in a document to which the maker's seal was attached and which was delivered as "his deed". See now L.P. (Misc. Provs.) A. 1989, s. 1.

contract, unenforceable. See UNENFORCEABLE CONTRACT.

contract, unilateral. See UNILATERAL CONTRACT.

contract, vicarious performance of. See VICARIOUS PERFORMANCE OF CONTRACT.

contract, wagering. See WAGERING CONTRACT.

contra proferentem **rule.** See VERBA CHARTARUM (ETC).

contravention. The violation of an order. For planning contravention notices, see T.C.P.A. 1990, s. 171C, inserted by Planning and Compensation Act 1991, s.1.

contribution. 1. Payment imposed on, or made by, some person. 2. Payment of the share of an individual relating to a loss for which several persons are jointly liable, e.g., joint tortfeasors (q.v.). See Civil Liability (Contribution) Act 1978; and O. 16, r. 10 (offer of contribution before trial of an action).

contributories, liability on winding-up. Obligation of every past and present member of a company to contribute to its assets to any amount sufficient for payment of its debts and liabilities, and the expenses of winding-up, and for the adjustment of contributories' rights among themselves: Ins.A. 1986, s. 74(1). Maximum liability is limited in the case of a company limited by shares to the amount unpaid on the shares, and, in the case of a company limited by guarantee, to the amount of the guarantee: s. 74(2), (3). A past member is not liable to contribute if he has ceased to be a member for one year or more before the commencement of the winding-up: s. 74(2)(*a*).

contributory negligence. "A man's carelessness in looking after his own safety." A defence established where it is proved that an injured party failed to take reasonable care of himself, thus contributing materially to his own injury: *Nance* v *British Columbia Electric Rlwy* [1951] AC 601. Under Law Reform (Contributory Negligence) Act 1945 a claim in respect of damage is reduced to such extent as the court thinks just and equitable having regard to the claimant's share in responsibility for damage. "Damage" includes loss of life and personal injury. See *Tremayne* v *Hill* [1987] RTR 131 – no duty on a pedestrian who is crossing a multiple road junction to keep a lookout. See Animals Act 1971, s. 10; Fatal Accidents Act 1976, s. 5; *Harrison* v *British Railways* [1981] 3 All ER 679. The 1945 Act does not apply to contract (see *Basildon DC* v *Lesser Ltd* [1985] QB 839), or to a claim based on a breach of the duty of utmost good faith (see *Banque Keyser Ullmann* v *Skandia Ltd* [1987] 2 WLR 1300). For contributory negligence as a defence in contract, see Law Commission Working Paper (1990) No. 114. See *Pitts* v *Hunt* [1991] 1 QB 24. See NEGLIGENCE.

controlled drugs. See DRUGS, CONTROLLED.

controlled trust. Means, in relation to a solicitor, a trust of which he is a sole trustee or co-trustee with one or more of his partners or employees: Solicitors Act 1974, s. 87(1). See TRUST.

controller. A managing director, chief executive, or a person who, either alone or with associates, controls the exercise of 15 per cent or more of voting power: Banking Act 1987, s. 105(3). See also C.C.A. 1974, s. 189(1).

controlling director. A director of a company, the directors of which have a controlling interest therein, who is the beneficial owner of, or who is able either directly or through the medium of other companies or by any other in-direct means to control more than 5 per cent of the ordinary share capital of the company.

convention. 1. A treaty between states. In interpreting a statute designed to enact a convention, the court may look at it in the event of an ambiguity: *The Banco* [1971] P 137; *R v Chief Immigration Officer, ex p Salamat Bibi* [1976] 1 WLR 979. 2. Agreed usage or practice. 3. A convention of the constitution is one of the "rules for determining the mode in which the discretionary powers of the Crown (or of ministers or servants of the Crown) ought to be exercised": Dicey. Conventions are un-derstandings, tacitly agreed, resulting from long practice by which the con-duct of the Crown and Parliament is regulated in the absence of formal legal rules ("constitutional morality": Dicey). Example: the party with a ma-jority in the Commons is entitled to have its leader made Prime Minister (q.v.). The courts recognise, but do not enforce, conventions. See, e.g., *A.-G. v Jonathan Cape Ltd* [1976] QB 752. For example of convention incor-porated into statute, see Statute of Westminster 1931.

convention, estoppel by. *See* ESTOPPEL..

conversion. 1. In criminal law, "fraudu-lent conversion" to one's use or benefit was formerly an offence under Larceny Act 1916, s. 20. See now Th.A. 1968, s. 1. 2. In equity, conversion is a notional change, under certain condi-tions, of land into money, or money into land, which arises as soon as the duty to convert arises. Example: P gives personalty on trust to Q to purchase land and hold it for R – the personalty is notionally considered as realty. See *Fletcher v Ashburner* (1779) 1 Bro CC 497; *Irani Finance Ltd v Singh* [1971] Ch. 59. *See* CONVERSION, TORT OF; RECON-VERSION.

conversion of title. Rules set out in L.R.A. 1925, s. 77 (as substituted by L.R.A. 1986, s. 1) whereby: good lease-hold title may be upgraded to absolute title at any time; possessory title may be upgraded to absolute (if freehold) or good leasehold (if leasehold); quali-fied title may be converted to absolute (if freehold) or good leasehold (if leasehold) at any time.

conversion, tort of. An act in relation to a person's goods which constitutes a serious and unjustifiable denial of his title to them. Plaintiff must show pos-session or the right to immediate pos-session. See, e.g.: *Chubb Cash v Crilley & Son* [1983] 1 WLR 599; *BBMB v Eda Holdings* [1990] 1 WLR 409. An action lies in conversion for loss or destruc-tion of goods which a bailee has allowed to happen in breach of his duty to his bailor (that is to say, it lies in a case which is not otherwise con-version, but would have been detinue (q.v.) before detinue was abolished): Torts (Interference with Goods) Act 1977, s. 2. *See* BAILMENT; DELIVERY UP OF GOODS.

convert, duty to. A trustee's responsi-bility to convert, imposed by statute (see A.E.A. 1925, s. 3), or by the trust instrument, or the rule in *Howe v Lord Dartmouth* (1802) 7 Ves 137, under which, where there is in a will a resi-duary bequest of personal estate which is to be enjoyed by persons in possess-ion, and there is no intention on the part of the settlor that the property is to be enjoyed *in specie*, then the trus-tees are under a duty to convert all the property of a wasting, hazardous, reversionary or unauthorised charac-ter into authorised investments.

conveyance. 1. Transfer of ownership of property. 2. The instrument effecting the transfer. 3. Under L.P.A. 1925, s. 205(1), includes "mortgage, charge, lease, asset, vesting declaration, dis-claimer, release and every other assur-ance of property or of an interest therein by any instrument, except a will". See also L.C.A. 1972, s. 17(1). 4. Under Th.A. 1968, s. 12(1), as amended by C.J.A. 1988, s. 32, it is an offence to take a conveyance (i.e., one constructed or adapted for the car-riage of persons by land, water or air) for one's own or another's use without having the consent of the owner or other lawful authority. *See* JOY RIDING.

conveyance, deed of. *See* DEED.

conveyancer, licensed. One who holds a licence in force under A.J.A. 1985, Part II, allowing him to provide conveyanc-ing services (see C.L.S.A. 1990, s. 119(1)), e.g., preparation of transfers, conveyances, contracts and other documents in connection with, and other services ancillary to, the disposition or acquisition of estates or interests in land: A.J.A. 1985, s. 11.

conveyance, voluntary. *See* VOLUNTARY DISPOSITION.

Conveyancing Appeal Tribunals. Established under C.L.S.A. 1990, s. 41, to consider appeals from decisions of the Authorised Practitioners Board to refuse, or suspend applications for, authorisation under s. 37: s. 41. Appeal on points of law may be heard by the High Court: s. 42.

conviction. Defined under the Bail Act 1976, s. 2(1), as: a finding of guilt; a finding that a person is not guilty by reason of insanity; a finding under M.C.A. 1980, s. 30, that the person in question did the act or made the omission charged; a conviction of an offence for which an order is made placing the offender on probation or discharging him absolutely or conditionally.

conviction, proof of. The establishing of the fact of a person's conviction. Certified copies of extracts from court records are admissible. See, e.g., P. & C.E.A. 1984, ss. 73(1), 74. Fingerprints (q.v.) or palm prints (q.v.) may suffice under C.J.A. 1948.

convictions, evidence of previous. *See* PREVIOUS CONVICTIONS, EVIDENCE OF.

cooling-off period. Period during which a regulated agreement (q.v.) may be cancelled by a debtor or hirer: see C.C.A. 1974, ss. 67–74. See Consumer Protection (Contracts Concluded away from Business Premises) Regulations (SI 1987/2117) allowing a customer who contracts to buy goods or services during a trader's unsolicited visit to his home or place of work, a seven-day cooling-off period. The regulations do not apply, e.g., to the buying or leasing of land.

co-ownership of real property. Subsists, as in a joint tenancy (q.v.) and a tenancy in common (q.v.), where two or more persons simultaneously enjoy concurrent interests in the same property. *See also* COPARCENARY.

coparcenary. Where two or more persons together constituted a single heir, e.g., tenant in tail (q.v.) who has died intestate and left female heirs only. The heirs (coparceners) held in undivided shares. Abolished, save in the case of a tenant in tail who dies without having barred the entail, by A.E.A. 1925, s. 45(1). *See* BARRING OF ENTAILED INTEREST.

copyhold. Tenure at the will of the lord of the manor. Converted into socage tenure (q.v.) as from 1st January 1926: L.P.A. 1922, s. 128. See also L.P.A. 1925; L.P. (Amendment) A. 1926.

copyright. A property right (which is transmissible by assignment or will as personal property) which subsists in original literary, dramatic, musical or artistic works, sound recordings, films, broadcasts or cable programmes, and the typographical arrangement of published editions: Copyright, Designs and Patents Act 1988, s. 1(1). "Original" means originating from the author, not copied: see *Interlego* v *Tyco Industries* [1989] 3 WLR 678. "Author" means the person who creates the work: s. 9(1); he is the first owner of the copyright. Usually continues for the holder's life plus 50 years: s. 12(1). An author has the right to be identified as such: s. 77. Remedies for infringement include damages, injunctions: s. 96. For Copyright Tribunal, see Ch. VIII, See *BBC Enterprises* v *High-Tech Extravision Ltd* [1991] 3 WLR 1.

copyright, acts restricted by. These comprise: copying of the work (s. 17); issuing copies to the public (s. 18); performing, showing or playing the work in public (s. 19); broadcasting the work (s. 20): Copyright, Designs and Patents Act 1988, s. 16(1). For permitted acts (involving, e.g., research and private study), see Ch. III, 1988 Act. See *Express Newspapers* v *News (UK) Ltd* [1990] 3 All ER 376. Chancery Division has exclusive jurisdiction in all copyright matters: *Apac Rowena* v *Norpol Packaging* [1991] 4 All ER 516.

copyright, Crown. *See* CROWN COPYRIGHT.

copyright works, moral rights in. Stated in Copyright, Designs and Patents Act 1988, Ch. IV, as the right to be identified as: author or director ("right of paternity"); right to object to derogatory treatment of work ("right of integrity"); right to object to false attribution; right to privacy of certain photographs and films. Duration of moral rights is for the author's life plus 50 years: s. 86.

coram. In the presence of, e.g., *coram judice* (in the presence of the judge, i.e., before the court).

co-respondent. Generally refers to an alleged adulterer in relation to a petition for divorce or judicial separation and made, jointly with the wife, respondent to the suit. He need not be named in the petition: Family Proceedings Rules 1991, r. 2. See Mat.C.A. 1973, s. 49(1). *See* DIVORCE.

coroner. A person appointed under the Coroners Act 1988 from barristers, solicitors and registered medical practitioners of at least five years' standing. He has jurisdiction over treasure trove found in his district (s. 30), and, principally, inquests into deaths of persons dying within his district where there is, e.g., reasonable cause for suspecting violent or unnatural death: s. 8. His court is essentially a fact-finding body. In some cases the coroner's office must summon a jury whose verdict is termed an "inquisition" (q.v.). See also A.J.A. 1982, s. 62; C.L.S.A. 1990, Sch. 10; *A.-G.* v *Hampshire Coroner* [1991] COD 11. *See* POST-MORTEM.

corporal punishment. *See* PUNISHMENT, CORPORAL.

corporate body. *See* BODY CORPORATE.

corporate liability. The extension of liability for the commission of offences to companies and corporations. See *Bolton Engineering Co* v *Graham & Sons* [1957] 1 QB 159 – "In cases where the law requires a guilty mind as a condition of a criminal offence, the guilty mind of the directors or managers will render the company itself guilty": *per* Lord Denning. See Th.A. 1968, s. 18; T.C.P.A. 1990, s. 331; *Richmond BC* v *Pinn* (1989) 87 LGR 659; *R* v *P & O European Ferries Ltd* (1991) 93 Cr App R 72 (corporate manslaughter).

corporate veil. *See* LIFTING THE CORPORATE VEIL.

corporation. A body of persons associated for some purpose and considered as having rights and duties and the capacity of succession. A *corporation aggregate* is made up of groups of persons, e.g., incorporated companies. A *corporation sole* consists of one person and his successors in some public office, e.g., a bishop. A *corporation by prescription* (e.g., The City of London) is founded on the presumption that a charter was

granted but has been lost. A corporation is domiciled in its place of incorporation: *Gasque* v *IRC* [1940] 2 KB 80. *See* BODY CORPORATE.

corporation, public *See* PUBLIC CORPORATION.

corporation, statutory. *See* PUBLIC CORPORATION.

corporation tax. Tax paid on profits by companies and unincorporated associations other than partnerships. See I.C.T.A. 1988, ss. 8, 393; *Blackpool Marton Rotary Club* v *Martin* [1990] STC 1.

corporeal hereditaments. Visible, tangible property, e.g., houses, goods. *See* HEREDITAMENTS.

corpus delicti. The body of an offence, i.e., the aggregation of fundamental facts constituting an offence.

corpus juris. 1. A body of law. 2. Specifically, the collective designation of Justinian's sixth-century codification of sections of Roman law – *Corpus Juris Civilis*.

corrective justice. *See* JUSTICE, COMMUTATIVE, DISTRIBUTIVE AND CORRECTIVE.

correspondence, contract by. A contract, the terms of which are set out in letters which have passed between the parties or their agents. See L.P.A. 1925, s. 46; *Stearn* v *Twitchell* [1985] 1 All ER 631 (a single letter is not "correspondence").

correspondent. "In relation to a letter or other communication, means the sender or the addressee": British Telecommunications Act 1981, s. 66(5).

corroboration. Independent, admissible and credible evidence tending to confirm that the principal evidence is true. "Perhaps the best synonym is 'support'": *DPP* v *Hester* [1972] 3 All ER 1056. In a criminal case it must confirm that the crime has been committed and that the accused committed it. See, e.g., Perjury Act 1911, s. 13. It is required, usually, in some civil cases, e.g., affiliation proceedings, and in some criminal cases involving, e.g., perjury, evidence of an accomplice, some sexual offences. See Civil Evidence Act 1968, s. 6(4); Law Comm (1992) No. 202; *DPP* v *Kilbourne* [1973] AC 729; *Crossland* v *DPP* [1988] 3 All ER 712.

corroboration, rationale of. "Any risk of the conviction of an innocent person is lessened if conviction is based upon the testimony of more than one acceptable witness . . . The purpose of corroboration is not to give validity or credence to evidence which is deficient or suspect or incredible, but only to confirm and support that which as evidence is sufficient and satisfactory and credible": *per* Lord Morris in *DPP v Hester* [1973] AC 296.

corruption. Generally refers to an inducement by means of an improper consideration to violate some duty. See Prevention of Corruption Act 1916; *R v Parker* (1985) 82 Cr App R 60; *R v L G Election Commissioner ex p Mainwaring* (1991) The Times, 21 Jan. Representation of the People Act 1983, ss. 106–115, 158–160; C.J.A. 1988, s. 47. *See* BRIBERY; TREATING.

corruption of public morals. The term "suggests conduct which a jury might find to be destructive of the very fabric of society": *Knuller Ltd v DPP* [1972] 2 All ER 898.

costs. The expenses relating to an action. See, generally, S.C.A. 1981, s. 51, and O. 62. Includes "fees, charges, disbursements, expenses and remuneration": O. 62, r. 1. Each party must pay his solicitor's costs and the unsuccessful party may be ordered to pay costs to his opponent. Costs are usually in the discretion of the court and are normally dealt with at the conclusion of the cause of matter concerned (which is also the time when taxation normally occurs: O. 62, r. 8). See also Solicitors Act 1974, s. 87(1). For magistrates' powers to award costs see M.C.A. 1980, s. 64. For costs out of central funds (q.v.) in criminal proceedings, see *Practice Direction* [1991] 1 WLR 498; in civil proceedings see *Holden v CPS (No. 2)* (1991) NLJ 1626. See Prosecution of Offenders Act 1985, Part II. *See* COSTS, TAXATION OF.

costs, contentious. Costs incurred in or for the purposes of proceedings begun before a court or arbitrator. See Solicitors Act 1974, s. 61.

costs, discretion in relation to. Element of latitude allowed to the court in dealing with the questions of costs. There should be taken into account: offer of contribution (q.v.); payment into court (q.v.); and amount of such payment, any offer made on liability in connection with a split trial, and any offer contained in a "*Calderbank* let-

ter" (q.v.) (O. 62, r. 9). The discretion "must be exercised judicially and the judge ought not to exercise it against the successful party, except for some reason connected with the case": *Donald Campbell & Co Ltd v Pollak* [1927] AC 732.

costs follow the event. Success in litigation is generally followed by the award of costs (a discretionary matter) to the successful party (see O. 62, r. 3(3)). For security for costs see, e.g., *De Bry v Fitzgerald* [1990] 1 All ER 560.

costs in any event. Order made by the court suggesting its disapproval of a party's conduct, e.g., where that party has refused to disclose relevant documents. The party is ordered to pay costs of the application whether or not he eventually wins the case (see O. 62, r. 3(6)). Costs of this kind are (normally) payable only after the actual case has been determined.

costs in criminal cases. An acquitted defendant may be awarded costs out of central funds by a magistrates' court or the Crown Court, as compensation for properly-incurred expenses, where, e.g., an information has been laid but not proceeded with or the magistrates dismiss the information: Prosecution of Offenders Act 1985, s. 16, as amended by C.J.A. 1987, Sch. 2. A successful private prosecutor (but not a public authority) may be awarded just and reasonable costs: s. 17. For award of costs out of central funds against an accused person, see s. 18.

costs in the cause. "Means that the costs of . . . interlocutory proceedings are to be awarded according to the final award of costs in the action": *Stratford & Son Ltd v Lindley (No. 2)* [1969] 1 WLR 1547; see O. 62, r. 3(6).

costs, recovery of. An action cannot be brought to recover costs due to a solicitor until one month after the delivery of a bill signed by the solicitor or a partner in the firm: Solicitors Act 1974, ss. 69, 70.

costs reserved. Order in interlocutory proceedings whereby the master leaves to the trial judge the decision as to payment of costs (see O. 62, r. 3(6)).

costs, taxation of. An examination by an officer of the court of the lawyers' bills of costs in litigation, conducted with a view to ensuring that the claims for costs are for fair sums in relation to the work necessary to be done; see O. 62. Decisions may be reviewed, first by the taxing officer, then by a judge: O. 62, rr. 33–35. See e.g., *Harrison* v *Tew* [1990] 1 All ER 321. *See* INDEMNITY BASIS FOR COSTS; SOLICITOR AND OWN CLIENT BASIS OF COSTS; STANDARD BASIS FOR COSTS; TRUSTEES' COSTS BASIS.

costs, trustees', basis. *See* TRUSTEES' COSTS BASIS.

costs, wasted. Any costs incurred by a party as a result of any improper, unreasonable or negligent act or omission on the part of any legal or other representative or any employee of such a representative; or, which in the light of any such act or omission occurring after they were incurred, the court considers it is unreasonable to expect that party to pay: S.C.A. 1981, s. 51, substituted by C.L.S.A. 1990, s. 4. See *Wasted Costs Order, No.1 of 1991* (1992) The Times, 6 May.

costs, with. *See* WITH COSTS.

Council of Legal Education. Body, set up in 1852, responsible to the Senate of the Inns of Court and the Bar (q.v.) for the examinations and prescribed courses leading to call to the Bar (q.v.).

Council of Ministers. The body of representatives of the member states of the EEC, made up of government delegates. Its task is to ensure coordination of the general economic policies of member states: Treaty of Rome 1957, art. 145. The office of President is held by each member of the Council in turn. Business is prepared by the Committee of Permanent Representatives. *See* EEC.

Council on Tribunals. Body of 10–15 independent persons appointed by the Lord Chancellor and Secretary of State to keep under review the constitution and working of tribunals (q.v.). The Parliamentary Ombudsman (q.v.) is an *ex officio* member. See Tribunals and Inquiries Act 1992, ss. 1–3.

councils, county. Elected bodies for defined areas within the local government system comprising councillors (elected for four years) presided over by chairman. They are responsible for, e.g., lighting, police and fire services.

councils, district. Bodies corporate set up to administer local government in the divisions of counties known as districts (q.v.).

council tax. Tax, which replaced "community charge" (q.v.), payable in respect of chargeable dwellings: see Local Government Finance Act 1992, s. 1. Dwellings are placed in valuation bands: s. 5. Provision is made for discounts where there are fewer than two residents: s. 11. The tax is set with reference to calculations relating to local authorities' budget requirements and precepts. See SI 1992/550.

counsel. 1. A practising barrister (q.v.). 2. To advise. See Accessories and Abettors Act 1861, as amended; *R* v *Calhaem* [1985] QB 808.

Counsellors of State. Appointed by virtue of the Regency Act 1937. Royal functions are delegated to them in the event of the Sovereign's illness or absence abroad. See also Regency Acts 1943 and 1953.

counsel's duty in course of trial. Prosecuting counsel "ought not to struggle for the verdict against the prisoner, but they ought to bear themselves rather in the character of ministers of justice assisting in the administration of justice": *per* Avery J in *R* v *Banks* [1916] 2 KB 62. "It is not the duty of prosecuting counsel to obtain a conviction by all means at his command but rather to lay before the jury fairly and impartially the whole of the facts which comprise the case for the prosecution and to see that the jury are properly instructed in the law applicable to those facts": *Code of Conduct for the Bar.*

counterclaim. A cross-action (q.v.) which is not a defence, but, in effect, the defendant's statement of claim. If claim and counterclaim are of an entirely different nature and cannot be tried together conveniently, the court may order that the counterclaim be tried separately. It must always claim relief against the plaintiff: *Furness* v *Booth* (1876) 4 Ch D 587. See O. 15, r. 2; O. 18, r. 17; *The Gniezno* [1968] P 418.

counterclaim, discontinuance of. Procedure under O. 21, r. 3, whereby notice of discontinuance is served upon the plaintiff with leave (applied for by summons or motion or notice under O. 25, r. 7) or without leave if served within 14 days of service of the plaintiff's defence to the counterclaim, or within 14 days of expiration of the time intended for service if no defence was served.

counterfeit. A thing is a counterfeit of a currency note or of a protected coin (q.v.) if it is not a currency note or protected coin, but resembles them (whether on one side only or both) to such an extent that they are reasonably capable of passing for currency notes or protected coins, or if it is a currency note or protected coin which has been so altered that it is reasonably capable of passing for a currency note or protected coin of some other description: Forgery and Counterfeiting Act 1981, s. 28(1).

counterfeiting. It is an offence for a person to make a counterfeit of a currency note or of a protected coin (q.v.) intending that he or another shall pass or tender it as genuine: Forgery and Counterfeiting Act 1981, s. 14(1). It is an offence to make a counterfeit of a currency note or of a protected coin without lawful excuse or authority: s. 14(2). See COUNTERFEIT.

counterfeit notes. It is an offence to have in one's custody counterfeit notes and coins intending to pass or tender them as genuine; to have in one's custody and control things intended to be used for the purpose of counterfeiting; to import or export counterfeit notes or coins without Treasury consent: Forgery and Counterfeiting Act 1981, ss. 16–21.

counter-offer. See OFFER, COUNTER-.

counties palatine. The counties of Chester, Durham, Lancaster. Courts of these counties exercised chancery jurisdiction until their abolition by the Courts Act 1971, s. 41.

counts. The sections of an indictment (q.v.) containing separate allegations and charges. "Every count in an indictment is equivalent to a separate indictment; the prisoner can be tried on one or all of the counts": *R* v *Boyle* [1954] 2 QB 292.

counts, alternative. Separate clauses in an indictment (q.v.) each charging a separate offence, where the charges are based on the same facts or form part of a series of offences of the same

or a similar nature. See Indictment Rules 1971.

counts, general. Counts (q.v.) which are too general and insufficient may be quashed.

counts, separate. Where more than one offence is charged in an indictment (q.v.) each must generally be stated in a separate count (i.e., section) and each must be numbered separately. A count which charges more than one offence may be void for duplicity: *R* v *Molloy* [1921] 2 KB 364. See *DPP* v *Shah* [1984] 1 WLR 886; *R* v *GMC, ex p Gee* [1987] 1 WLR 564. See DUPLICITY.

county. Territorial division. See L.G.A. 1972. England is divided into a collection of borough councils and similar bodies for London, six metropolitan district councils (see L.G.A. 1985) and 39 counties. Wales has eight counties.

county councils. See COUNCILS, COUNTY.

county court registrar. See REGISTRAR, COUNTY COURT.

county courts. The main civil courts, established by the County Courts Act 1846. Their jurisdiction is statutory and includes: actions founded on contract and tort where the amount claimed is not more than an amount stated by Order in Council (see County C.A. 1984, s. 145); equity matters, e.g., trusts and mortgages where the amount does not exceed a statutory limit; actions for the recovery of land. All judges of the Supreme Court, circuit judges and recorders are empowered to sit in county courts. Rules of procedure are made by a rule committee (appointed by the Lord Chancellor) and are printed in the current "Green Book". Trial by jury may be ordered in an exceptional case. Each court sits at least once a month. Appeals on matters of law, evidence, fact, lie to the Court of Appeal or, in some few cases (involving, e.g., bankruptcy) to the High Court. See County C.A. 1984, amended by C.L.S.A. 1990, ss. 2, 3; Courts Act 1971; the I.A. 1978, Sch. 1; County Court Rules 1981; A.J.A. 1982, Part V; Matrimonial and Family Proceedings Act 1984, ss. 33, 34; High Court and County Courts Jurisdiction Order 1991 (SI 1991/724); SI 1991/1877 (appeals); Practice Direction [1991] 1 WLR 695; *Howes* v *Howes*

(1992) NLJ 753 (committal by county court).

county courts, choice of. In general, a plaintiff must commence proceedings in the court for the district in which the defendant resides or carries on business or in the court for the district where the cause of action arose wholly or in part. See County Court Rules 1981, O. 2, r. 1(1); O. 16, r. 4.

course of employment. The scope of a person's employment. Thus, a wrong committed falls within the scope of employment if expressly or impliedly authorised by the master or if necessarily incidental to something which the person who has committed the wrong is employed to do. See *Heatons Transport Ltd* v *TGWU* [1973] AC 15; *Kooragang Investments* v *Richardson & Wrench* [1982] AC 482.

court. 1. Residence of the Sovereign. 2. Formal assembly of a Sovereign's councillors. 3. A place where justice is administered. 4. Persons assembled under the authority of the law for the purpose of administering justice, i.e., the judge or judges. See also C.J.J.A. 1982, s. 50; C.L.S.A. 1990, s. 119(1); and *AEWU* v *Devanayagam* [1986] AC 356.

Court, Admiralty. *See* ADMIRALTY COURT.

court, attributes of a. Created by the state; conducts its procedure in accordance with rules of natural justice; procedure includes public hearing, reception of oral evidence, hearing of argument, oral examination and cross-examination of witnesses; has before it at least two parties, one of whom may be the Crown; and arrives at a decision concerned with legal rights which is final and binding for so long as it stands: *per* Eveleigh LJ in *A.-G.* v *BBC* [1981] AC 303. "The fundamental human right is not to a legal system that is infallible but to one that is fair": *per* Lord Diplock in *Maharaj* v *A.-G. of Trinidad (No. 2)* [1978] 1 WLR 902.

Court, Companies. *See* COMPANIES COURT.

Court, Consistory. *See* CONSISTORY COURT.

Court, Crown. *See* CROWN COURT.

court, election. *See* ELECTION COURT.

Court for Consideration of Crown Cases Reserved. Established in 1888 so as to decide questions of law reserved for

consideration by a judge or magistrate. Superseded by Court of Criminal Appeal (q.v.).

court-house, petty sessional. A court-house or place at which justices are accustomed to assemble for holding special or petty sessions (q.v.) (or for the time being appointed as a substitute place) or at which a stipendiary magistrate (q.v.) is authorised to do alone any act authorised to be done by more than one justice of the peace: M.C.A. 1980, s. 150(1).

court leet. (*Lathe* = land.) Ancient court of record, now virtually obsolete, which met annually within a manor or hundred (q.v.) to review trivial misdemeanours. See Sheriffs Act 1887, s. 40; L.P.A. 1922, s. 128.

Court of Appeal. It consists of the Lord Chancellor, Lord Chief Justice, Master of the Rolls, President of the Family Division, former Lord Chancellors, Lords of Appeal in Ordinary, Lords Justices of Appeal. There are two divisions: (1) *Criminal Division.* Successor of the Court of Criminal Appeal (q.v.) which was created in 1907. It exists "to correct demonstrable errors and to develop and clarify the law", and hears, e.g., appeals by persons convicted on indictment, or against sentence from the Crown Court (q.v.). Appeal is from the Criminal Division to the House of Lords. (2) *Civil Division.* Hears, e.g., appeals from the High Court, county courts, various tribunals. Appeal is usually by way of re-hearing. The work of the Civil Division is administered by the Registrar of Civil Appeals (see S.C.A. 1981, s. 89). Appeal is from the Civil Division to the House of Lords. See S.C.A. 1981; C.J.A. 1988, s. 43; Supreme Court Practice 1991, para 59; *R* v *McIlkenny and Others* (1991) The Guardian, 28 Mar. *See* APPEAL.

Court of Appeal, reception of fresh evidence by. "First, it must be shown that the evidence could not have been obtained with reasonable diligence for use at the trial; secondly, the evidence must be such that, if given, it would probably have an important influence on the result of the case, though it need not be decisive; thirdly, the evidence must be such as is presumably to be believed, or, in other words, it must be apparently credible though it need not be incontrovertible": *per* Denning LJ in *Ladd* v *Marshall* [1954] 1 WLR 1489. See *Skone* v *Skone* [1971] 1 WLR 812.

Court of Arches. Ecclesiastical court which has the jurisdiction of the former Provincial Court of Archbishop and hears appeals from the consistory court (q.v.). See, e.g., *Re St. Mary's, Banbury* [1987] 1 All ER 247.

Court of Chancery. Originally a court of equity consisting of Lord Chancellor, Master of the Rolls and vice-chancellors. Merged in the Supreme Court of Judicature by J.A. 1873 and became known as the Chancery Division (q.v.).

Court of Chivalry. Ancient feudal court, presided over by the Earl Marshal, which decided disputes concerning, e.g., the right to use armorial bearings. Last sat in 1955: *Manchester Corporation* v *Manchester Palace of Varieties (Ltd)* [1955] P 133.

Court of Common Pleas. Also known as the Court of Common Bench. A part of Curia Regis (q.v.) having extensive jurisdiction in civil actions, other than those concerning royal rights. It followed the King in his travels through the realm, before Magna Carta (q.v.). Transferred to High Court by J.A. 1873.

Court of Criminal Appeal. Created in 1907 by Criminal Appeal Act 1907. Consisted of the Lord Chief Justice and judges of the QBD. It heard appeals from, e.g., quarter sessions, assizes, Central Criminal Court. Abolished by Criminal Appeal Act 1966. *See* COURT OF APPEAL.

Court of Ecclesiastical Causes Reserved. Court composed of five judges, including two who have held high judicial office and three diocesan bishops, exercising jurisdiction over clergy in matters relating to ritual and doctrine. Petition lies to a Commission of Review (q.v.).

Court of Exchequer. 1. A division of Curia Regis (q.v.) with jurisdiction relating principally to public revenue matters. Jurisdiction was transferred to High Court of Justice, Exchequer Division, under J.A. 1873. 2. A Court of Exchequer Chamber was set up in 1830 to hear appeals from all common law courts. Jurisdiction passed to Court of Appeal (q.v.) in 1875.

Court of Faculties. An office administered by the Archbishop and responsible for the granting of faculties. See Public Worship Regulation Act 1874. *See* FACULTY.

court of first instance. Court in which proceedings are initiated.

Court of First Instance of EC. Inaugurated in 1989. Sits in Luxembourg in divisions of 3–5 judges to hear disputes between the EC and its staff, applications for judicial review against the Council or Commission in matters concerning, e.g., levies and prices. Appeal to the Court of Justice of the EC (q.v.) from CFI lies on grounds of CFI's lack of competence, breach of procedure and infringement of Community law. See, e.g., Case 51/89.

Court of High Commission. *See* HIGH COMMISSION, COURT OF.

Court of Human Rights, European. *See* EUROPEAN COURT OF HUMAN RIGHTS.

Court of Justice, International. *See* INTERNATIONAL COURT OF JUSTICE.

Court of Justice of the European Communities. Institution set up under Treaty of Rome to ensure that in interpretation and application of the Treaty the law is observed. It consists of judges from each member state, appointed for 6-year periods, assisted by three Advocates General (q.v.). It sits in Luxembourg, expressing itself in judgments when called upon to do so in proceedings initiated by member states, institutions of the EEC and natural or legal persons. Procedures are generally inquisitorial. Art. 173 provides for annulment by the Court of acts of the Council or Commission based on lack of competence, misuse of powers, infringement of the Treaty or of an essential procedural requirement. On all matters of Community law (q.v.), courts of the UK defer to relevant decisions of the Court of Justice. See Treaty of Rome 1957; *Van Duyn* v *Home Office* [1974] 3 All ER 178; O. 114. *See* COMMUNITY LAW, SOURCES OF; EEC.

Court of Justice of the European Communities, references to. See O. 114. The following principles relating to references from English courts were set out in *HP Bulmer Ltd* v *J. Bollinger SA* [1974] Ch 401: (1) only questions of Community law may be referred;

(2) questions will not be referred if a decision is not needed to enable the English court to give judgment; (3) questions will not be referred if free from doubt and generally clear; (4) points will not be referred if already decided by the Court of Justice; (5) all circumstances, including, e.g., time, interests of justice, must be taken into account. See EEC Treaty, art. 177. For actions heard directly by the Court of Justice see arts. 173, 175, 178, 215. See, e.g., *R v Henn and Darby* [1980] 2 WLR 597.

Court of King's (Queen's) Bench. Superior court of common law having concurrent jurisdiction in civil actions with the Court of Common Pleas (q.v.), and criminal jurisdiction. It heard pleas of the Crown, i.e., matters relating to wrongs committed against the peace of the King. Merged in the Supreme Court by J.A. 1873.

court of last resort. A court from which there can be no appeal.

Court of Pie Poudre. *Pieds poudrés* = dusty feet (probably reference to feet of litigants). Also known as the Piepowder Court. Originally a court of record with jurisdiction in commercial matters arising out of fairs and markets. Survived in the Bristol Tolzey Court until 1971.

Court of Probate. Usually the Family Division of the High Court. *See* PROBATE.

Court of Protection. Administers the property of mentally disordered persons (within the meaning of M.H.A. 1983), and consists of a master and other officers. Where the property is of small value, the power of administration may be exercised by the High Court. See Court of Protection Rules 1984; Public Trustee and Administration of Funds Act 1986, s. 2; Enduring Powers of Attorney Act 1985, Rules 1986, 1990; *Re W.* [1971] Ch 123; *Re B.* [1987] 1 WLR 552; and M.H.A. 1983, s. 93; SI 1992/1899.

court of record. Phrase used to refer to a court, the records of which are maintained and preserved, and which may punish for contempt of court (q.v.). See, e.g., S.C.A. 1981, s. 15(1).

Court of Requests. 1. A court of equity which grew out of the jurisdiction of the King's Council, concerned in particular, with petitions from the poor. It was suspended in 1642. See *Stepney v Flood* (1598) Cro Eliz 646. 2. Courts of Requests, or of Conscience, were set up to hear small causes. Abolished by County C.A. 1846.

Court of Session. The supreme civil court of Scotland. See Court of Session Act 1988.

court of summary jurisdiction. Obsolescent expression, now superseded by the term "magistrates' court" (q.v.).

Court of Tynwald. *See* TYNWALD, COURT OF.

Court, Patents. *See* PATENTS COURT.

court, payment into. *See* PAYMENT INTO COURT.

court, requesting. *See* REQUESTING COURT.

Court, Rules of. *See* RULES OF COURT.

court, sale by the. *See* SALE BY THE COURT.

courts, county *See* COUNTY COURTS.

courts' decisions, statement of reasons for. There is a general duty to state a reason for a judicial decision: see, e.g., *Davies v Price* [1958] 1 WLR 434. See also C.J.A. 1982, s. 2; *Medical Appeal Tribunal, ex p Gilmore* [1957] 1 QB 574; *Padfield v Minister of Agriculture* [1968] AC 997.

Courts, Divisional. *See* DIVISIONAL COURTS.

courts, inferior. *See* INFERIOR COURTS.

courts, juvenile. *See* JUVENILE COURTS.

courts, magistrates'. *See* MAGISTRATES' COURTS.

courts-martial. Courts governed by Army and Air Force Acts 1955, Naval Discipline Act 1957, and Armed Forces Acts 1971–91, exercising jurisdiction over members of HM Forces. Murder, manslaughter, rape and treason committed within the UK are tried by the ordinary criminal courts. Trial at a court-martial is generally preceded by an inquiry and takes place before 3–5 officers assisted by a judge-advocate. A finding of guilt must be confirmed by a superior officer. A Courts-Martial Appeal Court was created in 1951; appeal lies from it to the House of Lords. See Courts-Martial (Appeals) Act 1968; A.J.A. 1977, s. 5; S.C.A. 1981, s. 145; A.J.A. 1982, Sch. 8; *R v Aitken* (1992) The Times, 10 June.

courts of civil jurisdiction. These include county courts, Queen's Bench Division, Chancery Division, Family Division, Court of Appeal (Civil Division) and House of Lords.

courts of criminal jurisdiction. These include magistrates' courts, Crown Court, Divisional Courts, Court of Appeal (Criminal Division) and House of Lords.

courts of special jurisdiction. Courts exercising a jurisdiction within specialised fields, e.g., courts-martial, ecclesiastical courts.

Courts of the Staple. *See* STAPLE.

courts palatine. *See* PALATINE COURTS.

Courts, prize. *See* PRIZE COURTS.

courts, remedies and. "Courts of justice do not act of their own motion. In our legal system it is their function to stand idly by until their aid is invoked by someone recognised by law as entitled to claim the remedy in justice that he seeks": *per* Lord Diplock in *Gouriet v UPW* [1978] AC 435.

courts, superior. *See* SUPERIOR COURTS.

court, suit of. *See* SUIT OF COURT.

Court, Supreme. *See* SUPREME COURT.

court, ward of. *See* WARD.

covenant. A promise usually contained in a deed. See, e.g., *Hagee v Cooperative Insurance Society* [1991] NPC 92. No technical words are necessary to constitute a covenant: *Lant v Norris* (1775) 1 Burr 287. It will be implied only where it is apparently necessary to carry out the intention of the deed.

covenant, restrictive. *See* RESTRICTIVE COVENANT.

covenant running with the land. A covenant which ran with (or "touched and concerned") land was one which had direct reference to the land, e.g., to renew a lease, to repair property, not to build on adjoining land. A covenant of this nature may be enforced if the entire interest in the land is transferred and there is privity of contract (q.v.) between the parties. See *Kumar v Dunning* [1987] 2 All ER 801; *Federated Homes v Mill Lodge Properties* [1980] 1 WLR 594.

covenants, implied. Covenants (q.v.) which, although not stated directly, arise in certain types of conveyance. Examples: in a conveyance as beneficial owner, implied covenants include a good right to convey, quiet enjoyment, freedom from incumbrances. See L.P.A. 1925, ss. 76, 77, Sch. 2.

covenants, onerous. Covenants which impose obligations on a tenant which, at common law, he would not otherwise have, e.g., to insure or not to exercise a particular trade. See *Cosser v Collinge* (1832) 3 My & K 283; *Propert v Parker* (1832) 3 My & K 280. *See* ONEROUS.

covenants, usual. Where the phrase is contained in a lease it refers, generally, to covenants to pay rent, to pay the tenant's taxes and rates, to keep and deliver up premises in repair, to allow the lessor to enter and view the state of repairs: *Hampshire v Wickens* (1878) 7 Ch D 555. The list, however, is not closed; *Flexman v Corbett* [1930] 1 Ch 672. See *Chester v Buckingham Travel Ltd* [1981] 1 WLR 96.

cover note. Document issued by insurer to insured, covering risks until the issue of a policy. See *Mackie v European Assurance Society* (1869) 21 LT 102.

coverture. Legal status of a woman during marriage (i.e., under the authority (cover) of her husband).

credit. 1. Usually an agreed period of time given by a seller to a buyer for payment for goods. As used in C.C.A. 1974, the word covers all types of loan and financial accommodation, no matter the form in which made. "Running account credit" refers in the Act to facilities under a personal credit agreement, e.g., an overdraft or shop budget. "Fixed sum credit" refers to a hire-purchase agreement, or a loan of a fixed amount. "Credit brokerage" is used in the Act to refer to the introduction of individuals desiring to obtain credit or goods on hire to persons who carry on a consumer credit or hire business. See also S.G.A. 1979, s. 61. "Credit bargain" is any personal credit agreement (q.v.). 2. A "witness's credit" is his credibility. *See* CREDIT UNION.

credit business, ancillary. *See* ANCILLARY CREDIT BUSINESS.

credit card. *See* CREDIT TOKEN.

credit, cross-examination as to. Cross-examination (q.v.) of a witness designed to discredit him by showing, e.g., that his character or background is such that he ought not to be believed. Generally, cross-examination *as to credit* relates to the character of the witness, cross-examination *as to credibility* may be concerned with attributes likely to affect his credibility (e.g., some physical characteristic). See, e.g.,

R v *Sweet-Escott* (1971) Cr App R 316; *R* v *Funderburk* [1990] 2 All ER 482. *See* EVIDENCE.

creditor. One to whom a debt is owing. 1. A secured creditor is one who holds a mortgage (q.v.) or charge on the debtor's property. An unsecured creditor holds no such charge. 2. A judgment creditor is one in whose favour a judgment for a sum of money has been entered against a debtor. 3. Under C.C.A. 1974, s. 189(1), a creditor is a person providing credit under a consumer credit agreement or the person to whom his rights and duties under the agreement have passed by assignment or operation of law.

creditors' meeting. In relation to bankruptcy (q.v.), the summoning of every person who is a creditor of the bankrupt in respect of a bankruptcy debt, and every person who would be such a creditor if the bankruptcy had commenced on the day on which notice of the meeting is given: Ins. A 1986, s. 257. The meeting may approve or modify a proposed voluntary arrangement and must report its decisions to the court: ss. 258, 259. The approval of a voluntary arrangement binds all persons who had notice of the meeting and are entitled to vote: s. 260

creditors' meeting, in relation to companies. Meeting of creditors summoned under Ins. A. 1986, s. 23, to decide whether to approve the proposals of an administrator (q.v.): s. 24(1). A creditors' committee may be established under s. 26.

creditor's petition. A bankruptcy petition presented against a debtor by a creditor (or creditors) where: the amount of the debt is equal to or exceeds the bankruptcy level (set by the Secretary of State); each debt is for a liquidated sum payable to one or more of the creditors, immediately or at some certain future time, and is unsecured; each debt is one which the debtor appears unable to pay or to have no reasonable prospect of being able to pay; and there is no outstanding application to set aside a statutory demand served in respect of the debts: Ins. A. 1986, s. 267. *See* BANKRUPTCY PETITION; PAY, INABILITY TO.

creditor's petition, proceedings on. The court will not make a bankruptcy order (q.v.) on such a petition unless satisfied that the debt has been neither paid nor secured or compounded for, or the debtor has no reasonable prospect of being able to pay when it falls due: Ins. A. 1986, s. 271 (1). See *Re Marr* [1989] 3 WLR 674. The petition will be dismissed if the court is satisfied that the debtor is able to pay, or has made an offer to compound, and that acceptance of the offer would have required dismissal of the petition and has been unreasonably refused: s. 272 (3).

creditors, transactions defrauding. Phrase used in Ins. A. 1986, Part XVI, relating to transactions entered into at an undervalue, as where a person makes a gift to another on terms that provide for him to receive no consideration, or he enters into a transaction with the other in consideration of marriage or for a consideration the value of which is significantly less than the value of the consideration provided by himself: s. 423(1). The court can make an order protecting victims of the transaction if satisfied that its purpose was to put assets beyond the reach of a claimant: s. 423 (2), (3). See *Arbuthnot Leasing* v *Havelet Leasing* (No. 2) [1990] BCC 636.

credit reference agency. A business set up to supply information it has collected on a consumer's financial standing. Under C.C.A. 1974 a consumer is entitled to obtain from a creditor details of any agency from which information was sought. The agency is also obliged to give the consumer a copy of any file kept about him. A consumer can ask the agency to remove any offending entry. See C.C.A. 1974, ss. 145(8), 189(1).

credit, restricted-use. *See* RESTRICTED-USE CREDIT AGREEMENT.

credit sale agreement. "An agreement for the sale of goods, under which the purchase price or part of it is payable by instalments, but which is not a conditional sale agreement": C.C.A. 1974, s. 189.

credit token. Defined under C.C.A. 1974, s. 14, as "a card, cheque, voucher, coupon, stamp, form, booklet, or other document or thing" whereby a creditor undertakes, on its production, that he or a third party will supply goods, services or cash.

Under s. 51 it is an offence to give a person a credit token if he has not asked for it in writing. A credit token agreement is a regulated agreement (q.v.) under C.C.A. 1974, s. 14(2). See I.C.T.A. 1988, s. 142; *R* v *Lambie* [1981] 2 All ER 776; *Re Charge Card Services* [1988] 3 All ER 702; *R* v *Bumrungpruik* (1922) The Times, 5 June (custodial sentence for credit card theft).

credit, total charge for. The true cost to the debtor of credit provided or to be provided under an actual or prospective consumer credit agreement (q.v.): C.C.A. 1974, s. 20(1).

credit union. Financial savings and loans co-operative owned and run by its members, who share a common bond or link, e.g., residing in the same locality or being employed in a particular employment: Credit Unions Act 1979. Its objects include the promotion of thrift by savings, making loans to members: s. 1(3).

crime. Any act or omission resulting from human conduct which is considered in itself or in its outcome to be harmful and which the State wishes to prevent, which renders the person responsible liable to some kind of punishment, generally of a stigmatic nature, as the result of proceedings which are usually initiated on behalf of the State and which are designed to ascertain the nature, extent and legal consequence of that person's responsibility. In *Board of Trade* v *Owen* [1957] AC 602, the House of Lords adopted as a definition that given in Halsbury's *Laws of England*: a crime is an unlawful act or default which is an offence against the public and renders the person guilty of the act liable to legal punishment.

criminal. 1. One charged with a crime (q.v.) and found guilty. 2. Pertaining to a crime, or the character of a crime.

Criminal Appeal, Court of. *See* COURT OF CRIMINAL APPEAL.

criminal conversation. Common law action, abolished in 1857, by which a husband could recover damages against an adulterer.

criminal damage. The offence of destroying or damaging any property belonging to another, intentionally or recklessly and without lawful excuse: Criminal Damage Act 1971, s. 1(1). It

is also an offence to threaten without lawful excuse, to destroy or damage property, or to possess anything with intent to destroy or damage property without lawful excuse: ss. 2, 3. See *R* v *Caldwell* [1982] AC 341; *R* v *Dudley* [1989] Crim LR 57; *Lloyd* v *DPP* [1991] Crim LR 904.

criminal deception. *See* DECEPTION, OBTAINING PROPERTY BY.

criminal information. Proceedings in the QBD at the suit of the Crown without any previous indictment commenced by the Attorney-General *ex officio* or at the suit of a relator (q.v.). Generally abolished under A.J. (Misc. Provs.) A. 1938, s. 12 and C.LA 1967, s. 6.

Criminal Injuries Compensation Board. Set up in 1964 to consider applications for *ex gratia* payments of compensation to victims of crimes of violence. See C.J.A. 1988, ss. 108–112, Sch. 6. The Board consists of a chairman and eight legally qualified members appointed by the Home Secretary. Application is made by the injured party, or, if he is dead, the spouse or dependants. For definition of "criminal injury", see s. 109. See *R* v *CICB* (1992) The Times, 21 Jan. *See* COMPENSATION.

criminal jurisdiction, courts of. *See* COURTS OF CRIMINAL JURISDICTION.

Criminal Law Revision Committee. Committee of judges and lawyers, including the DPP (q.v.), established in 1959 to advise the Home Secretary on aspects of criminal law and to consider revisions.

criminal libel. *See* LIBEL.

criminal lunatic. Phrase used under Criminal Lunatics Act 1884, s. 16, replaced by "Broadmoor patient" under C.J.A. 1984, s. 62(2). *See* BROADMOOR.

criminal negligence. "A higher degree of negligence has always been demanded in order to establish a criminal offence than is sufficient to create civil liability. An obvious illustration is the difference between the degree of negligence in accident cases required to prove the crime of manslaughter and that sufficient to create civil liability": *per* Lord Porter in *Riddell* v *Reid* [1943] AC 1. See also *R* v *Bateman* (1925) 94 LJ KB 791; *Andrews* v *DPP* [1937] AC 576.

cross-action. An action brought by X against Y in reference to a transaction on the basis of which Y has brought an action against X. See *Davies v Hedges* (1871) LR 6 QB 687.

cross-appeals. Appeal against judgment by both parties to a case. See O. 59.

cross-examination. A stage in the examination of a witness (q.v.) designed to elicit information concerning facts in issue favourable to the party on whose behalf it is conducted, and to throw doubt on the accuracy of evidence given against that party. Known also as "cross-examination to the issue". Counsel may ask in cross-examination leading questions (q.v.) and questions designed to test knowledge, memory or to elicit existence of bias or previous contradictory statements. For cross-examination of alleged child victim, see C.J.A. 1988, s. 34, amended by C.J.A. 1991, s. 55(7). *See* CREDIT, CROSS-EXAMINATION AS TO.

cross-holdings. Situation in which two companies own shares in each other. Lawful unless the companies constitute a "group", i.e., a relationship of holding and subsidiary to each other. See Cos.A. 1985, s. 23. *See* HOLDING COMPANY.

cross-offers. *See* OFFERS, CROSS-.

Crown. The monarch, or monarchy (q.v.). Held also to mean ministers and their departments: *Town Investments v Department of the Environment* [1979] 1 All ER 813. "A corporation aggregate . . . headed by the Queen": *per* Lord Simon. Title to the Crown derives from the Act of Settlement 1701 and common law rules of descent. For the domicile and seat of the Crown, see C.J.J.A. 1982, s. 46, as amended by C.J.J.A. 1991, Sch. 2. *See* SOVEREIGN.

Crown Agents. The Crown Agents for Oversea Governments and Administrations. They provide commercial, financial and professional services for governments of independent countries, overseas public bodies and international bodies. See Crown Agents Act 1979; and Crown Agents (Amendment) Act 1986.

Crown, Commonwealth and. The Crown is not single and indivisible, but separate in respect of each self-governing territory within the Commonwealth: *R v Secretary of State, ex p Indian Association of Alberta* [1982] QB 892.

Crown copyright. Where a work is made by a Crown servant in the course of his duties it is protected by copyright for a maximum period of 125 years: Copyright, Designs and Patents Act 1988, s. 163.

Crown Court. Created by the Courts Act 1971 as part of the Supreme Court (see S.C.A. 1981, s. 1 (1)) and a superior court of record. Its jurisdiction, in relation to criminal charges on indictment (see S.C.A. 1981, s. 46), is exercised by any High Court judge, circuit judge or recorder (qq.v.), or a judge of the High Court, circuit judge or recorder sitting with not more than four JPs: S.C.A. 1981, s. 8. It sits regularly at 90 centres. "There is one Crown Court which is indivisible": *R v Slatter* [1975] 1 WLR 1084. It may hear appeals from magistrates' courts and may sentence persons committed for sentencing by those courts. Appeal lies to the Court of Appeal: see Criminal Appeal Act 1968, s. 45.

Crown Court, appeal to. The defendant may appeal against conviction in a magistrates' court. He may appeal only against sentence if he pleaded guilty, or against conviction and sentence if he pleaded not guilty. See M.C.A. 1980, s. 108. Proceedings involve a complete rehearing of the case. See S.C.A. 1981, s. 48.

Crown Court, distribution of business in. See S.C.A. 1981, s. 75. Offences are grouped in four classes: Class 1, to be tried by a High Court judge, including murder, genocide, offences under Official Secrets Act 1911, s. 1; Class 2, to be tried by a High Court judge, including manslaughter, rape, sedition; Class 3, to be tried by a High Court judge, or circuit judge or recorder, comprising all offences triable only on indictment other than those in classes 1, 2, 4; Class 4, to be tried by a High Court judge, circuit judge or recorder, including all offences triable either way, and a number of specific offences including, wounding, robbery (see *Practice Direction* [1987] 1 WLR 1671). See C.J.A. 1988, s. 41.

Crown employment. Employment under or for the purposes of a government department or any officer or body exercising on behalf of the Crown functions conferred by any statutory provision: see Employment Act 1990, s. 30; T.U.L.R.(C.)A. 1992, s. 273.

Crown interest. An interest "belonging to Her Majesty in right of the Crown or belonging to a government department or held in trust for Her Majesty for the purposes of a government department": T.C.P.A. 1990, s. 293.

Crown Land. Land in which an interest belongs to Her Majesty in right of the Crown or of the Duchies of Lancaster or Cornwall, or which belongs to a government department or is held in trust for the purposes of such a department: see T.C.P.A. 1990, s. 293.

᛫ **Crown, liabilities in tort of.** "The Crown shall be subject to all those liabilities in tort to which, if it were a private person of full age and capacity, it would be subject in respect of torts committed by its servants or agents or for any breach of those duties which a master owes to his servants or agents at common law or in respect of any breach of the duties attaching at common law to the ownership, occupation, possession or control of property": Crown Proceedings Act 1947, s. 2. A Crown servant, for whose acts the Crown is liable, is defined in s. 2(5) as an officer appointed directly or indirectly by the Crown who is paid out of the Consolidated Fund (q.v.) or money provided by Parliament, or any other fund certified by the Treasury for the purposes of the Act. See O. 42; O. 77; *Pearce* v *Secretary of State* [1988] 2 WLR 144; Crown Proceedings (Armed Forces) Act 1987.

Crown Office, Master of. See MASTER OF THE CROWN OFFICE.

Crown privilege. The principle of exclusion of evidence, the disclosure of which would be prejudicial to the interest of the Crown. Even where neither party raises objections, the judge may exclude that evidence. See Crown Proceedings Act 1947; *Duncan* v *Cammell Laird & Co* [1942] AC 624; *Conway* v *Rimmer* [1968] AC 910; *Burmah Oil Co* v *Bank of England* [1980] AC 1090. *See* PRIVILEGE.

Crown property. "Includes property in the possession or under the control of the Crown and property which has been unlawfully removed from its possession or control": Ministry of Defence Police Act 1987, s. 2(5).

Crown Prosecution Service. An integrated national service, headed by the DPP (q.v.), including, for each designated area, Chief Crown Prosecutors, assisted by Crown Prosecutors (solicitors or barristers). It is the principal duty of the Service to take over the conduct of all criminal proceedings, other than those of a specified nature, instituted on behalf of a police force, and to advise police forces on matters related to criminal offences: Prosecution of Offences Act 1985, s. 3(1); C.L.S.A. 1990, Sch. 10. See *R* v *Pawsey* [1989] Crim LR 152.

Crown road. "A road other than a highway to which the public has access by permission granted by the appropriate Crown authority or otherwise granted by or on behalf of the Crown": Road Traffic Regulation Act 1984, s. 131(7). *See* ROAD.

Crown servant. An individual who holds office under, or is employed by, the Crown. See, e.g., Company Securities (Insider Dealing) Act 1985, s. 16(1); F.S.A. 1986, s. 173; Official Secrets Act 1989, s. 12(1); *R* v *Lord Chancellor's Department, ex p Nangle* [1991] IRLR 343. For "public servant", see F.S.A. 1986, s. 173(2).

Crown servants, dismissal of. "Any appointment as a Crown servant, however subordinate, is terminable at will unless it is expressly otherwise provided by statute": *Kodeeswaran* v *A.-G. of Ceylon* [1970] AC 1111. See e.g., E.P.(C.) A. 1978, s. 138.

Crown service. The service of the Crown, whether within HM dominions or elsewhere: B.N.A. 1981, s. 50(1).

Crown, statutes affecting the. There is a presumption that the Crown is not bound by a statute unless reference is made to it in express terms or by some necessary implication. See *BBC* v *Johns* [1965] Ch 32.

cruelty. Behaviour which when considered in the context of the hearing of a petition for divorce indicates that the respondent has behaved in such a way that the petitioner cannot reasonably be expected to live with the respondent, i.e., that the marriage has broken down irretrievably. See Mat.C.A. 1973, s. 1(2)(*b*). Cruelty has no artificial meaning in relation to proceedings for divorce, but it must be constituted by "grave and weighty matters". See *Le Brocq* v *Le Brocq* [1964] 1 WLR 1085. For cruelty to a child, see *R* v *Burcher* (1988) 10 Cr App R (S.) 72; *R* v *Ace* (1990) 12 Cr App R (S.) 533. *See* DIVORCE.

crystallisation of charge. *See* CHARGE, CRYSTALLISATION OF.

cujus est solum ejus est usque ad coelum et ad inferos. Whose is the soil, his it is even to the heaven and the depths of the earth. (Attributed to Accursius of Bologna, b. 1182.) Exceptions to this general presumption, as a result of which the owner of the soil has a restricted freedom, include, e.g., rights of others over his land, statutory restrictions on the use of his land, limitation of the right to the ownership of minerals. See *Bernstein* v *Skyviews Ltd* [1978] QB 479; *Anchor Developments* v *Berkley House* (1987) 38 Build. R. 82.

culpable. 1. Involving the breach of a legal duty. 2. Blameworthy.

cum div. 1. Reference to a quotation relating to stocks and shares showing that the price includes dividends and interest accrued to date. 2. A transfer *cum div.* refers to a transfer of shares near the time of the declaration of the dividend by which the transferor is to obtain benefit of that dividend (as contrasted with a transfer *ex div.* (q.v.)).

cum testamento annexo. *See* GRANT OF REPRESENTATION.

cumulative legacy. *See* LEGACY, CUMULATIVE.

cur. adv. vult. Curia advisari vult. The court wishes to be advised. An abbreviation used in law reports indicating that the court has not given judgment immediately, but has deliberated further.

curator bonis. Trustee appointed to take care of the property and affairs of, e.g., absent persons. Not recognised in English law: *Kamouh* v *Associated Electrical Industries* [1980] QB 177.

curfew order. A community sentence under C.J.A. 1991, s. 12, ordering a person of or over 16, convicted of an offence, to remain, for specified periods, at a specified place. Electronic monitoring of the offender's whereabouts is possible under s. 13.

Curia Regis. The King's Court. The term was applied after the Norman Conquest to a body of the King's tenants-in-chief who assisted in the centralisation and administration of

judicial power. It later developed into the King's Council, "the mother of the common law courts". Its last full meeting was in 1640.

current. As applied to legislation, means "for the time being in force."

curriculum, school. Under the Education Reform Act 1988, s. 1(2), a "balanced and broadly based curriculum" is one which promotes the spiritual, moral, cultural, mental and physical development of pupils and society and prepares pupils for the opportunities, responsibilities and experiences of adult life. For "National Curriculum", see s. 2. For Curriculum and Assessment Councils, see Sch. 2.

curtain clauses. Those provisions of the land legislation of 1925 by which certain equitable interests (q.v.) are placed "behind a legal curtain", i.e., those equities are transferred from land to the purchase money or to rents and profits where the land is leased. See S.L.A. 1925, s. 110(2).

curtesy. A right to tenure "by the curtesy of England" possessed by a widower, giving him a life estate in the land of his deceased wife. See A.E.A. 1925, s. 45(1); L.P.A. 1925, s. 130(4).

curtilage. Garden, field or yard included within an area surrounding a dwelling-house. See *Dyer* v *Dorset CC* [1988] 3 WLR 213; *Barwick* v *Kent CC* [1992] EGCS 12.

custodial sentence. *See* SENTENCE, CUSTODIAL.

custodian trustee. Office created by the Public Trustee Act 1906. For greater security, trust property can be vested in a custodian trustee who has custody of all securities and documents of title relating to the property and who pays or receives all sums payable to or out of income or capital of the property. Among those who may act as custodian trustee are the Treasury Solicitor (q.v.) and trust corporations (q.v.). *See* TRUST.

custody. 1. Control of some thing or person (e.g., a child) and possession (actual or constructive) in accordance with a law or duty. 2. Confinement or imprisonment of a person. See *R* v *Coroner for Inner London District ex p Linnaine* [1989] 1 WLR 395 (meaning of "police custody"); *R* v *Kerawalla* [1991] Crim LR 451.

custody, commit to. *See* COMMIT TO CUS-
TODY.

custody disputes. Proceedings relating
to disputes between parents of a child,
a parent and a third party, persons not
related to the child (e.g., local authority and foster parents). *See* WELFARE
OF A CHILD.

custody officer. A police officer (sergeant or above) appointed for a designated police station whose duties
relate to the charging of detained and
arrested persons: see the P. & C.E.A.
1984, ss. 36–39, as amended by C.J.A.
1991, s. 59. *See Vince v Dorset Police*
[1992] 1 WLR 47. *See* DETENTION,
POLICE.

custody record. Statement which must
be compiled for a person brought
under arrest to a police station, or arrested there, having attended voluntarily. A copy must be supplied on
request, up to 12 months after release,
to a detained person or his legal representative: *Code of Practice*, issued under
the P. & C.E.A. 1984, and revised in
April 1991.

custody, surrender to. Means "in relation to a person released on bail, surrendering himself into the custody of
the court or of the constable (according to the requirements of the grant of
bail) at the time and place for the time
being appointed for him to do so":
Bail Act 1976, s. 2(2). *See* BAIL.

custom. Long established practice considered as unwritten law. In order that
a practice might be considered as a
valid custom it should have been exercised from time immemorial (q.v.);
have been exercised continuously;
have been observed as of right; be reasonable; be contrary neither to statute
nor common law; be not inconsistent
with other accepted customs. Existence of a custom may be proved: by direct evidence by a witness of his
personal knowledge of its existence; by
a witness testifying to its exercise; by

evidence of a comparable custom in a
similar trade or locality. See *Mills* v
Mayor of Colchester (1867) LR 2 CP 567;
North and South Trust Co v *Berkeley*
[1971] 1 All ER 980. For local customary rights, see, e.g., *New Windsor Corporation* v *Mellor* [1975] Ch 380. *See*
CONTRACT, CUSTOM AND.

customs duties. Taxes on imports and
exports, collected and administered by
the Commissioners of Customs and
Excise. See, e.g., Customs and Excise
Management Act 1979.

customs union. An objective of the
Treaty of Rome, art. 9, calling on
member states of EEC to form a customs union and prohibiting, as between them, customs duties and
equivalent charges, and the adoption
of a common customs tariff in relation
to other countries. See also arts. 18–29
(common customs tariff). See Cases
195/76 and 70/77.

cycling, dangerous. An offence committed by a person who rides a cycle
on the road dangerously, i.e., in a way
that falls far below what would be expected of a careful and competent cy-
clist to whom it would be obvious that
riding in such a way would be dangerous to persons or property: see Road
Traffic Act 1988, s. 28, as substituted
by Road Traffic Act 1991, s. 7.

cy-près doctrine. *Si près* = so near, as
near. A charitable trust (q.v.) which by
its terms is impossible initially or is impracticable, or becomes so subsequently, will not necessarily fail; the
court may apply the trust property cy-
près by means of a scheme (q.v.) to
some other charitable purpose which
resembles the original purpose as
nearly as possible. See Charities Act
1960, s. 14 as amended by Charities
Act 1992, s. 15. *Re Lysaght* [1966] Ch
191; *Re Woodhams* [1981] 1 WLR 493;
Re J W Laing Trust [1984] 1 All ER 50.
See TRUST.

D

daily. Means, generally, every day including Sunday. See, e.g., *LCC* v *Metropolitan Gas Co* [1903] 2 Ch 532.

damage. Loss or harm, physical or economic, resulting from a wrongful act or default and generally leading to the award of a measure of compensation. Includes the death of, or injury to, any person, including the impairment of physical or mental condition: Animals Act 1971, s. 11. "The word is sufficiently wide in its meaning to embrace injury, mischief or harm done to property, and that in order to constitute 'damage' it is unnecessary to establish such definite or actual damage as renders property useless or prevents it from serving its normal function": *per* Walters J in *Samuels* v *Stubbs* [1972] 4 SASR 200.

damage, criminal. *See* CRIMINAL DAMAGE.

damage feasant. Doing damage. Usually applied to animals belonging to X which were wrongfully on Y's land and were doing damage to it. Seizure by Y of X's animals was known as distress damage feasant (q.v.) which generally suspends the alternative remedy of damages: *Boden* v *Roscoe* [1894] 1 QB 608. Abolished in relation to animals: Animals Act 1971, s. 7.

damage, latent. Damage which does not appear until some time after it has been caused. See, e.g., *Cartledge* v *Jopling & Sons* [1963] AC 758. Time limits for negligence actions in respect of latent damage not involving personal injuries are now: three years from the earliest date on which plaintiff had the knowledge required for bringing an action, and the right to bring such an action; fifteen years ("long stop") period: Limitation Act 1980, ss. 14A, 14B, inserted by Latent Damage Act 1986, s. 1. The 1986 Act applies in cases of negligence only, and not to actions for breach of contract. See *Iron Trade Mutual Insurance.* v *Buckenham Ltd* [1990] 1 All ER 808.

damages. The court's estimated compensation in money for detriment or injury sustained by plaintiff in contract or tort. They can be classified as: (1) *nominal,* where no actual damage has been suffered; (2) *contemptuous,* where the amount awarded is derisory (see *Dering* v *Uris* [1964] 2 QB 669); (3) *substantial,* representing compensation for loss actually sustained; (4) *exemplary,* or *vindictive,* or *punitive,* given so as to "punish" defendant (but not generally awarded in contract); (5) *liquidated,* based on the pre-estimate for anticipated breach of contract; (6) *unliquidated,* dependent on the circumstances of the case. See *Rookes* v *Barnard* [1964] AC 1129; *Cassell & Co Ltd* v *Broome* [1972] 1 All ER 801; *Bradford CMC* v *Arora* [1991] 2 WLR 1377; *Marks* v *Chief Constable of Manchester Police* (1992) The Times, 28 Jan.; and S.G.A. 1979, Part VI. *See* GENERAL AND SPECIAL DAMAGES; MEASURE OF DAMAGES.

damages and supervening event. In assessing the quantum of damages, account is to be taken of the effects of a supervening, although unrelated, condition or illness: *Jobling* v *Associated Dairies* [1982] AC 794. *See* SUPERVENING EVENT.

damages, exemplary, justification of. "There are certain categories of case in which an award of exemplary damages can serve a useful purpose in vindicating the strength of the law, and thus affording a practical justification for admitting into the civil law a principle which ought logically to belong to the criminal": *Rookes* v *Barnard* [1964] AC 1129. See *Riches* v *News Group Newspapers* [1985] 2 All ER 845.

damages, inflation and. "Inflation and the high rates of interest to which it gives rise is automatically taken into account by the use of multipliers based on rates of interest related to a stable currency. It would therefore be wrong for the court to increase the award of damages by attempting to make a further specific allowance for future inflation": *per* Lord Fraser in *Cookson v Knowles* [1979] AC 556. See, however, *Robertson v Lestrange* [1985] 1 All ER 950.

damages, measure of, in contract. *See* MEASURE OF DAMAGES IN CONTRACT.

damages, measure of, in tort. *See* MEASURE OF DAMAGES IN TORT.

damages, mitigation of. *See* MITIGATION.

damages, multiple. *See* MULTIPLE DAMAGES.

damages, provisional assessment of. *See* PERSONAL INJURIES, PROVISIONAL DAMAGES FOR.

damnum absque injuria. Also *damnum sine injuria.* Damage without wrong, i.e., damage or loss for which no action can be maintained.

danger, alternative, principle of. *See* ALTERNATIVE DANGER, PRINCIPLE OF.

dangerous machinery. "A part of machinery is dangerous if it is a possible cause of injury to anybody acting in a way in which a human being may be reasonably expected to act in circumstances which may be reasonably expected to occur": *Walker v Bletchley Flettons Ltd* [1937] 1 All ER 170. See Factories Act 1961, s. 14 (under which such machinery must be securely fenced); *Wearing v Pirelli* [1977] 1 WLR 48 (employers may be liable under the Factories Act 1961, s. 14(1), where an injury is caused by dangerous machinery even though the injured person did not come into contact with it).

dangerous species. A species not commonly domesticated in the UK, and whose fully grown animals normally have such characteristics that they are likely, unless restrained, to cause severe damage or that any damage they may cause is likely to be severe: Animals Act 1971, s. 6(2). Where damage is caused by an animal of this type, the keeper is liable: s. 2(1). See Dangerous Wild Animals Act 1976; *Cummings v Granger* [1975] 1 WLR 1330; *Curtis v Betts* [1990] 1 All ER 769. *See* DANGEROUS WILD ANIMALS.

dangerous things, liability relating to. Things likely to do mischief and the resulting liability were considered in *Rylands v Fletcher* (1868) LR 1 Ex 265, in which it was stated that "the person who for his own purposes brings on his lands and collects and keeps there anything likely to do mischief if it escapes, must keep it in at his peril, and, if he does not do so, is prima facie answerable for all the damage which is the natural consequence of its escape". Exceptions to this rule of strict liability include the plaintiff's default or consent; *vis major* (q.v.); Act of God (q.v.); and the act of a stranger. See *British Celanese Ltd v A.H. Hunt Ltd* [1969] 1 WLR 959; *Rigby v Chief Constable of Northants* [1985] 1 WLR 1242.

dangerous wild animals. Animals enumerated in the Dangerous Wild Animals Act 1976, including, wild dog, wolf, baboon, crocodile, cobra, lion, tiger, leopard, panther, chimpanzee. No person may keep any dangerous wild animal except under the authority of a licence granted by a local authority: s. 1. The list was revised by Dangerous Wild Animals Act 1976 (Modification) Order 1981, S.I. 1981/1173.

data. 1. Organised information. 2. "Information recorded in a form in which it can be processed by equipment operating automatically in response to instructions given for that purpose": Data Protection Act 1984, s. 1(2). See Access to Health Records Act 1989. 3. "Personal data" is information relating to a living person who can be identified from it: s. 1(3). 4. "Data user" is one who holds, controls and uses data: s. 1(5). Data users and computer bureaux must be registered: s.4.

data subjects, rights of. An individual is entitled to be informed by any data user whether the data held by him include personal data of which that individual is the data subject, and to be supplied by any data user with a copy of the information constituting any such personal data held by him: Data Protection Act 1984, s. 21(1).

day. A period of 24 hours, from midnight to midnight. "The law maketh no fraction of a day": Coke. See *Re Shurey* [1918] 1 Ch 266. For "time of day", see I.A. 1978, s. 9. For "any day", see *Carey v DPP* [1989] Crim LR 368.

day, business. *See* BUSINESS DAY.

day certain. Fixed or appointed day. See S.G.A. 1979, s. 49(2); *Hyundai Ltd v Papadopoulos* [1980] 1 WLR 1129.

days, clear. *See* CLEAR DAYS.

days of grace. The days immediately following the day on which a payment becomes due, allowed for payment to be made. Usually three days in the case of a bill of exchange (q.v.). See *Salvin* v *James* (1805) 6 East 571.

day, year and waste. A right of the Crown, now abolished, to the profits of land of a person convicted of treason or felony, and the right to commit waste (q.v.).

D.C. Divisional Court (q.v.).

dead rent. Rent which must be paid under a mining lease even though the mine is not worked.

dealer. "A person carrying on a business of selling goods, whether by wholesale or by retail": Resale Prices Act 1976, s. 24(1).

dealings, commercial. Transactions (q.v.) relating to business. May also include "the communings, the negotiations, verbal and by correspondence, and other relations which occur in a business or commercial setting": *Gye* v *McIntyre* (1991) 65 ALJR 221.

death. Cessation of life processes and all vital signs. Not defined by statute. (Note, however, an American definition: "A person will be considered medically and legally dead if, in the opinion of a physician, based on ordinary standards of medical practice, there is the absence of spontaneous brain function . . .": *Kansas Statutes* 1971.) See, e.g., Human Tissue Act 1961 (amended by Corneal Tissue Act 1986).

death duties. Estate duty paid on property which passed at death. Replaced by capital transfer tax (q.v.) and inheritance tax (q.v.).

death penalty. *See* CAPITAL PUNISHMENT.

death, presumption of. *See* PRESUMPTION OF DEATH.

death, proof of. Procedure whereby death is established in evidence: by the production of the death certificate and proof of identity; by presumption of death (q.v.); by someone who has identified the corpse; by someone present at its occurrence.

death, registration of. Procedure which must be completed within five days (or four days if the registrar has been notified in writing of the death), consisting of the furnishing of the following particulars: date and place of death; name, surname, sex, date, place of birth, address and occupation of the deceased; cause of death; name, surname, qualifications, address and signature of informant; signature of registrar; date of registration. See Births and Deaths Registration Act 1953.

death, survival of causes of action on. In general, on the death of a person, all causes of action subsisting against or vested in him, survive against, or for the benefit of, the estate (save causes of action for defamation). Exemplary damages will not be awarded in favour of a deceased plaintiff's estate. See Law Reform (Misc. Provs.) Act 1934, s. 1; and Law Reform (Misc. Provs.) Act 1970.

de bene esse. (Of well-being.) Used in relation to that which is done conditionally, provisionally, subject to some possible future challenge or exception. Example: the taking of evidence for future use (see O. 39, r. 1). *See* DEPOSITION.

debenture. Document under a company's seal acknowledging indebtedness for a capital sum, undertaking to repay on an ascertainable date and to pay interest at a fixed rate. They include, under F.S.A. 1986, Sch. 1, debenture stock, loan stock, bonds, certificates of deposit and other instruments creating or acknowledging indebtedness. Debentures are not part of a company's capital. They rank first for capital and interest and are usually secured by a charge (q.v.) on company assets. Debenture holders are creditors of the company. Power to issue debentures is usually stated in express terms in the memorandum of association (q.v.). *Mortgage debentures* give the holder security by way of charge on company's property; *naked debentures* are simply undertakings to repay; *bearer debentures* are made payable to bearer (see *Edelstein* v *Schuler* [1902] 2 KB 144). See Cos. A. 1985, ss. 190–197, 744; Cos. A. 1989, ss. 191, 419(1).

debenture stock. An obligation or debt due from a company and secured by trust deed. See Cos.A. 19

debenture trust deed. *See* TRUST DEED, DEBENTURE.

de bonis asportatis. Of goods carried away. A writ of trespass (q.v.) in relation to chattels wrongfully taken.

de bonis non administratis. Of goods which have not been administered. Grant made where an administrator, with or without a will annexed, dies, or where an administrator cannot be found; *Re Loveday* [1900] P 154. In effect, a grant limited to unadministered property when a previous grant has ceased prematurely. *See* GRANT.

de bonis propriis. From one's own goods. Refers to a judgment against, e.g., an executor, to be satisfied "out of his own pocket".

debt. A sum that one person is bound to pay to another. "Debt normally has one or other of two meanings: it can mean an obligation to pay money or it can mean a sum of money owed": *DPP v Turner* [1973] 3 All ER 124. A *specialty debt* is created by deed; a debt of *record* is, e.g., a judgment debt. See T.C.G.A. 1992, s. 251.

debt-adjusting. Under C.C.A. 1974, ss. 145(5), 189(1), the activities carried on by a person who acts as an intermediary between an individual and the creditor with a view to the discharge of a debt due.

debt-collecting. Under C.C.A. 1974, ss. 145(7), 189(1), the taking of a step to procure payment of debts due under regulated and exempt consumer credit or hire agreements (qq.v.).

debt, imprisonment for. Generally abolished under Debtors Act 1869. See also A.J.A. 1970, s. 11.

debtor. One who owes a debt. Under C.C.A. 1974, s. 189(1), it means "the individual receiving credit under a consumer credit agreement or the person to whom his rights and duties under the agreement have passed by assignment or operation of law, and in relation to a prospective consumer credit agreement (q.v.) includes the prospective debtor."

debtor–creditor agreement. Under C.C.A. 1974, s. 13, a regulated consumer credit agreement (q.v.) is a restricted use credit agreement falling within s. 11(1) (*b*) of the Act, but not made by a creditor under pre-existing arrangements in contemplation of future arrangements, between himself and the supplier, or a restricted-use agreement within s. 11(1)(*c*), or an unrestricted-use credit agreement, which is not made by a creditor under pre-existing arrangements between himself and a person (the "supplier") other than the debtor in the knowledge that the credit is to be used to finance a transaction between the debtor and supplier.

debtor–creditor–supplier agreement. Agreement, under C.C.A. 1974, s. 12, whereby a creditor and supplier are the same person, or who have a business link.

debtor, judgment. *See* JUDGMENT DEBTOR.

debtors, harassment of. *See* HARASSMENT OF DEBTORS.

debtor's petition. Exercise of the right of a debtor to petition for his adjudication as a bankrupt on the sole ground of inability to pay his debts: Ins. A. 1986, s. 272(1). The petition must be accompanied by a statement of affairs. No order will be made if it appears, e.g., that if the order were made, the aggregate amount of bankruptcy debts, so far as unsecured, would be less than the prescribed small bankruptcies level: s. 273(1). An insolvency practitioner (q.v.) may be appointed to prepare a report: s. 273. *See* BANKRUPTCY.

deceit. A tort arising from a false statement of fact made by one person, knowingly or recklessly, with the intent that it shall be acted on by another who, as a result, suffers damage. See Misrepresentation Act 1967, s. 2(1); *Derry v Peek* (1889) 14 App Cas 337; *Archer v Brown* [1985] QB 401; *East v Maurier* [1991] 1 WLR 461 (damages for deceit). *See* DECEIVE.

deceit, writ of. Writ, which originated in the thirteenth century, used against one who had utilised legal proceedings in order to deceive another. See *Bailey v Merrell* (1616) 3 Bulstr 94. Abolished by Real Property Limitation Act 1833, s. 36.

deceive. To induce a person to believe that a thing is true which is false, or a thing is false which is true, contrary to that which the person practising such deceit knows or believes to be the case. See *Re London & Globe Finance Corp Ltd* [1903] 1 Ch 728; *Welham v DPP* [1961] AC 103.

deception, evasion of liability by. Where a person by any deception dishonestly secures the remission of the whole or part of any existing liability to make a payment, whether his own liability or another's, or with intent to make permanent default in whole or part on any existing liability to make a payment, or with intent to let another do so, dishonestly induces the creditor or any person claiming payment on behalf of the creditor to wait for payment (whether or not the due date for payment is deferred) or to forgo payment; or dishonestly obtains any exemption from or abatement of liability to make a payment; he shall be guilty of an offence: Th.A. 1978, s. 2. See *R* v *Attewell Hughes* [1991] 1 WLR 955.

deception, obtaining property by. It is an offence under the Th.A. 1968 dishonestly to obtain property by deception or to obtain a pecuniary advantage by deception: ss. 15, 16. Deception means, in this context, "any deception (whether deliberate or reckless) by words or conduct as to fact or as to law, including a deception as to the present intentions of the person using the deception or any other person": s. 15(4). The question for the jury, to be answered as a question of fact by the application of commonsense, is: was the deception an operative cause of the obtaining of the property? See *R* v *Woolven* (1984) 77 Cr App R 231; *R* v *Hamilton* (1991) 92 Cr App R 54; *R* v *O'Connell* [1991] Crim LR 771. *See* PECUNIARY ADVANTAGE.

deception, obtaining services by. A person who by any deception dishonestly obtains services from another is guilty of an offence: Th.A. 1978, s. 1(1). It is an obtaining of services where the other is induced to confer a benefit by doing some act, or causing or permitting some act to be done, on the understanding that the benefit has been or will be paid for: s. 1(2). (This replaces Th.A. 1968, s. 16(2)(a).) See *R* v *Halai* [1983] Crim LR 624; *R* v *Widdowson* [1986] RTR 124.

decision, judicial. *See* JUDICIAL DECISION REQUISITES OF.

decisions of EEC. *See* COMMUNITY LEGISLATION, FORMS OF.

declaration. 1. A statement of claims in proceedings. 2. A decision of the court. 3. A discretionary remedy declaring the position in law based on given facts: *Vine* v *National Dock Labour Board* [1957] AC 488. See O. 15, r. 16; and *Imperial Tobacco* v *A.-G.* [1981] AC 718. 4. A formal statement, e.g., to assert a right. 5. A statement or testimony made by a witness not under oath. 6. A declaration of trust is an acknowledgement by a person that he holds property in trust (q.v.) for another. It may be implied from conduct. See *Gee* v *Liddell* (1866) 35 Beav 621. 7. A statutory declaration is one made before a Commissioner for Oaths (q.v.) in prescribed form. See Statutory Declarations Act 1835; and Th.A. 1968, s. 27(4).

declaration against interest. Statements of a deceased person are generally admissible as evidence if against his proprietary or pecuniary interests. See *Ward* v *H. S. Pitt & Co* [1913] 2 KB 130.

declaration concerning pedigree. An exception to the hearsay rule, whereby an oral or written statement of a deceased person relating to the pedigree of a relative, which is the subject of dispute, is admissible in evidence. The declarant must be a blood relation, or the spouse of a blood relation, of the person whose pedigree is in dispute. See Civil Evidence Act 1968, s. 9; *Johnson* v *Lawson* (1824) 2 Bing 86.

declaration concerning public or general rights. An exception to the hearsay rule, whereby an oral or written statement by a deceased person concerning the reputed existence of a right, public or general, is admissible in evidence provided it was made before the proceedings had commenced and the declarant had competent knowledge. See, e.g., *R* v *Bedfordshire (Inhabitants)* (1855) 4 E & B 535. *See* EVIDENCE, HEARSAY.

declaration in course of duty. An exception to the hearsay rule, whereby a written or oral statement of a deceased person made in pursuance of a duty to act and record those acts, and made contemporaneously with those acts, may be admissible in evidence. See, e.g., *Price* v *Torrington* (1703) 1 Salk 285. *See* EVIDENCE, HEARSAY.

declaration of intention. In relation to contract, this means merely that an offer will be made or invited in the future. It does not imply that an offer is made now. See *Harris* v *Nickerson* (1873) LR 8 QB 286.

declaratory judgment. A judgment which merely states the court's opinion on a question of law, or declares the rights, existing or future, of the parties. It does not generally carry an order for enforcement. Action for declaration may be commenced by writ or originating summons. See O. 15, r. 16.

declaratory theory of common law. The theory "that every case was governed by a relevant rule of law, existing somewhere and discoverable somehow, provided sufficient learning and intellectual rigour were brought to bear": *Jones* v *Secretary of State for Social Services* [1972] AC 944. "The decisions of courts of justice are the evidence of what is common law": Blackstone. *See* COMMON LAW; JUS DICERE.

decree. 1. A law. 2. A judgment or order of the court. 3. In relation to dissolution of marriage, *decree absolute* is the decree which finally dissolves the marriage. It may be issued after six clear weeks from the day following the grant of a *decree nisi* (*nisi* = unless) – a type of conditional decree requiring something further to be done to make it absolute. The registrar must be satisfied that, e.g., no proceedings have been commenced to appeal against the decree nisi. It must be pronounced in open court: Family Proceedings Rules 1991. (The period may be shortened for some substantial reason.) See Mat.C.A. 1973, ss. 1(5), 10(1), 41(2) (amended by Ch.A. 1989); Matrimonial Causes Rules 1977, rr. 65–67; *Dackham* v *Dackham* (1987) Fam Law 345; *Callaghan* v *Andrew-Hanson* [1991] 3 WLR 464 (once decree absolute is granted it may not subsequently be challenged by one of the parties); *Garcia* v *Garcia* [1991] 3 All ER 451 (delaying decree absolute).

dedication of way. The creation of a public right of way by "dedication and acceptance". It may be established at common law on proof of dedication by the owner to the public and of acceptance by the public, usually shown by user: *Cubitt* v *Lady Maxse* (1873) LR 8 CP 704. Under Highways Act 1980, s. 31, the way was deemed to have been dedicated on proof of 20 years' enjoyment of way over land as of right and without physical obstruction.

de donis conditionalibus. The Statute of Westminster II 1285 provided that a grant of an estate "to X and the heirs of his body" would create a fee tail (q.v.) which descended on the death of the tenant in tail to his lineal heirs. The fee ceased to exist if the issue of the original tenant died out.

deed. 1. An act performed consciously. 2. Originally, and before August 1991, a sealed contract or covenant. Now an instrument which makes it clear on its face that it is intended to be a deed by the person making it or the parties to it and is validly executed as a deed: L.P. (Misc. Provs.) A. 1989, s. 1(1). Sealing is no longer required. 3. A *deed poll* is a unilateral declaration of a party's intention, e.g., to alter his name. 4. A *deed of conveyance* comprises: exordium (commencement); recitals; testatum; parcels; general words; habendum; tenendum; reddendum; conditions; powers; covenants; testimonium (qq.v.). For alterations rendering a deed void, see *Lombard Finance* v *Brookplain Trading* [1991] 2 All ER 762.

deed, valid execution of. Valid execution of a deed by an individual requires that he shall sign in the presence of a witness who attests the signature; or at his direction and in his presence and the presence of two witnesses who each attest the signature; and it is delivered as a deed by him or a person authorised to do so on his behalf: L.P (Misc. Provs.) A. 1989, s. 1(3). "Sign" includes making one's mark on the instrument: s. 1(4).

deeds of arrangement. *See* ARRANGEMENT, DEEDS OF.

deemed. Supposed. "Sometimes the word is used to impose for the purpose of a statute an artificial construction of a word or phrase that would otherwise not prevail. Sometimes it is used to put beyond doubt a particular construction that might otherwise be uncertain. Sometimes it is used to give a comprehensive description that includes what is obvious, what is uncertain and what is, in the ordinary sense, impossible": *St. Alwyn* v *A.-G. (No. 2)* [1952] AC 15. See *Barclays Bank* v *IRC*

[1961] AC 509. For "deemed notice" see, e.g., Cos. A. 1989, s. 142.

de facto. In fact, in reality.

defalcation. "Essentially involves the presence of fraudulent or dishonest dealing": *per* Samuels J in *Daly* v *Sydney Stock Exchange* (1982) 2 NSWLR 421.

defamation. The publishing of a statement which tends to lower a person in the estimation of right-thinking members of society. It may be actionable without proof of special damage where it involves, e.g., imputation of a criminal offence punishable with imprisonment. Defences may be based on justification (or truth), privilege (absolute or qualified), fair comment (qq.v.). See Defamation Act 1952; O. 82; *Youssoupoff* v *Metro-Goldwyn-Mayer Pictures Ltd* (1934) 50 TLR 58; *Khashoggi* v *IPC Ltd* [1986] 1 WLR 1412; *Derbyshire CC* v *Times Newspapers* [1992] 3 All ER 65. *See* LIBEL; SLANDER.

defamation, unintentional. *See* UNINTENTIONAL DEFAMATION.

default. Failure to do something required by law, e.g., non-appearance in court on the required day. Judgment in default may be given against a party by reason of non-acknowledgement of service within the time limit (14 days from service of the writ). A default judgment may be *interlocutory* (i.e., final as to liability, but leaving the amount due to the plaintiff to be assessed) or *final* (as to liability and quantum). The procedure is not generally available (unless leave is obtained) in cases relating to: hire-purchase and conditional sale agreement (see O. 83); mortgage actions commenced by writ (see O. 88, r. 7); tort actions between spouses during the subsistence of the marriage (see O. 89, r. 2); cases against the Crown (see O. 77, r. 9). See O. 13, O. 14. For imprisonment for default on payment of fines see M.C.A. 1980, s. 82, and P.C.C.A. 1973, s. 31 as amended by C.J.A. 1982, s. 69, and C.J.A. 1991, Sch. 11. Default action may be commenced in any county court: County Court (Amendment No. 2) Rules 1991.

default. notice. Term used under C.C.A. 1974, s. 87, relating to a debtor's breach of agreement, whereby he must be issued with a default notice in the prescribed form if the creditor wishes to terminate the agreement, to recover possession or to enforce a security. Under s. 88(1) the notice must specify: the nature of the alleged breach; the action required to remedy it; the date before which that action is to be taken; the sum payable as compensation for breach.

default of acknowledgement of service. *See* DEFAULT.

default summons. Procedure by which a debt may be recovered in the county court (q.v.).

default, wilful. *See* WILFUL DEFAULT.

defeasance. Ending of an interest in property in accordance with conditions stipulated in a separate instrument.

defeasible. Capable of being annulled.

defect. Irregularity or fault. "Lack or absence of something essential to completeness": *Tate* v *Latham* (1897) 66 LJQB 351. A *patent defect* is one that ought to be discovered by ordinary vigilance. A *latent defect* is one that could not be discovered by reasonable examination. See Latent Damage Act 1986; *Ashburner* v *Sewell* [1891] 3 Ch 405.

defect in a product. There is a defect, for the purposes of C.P.A. 1987, "if the safety of the product is not such as persons generally are entitled to expect": s. 3(1). The circumstances to be taken into account include: the manner in which, and purposes for which, the product has been marketed; what might reasonably be expected to be done with or in relation to the product; and the time when the product was supplied by its producer (q.v.) to another: s. 3(2). *See* PRODUCTS, DEFECTIVE, LIABILITY FOR.

defective. One suffering from severe subnormality, arrested or incomplete development of mind so that he is incapable of living an independent life. See M.H.A. 1983, Part I.

defective dwellings. *See* DWELLINGS, DEFECTIVE.

defective equipment, liability for. Under Employers' Liability (Defective Equipment) Act 1969 an employer may be liable for defective equipment and liable in damages to an employee injured by it.

defective premises, liability for. Under Defective Premises Act 1972 there is a duty to build premises properly and that duty is not abated by the subsequent disposal (including letting, assignment or surrender of the tenancy) of those premises by the person who owes that duty. "Premises" in the 1972 Act means the whole premises, land and buildings, unless there is clear language to restrict its meaning: *Smith v Bradford Metropolitan Council* (1982) 44 P & CR 171. For demolition of defective premises, see Building Act 1984, s. 76. See *Andrews v Schooling* [1991] 1 WLR 783; *McAuley v Bristol CC.* [1992] 1 All ER 749.

defective products, liability for. *See* PRODUCTS, DEFECTIVE, LIABILITY FOR.

defectum sanguinis. Failure of issue. *See* ESCHEAT.

defence. Generally, the defendant's opposing or denying the truth of the prosecutor's or plaintiff's case. For service of a defence, see O. 18, r. 2. For "improbable defence", see *Rafidain Bank v Agom Sugar Co* [1987] 1 WLR 1606. For alternative defences, see *R v Johnson* (1989) 89 Cr App R 148. *See* STATEMENT OF DEFENCE.

defence, withdrawal of. *See* WITHDRAWAL OF DEFENCE.

defendant. Includes any person served with a writ of summons or process, or served with notice of, or entitled to attend, any proceedings. Applied also to person charged with offences.

defendant, compelling appearance of. Appearance may be compelled by summons, warrant for arrest and arrest without warrant. See M.C.A. 1980, s. 1.

defend, leave to. *See* LEAVE TO DEFEND.

defer. To delay; to postpone. A decision to defer is not necessarily a refusal: *R v Middlesbrough DC ex p Cameron Holdings Ltd* (1991) The Times, 19 Nov.

deferred debts. Debts deferred under statute until those with priority are paid in full.

deferred shares. Shares, now rarely issued, carrying a right to all, or a substantial proportion of, profits after ordinary shares have received a dividend. Known also as "founders' shares". The number of such shares must usually be stated in the prospectus (q.v.): see F.S.A. 1986, ss. 146–148, 162–164.

deferring of sentence. Under P.C.C.A. 1973, s. 1 (as amended by C.J.A. 1982, s. 63), the Crown Court (q.v.) or magistrates' court (q.v.) can defer passing sentence on an offender (with his consent) to enable the court, in determining his sentence, to consider any change in his circumstances or conduct after conviction (q.v.). See also *R v George* [1984] 3 All ER 13.

defraud. "To deprive a person dishonestly of something which is his or of something to which he is or would or might but for the perpetration of the fraud be entitled": *Scott v Metropolitan Police Commissioner* [1974] 3 All ER 1032. *See* CONSPIRACY TO DEFRAUD.

defunct company. A company (q.v.) which the Registrar of Companies has reasonable cause to believe is non-operational or not carrying on business. He may strike it off the register: Cos.A. 1985, s. 652.

degrees, bogus. It is an offence under the Education Reform Act 1988, s. 214, to grant or offer to grant unrecognised degrees, i.e., those not made or sanctioned by universities or other authorised bodies.

dehors. Beyond; unconnected with; foreign to. *See* EXTRINSIC.

de jure. By right; by lawful title.

del credere **agent.** *Del credere* = of belief; of trust. An agent who receives a higher rate of commission than that which is usual, in return for a guarantee that his principal will receive due payment for goods sold. See, e.g., *Harburg India Rubber Comb Co v Martin* [1902] 1 KB 778.

delegated legislation. Legislation made by some person or body (e.g., a minister or local authority) under authority delegated by Parliament under statute. See, e.g., Planning and Compensation Act 1991, s. 84(2). It may take the form of statutory instruments (q.v.) (based commonly on Orders in Council (q.v.)), departmental orders, regulations, rules, circulars, codes of practice. Known also as "subordinate legislation". Can be controlled by judicial review, pre-promulgation consultation, supervision by Parliament.

delegated legislation, justification of. Stated in the *Report on Ministers' Powers* 1932, to be: pressure on Parliament's time; technicality of much legislation; ease of modification in light of experience; the need for occasional arbitrary and swift action in administrative matters.

delegated legislation, sub-. A "three-tier" process of legisation: an enabling ("parent") Act is made; regulations are made under that Act; those regulations are utilised so as to create further regulations. See Emergency Powers (Defence) Act 1939, s. 1(3); European Communities Act 1972, s. 2(2), Sch. 2; *Jackson, Stansfield & Sons v Butterworth* [1948] 2 All ER 558.

delegation. The investing of one person with appropriate and sufficient authority to act for another.

delegation, principle of. An aspect of vicarious and strict liability (qq.v.). "When an absolute offence has been created by Parliament, then the person on whom a duty is thrown is responsible, whether he has delegated or whether he has acted through a servant; he is absolutely liable regardless of any intent or knowledge or *mens rea*. The principle of delegation comes into play, and only comes into play, in cases where, though the statute uses words which import knowledge or intent such as in this case 'knowingly'; or in some other cases 'permitting' or 'suffering' and the like, cases to which knowledge is inherent, nevertheless it has been held that a man cannot get out of the responsibilities which have been put on him by delegating those responsibilities to another": *R v Winson* [1968] 1 All ER 197. For delegation by a government minister to his officials, see *Carltona Ltd v Commrs of Works* [1943] 2 All ER 560; *Oladehinde v Secretary of State for Home Dept.* [1990] 3 All ER 393. See also *Vane v Yiannopoulos* [1964] 3 All ER 820. *See* MENS REA.

delegatus non potest delegare. A delegate cannot delegate. A trustee (q.v.), however, may appoint an agent, subject to the terms of the trust instrument, to carry out trust business: Tr.A. 1925, ss. 23, 25. "The law is not that trustees cannot delegate: it is that trustees cannot delegate unless they have authority to do so": *Pilkington v IRC* [1962] 3 All ER 622. See also L.P.A. 1925, ss. 29, 30; Powers of Attorney Act 1971, s. 9; *De Bussche v Alt* (1878) 8 Ch D 286.

delict. A wrongful act.

deliverable state. *See* GOODS, DELIVERABLE STATE.

delivery. The voluntary transfer of possession, i.e., the putting of property into the legal possession of another. It may be actual or constructive, e.g., by symbolic delivery (of a bill of lading). See S.G.A. 1979, s. 61; *The Naxos* [1990] 1 WLR 1337.

delivery of a deed. Formerly performed by the person executing the deed placing his finger on the seal, saying at the same time: "I deliver this as my act and deed;" Requirement of sealing is now abolished; delivery is denoted in any way by which a party indicates that he regards the deed as binding on him. See L.P. (Misc. Provs.) A. 1989, s.1; *Longman v Viscount Chelsea* (1989) 2 EGLR 242. *See* DEED.

delivery of goods. It is the duty of the seller to deliver the goods, and of the buyer to accept and pay for them, in accordance with the terms of the contract of sale: S.G.A. 1979, s. 27. Whether it is for the buyer to take possession of the goods or for the seller to send them to the buyer is a question depending in each case on the contract, express or implied, between the parties: S.G.A. 1979, s. 29(1). *See* TIME AS ESSENCE OF CONTRACT.

delivery up of goods. Remedy, in a case of conversion (q.v.) or trespass to goods, by which the plaintiff recovers his goods from the defendant who is interfering with them, under Torts (Interference with Goods) Act 1977. See *Howard Perry & Co v British Rlwy Board* [1980] 1 WLR 1375.

delivery, writ of. Writ of execution enforcing a judgment for delivery of goods by directing the sheriff (q.v.) to seize goods and deliver to the plaintiff, or for recovery of their assessed value. See O. 45, r. 4. A writ of *specific delivery* directs the seizure of goods stated in the writ, but with no alternative for payment of assessed value. *See* JUDGMENTS, ENFORCEMENT OF.

delusion. Continuing self-deception relating to some matter, in spite of evidence to the contrary. 1. In the case of a testator (q.v.), where the delusion does not result in the impairing of his understanding and where it relates to matters which do not involve his property, he may make a valid will: *Smee v Smee* (1879) 28 WR 703. See also *Banks v Goodfellow* (1870) LR 5 QBD

549 2. For criminal acts committed under an insane delusion, see the M'Naghten Rules (q.v.).

demanding with menaces. *See* BLACKMAIL.

demand, liquidated. *See* LIQUIDATED DEMAND.

demesne. A term used in old land law to signify the lands of a manor which the lord occupied.

demesne, ancient. *See* ANCIENT DEMESNE.

de minimis non curat lex. The law does not concern itself with trifles. The so-called *de minimis principle.* refers, e.g., to some circumstances in which the police tend to refrain from prosecuting: *Delaroy-Hall* v *Tadman* [1969] 2 QB 208; *Putnam* v *Calvin* [1984] RTR 150; *Regent OHG* v *Francesca* [1981] 3 All ER 327 (maxim used in relation to delivery of goods).

demise. 1. Transference, on the death of a monarch, of the royal dignity. 2. Transfer by grant of a lease (q.v.) of lands as in a mortgage by a long lease (e.g., 3000 years): See L.P.A. 1925, ss. 85, 86. 3. Death.

demolition order. An order requiring that premises be vacated within a specified period of at least 28 days from the date on which the order becomes operative, and be demolished within six weeks after the end of that period, or within a longer period considered reasonable by the local housing authority (q.v.): H.A. 1985, s. 267(1). See T.C.P.A. 1990, s. 55; Planning and Compensation Act 1992, s. 13.

demonstrative legacy. A gift, in its nature general, directed to be satisfied or paid out of a specified fund or specified part of the testator's property. Example: "£1,000 out of my account with Barclays". See *Re Webster* [1937] 1 All ER 602. *See* LEGACY.

demur. To deliver a plea by demurrer, i.e., an allegation that a pleading shows no good cause of action. Now virtually obsolete. See O. 18; *R* v *Deputy Chairman of Inner London QS, ex p Metropolitan Police Commissioner* [1969] 3 All ER 1537. *See* PLEADINGS.

demurrage. An agreed sum to be paid by the charterer to the shipowner as liquidated damages (q.v.) for any delay beyond a time stipulated in the contract. See *The Notos* [1987] 1 Lloyd's Rep 503.

de novo. Anew.

deodand. (*Deo dandum* = that must be given to God.) Any inanimate instrument by which a killing had been effected, which was forfeit to the Crown. Abolished in 1846.

departure. A party's pleading containing an allegation of fact, or raising a new ground or claim, inconsistent with a previous pleading of his. See O. 18, r. 10(1); *Herbert* v *Vaughan* [1972] 1 WLR 1128.

dependant. One who relies for his support on another. Under the Inheritance (Provision for Family and Dependants) Act 1975, those who may apply for reasonable financial provision from the deceased's estate include: wife or husband, or former wife or husband who has not remarried, or child of the deceased; any person (not being a child of the deceased) who, in the case of any marriage to which the deceased was at any time a party, was treated by the deceased as a child of the family in relation to that marriage; any other person who immediately before the death of the deceased was being maintained, either wholly or partly by the deceased: s. 1. See I.C.T.A. 1988, s. 263 (tax claim for dependants); *Bishop* v *Plumley* [1991] 1 All ER 236.

dependent relative revocation. Where the revocation of a will is relative to another will and is intended to be dependent upon the fact of that other will being valid, then unless that other will takes effect, the revocation is ineffective. Example: the testator (q.v.) destroys his will with the intention of making another one, but then fails to make another will. The original will is considered as unrevoked. See *Dixon* v *Solicitor to the Treasury* [1905] P 42; *Re Finnemore* [1991] 1 WLR 793. *See* REVOCATION OF WILL.

dependent territory. Any territory outside the British Isles for whose external relations the Government of the UK is responsible.

deponent. One who gives evidence by deposition (q.v.) on affidavit (q.v.).

deportation. Expulsion from a country. "The taking of the person in question from the country from which he is deported to some other place": *R* v *Secretary of State for Foreign Affairs, ex p Greenberg* [1947] 2 All ER 550.

deportation from the UK. Persons who do not have a right of abode are liable to be removed from the UK under the following circumstances: where over 17, following conviction for an offence punishable with imprisonment where the court recommends deportation; where another member of their family is to be deported; where the Home Secretary deems deportation conducive to the public good; where they have remained beyond the time limit on a stay or failed to comply with a condition of admission. The court's recommendation for deportation of an offender who comes from any EEC country is subject to EEC restrictions on interference with free movement of workers: *R* v *Bouchereau* [1978] QB 732. See Immigration Act 1971, s. 3, Sch. 3 (as amended by C.J.A. 1982, Sch. 10); *R* v *Immigration Appeal Tribunal, ex p Patel* [1988] 1 WLR 375 (deportation for deception after entry); *R* v *Secretary of State ex p Cheblack* [1991] 2 All ER 319 (deportation on grounds of national security); *R* v *Villa* (1992) The Times, 6 May.

deportation, right of appeal against. Procedure whereby the person against whom the deportation order has been made exercises the right of appeal, in the first instance, to the adjudicators appointed by the Home Secretary. If dissatisfied with the adjudication, the appellant or Home Secretary may appeal to the Immigrants Appeal Tribunal. See Immigration Act 1971, ss. 12–22.

depose. To make a deposition (q.v.) or a statement on oath.

deposit. 1. A sum of money paid on terms under which it will be repaid, with or without interest or a premium, and either on demand or at a time or in circumstances agreed by or on behalf of the person making the payment and the person receiving it, and which are not referable to the provision of property or the giving of security: Banking Act 1987, s. 5(1). For fraudulent inducement to make a deposit, see s. 35. 2. Payment made in a contract for sale of land, so as to bind a bargain. See L.P.A. 1925, s. 49(2); *Barrington* v *Lee* [1971] 3 All ER 1231. 3. Use of title deeds as security for a loan (which creates an equitable charge

(q.v.)). 4. In a contract for sale of goods, "a guarantee that the purchaser means business": *Soper* v *Arnold* (1889) 61 LT 702. 5. Any sum payable by a debtor or hirer by way of deposit or down payment: C.C.A. 1974, s. 189(1). 6. Includes the sense of leaving, remaining or leave lying: *Craddock* v *Green* [1983] RTR 479.

deposition. A statement made on oath before a magistrate or other official of the court by a witness. 1. In civil cases, depositions *de bene esse* (q.v.) may be read at the trial by consent or if the witness is dead or unable to attend because of sickness. See O. 39. 2. In criminal cases, depositions may be read, e.g., if the witness is insane, or too ill to attend. See, e.g., *Henriques* v *R* [1991] Crim LR 912. In the case of certain types of offences against children, the child's deposition may be read if signed by an examining magistrate or if the court is satisfied that the child's attendance would involve serious risk to health. See M.C.A. 1980, ss. 103, 105; Magistrates' Courts Rules 1981, rr. 7, 33. See also Civil Evidence Act 1972, s. 1. *See* EVIDENCE.

Deposit Protection Board. Constituted under the Banking Act 1987, s. 50 and Sch. 4, to administer the Deposit Protection Fund (established by Banking Act 1979, s. 21 (now repealed)). If at any time an authorised institution becomes insolvent (see 1987 Act, s. 59(1)) the Board will pay to each depositor who has a protected deposit (see s. 60) three-quarters of such deposit: s. 58. *See* BANK, AUTHORISED.

deposit-taking business. Business in the course of which money received by way of deposit (q.v.) is lent to others or any other activity of the business is financed out of the capital of or interest on money received by way of deposit. In general, deposit-taking is prohibited except in the case of the Bank of England, authorised banks (q.v.), licensed institutions: Banking Act 1987, ss. 3–7. For the minimum criteria, see Sch. 3. See I.C.T.A. 1988, s. 481; *SCF Finance Co* v *Masri* [1987] QB 1028. *See* BANK, AUTHORISED.

deprave. To corrupt. "If someone is made or kept morally bad or worse by something they are depraved by it": *R* v *Sumner* [1977] Crim LR 362. See Ob-

scene Publications Act 1959. *See* OB-
SCENITY.

deprivation of citizenship. Procedure
whereby the Secretary of State may
remove the status of British and British
Dependent Territories citizenship
from those registered or naturalised as
such if he is satisfied that the registration or naturalisation was obtained by
fraud, false representation or concealment of a material fact, or if he is satisfied of their disloyalty, disaffection or
where the person has served a year's
imprisonment within five years of registration or naturalisation: B.NA. 1981,
s. 40.

deprivation of property, order for.
Where a person is convicted of an offence punishable with not less than
two years' imprisonment and the court
is satisfied that the property in his possession or control at the time of his apprehension had been used to commit
or facilitate the commission of the offence or was intended by him to be
used for that purpose, an order depriving him of that property may be made:
P.C.C.A. 1973, s. 43. See Road Traffic
Act 1991, s. 36 (forfeiture of vehicles);
R v *Khan* [1982] 1 WLR 1403 (the
order cannot be made to deprive a
convicted person of any interest in real
property); Drug Trafficking Offences
Act 1986, s. 1.

derelict. A thing voluntarily abandoned
or thrown away by its owner.

derivative action. A company's action,
the right to which is derived from the
company, brought by minority share-
holder(s). It is an exception to the
rule that the proper plaintiff in respect
of a wrong alleged to be done to a
company is, prima facie, the company.
See *Foss* v *Harbottle* (1843) 2 Hare 461;
Fargo v *Godfroy* [1986] 1 WLR 1134.

derivative deed. One deed of settlement
or conveyance (q.v.) related to another document of settlement or conveyance, which enlarges, confirms or
otherwise alters it.

derivative trust. A sub-trust (q.v.).

derogate. To annul or restrict the
strength of an obligation or right by
some subsequent act. "No man may
derogate from his own grant": *Wheeldon* v *Burrows* (1879) 12 Ch D 31. A
landlord has an implied obligation not
to derogate from his grant (see *Ward* v

Kirkland [1967] Ch 194); derogation
may occur if the property is "rendered
unfit or materially less fit to be used
for the purposes for which it was demised": *per* Parker J in *Browne* v *Flower*
[1911] 1 Ch 219. See *British Leyland* v
Armstrong [1986] AC 577.

descendant. A person descended from
an ancestor (q.v.). See *Re Eyton* [1876]
WN 142. Generally refers to lineal descendants only.

descent. Devolution (q.v.) of an estate
by inheritance and not by will. Prior to
their abolition by A.E.A. 1925, s. 45,
the rules were: descent was traced
from the last purchaser (q.v.); priority
of males, so that the eldest took to exclusion of others in the same degree;
lineal descendants of purchaser represented him; lineal ancestors took after
lineal descendants; paternal were
preferred to maternal ancestors.

descent, citizenship by. *See* CITIZENSHIP,
BRITISH, ACQUISITION BY DESCENT.

description, sale by. Refers to a specific
article sold as an article which corre-
sponds to a description, or to articles
to be identified by reference to a certain description. (Description involves
"an account of an object by a recital of
its characteristics and qualities":
Black.) There is an implied condition
(q.v.) that, where there is a sale of
goods, they shall correspond with their
descriptions: S.G.A. 1979, ss. 13, 14.
See *Beale* v *Taylor* [1967] 1 WLR 1193;
Harlington Enterprises v *Christopher Hull
Ltd* [1990] 1 All ER 737.

desertion. 1. Continual absence from
cohabitation (q.v.), which may be a
ground for a decree of divorce or judicial separation (q.v.). "Separation
without consent and just cause": *Pheasant* v *Pheasant* [1972] 1 All ER 587.
Characterised by the fact that the common life and common home have
ceased to exist: *Walker* v *Walker* [1952]
2 All ER 138. Cessation of cohabitation
and the respondent's intention permanently to desert the petitioner must be
proved. For the case of cohabitation
during desertion, see Mat. C.A. 1973, s.
2(5). Desertion for a period of two
years may be a proof of irretrievable
breakdown of marriage. See Mat. C.A.
1973, s. 1(2) (*c*). 2. Improper absence
from one's place of duty with HM
Forces, with the intention of remain-

ing permanently absent. See Armed Forces Act 1976; and Reserve Forces Act 1980, s. 73, Sch. 5.

desertion, constructive. *See* CONSTRUCTIVE, DESERTION.

desertion, mutual. *See* MUTUAL DESERTION.

design right. A property right in an original design, i.e., the design of any aspect of the shape or configuration of the whole or part of an article: Copyright, Designs and Patents Act 1988, s. 213. The designer is the first owner of the right: s. 215. Maximum period of protection is just under 16 years: s. 216. Remedies for infringement include damages, injunction: s. 229. See also Registered Designs Act 1949, as amended by the 1988 Act, Sch. 4.

de son tort. See EXECUTOR DE SON TORT; TRUSTEE DE SON TORT.

destroy. Appears to imply, not necessarily demolition, but rather the rendering of property useless for its intended purpose: *Samuels v Stubbs* [1972] 4 SASR 200.

desuetude. Disuse, as in reference to "practices which have fallen into desuetude". A statute does not become inoperative merely through desuetude: *Rv LCC* [1931] 2 KB 215.

detain. To hold or retain as though in custody. While every arrest involves a deprivation of liberty, the converse is not necessarily true in that arrest can only be effected in the exercise of an asserted authority: *R v Brown* [1977] RTR 160. *See* ARREST.

detainer, forcible. *See* FORCIBLE DETAINER.

detention, police. A person is in police detention if he has been taken to a police station after being arrested for an offence, or he is arrested at a police station after attending there voluntarily or accompanying a constable to it, and is detained there, or is detained elsewhere in charge of a constable: P. & C.E.A. 1984, s. 118. See *Revised Code C* (1991). He must not be kept in police detention except in accordance with the provisions of Part IV of the Act: s. 34(1). In general, he must not be kept in detention for more than 24 hours before being charged: s. 41(1); he must be brought before a magistrates' court as soon as practicable and not later than the first sitting after he is charged: s. 46(1). See Northern Ireland (Emergency Provisions) Act 1991, Part IV.

determinable fee. A fee (q.v.) which may determine by an event, stated in express terms, before completion of the period for which it could continue. Example: "Blackacre to X in fee simple until he shall qualify as a doctor of medicine." An instrument under which a determinable fee is created constitutes a *settlement* (q.v.): S.L.A. 1925, s. 1. See *Hopper v Liverpool Corporation* (1944) 88 SJ 213; *Re Rowhook Mission Hall* [1985] Ch 82; Highways Act 1980, s. 263 (statutory creation of determinable fee simple).

determinable interests. Interests which are terminable on the happening of specified contingencies. See, e.g., *Re Leach* [1912] 2 Ch 422. For determinable life interest, see Co. Litt. 420a; for determinable term of years, see LPA 1925, s. 149(6).

determine. To come, or to bring, to an end.

detinue. An action by which the plaintiff sought the return of an unlawfully detained chattel. Judgment for the plaintiff was that he recovered either the chattel or its value, and damages for detention. See *Strand Electric Co. v Brisford Entertainments* [1952] 2 QB 246. Abolished under Torts (Interference with Goods) Act 1977, s. 2(1).

detriment. 1. Injury, damage or loss suffered. 2. In the law of contract, means that the promisee, in return for a promise, has foregone a legal right which he might otherwise have exercised.

devastavit. He has wasted. A personal representative (q.v.) who misapplies or mismanages the assets of a deceased person is answerable for that waste, which is said to constitute a *devastavit.* Examples: acting fraudulently in paying legacies out of the correct order or conveying an estate to the personal representative's own use. See *Re Parry* [1969] 2 All ER 512.

development. Concept of planning law, defined by the T.C.P.A. 1990 as "the carrying out of building, engineering, mining or other operations (q.v.) in, on, over or under land, or the making of any material change in the use of any buildings or other land": s. 55. See also Town and Country Planning (Use

Classes) Order 1987 (S.I. 1987/764), listing "use classes", changes within which are not classed as "development". For "development order", see 1990 Act, s. 59; for "established use", see s. 191; for "certificate of lawful use or development", see Planning and Compensation Act, 1991, s. 10. See *Secretary of State for the Environment* v *Cambridge CC* (1992) The Times, 12 Feb. (demolition is not development.) See SI 1991/2805. *See* PLANNING PERMISSION.

development land. "If the Secretary of State directs an authority to do so, it shall make an assessment of land which is in its area and which is in its opinion available and suitable for development for residential purposes": L.G.P.L.A. 1980, s. 116(1).

development, permitted. Categories of development (q.v.) for which individual applications for permission are not necessary, e.g., certain developments within the curtilage (q.v.) of a dwelling house: see Town and Country Planning General Development Order 1977, art. 3: T.C.P.A. 1990, s. 55(2). See Planning and Compensation Act 1991.

deviation. Departure from the norm, or from the method of performance agreed in a contract. See *Edwards* v *Newland* [1950] KB 534.

deviation of ships. Where a ship deviates from a voyage contemplated by the voyage policy, or goes past the destination, the insurer is discharged from liability as from the time of deviation, except, e.g., where the deviation was caused by circumstances beyond control of the ship's master, or where it was necessary for the ship's safety. See *The Al Taha* [1990] 2 Lloyd's Rep 117 (deviation not unreasonable because unplanned).

devilling. An arrangement whereby one barrister obtains the assistance of another in preparing the paperwork relating to a case. The first barrister retains responsibility for the case and remunerates the other for his assistance.

devise. A gift of real property by will made by a devisor to a devisee. May be *general*, e.g., "all my realty to X", or *specific*, e.g., "Blackacre to Y", or *residuary*, e.g., "all the rest of my real property to Z": *Re Wilson* [1967] Ch 53. For "specific disposition", see I.C.T.A. 1988, s. 701(5).

devolution. 1. The passing of property or rights from one person to another, e.g., on death. 2. The transfer, or delegation, of powers and authority held by the central government to local or regional authorities.

dictionary in interpretation of statutes, use of. A dictionary may be used by the court to ascertain words to which no particular legal interpretation attaches. See, e.g., *R* v *Peters* (1866) 16 QBD 636 (Dr Johnson's definition of "credit"); *Re Ripon Housing Confirmation Order* [1939] 2 KB 838 (meaning of "park"); and *Gravesham BC* v *Wilson* [1983] JPL 607 (meaning of "commodious"). See *R* v *Wallace* [1990] Crim LR 433 (dictionary supplied to jury after retirement).

dictum. An observation by a judge on a matter arising during the hearing of a case. *See* OBITER DICTUM.

differences, contract for. A contract, the purpose or pretended purpose of which is to secure a profit or avoid a loss by reference to fluctuations in the value or price of property of any description or in an index or other factor designated for that purpose in the contract: F.S.A. 1986, Sch. 1. See *Universal Stock Exchange Ltd* v *Strachan* [1896] AC 116; *City Index Ltd* v *Leslie* [1991] 3 WLR 207 (a contract for differences involves "related contracts for the sale and purchase of shares or commodities to be fulfilled by the payment of differences in price and not by delivery": *per* Lord Donaldson).

digest. 1. A collection of rules of law, e.g., the *Digest of Justinian*, published in AD 533. 2. A précis of cases, in the form of head-notes or main points, arranged in alphabetical order.

dilapidation. 1. Repairs needing to be made to premises at the end of a tenancy (q.v.). 2. A state of disrepair, relating to land and buildings, where legal liability is imposed on those responsible. See, e.g., *Post Office* v *Aquarius Properties* (1985) 276 EG 923.

diligence, due. *See* DUE CARE.

diminished responsibility. Where a person kills or is party to the killing of another, he will not be convicted of murder if suffering from such abnormality of mind (whether arising from a condition of arrested or retarded development of mind or any inherent causes or induced by disease or injury) as substantially impaired his mental responsibility for his acts and omissions in doing or being a party to the killing. Such a person is liable to be convicted of manslaughter: Homicide Act 1957, s. 2. See Criminal Procedure (Insanity) Act 1964; *R* v *Byrne* [1960] 2 QB 396; *R* v *Au-Yeung* (1989) 11 Cr App R (S.) 502; *R* v *Sanders* (1991) 93 Cr App R 245. For effect of alcohol on defence of diminished responsibility, see: *R* v *Gittens* [1984] QB 698; *R* v *Atkinson* [1985] Crim LR 314; *R* v *Egan* (1992) The Times, 5 June.

Diplock Court. Trial by judge alone of certain scheduled offences (in N. Ireland), set up following recommendations of the Diplock Commission (Cmnd 5185) in 1972. See N. Ireland (Emergency Provisions) Act 1991, s. 1, Sch. 1 (enumerating the "scheduled offences").

diplomatic privilege. The right extended to a foreign diplomat, or to certain members of his staff, whose government does not waive privilege, not to be prosecuted in an English criminal court. See Diplomatic Privileges Act 1964; European Communities Act 1972, s. 4; State Immunity Act 1978, ss. 16–20; Diplomatic and Consular Premises Act 1987; Arms Control and Disarmament (Privileges and Immunities) Act 1988. *See* PRIVILEGE.

direct evidence. *See* EVIDENCE, DIRECT.

direct examination. Examination-in-chief (q.v.).

directions appointment. Preliminary hearing in relation to family proceedings, with a view to issuing directions on the conduct of proceedings, by the justices' clerk, a single justice or the full court: Family Proceedings Courts Rules 1991, r. 14 (see also SI 1991/1395).

directions, summons for. A summons, marking the end of preliminaries to an action, taken out by the plaintiff within one month of the close of pleadings (q.v.), for directions relating to, e.g., discovery and inspection of documents (q.v.), so that all matters which must or can be dealt with on interlocutory

application and have not been dealt with may be disposed of. See O. 25; *Nagy* v *Co-operative Press* [1949] 2 KB 188.

directives of EEC. *See* COMMUNITY LEGISLATION, FORMS OF.

director. An officer of a company (q.v.) who is responsible for its management. Described in Cos. A. 1989, s. 53(1) as, in relation to a body corporate, any person occupying in relation to it the position of director (by whatever name called) and any person in accordance with whose directions or instructions (not being advice given in a professional capacity) the directors of the body are accustomed to act. A director is a trustee (q.v.) for the company but not for individual shareholders, and an agent for the company. A *board of directors* is appointed, in accordance with the articles of association (q.v.), by shareholders to run the company. See Cos.A. 1985; Cos.A. 1989, s. 108; Table A, art. 81; Banking Act 1987, s. 105(2); I.C.T.A. 1988, ss. 417(5), 612(1); *Guinness* v *Saunders* [1990] 1 All ER 652.

director, controlling. *See* CONTROLLING DIRECTOR.

director, disqualification order. An order of the court, under the Company Directors Disqualification Act 1986, prohibiting a person, without leave of the court, from being a director for a specified period. The prohibition may arise on conviction of an indictable offence (s. 2), for persistent breach of companies legislation (s. 3), etc. See ss. 2–11; *Re Melcast* [1991] BCLC 288; *In Re Samuel Sherman plc* [1991] 1 WLR 1070.

Director General of Fair Trading. Appointed under Fair Trading Act 1973. General functions are: to keep under review commercial activities in the UK relating to the supply of goods and services to the consumer; collecting and receiving information about activities and practices that may adversely affect consumers' economic and other interests; reviewing commercial activities relating to monopoly situations; making recommendations to the Secretary of State on these matters. Under C.C.A. 1974, s. 1, he has the duty to administer the licensing system set up under that Act and generally to superintend the workings of the Act. See also Competition Act 1980, ss. 9, 21–41. *See* FAIR TRADING, PROCEEDINGS RELATING TO.

director, managing. *See* MANAGING DIRECTOR.

Director of Public Prosecutions. An officer (who must possess a 10-year general qualification: see C.L.S.A. 1990, s. 71), who works under the general supervision of the Attorney-General (q.v.). Also heads the Crown Prosecution Service (q.v.) and may appear for the Crown in a criminal appeal to the House of Lords. Some statutes require DPP's consent to a prosecution: e.g., O.S.A. 1989, s. 9. See Prosecution of Offences Act 1985 (as amended by C.J.A. 1987, Sch. 2, para. 13).

director, persons connected with. *See* CONNECTED PERSONS.

directors' duty of care. Directors have a fiduciary duty to the company (as a whole: see *Balstone* v *Headline Filters* [1990] FSR 385), and a duty of care, but are not liable for mere errors of judgment. See *Re City Equitable Fire Insurance Co Ltd* [1925] Ch 407. In the performance of their functions they should have regard to the interests of the company employees as well as the interests of company members: Cos.A. 1985, s. 309. See *Kuwait Asia Bank* v *National Mutual Life Nominees* [1991] AC 187. For directors' powers to bind a company, see Cos.A. 1985, s. 35, and Cos.A. 1989, s. 108.

directors, enforcement of fair dealing by. Provisions in Cos.A. 1985, Part X, imposing restrictions on company directors taking financial advantage by, e.g., prohibition of tax-free payments (s. 311), imposition of duty on directors to disclose interests in contracts (s. 317), etc.

director, shadow. "A person in accordance with whose directions or instructions the directors of a company are accustomed to act": Cos.A. 1985, s. 741(2).

directors' interests, register of. Under Cos.A. 1985, s. 325, a company must keep a register recording information relating to notification by a director of any matter related to listed shares or debentures. See also ss. 288, 289, as amended. Substantial contracts with directors must be disclosed in ac-

counts: Cos.A. 1985, s. 232.

directors, loans to. A company may not make a loan to its directors or the directors of its holding company or enter into a guarantee for a loan made by another person to any of its directors: Cos.A. 1985, s. 330. For exceptions, see s. 334.

directors, register of. A company must keep at its registered office a register of directors and must notify the registrar within 14 days of changes in its contents: see Cos.A. 1985, s. 288.

directors, remuneration of. Unless the articles so provide, directors may not be paid for their services. See Cos.A. 1989, s. 6(3)(4), Sch. 4.

directors' report. Report to be attached to a company's balance sheet (q.v.), stating, e.g., changes in fixed assets, and giving a "fair review of the development of the business of the company and its subsidiaries", and recommending dividend. See Cos.A. 1985, Sch. 7; Cos.A. 1989, s. 234. *See* COMPANY.

directors, service. Directors employed by the company in some capacity. Remuneration may be governed by Table A, art. 82. See Cos.A. 1985, Part IX.

disability, person under. Phrase applied to, e.g., an infant (q.v.) or mental patient (q.v.), i.e., one who lacks some legal capacity or qualification.

disabled person. One who is blind, deaf or dumb or who is substantially and permanently handicapped by illness, injury or congenital deformity or any other disability for the time being statutorily prescribed. See: Disabled Persons (Employment) Acts 1948–58, imposing on those employing a substantial number of persons a duty to employ a quota of registered disabled persons; Inland Revenue Statement of Practice SP 10/81, in which "disability" includes continuing incapacity to perform duties arising from culmination of process of deteriorating physical or mental illness. For disablement allowances, see S.S. Contributions and Benefits Act 1992, ss. 68–76.

disabling statute. A statute which deprives persons or bodies of legal rights or qualifications.

disaffection, incitement to. It is an offence, maliciously and advisedly to endeavour to seduce any member of the

Forces from his duty or allegiance to the Crown: Incitement to Disaffection Act 1934. See also Police Act 1964, s. 53.

disbar. To expel a barrister (q.v.) from his Inn of Court (q.v.).

discharge. Generally, a release from an obligation. 1. Discharge of contract refers to the freeing of parties from their mutual obligations by performance, express agreement, breach, or under the doctrine of frustration (qq.v.). 2. Release of a prisoner. 3. Release of a surety (q.v.) from liability. 4. Absolute or conditional discharge (q.v.), i.e., freeing of a person found guilty of an offence. See P.C.C.A. 1973, s. 7; C.J.A. 1991, Sch. 1. 5. Freeing of a bankrupt from debts and liabilities, by order of discharge. See Ins.A. 1986, s. 280. 6. Dismissal of a jury on their having given a verdict. 7. Nullifying of rights and liabilities on a bill of exchange (q.v.). 8. Expulsion of a charge from a weapon: see *Flack* v *Baldry* [1988] 1 WLR 393.

discharge and modification of restrictive covenants. *See* RESTRICTIVE COVENANTS, DISCHARGE AND MODIFICATION OF.

disclaimer. Denial or disavowal of a claim; renunciation of title or interest. 1. A power (q.v.) may be disclaimed by deed: L.P.A. 1925, s. 156. 2. Where two gifts are made by a testator (q.v.), if one is onerous and the other beneficial, the beneficiary can disclaim the former: *Re Loom* [1910] 2 Ch 230. 3. A trustee in bankruptcy may disclaim unprofitable contracts, land burdened with very onerous covenants, etc. See A.E.A. 1925, s. 23; *Re Lister* [1926] Ch 149; *Lewin* v *Fuell* [1990] Crim LR 658 (oral disclaimer concerning brand names).

disclosure, non-. Failure to perform a duty to make known relevant material information. See *Hill* v *Harris* [1965] 2 QB 601; and *Williams & Glyn's Bank Ltd* v *Boland* [1981] AC 487. *See* INSURANCE.

disclosure of documents. *See* DISCOVERY AND INSPECTION OF DOCUMENTS.

discontinuance, notice of. The voluntary ending of an action by the plaintiff giving written notice to the defendant, in proceedings commenced by a writ of summons. See O. 21.

discontinuance of action. *See* WITHDRAWAL OF DEFENCE.

discontinuance of counterclaim. *See* COUNTERCLAIM, DISCONTINUANCE OF.

discontinuance of prosecution in magistrates' courts. Where the DPP (q.v.) has the conduct of proceedings, then, in relation to the preliminary stages (i.e., in the case of a summary offence, before evidence for the prosecution has been given, or, in the case of an indictable offence, before committal of the accused or evidence for the prosecution has been given), he may give notice of discontinuance to the clerk of the court. The accused has the right to require that proceedings shall continue. See Prosecution of Offences Act 1985, s. 23; *R* v *DPP ex p Cooke* (1991) The Times, 18 Dec.

discount. 1. Deduction from the catalogue price often allowed, e.g., by a wholesaler to a retailer (known as a "trade discount"). 2. Inducement offered by a creditor to a debtor to pay swiftly (known as a "cash discount"). 3. Procedure whereby a bill of exchange (q.v.) is acquired for a sum less than its face value.

discount, issue of shares at a. Prohibited under Cos.A. 1985, s. 100(1), in the case of public or private companies.

discount securities, deep. Redeemable stock issued by a corporation, with a discount greater than one half per cent for each completed year of the life of the stock or 15 per cent where the life of the stock is greater than 30 years: see Finance Act 1984, s. 36; I.C.T.A. 1988, s. 57, Sch. 4.

discovery and inspection of documents. Disclosure by a party of the relevant documents in the action which are in his custody or possession. See also S.C.A. 1981, ss. 33–35. A party may require inspection of any document referred to in the other party's pleadings: O. 24, r. 10. In an action commenced by writ, discovery without order must be made by exchanging lists of documents within 14 days of the close of proceedings: O. 24, r. 2. Discovery by order follows where a party is not satisfied with the opponent's list, or where a party fails to comply with a rule of discovery without order: O. 24, r. 3; County Court Rules

1981, O. 14; for specialised provision for discovery and inspection see O. 24, rr. 11A and 14A. See also *Norwich Pharmacal Co* v *Customs and Excise Commissioners* [1974] AC 133; *Black and Decker* v *Flymo Ltd* [1991] 1 WLR 753; *Lubrizol Corporation* v *Esso Ltd* (1992) The Times, 13 May (copies of documents liable to disclosure). See DOCUMENTS, LIST OF.

discovery, failure to make. Failure of a party to make a discovery of documents (q.v.) or to produce them for inspection when required. The master may then make an appropriate order for production for inspection under O. 24, r. 11. See *Chipchase* v *Rosemund* [1965] 1 WLR 153.

discretion. A right to act in certain circumstances and within given limits and principles on the basis of one's judgment and conscience.

discretionary trust. A trust under which trustees are allowed discretion to pay or apply income for beneficiaries, but no beneficiary is able to claim of right that any part or all of the income is to be paid to him or applied in any way for his benefit. Example: land is conveyed to trustees upon trust to apply rent and profits "for the benefit of X in the absolute discretion of the trustees". See, e.g., *Gartside* v *IRC* [1968] 1 All ER 121; *Turner* v *Turner* [1983] 2 All ER 745. See TRUST.

discretion, judicial. The power, residing in the court, of deciding a question where latitude of judgment is allowed. A discretionary remedy is, therefore, one which may or may not be granted. "A person entrusted with a discretion must direct himself properly in law. He must call his own attention to the matters which he is bound to consider. He must exclude from his consideration matters which are irrelevant to the matter that he has to consider": *Associated Picture Houses Ltd* v *Wednesbury Corporation* [1947] 2 All ER 680. See also P. & C.E.A. 1984, s. 78; *R* v *Metropolitan Police Commissioner, ex p Blackburn (No. 3)* [1973] QB 241 (relating to police discretion).

discretion, judicial, relating to admissibility of evidence. "In every criminal case the judge has a discretion to disallow the evidence even if in law relevant, and, therefore, admissible, if admissibility would operate unfairly against the defendant": *Callis* v *Gunn* [1964] 1 QB 495. See Civil Evidence Act 1968, s. 8; O. 38, r. 29; P & C.E.A. 1984, ss. 78, 82(3). See EXCLUSIONARY RULES OF EVIDENCE.

discretion to arrest or prosecute. "It is for the Commissioner of Police or the Chief Constable . . . to decide in any particular case whether enquiries should be pursued, or whether an arrest should be made, or a prosecution brought": *per* Lord Denning in *R* v *Chief Constable of Devon and Cornwall, ex p CEGB* [1982] QB 458. See CROWN PROSECUTION SERVICE.

discrimination. The according of some differential treatment to persons or bodies in the same position, e.g., sex or racial discrimination. Discrimination on grounds of nationality is prohibited under Treaty of Rome 1957, art. 7.

discrimination, racial. Discrimination by one person against another so that, on racial grounds (colour, race, nationality, ethnic or national origins), he treats the other less favourably than he treats or would treat others, or applies to that other a requirement which he applies or would apply equally to persons not of the same racial group as that other but which is such that the proportion of persons who can comply with it is considerably smaller than the proportion of persons not of that racial group who can comply with it and which he cannot show to be justifiable and which is to the detriment of that other because he cannot comply with it: Race Relations Act 1976, s. 1. Unlawful in the employment and other fields, under the 1976 Act. See also L.G.A. 1988, s. 18; *Mandla* v *Lee* [1983] 2 AC 548; *Dhatt* v *Macdonalds Ltd* [1991] 1 WLR 527.

discrimination, reverse. Social and legal policies intended to correct existing patterns of discrimination against certain groups. "It is a call to offset the effects of past acts of bias by skewing opportunity in the opposite directions" (Katzner, 1991). Known also as "positive discrimination" and "affirmative action". See Cmnd 8427 (Lord Scarman's *Report on the Brixton Disorders 1981*), para 6.32.

discrimination, sex. Unfavourable treatment, direct, indirect, or by victimisation, of a person because of sex or marital status. May be unlawful under the Sex Discrimination Acts 1975, 1986, e.g., when taking on staff or affording access to promotion. See Employment Act 1989. See, e.g., *Gloucester Working Men's Club* v *James* [1986] ICR 603; *James* v *Eastleigh BC* [1990] 2 AER 607 (test for direct discrimination is objective); *Webb* v *Emo Air Cargo Ltd* (1991) The Times, 30 Dec. (dismissal on grounds of pregnancy). *See* EQUAL PAY.

disease. Includes injury, ailment or adverse condition whether of body or mind: Medicines Act 1968, s. 132(1).

disease of the mind. "Mind" in the M'Naghten Rules (q.v.) is used in the ordinary sense of the mental faculties of reason, memory and understanding. "If the effect of a disease is to impair these faculties so severely as to have either of the consequences referred to in the latter part of the Rules, it matters not whether the aetiology of the impairment is organic, as in epilepsy, or functional, or whether the impairment itself is permanent or is transient and intermittent, provided that it subsisted at the time of the commission of the act": per Lord Diplock in *R* v *Sullivan* [1984] AC 156.

disentailing deed. *See* BARRING OF ENTAILED INTEREST.

disentailment. Mode of barring of an entailed interest (q.v.) by deed, known as a distentailing assurance, so that the rights of the tenant's issue and of persons whose estates should take effect after the determination or in defeasance of the entailed interests are defeated. Interests ranking prior to entailed interests cannot be defeated in this way. See L.P.A. 1925, s. 133.

disfranchise. To deprive of a right.

disherison. Debarring from an inheritance, i.e., disinheriting.

dishonest. Lacking intentionally in an element of truth or probity. The "dishonest appropriation" of property is an essential element in the offence of theft: Th.A. 1968, s. 1(1). Appropriation is not to be regarded as dishonest if, e.g., a person appropriates property in the belief that he has in law the right to deprive another of it: s. 2(1). See *Anderton* v *Burnside* [1984] AC 320; *R* v *Navvabi* [1986] 3 All ER 102: *R* v

Gomez [1991] 3 All ER 394.

dishonest suppression of documents. *See* SUPPRESSION OF DOCUMENTS, DISHONEST.

dishonesty, proper test for. The test is a dual one: did the accused act dishonestly by the standards of "ordinary decent people" and, if so, must he have realised that his acts were by the standards of those people dishonest? An accused can be convicted only if the answer to both questions is affirmative. See *R* v *Ghosh* [1982] QB 1053. See also *R* v *Morris* [1983] QB 587; *R* v *Brennen* [1990] Crim LR 118.

dishonour of bill. Refusal by the drawee of a bill of exchange (q.v.) to accept it, or failure to pay after acceptance. See B. Ex.A. 1882, s. 47; A.J.A. 1977, s. 4; *Rae* v *Yorkshire Bank plc* (1987) The Times, 12 Oct. (damages for dishonour of cheque).

dismissal, constructive. *See* CONSTRUCTIVE DISMISSAL.

dismissal, fair. *See* FAIR DISMISSAL.

dismissal from employment. Means, under E.P.(C.)A. 1978, s. 55, the termination of an employee's contract of employment by the employer with or without notice; where under that contract an employee is employed for a fixed term, the expiry of that term without its renewal under the same contract; termination of a contract by an employee, with or without notice, in circumstances such that he is entitled to terminate it without notice by reason of the employer's conduct. An employee is not entitled to a written statement from his employer of the reasons for his dismissal unless continuously employed for not less than two years: E.P.(C.)A. 1978, s. 53(2) as substituted by Employment Act 1989, s. 15(1). See T.U.L.R.(C.)A. 1992, s. 156.

dismissal of action. Result of a successful application to the court by the defendant requesting that an action be dismissed, e.g., because of default in service of a statement of claim: O. 19, r. 1. Generally the plaintiff must be guilty of inexcusable, inordinate and prejudicial delay: *Allen* v *McAlpine & Sons Ltd* [1968] 1 All ER 543. For dismissal for want of prosecution, see *Birkett* v *James* [1977] 2 All ER 801; *James Investments* v *Phillips* (1987) The Times, 16 Sept.

dismissal procedures agreement. "An agreement in writing with respect to procedures relating to dismissal made by or on behalf of one or more independent trade unions and one or more employers or employers' associations". E.P.(C.)A. 1978, s. 153(1).

dismissal statement. A written statement, to which an employee with at least 26 weeks of continuous service is entitled, giving reasons for dismissal: E.P.(C.)A. 1978, s. 53. See *Harvard Securities* v *Younghusband* [1990] IRLR 17. A complaint to a tribunal may be made if the statement is refused or is untrue.

dimissal, summary. *See* SUMMARY DISMISSAL.

dismissal, unfair. Dismissal, where e.g., the employee was or proposed to become a member of an independent union, or had taken part in its activities, or where he refused to join a union (where there is a union membership agreement (q.v.)) because of a genuine objection on grounds of conscience or deeply-held personal conviction. The determination of whether dismissal is fair or unfair is related to the question of whether in the circumstances the employer had acted reasonably or not. See T.U.L.R.(C.)A. 1992, s. 152. In general, an employee has the right not to be unfairly dismissed by his employer: E.P.(C.)A. 1978, s. 54(1). See *W. Midlands Co-op Society* v *Tipton* [1986] AC 536; *Brooks* v *British Telecommunications* [1992] IRLR 66. *See* FAIR DISMISSAL.

disorderly house. A brothel (q.v.). See the S.O.A. 1956, ss. 33–36; *Moores* v *DPP* [1991] 3 WLR 549 (persistent disorderly use has to be shown).

disorder, violent. Where three or more persons who are present together use or threaten unlawful violence and the conduct of them (taken together) is such as will cause a person of reasonable firmness present at the scene to fear for his personal safety, each of the persons using or threatening personal violence is guilty of violent disorder; P.O.A. 1986, s. 2(1). See *R* v *McGuigan* [1991] Crim LR 719.

disparagement of goods. *See* SLANDER OF TITLE.

dispensing power. The right to dispense with statute law, exercised by the Crown under the Tudor and Stuart dynasties. Effectively ended by Bill of Rights 1688 (q.v.).

disposal of premises. Includes a letting, assignment or surrender of a tenancy of the premises and the creation by contract of any other right to occupy the premises: Defective Premises Act 1972, s. 6(1).

disposal of uncollected goods. The bailee may give the bailor written notice (by delivery to the bailor), by post, by leaving it at his proper address, specifying goods, stating that they are ready for delivery and specifying the amount payable by the bailor in respect of the goods: Torts (Interference with Goods) Act 1977, Sch. 1. If the bailee has given notice and has failed to trace the bailor, he is entitled to sell the goods: s. 12(3). *See* BAILMENT.

disposition. 1. The passing of property, whether by act of parties or act of the law: *Northumberland* v *A.-G.* [1905] AC 406; *Re Billson's ST* [1984] Ch 407. See L.P.A. 1925, s. 15(1)(c); Legitimacy Act 1976, s. 10(1). Includes "a conveyance and also a devise (q.v.), bequest or an appointment of property contained in a will": L.P.A. 1925, s. 205(1) (ii). See *Rye* v *Rye* [1962] AC 496. 2. Term used in the law of evidence to indicate a person's general tendencies to think or act in a particular way. It may be proved by evidence of character, previous convictions, conduct on other occasions. See *Selvey* v *DPP* [1970] AC 304; *Boardman* v *DPP* [1974] 3 All ER 887.

disposition, voluntary. *See* VOLUNTARY DISPOSITION.

dispossess. To oust from land. See H.A. 1985, s. 389. *See* OUSTER.

dispute. A conflict of claims or rights. Whenever one party to a contract requests something from the other party under the terms of their contract and that request is not complied with, there is a dispute: *Ellerine Bros Ltd* v *Klinger* [1982] 2 All ER 737.

dispute, trade. *See* TRADE DISPUTE.

disqualification. Deprivation of a right, power or privilege. See, e.g., Company Directors Disqualification Act 1986; *Re Sevenoaks Stationers Ltd* [1991] Ch. 164. Thus, where a person is convicted of certain driving offences, he may be ordered by the court to be disqualified from driving for a period. See Road Traffic Act 1991, ss. 19, 25; Road Traffic Offenders Act 1988, ss. 36–38, 42.

disseisin. The wrongful putting out of a person seised of a freehold. *See* SEISIN.

dissentiente. Generally abbreviated to *diss.* Delivering a dissenting judgment.

dissolution. Breaking up; bringing to an end. 1. Dissolution of Parliament means bringing the life of an existing Parliament to an end, e.g., proroguing Parliament, which is then dissolved by proclamation of the Queen. 2. Dissolution of a marriage, e.g., by decree of divorce (q.v.). 3. Termination of existence of a company by legal process resulting from, e.g., being struck off the register.

distinguishing a case. Where the court has been invited to follow a previous decision, but feels that there are important points of difference between that decision and the case on which it was based and the case it is considering, the case is said to have been "distinguished".

distrain. To levy a distress (q.v.).

distress. The seizing of a personal chattel (q.v.) from a debtor or wrongdoer so as to obtain payment for a debt (e.g., arrears of rent) or satisfaction for a wrong committed. See Rent Act 1977, s. 147; M.C.A. 1980, ss. 76–78. Chattels may be privileged from distress *absolutely* (fixtures, goods of a third party, etc) or *conditionally* (e.g., beasts of the plough).

distress damage feasant. A form of self-help taking the form of the seizure by X of a chattel or animal belonging to Y which is wrongfully on X's land and damaging it. See *Burt* v *Moore* (1973) 5 TR 329. Abolished in relation to animals by the Animals Act 1971, which created a general right to detain and sell, after 14 days, trespassing livestock not under control: s. 7. *See* DAMAGE FEASANT.

distribution. The division of property of an intestate among the next of kin. See A.E.A. 1925, ss. 33, 46, 47; Intestates' Estates Act 1952; Family Provision Act 1966; F.L.R.A. 1969; Inheritance (Provision for Family and Dependants) Act 1975; *Re Collens* [1986] 1 All ER 611.

distribution of company assets. Distribution of company assets, in cash or otherwise to members out of profits is prohibited except when made by way of issue of fully or partly-paid bonus shares, redemption of preference shares from the proceeds of fresh issue, reduction of share capital by reducing or writing off members' liability in respect of unpaid share capital, distribution or winding up: Cos.A. 1985, s. 263. For restrictions, see ss. 263, 264.

distribution of company assets on liquidation, order of. The order is generally: secured creditors with fixed charges; liquidation costs; preferential creditors; secured creditors with floating charges; unsecured creditors; debts due to company members as members; repayment of capital to members; division of surplus assets among members.

distributive justice. *See* JUSTICE, COMMUTATIVE, DISTRIBUTIVE AND CORRECTIVE.

district councils. *See* COUNCILS, DISTRICT.

district judges. *See* JUDGES, DISTRICT.

district registries. Registries in England and Wales which function as branch offices of the Supreme Court (q.v.) allowing procedings to be commenced in many parts of the country by writ of summons. See S.C.A. 1981, s. 99.

districts. The six former metropolitan counties in England were divided into 36 metropolitan districts which have been, to a large extent, continued (see L.G.A. 1985, Parts I and II); the 39 non-metropolitan counties were divided into 296 districts; Wales had 37 districts; Scotland had 53 (based on nine regions).

distringas. That you distrain. Writ commanding the sheriff (q.v.) to distrain on a person. A *distringas notice* was issued so as to prevent the transfer of shares in a company (q.v.); it was replaced later by a stop notice. See O. 50, rr. 11–15. *See* DISTRAIN.

disturbance. Interference with the existence or exercise of a right by, e.g., "trespass or nuisance, or in any other substantial manner": *Fitzgerald* v *Forbank* [1897] 2 Ch 96.

divest. To deprive, dispossess. "The taking away of the possession of a thing": *Termes de la Ley.*

dividend. 1. Amount payable to a bankrupt's creditors after payment of expenses and preferential debts. 2. A part of a company's net profit distributed by means of "dividend warrants" among shareholders in proportion to their shareholdings. See I.C.T.A. 1988, ss. 45, 128 (foreign dividends); T.C.G.A. 1992, s.177 (dividend stripping). Must, generally, be paid out of profits. See Table A, arts. 102–7. See PROFITS AVAILABLE FOR DISTRIBUTION.

dividend, interim. See INTERIM DIVIDEND.

Divine Right of Kings. "The State of monarchy is the supremest theory upon earth; for kings are not only God's lieutenants upon earth and sit upon God's throne, but even by God himself they are called gods . . . Kings are justly called gods for that they exercise a manner or resemblance of divine power on earth . . . it is seditious in subjects to dispute what a king may do in the height of his power . . .": James I, in a speech to Parliament, March 1610.

divine service, tenure by. Tenure involving fealty and obligation to say a mass at regular intervals. Abolished in 1660.

divisible contract. A contract in which the parties intend that their promises are to be independent of each other: *Taylor* v *Webb* [1937] 2 KB 283. An *entire* (or *indivisible*) contract is one in which there is agreement, implicit or explicit, that neither party may demand performance until he is ready to fulfil, or has fulfilled, his promise. See CONTRACT.

Divisional Courts. Term applied collectively to the Queen's Bench Divisional Court, the Chancery Divisional Court and the Family Divisional Court. The Queen's Bench Divisional Court hears appeals on points of law by way of case stated from decisions of magistrates or from the Crown Court, hears appeals by solicitors from decisions of the Solicitors' Disciplinary Tribunal and exercises supervisory jurisdiction over inferior courts and tribunals. It consists of 2–3 judges. The Chancery Divisional Court consists of 1–2 judges and hears appeals from county courts concerning, e.g., land registration matters and bankruptcy and appeals from the Commissioners of Inland Revenue. The Family Divisional Court usually consists of two judges and hears appeals from decisions of the Crown Court, county court and magistrates in

matters of domestic law. See S.C.A. 1981, s. 66.

Divisions of the High Court. The Chancery Division, Queen's Bench Division and Family Division (qq.v.). See S.C.A. 1981, s. 5(1).

divorce. Dissolution of marrriage on the ground of its irretrievable breakdown (q.v.). Proceedings commence with the filing of a petition (after at least one year from the date of marriage) in the prescribed form, which sets out the facts on which the petitioner (i.e., the person seeking a decree of divorce against the respondent) relies as proof of irretrievable breakdown of marriage, and which concludes with a prayer "that the said marriage may be dissolved". Proceedings may take place in divorce county courts and Family Hearing Centres: see SI 1991/1677. See Mat.C.A. 1973, s.1(1); Family Law Act 1986, Part II; Ch. A. 1989. Sch. 12, para 31; Family Proceedings Rules 1991; Law Comm. Report (1990) No. 192.

divorce and judicial separation, special procedure for. Procedure whereby, if a petition is based on either adultery or desertion or two years' separation, etc, and it is undefended, the petitioner can apply to put the case in the Special Procedure List. If the registrar agrees, evidence is considered and, if he finds the facts proved, he will announce a day for the pronouncement of the decree in open court. The parties need not attend. Known also as "postal divorce."

divorce, bars to. The Divorce Reform Act 1969 abolished most existing bars (e.g., connivance, condonation) to divorce. The defence now available to the respondent is that no irretrievable breakdown of marriage (q.v.) has taken place. A decree nisi may be refused where the respondent would be caused grave financial hardship (see Mat.C.A. 1973, s. 1(2) (*e*)) or other hardship. Decree absolute will not be made until the court has considered the position of the children of the family: Mat.C.A. 1973, s. 41. See QUEEN'S PROCTOR.

divorce by mutual consent. Term applied to a decree of divorce after two years of separation immediately preceding the presentation of the petition, where the respondent consents to the grant of a decree: Mat.C.A. 1973, s. 1(2) (d).

divorce, ground for. The sole ground, after 1970, is the irretrievable breakdown of marriage (q.v.): Mat.C.A. 1973, s. 1(1).

divorce, petition for. Statement by the petitioner setting out the facts relating to the breakdown of marriage (q.v.) and praying for relief by way of dissolution of the marriage. No petition for divorce can be presented to the court within one year from the date of marriage. See Mat.C.A. 1973, s. 3; Family Proceedings Rules 1991, r. 2, App. 2 (contents of petition). *See* DIVORCE AND JUDICIAL SEPARATION, SPECIAL PROCEDURE FOR.

divorce procedure, supporting documents. Together with the petition there should be filed the marriage certificate, reconciliation certificate, any previous relevant court orders and a statement of arrangements concerning the care of children of the family and to whom Mat.C.A. 1973, s. 41, applies.

DNA profiling. The examination of bodily samples in order to reveal and assess the composition of the human genetic coding material, allowing deductions as to whether or not two or more samples have come from the same person, or whether there is a parent–child relationship between persons from whom samples have been taken. See *Re I.* (1987) The Times, 22 May; *Welsh* v *HM Advocate* (1991) The Times, 13 Dec.; *R* v *Secretary of State for Home Department ex p Rosed* [1991] Imm AR 349.

dock brief. Name of the procedure whereby a prisoner, on trial on indictment, could directly instruct from the dock and for a nominal fee any barrister sitting robed in the court. The process is largely obsolete.

dock identification. Identification of witness for the first time in court. See *R* v *Horsham Justices ex p Bukhari* (1982) 74 Cr App R 291; *R* v *Fergus* [1992] Crim LR 363.

dock statements. Unsworn statements (q.v.) from the dock in criminal trials. See *R* v *Farnham Justices ex p Gibson* [1991] RTR 309 (defendant required to give evidence from dock).

document. A paper which can be relied upon as proof, or in support, of something. Under the Civil Evidence Act 1968, s. 10, a document was defined as, in addition to a document in written form: "(a) any plan, map, graph or drawing; (b) any photograph; (c) any disc, tape, soundtrack or other device in which sounds or other data (not being visual images) are embodied so as to be capable (with or without the aid of some other equipment) of being reproduced therefrom; and (d) any film, negative, tape or other device in which one or more visual images are embodied so as to be capable (as aforesaid) of being reproduced therefrom."

document, ancient. *See* ANCIENT DOCUMENT.

documentary evidence. Documents produced with the intention that they be inspected by judge and jury. See C.J.A. 1988, Part II. *See* EVIDENCE.

document exchange. A private form of postal service, now authorised to be used for the service of writs and summonses, etc, between solicitors: see O. 6, r. 5(2) and O. 65, r. 5(1) (c). *See* SERVICE.

document, intention of a. *See* INTENTION OF A DOCUMENT.

document, private, proof of execution of. Procedure involving: proof of handwriting; or proof of attestation (q.v.); or a presumption that a document produced from proper custody, which is not less than 20 years old, is validly executed. See Evidence Act 1938, s. 4.

document, public. *See* PUBLIC DOCUMENT.

documents, affidavit of. *See* AFFIDAVIT OF DOCUMENTS.

documents, discovery of. See DISCOVERY AND INSPECTION OF DOCUMENTS.

documents, dishonest suppression of. *See* SUPPRESSION OF DOCUMENTS, DISHONEST.

document, secondary evidence of. Exceptions to the general rule that the original of a document must be put in evidence include the following cases: where the original is lost or destroyed; where the original is in possession of a third party who justifiably declines to produce it; where production of the original is highly inconvenient; where the document is a public document (q.v.); where (in civil proceedings) a party has failed to comply with a notice to produce, so that the party serving notice can put a copy of the document in evidence. See EVIDENCE, SECONDARY.

documents, inspection of. See DISCOVERY AND INSPECTION OF DOCUMENTS.

documents, list of. List of documents to be served by one party on the other, drawn up in accordance with O. 24. Documents are enumerated and identified by short descriptions. There is a further enumeration of documents which the party objects to producing. Other documents which have been in the party's possession, but which are no longer so, are also listed. See also O. 27, r. 4; *Rafidain Bank* v *Agom Sugar Co* [1987] 1 WLR 1606.

documents of title to goods. "Any bill of lading, dock warrant, warehouse-keeper's certificate, any warrant or order for the delivery of goods, and any other document used in the ordinary course of business as proof of the possession or control of goods, or authorising or purporting to authorise, either by endorsement or by delivery, the possessor of the documents to transfer or receive goods thereby represented": Factors Act 1989, s. 1(4).

documents, trust. See TRUST DOCUMENTS.

documents, withholding of. It is wrong to allow the prosecution to withhold material documents without giving any notice of that fact to the defence: *R* v *Ward* (1992) The Times, 8 June.

Doe, John. Name of the fictitious plaintiff formerly used in the action of ejectment (q.v.). See the comments of Donaldson LJ in *Barrett* v *French* [1981] 1 WLR 848.

dogs, dangerous. "Dangerous" refers not only to danger to persons, but also, e.g., cattle: see Dogs Act 1906, s. 1(4). Magistrates may order a dangerous dog to be kept under control or destroyed: Dogs Act 1871, s. 2, as amended by Dogs Act 1989. The Dangerous Dogs Act 1991 restricts the owning of designated breeds bred for fighting: s. 1. If a dog is dangerously out of control in a public place, the owner or person in charge of the dog is guilty of an offence if the dog injures any person: s. 3. For seizure of stray dogs, see En. P.A. 1990, s. 149. See also

Animals Act 1971.

dogs injuring livestock. See LIVESTOCK.

dogs, killing or injuring of. See LIVESTOCK, PROTECTION OF.

doli capax. Capable of fraud or deceit. Phrase used to signify that a young person is old enough, or sufficiently intelligent, to be responsible in law for the wrongful acts of which he is accused. There is a conclusive presumption that a child under 10 is *doli incapax* (i.e., incapable of crime). Between 10–14, he may be shown to be capable of discriminating between good and evil and, therefore, may be held responsible for his actions (the maxim is *malitia supplet aetatem* – malice supplements age). See *R* v *B.* [1979] 1 WLR 1185 (where evidence of previous convictions was held admissible); *J.M.* v *Runeckles* (1984) 79 Cr App R 255; *A.* v *DPP* [1992] Crim LR 34.

domain. 1. Concept involving absolute right to and authority over property. 2. Territory over which authority is exercised.

domain, eminent. See EMINENT DOMAIN.

Domesday Book. A record of William the Conqueror's "description of England", carried out in 1081–6 by panels of commissioners who based their survey of the lands of England on the accounts of the estates of the King and his tenants-in-chief (q.v.).

domestic agreements. Agreements made within the course of family life. They are considered as not normally made in contemplation of the creation of a legal relationship. See, e.g., *Balfour* v *Balfour* [1919] 2 KB 571 ("In respect of these promises each house is a domain into which the King's writ does not seek to run": *per* Aitkin LJ); *Pettitt* v *Pettitt* [1970] AC 777.

domestic animal. See ANIMAL.

domestic arbitration agreement. See ARBITRATION AGREEMENT, DOMESTIC.

domestic premises. Premises occupied as a private dwelling-house, including any garden, yard, garage, outhouse or other appurtenance of such premises not used in common by the occupants of more than one such dwelling. See the H.S.W.A. 1974, s. 53(1).

domestic tribunals. Disciplinary committees exercising judicial or quasi-judicial functions, e.g., disciplinary committee of The Law Society (see Solicitors Act 1974, s. 46). The High Court exercises a supervisory jurisdiction over these tribunals (q.v.).

domestic violence. *See* INJUNCTIONS, MATRIMONIAL.

domicile. Generally, the country where a person has his permanent home: *Whicker* v *Hume* (1858) 7 HL Cas 124. Under C.J.J.A. 1982, s. 41(1), "an individual is domiciled in the UK if and only if he is resident in the UK and the nature and circumstances of his residence indicate that he has a substantial connection with the UK." A person's *domicile of origin* is that which he receives at birth (usually the domicile of his father); this is preserved until he acquires another. See *IRC* v *Bullock* [1976] 1 WLR 1178. A *domicile of choice* is acquired by a person establishing his residence in a chosen country, intending to remain there permanently. A *domicile of dependence* is that of a child under 16, which changes with that of its parents. No person can be without a domicile or have more than one at the same time. Under Domicile and Matrimonial Proceedings Act 1973, a wife's "domicile of dependence" (i.e., a domicile dependent on the domicile of some other person) was abolished and her domicile is ascertained by reference to the same factors as in the case of any other individual capable of having an independent domicile: s. 1(2). See Family Law Act 1986, s. 46; *Plummer* v *IRC* [1988] 1 WLR 292.

dominant position. Phrase used in EEC decisions (q.v.) to refer to "a position of economic strength enjoyed by an undertaking which enables it to prevent effective competition being maintained on the relevant market by giving it the power to behave to an appreciable extent independently of its competitors, customers and ultimately of its consumers": *United Brands* v *Commission* (Case 27/76).

dominant tenement. Land to which there is attached the benefit of a right. Example: X owns Blackacre and grants to Y, his neighbour, owner of Whiteacre, a right to use a footpath over Blackacre. Whiteacre is the *dominant tenement*; Blackacre is the *servient tenement.*

Dominions. Name formerly applied to the British Commonwealth countries of, e.g., Australia, Canada, New Zealand. These countries, former dependencies of the UK, had, generally, complete self-government, usually modelled on the UK. See Statute of Westminster 1931, s. 1: *Manuel* v *A.-G.* [1983] Ch 77.

dominium. Ownership. (In its original sense, single and indivisible, absolute and exclusive.)

domitae naturae. See ANIMALS, CLASSIFICATION OF.

domus sua cuique est tutissimum refugium. To every person his house is his surest refuge. See *Seymayne's Case* (1605) 5 Co Rep 91; *Swales* v *Cox* [1981] QB 849.

donatio mortis causa. A gift of property by a donor in anticipation of his death. (Plural: *donationes mortis causa.*) To be effective: the property must be capable of passing by *donatio*; death in the near future must be contemplated by the donor; *donatio* must have been made conditional on the donor's death; delivery is essential. See *Wilkes* v *Allington* [1931] 2 Ch 104; *Woodward* v *Woodward* [1991] Fam Law 470; *Sen* v *Headley* [1991] 2 All ER 636 (land may pass in this way).

doom. Judgment (Anglo-Saxon).

dormant company. A company is treated as dormant for any period during which it does not enter into any significant accounting transaction, i.e., which it would be obliged by law to enter in its accounting records, other than receipt of issue price for subscribers' shares. See Cos.A. 1985, s. 252(5); Cos.A. 1989, s. 14.

dormant partner. A "sleeping partner", i.e., a member of a partnership (q.v.) who does not play an active part in the running of the business.

dotards. Dead or decayed trees, that cannot be used as timber. A tenant for life (q.v.) may, in general, cut dotards and all the trees which are not timber; *Re Harker's WT* [1938] Ch 323.

double insurance. *See* INSURANCE, DOUBLE.

double jeopardy. Possibility of repeated prosecution for the same offence. See *R* v *Police Complaints Board, ex p Madden* [1983] 2 All ER 353; *R* v *Griffiths* [1990] Crim LR 191; *R* v *King* [1992] Crim LR 47. *See* AUTREFOIS ACQUIT.

double portions, rule against. A child is generally prohibited from taking both a sum paid to him as a portion and a legacy which has been bequeathed to him as a portion. The general principle is: "Equity leans against double portions." See *Fowkes* v *Pascoe* (1875) 10 Ch App 343. *See* PORTION.

double probate. A grant of probate made to an executor (q.v.) to whom power has been reserved to prove at a later date, or on the happening of a specified event, and who has proved. Example: an executor who was an infant (q.v.) and who has later attained his majority. See *Re Griffin* (1910) 54 SJ 378. *See* GRANT; PROBATE.

double renvoi. *See* RENVOI.

double value, action for. Action brought under Landlord and Tenant Act 1730 by landlord for double the yearly value of premises where a tenant holds over wilfully, and not by mistake, or under a *bona fide* claim of right, and not by mistake, after notice has been given before the expiry of possession. See *French* v *Elliott* [1960] 1 WLR 40. An action for double rent may be brought under the Distress for Rent Act 1737, s. 18, against a tenant under a periodic tenancy who gives notice to quit and then fails to give up possession.

doubt, reasonable. *See* REASONABLE DOUBT.

dower. The right of a widow to a life interest in the realty of her deceased husband. Abolished by L.P.A. 1925 and A.E.A. 1925, s. 45.

DPP. Director of Public Prosecutions (q.v.).

draft. 1. An order for the payment of a sum of money. (A "banker's draft" is a draft drawn by a bank upon itself, e.g., by a branch or head office or on another branch. It is not a cheque or bill. See e.g., *Bank of Montreal* v *Dominion Gresham Guarantee Co* [1930] AC 659); *Citibank N.A.* v *Brown Shipley & Co* [1991] 2 All ER 690. 2. An outline copy of a document.

driver. One who is in charge of a vehicle and, if a separate person acts as a steersman, the term includes that person as well as any other person in charge of the vehicle or engaged in the driving of it. Driving means "imparting motion to a vehicle and endeavouring to control it": *Rowan* v *Chief Constable of Merseyside* (1985) The Times, 10 December; *McKoen* v *Ellis* [1987] Crim LR 54.

driving, careless and inconsiderate. It is an offence for a person to drive a mechanically propelled vehicle on a road or other public place without due care and attention, or without reasonable consideration for other persons using the road or place: Road Traffic Act 1991, s. 2 (amending Road Traffic Act 1988, s. 3).

driving, careless, influence of drink or drugs, causing death by. If a person causes the death of another by careless and inconsiderate driving (q.v.) and he is, at the time of driving unfit to drive through drink or drugs or the proportion of alcohol in his breath, blood, urine, exceeds the prescribed limits, or he fails, within 18 hours of being required to produce a specimen, to do so, he is guilty of an offence: Road Traffic Act 1988, s. 3A, inserted by Road Traffic Act 1991, s. 3. *See* BREATH TEST.

driving, dangerous. A person is to be regarded as driving dangerously if the way he drives falls far below what would be expected of a competent and careful driver and it would be obvious to a competent and careful driver that driving in that way would be dangerous. "Dangerous" refers to the danger of injury to a person or of serious damage to property. See Road Traffic Act 1988, s. 2A, substituted by Road Traffic Act 1991, s. 1. It is an offence: to drive a mechanically propelled vehicle dangerously on a road or other public place (Road Traffic Act 1988, s. 2, as substituted by Road Traffic Act 1991, s. 1); to cause death by dangerous driving (1988 Act, s. 1, substituted by 1991 Act, s. 1). For offence of motor racing on public ways, see 1988 Act, s. 12.

driving, faulty. *See* FAULTY DRIVING.

driving licence. Authority to drive a motor vehicle. An applicant for a licence must be physically fit and pass a driving test (unless he already possesses a licence). It is an offence to drive on a road without holding a licence. See, e.g., Road Traffic Act 1988, Part III.

driving test order. An order disqualifying an offender from driving until he passes a test showing his competence to drive.

driving with alcohol concentration above prescribed limit. If a person drives or attempts to drive a motor vehicle on a road or other public place or is in charge of a motor vehicle on a road or other public place after consuming so much alcohol that the proportion of it in his breath, blood or urine exceeds the prescribed limit (q.v.), he is guilty of an offence: Road Traffic Act 1988, s. 5. *See* BREATH TEST.

drug addict. "A person shall be regarded as being addicted to a drug if, and only if, he has as a result of repeated administration become so dependent upon the drug that he has an overpowering desire for the administration of it to be continued": SI 1973/799, as amended by SI 1989/1909. See also Misuse of Drugs Act 1971, s. 10(2)(i); *R* v *Crampton* (1991) 92 Cr App R 369.

drugs, controlled. Drugs, classified by the Misuse of Drugs Act 1971 as: Class A (opium, etc); Class B (amphetamine, etc); Class C (pemoline, etc). Classification affects the maximum penalties for the offence of having possession of a controlled drug. It is an offence for one who is an occupier of premises or concerned in their management to knowingly permit the smoking of opium or cannabis (q.v.) on those premises: s. 8. For restriction of production, see s. 4(2); "production" refers to manufacture, cultivation, or any other method: s. 37(1); *R* v *Russell* [1992] Crim LR 362 (conversion of drug is "production"). For "preparation" containing a drug, see Sch. 2, Part 1, para 1. See *Hodder* v *DPP* [1990] Crim LR 261. See also Transport and Works Act 1992, s. 27. See the Controlled Drugs (Penalties) Act 1985; *A.-G.'s Reference No 16 of 1992* [1992] Crim LR 456. *See* DRUG TRAFFICKING; POSSESSION, UNLAWFUL, OF DRUGS.

drugs, supply of. It is an offence under the Misuse of Drugs Act 1971, s. 4(1), "to supply or offer to supply a controlled drug to anyone". It is not a necessary element in the concept of "supply" that the provision should be made out of the personal resources of the person who does the supplying: see *R* v *Maginnis* [1987] AC 303. See also *R* v *Connelly* (1991) The Times, 6 Nov. *See* POSSESSION, UNLAWFUL, OF DRUGS.

drug trafficking. Producing, supplying, transporting, storing, importing or exporting a controlled drug in contravention of the Misuse of Drugs Act 1971 or some other law: Drug Trafficking Offences Act 1986, s. 38(1), as amended by Criminal Justice (International Cooperation) Act 1990, Sch. 4. See C.J.A. 1988, Sch. 5. A confiscation order, based on the Crown Court's assessment of the value of a defendant's proceeds of drug trafficking, can be issued: s. 4. It is an offence to assist another to retain the benefits of drug trafficking (s. 24(1)), or to prejudice investigations of trafficking (s. 31(1)), or to supply articles for administering or preparing controlled drugs (s. 34(1)). See, e.g., *R* v *Redbourne* (1992) The Times, 26 June.

drunkenness. *See* INTOXICATION.

dry rent. Known also as rent seck. A rent not supported by a right of distress (q.v.). Ceased to exist after Landlord and Tenant Act 1730.

dubitante. Doubting. A word found in the law reports indicating that a judge is doubting the correctness of some proposition relating to the decision he has to take.

duces tecum. Bring with you. A subpoena ordering a person to attend a trial and to bring with him documents or other things to be produced in evidence. See O. 38, rr. 14–19. *See* SUBPOENA.

due. Owed, e.g., as a debt. A debt is due when it is payable.

due care. Adequate caution in all the circumstances obtaining at a given time. See *Milkins* v *Roberts* [1949] SASR 251. For the statutory defence of "due diligence" (i.e., that the accused "took all reasonable steps and exercised all due diligence to avoid committing the offence"), see, e.g., C.P.A. 1987, s. 39.

due course, payment in. *See* PAYMENT IN DUE COURSE.

due process of law. The regular and orderly course of the law through the courts.

dum bene se gesserit. So long as he shall conduct himself well. Phrase used in relation to offices, the tenure of which depends on the holder's conducting himself well, as in the case of a judge. *See* DURANTE BENE PLACITO NOSTRO.

dum casta vixerit. As long as she shall live chaste. See, in relation to this clause in a deed of separation, *P. v P.* [1957] NZLR 854.

dum sola. While single.

duplicated offences. Where an act or omission constitutes an offence under two or more Acts, or both under an Act and at common law, the offender shall, unless the contrary intention appears, be liable to prosecution and punishment under either or any of those Acts or at common law, but shall not be liable to be punished more than once for the same offence: I.A. 1978, s. 18.

duplicity. 1. Deception, fraud. 2. The fault of uniting two or more causes of action in one count, or two or more grounds of defence in one plea, or distinct, unrelated crimes in one indictment. See, e.g., *R v Fyffe and Others* [1992] Crim LR 442. *See* COUNTS, SEPARATE.

durante absentia. During absence. Administration (q.v.) is granted *durante absentia* when an executor is out of the realm.

durante bene placito nostro. During our (i.e., the Crown's) good pleasure. Phrase used to describe the tenure of offices of judges during, e.g., the reigns of James I and Charles I. Independence of judges was assured by the Act of Settlement 1701.

durante minore aetate. During minority.

durante viduitate. During widowhood. See *Jordan v Holkham* (1753) Amb 209.

duress. 1. Restraint by force, e.g., imprisonment. 2. Actual violence or threats of violence to the person. Known also as *duress per minas* (by threats). A contract obtained by duress is voidable. "Duress, whatever form it takes, is a coercion of will so as to vitiate consent": *per* Lord Scarman in *Pao On v Lau Yiu Long* [1980] AC 614. 3. Duress may be made the basis of a defence in some criminal proceedings; but see, however, *R v Sharp* [1987] QB 853. It is not available on a charge of murder: *R v Howe* [1987] AC 417 or attempted murder (*R v Gotts* [1992] 2 WLR 284). See *R v Shepherd* (1988) 86 Cr App R 47. For duress vitiating a marriage, see *Szechter v Szechter* [1971] P 286. *See* NECESSITY; UNDUE INFLUENCE.

duress, economic. Recovery of money paid under duress (i.e., illegitimate pressure resulting in compulsion),

other than to the person, is not limited to duress to goods; it can include economic duress where that is constituted by a threat to break a contract, even though there is good consideration for that further contract: *North Ocean Shipping Co v Hyundai Construction Co* [1978] 3 All ER 1170; *The Universe Sentinel* [1983] AC 366. ("The victim's silence will not assist the bully, if the lack of any practicable choice but to submit is proved": *per* Lord Scarman); *Dimskal Shipping Co. v ITWF* [1991] 4 All ER 871.

duress of goods. Where X is in a strong bargaining position by being in possession of Y's goods by virtue of a legal right (e.g., by way of pawn), and Y is in a weak position because he needs the goods urgently, so that X demands from Y more than is justly due and Y pays. "Such a transaction is voidable. [Y] can recover the excess": *per* Lord Denning MR in *Lloyds Bank v Bundy* [1975] QB 326.

during Her Majesty's pleasure. Following a verdict of "not guilty by reason of insanity" the offender may be ordered by the court to be detained indefinitely in a specified hospital during Her Majesty's pleasure. See Criminal Procedure (Insanity) Act 1964, s. 1; M.H.A. 1983, s. 46. A person convicted of murder who was under 18 at the time of the commission of the offence is also detained in similar fashion: C. & Y.P.A. 1933, s. 53(1) (as amended by Murder (Abolition of Death Penalty) Act 1965, s. 1(5)). See also Criminal Procedure (Insanity and Unfitness to Plead) Act 1991.

Dutch auction. An auction (q.v.) at which property is offered at a relatively high price, then at a price which is gradually lowered, until an offer is made which is accepted. See Mock Auctions Act 1961, s. 3.

duties, absolute. *See* ABSOLUTE DUTIES.

duty. 1. An act that is due by legal or moral obligation. "A man is subject to a duty when the law commands or forbids him to do an act . . . A duty is to act or not to act so as to produce certain consequences": Terry. 2. The correlative of a right. 3. Payment levied on, e.g., imports and exports.

duty of care. "You must take reasonable care to avoid acts or omissions which you can reasonably foresee would be likely to injure your neighbour. Who, then, in law is my neighbour? The answer seems to be – persons who are so closely and directly affected by my act that I ought reasonably to have them in contemplation as being affected when I am directing my mind to the acts or omissions which are called in question'': *per* Lord Atkin in *Donoghue* v *Stevenson* [1932] AC 562. See *Murphy* v *Brentwood DC* [1990] 2 All ER 908 (overriding *Anns* v *Merton LBC* [1978] AC 728) – a builder is not liable in negligence for pure economic loss to the occupier caused by the defective nature of the building works. *See* CARE, COMMON DUTY OF; OCCUPIERS' LIABILITY, PRINCIPLE OF; OCCUPIER'S LIABILITY TO NON-VISITORS.

duty of care, directors' *See* DIRECTORS' DUTY OF CARE.

duty solicitors. Solicitors on duty on a rota basis at magistrates' courts who provide services to defendants appearing without representation. Initiated by the Bristol Law Society in 1972.

dwelling. A building or part of a building occupied or intended to be occupied as a separate dwelling, together with any yard, garden, out-houses and appurtenances belonging to or usually enjoyed with it: see, e.g., Housing Associations Act 1985, s. 106; Common Land (Rectification of Registers) Act 1989, s. 3. For ''new dwelling'', see C.P.A. 1987, s. 23(3).

dwellings, defective. The Secretary of State may designate as a class buildings, each of which consists of or includes one or more dwellings, if it appears to him that buildings in the proposed class are defective by reason of their design or construction and, as a result, the value of some or all of the dwellings has been substantially reduced: H.A. 1985, s. 528.

dying declaration. As an exception to the rule that hearsay is not admissible, the oral or written declaration of a dying person may be admissible evidence of the cause of his death in a trial for his manslaughter or murder if he would have been a competent witness had he lived, and if he had been in settled hopeless expectation of death at the time of making the declaration. ''The principle on which this species of evidence is admitted is, that they are declarations made in extremity, when the party is at the point of death, and when every hope of this world is gone; when every motive to falsehood is silenced, and the mind is induced by the most powerful considerations to speak the truth: a situation so solemn and so awful is considered by law as creating an obligation equal to that which is imposed by a positive oath administered in a court of justice'': *R* v *Woodcock* (1789) 1 Leach 500. See also *R* v *Turnbull* (1985) 80 Cr App R 104; *R* v *Andrews* [1987] AC 281 (overruling *R* v *Bedingfield* (1879) 14 Cox CC 341). *See* EVIDENCE.

dying without issue. Construed, when used in a will (q.v.), to mean a want or failure of issue in the lifetime or at the time of the death of the stated person, and not an indefinite failure of his issue, unless a contrary intention shall appear by the will: W.A. 1837, s. 29. *See* ISSUE.

E

earned income. Income arising in respect of remuneration for any office or employment or in respect of a pension, superannuation, deferred pay, compensation for loss of office, income from property forming part of emoluments of any office or employment of profit, and income charged under Schedules A, B, D, derived from the carrying on of a trade, profession or vocation. See I.C.T.A. 1988, ss. 15–20, as amended.

earner, employed. A person who is gainfully employed in Great Britain either under a contract of service, or in an office (including elective office) with emoluments chargeable to income tax under Schedule E: S.S. Contributions and Benefits Act 1992, s. 2.

earning capacity, loss of. Compensation may be made to plaintiff if he would be at a disadvantage in the labour market were he to lose his job. "It is necessarily a matter of weighing up risks and chances in all the circumstances of a particular case": *per* Lloyd LJ in *Foster* v *Tyne and Wear CC* [1986] 1 All ER 567.

earnings. Sums payable to a person by way of wages or salary (including fees, bonus, overtime pay, commission) and by way of pension, but not, e.g., a disablement pension: A.J.A. 1970, s. 54. "Any remuneration or profit derived from an employment": S.S.A. 1975. s. 3(1). See S.S.A. 1989, s. 7, Sch.1 (abolition of earnings rule in relation to retirement pensions). *See* WAGES.

easement. An incorporeal hereditament, involving a right capable of forming the subject-matter of a grant which is appurtenant to the land of one person and exercisable over the land of another. See I.C.T.A. 1988, s. 119(3). Example: A, the owner of Blackacre, grants B, owner of adjoining Whiteacre, the right to walk across Blackacre. The right of way granted to B is

in the *nature of an easement*; Blackacre is the *servient tenement*; Whiteacre is the *dominant tenement*; A is the *servient owner*; B is the *dominant owner*. An easement is *affirmative* (e.g., as where A must allow B to perform a certain act); it is *negative* where the servient owner can be compelled by the dominant owner not to perform certain acts. See L.P.A. 1925, s. 62 (unless a contrary intention is expressed, a conveyance of land includes and conveys all easements); *Simmons* v *Dobson* [1991] 1 WLR 720. For easements of necessity, see *Wong* v *Beaumont Property Trust* [1965] 1 QB 173. *See* EQUITABLE EASEMENT.

easement of necessity. Where, e.g., a grantor grants the whole of a plot of land save for an area which is surrounded by the part granted, there will be implied in favour of the part retained an easement of necessity: *Pinnington* v *Galland* (1853) 9 Exch 1; *Nickerson* v *Barraclough* [1980] Ch 325.

easement, right as. A right is an easement only where it has the following qualities: there must be a dominant and servient tenement (qq.v.); the tenements must be owned by different persons; the easement must have some natural connection with the estate as being for its benefit; the right must lie in grant. See *Marchant* v *Capital and Counties Property* (1982) 263 EG 661.

easements, extinguishment of. Easements may be extinguished by: statute (see, e.g., T.C.P.A. 1990, s. 236(1)); release, express or implied; unity of seisin (q.v.), i.e., where the fee simple of the dominant and servient tenements unite under one owner. See *Huckvale* v *Aegean Hotels* (1989) 58 P & CR 163.

easements, implied. Easements implied into a lease so as to enable the tenant to carry out effectively those of his purposes known to the landlord: *Wong* v

Beaumont Property Trust Ltd [1965] 1 QB 173.

EC. The EEC (q.v.).

Ecclesiastical Causes Reserved, Court of. *See* COURT OF ECCLESIASTICAL CAUSES RESERVED.

ecclesiastical courts. These include: consistory courts (in each diocese); the Provincial Courts (Arches Court and the Chancery Court of York). Appeal is to the Judicial Committee of the Privy Council (q.v.). *See* COMMISSION OF REVIEW; COURT OF ECCLESIASTICAL CAUSES RESERVED.

economic duress. *See* DURESS, ECONOMIC.

ecu. European currency unit based on the European unit of account. Its value is based on a "basket of currencies". It is legal tender in Belgium. See Regulation 3180/70. *See* EEC.

education. "Education includes . . . not only teaching, but the promotion or encouragement of those arts and graces of life which are, after all, perhaps the finest and best part of the human character": *per* Vaisey J in *Re Shaw* [1952] Ch 163. See also *Hopkins' WT* [1965] Ch 669.

EEC. European Economic Community, consisting, in 1992, of Belgium, France, Germany, Italy, Luxembourg, the Netherlands (all original members), Britain, Irish Republic, Denmark, Greece, Portugal and Spain. The Treaty of Accession was signed by the original member states in January 1972. The EEC was created by the Treaty of Rome 1957. Its aims include the harmonious development of economic activities, an increase in stability and an accelerated raising of the standard of living: Treaty of Rome 1957, art. 2. The objects of the EEC are to be attained through the establishment of a common market. *See* COMMON MARKET; COMMUNITY LAW; EUROPEAN COMMUNITIES; SINGLE EUROPEAN MARKET.

EEC, amendment of Treaty of Rome. "The Government of any Member State or the Commission may submit to the Council proposals for the amendment of this Treaty . . . The amendments shall enter into force after being ratified by all the Member States in accordance with their respective constitutional requirements": Treaty of Rome 1957, art. 236.

effectiveness, rule of. Concept used in interpretation of international law, suggesting that preference in interpretation should be given to that construction which allows a rule its widest effect and maximum practical value. See, e.g., *Commission v Germany* [1973] ECR 829.

effects. Generally, a person's property. See *Mitchell v Mitchell* (1820) 5 Madd 69.

egg-shell skull principle. A defendant must take his victim as he finds him. "If a man is negligently run over or otherwise negligently injured in his body, it is no answer to the sufferer's claim for damages that he would have suffered less injury, or no injury at all, if he had not had an unusually thin skull or an unusually weak heart": *per* Kennedy J in *Dulieu v White* [1901] 2 KB 669. See *Brice v Brown* [1984] 1 All ER 997 (psychiatric injury); *R v Ruby* (1988) 86 Cr App R 186 (manslaughter).

ei qui affirmat non ei qui negat incumbit probatio. The burden of proof lies upon the person who affirms, not upon the person who denies. ". . . An ancient rule founded on considerations of good sense and it should not be departed from without strong reasons": *Joseph Constantine Steamship Line Ltd v Imperial Smelting Corp* [1942] AC 154. *See* BURDEN OF PROOF.

ejectione firmae, de. Writ of ejectment, introduced in 1500, which commenced an action against one who had been ejected *firma sua* (from his term).

ejectment. Remedy available originally to leaseholders, and later to freeholders, wrongfully dispossessed. A person claiming a freehold was held, by a fiction (q.v.) to have leased to a fictitious person, John Doe (q.v.) who was held to have been ejected by the casual ejector, the fictitious Richard Roe. The person in possession admitted to the fiction and relied on his real title as the basis of his defence. The title of the action was, e.g., *Doe d. Smith v Jones* (i.e., Doe, on the demise of *Smith* v *Jones*). Abolished under Common Law Procedure Act 1852.

ejusdem generis. Of the same kind or nature. Rule of construction whereby if particular words forming a genus or kind are followed by general words, the general words are constructed *ejusdem generis*, i.e., are held to be intended to describe only other things of the same kind as those enumerated by the particular words. Example: "To A, I leave my coats, suits, hats and other wearing apparel"; "other wearing apparel" would include shirts but not the testator's fob watch. The rule does not apply where a contrary intention is shown, or where the particular words exhaust the genus. See *Re Miller* (1889) 61 LT 365; *Le Cras* v *Perpetual Trustee Co* [1967] 3 All ER 915. See CONSTRUCTION, RULES OF.

Elder Brethren. See ADMIRALTY COURT.

election. 1. The act of choosing among alternatives, e.g., as to mode of trial. See, e.g., M.C.A. 1980, s. 20(3); *Nicholls* v *Brentwood Justices* [1991] 3 All ER 359. 2. Procedure whereby a constituency returns a member to Parliament. See Representation of the People Acts 1983–91. 3. The equitable doctrine whereby he who takes a benefit under an instrument must accept or reject the instrument as a whole. Example: A, under his will, gives B £50,000 and gives C Blackacre, which belongs to B. B must elect. He may either take the £50,000 and allow C to take Blackacre, or he may retain Blackacre and claim the £50,000, but in such a case he will be obliged to compensate C by paying him the value of Blackacre out of the £50,000. See *Re Gordon's WT* [1978] Ch 145; and *Barclays Ltd* v *Bluff* [1981] 3 All ER 232.

election court. A special court, comprising two High Court judges, for the trial of controversial Parliamentary elections. It may order, e.g., a recount, a fresh election. Its decision is communicated to the Commons by the Speaker (q.v.). See Representation of the People Act 1983, ss. 120, 147(7), 159.

elections, parliamentary. There are two types: (1) general elections, held following the dissolution of Parliament and the summoning of a new one by the Sovereign; and (2) by-elections, held when a vacancy occurs in the House of Commons (q.v.) following the resignation or death of a member or his elevation to the House of Lords (q.v.). See PARLIAMENT.

elective resolution. An election by a private company (q.v.) for purposes such as those relating to directors' authority to allot unissued shares or to dispense with the annual appointment of auditors: Cos.A. 1985, s. 379(1), inserted by Cos.A. 1989, s. 116. It requires at least 21 days' written notice and must be agreed to at the meeting, in person or by proxy, by all the members entitled to attend and vote: s. 379A (2).

elector. 1. One whose name is shown on the register to be used at an election, excluding those shown on that register as below voting age (18) on polling day: Representation of the People Act 1983, ss. 1, 202. For postal and proxy voting, see Representation of the People Act 1985, ss. 5, 6. 2. One who, taking a benefit under an instrument, either accepts or rejects the instrument as a whole.

electors, registration of. A person is entitled to be registered as an elector if he will attain voting age (i.e., 18 or over) before the end of the 12 months following the day by which the register is required to be published. See Representation of the People Acts 1983–91. Aliens, convicted persons in prison, peers (other than Irish peers) are among those who cannot be registered because of disqualification.

electricity, dishonest abstraction of. The dishonest use without due authority or dishonestly causing to be wasted or diverted, any electricity. An offence under Th.A. 1968, s. 13. See *Low* v *Blease* [1975] Crim LR 513 (electricity held not to be "property" within Th.A. 1968, s. 4); *Boggeln* v *Williams* [1978] 1 WLR 873; *Collins and Fox* v *Chief Constable of Merseyside* [1988] Crim LR 247; *R* v *McCreadie* (1992) The Times, 10 June.

electricity, supply of. It is an offence for an unlicensed person to generate electricity for supply to premises, to transmit electricity for that purpose, or to supply electricity to any premises: Electricity Act 1990, s. 4.

electronic surveillance. The use of concealed microphones, etc. to intercept communications. Evidence obtained in this way is generally admissible. See Interception of Communications Act 1985; *R* v *Secretary of State, ex p Ruddock* [1987] 1 WLR 1482; *R* v *Preston* (1992) The Times, 13 May.

eleemosynary corporation. (*Eleemosyna* = alms.) A corporation organised for charitable purposes, usually for the distribution of alms in the name of the founder. See *Re Armitage's WT* [1972] 1 All ER 78.

elegit. He has chosen. Writ of execution allowing a judgment creditor (q.v.) to enter into possession of the debtor's land and hold it until the debt is satisfied. Replaced by an order creating a charge over land or over an interest in the land. Abolished by S.C.A. 1981, s. 141.

emancipation. The act of setting free from the power and control of another.

embezzlement. Offence committed by a clerk or servant who fraudulently appropriated to his own use property delivered to or taken into possession by him on account of his master or employer: see Larceny Act 1916, s. 17. No longer a separate offence under Th.A. 1968.

emblements. (*Emblaer* = to sow a field.) The profits from sown lands. A lessee (q.v.) or his personal representatives may enter, after the determination of the lease, so as to reap certain cultivated crops which he has sown. See *Graves* v *Weld* (1833) 110 ER 731.

embody. A document is said to embody a provision if the provision is set out either in the document itself or in another document referred to in the document: C.C.A. 1974, s. 189(1).

embracery. The obsolescent common law offence of perverting the course of justice by attempting to influence or instruct a juror by corrupt means. See *R* v *Owen* [1976] 1 WLR 840.

embryo. Under the Human Fertilisation and Embryology Act 1990, s. 1, refers to "a live human embryo where fertilisation is complete", including "an egg in the process of fertilisation". An embryo becomes a foetus (q.v.) when the process of development ends and the organs are formed. The creation of an embryo outside the body, except in pursuance of a licence from the Human Fertilisation and Embryology Authority, is prohibited: s. 3. A licence cannot authorise the keeping or using of an embryo after the appearance of the primitive streak (i.e., the heaping up of cells of the inner cell mass about the 15th day): s. 3(3). For licence conditions, see ss. 12–22. See Human Fertilisation and Embryology (Disclosure of Information) Act 1992.

emergency powers. Powers conferred by statutes such as Emergency Powers Acts 1920 and 1964, allowing the Crown to issue a proclamation of a state of emergency whenever it appears, e.g., that action is threatened or has been taken, calculated to deprive the community or any substantial portion of it of the essentials of life. The proclamation is in force for one month only, but may be renewed.

emergency protection order. Available under Ch.A. 1989, s. 44, limited to 8 days, to ensure a child's safety where he might otherwise suffer significant harm if not removed to accommodation provided by or on behalf of the applicant. See s. 46 for police powers to take a child into protection for up to 72 hours.

eminent domain. Term first used by Grotius in the seventeenth century. The right and inherent power of the state (apparently unknown to the common law) to appropriate private property within its boundaries to public use (i.e., to expropriate). *See* EXPROPRIATION.

emoluments. Some profit or advantage, i.e., anything by which a person is benefited: *R* v *Postmaster General* (1878) 3 QBD 428. All salaries, fees, wages, perquisites and profits whatsoever: I.C.T.A. 1988, s. 131(1). See *Bird* v *Martland* (1982) 56 TC 89. *See* FOREIGN EMOLUMENTS.

emphyteusis. Term used in Roman law referring to a grant of rights of ownership over land in perpetuity subject to payment of a yearly rent and forfeiture in certain circumstances.

employed earner. One who is gainfully employed in Great Britain under a contract of service or in an office with emoluments chargeable to income tax under Sch. E. *See* INCOME TAX; SELF-EMPLOYED.

employee. An individual who has entered into or works under a contract of employment: T.U.L.R.(C.)A. 1992, s. 295. The test of whether a person is or is not an employee may be answered by reference to the question: "Was the contract a contract of services within the meaning which an ordinary person would give to these words?": *Cassidy* v *Minister of Health* [1951] 2 KB 348. *See* SERVANT.

employee and order to work. No court may compel any employee to do any work or attend at any place for the performance of any work by way of an order for specific performance (q.v.) or an injunction (q.v.): T.U.L.R.(C.)A. 1992, s. 236.

employee's duties. Generally: to obey a lawful order within the terms of the contract (see *Turner* v *Mason* (1845) 14 M & W 112); to serve faithfully (i.e., to co-operate with his employer); to perform his duties with proper care and diligence and indemnify his employer in appropriate cases (see *Lister* v *Romford Ice and Cold Storage Co Ltd* [1957] AC 555).

employer. The master of a servant. A person (corporate or incorporate) who employs the services of others whose wages and salaries he pays. See, e.g., T.U.L.R.(C.)A. 1992, s. 295. *See* MASTER AND SERVANT; SERVANT; WORKER.

employer and employee. *See* MASTER AND SERVANT.

employers, associated. *See* ASSOCIATED EMPLOYERS.

employers' association. An organisation representing employers and any associations of such organisations or of employers and such organisations: Wages Councils Act 1986, s. 21. See also T.U.L.R.(C.)A. 1992, s. 122.

employer's duties. Generally: to provide "a reasonable amount of work to enable [the employee] to earn that which the parties must be taken to have contemplated" (*Bauman* v *Hulton Press* [1952] 2 All ER 1121); to indemnify the employee against liabilities and losses properly incurred in the performance of his work; to provide adequate material and a proper system and effective supervision. See *Scally* v *Southern Health and Social Services Board* [1991] 4 All ER 563 (employers' duties to explain employees' rights).

employer's liability. The liability of an employer to pay damages to employees for personal injuries sustained in the course of employment. In general, an accident arising out of the course of employment will be deemed, in the absence of evidence to the contrary, to

have arisen out of that employment.

employment. Usually taken to include business, profession, vocation, trade, etc. "Employment under a contract of employment": T.U.L.R.(C.)A. 1992, s. 143. *See* CONTRACT OF EMPLOYMENT.

Employment Appeal Tribunal. Body set up under E.P.A. 1975, s. 87, Sch 6 (now repealed and replaced by E.P.(C.)A. 1978, s. 135), consisting of judges of the High Court and Court of Appeal, Court of Session and lay members, to hear appeals on questions of law relating to decisions of tribunals on, e.g., Redundancy Payments Act 1965, Equal Pay Act 1970, Sex Discrimination Act 1975, E.P.A. 1975 and E.P.(C.)A. 1978. Appeal on a point of law lies to the Court of Appeal (q.v.), following leave of the court: E.P.(C.)A. 1978, s. 136(4). See SI 1980/2035.

employment, common. *See* COMMON EMPLOYMENT.

employment, contract of. *See* CONTRACT OF EMPLOYMENT.

employment, course of. *See* COURSE OF EMPLOYMENT.

employment, expenses incurred in. Claim for such expenses, under Taxes Act 1988, s. 198, must establish: expenses were incurred in performance of duties of employment; employee was necessarily obliged to incur the expenses in performing his duties; expenses must be wholly and exclusively incurred in performing the duties. See, e.g., *Smith* v *Abbott* [1991] BTC 414.

enabling statute. 1. A statute which makes legal that which was illegal. 2. A statute giving obligatory or discretionary powers.

enacting words. The introductory part of a statute, stating the authority by which it was made, which runs: "Be it enacted by the Queen's most Excellent Majesty, by and with the advice and consent of the Lords Spiritual and Temporal, in this present Parliament assembled, and by the authority of the same, as follows . . .".

enactment. An Act of Parliament (q.v.) or part of an Act. Includes any by-law or regulation having effect under an enactment. *See* LEGISLATIVE HISTORY OF AN ENACTMENT.

enclosure. Also "inclosure". The discharge of land from all rights of common. Regulated by Commons Acts

1876 and 1879; requires approval of application by the Secretary for the Environment. See Highways Act 1980, s. 45(12). *See* COMMONS, REGISTRATION OF.

encourage. To urge to a course of action; to incite. "There can be no incitement of anyone whether by words or written matter unless the incitement reaches the man whom it is said is being incited": *Wilson v Danny Quastel Ltd* [1965] 2 All ER 541. *See* INCITEMENT.

encroachment. Unlawfully entering upon another's rights or possessions. See *Ankerson v Connelly* [1907] 1 Ch 678.

encumbrance. A liability which burdens property, e.g., a lease, mortgage, easement, restrictive covenant, rentcharge (qq.v.). One who has the right to enforce an encumbrance is known as an "encumbrancer". See L.P.A. 1925, s. 205 (1)(vii); S.G.A. 1979, s. 12(2).

encumbrance, freedom from. Warranty, under S.G.A. 1979, s. 12(2)(*a*), "that the goods are free and will remain free, until the time when the property is to pass, from any charge or encumbrance not disclosed or known to the buyer before the contract is made".

endorsement. 1. A signature, usually on the reverse side of a document, generally operating as a transfer of rights arising from the document. An *endorsement in blank* is a simple signature usually rendering a bill of exchange (q.v.) payable to bearer. A *special endorsement* specifies the name of the person to whom or to whose order the bill is to be made payable. A *conditional endorsement* transfers the property in a bill subject to the fulfilment of a stipulated condition. A *restrictive endorsement* prohibits further negotiation (e.g., "pay X only"). See B.Ex.A. 1882, s. 32. 2. Endorsement of a driving licence is a procedure whereby a person convicted of certain offences will have particulars of the conviction noted on that licence. See Road Traffic Offenders Act 1988, ss. 44, 45.

endorsement of claim. A writ must be endorsed either with a full statement of claim (known formerly as "special endorsement") or a short statement of the nature of the claim or remedy or relief required. The writ must be endorsed with a claim for fixed costs where the claim is for a debt or liquidated demand (q.v.), and with the plaintiff's address and, where appropriate, his solicitor's name and address. Claims for interest must be specifically pleaded (O. 18, r. 8(4)). See O. 6, r. 2. *See* WRIT.

endorsement of service. Particulars of time, place and method of service endorsed on a writ within three days after personal or substituted service has been made. See O. 10, r. 1.

endorsement of writ, formal. A writ must be endorsed with the plaintiff's address, solicitor's name and address, etc. A writ lacking the appropriate formal endorsements will not be issued until they have been completed.

endowment. 1. Giving of dower (q.v.). 2. Provision for a charity (q.v.).

enemy. States and persons engaged in armed operations against Her Majesty's Forces. See Army Act 1955, s. 225. *See* WAR.

enforcement notice. Notice served, e.g., under T.C.P.A. 1990, s. 172, Planning and Compensation Act 1991, ss. 5–8, by a local planning authority on the owner and occupier of land on which there has been a breach of planning control, i.e., where development (q.v.) has taken place without permission, or in disregard of the limitations of such permission. The notice specifies the breach and the steps required to remedy it and states a time for compliance. Appeal is to the Secretary of State. See also En.P.A. 1990, s. 13; *R v Secretary of State for Environment, ex p Davies* (1990) 61 P & CR 487.

enforcement of judgments. *See* JUDGMENTS, ENFORCEMENT OF.

enfranchise. 1. The conferring of a right to vote at an election. 2. The conferring on a constituency of a right to return a member to Parliament. 3. The conversion of copyhold land into socage (q.v.).

enfranchisement of tenancy. Process whereby a tenant is entitled to acquire a freehold or extended long lease. The tenant must hold a tenancy exceeding 21 years at a rent less than two-thirds of the rateable value of the premises: Leasehold Reform Acts 1967 and 1979. See H.A. 1980, Sch. 21. *See* LONG TENANCY.

engage. 1. To engage to do something has the same force as "to covenant"(q.v.). 2. To be engaged in an occupation is to be occupied therein. It "connotes such a degree of employment as occupies the whole or at least a substantial part of the [employee's] time": *Buntine* v *Hume* [1943] WLR 123.

engagement to marry. Under common law this was considered as a contract, the breaking of which could lead to an action for breach of promise (q.v.). The action was abolished under Law Reform (Misc. Provs.) Act 1970. (The engagement ring is now presumed to be an absolute gift.) See also Matrimonial Proceedings and Property Act 1970, s. 37.

Englishry, presentment of. In the Norman era, proof (usually by inquest and declaration by a dead person's four nearest relatives) that a slain person was English. This meant that a heavy fine on the community (known as *murdrum = morth*, a secret killing) was avoided. (The original law may have been introduced by Canute in 1016, for the protection of his Danish courtiers.) Abolished in 1340.

engross. 1. To prepare the text of a document. An engrossment is a deed prior to its execution. 2. To buy up, e.g., corn, so as to sell it at a higher price (an offence abolished in 1843).

enjoyment. The taking of the benefit of some right. "The amenity or advantage of using": *per* Stirling J in *Smith* v *Baxter* [1900] 2 Ch 138.

enlarge. 1. To free. 2. To extend a period of time, e.g., in which a person may appeal. 3. A mortgagee (q.v.) who has obtained title to the land free from the mortgage by remaining in possession for 12 years may enlarge the term of years into a fee simple (q.v.) by deed: L.P.A. 1925, ss. 88, 153.

enquiry, writ of. In a common law action, after a judgment of default was given for the plaintiff, the sheriff (q.v.) would enquire, with a jury of 12 persons, into the damages sustained by the plaintiff. The procedure commenced by a writ.

enrolment. The registration or recording on an official record of an act. See S.C.A. 1981, s. 133.

entailed interest. *See* FEE TAIL.

enter. 1. To record in an account. 2. To go on land so as to assert some right. 3. The entrance of any part of the offender's body or of an instrument for removing any goods, into a house, during commission of the offence of burglary (q.v.).

entering appearance. *See* APPEARANCE, ENTERING.

entering judgment. *See* JUDGMENT, ENTERING.

enterprise zones. Designated areas in which some fiscal and administrative burdens may be removed, e.g., exemption from rates of industrial buildings: see L.G.P.L.A. 1980, s. 179, Sch. 32; Capital Allowances Act 1990, s. 1; T.C.P.A. 1990, ss. 6, 88; SI 1992/571; Finance Act 1992, Sch. 13.

enticement of spouse. *See* CONSORTIUM.

entire contract. *See* DIVISIBLE CONTRACT.

entireties, tenancy by. *See* TENANCY BY ENTIRETIES.

entrapment. The enticing of a person into the commission of a crime so that he may be prosecuted. English law has no such doctrine of defence: *R* v *McEvilly* (1975) 60 Cr App R 59. Offences must not be committed so as to trap criminals: See also *R* v *Sang* [1980] AC 402; *R* v *Gill and Ranvanna* [1989] Crim LR 358; *R* v *Christou* (1992) NLJ 823. *See* AGENT PROVOCATEUR.

entry clearances. Comprise, under Immigration Rules 1990, ss. 14–18, visas, letters of consent (from non-visa foreign nationals), entry certificates (for non-visa Commonwealth citizens). *See* IMMIGRATION.

entry, forcible. *See* FORCIBLE ENTRY.

entry into possession. Right of a legal mortgagee to enter into possession of the mortgaged property. An action for possession of a dwelling-house can be adjourned by the court, or the possession order suspended or postponed, if it appears that the mortgagor is likely, within a reasonable period, to pay any sums due under the mortgage or to remedy a default consisting of a breach of any other obligation. See A.J.A. 1970, s. 36 and A.J.A. 1973, s. 8; *Four Maids Ltd* v *Dudley Marshall Ltd* [1957] 2 All ER 35; *Britannia BS* v *Earl* (1989) 22 HLR 98. *See* MORTGAGE.

entry, right of. *See* RIGHT OF ENTRY.

entry, violence for securing. It is an offence for a person who unlawfully uses or threatens violence to secure entry into premises for himself or some other person, provided that there is someone present on the premises who is opposed to the entry and the person using or threatening violence knows that that is the case: C.L.A. 1977, s. 6(1). For defences, see s. 6(3).

entry, without warrant. See WARRANT, ENTRY WITHOUT.

entry, writ of. Writ by which the party claiming possession to the land disproved the possessor's title by showing, e.g., that he had entered unlawfully. Abolished in 1834.

enure. Also "inure". To take effect.

en ventre sa mère In his mother's womb. Refers to a conceived but unborn child. See FOETUS.

environment. "The air, water and land; and the medium of air includes the air within buildings and the air within other natural or man-made structures above or below ground": En.P.A. 1990, s. 1(2). See EEC Directive 85/337.

environmental protection. Under SI 1991/472 (Environmental Protection Regulations 1991) made under En.P.A. 1990, processes which pose the highest pollution threat are subject to control by HM Inspectorate of Pollution who have overall responsibility for control of emissions to all environmental media. Processes involving emissions to the atmosphere only are subject to local authority control. Key control concepts include "best practicable environment option" and "best available techniques not entailing excessive cost": see 1990 Act, s. 7. See AIR POLLUTION.

epitome of title. See ABSTRACT AND EPITOME OF TITLE.

equality clause. A provision relating to terms of a contract under which a woman is employed, having the effect that, where she is employed on like work with a man in the same employment or on work rated as equivalent with that of a man in the same employment, her contract is to be treated as modified, if necessary, so that it is no less favourable than that of the man or so that it includes any terms corresponding to those benefiting the man. See Equal Pay Act 1970, s. 1; and Sex Discrimination Act 1975, s. 8.

Equal Opportunities Commission. Body of 8–15 persons set up under Sex Discrimination Act 1975, s. 53, to work towards the elimination of discrimination and to promote equality of opportunity between men and women generally and to review working of 1975 Act and Equal Pay Act 1970. See DISCRIMINATION, SEX.

equal pay. Under Equal Pay Act 1970 (as amended) it was provided that, as from the end of 1975, women doing the same or broadly similar work to men would qualify for equal pay and conditions of employment. The Treaty of Rome 1957, art. 119, calls for member states to apply the principle that men and women shall receive equal pay for equal work. The principle may be invoked before national courts: *Defresne* v *Sabena* [1981] 1 All ER 122. See *Hayward* v *Cammell Laird Ltd* [1988] QB 12; *Finnegan* v *Clowney Youth Training Programme* [1990] 2 All ER 546; *Financial Times Ltd* v *Byrne (No. 2)* [1992] IRLR 163.

equitable. 1. Fair and just. 2. In accordance with rules of equity (q.v.). 3. In accordance with the practice and procedure of the courts of equity.

equitable apportionment. See APPORTIONMENT.

equitable assignment. See ASSIGNMENT.

equitable charge, general. An equitable charge which is not secured by a deposit of documents relating to the legal estate affected, and does not arise or affect an interest arising under a trust for sale or a settlement, and is not a charge given by way of indemnity against rents, and is not included in any other class of land charge: L.C.A. 1972, s. 2. Example: an equitable mortgage not protected by the deposit of title deeds. "The equitable charge does not pass an absolute or special property to the creditor or any right of possession, but only a right of realisation by judicial process in case of non-payment of the debt": *London County and Westminster Bank* v *Tompkins* [1918] 1 KB 515. Registrable under Class C as a land charge: s. 2(4) (*i*). See LAND CHARGES.

equitable easement. "Any easement right or privilege over or affecting land created or arising after the commencement of this Act and being merely an equitable interest": L.C.A. 1972, s. 2. Registrable as a land charge under Class C. Example: an easement for the grantee's life. See *Shiloh Spinners Ltd v Harding* [1973] AC 691. *See* EASEMENT.

equitable estate or interest. An estate, interest or charge in or over land which is not a legal estate and which takes effect as an equitable interest or right. It involves a right *in personam* (q.v.). Examples: equity of redemption (q.v.), restrictive covenant (q.v.). See L.P.A. 1925, s. 1(3).

equitable estoppel. *See* ESTOPPEL.

equitable execution. Procedure whereby equitable relief is obtained by the appointment of a receiver (q.v.) or by injunction (q.v.). See O. 51 (receiver) and O. 29, r. 1 (injunction).

equitable fraud. A wider concept than common law fraud, embracing, e.g., the unfair and unconscientious exploitation of another's weakness or ignorance, the abuse of a fiduciary relationship. See *Nocton v Lord Ashburton* [1914] AC 932; *O'Sullivan v Management Agency Ltd* [1985] QB 528.

equitable interests. Interests, the recognition and protection of which were originally within the province of the courts of equity. See, e.g., L.P.A. 1925, s. 1(1)–(3), in which they are defined by exclusion. *See* EQUITABLE RIGHTS.

equitable lease. A lease (q.v.) which does not satisfy the necessary requirements for a legal lease but is, nevertheless, valid in equity. There must be a valid contract to create a lease and the contract must be specifically enforceable. See *Walsh v Lonsdale* (1882) 21 Ch D 9; L.P. (Misc. Provs.) A. 1989.

equitable lien. *See* LIEN.

equitable mortgage. A mortgage which transfers an equitable interest only, either because the mortgagor's interest is equitable, or because the conveyance or other mode of transfer is equitable. See L.P.A. 1925, s. 53(1)(c). It may be created, e.g., by agreement to create a legal mortgage (q.v.), creation of an equitable charge (i.e., where property is charged with payment of the debt, but there is no transfer of possession or ownership of the property). Deposit of title deeds alone no longer suffices to create an equit-

able mortgage, by virtue of L.P. (Misc. Provs.) A. 1989. See *Matthews v Goodday* (1861) 31 LJ Ch 282. The equitable mortgagee's remedies include foreclosure, appointment of a receiver, power of sale. *See* MORTGAGE.

equitable presumptions. Presumptions raised in equity in certain cases, e.g., as where a testator bequeaths two legacies to the same person under the same will (so that if the legacies are of unequal amounts, both will be payable). See *Re Davies* [1957] 1 WLR 922.

equitable remedies. Those remedies principally evolved by equity, e.g., specific performance, rescission, delivery up and cancellation of documents, injunctions, account, receivers.

equitable rights. 1. Those rights originally recognised and enforced only in the courts of equity. 2. Those rights which are good against all persons save the *bona fide* purchaser of a legal estate for value without notice, and those who claim under such a person. (In contrast, legal rights are "good against the whole world".)

equitable waste. The malicious or wanton destruction of property by a lessee (q.v.), e.g., stripping a house of its doors. So-called because it could be remedied before J.A. 1873 only in a court of equity. A tenant who commits waste of this nature can be restrained by an injunction and ordered to rehabilitate the premises. See *Turner v Wright* (1860) 2 De G F & J 234. *See* WASTE.

equity. *Aequus* = fair. 1. Impartiality. 2. Natural justice (q.v.). 3. "Any body of rules existing by the side of the original civil law, founded on distinct principles and claiming incidentally to supersede the civil law in virtue of a superior sanctity inherent in those principles": Maine. 4. A system of doctrines and procedures which developed side by side with the common law and statute law, having originated in the doctrines and procedures evolved by the Court of Chancery in its attempts to remedy some of the defects of common law. 5. A right to enforce an equitable remedy. 6. The issued share capital of a company: Cos.A. 1985, s. 744.

equity and law, conflict of. *See* LAW AND EQUITY, CONFLICT OF.

equity and law, fusion of. *See* LAW AND EQUITY, FUSION OF.

equity, maxims of. Aphorisms purporting to state some of the fundamental principles of equity. A collection was made by Richard Francis in *Maxims of Equity* (1725). They include: equity acts *in personam*; equity follows the law; equity acts on the conscience; equity aids the vigilant; equity looks to the intent rather than the form; he who comes to equity must come with clean hands, etc. See *Tinsley* v *Milligan* [1991] NPC 100.

equity, nature of. "Now equity is no part of the law, but a moral virtue, which qualifies, moderates and reforms the rigour, hardness and edge of the law, and is a universal truth; it does also assist the law where it is defective and weak in the constitution (which is the life of the law) and defends the law from crafty evasions . . . and this is the office of equity, to support and protect the common law from shifts and crafty contrivances against the justice of the law. Equity therefore does not destroy the law, nor create it, but assists it": *per* Lord Cowper in *Dudley* v *Dudley* (1705) Prec Ch 241.

equity of a statute. Sixteenth-century doctrine expounded by, e.g., Plowden (see *Eyston* v *Studd* (1574) Plow 459): "It is not the words of the law but the internal sense of it that makes the law, and our law consists of two parts . . . the letter of the law is the body of the law, and the sense and reason of the law is the soul of the law . . . and Equity enlarges or diminishes the letter according to its discretion."

equity of redemption. The sum total of the mortgagor's rights in equity, i.e., his rights of ownership of the property subject to the mortgage: *Re Wells* [1933] Ch. 29. The right of redemption is inviolable and may not be restricted unduly. See *Kreglinger* v *New Patagonia Meat Co Ltd* [1914] AC 25; *Knightsbridge Estates Trust Ltd* v *Byrne* [1939] Ch 441 (postponement of right to redeem). *See* MORTGAGE; REDEMPTION.

equity's darling. Maitland's description of a *bona fide* purchaser for value of the legal estate without notice.

equity security. A relevant share in the company (other than a share shown in the memorandum to have been taken by a subscriber to the memorandum or a bonus share) or a right to subscribe for, or to convert securities into, relevant shares in the company: Cos.A. 1985, s. 94(2).

equity share capital. *See* SHARE CAPITAL, EQUITY.

equivocation. An ambiguity in a document, e.g., where a person is described in terms which could apply equally to another. Example: "Blackacre to my nephew John", where the testator has two nephews named John. Evidence of the testator's intention may be admissible in explanation. See A.J.A. 1982, ss. 20–22; and *Richardson* v *Watson* (1833) 4 B & Ad 787. *See* AMBIGUITY.

error. 1. "A fault in a judgment, or in the process or proceeding to judgment or in execution upon the same": *Termes de la Ley*. 2. Writ of error was used to instruct an inferior court (q.v.) to send records of proceedings for review by a superior court (q.v.). Abolished in civil cases by J.A. 1875 and in criminal cases by Criminal Appeal Act 1907.

error, jurisdictional. *See* JURISDICTIONAL ERROR.

error of law on the face of the record. An error which may be ascertained without recourse to any evidence other than examination of the record of the proceedings. The record "must contain at least the document which initiates the proceedings, the pleadings, if any, and the adjudication; but not the evidence, nor the reasons, unless the tribunal chooses to incorporate them": *R* v *Northumberland Compensation Appeal Tribunal, ex p Shaw* [1952] 1 KB 338.

escape. The common law offence committed by one who, being lawfully confined in connection with a criminal offence, breaks out of any place in which he is confined with the intention of escaping from custody. See Prison Act 1952, s. 39, as amended by C.J.A. 1961 s. 22, and Prison Security Act 1992 s. 2, by which it is an offence to aid the escape of a prisoner.

escape of dangerous things. *See* DANGEROUS THINGS, LIABILITY RELATING TO.

escheat. Procedure whereby land reverted on the extinction of a tenancy (q.v.). 1. *Escheat propter delictum tenentis* (for the tenant's crime), i.e., where the tenant was convicted and sentenced to death, the land reverted to the lord. 2. *Escheat propter defectum sanguinis* (for failure of blood), i.e., where the tenant died without an heir, the land escheated to the lord. Abolished under Inheritance Act 1833, s. 10 and A.E.A. 1925, s. 45(1).

escrow. A deed (q.v.) or bond delivered to a person who is not a party to it, to be held by that party until a future fixed date when conditions are performed, after which it is delivered and becomes absolute. See *Alan Estates Ltd v WG Stores Ltd* [1982] Ch 511.

espionage, industrial. The obtaining of industrial intelligence by illegal means. See *Ansell Rubber* v *Allied Rubber* [1972] RPC 811.

essence of a contract. The essential conditions, the very basis, of a contract, without which no agreement would have been entered into. See S.G.A. 1979, s. 10. *See* CONDITION; CONTRACT.

establishment, right of. The right to take up and pursue activities as self-employed persons and to set up and manage undertakings in the member states of the EEC: Treaty of Rome 1957, art. 52. See Directive 75/363; *R* v *Southwark Crown Court, ex p Watts* [1991] COD 260. *See* EEC.

estate. 1. An area of land. 2. An expression in land law which applies to the period of time for which a tenant (q.v.) was entitled to hold the land. "All estates are but times of their continuances": Bacon. Common law recognised the following estates: (1) freehold (i.e., estates whose duration is not known) – estate in fee simple, estate in fee tail, estate for life, estate *pur autre vie*, (2) less than freehold (i.e., where the duration is certain) – leaseholds for a fixed term of years, tenancies from year to year.

estate agency work. Things done by a person in the course of a business pursuant to the instructions of a client who wishes to dispose of or acquire an interest in land, relating to introductions of third persons to the client and the disposal or acquisition of that interest: Estate Agents Act 1979, s. 1(1). The Director General of Fair Trading (q.v.) is empowered under s. 3(1) to make orders prohibiting unfit persons

from doing estate agency work. See *Robinson Scammel* v *Ansell* (1985) NLJ 752; SI 1991/860/1032.

estate contract. Contracts by estate owners or persons entitled at the date of contract to have a legal estate conveyed to them, to convey or create a legal estate, including a contract conferring valid options to purchase, rights of pre-emption (q.v.) or similar rights. A Class C charge under L.C.A. 1972, s. 2(4). See *Barrett* v *Hilton Developments Ltd* [1974] Ch 237; *Phillips* v *Mobil Oil* [1989] 1 WLR 888.

estate duty. Tax on the value of property passing on death. Abolished under Finance Act 1975, s. 49.

estate, future. *See* FUTURE INTEREST.

estate, net. *See* NET ESTATE.

estate owner. The owner of a legal estate, i.e., the person in whom there is vested the fee simple absolute in possession (q.v.) in the case of a freehold or the term of years absolute (q.v.) in the case of a leasehold.

estate, real. *See* REAL ESTATE.

estate rentcharge. *See* RENTCHARGE.

estates, administration of. Procedure relating to assets of a deceased person, whereby they are collected, debts are paid and the surplus distributed to those beneficially entitled. Order of the application of assets (in the case of a solvent estate and subject to the testator's directions) is: property undisposed of by will; property not specifically devised or bequeathed but included in residuary gift; property specifically appropriated for payment of debts; property charged with payment of debts; fund retained to meet legacies; property specifically devised or bequeathed; property appointed under will by general power. See A.E.A. 1925, s. 34(1), Sch. 1, Part II; SI 1991/1876, amending Non-Contentious Rules 1987. Funeral, testamentary and administration expenses have priority; A.E.A. 1925, Part I, Sch. 1. For appropriation of assets, see s. 41.

estates, legal. Estates capable of subsisting at law (q.v.).

estates of the realm. Originally clergy, baronage, commons. The term is now applied to the Lords Spiritual and Temporal, i.e., the House of Lords (q.v.) and the Commons, i.e., the House of Commons (q.v.).

estates subsisting at law. Under L.P.A. 1925, s. 1, the only estates in land capable of subsisting or of being conveyed or created at law, i.e., "legal estates" are, as from January 1926: an estate in fee simple absolute in possession (q.v.); a term of years absolute (q.v.). All other estates take effect as equitable interests (q.v.).

estoppel. A rule of evidence (and not a cause of action) preventing a person from denying the truth of a statement he has made previously, or the existence of facts in which he has led another to believe. 1. *Estoppel in pais* (or by conduct). Thus, a tenant who has accepted a lease (q.v.) cannot dispute the lessor's title. 2. *Estoppel by deed.* A party to a deed "is estopped in a court of law from saying that the facts stated in the deed are not truly stated": *Baker v Dewey* (1823) 1 B & C 704. 3. *Estoppel by record.* A person cannot deny the facts upon which the judgment against him has been given. 4. *Equitable estoppel.* (i) Under the doctrine of *Promissory estoppel,* where X, by words or conduct, makes to Y an unambiguous representation by promise or assurance concerning his (X's) future actions, intended to affect the legal relationship between X and Y, and Y alters his position in reliance on it, X will not be allowed to act inconsistently with that representation. (ii) *Proprietary estoppel.* X may be estopped from denying Y's rights in X's property, e.g., where Y has incurred expenditure in the property. See *J T Developments v Quinn* [1991] 62 P & CR 33. It has been described as involving "an assurance, a reliance and a resulting detriment". For "estoppel by convention", see *Troop v Gibson* (1986) 277 EG 1134. See *E.R. Ives Investments Ltd v High* [1967] 2 QB 379; *Voyce v Voyce* (1991) 62 P & CR 290. See S.G.A. 1979, s. 21(1). *See* RES JUDICATA.

estoppel, agency by. *See* AGENCY BY ESTOPPEL.

estoppel, cause of action. It "arises where the cause of action in the later proceedings is identical to that in the earlier proceedings, the latter having been between the same parties or their privies and having involved the same subject matter . . . The bar is absolute in relation to all points decided unless fraud or collusion is alleged": *per* Lord Keith in *Arnold v National Westminster Bank plc* [1991] 2 WLR 1177.

estoppel, issue. *See* ISSUE ESTOPPEL.

estoppel, licence by. *See* LICENCE BY ESTOPPEL.

estoppel, partnership by. *See* PARTNERSHIP BY ESTOPPEL.

estoppel, remedies in relation to. These include: grant of monetary compensation, right to occupy (see *Greasley v Cooke* [1980] 1 WLR 1306), right of occupation plus compensation, order directing transfer of freehold (see *Pascoe v Turner* [1979] 1 WLR 431).

estovers. (*Estovoir* = to be necessary.) Rights of a lessee (q.v.) to woodland timber for certain necessary or immediate repairs, e.g., hay bote (or "bot") (for repair of fences), house bote (for repair of dwelling). *See* BOTE.

estreat. 1. A true copy of a record, relating to recognisances and fines. 2. The enforcement of a fine or the forfeiture of a recognisance. For estreatment of a recognisance, see *R v Warwick Crown Court, ex p Smalley* [1987] 1 WLR 237.

et al. 1. *Et alibi* = and elsewhere. 2. *Et alii,* or *et aliae,* or *et alia* = and others.

ethnic. "In my opinion the word still retains a racial flavour but is used nowadays in an extended sense to include other characteristics which may be commonly thought of as being associated with common racial origin. For a group to constitute an ethnic group in the sense of the 1976 Act it must, in my opinion, regard itself and be regarded by others, as a distinct community by virtue of certain characteristics": *per* Lord Fraser in *Mandla v Lee* [1983] 2 AC 548. See Race Relations Act 1976, s. 3(1). *See* ETHNIC GROUP.

ethnic group. Considered by Lord Fraser in *Mandla v Lee* [1983] 2 AC 548 as a community, distinct because it has a long shared history, cultural tradition of its own, common geographical origin, common language, common literature, and is a minority or dominant group within a larger community. See *Crown Suppliers v Dawkins* [1991] ICR 583.

et seq. *Et sequentes.* And those which follow.

Eurobonds. Bearer bonds issued by a consortium of issuing houses and banks in London, France, Germany and Italy, paid without deduction of tax on interest. For "quoted Eurobonds", see I.C.T.A. 1988, s. 124.

European Communities. They comprise: the European Economic Community (EEC) (q.v.) (set up in 1957) (see Treaty of Rome 1957); the European Coal and Steel Community (set up in 1951); European Atomic Energy Authority (Euratom) (set up in 1957). See European Communities Act 1972, s. 1; European Communities (Amendment) Act 1986; European Communities (Finance) Act 1988. *See* COMMUNITY LAW.

European Communities, Court of Justice of the. *See* COURT OF JUSTICE OF THE EUROPEAN COMMUNITIES.

European Convention on Human Rights. *See* HUMAN RIGHTS, EUROPEAN CONVENTION ON.

European Council. A twice-yearly meeting of Heads of State (representing members of EEC) and their foreign ministers.

European Court. Name given to the Court of Justice of the European Communities (q.v.).

European Court of Human Rights. The judicial body of the Council of Europe which can hear cases involving alleged breaches of basic rights and freedoms. There is no obligation binding member states to accept its jurisdiction. It consists of a number of judges equal to the number of members of the Council. See *Convention on Human Rights* 1950; *Rules of Procedure* 1959 (revised 1982). The Convention is not part of English law: see, e.g., *A.-G.* v *BBC* [1981] AC 303; *Brind* v *Secretary of State for Home Department* [1991] 1 All ER 720.

European Economic Community. *See* EEC.

European Economic Community law. *See* COMMUNITY LAW.

European Parliament. Formerly the "Assembly" of EEC. Comprises some 520 "representatives of the peoples" of European Community states, directly elected, and based in Strasbourg. Exercises advisory and supervisory powers; debates and passes resolutions and may veto admission of new member states. See Single European Act 1986; European Parliament Elections Act 1978 (by which UK representatives are elected for a five-year term); SI 1992/233. *See* EEC.

euthanasia. Euphemism applied to the (illegal) practice of painlessly bringing about the death of those suffering from incurable diseases. See *A.-G.* v *Able* [1984] QB 795. *See* MERCY KILLING.

evasion of liability by deception. *See* DECEPTION, EVASION OF LIABILITY BY.

eviction. 1. The recovery of lands from possession of another by the course of law. 2. Dispossession of a tenant (q.v.) by his landlord. 3. Dispossession by virtue of paramount title.

eviction of occupier, unlawful. It is an offence to unlawfully deprive or attempt to unlawfully deprive residential occupier (q.v.) of any premises, of his occupation of the premises or any part thereof unless the accused can show that he reasonably believed that the residential occupier has ceased to reside therein: Protection from Eviction Act 1977, s. 1(2). See H.A. 1988, ch. IV (measure of damages); *Tagro* v *Corfane.* [1991] 1 WLR 378. *See* HARASSMENT OF OCCUPIER.

evidence. Testimony and production of documents and things relating to the facts into which the court enquires and the methods and rules relating to the establishing of those facts before the court. "That which demonstrates, makes clear, or ascertains the truth of the very fact or point in issue": Blackstone. Evidence may be classified as: direct and circumstantial; primary and secondary; conclusive and inconclusive.

evidence, admissibility of. *See* ADMISSIBILITY OF EVIDENCE.

evidence, advice on. *See* ADVICE ON EVIDENCE.

evidence as to character. *See* CHARACTER, EVIDENCE AS TO.

evidence, best. *See* BEST EVIDENCE RULE.

evidence, burden of adducing. *See* BURDEN OF ADDUCING EVIDENCE.

evidence by certificate. The use of certificated documents as evidence. See e.g., Video Recordings Act 1984, s. 19.

evidence, circumstantial. Evidence of facts not in issue from which can be inferred a fact in issue, e.g., evidence that skid-marks made by the defendant's motor cycle were on the wrong side of the road. "It is no derogation of evidence to say that it is circumstantial": *R v Taylor* (1928) 21 Cr App R 20. See, e.g., *Coles v Underwood* (1984) 148 JP 178; *Teper v R* [1952] AC 480.

evidence, conclusive. Evidence which must be taken by the court as sufficient proof of a fact, i.e., evidence which may not be disputed. Thus, a certificate of incorporation of a company (q.v.) is conclusive evidence of its registration.

evidenced in writing. Some contracts are unenforceable unless evidenced in writing, e.g., contracts of guarantee (Statute of Frauds 1677). The phrase means that the writing should contain, e.g., the signature of the party to be charged, names or other identification of the parties, description of the subject-matter and price. See L.P. (Misc. Provs.) A. 1989 (contracts for sale of land). *See* CONTRACT.

evidence, direct. Used in two senses. (1). Testimony, as contrasted with hearsay, i.e., an assertion by a witness offered as proof of the truth of a fact he asserts. (2). Statement by a witness that he perceived with one of his senses a fact in issue. Example: production of a document constituting a fact in issue, when its existence is disputed.

evidence, documentary. *See* DOCUMENTARY EVIDENCE.

evidence, exclusion of. *See* DISCRETION, JUDICIAL, RELATING TO ADMISSIBILITY OF EVIDENCE; EXCLUSIONARY RULES.

evidence, expert. *See* EXPERT OPINION.

evidence, extrinsic. Evidence of statements of circumstances or facts not referred to in a document which may explain or vary its meaning. Not generally admissible except in the case of, e.g., parol evidence to contradict express terms of a document, parol evidence to supplement the omitted terms of a private formal document, to show the real nature of a transaction, to explain a latent ambiguity (q.v.).

evidence, first-hand and second-hand hearsay. Statement made by X which is proved by producing a document wherein X made it, or by oral evidence of Y who heard X making the statement, is first-hand evidence. Where a witness, Y, states on oath that X told him that Z had made a statement, that

hearsay statement is second-hand evidence. See C.J.A. 1988, s. 23.

evidence, hearsay. The oral or written statements of one who is not called as a witness which are narrated to the court by a witness or through a document, for the purpose of establishing the truth of what was asserted. Such evidence is generally inadmissible. Exceptions to the rule include: statutory exceptions; declarations of deceased persons (in very restricted circumstances); evidence given in former trials; depositions by witnesses; informal admissions and confessions. First-hand hearsay evidence (q.v.) was made admissible in civil proceedings by the Civil Evidence Act 1968, s. 2(1) (see also ss. 4, 5). See Civil Evidence Acts 1968, 1972, 1988; SI 1991/143/1115; O. 38; *Sparks v R* [1964] AC 964; *R v Harry* [1987] Crim LR 325; *R v Cole* [1990] 2 All ER 108; *R v Beckford* [1991] Crim LR 835; *R v Kearley* [1992] 2 All ER 345.

evidence, hearsay, and documentary statements. A documentary statement is admissible as an exception to the hearsay rule (q.v.) if direct/oral evidence would have been admissible, if the document was part of a record compiled under a duty from information derived from one who had personal knowledge of the matters in the information, and if the person supplying the information in the record is dead, or unfit to attend as a witness, or outside the UK, or cannot be expected to recollect the matter, or cannot be identified or found: P. & C.E.A. 1984, s. 68 (replacing Criminal Evidence Act 1965, s. 1).

evidence, hearsay, common law exceptions applicable to criminal cases. These include: admissions and confessions; statements concerning the maker's physical condition, emotion or state of mind; statements relating to an event in issue; statements accompanying and explaining some relevant act; statements in former proceedings; statements by deceased persons; statements in public documents.

evidence, hearsay, statutory exceptions applicable to criminal cases. These include: C.J.A. 1967, s. 9; Th.A. 1968, s. 27 (4); and P. & C.E.A. 1984, s. 68. See *R v Iqbal* [1990] 3 All ER 787.

evidence in civil proceedings, hearsay. Statements other than those made by a person while giving oral evidence in civil proceedings which are tendered as evidence of the facts stated therein. Under Civil Evidence Act 1968, ss. 1, 2, such evidence is admitted in civil proceedings by agreement of the parties, or under the rules of the court, or under the Act or any other statute.

evidence, indirect. Hearsay or circumstantial evidence.

evidence in rebuttal. May be given, subject to the control of the judge, to counter what has been said in cross-examination relating to a fact in issue.

evidence, insufficient. Evidence which is so weak that a reasonable man would be unable to decide the issue in favour of the party on whose behalf it is adduced. See, e.g., *Hawkins* v *Powells Tillery Steam Coal Co* [1911] 1 KB 988.

evidence, intrinsic. Evidence from within a document, needing no external matter to explain it.

evidence, irrelevant. See IRRELEVANT EVIDENCE.

evidence, judicial. The testimony, admissible hearsay, things, facts, documents, acceptable to a court as evidence of facts in issue. Divided into testimonial, circumstantial and real evidence (qq.v.).

evidence obtained illegally. Evidence obtained by some tort or criminal act or by an infringement of rules relating to police investigation. "It matters not how you get it, if you steal it even, it would be admissible in evidence": *R* v *Leathem* (1861) 8 Cox CC 498. See *R* v *Sang* [1980] AC 402; *ITC Film Distributors* v *Video Exchange* [1982] 2 All ER 241; P. & C.E.A. 1984, s. 78.

evidence of child in civil proceedings. Where the court is of the opinion that the child does not understand the nature of an oath, the child's evidence may be heard if the court is of the opinion that he understands that it is his duty to speak the truth and that he has sufficient understanding to justify his evidence being heard: Ch. A. 1989, s. 96. For privacy for children involved in certain proceedings, see s. 97. See SI 1990/143 (admissibility of children's hearsay evidence).

evidence of child in criminal proceedings. Under C.J.A. 1991, s. 52, amending C.J.A. 1988, s. 33, the evidence of a child under 14 in criminal proceedings shall be given unsworn. The deposition of a child's unsworn evidence may be taken for the purposes of criminal proceedings as if that evidence had been given on oath. For use of video recordings, see 1991 Act, s. 54, amending 1988 Act, s. 32. The trial judge's decision as to the competency of a child to give evidence should be decided in the presence of the jury: *R* v *Norbury* (1992) NLJ 788.

evidence of disposition. See DISPOSITION.

evidence of opinion. See OPINIONS IN EVIDENCE.

evidence of previous convictions. See PREVIOUS CONVICTIONS, EVIDENCE OF.

evidence of system. See SYSTEM, EVIDENCE OF.

evidence, oral. That given in court by word of mouth. It may be testimony (i.e., what the witness perceived through his senses) or hearsay (q.v.).

evidence, original. May mean "direct evidence", or proof of some fact by first-hand means. Example: the production of a letter containing a libel is evidence of the words constituting that libel.

evidence, parol. 1. Testimony given by word of mouth of witness. 2. Extrinsic evidence (q.v.).

evidence, power to receive fresh. Power of the Court of Appeal (q.v.) to receive fresh evidence which is admissible and likely to be credible. See, e.g., *R* v *Melville* [1976] 1 All ER 395.

evidence, presumptive. Prima facie evidence (q.v.).

evidence, prima facie. "In its usual sense is used to mean prima facie proof of an issue, the burden of proving which is upon the party giving that evidence. In the absence of further evidence from the other side, the prima facie proof becomes conclusive proof and the party giving it discharges his onus": *R* v *Jacobson and Levy* [1931] App D 466. Thus, a share certificate is prima facie evidence of a member's title.

evidence, primary. Evidence which by its nature does not suggest that better evidence might be available. Example: the original of a document.

evidence, propensity. Evidence relying on alleged striking similarities or the "underlying unity" of facts: see *R* v *P* (1991) The Independent, 28 June. Often used synonymously with "similar fact evidence" (q.v.).

evidence, psychiatric. Evidence concerning a defendant's state of mind, usually given by a specialist medical practitioner. "It is for the jury and not for medical men of whatever eminence to determine the issue [relating to a defence of insanity or diminished responsibility]": *R* v *Rivett* (1950) 34 Cr App R 87. See Criminal Procedure (Insanity and Unfitness to Plead) Act 1991, s. 6(1). See *R* v *Weightman* (1991) 92 Cr App R 291. *See* SPECIAL VERDICT; UNFITNESS TO PLEAD.

evidence, real. Known also as "demonstrative" and "objective" evidence, which is afforded by production and inspection of material objects. Examples: an exhibit (q.v.) of goods alleged to have been stolen by the accused; a person's physical appearance (e.g., his wounds); a view (q.v.); a witness's demeanour. See *Castle* v *Cross* [1985] 1 All ER 87. *See* INSPECTION BY JUDGE.

evidence, relevant. *See* RELEVANT EVIDENCE.

evidence rule, parol. *See* PAROL EVIDENCE RULE.

evidence, secondary. That evidence which suggests the existence of better evidence and which might be rejected if that better evidence is available. Example: the copy of a document. Where an original document is destroyed, secondary evidence of its contents may be given. See Civil Evidence Act 1968; O. 38, r. 3. *See* DOCUMENT, SECONDARY EVIDENCE OF.

evidence, second-hand. Hearsay evidence (q.v.).

evidence, similar fact. Evidence which is adduced in an attempt to suggest, through its striking similarity, that there is an underlying link between the matters with which it purports to deal – which relate essentially to occasions other than those specifically in question – and the matter presently before the court. It may be used to establish identity by reference to a distinguishing characteristic, to rebut a defence of accident or coincidence, to suggest some propensity (i.e., inclination): see *Lanford* v *GMC* [1990] AC 13. Its admissibility depends on its logical, probative value. See *R* v *Kilbourne* [1973] AC 729; *Boardman* v *DPP* [1975] AC 421; *R* v *Mather* [1991] Crim LR 285. *See* SIMILARITY OF FACTS.

evidence, testimonial. Assertions offered as proof of the truth of that which is being asserted. It includes a testimony (i.e., an account by a witness of what he perceived with his senses) and hearsay (q.v.).

evidence, unsworn. Evidence not given on oath or by affirmation. In the case of children, their evidence in criminal proceedings shall be given unsworn: C.J.A. 1988, s. 33, inserted by C.J.A. 1991, s. 52(1). An accused person might formerly have made an unsworn statement (q.v.) (see Criminal Evidence Act 1898, s. 1(h)) but, generally, he could not be cross-examined on it. The "right" to make such a statement was abolished by C.J.A. 1982, s. 72.

evidential facts. *See* FACTS, RELEVANT.

ex abundanti cautela. From an excess of caution. See, e.g., *R* v *Thompson* [1982] QB 647.

examination. Interrogation on oath.

examination-in-chief. Known also as "direct examination". The object of examination-in-chief is to put the witness's story before the court so as to obtain a testimony in support of the version of the facts for which the party calling the witness is contending. It is conducted by the witness's own counsel. In general, it may not be based on leading questions (q.v.), save, e.g., where the matter is merely introductory or where it has already been put in evidence by the other side, or where the judge considers the witness hostile (q.v.) and gives leave. *See* EVIDENCE.

examination of goods, buyer's right. Where goods are delivered to the buyer, and he has not previously examined them, he is not deemed to have accepted them until he has had a reasonable opportunity of examining them for the purpose of ascertaining whether they are in conformity with the contract: S.G.A. 1979, s. 34(1).

examiners. Barristers appointed by the Lord Chancellor to take evidence out of court: see O. 39. See, e.g., *R* v *Rathbone, ex p Dikko* [1985] QB 630.

examining justices. Magistrates who conduct a preliminary investigation of a charge made against a prisoner so as to determine whether there is sufficient evidence to justify a committal of the accused. The functions of examining justices may be discharged by a single justice: M.C.A. 1980, s. 4(1).

examples in statutes, use of. A recent innovation in the drafting of statutes, whereby the schedule of an Act contains examples illustrating applications of the terminology and provisions of the Act. See, e.g., C.C.A. 1974, s. 188(1), Sch. 2.

excepted perils. Term used in contracts of carriage to which the Hague Rules do not apply, whereby a carrier's liability is excluded for loss or damage to goods caused by: Act of God (q.v.); act of the Queen's enemies; restraint of princes and rulers; perils of the seas; fire; barratry; piracy; robbery and theft; collisions, strandings and other accidents of navigation.

exception. 1. An objection taken to an answer, or some other challenge to it. 2. A clause in a deed preventing some thing passing which might otherwise pass under the deed. See *Suisse Atlantique Société* v *NV Rotterdamsche Kolen Centrale* [1967] 1 AC 361.

exchange. 1. Reciprocal transfer of ownership or possession. For the exclusion of exchange from the S.G.A. 1979, see s. 61; *Harrison* v *Luke* (1845) 14 M&W 139. 2. A place for the business transactions of brokers, e.g., London Stock Exchange. 3. A transfer of settlement land for other land. An exchange of settled land or any part of it or easements may be made for other land or easements: S.L.A. 1925, s. 38(iii).

exchange contracts. Contracts, within art. VIII of s. 2(b), Bretton Woods Agreement Order in Council 1946, by which the currency of one country is exchanged for that of another. See *United City Merchants Ltd* v *Royal Bank of Canada* [1982] QB 208; *Mansouri* v *Singh* [1986] 2 All ER 619.

exchange, investment. *See* INVESTMENT EXCHANGE.

Exchequer. The government department which receives and has the care of the national revenues. *See* CHANCELLOR.

Exchequer, Court of. *See* COURT OF EXCHEQUER.

excise. Tax levied on goods produced in the UK.

excise dealer, registered. An approved revenue trader who may import and pay excise duties on goods from other member states of EEC (q.v.) without having to make customs entries for goods clearance: see Customs and Excise Management Act 1979, s. 1(1), inserted by Finance Act 1991, s. 11.

exclusionary rules of evidence. "I would hold that there has now developed a general rule of practice whereby in a trial by jury, the judge has a discretion to exclude evidence which, though technically admissible, would probably have a prejudicial influence on the minds of the jury, which would be out of proportion to its true evidential value": *per* Lord Diplock in *R* v *Sang* [1980] AC 402. *See* EVIDENCE.

exclusion clause. "One which excludes or modifies an obligation, whether primary, general secondary or anticipatory secondary, that would otherwise arise under the contract by implication of law": *per* Lord Diplock in *Photo Productions Ltd* v *Securicor Transport Ltd* [1980] AC 827. See S.G.A. 1979, s. 55; and *George Mitchell* v *Finney Lock Seeds* [1983] 2 AC 803.

exclusion clauses, restriction of. Under the Unfair Contract Terms Act 1977: liability for death resulting from negligence cannot be excluded or restricted by contractual terms (s. 2(1)); liability for loss or damage resulting from negligence cannot be excluded or restricted by a term which fails to satisfy a reasonableness test (s. 2(2)); a consumer cannot, by contract, be made to indemnify another person in respect of liability that may be incurred by that other for breach of contract or negligence except where the contract satisfies the reasonableness test (s. 4); liability for loss or damage from negligent manufacture of consumer goods (q.v.) cannot be restricted or excluded in a guarantee (s. 5).

exclusion order. 1. An order under Prevention of Terrorism (Temporary Provisions) Act 1989, Part II, whereby the Secretary of State excludes from the UK persons whom he is satisfied are or have been concerned in the commission, preparation or instigation of acts of terrorism (q.v.) or who attempt to enter the country for such a purpose. 2. Order under D.P.A. 1978, s. 16, instructing the respondent to leave the matrimonial home and/or prohibiting him from entering it. See *R* v *Sharples* [1990] Crim LR 198. For exclusion of adult child from parental home, see *Egan* v *Egan* [1975] Ch 218. 3. Order prohibiting a convicted person from entering licensed premises: see the Licensed Premises (Exclusion of Certain Persons) Act 1980; *R* v *Grady* (1990) 12 Cr App R (S) 152. 4. For power to exclude pupils from a school, see Education (No. 2) Act 1986, ss. 22–28. *See* OUSTER ORDER.

exclusive possession. *See* POSSESSION, EXCLUSIVE.

ex contractu. Arising out of a contract.

excusable homicide. 1. Homicide in reasonable self-defence of person or property. See C.L.A. 1967, s. 3; *Palmer* v *R* [1971] AC 814. 2. Homicide by misadventure. See *R* v *Bruce* (1847) 2 Cox CC 262. *See* HOMICIDE; MURDER.

ex debito justitiae. Arising as a matter of right. A remedy available to the applicant as of right (in contrast to a discretionary remedy).

ex div. Ex dividend. Stock Exchange quotation relating to stocks and shares, stating that the price does not include dividends or interest accrued to date. *See* CUM DIV.

ex dolo malo non oritur actio. A right of action cannot arise out of fraud.

exeat. Let him go. Permission to leave. *See* NE EXEAT REGNO.

executed. That which is done or completed, as in, e.g., *executed consideration* (q.v.). Thus, an *executed trust* is one in which the settlor has declared and perfected in the trust instrument the limitations of the estate of the trustees and the beneficiaries so that no further instrument is needed to define those interests. See *Egerton* v *Brownlow* (1853) 4 HL Cas 1. An *executed agreement*, under C.C.A. 1974, s. 189(1), is a document signed by or on behalf of the parties, embodying the terms of a regulated agreement (q.v.) or such of them as have been reduced to writing.

execution. 1. The signing of an instrument in a manner which gives it a legally valid form. 2. The carrying out of a court's sentence of death. 3. Enforcing the rights of a judgment creditor (q.v.). See Ins. A. 1986, s. 183. 4.

Carrying out of the terms of a trust (q.v.).

execution of valuable security. Signifies, within Th.A. 1968, s. 20(2), doing something to the face of a document, e.g., signing it, or the due performance of all formalities necessary to give it validity. It does not mean "give effect to": *R* v *Kassim* [1991] 3 WLR 254. See *R* v *King* [1991] 3 WLR 246.

execution of wills. No will is valid unless in writing and signed in order to give effect to it by the testator or by some other person in his presence and by his direction; and the signature must be made or acknowledged by the testator in the presence of two or more witnesses present at the same time, and each witness must attest and subscribe the will in the presence of the testator but not necessarily in the presence of any other witness: W.A. 1837, s. 9 (as substituted by A.J.A. 1982, s. 17). *See* WILL.

execution, stay of. *See* STAY OF EXECUTION.

execution, writ of. Procedure relating to the enforcing of judgments by, e.g., a writ of sequestration (q.v.). The writ will issue: after a *praecipe* (q.v.) is filed; after judgment upon which the writ is to issue is produced; after the officer authorised to seal the writ is satisfied that the period specified for payment has expired. See O. 46.

executive. The branch of government which carries out the general policy determined by the Cabinet (q.v.). It includes the Government, Cabinet, government departments, local authorities and public corporations.

executor. One appointed by a will (q.v.) to administer the testator's property and to carry out provisions of that will. In general the office can be exercised only by the person so appointed: *Re Skinner* [1958] 3 All ER 273. If a minor (q.v.) is appointed, however, probate will not be issued until he reaches the age of 18. An executor (*f.* "executrix") who is appointed by implication is known as an executor "according to the tenor [of the will]".

executor *de son tort.* Executor "in his own wrong". One who is not an executor, either by express or implied appointment, and who has not obtained a grant of administration, and intermeddles with the goods of the deceased or carries out an act which is characteristic of the office of executor. He may be sued by the rightful executor, administrator, creditor or beneficiary (q.q.v.). See A.E.A. 1925, ss. 28, 55(1) (xi); *Re Clore* [1982] Ch 456.

executor, duties of. Getting in the assets of the deceased; paying funeral expenses; paying legacies; accounting for residual estate: *Re Adamson* (1875) LR 3 P & D 253.

executor's year. The period of one year from the death of the deceased in which the executor (q.v.) must complete the administration of the assets. Generally, until the end of that period, he is not bound to distribute the estate of deceased: A.E.A. 1925, s. 44. See *Brooke v Lewis* (1822) 6 Madd 358.

executory. That which remains to be done, as in executory consideration (q.v.). Thus, an executory trust is an agreement or covenant for the execution of a trust instrument, the terms of which are not defined precisely, at some future time, or directions on the basis of which the trustee is expected to prepare a final settlement at a future date. See *Miles v Harford* (1879) 12 Ch D 691.

executory interest. A future interest in land or personal property, except reversions (q.v.) or remainders (q.v.).

exemplary damages. *See* DAMAGES.

exemption clauses. Clauses in an agreement seeking to exempt the parties from general liability or excluding or modifying their liability in certain contingencies. *See* EXCLUSION CLAUSE.

ex gratia As of favour. As in *ex gratia* payment – a payment not compelled by any legal right. See *Edwards v Skyways Ltd* [1964] 1 WLR 349; *R v Secretary of State for Home Department, ex p Harrison* [1988] 3 All ER 96. See Charities Act 1992, s. 17.

exhibit. Something produced to be viewed by a judge or jury, or shown to a witness who is giving evidence, or an object referred to in an affidavit (q.v.). *See* EVIDENCE, REAL.

exhumation. Disinterring of a buried corpse. Unlawful unless authorised. See Coroners Act 1988, s. 23; *Re St Lukes* [1990] 2 All ER 749.

ex improviso. Unexpectedly, without preparation. See *R v Hutchinson* (1986)

82 Cr App R 51 (right of prosecution to call additional evidence in rebuttal of matters introduced by defence *ex improviso*).

ex lege, right. *See* RIGHT EX LEGE.

ex nudo pacto non oritur actio. A right of action cannot arise out of a bare pact, i.e., an agreement made without consideration (q.v.). *See* CONTRACT.

ex officio. By virtue of office. *Ex officio information* is a criminal information (q.v.) filed by the Attorney-General (q.v.) on behalf of the Crown.

exonerate. 1. To clear of an accusation. 2. To relieve from a liability.

ex parte. On behalf of. 1. An *ex parte* injunction (q.v.) may be granted after hearing only one party and in a case of great urgency. See *Bates v Lord Hailsham of Marylebone* [1972] 1 WLR 1373; *In re First Express Ltd* (1991) The Times, 10 Oct. 2. "*Ex p Jones*" in the title of a case indicates the name of the party on whose application the hearing has taken place. For *ex parte* originating summons, see, e.g., *Practice Direction* [1987] 1 WLR 251.

ex parte inspection order. *See* INSPECTION ORDER, EX PARTE.

expatriation. 1. The voluntary act of renouncing allegiance to one's own country so as to take up residence permanently in a foreign country. 2. The act of forcing a person to leave his native country, e.g., by exile.

expectancy, interest in. *See* INTEREST IN EXPECTANCY.

expectant heir. One who has a vested remainder or contingent remainder in property, or one who has a hope of succeeding to property. Catching bargains (q.v.) with expectant heirs may be set aside by the court: *Benyon v Cook* (1875) LR 10 Ch 391. *See* REMAINDER.

expectation, legitimate or reasonable. Concept developed by the courts in relation to natural justice and first used in *Schmidt v Secretary of State for Home Affairs* [1969] 2 Ch 149. The expectation may arise "either from an express promise given on behalf of a public authority or from the existence of a regular practice which the claimant can reasonably expect to continue": *per* Lord Fraser in *CCSU v Minister for the Civil Service* [1985] AC 374. It was considered in *R v ITC ex p TV South West* (1992) The Times, 7 Feb., as an aspect of procedural propriety. For its use in EEC legislation, see Cases 2/75 and 338/85.

expectation of life, loss of. In an action for damages for personal injuries, no damages are recoverable in respect of loss of expectation of life caused to the injured person by the injuries, but account is taken of any suffering caused by awareness of reduction in expectation of life: A.J.A. 1982, s. 1.

expenses, living. *See* LIVING EXPENSES.

expert opinion. Expert opinion is admissible evidence when the subject is one "upon which competency to form an opinion can only be acquired by a course of special study or experience": *R* v *Kusmack* (1955) 20 CR 365. The expert's duty is to "furnish the judge or jury with the necessary scientific criteria for testing the accuracy of their conclusions so as to enable the judge or jury to form their own independent judgment by the application of these criteria to the facts proved in evidence": *Davie* v *Edinburgh Magistrates*, 1953 SC 34. See Civil Evidence Act 1972, s. 3 (admissibility of expert's opinion on matter in issue in civil proceedings); P. & C.E.A. 1984, s. 81; O. 38; C.J.A. 1988, s. 30. "Expert evidence presented to the court should be seen to be the independent product of the expert, uninfluenced as to form or content by the exigencies of the litigation": *per* Lord Wilberforce in *Whitehouse* v *Jordan* [1981] 1 WLR 246. See *Providential Assurance Co.* v *Fountain Page Ltd* [1991] 1 WLR 756. *See* EVIDENCE.

Expiring Laws Continuance Acts. Acts passed to continue other Acts which would have expired otherwise.

explosion. An extremely rapid expansion of gas or vapour under pressure caused by chemical or nuclear means; it does not include centrifugal disintegration: *per* Staughton J in *Commonwealth Smelting* v *Guardian Royal Exchange Assurance* [1984] 2 Lloyd's Rep 608.

explosive. "Any article manufactured for the purpose of producing a practical effect by explosion, or intended by the person having it with him for that purpose": Th.A. 1968, s. 10(1) (*c*) O.P.A. 1861, ss. 28–30; Explosive Substances Act 1883; Aviation and Maritime Security Act 1990, s. 46; *R* v *Byrne* (1975) 63 Cr App R 33; *R* v *Bouch* [1983] QB 246 (petrol bomb as "explosive substance"); *R* v *Berry* [1985] AC 246.

exporter. Includes, in relation to goods being sent abroad, the shipper of the goods; see e.g., Customs and Excise Management Act 1979, s. 1(1), as amended.

expose. 1. To display, e.g., food for sale. An offence if unfit for human consumption. See Food Safety Act 1990, s. 8. 2. It is an offence (known as "indecent exposure") for a person wilfully and obscenely to expose his penis with intent to insult a female: Vagrancy Act 1824, s. 4. See *Evans* v *Ewels* [1971] 1 WLR 671; *Cheeseman* v *DPP* [1991] (see Town Police Clauses Act 1847, s. 28).

ex post facto. By a subsequent act. An *Ex post facto* statute has a retrospective effect. See *Phillips* v *Eyre* [1870] QB 1. *See* RETROSPECTIVE LEGISLATION.

express. Distinctly stated, rather than implied.

expressio unius personae vel rei est exclusio alterius. The express mention of one person or thing is the exclusion of another. The rule does not operate where an expression was incomplete due to accident. See, e.g., *Dean* v *Wiesengrund* [1955] 2 QB 120; *D.* v *NSPCC* [1977] 1 All ER 589.

express term. An express statement of undertakings and promises contained in a contract or other written instrument. A deviation from such a term may constitute a breach of contract (q.v.): see e.g., *The Hansa Nord* [1976] QB 44. See *Johnstone* v *Bloomsbury HA* [1991] 2 WLR 1362.

express trust. A trust created as the result of a settlor's expressed intention, e.g., as where A conveys property to B on trust for C. In general, an express declaration will suffice for the creation of an express trust, e.g., by will, deed, writing not under seal, spoken word. *See* TRUST.

expressum facit cessare tacitum. That which is expressed puts an end to that which is silent; i.e., if something can be expressed, there is no room for implication. Where there is an express mention of certain things, anything of the same class not mentioned is excluded. See *R* v *Caledonian Rwy* (1850) 16 QB 19.

expropriation. The act, usually of a state, in enforcing the compulsory surrender of private property for the state's purposes, without compensation. For recognition of the validity of a foreign government's expropriation, see, e.g., *A/S Tallinna Laevauhisus* v *Tallinna Shipping Co* (1946) 80 Ll L Rep 99. *See* EMINENT DOMAIN.

ex proprio motu. Of his own motion. Term applied to an action taken by the court on its own initiative.

ex rel. (*Ex relatione.* From a narrative.) Applied to a person's report of proceedings usually not as the result of his having been present, but compiled from information given by another.

ex rights. Term relating to the issue of new shares to shareholders (q.v.) in proportion to their existing holdings, in which the price has been adjusted by deducting the value of the right to subscribe. *See* RIGHTS ISSUE.

extinguishment. An obligation or right is extinguished when it ceases its existence, e.g., as when a debt is paid.

extortion. The obtaining of some benefit by intimidation or physical force applied to another. The unwarranted demanding of money by threats may be blackmail (q.v.).

extortionate. Oppressive. Under C.C.A. 1974, ss. 137–140, as amended, a credit bargain is considered extortionate (and may be reopened by the court) if the debtor, or relatives, are required to make grossly extortionate payments or payments which contravene in gross fashion the ordinary principles of fair dealing. If a debtor alleges that a credit bargain is extortionate, the onus of proving the contrary is on the creditor: s. 171(7). See *Ketley* v *Scott* [1981] ICR 241; *Davis* v *Direct Loans* [1986] 1 WLR 823.

extradition. The surrendering by one state, at the request of another, of a person accused of a crime or alleged to be unlawfully at large after conviction, under the laws of the requesting state. It is usually regulated by reciprocal extradition treaties between states. Extradition may be barred unless for an offence punishable in the surrendering state by a period of one year's imprisonment or more. See the Extradition Act 1989. "Extradition crimes" are defined in s. 2. For procedure, see Part III. See *Re Farinha* [1992] Crim LR 438; *R* v *Governor of Brixton Prison, ex p Osman (No. 4)* [1992] 1 All ER 579.

extraordinary general meeting. Meeting of a company (q.v.) called, e.g., before the next ordinary meeting. The holders of not less than one-tenth of paid-up capital carrying voting rights can compel the directors to call such a meeting. See Cos.A. 1985, s. 368; Cos A. 1989, s. 145, Sch. 19, para 9.

extraordinary resolution. Resolution (q.v.) usually passed by a three-quarters majority at a general meeting of which notice declaring an intention to propose the resolution as an extraordinary resolution has been given. It may be used, e.g., to wind up a company voluntarily. See Ins.A. 1986, s. 84.

extra-territoriality. Doctrine of international law under which some persons (e.g., ambassadors) are considered to be outside the territory of the state in which they are living so as to carry out their duties. In effect, therefore, they are not within the jurisdiction of that state. *See* DIPLOMATIC PRIVILEGE.

extrinsic. Lying outside; derived from some external source.

extrinsic evidence. *See* EVIDENCE, EXTRINSIC.

ex turpi causa non oritur actio. A right of action will not arise from a base cause. Thus, an illegal contract is generally unenforceable. See, e.g., *Saunders* v *Edwards* [1987] 1 WLR 1116; *Tinsley* v *Milligan* [1991] NPC 100.

eye witness. One who has seen that to which he testifies.

eyre. *Eyre* = a hearing. A court of itinerant justices, established in 1176. A King's Justice acting under the commission *ad omnia placita* presided over each eyre. The last eyre was held in the reign of Richard II.

F

fact. A circumstance or incident relating to a case which is being heard. In general, questions of fact are decided by the jury; questions of law are for the judge.

factor. A mercantile agent who in the course of his business has authority to sell or buy goods, to consign goods for the purpose of sale, or to raise money on the security of goods: see S.G.A. 1979, s. 26. See Factors Act 1889.

factory. Premises in which persons are employed in manual labour in any process for or incidental to, purposes, such as, the making of any article or any part of an article, the altering, repairing, ornamenting, cleaning, demolition, adapting for sale, of any article. See Factories Act 1961, s. 175 as amended; and H.S.W.A. 1974.

facts, evidential. *See* FACTS, RELEVANT.

facts, inferential. Facts established indirectly by conclusions drawn from the evidence.

facts in issue, main. Those facts which must be proved by the party making an allegation (i.e., by the plaintiff or prosecutor) in order to succeed, and the facts that the defendant must prove in order to establish his defence. "Whenever there is a plea of not guilty, everything is in issue": *R* v *Sims* [1946] 1 All ER 697. *See* EVIDENCE.

facts in issue, subordinate or collateral. Facts affecting the admissibility of evidence and the credibility of witnesses. See *R* v *Mendy* (1976) 64 Cr App R4.

facts, investitive. Facts which invest persons with particular rights, e.g., a breach of contract investing the plaintiff with the right to claim damages. "Divestitive facts" modify or extinguish rights, as in the case of payment of a debt.

facts, means of proof of. Generally: testimony of witnesses; real evidence; documentary evidence.

facts, notorious. *See* NOTORIOUS FACTS.

facts, primary. "Primary facts are facts which are observed by witnesses and proved by oral testimony, or facts proved by the production of a thing itself, such as original documents. Their determination is essentially a question of fact for the tribunal of fact, and the only question of law that can arise on them is whether there was any evidence to support the finding. The conclusions from the primary facts are, however, inferences deduced by a process of reasoning from them": *British Launderers' Research Association* v *Hendon Rating Authority* [1949] 1 KB 462.

facts, probative. Facts which have a natural and logical tendency to prove or disprove a fact in issue.

facts, relevant. Facts from which facts in issue may be inferred. Known also as "evidential facts".

facts which can be established by other means than proof. The following do not generally require affirmative proof: formal admissions (see e.g., C.J.A. 1967, s. 10); facts judicially noted; presumptions (q.v.).

factum probandum. (Plural: *facta probanda.*) Principal fact; fact in issue. A fact which has to be proved. *See* EVIDENCE.

factum probans. (Plural: *facta probantia.*) Evidentiary fact; fact related to the issue. Fact given in evidence intended to prove those other facts which are in issue. May be proved by testimony, documents, other things, admissible hearsay, other evidentiary facts.

faculty. A term used in ecclesiastical law to denote a special licence granted to a person to do that which was not allowed by common law, e.g., to marry without publication of banns (q.v.). See also Faculty Jurisdiction Measure 1964; Faculty Jurisdiction Rules 1967, which regulate the grant of faculties for, e.g., making changes in the fabric of a church, selling certain church equipment.

fair. 1. "A concourse of buyers and sellers for the purchase and sale of commodities pursuant to a franchise with an optional addition of provision for amusement": *Wyld* v *Silver* [1963] 1 QB 169. See Fairs Act 1871. 2. Reasonable, impartial.

fair comment. Defence to an action for defamation (q.v.), in which the defendant shows that words complained of were not actuated by malice and were comment, were fair (in the sense of "honest") and amounted to comment on a matter of public interest. The defence will not extend to a misstatement of fact. See Defamation Act 1952, s. 6; *London Artists Ltd* v *Littler* [1969] 2 QB 375; *Control Risks Ltd* v *New English Library Ltd* [1990] 1 WLR 183; *Telnikoff* v *Matusevitch* [1991] 3 WLR 952.

fair-dealing rule. A principle related to the nature of trusteeship, whereby a trustee (q.v.) may not buy from his *cestui que trust* (q.v.), unless this was intended by the latter, and there is no concealment or fraud. See, e.g., *Coles* v *Trecothick* (1804) 9 Ves 233. The principle applies generally to any person in a fiduciary position (e.g., solicitor and client): see *Tate* v *Williamson* (1866) 2 Ch App 55.

fair dismissal. Dismissal from employment on the following grounds; capability or qualifications for the job; conduct; redundancy; where continued employment of an employee results in a contravention of law; other substantial reasons. *See* DISMISSAL FROM EMPLOYMENT.

fair rent. That fixed under the Rent Acts of 1974 and 1977, when regard is had "to all the circumstances (other than personal circumstances) and in particular to the age, character, locality and state of repair of the dwelling-house, and if any furniture is provided for use under the tenancy, to [its] quantity, quality and condition". For certificates of fair rent issued to landlords, see Rent Act 1977, s. 69 (as modified by H. & P.A 1986, s. 7). See *BTE Ltd* v *Merseyside RAC* [1992] 16 EG 111.

fair trading, proceedings relating to. Under the Fair Trading Act 1973, where a firm fails to give an assurance to the Director General of Fair Trading (q.v.) that an unfair consumer practice or one detrimental to the interests of consumers will cease, the Director General can take proceedings against that firm in the Restrictive Practices Court (q.v.). See F.S.A. 1986, s. 124, as amended by Cos.A. 1989, Sch. 23. *See* UNFAIR CONSUMER PRACTICES.

fair wear and tear. Where a repairing covenant exempts the covenantor from liability for fair (or "reasonable") wear and tear, "the tenant is bound to do such repairs as may be required to prevent the consequences flowing originally from the wear and tear from producing others which wear and tear would not directly produce": *Haskell* v *Marlow* [1928] 2 KB 45. *See* WEAR AND TEAR.

false demonstratio non nocet cum de corpore constat. A false description does not vitiate a document when the thing is described with certainty. Thus, in *Pratt* v *Mathew* (1856) 22 Beav 328, the testator (q.v.) made a gift as follows: "to my wife, Caroline". He had a wife, Mary, but lived with Caroline with whom he had contracted a void marriage. It was held that the word "wife" did not affect the validity of the gift to Caroline. See also *Maxted* v *Plymouth Corporation* [1957] CLY 243.

false. Untrue, or designedly incorrect and intended to deceive. A statement, although literally true, may be false if it is used so as to convey a false impression: see, e.g., *R* v *Kylsant* [1932] 1 KB 442.

false accounting. *See* ACCOUNTING, FALSE.

false imprisonment. The direct, intentional (or negligent) infliction of some bodily restraint involving complete deprivation of liberty for any time no matter how short, which is neither expressly nor impliedly authorised by law. A common law offence and also a tort. See *John Lewis & Co* v *Tims* [1952] AC 676; *Weldon* v *Home Office* [1990] 3 All ER 672 (prisoner in lawful custody entitled to protection of law in respect of residual liberty); *Hague* v *Deputy Governor of Parkhurst Prison* [1991] 3 All ER 733. *See* RESTRAINT, BODILY.

false instrument. *See* INSTRUMENT, FALSE.

false judgment, writ of. A writ which was available to correct errors in an inferior court (q.v.).

false personation. It is an offence to personate another in certain circumstances, e.g., for the purpose of voting at an election or where the other person is a juryman. See Representation of the People Act 1983, s. 60; *R* v *Phillips* (1984) 6 Cr App R (S) 293. *See* PERSONATION.

false plea. Known also as a "sham plea"; obviously absurd or merely frivolous, entered only to delay the course of an action. See O. 18, r. 19.

false pretence. Phrase relating originally to an offence under Larceny Act 1916, s. 32. Now relates to the offence of obtaining property by deception under Th.A. 1968. *See* DECEPTION, OBTAINING PROPERTY BY.

false statement. *See* PERJURY.

false trade description. A trade description which is false or misleading to a material degree applied by a person to goods in the course of a trade or business: Trade Descriptions Act 1968. Any person who in the course of a trade or business applies a false trade description to goods or supplies or offers to supply any goods to which a false trade description is applied, is guilty of an offence: s. 1(1). See *Holloway* v *Cross* [1981] 1 All ER 1012; *Olgeirsson* v *Kitching* [1986] 1 WLR 304 (conviction of private individual). *See* TRADE DESCRIPTION.

falsification of accounts. *See* ACCOUNTING, FALSE.

falsify. 1. To alter a document, e.g., by obliteration, with intent to deceive. 2. To show that some matter, e.g., an item in an account, is false.

family. Social unit, usually consisting of a male and female adult living in one household and caring for their children. For an extended definition in relation to social security, see S.S. Contributions and Benefits Act 1992, s. 137 (1). See also Ch. A. 1989, s. 17 (10); *Re Collins* [1990] 2 All ER 47; T.C.G.A. 1992, Sch. 6, para 1. *See* HOUSEHOLD.

family assistance order. Order requiring a probation officer or officer of a local authority to advise, assist and (where appropriate) befriend any person named therein: Ch.A. 1989, s. 16 (1).

family company. Means, for the purpose of claiming relief from capital gains tax (q.v.), a company in which not less than 25 per cent of the voting rights are held by the person claiming relief or 10 per cent by himself and 75 per cent by his family, including himself. ("Family" means here the person's spouse, and the brother, sister, ancestor or lineal descendant of that person or spouse.)

family credit. Benefit under S.S. Contributions and Benefits Act 1992, s. 128, paid for 26 weeks, or other prescribed period, to a person who is (or whose partner is) engaged in full-time work whose income does not exceed the amount applicable and provided that there is a child of the same household of which the claimant is a member.

Family Division. Formerly, the Probate, Divorce and Admiralty Division, renamed under A.J.A 1970, s. 1. A division of the High Court (q.v.) consisting of a President and other judges. Its original jurisdiction includes hearing defended matrimonial cases, adoption, family proceedings; its appellate jurisdiction includes hearing appeals from magistrates' courts and county courts and the Crown Court. Under the Matrimonial and Family Proceedings Act 1984, s. 39, the county court may transfer family proceedings to the High Court (and, under s. 38, vice versa); see *President's Direction* (1992) NLJ 863. See now S.C.A. 1981, s. 5, Sch. 1; Matrimonial and Family Proceedings Act 1984, s. 32; C.L.S.A. 1990, s. 9.

Family Health Services Authorities. An Authority comprises a chairman, the Authority's chief officer and a prescribed number of members appointed by the Regional Health Authority: NHS and Community Care Act 1990, Sch. 1. For functions, see s. 12.

family name. *See* SURNAME.

family proceedings. Formerly "domestic proceedings". Proceedings in relation to children under the inherent jurisdiction of the High Court; see also Ch.A. 1989, Parts I, II, IV; Mat.C.A. 1973; Adoption Act 1976; D.P.A. 1983, etc. The Lord Chancellor may allocate such proceedings to specified judges or specified descriptions of judges: C.L.S.A. 1990, s. 9. See also Ch.A. 1989, s. 92.

Family Proceedings Department. Formerly the Divorce Department of the Family Division: *Practice Direction* [1991] 3 All ER 877. It will also contain a Children Branch, responsible for wardship, adoption and all proceedings under Ch.A. 1989.

family provision. The provision for a family which can be ordered by the court out of the net estate of the deceased. See Inheritance (Provision for Family and Dependants) Act 1975; *Re Coventry* [1980] Ch 461. *See* DEPENDANT.

farming. "Carrying on of activities appropriate to land recognisable as farm land. It must at least include the raising of beasts, the cultivation of land and the growing of crops": *Lowe* v *Ashmore Ltd* [1971] 1 All ER 1057. See I.C.T.A. 1988, s. 832 (1).

fatal accident, right of action relating to. "If death is caused by any wrongful act, neglect or default which is such as would (if death had not ensued) have entitled the person injured to maintain an action and recover damages in respect thereof, the person who would have been liable if death had not ensued shall be liable to an action for damages, notwithstanding the death of the person injured": Fatal Accidents Act 1976, s. 1(1) (as substituted by A.J.A. 1982, s. 3). An action must be for the benefit of, e.g., the wife or husband, certain dependants, parent or grandparent, child or grandchild, issue of a brother, sister, uncle, aunt, of the deceased: s. 1(3). See also Lim.A. 1980, s. 33, *Black* v *Yates* [1991] 3 WLR 90; *Wood* v *Bentall Simplex Ltd* (1992) The Times, 3 Mar. *See* BEREAVEMENT, DAMAGES FOR.

father. Male parent. The rule of law that a father is the natural guardian of his legitimate child was abolished by Ch. A. 1989, s. 2 (4). See also s. 4; Human Fertilisation and Embryology Act 1990, s. 28. *See* PARENTAL RESPONSIBILITY; PUTATIVE FATHER.

fealty. Fidelity. The tie, based on oath, which bound a feudal tenant or vassal to his lord.

fear, and damages. "Fear by itself, of whatever degree, was a normal human emotion for which no damages could be awarded . . . Fear of impending death felt by the victim of a fatal injury before that injury was inflicted could

not by itself give rise to a cause of action that survived for the benefit of the victim's estate": *per* Lord Bridge in *Hicks* v *S Yorks Police* [1992] 1 All ER 690.

fear or provocation of violence. A person is guilty of an offence if he uses towards another person threatening, abusive or insulting words or behaviour, or distributes or displays to another person any writing, sign or other visible representation which is threatening, abusive or insulting, with intent to cause that person to believe that immediate unlawful violence will be used against him or another by any person, or to provoke the immediate use of unlawful violence by that person or another, or whereby that person is likely to believe that such violence will be used or it is likely that such violence will be provoked: P.O.A. 1986, s. 4(1).

federalism. Doctrine underlying a political organisation based on a compact between two or more separate states to achieve unity under one central government while allowing each state to remain an entity.

fee. *Feodum* = a fief (q.v.). Originally a benefice granted to a man and his heirs in return for services. Used in land law to indicate that an estate (q.v.) is capable of being inherited.

feeble minded. Extremely sub-normal in intelligence. See now M.H.A. 1983, Part I.

fee, movable. "The fee itself is a continuing estate, but it is an estate in land which from time to time changes its position": *per* Megarry V.-C. in *Baxendale* v *Instow Parish Church* [1982] Ch 14 (strip of land revealed when sea receded).

fee farm rent. *See* CHIEF RENT.

fee simple absolute in possession. One of the two estates in land which, after 1925, are capable of subsisting or being conveyed or created at law. *Fee* denotes an estate of inheritance. *Simple* denotes a fee which can pass to the general heirs of the tenant. *Absolute* means that the estate is not subject to determination by an event other than that which is implied in the words of limitation. *In possession* denotes an estate that is immediate, i.e., neither in reversion nor in remainder. In effect, absolute ownership of land. See L.P.A. 1925, s. 1(1).

fee simple conditional. A conditional fee (q.v.).

fee simple held by public sector landlord. Under H.A. 1988, Part IV, approved persons may acquire from a public sector landlord (e.g., local housing authorities) the fee simple in any buildings each of which contains one or more dwelling-houses occupied by secure tenants whose tenancies are held directly from the landlord as owner of the fee simple: s. 93(4).

fee tail. *Feodum talliatum* = a fee cut down. An entailed interest. Refers to land descending neither to an ancestor nor to a collateral relative, but only to the lineal descendants of the first tenant in tail, e.g., "to X and the heirs of his body". The estate endures for as long as the original tenant or his lineal descendants survive. Under L.P.A 1925, an entailed interest exists only as an equitable interest behind a trust. Types of fee tail include: fee tail male general; fee tail female general; special tail (where the heir may be selected only from descendants of a specified spouse).

felo de se. Felon of himself. Term which was used to refer to one who committed suicide (*felonia de se*). See SUICIDE.

felony. An offence which had been made such by statute or which, at common law, carried on conviction the penalties of death and forfeiture of property (abolished in 1870). All other offences were misdemeanours (q.v.). Under C.L.A. 1967, s. 1, all distinctions between felony and misdemeanour were abolished; indictable offences are now regulated by those rules applying to misdemeanours.

felony, appeal of. Ancient procedure whereby the defendant could call for trial by battle (q.v.). Obsolescent by the sixteenth century and abolished in 1819.

feme covert. A married woman.

feme sole. An unmarried woman, e.g., spinster, widow, divorced woman.

fence. Any type of barrier, e.g., hedge, bank, wall, cattle grid: Animals Act 1971, s. 11. Right to have a fence maintained by an adjoining owner may be an easement (q.v.): *Crow* v *Ward* [1971] 1 QB 77. See L.P.A. 1925, s. 194; Highways Act 1980, s. 165(1).

feoffee to uses. One to whom a feoffment (q.v.) was made to the use of another person. *See* USE.

feoffment. A conveyance, in feudal times, with livery of seisin (q.v.). Abolished in 1845.

ferae naturae. See ANIMALS, CLASSIFICATION OF.

fermor. One who held "by lease for life or lives or for years, by deed or without deed": Coke. See Statute of Marlbridge 1267, s. 2; *Woodhouse* v *Walker* (1880) 5 QBD 404.

feudal system. A political and social system developed in England by the Normans in 1066, based on duties and rights resting essentially on land ownership, tenure and resultant, reciprocal relationships. It was characterised by a hierarchy dominated by a King and Lords from whom vassals held land in fief (q.v.) and to whom they owed services, some of which continued until the Tenures Abolition Act 1660.

fiat. Let it be done. A command, endorsement, sanction, e.g., a warrant of a judge.

fiat justitia, ruat coelum. Let justice be done, though the heavens fall.

fiction, legal. "Any assumption which conceals, or affects to conceal, the fact that a rule of law has undergone alteration, its letter remaining unchanged, its operation being modified": Maine. Used to extend the courts' jurisdiction and to increase the scope of available remedies. Example: action of ejectment (q.v.). "A legal fiction is always consistent with equity": Coke.

fidelity guarantee insurance. Insurance taken out by an employer as indemnification against misappropriation by an employee. All the material facts must be disclosed in such a case: *London General Omnibus Co* v *Holloway* [1912] 2 KB 77.

fiduciary. Involving trust or confidence, e.g., as describing the relationship between a trustee (q.v.) and beneficiary (q.v.). In general, where a fiduciary relationship between parties to a transaction exists, undue influence (q.v.) leading to some agreements, such as contract, may be presumed. See, e.g., *Lancashire Loans Ltd* v *Black* [1934] 1 KB 380 (mother and daughter); *Allcard* v *Skinner* (1887) 36 Ch D 145 (member of religious order and her Superior).

fief. Land which, under a feudal system, is held by an inferior as tenant of his superior. *See* FEUDAL SYSTEM.

fieri facias. Abbreviated to *fi. fa.* Cause to be made. Writ directed to sheriff (q.v.) of the county in which is situated property to be seized so as to enforce a judgment for payment of money. Sheriff is commanded to cause to be made out of debtor's property a sum of money sufficient to satisfy judgment debt, plus interest and costs of execution. Goods exempted from seizure include, e.g., tools, vehicles, clothing, for the domestic needs of the person and his family. See S.C.A 1981, s. 138, as amended by C.L.S.A. 1990, s. 15; O. 45, O. 47. *See* JUDGMENTS, ENFORCEMENT OF.

fieri feci. I have caused to be made. The report of a sheriff (q.v.) after enforcement of a writ of execution.

fi. fa. See FIERI FACIAS.

fifteens. Term used in Statute of Charitable Uses 1601. A tax levied on movable property.

file. Term used in C.C.A. 1974 to refer to all the information about an individual which is kept by a credit reference agency (q.v.).

filius nullius. A son of no man. A bastard (q.v.).

film. Any record, however made, of a sequence of visual images, which is a record capable of being used as a means of showing that sequence as a moving picture: Films Act 1985, Sch. 1. See also Copyright, Designs and Patents Act 1988, s. 5(1). For "film exhibition", see Cinemas Act 1985, s. 21(1).

finality clause. Clause in a statute providing, e.g., that "the decision of the Minister shall be final". "Parliament only gives the impression of finality to the decisions of a tribunal on condition that they are reached in accordance with the law": *per* Denning LJ in *R v Medical Appeal Tribunal, ex p Gilmore* [1957] 1 QB 574.

final judgment. Judgment awarded when an action is ended.

final process. Writ of execution relating to a judgment.

Finance Bill. Introduced into Parliament following a budget (q.v.) so as to give effect to its proposals.

financial provision, enforcement of orders for. Enforcement by the High Court by means of garnishee, charging and attachment of earnings orders; writs of *fieri facias* (q.v.) and sequestration; judgment summons (Debtors Act 1869); appointment of receiver. See *Levermore v Levermore* [1980] 1 WLR 1277.

financial provision for children of the family. The court may make orders under M.C.A. 1973, s. 23, concerning lump sums, secured or unsecured periodical payments, transfer or settlement of property and variation of nuptial settlements. See *Gojkovic v Gojkovic* [1992] 1 All ER 267.

financial provision order during marriage. Either party to a marriage may apply for an order on the ground that the other party has failed to provide reasonable maintenance for the applicant, or has failed to provide, or to make a proper contribution towards, reasonable maintenance for any child of the family, or has behaved in such a way that the applicant cannot reasonably be expected to live with the respondent, or has deserted the applicant: D.P.A. 1978, s. 1. See M.C.A. 1980, ss. 59–61 for the basic procedures in a magistrates' court. There are comparable provisions for the High Court and county courts: Mat.C.A. 1973, ss. 27–36 (as modified by Matrimonial and Family Proceedings Act 1984, Part II).

financial provision, reasonable. Term used in Inheritance (Provision for Family and Dependants) Act 1975 to refer to such provision as it would be reasonable in all the circumstances of the case for a husband or wife to receive, whether or not that provision is required by his or her maintenance: s. 1(2). The court is empowered to make an order for reasonable financial provision out of the deceased's estate: s. 2. See also Matrimonial and Family Proceedings Act 1984, s. 25 (extending the 1975 scheme to *former* spouses); *Rajabally v Rajabally* (1987) 17 Fam Law 314.

financial relief. Term relating to orders, e.g., for maintenance pending a suit in divorce proceedings. See Mat.C.A. 1973, ss. 21–40 (as modified by Matrimonial and Family Proceedings Act

1984, Part II). Magistrates' courts have separate schemes: see D.P.A. 1978, Part I (also modified by the 1984 Act, ss. 10, 11) for matrimonial cases. See Ch. A. 1989, s. 15 (financial relief with respect to children).

financial services. "Banking, insurance, investment, trusteeship and executorship": Building Societies Act 1986, s. 34(11). See F.S.A. 1986. For Financial Services Tribunal, see F.S.A. 1986, Chap. IX. For modification of 1986 Act, see Cos.A. 1989, Part VIII.

financial year. Usually refers to the period of 12 months ending on 31 March: I.A. 1978. See ACCOUNTING REFERENCE PERIOD; FISCAL YEAR.

financial year, in relation to body corporate. Where Cos.A. 1985, Part VII, applies, it means a period in respect of which a profit and loss account under s. 227 is made up. The first financial year begins with the first day of its first accounting reference period (q.v.) and ends with the last day of that period, or other such date, not more than seven days before or after the end of that period, as the directors (q.v.) may determine: Cos.A. 1985, s. 223, as inserted by Cos.A. 1989, s. 3. In relation to any other body corporate, means a period in respect of which a profit and loss account of the body placed before it in general meeting is made up (whether, in either case, that period is a year or not): Cos.A. 1985, s. 742(1).

finding is keeping. Popular misconception that the finder of chattels acquires title as against all other persons, including the rightful owner. See Th.A. 1968, ss. 1, 2; *Armoury* v *Delamirie* (1721) 1 Stra 505; and *Parker* v *British Airways Board* [1982] QB 1004.

findings. The conclusions of an enquiry.

finding, theft by, immunity from. "A person's appropriation of property belonging to another is not to be regarded as dishonest . . . if he appropriates the property in the belief that the person to whom the property belongs cannot be discovered by taking reasonable steps": Th.A. 1968, s. 2(c).

fine. (*Finis* = end.) 1. Monetary penalty payable on conviction. See M.C.A. 1980, ss. 34, 150(1) (see *Chief Constable*

of Kent v *Mather* [1986] RTR 36); P.C.C.A. 1973, ss. 30–32; and C.L.A. 1977, Sch. 6. For imprisonment in default, see C.J.A. 1988, s. 60. For the relevance of means in the assessment of a fine, see C.J.A. 1988, ss. 20, 21. See also C.J.A 1982, ss. 36–37 (standard scale of fines); C.J.A. 1988, s. 59; C.J.A. 1991, s. 18 (system of unit fines). 2. Process used in conveyance by entry on court rolls. A writ was issued, followed by agreement of parties (*finalis concordia*) which was recorded on the rolls. Abolished in 1833. 3. Lump sum payment, a premium for the grant or renewal of a lease: L.P.A. 1925, s. 205(1) (xxiii). See *Binion* v *Evans* [1972] Ch 359. 4. Money paid in early times by a tenant to his lord when land was alienated.

fine, payment in instalments of. A magistrates' court may order payment of a fine by instalments: M.C.A. 1980, s. 85. Variation of an order was allowed under s. 85A (added by the C.J.A. 1982, s. 51(1)).

fine, remission of. Power of a court to remit whole or part of a fine imposed by a magistrates' court, after enquiry into an offender's means, if the court thinks it just to do so, having regard to any change in his circumstances since the conviction: M.C.A. 1980, s. 85. See C.J.A. 1991, s. 22.

fine, responsibility of parent or guardian. The court may order a parent or guardian to pay the financial penalties imposed on a child or young person, unless it is unreasonable, or he or she cannot be found: see C. & Y.P.A. 1933, s. 55, as amended by C.J.A. 1991, s. 57.

fingerprints. Impressions made by ridges at the end of the thumb and fingers, used as a means of identification. Under C.J.A. 1948, s. 39, proof of previous convictions in criminal proceedings by reference to fingerprints was admissible. See also P. & C.E.A. 1984, ss. 27, 61, 64 as amended by C.J.A. 1988, s. 148 (computer data concerning fingerprints). *See* PALM PRINTS.

firearm. Defined under Firearms Act 1968 as "a lethal barrelled weapon of any description from which any shot, bullet or other missile can be discharged, and includes any prohibited weapon, whether it is such a lethal weapon or not". It is an offence to purchase, acquire or possess such a weapon without a certificate. An imitation firearm is any object having the appearance of a firearm whether or not it is capable of discharging a missile. See Th.A. 1968, s. 10(1) (*a*); Criminal Damage Act 1971, s. 3; Firearms Act 1982 (applying the provisions of the 1968 Act to imitation firearms readily convertible into firearms); C.J.A. 1988, s. 44; Firearms (Amendment) Acts 1988 and 1992; *R* v *Bradish* [1990] 1 All ER 460; *R* v *Waller* [1991] Crim LR 381.

firearms, imitation, convertible. An imitation firearm is regarded as readily convertible into a firearm to which the Firearms Act 1968, s. 1, applies if it can be converted without any special skill on the part of the person converting it in the construction or adaptation of firearms of any description, and the work of conversion does not require special equipment or tools other than such as are in common use by persons carrying out construction and maintenance work in their own homes: Firearms Act 1982, s. 1(6).

fire damage, responsibility for. In general, the owner of a house in which a fire begins by accident, and not by negligence, is not responsible for damage caused to others. See Fire Prevention (Metropolis) Act 1744, s. 86; Highways (Amendment) Act 1986, s. 1.

fire ordeal. *See* ORDEAL, TRIAL BY.

firm. A partnership (q.v.). The name under which a partnership is carried on is known as "the firm-name": Partnership Act 1890, s. 4(1).

first instance, court of. *See* COURT OF FIRST INSTANCE.

First Lord of the Treasury. *See* TREASURY.

fiscal year. The financial year, reckoned, e.g., for income tax purposes, as from 6th April in one year to 5th April in the following year.

fishery. Known also as "piscary". A right of fishing. 1. *A several fishery.* "A right to take fish *in alieno solo*, and to exclude the owner of the soil from the right of taking fish himself": *per* Lord Coleridge in *Foster* v *Wright* (1878) LR 4 CPD 438. See *Loose* v *Castleton* (1978) 41 P & C R 19. 2. *A free fishery.* Exclusive right to fish. It may be a *Royal fishery*, i.e., exclusive right of the Crown, or a right granted to a subject. 3. *A*

public or common fishery. Right to fish in another's waters, in common with the owner of the soil.

fishing interrogatories. *See* INTERROGATORIES, FISHING.

fish, Royal. Whale and sturgeon thrown ashore or caught near to the coast are considered the property of the Sovereign. See Wild Creatures and Forest Laws Act 1971, s. 1.

fitness for purpose. Where goods are sold in the course of a business, and the buyer expressly or impliedly makes known to the seller any particular purpose for which the goods are being bought, there is an implied condition that they are fit for that purpose: S.G.A. 1979, s. 14(3). See *Aswan Engineering Co.* v *Lupdine Ltd* [1987] 1 WLR 1; *Business Appliances Ltd* v *Nationwide Credit Ltd* [1988] RTR 332.

fixed charge. *See* CHARGE.

fixed penalty notice. Notice (which may be affixed to a stationary vehicle) offering the opportunity of the discharge of any liability to conviction of the offence to which the notice relates by payment of a fixed penalty: introduced by Transport Act 1982, s. 27, Sch. 1.

fixed sum credit. *See* CREDIT.

fixed term. Expression relating to a lease (q.v.) for a fixed period. "In my opinion a 'fixed term' is one which cannot be unfixed by notice. To be a 'fixed term', the parties must be bound for the term stated in the agreement and unable to determine it on either side": *per* Lord Denning in *BBC* v *Ioannou* [1975] 2 All ER 999.

fixtures. Chattels affixed to land or to a building so that they are part thereof. Generally the degree of annexation required is such that the chattel must be connected to the land or to a building on the land in some substantial way. See *Berkley* v *Poulett* (1976) 120 SJ 836; *Deen* v *Andrews* (1985) 135 NLJ 728; *Mancetter Developments* v *Garmanson* [1986] QB 1212. For mortgagee's right to fixtures, see *Lyon and Co* v *London City and Midland Bank* [1903] 2 KB 135. See Capital Allowances Act 1990, s. 51. *See* QUICQUID PLANTATUR.

flagrante delicto. Literally: while the crime is flagrant. In the very act of committing an offence.

flat. A separate set of premises, whether or not on the same floor, which forms part of a building, is divided horizontally from some other part of the building, and is constructed or adapted for use for the purposes of a dwelling: Landlord and Tenant Act 1987, s. 60. "A dwelling-house which is not a house is a flat": H.A. 1985, s. 183. A "block of flats" means a building containing two or more flats held on leases or other lettings and occupied or intended to be occupied wholly or mainly for residential purposes: H.A. 1988, s. 48. See *R* v *Lambeth LBC, ex p Clayhope Properties* [1987] 3 WLR 854.

floating charge. *See* CHARGE.

flood. Term used in, e.g., insurance policies to mean a large and temporary movement of water having an element of violence and suddenness: *Young* v *Sun Alliance and London Insurance Ltd* [1976] 3 All ER 561. See *Home Brewery Ltd* v *Davis & Co* [1987] QB 339.

flotsam. Wreckage of a cargo floating on the sea. It may go to the Crown if unclaimed.

flying freehold. "A man may have an inheritance in an upper chamber though the lower building and soil be in another": Co.Litt. 48 b. A fee simple may exist in the above-ground-level storey of a building distinct from the rest. See *Grigsby* v *Melville* [1974] 1 WLR 80. *See* COMMONHOLD.

f.o.b. contract. Free on board. Goods are to be delivered on board by the seller, free of expense to the purchaser; they are not at the purchaser's risk until actually delivered on board, when property in them generally passes. See, e.g., *Mitsui Ltd* v *Flota Mercante* [1989] 1 All ER 951.

foetus. An unborn infant that has developed to the stage of being recognisably human (i.e., from the 6th–8th week of pregnancy) with all its organs formed. See Infant Life (Preservation) Act 1929; Abortion Act 1967, s. 5; *R* v *Tait* [1989] 3 WLR 391 (threat to kill a foetus); *B* v *Islington H.A.* (1992) The Times, 25 Mar. (duty of care to foetus and right to sue for pre-birth harm). *See* BORN ALIVE.

folcland. Folkland. Term used in Anglo-Saxon times to describe land held by customary law without written title.

following trust property. There is a right to follow trust property, recog-

nised by common law and equity, where that property is in the hands of some person (e.g., as the result of a disposition of trust property in breach of trust) and is in an identifiable form. Under common law, property was considered identifiable only if not mixed with other property. *See* TRUST.

food. "The word must be interpeted in its primary sense – namely as something taken into the system as nourishment, and not merely as a stimulant": *Hinde* v *Allmand* (1918) LJ KB 893. See Food Act 1984, Food Safety Act 1990, s. 1, in which "food" includes drink, articles and substances of no nutritional value used for human consumption, articles used as ingredients in the preparation of food and drink. For "sale of food", see 1990 Act, s. 2.

food, offences in relation to. It is an offence to add any substance to food, to use any substance as an ingredient in the preparation of food, to abstract any constituent from food or to subject food to any treatment, so as to render the food injurious to health, with intent that it shall be sold for human consumption in that state: Food Safety Act, 1990, s. 7. It is an offence to sell, or advertise for sale, for human consumption, any food rendered injurious to health by means of an operation described in s. 7(1): s. 8.

food, preparation of. Includes, for the purposes of the Food Safety Act 1990, manufacture and any form of treatment. "Preparation for sale" includes packaging: s. 53(1). See *Leeds CC* v *Dewhurst* [1990] Crim LR 725.

football matches, offences by spectators. These include, under the Football (Offences) Act 1991, ss. 1–4, throwing of missiles, racialist or indecent chanting (q.v.), going onto the playing area without lawful authority or excuse.

footpath. Way over which the public have a right of way not associated with a carriageway (q.v.): Horses (Protective Headgear etc.) Act 1990, s. 3.

forbearance. Refraining from enforcing, e.g., a debt. Generally a forbearance to sue may be adequate consideration (q.v.) See *Alliance Bank* v *Broom* (1864) 2 D & S 289.

force. 1. Violence, generally of an unlawful nature. 2. "The application of any energy to the obstacle with a view to removing it": *per* Donaldson LJ in *Swales* v *Cox* [1981] QB 849.

force majeure. An event that can generally be neither anticipated nor controlled, e.g., an industrial strike which leads to loss of profits. See *André et Cie* v *Tradax* [1983] 1 Lloyd's Rep 254.

force, reasonable. *See* REASONABLE FORCE.

forcible detainer. 1. Refusal to restore the goods of one who has tendered amends, the remedy for which was trover (q.v.). 2. The offence of detaining land by violence or threats, after having entered peacefully. See *R* v *Mountford* [1972] 2 QB 28. Generally abolished under C.L.A. 1977, s. 13.

forcible entry. The crime (and tort) of entering land in a violent manner, in order to take possession thereof. It is immaterial whether those concerned had or had not a right to enter. Generally abolished under C.L.A. 1977, s. 13. *See* ENTRY, VIOLENCE FOR SECURING.

foreclosure. The judicial procedure whereby a mortgagee acquires the property freed from the mortgagor's equity of redemption (q.v.). The mortgagee's right to foreclose arises after the date for redemption has passed, or on the breach of a term in the mortgage, e.g., failure to pay interest. It is carried out by order of the court and all those interested in the equity of redemption must be made parties to the action. See L.P.A. 1925, ss. 88, 89, 91; Lim.A. 1980, s. 29. *See* MORTGAGE.

foreign agreement. An agreement of which the proper law (q.v.) is the law of a country outside the UK: C.C.A. 1974, s. 145.

foreign bill. *See* INLAND BILL.

foreign country. A country other than the UK, a dependent territory, the Republic of Ireland, or a country mentioned in Sch. 3: B.N.A. 1981, s. 50(1).

foreign currency. Any currency other than sterling, including special drawing rights and any other units of account defined by reference to more than one currency: Export and Investment Guarantees Act 1991, s. 6(5).

foreign emoluments. "The emoluments of a person not domiciled in the UK from an office or employment under or with any person, body of persons or partnership resident outside the UK": I.C.T.A. 1988, s. 192(1).

foreign judgments, enforcement of. In the case of contract, a foreign judgment is enforceable in an English court if the foreign court is competent, judgment is for a definite sum and is final and conclusive. "In actions *in personam* there are five cases in which the courts of this country will enforce a foreign judgment: (1) where defendant is a subject of the foreign country in which judgment has been obtained; (2) where he was resident in the foreign country when the action began; (3) where plaintiff has selected the forum in which he afterwards sues; (4) where defendant has voluntarily appeared; (5) where defendant has contracted to submit himself to the forum in which judgment was obtained": *Emanuel* v *Syman* [1908] 1 KB 302. See Foreign Judgments (Reciprocal Enforcement) Act 1933; European Communities (Enforcement of Community Judgments) Order 1972; C.J.J.A. 1982 and 1991.

foreign law. All law except English law. Thus, the law of Scotland, of the Republic of Ireland, comes under the heading of "foreign law". What the rule of the particular foreign law which applies in a case states, will be determined by the judge after considering, where appropriate, the evidence of expert witnesses. See Civil Evidence Act 1972, s. 4(1); S.C.A. 1981, s. 69(5).

foreign law, execution of. The courts of no country execute the penal laws of another: *Huntington* v *Attrill* [1893] AC 150. For foreign revenue laws, see *Government of India* v *Taylor* [1955] AC 491; for other public laws, see *A.-G. of New Zealand* v *Ortiz* [1984] AC 1.

foreign law, proof of. The burden rests on the party who is basing his claim or defence on it: *Guaranty Trust Corp* v *Hannay* [1918] 2 KB 623. For judicial notice (q.v.) see *Saxby* v *Fulton* [1909] 2 KB 208.

foreign law, theory of vested rights in. "The courts never in strictness enforce foreign law; when they are said to do so, they enforce not foreign laws, but rights acquired under foreign laws": Dicey.

foreman of jury. Member of a jury (q.v.) who is chosen as its chairman and announces its verdict. See *R* v *Williams* (1987) 84 Cr App R 274 (dissent between foreman and jurors).

forensic. Relating to legal matters. Forensic medicine (known also as "medical jurisprudence") deals with medical facts used in the interpretation of legal problems. For duties of forensic scientists, see *R* v *Ward* (1992) NLJ 859.

foreshore. Includes "the shore and bed of the sea and of every channel, creek, bay, estuary and navigable river as far up it as the tide flows": Salmon and Freshwater Fisheries Act 1975, s. 41(1). See *Baxendale* v *Instow PC* [1982] Ch 14. *See* BEACH.

foresight. Looking forward to some event. In determining whether a person has committed an offence, the court is not bound to infer that he intended or foresaw a result of his actions by reason only of it being a natural and probable consequence of those actions, but shall decide whether he did intend or foresee that result by reference to all the evidence, drawing such inferences from the evidence as appear proper in the circumstances: C.J.A. 1967, s. 8. *See* NEGLIGENCE, FORESEEABILITY AND.

forestry. Includes the felling of trees and the extraction and primary conversion of trees within the wood or forest in which they were grown, and the use of land or woodlands ancillary to the use of land for other agricultural purposes: H.S.W.A. 1974, s. 53(1). "The growing of a utilisable crop of timber": T.C.P.A. 1990, Sch. 5. See also, e.g., Forestry Acts 1979 and 1986; T.C.P.A. 1971, s. 30A (added by T.C.P. (Minerals) A. 1981, s. 5).

forfeiture. 1. A punishment whereby the offender lost all his interests in his property. Thus, the goods and chattels of a felon were, prior to Forfeiture Act 1870, s. 1, forfeited to the Crown. 2. The P.C.C.A. 1973, s. 43, empowers the court to deprive an offender of property used, or intended to be used, for purposes of crime. See also Misuse of Drugs Act 1971, s. 27; *R* v *Slater* [1986] 1 WLR 1340. 3. In a lease (q.v.) a forfeiture clause reserves to the lessor a right of re-entry, upon which the lease is forfeited. See L.P.A. 1925, s. 146; and Protection from Eviction Act 1977, s. 2; *Fuller* v *Judy Properties* (1991) The Times, 30 Dec. (object of relief against forfeiture is continuation of

lease); *Billson* v *Residential Apartments Ltd* [1992] 2 WLR 15. *See also* DRUG TRAFFICKING.

forfeiture of benefit under will. "A man shall not slay his benefactor and thereby take the bounty." See *Re Crippen* [1911] P 108; and *Re Hall* [1914] P 1. See now Forfeiture Act 1982, giving the court a discretion to modify the rule in respect of certain forfeited property rights in given circumstances in respect of one who has unlawfully killed another. Murderers are excluded from the operation of the Act: s. 5. See *Re K.* [1986] Ch 180; *Re H.* (1990) 1 FLR 441.

forfeiture of shares. Shares may be forfeited (i.e., taken away from company members) by resolution of the board of directors if such a power is given in the articles of association (q.v.). The object of forfeiture must be for the company's benefit. Shares may be forfeited, e.g., where a member fails to pay a call properly made on him. See *Re Esparto Trading Co* (1879) 12 Ch D 191. *See* COMPANY; SHARE.

forgery. "A person is guilty of forgery if he makes a false instrument, with the intention that he or another shall use it to induce somebody to accept it as genuine, and by reason of so accepting it to do or not to do some act to his own or any other person's prejudice": Forgery and Counterfeiting Act 1981, s. 1. See Road Traffic Act 1988, s. 173; *Lombard Finance* v *Brookplain Trading* [1991] 1 WLR 271. *See* INSTRUMENT, FALSE.

forgiveness of victim. This makes no difference to the seriousness of an offence; the public, not merely the victim, must be considered: *R* v *Gainford* (1989) The Times, 31 Jan.

formal contract. Term applied to a contract, e.g., for the sale of land, comprising particulars (describing property); special conditions (relating to sale in question); general conditions (standardised and incorporated into contract by reference to, e.g., "national conditions of sale"). See LPA 1925, ss. 52, 54(2); C.C.A. 1974, s. 61; L.P. (Misc. Provs.) A. 1989, s. 2. *See* CONTRACT.

forthwith. Immediately, or, more generally, when used in a statute, within a reasonable time. See *Hillingdon LBC* v *Cutler* [1968] Crim LR 109.

fortune telling. It is an offence to purport to "exercise powers of telepathy, clairvoyance or other similar powers". See Vagrancy Act 1824, s. 4 (amended by Fraudulent Mediums Act 1951, s. 2(*b*)); *R* v *Martin* [1981] Crim LR 109.

forum. 1. A judicial assembly. 2. Country in which jurisdiction is exercised. If, e.g., X is sued in England on a contract made in Italy, England is the forum, and the *lex fori* (q.v.) is the law of England.

forum non conveniens. Doctrine whereby the court refuses to exercise its right of jurisdiction because, for the convenience of parties and in the interests of justice, an action should be brought elsewhere. The phrase means, not that the English court is "not convenient", but that some other court is more suitable: *Spiliada Maritime Corporation* v *Cansulex Ltd* [1987] AC 460. See *Re Harrods Ltd* (No. 2) [1991] 4 All ER 348.

forum rei. The court of the country in which the subject-matter of the action is situated.

foster-child. See PRIVATELY FOSTERED CHILDREN.

founders' shares. See DEFERRED SHARES.

four-day order. Supplemental order, based on O. 42, r. 2, by which, if a time within which an act to be done is not specified, four days (or some other suitable period) will be given for compliance.

four unities, the. See JOINT TENANCY.

franchise. 1. The right of voting in a parliamentary or local election. 2. A privilege belonging to the Crown, or by virtue of a grant, expressed or implied, to a subject. Example: the right to hold markets. Known also as a "liberty". See Wild Creatures and Forest Laws Act 1971, s. 1; *Iveagh* v *Martin* [1961] 1 QB 232.

franchise clause. Clause in an insurance policy relieving the insurer from total liability in respect of losses below a standard percentage or other figure. See *Stewart* v *Merchants' Marine Insurance Co* (1885) 16 QBD 619.

frankalmoign. Free alms. Land tenure originating in the Anglo-Saxon era, when lands were granted to the church in return for prayers for the grantor's soul. Abolished under A.E.A. 1925, Sch. 2.

fraud at common law. Intentional deceit. A false representation by the defendant of an existing fact, made knowingly, or without belief in its truth, or recklessly, careless whether it be true or false, with the intention that the plaintiff should act on it, and which results in damage to the plaintiff. See *Horsfall* v *Thomas* (1862) 10 WR 650; *Redgrave* v *Hurd* (1881) 20 Ch D 1; *Midland Bank Trust* v *Green* [1981] AC 513 (discussion of fraud "unravelling everything").

fraud, concealed. See CONCEALED FRAUD.

fraud, constructive. See CONSTRUCTIVE FRAUD.

fraud in equity. See EQUITABLE FRAUD.

fraud on a power. "The term . . . merely means that the power has been exercised for a purpose, or with an intention, beyond the scope of or not justified by the instrument creating the power": *Vatcher* v *Paull* [1915] AC 372. Example: an appointment made for a corrupt purpose (see *Lord Hinchinbroke* v *Seymour* (1789) 1 Bro CC 385). See APPOINTMENT, POWER OF.

fraud on minority. See MINORITY SHAREHOLDERS, OPPRESSION OF.

fraud, serious. See SERIOUS FRAUD OFFICE.

frauds, relating to theft. Under Th.A. 1968, the following offences relating to fraud exist: obtaining property by deception, s. 15; obtaining a pecuniary advantage by deception, s. 16; false accounting, s. 17; false statements by company directors, s. 19; dishonest suppression of documents, s. 20(1); dishonest procuring by deception of the execution of a valuable security, s. 20(2). Each is an arrestable offence (q.v.).

fraudulent conversion. See CONVERSION.

fraudulent conveyance. A voluntary disposition of land made with intent to defraud a subsequent purchaser is voidable at the instance of the purchaser: L.P.A. 1925, s. 173. See Ins.A. 1986, s. 357, for offences relating to the fraudulent disposal of property (replacing the (repealed) L.P.A 1925, s. 172).

fraudulent mediums. See WITCHCRAFT.

fraudulent misrepresentation. See MISREPRESENTATION, FRAUDULENT.

fraudulent preference. A conveyance or transfer of a debtor's property intended to give a creditor or surety any preference over other creditors and made by a person insolvent at the time.

fraudulent trading. Trading by a company (q.v.) with intent to defraud creditors or other persons. See Cos.A. 1985, s. 458, and Ins.A. 1986, s. 213. See also *R* v *Cox and Hedges* (1982) 75 Cr App. R. 291.

freehold. An estate of an uncertain length of duration. The fee simple absolute in possession (q.v.) is the sole surviving legal freehold estate. Originally an estate held by a "free man". *See* ESTATE.

free movement. Phrase used in the Treaty of Rome 1957, which set up the EEC (q.v.), referring to the movement of persons, services and capital within the EEC, which is to be without limitations. See *R* v *Saunders* [1979] 2 All ER 267.

freight. A consideration paid to a carrier for the carriage of goods. *Lump sum freight* is paid by the charterer as a sum for the use of a ship for one service. *Pro rata freight* is the amount recoverable by a carrier when the owner of goods agrees to take delivery at a port short of the agreed destination, or when the carrier delivers only part of the cargo. *Advance freight* is payable before delivery of goods.

frequenting. Term used in relation to a suspected person (q.v.), to suggest visiting a place repeatedly. It involves the notion of more than mere physical presence and something which is to some degree continuous: *Nakhla* v *The Queen* [1976] AC 1.

friend in court. *See* LITIGANT, ASSISTANCE BY ADVISER.

friendly society. A society registered by the Chief Registrar of Friendly Societies under the Friendly Societies Acts 1974–92, being a society which, as part of its ordinary business, provides benefits during sickness or other infirmity, or in old age, or in widowhood, or for orphans: S.S.A. 1975, Sch. 20. See F.S.A. 1986, ss. 23, 140–141; Finance Act 1987 s. 30. For criteria of prudent management, see 1992 Act, s. 50; for accounts and audit, see Part VI.

fringe benefits. Benefits granted by an employer to an employee which do not enter into his basic wage. See Finance Act 1976, ss. 60–72.

frivolous action. *See* VEXATIOUS ACTION.

fructus industriales. That which is the produce of "labour and industry". Example: corn, as compared with *fructus naturales* (crops which grow naturally). See S.G.A. 1979, s. 61; *Marshall* v *Green* (1875) 1 CPD 35.

frustration of contract. Where there is an event or change of circumstances so fundamental as to strike at the root of a contract as a whole and beyond what was contemplated by the parties, that contract is considered frustrated. Under the Law Reform (Frustrated Contracts) Act 1943, all sums payable under a frustrated contract are recoverable and sums payable cease to be payable. The Act does not apply, e.g., to a contract containing a provision to meet a case of frustration, to a contract of insurance or carriage of goods by sea, or to a contract not governed by English law. See *Fibrosa Case* [1943] AC 32; *BP Exploration Corp* v *Hunt (No. 2)* [1983] 2 AC 352; *The Super Servant Two* [1990] 1 Lloyd's Rep 1. For frustration of a lease, see *National Carriers* v *Panalpina* [1981] AC 675. See also S.G.A. 1979, s. 7. *See* CONTRACT; NON HAEC.

frustration, self-induced. Frustration of a contract due to one's own conduct or to the conduct of those for whom one is responsible: *Bank Line Ltd* v *Arthur Capel & Co* [1919] AC 435. See *The Eugenia* [1964] 2 QB 226.

fugitive criminal. Any person accused or convicted of an extradition crime committed within the jurisdiction of any foreign state who is in or is suspected of being in some part of HM dominions. "Fugitive criminal of a foreign state" means a fugitive criminal accused or convicted of an extradition crime committed within the jurisdiction of that state: Extradition Act 1989, Sch. 1, para 20. *See* EXTRADITION.

full age. Age of majority: 18 since the F.L.R.A. 1969, s. 1. *See* INFANT.

functus officio. A task performed. Refers to one who has exercised his authority and brought it to an end in a particular case. Thus, a judge who has convicted a person charged with an offence is *functus officio*. See *Re VGM Holdings* [1941] 3 All ER 417; *R* v *Dwight* [1990] 1 NZLR 160.

fund-raising business. "Any business carried on for gain and wholly or primarily engaged in soliciting or otherwise procuring money or other property for charitable, benevolent or philanthropic purposes": Charities Act 1992, s. 58(1). For prohibitions on professional fund-raising, see s. 59. *See* PUBLIC CHARITABLE COLLECTION.

funds, payment into court. *See* PAYMENT INTO COURT.

funeral expenses. Reasonable expenses involved in burying a deceased person must be paid out of his estate prior to any other duty or debt: *R v Wade* (1818) 5 Pr 621.

fungibles. Movable goods which are ordinarily dealt with by number, measurement or weight. "Fungible assets" are assets of a company "substantially indistinguishable one from another": see Cos.A. 1985, Sch.4, para. 31.

furniture. "For articles to be furniture . . . I do not think it is essential that they shall be movable, and though, of course, articles of furniture are commonly movable, I do not think they pass out of the popular meaning of furniture because they are fixed by a nail or a screw to a wall or floor": *per* Stamp J in *F. Austin Ltd* v *Commissioners of Customs & Excise* [1968] 2 All ER 13.

future goods. *See* GOODS.

future interest. An interest limited so that it confers a right to the enjoyment of property at some time in the future. Example: grant "to A for his life and then to the first of his sons who shall attain the age of 21" – in the case of the first of A's sons, the interest takes effect in the future.

future lease. An existing lease carrying the right to possession at a specified time in the future. *See* LEASE.

futures. "Rights under a contract for the sale of a commodity or property of any other description under which delivery is to be made at a future date and at a price agreed upon when the contract is made": F.S.A. 1986, Sch. 1.

G

gage. A pledge. Something given as security for some act. In the twelfth century the *vivum vadium* (living pledge) allowed a mortgagee to take possession of land rents and profits in discharge of principal and interest. The *mortuum vadium* (dead pledge) allowed him to take rents and profits in discharge of the interest only.

gain. "The most appropriate definition to be found in a dictionary may be 'increase in resources or business advantages resulting from business transactions or dealings' ": *Re Riverton Sheep Dip* (1943) SASR 344.

game. Animals *ferae naturae*, hunted for sport or food, including hares, pheasants, partridges, grouse, heath or moor game, woodcock, etc. See Game Laws (Amendment) Act 1960, by which a constable may arrest a person trespassing in pursuit of game. See also Wild Creatures and Forest Laws Act 1971. *See* ANIMAL; POACHING.

gaming. Known also as "gambling". "The playing of a game of chance for winnings in money or money's worth, whether any person playing the game is at risk of losing any money or money's worth or not": Gaming Act 1968, s. 52. The 1968 Act prohibited gaming in public bars and wherever a charge is made. It also prohibits gaming involving playing or staking against a bank or where the chances are unequal. Commercial gaming may be permitted under licence. See Betting, Gaming and Lotteries Act 1963; Gaming Act 1968; Lotteries and Amusements Act 1976; Gaming (Amendment) Acts 1982, 1987, 1990; Bingo Act 1992. (For a definition of "gaming machine", see Betting and Gaming Duties Act 1981, s. 25, as amended by Finance Act 1982, Sch 6, Part V.)

gaming contracts. Contracts which are wagers upon a game, e.g., a horse race. They involve "the playing of a game of chance for winnings in money or money's worth": Betting, Gaming and Lotteries Act 1963, as amended by Gaming Act 1968. Generally null and void; no action can be brought to recover money relating to a wager. Securities given for gaming contracts are, in effect, given for an illegal consideration (q.v.) and are void as between the parties. See Gaming Act 1968; F.S.A. 1986, s. 63; *C.H.T.* v *Ward* [1963] 3 All ER 835; *Crockfords* v *Mehta* [1992] 1 WLR 355 (licensed gaming club suing on cheques).

garnishee. One who has been warned by a court order that a debt is to be paid to some person who has obtained a garnishee order against his creditor, and not to that creditor. See O. 49; *Llewellyn* v *Carrickford* [1970] 1 WLR 1124.

garnishee proceedings. Proceedings enabling a judgment creditor (q.v.) to have assigned to him the benefit of any debt owed by the garnishee (q.v.) to the judgment debtor (q.v.). Example: A owes B £1,000 and C owes A £1,000. B may commence proceedings to obtain a garnishee order so that C will pay the £1,000 directly to B. Where proceedings fail, the courts have a wide discretion as to costs and may order the judgment debtor to pay them: *Wright & Son* v *Westoby* [1972] 3 All ER 1078. See A.J.A. 1985, s. 52. See *Man* v *Miyazaki Commercial Agricola* [1991] 1 Lloyd's Rep 154. *See* JUDGMENTS, ENFORCEMENT OF.

gavelkind. (*Gafolcund* = yielding a rent.) Socage tenures (q.v.) in Kent, held under unique conditions, e.g., land could be alienated by a tenant at the age of 15, could be devised and was not liable to escheat (q.v.) for felony (q.v.). Abolished by A.E.A. 1925, s. 45(1) (*a*). See also L.P.A. 1922, Sch. 12.

Gazette. *See* LONDON GAZETTE.

gazump. Colloquial term used to refer to a situation in which the vendor of a house "subject to contract" (q.v.) withdraws from the bargain, or threatens to do so, in the expectation of receiving a higher price elsewhere.

general and special damages. For purpose of procedure, damages may be divided thus: 1. General damages, such as will be presumed to have resulted from the defendant's acts. They may include, e.g., damages for pain, inconvenience and generally need not be specifically pleaded. 2. Special damages, such as will not be presumed, e.g., loss of earnings, medical expenses. These must be pleaded specifically and proved. See DAMAGES.

general average. See AVERAGE.

General Council of the Bar. See BAR COUNCIL.

general devise. See DEVISE.

general equitable charge. See EQUITABLE CHARGE, GENERAL.

generalia specialibus non derogant. General things do not derogate from special things. See, e.g., *Harlow* v *Minister of Transport* [1951] 2 KB 98.

generalia verba sunt generaliter intelligenda. General words are to be understood generally.

generalibus specialia derogant. Special things derogate from general things.

general issue. A plea by the defendant who traversed or denied allegations in their entirety, e.g., "never indebted" in an action of debt. No longer admissible in a civil action, save where in accordance with the requirements of statute. See O. 18.

general legacy. A bequest which does not identify specifically the thing bequeathed. Example: "a horse to X and a gold watch to Y". The subject-matter of a general legacy need not form part of the testator's assets at the time of his death: *Bothamley* v *Sherson* (1875) LR 20 Eq 304. See LEGACY.

general lien. A right to retain possession of another's goods until all claims against that other are satisfied. It exists, e.g., in the case of bankers and solicitors. See *Halesowen Presswork & Assemblies Ltd* v *Westminster Bank Ltd* [1971] 1 QB 1. See LIEN.

general power. See APPOINTMENT, POWER OF.

general verdict. A finding on the point in issue; e.g., a verdict of guilty, or one of not guilty. See SPECIAL VERDICT.

general warrant. Warrant in which neither the persons nor the premises to be searched were named. Declared illegal in *Wilkes* v *Wood* (1765) 19 St Tr 1153. "By the law of England every invasion of private property be it ever so minute is a trespass. No man can set foot on my ground without my licence . . . he is bound to show by way of justification that some positive law has empowered or excused him": *Entick* v *Carrington* (1675) 19 St Tr 1030. See *Elias* v *Pasmore* [1934] 2 KB 164. See WARRANT.

general words. Words which were necessary in a conveyance (q.v.) to convey rights and easements (q.v.). Under L.P.A. 1925, s. 62, such words are implied, if no contrary intention is expressed.

genocide. The offence committed by one who, with intent to destroy a national, ethnic, racial or religious group, kills or causes serious bodily or mental harm to members of the group, inflicts on the group conditions of life intended to physically destroy it, or forcibly transfers children of that group to another group. See Genocide Act 1969; Extradition Act 1989, s. 23.

gentlemen's agreement. Colloquial term used to describe an agreement resting on the honour of the parties. It is not usually enforceable at law.

gestation. The time between conception and birth (around 267 days for humans). See *Preston-Jones* v *Preston-Jones* [1951] AC 391. See FOETUS.

gift. A gratuitous transfer of the ownership of property: Blackstone. See *Esso* v *Customs & Excise* [1976] 1 All ER 117.

gift, imperfect. A gift which has not been completely constituted. An apparently imperfect transfer may be effective: if the conditions for a *donatio mortis causa* (q.v.) are satisfied; under the rule in *Strong* v *Bird* (1874) LR 18 Eq 315; by statute, e.g., L.P.A. 1925, ss. 1, 19 and S.L.A. 1925, ss. 4, 9, 27; under the doctrine of equitable estoppel (q.v.).

gift *inter vivos*. A gratuitous grant or transfer of property between living persons. Validity of the gift necessitates the intention to give and appropriate acts to make the intention effective. See, e.g., *Dewar* v *Dewar* [1975] 2 All ER 728.

gift over. A gift which comes into existence when a particular preceding estate (q.v.) is determined.

Gillick child, competence of. Concept enunciated by the House of Lords in *Gillick* v *W Norfolk HA* [1986] AC 112: a child under 16 had the legal capacity to consent to medical examination and treatment if she had sufficient maturity and intelligence to understand the nature and implications of the treatment; parents' right to determine such matters ended when child achieved sufficient intelligence and understanding to make its own decision. "It is not enough that she should understand the nature of the advice which is being given: she must also have sufficient maturity to understand what is involved": *per* Lord Scarman See F.L.R.A. 1969, s. 8; Ch.A. 1989, s. 10(8); *Re R.* [1991] 3 WLR 592.

gilt-edged securities. Generally stock exchange securities carrying a minimum of risk regarding regular payment of interest on due date and redemption of stock (unless undated) at the stated time. For a list, see T.C.G.A. 1992, Sch. 9, Part II. *See* SECURITIES.

going concern. A business which is in continuous, uninterrupted operation. See *Gordon* v *IRC* [1991] BTC 130.

going equipped for stealing. "A person is guilty of an offence if, when not at his place of abode, he has with him any article for use in the course of or in connection with any burglary, theft or cheat": Th.A. 1968, s. 25(1). See *R* v *Doukas* [1978] 1 WLR 372; *A.-G.'s Ref. (No. 1 of 1985)* [1986] QB 491.

golden handshake. Phrase referring to payment (usually of considerable value) made *ex gratia* (q.v.) or as compensation for loss of office. See Finance Act 1986, s. 45; I.C.T.A. 1988, s. 148; *Sybron Corporation* v *Rochem Ltd* [1983] 2 All ER 707; *Shilton* v *Wilmshurst* [1990] STC 55.

golden rule. Rule for construing a statute: *Mattison* v *Hart* (1854) 14 CB 385. "The grammatical and ordinary sense of the words is to be adhered to unless that would lead to an absurdity or some repugnancy or inconsistency with the rest of the instrument, in

which case the grammatical and ordinary sense of the words may be modified so as to avoid such absurdity, repugnancy or inconsistency, but no further": *Grey* v *Pearson* (1857) 6 HLC 61. See *Federal Steam Navigation Co* v *Department of Trade and Industry* [1974] 2 All ER 97. *See* INTERPRETATION OF STATUTES.

good behaviour. A person may be ordered by a magistrate (q.v.) to keep the peace, or to be of good behaviour and may also be ordered to enter into recognisances (q.v.). If he fails to be of good behaviour for that period the recognisances may be estreated and he becomes liable to be sentenced for the original offence. See M.C.A. 1980, ss. 115, 116.

good consideration. Consideration founded on generosity, natural affection or normal duty. It is not regarded as "valuable consideration" (e.g., money, money's worth) so that, e.g., a settlement merely supported by good consideration is regarded as "voluntary". Because equity will not assist a volunteer, should A promise B that he will create a trust and should he fail to do so, B cannot compel performance if he has not given valuable consideration. See *Midland Bank Trust Co* v *Green* [1981] AC 513. *See* CONSIDERATION.

good faith. "The words, in my opinion, mean 'honestly'. A claim is not made honestly if made with the intention of committing a criminal offence, or of facilitating the commission of a future offence": *per* Phillimore LJ in *Central Estates Ltd* v *Woolgar* [1971] 3 All ER 647. See B.Ex.A. 1882, s. 90. *See* UBERRIMAE FIDEI.

good leasehold title. A title under L.R.A. 1925, whereby no guarantee as to the lessor's right to validly grant the lease is given, but in other respects the title is effectively equivalent to absolute leasehold title.

good repair. Such a state of repair as will satisfy a respectable occupant using the premises fairly. See *Dashwood* v *Magniac* [1891] 3 Ch 306.

goods. Under the S.G.A. 1979, all chattels personal, other than things in action and money: s. 61. In effect, therefore, all things in possession, save money used as currency of the realm.

"Every description of wares and merchandise": Merchant Shipping Act 1894, s. 492. "Future goods" are those to be manufactured or acquired by the seller following the making of the contract of sale. "Specific goods" are those "identified and agreed upon at the time a contract of sale is made": 1979 Act, s. 61. See C.P.A. 1987, s. 45(1). *See* SUPPLY.

goods, consumer. *See* CONSUMER GOODS.

goods, contamination of, or interference with. It is an offence for a person to contaminate or interfere with goods with the intention of causing public anxiety or causing injury to those using or consuming the goods, or of causing economic loss: P.O.A. 1986, s. 38(1). "Goods" include "substances whether natural or manufactured and whether or not incorporated in or mixed with other goods": s. 38(4). It is an offence to threaten to do, or claim to have done, any of the offences mentioned in s. 38(1) with the intention mentioned above: s. 38(2).

goods, deliverable state. Goods "in such a state that the buyer would under the contract be bound to take delivery of them": S.G.A. 1979, s. 61(5).

goods, delivery of. *See* DELIVERY OF GOODS.

goods, documents of title to. *See* DOCUMENTS OF TITLE TO GOODS.

goods, duress of. *See* DURESS OF GOODS.

goods, hire of, contract for. "A contract under which one person bails or agrees to bail goods to another by way of hire, other than an excepted contract": Supply of Goods and Services Act 1982, s. 6(1). "Excepted contract" refers to a hire-purchase agreement or a contract under which goods are bailed in exchange for trading stamps on their redemption: s. 6(2). For implied terms, see ss. 7–10.

goods, parting with possession of, and property in. "If a man intends to part not only with the possession of goods but also with the property in them or the power of disposing of them, or behaves as if he had that intention by arming the recipient with all the documents necessary to that end, he is not entitled to recover them from an innocent purchaser": *per* Denning LJ in *Central Newbury Car Auctions Ltd* v *Unity Finance Ltd* [1957] 1 QB 371.

goods, protected. *See* PROTECTED GOODS.

goods, quality of. *See* QUALITY.

goods, rejection of. *See* REJECTION OF GOODS.

goods, safe. Means that there is no risk, or minimum risk, that the death of, or any personal injury to, any person will be caused by the goods, their keeping, use or consumption, any emission or leakage from the goods, reliance on the accuracy of measurement made by the goods: C.P.A. 1987, s. 29(1). *See* CONSUMER SAFETY; DEFECT IN A PRODUCT.

goods, safety of. *See* CONSUMER SAFETY.

goods, slander of. *See* SLANDER OF GOODS.

goods, title to, transfer of. *See* TITLE TO GOODS, TRANSFER OF.

goods, transfer of, contract for. "A contract under which one person transfers or agrees to transfer to another the property in goods, other than an excepted contract": Supply of Goods and Services Act 1982, s. 1(1). "Excepted contract" refers to a contract of sale of goods, a hire-purchase agreement, a contract under which property is transferred on redemption of trading stamps, a contract intended to operate by way of mortgage, pledge, charge or other security: s. 1(2). For implied terms and warranties, see ss. 2–5.

goods, trespass to. *See* TRESPASS TO GOODS.

goods, wrongful interference with. *See* INTERFERENCE WITH GOODS, WRONGFUL.

goodwill. "The attractive force which brings in custom": *Inland Revenue* v *Muller* [1901] AC 224. "The whole advantage, wherever it may be, of the reputation and connection of the firm which may have been built up by years of honest work or gained by lavish expenditure of money": *Trego* v *Hunt* [1896] AC 7. It is measured by the amount by which the value of a business as a whole exceeds the value of assets less liabilities. See Cos.A. 1985, Sch. 4; *Kirby* v *Thorn EMI* [1987] STC 621.

go-slow. A form of industrial action by workers, taking the form of working more slowly than usual. Known also as "working to rule", i.e., reducing output by paying exaggerated attention to rules relating to working conditions. See *Secretary of State for Employment* v

ASLEF (No. 2) [1972] 2 QB 455.

government. 1. The exercise of authority. 2. The institutions, customs and laws through which government functions. 3. Her Majesty's Government, i.e., a body of ministers responsible for the administration of the nation's affairs.

grand assize. Introduced by Henry II as an alternative to trial by battle (q.v.). The plaintiff alleged in his writ of right that he had been dispossessed wrongfully. Twelve knights were called to deliver to the justices of assize a verdict as to whether the plaintiff's allegation of title was, in fact, truthful. Abolished by Civil Procedure Act 1833. *See* ASSIZE.

grand jury. *See* JURY, GRAND.

grand larceny. The offence of stealing goods worth more than twelve pence. *Petty larceny* referred to stealing goods below that value. The distinction was abolished in 1827.

grand serjeanty. A tenure originating in services rendered to the King by his courtiers and followers, e.g., officers of the King's household. The tenure enjoyed by the great nobles of the realm was *grand serjeanty*; the tenure involving only minor services was *petty serjeanty.* Grand serjeanty became the equivalent of knight service (q.v.); petty serjeanty, the equivalent of socage (q.v.).

grant. 1. Transfer of property under written instrument without immediate delivery. 2. The allocation of rights, etc, to persons.

grant, block. *See* BLOCK GRANT; AIDS.

grant in aid. *See* AIDS.

grant of representation. 1. Probate (q.v.). 2. *Cum testamento annexo,* made when the deceased left a valid will which has not been proved by an executor (q.v.). See S.C.A. 1981, s. 119. 3. Simple administration, when deceased died wholly intestate.

grants, special and limited. 1. Grants of representation may be limited as to property, e.g., where the testator (q.v.) has expressly limited the powers of his executor; in the case of grants as to specific settled land; grants *caeterorum* (where a grant has been made to a portion of the estate and it is necessary to apply for administration of the rest of the estate); *de bonis non administratis* (q.v.). 2. Grants may be limited as to time, e.g., until the will be found; for the use of infants (q.v.); during mental incapacity; *ad litem* (q.v.); *ad colligenda bona* (q.v.).

grants to attorney. When an executor or administrator entitled to a grant resides outside England and the grant is limited until that person shall obtain a grant, it may be made to the lawfully constituted attorney of the person entitled for his use and benefit: Non-Contentious Probate Rules 1987, r. 31.

gratuities. Money given in recognition of services rendered. See *Figael Ltd* v *Fox* [1992] STC 83 (liability for tax on tips); SI 1973/334.

gratuitous. Given freely, i.e., without legal consideration (q.v.).

grave hardship. In the case of divorce (q.v.) based on five years living apart, the respondent can object to the granting of a decree by showing that dissolving the marriage would result in "grave financial or other hardship to him": Mat.C.A. 1973, s. 5(1). "Grave" is given its ordinary meaning and "hardship" is to be determined objectively, according to the standard of sensible people. See *Rukat* v *Rukat* [1975] Fam 63. *See* HARDSHIP.

Gray's Inn. One of the four Inns of Court (q.v.). The site of the Inn was let by the Dean of St Paul's to Reginald de Grey, chief justice of Chester, in the thirteenth century. The Inn began to function as a legal institution *c.* 1320.

Great Britain. *See* UNITED KINGDOM.

Green Belt land. Land intended for preservation from industrial or building development. See Green Belt (London and Home Counties) Act 1938; T.C.P.A. 1990, s. 229; *Planning Policy Guidance Note 2 ("Green Belts"),* Dept. of Environment (Jan 1988); *Scottish and Newcastle Breweries plc* v *Secretary of State for the Environment* (1992) The Times, 6 Mar.

Green Book. *See* COUNTY COURTS.

Green Form scheme. *See* LEGAL AID SCHEME.

Green Paper. *See* PARLIAMENTARY PAPERS.

grievous bodily harm. *See* BODILY HARM, GRIEVOUS.

gross. Entire; exclusive of deductions. The term "in gross" means, when referring to a right, that it is not appendant (q.v.) or otherwise annexed to land.

gross indecency. 1. It is an offence for a

man to commit an act of gross indecency (a term not defined by statute: but see Wolfenden Committee Report 1957, Cmnd 247, p. 38) with another man in public or private, to be a party to the commission of such an act or to procure its commission. See S.O.A. 1956, s. 13; *Chief Constable of Hants* v *Mace* (1987) 84 Cr App R 40. The term is generally used in practice to refer to a sexual act, other than buggery (q.v.), between males. 2. It is an offence for a person to commit an act of gross indecency with or towards a child under the age of 14 or to incite such a child to do such an act with him or any other person. See Indecency with Children Act 1960; *R* v *Speck* [1977] 2 All ER 859; *R* v *Clayton* [1990] Crim LR 447.

gross negligence. Used colloquially to refer to negligence (q.v.) characterised by total indifference to the rights of others and the consequences of one's act. "The use of the expression 'gross negligence' is always misleading. Except in the one case when the law relating to manslaughter is being considered, the words 'gross negligence' should never be used in connection with any matter to which the common law relates because negligence is a breach of duty, and, if there is a duty and there has been a breach of it which causes loss, it matters not whether it is a venial breach or a serious breach": *Pentecost* v *London District Auditor* [1951] 2 KB 759.

gross negligence, killing by. In a case of alleged killing by gross negligence, the facts must be such "that in the opinion of the jury, the negligence of the accused went beyond a mere matter of compensation between subjects and showed such disregard for the life and safety of others as to amount to a crime against the State and conduct deserving of punishment": *R* v *Bateman* (1925) 133 LT 730. See *R* v *Lamb* [1967] 2 QB 981. See NEGLIGENCE.

gross value of premises. Phrase used in the Rent Acts to mean letting value of premises by the year, assuming that the cost of insurance and repairs is carried by the landlord.

gross weight. In relation to any goods, the aggregate weight of the goods and any container in or on which they are made up: Weights and Measures Act 1985, s. 94(1).

ground rent. *See* BUILDING LEASE.

group accounts. Accounts laid in general meeting before a company which has subsidiaries: Cos.A. 1985, s. 229. They must consist of a consolidated balance sheet and profit and loss account and must comply with requirements of the Cos.A. 1985, Sch. 4.

grundnorm. *See* LAW, PURE THEORY OF.

guarantee. A collateral engagement to answer for the debt, default or miscarriage of another person. To be enforceable, such a promise must be evidenced in writing: Statute of Frauds 1677, s. 4. "Miscarriage" refers here to "that species of wrongful act for the consequences of which the law would make the party civilly responsible": *Kirkham* v *Marter* (1819) 2 B & A 613. See Cos.A. 1985, s. 331(2); *TCB Ltd* v *Gray* [1986] Ch 621; *The Maria D* [1991] 2 Lloyd's Rep 311.

guarantee, company limited by. Company (q.v.) formed, e.g., for charitable or educational purposes. If it has share capital, a member is liable up to the amount unpaid on his shares and also up to the amount of guarantee; but if it has no share capital, he is liable only up to the amount of the guarantee. See Tables C and D; and Cos.A. 1985, s. 30. With effect from December 1980, a company cannot be formed as, or become, a company limited by guarantee with a share capital: Cos.A. 1985, s. 1(4).

guarantee payments. Payments made by an employer to an employee who has more than four weeks' service and who is laid off: E.P.(C.)A. 1978, ss. 12–18 (as modified by Employment Act 1980, s. 14). Employees hired for a period of less than 12 weeks are generally excluded. Amount of payment is regulated by a formula set out in s. 14(2).

guarantor. One who promises to answer for another; a surety (q.v.). See Minors' Contracts Act 1987, s. 2.

guardian. One appointed to take care of another person, his affairs and property. A guardian may be appointed if the child has no parent with parental responsibility (q.v.) for him: Ch. A. 1989, s. 5(1) (a). A parent who has parental responsibility may appoint another person to be the child's guardian in the event of his death: s. 5(4). For revocation and disclaimer, see s. 6. For guardian's allowance, see S.S. Contributions and Benefits Act 1992, s. 77.

guardian *ad litem.* *See* AD LITEM.

guardian removal of. The court may terminate the appointment of a guardian on the application of the child concerned or any person with parental responsibility (q.v.) for him or if the court considers that it should be ended even though no application has been made: Ch.A. 1989, s. 6(7). For disclaimer, see s. 6(5).

guilty. Confession by the defendant that he has committed the offence with which he is charged. He may plead guilty to one count in an indictment, but not guilty to another. A plea of guilty made under pressure upon counsel from the trial judge is not a proper plea, so that the ensuing trial is a nullity: *R* v *Inns* (1975) 60 Cr App R 231. For changing guilty plea, see *S.* v *Recorder of Manchester* [1969] 3 All ER 1230. For a mistaken plea of guilty, see *R* v *Phillips* [1982] 1 All ER 245. See *R* v *Newton* (1983) 77 Cr App R 13; *R* v *Challinor* (1985) 80 Cr App R 253; *R* v *Gent* [1990] 1 All ER 304; *R* v *R* (1992)

The Times, 16 Jan. (granting of "credit" for guilty plea). *See* NOT GUILTY.

guilty knowledge. That awareness by virtue of which a person's act or omission is rendered criminal in nature. In *Roper* v *Taylor's Central Garages (Exeter) Ltd* [1951] 2 TLR 284, it was categorised as (1) actual knowledge, which could be inferred from the accused's conduct; (2) knowledge in the eye of the law, where the accused has deliberately refrained from making enquiries; (3) constructive knowledge.

guilty mind. *See* MENS REA.

guilty, plea by post of. *See* POST, PLEA OF GUILTY BY.

gypsies. Described in Caravan Sites Act 1968 as "persons of nomadic habit of life, whatever their race or origin". They were prohibited under Highways Act 1980 from encamping on highways. Local authorities have the duty under the 1968 Act to provide adequate accommodation for gypsies residing in or resorting to their area. See L.G.P.L.A. 1980, s. 70. For purposes of the Race Relations Act 1976, they constitute a "racial group": *Commission for Racial Equality* v *Dutton* [1989] 2 WLR 17. See *Reigate BC* v *Brown* (1992) The Times, 3 Mar.

H

habeas corpus. That you have the body. A prerogative writ ("the great writ of liberty") used to command a person who is detaining another in custody to produce that person before the court. "The King is at all times entitled to have an account why the liberty of his subjects is restrained": Blackstone. The writ *habeas corpus ad subjiciendum* commands a person to produce the detainee, with details of the day and cause of his caption and detention, to do, submit to and receive what shall be directed by the court. The QBD has jurisdiction to issue the writ; an application takes precedence over other business. See Habeas Corpus Acts 1679 (q.v.), 1816 and 1862. See A.J.A. 1960, s. 14; O. 54, r. 9; Extradition Act 1989, s. 11. *R* v *Home Secretary, ex p Lees* [1941] 1 KB 72; and *Govt of USA* v *McCaffery* [1984] 1 WLR 867.

Habeas Corpus Act 1679. "An Act for the better securing the liberty of the subject and for prevention of imprisonment beyond the seas." Among its provisions were: that an unconvicted prisoner could demand from a judge a writ of habeas corpus (q.v.); that no person once delivered by habeas corpus should be recommitted for the same offence; and that no inhabitant of England should be sent to imprisonment out of England.

habendum. To have. The clause in a conveyance (q.v.) which defines the extent of the purchaser's interest or estate (e.g., "to hold unto the purchaser in fee simple").

habit, presumption from. The fact that a person was in the habit of acting in a certain way may be relevant to the issue of whether he acted in that way on the occasion which forms the basis of the court's enquiry. See *Joy* v *Phillips, Mill & Co Ltd* [1916] 1 KB 849 – evidence was admitted of a boy's practice of teasing a horse, in an action result-ing from his death caused by a kick from the horse. *See* EVIDENCE.

Hague Conventions. Agreements signed at the Hague Peace Conference in 1899 and 1907 relating to, e.g., the definition of a state of belligerency.

Hague Rules, application to goods of. Article I of the 1924 Rules, as amended in 1968 (by the Visby Protocol), defines goods to which the Rules apply, as including: "goods, wares, merchandise and articles of every kind whatsoever, except live animals and cargo which by the contract of carriage is stated as being carried on deck and is so carried". Carriage of goods "covers the period from the time when the goods are loaded on to the time when they are discharged from the ship". See *The Captain Gregos* [1990] 1 Lloyd's Rep 310.

half blood. *See* BLOOD RELATIONSHIP.

half-secret trust. Created where a will or other instrument discloses the existence of a trust, but not its terms, e.g., as where property is left to X " on the trusts I have discussed with him". Thus, where a sealed letter handed by the testator (q.v.) to the trustee (q.v.) is marked "not to be opened until after my death" and the trustee knows that it contains terms of a trust which he agrees to carry out, such a communication suffices to create a half-secret trust. See *Re Keen* [1937] Ch 326; *Re Bateman's WT* [1970] 3 All ER 817.

handling. "A person handles stolen goods if (otherwise than in the course of the stealing) knowing or believing them to be stolen goods he dishonestly receives the goods, or dishonestly undertakes or assists in their retention, removal, disposal or realisation by or for the benefit of another person, or if he arranges to do so": Th.A. 1968, s. 22(1). See *A.-G.'s Ref (No. 4 of 1979)* [1981] 1 All ER 1193; P. & C.E.A. 1984, s. 74; *R* v *Wood* [1987] 1 WLR

779; *R* v *Park* (1988) 87 Cr App R 164. For theft and handling as alternative charges, see *R* v *Shelton* (1986) 83 Cr App R 379.

handwriting, proof of. Types of relevant evidence include: direct evidence, e.g., testimony of the person whose writing has to be proved; opinion, e.g., by a handwriting expert; comparison (see, e.g., *Cobbett* v *Kilminster* (1865) 4 F & F 490). See also *R* v *Silverlock* [1894] 2 QB 766; *R* v *Ewing* [1983] QB 1039. See EVIDENCE.

hanging. Execution by the gallows, abolished in relation to murder by the Murder (Abolition of Death Penalty) Act 1965. See CAPITAL PUNISHMENT.

hanging, drawing and quartering. Formerly the penalty for treason. The sentence was ". . . that the offender be dragged to the gallows; that he be hanged by the neck and then cut down alive; that his entrails be taken out and burned while he is yet alive; that his head be cut off; that his body be divided into four parts and that his head and quarters be at the King's disposal." Abolished in 1870. The last offender to suffer the full penalty was Francis Towneley, a Jacobite, executed in 1746 on Kennington Common.

Hansard. Colloquial name for the *Official Report of Parliamentary Debates,* usually published daily, so-called after Luke Hansard, printer to the Commons. *Hansard* may never be referred to in construing a statute: *Davis* v *Johnson* [1979] AC 264. See also *Hadmor Productions* v *Hamilton* [1983] 1 AC 191. See INTENTION OF PARLIAMENT.

harassment, alarm or distress. The offence of using threatening, abusive or insulting words or behaviour, or disorderly behaviour, or displaying any writing, sign or other visible representation which is threatening, abusive or insulting, within the hearing or sight of a person likely to be caused harassment, alarm or distress thereby: P.O.A. 1986, s. 5(1). See *DPP* v *Clarke* [1992] Crim LR 60. Harassment is not a tort: *Patel* v *Patel* (1987) The Times, 21 August.

harassment of debtors. It is an offence for a person, with the object of coercing another to pay money claimed from the other as a debt due under a contract, to harass the other with demands for payments which are calculated to subject him or members of his family or household to alarm, distress or humiliation, or to falsely represent that criminal proceedings lie for failure to pay the money claimed: A.J.A. 1970, s. 40. See *R* v *Bokhari* [1974] Crim LR 559.

harassment of occupier. It is an offence to do acts likely to interfere with the peace or comfort of a residential occupier or member of his household or to persistently withdraw or withhold services reasonably required for occupation with intent to cause the occupier to give up occupation or refrain from exercising any right or pursuing any remedy in respect of the premises: Protection from Eviction Act 1977, s. 1(3), as amended by H.A. 1988, s. 29. See *R* v *Pheeko* [1981] 1 WLR 1117 (not an absolute offence); *R* v *Yuthiwattana* (1985) 80 CR App R 55; *R* v *Burke* [1990] 2 WLR 1313.

harassment, sexual. Causing annoyance to female employees at their place of work by pestering or taunting them in a manner involving unwelcome physical, verbal and non-verbal conduct of a sexual nature. Not specifically recognised under Sex Discrimination Acts 1975 and 1986, but a resignation consequent on sexual harassment could result in a claim for constructive dismissal (q.v.). See *Porcelli* v *Strathclyde Regional Council* [1986] ICR 564; *Cornelius* v *University College of Swansea* [1987] IRLR 141.

harbour. Port, estuary, haven, dock or other place containing waters, and controlled by the statutory harbour authorities. See Harbours Act 1964, s. 57.

harbouring. Providing shelter, with the object of concealing. At one time it was an offence to harbour a thief or reputed thief, under Prevention of Crimes Act 1871 (now repealed). The action which could be brought for harbouring a wife or child (which provided a method of seeking damages from the person with whom a spouse was committing adultery) was abolished under Law Reform (Misc. Provs.) Act 1970.

hard cases. Phrase used by Dworkin (see *Taking Rights Seriously*, 1978) to refer to cases in which the application by the court of a precise, unmodified legal rule would almost certainly produce injustice.

hardship. "The word 'hardship' is not a word of art . . . in my judgment the ordinary sensible man would take the view that there are two aspects of 'hardship' – that which the sufferor from the hardship thinks he is suffering and that which a reasonable bystander with knowledge of all the facts would think he was suffering": per Lawton J in *Rukat v Rukat* [1975] 1 All ER 343. "Undue hardship" means excessive hardship: per Brandon J in *The Pegasus* [1967] 2 QB 86. See GRAVE HARDSHIP.

harmonisation of laws. Phrase used to refer to the adjustment of legislation by member states of the EEC (q.v.) in a given area of social and economic policy.

hay bote. See ESTOVERS.

hazardous substances. Not defined by statute. Term generally includes inherently dangerous, unstable materials. The Secretary of State may make regulations specifying such substances: Planning (Hazardous Substances) Act 1990, s. 5. Consent for the presence of such substances is required under s. 4(1); for exceptions, see s. 4(2)(4). See also En.P.A. 1990, Sch. 13; SI 1992/725.

headings. Words prefixed to sections of a statute, regarded as preambles (q.v.). Reference to headings may be made so as to assist in resolving an ambiguity. See *DPP v Schildkamp* [1971] AC 1.

head lease. A lease (q.v.) from which lesser interests (i.e., sub-leases) have been created. See *Gratton-Storey v Lewis* (1987) 283 EG 1562.

head note. Summary of points decided in a case, placed at the head of a law report.

health record. Record consisting of information relating to the physical or mental health of an individual who can be identified from that information, or from that and other information in the possession of the record holder, and has been made by or on behalf of a health professional in connection with the care of that individual: Access to Health Records Act 1990, s. 1(1). For right of access, see s. 3.

Health Service, National. The health service established in England and Wales and in Scotland respectively in pursuance of s. 1 of National Health Services Act 1946 (for England and Wales), 1977, and National Health Service (Scotland) Act 1947. See Health Services Act 1980; Health and S.S.A. 1984; Health and Medicines Act 1988; NHS and Community Care Act 1990.

hearing. The trial of a cause or action.

hearsay evidence. See EVIDENCE, HEARSAY.

hearsay evidence, victim's statement as. Hearsay evidence of a statement made to a witness by the victim of an attack, naming or describing the attacker, is admissible in evidence at the trial of the attacker, as part of the *res gestae* (q.v.), if the statement was made in conditions which were sufficiently spontaneous and contemporaneous with the attack to preclude the possibility of concoction or distortion. See *R v Andrews* [1987] AC 281 (overruling *R v Bedingfield* (1879) 14 Cox CC 341).

hedge and ditch presumption. Where there is nothing else to identify a boundary (q.v.) and there is a ditch and a bank, the presumption is that the person who dug the ditch dug it to the extremity of his land and threw the soil on his own land to make the bank: *Fisher v Winch* [1939] 1 KB 666. The presumption may be rebutted by production of the title deeds. See *Falkingham v Farley* (1991) The Times, 22 Feb.

heir. One who succeeds by descent (q.v.). Under L.P.A. 1925, s. 132, a limitation of property in favour of the heir (special or general) which, prior to the Act, would have conferred on the heir an estate by purchase, confers a corresponding equitable interest (q.v.) on the person who would have answered the description of heir before the Act.

heir apparent. A person who, if he survives his ancestor, will be his heir. He is not the heir until after the death of the ancestor, since *nemo est heres viventis* (q.v.).

heirloom. "Any piece of household stuff which, by custom of some countries, having belonged to a house for certain descents, goes with the house, after the death of the owner, unto the heir and not to the executors": *Termes de la Ley*. The tenant for life can sell heirlooms, the money arising from the sale being capital money: S.L.A. 1925, s. 67.

heir presumptive. One who would be the heir (e.g., an eldest son) if his ancestor were to die immediately.

heirs of the body. Words of limitation in a conveyance which comprehends "all the posterity of the donee in succession": *Re Woodward Estate* [1945] 1 WLR 722. *See* LIMITATION, WORDS OF.

Henry VIII clause. Clause in a statute conferring powers, e.g., on a minister, to make some exceptions to the operation of that statute, or to make other alterations of detail. So-called because of that monarch's predilection for the exercise of personal powers. See, e.g., Banking Act 1987, s. 4(3).

hereditaments. Real property which devolved on an heir (q.v.) on an intestacy (q.v.). Classified as: *incorporeal* (rights of property, e.g., easements); *corporeal* (physical objects, e.g., land, buildings).

heresy. Deliberate and overt denial of some accepted dogma of the church. A capital offence until 1677. See the Ecclesiastical Jurisdiction Measure 1963; *Noble* v *Voysey* (1871) LR 3 PC 357.

High Commission, Court of. Originated in 1583 in commissions granted for enforcing the state's religious policies. Could fine, imprison, excommunicate. See *Chancey's Case* (1611) 12 Co Rep 82. Abolished in 1641.

High Court of Justice, the. A court of unlimited civil jurisdiction with appellate jurisdiction in civil and criminal matters. Part of the Supreme Court of England and Wales (S.C.A. 1981, s. 1). Consists of the Lord Chancellor, Lord Chief Justice, President of the Family Division, Vice-Chancellor, and up to eighty-five puisne judges. (High Court work generally involves one judge sitting alone.) It sits at the Royal Courts of Justice in London and at 26 first-tier Crown Court centres outside London. Its divisions are Chancery Div., Queen's Bench Div. and Family Div: S.C.A. 1981, ss. 4, 5. The Patents Court is part of Chancery Div.; the Admiralty Court and Commercial Court are part of Queen's Bench Div.: s. 6. For the general jurisdiction, see ss. 19, 25–31. For the distribution of business, see s. 61, Sch. 1. For the allocation of business between the High Court and

county courts, see C.L.S.A. 1990, s. 1; *Practice Direction* [1991] 1 WLR 695. For penalty for launching proceedings in the wrong court, see S.C.A. 1981, s. 51(8)(9), substituted by C.L.S.A. 1990, s. 4.

high seas. The seas lying more than 5 km beyond the coast of a country. The criminal law of England extends to all British ships upon the high seas (*Oteri* v *The Queen* [1976] 1 WLR 1272) and to acts of British subjects when passengers on foreign ships on the high seas (*R* v *Kelly* [1982] AC 665).

high treason. Formerly treason which was not *petit treason* (i.e., the killing of a master by his servant). In effect, treason against the Sovereign. *Petit treason* was abolished in 1828. High treason is now known merely as "treason". *See* TREASON.

highway. A road or way either on land or water (e.g., path, bridge) used by the public for passing and repassing as a matter of right. It may exist by statute, dedication (q.v.) or prescription (q.v.). See Highways Act 1980; T.C.P.A. 1990, s. 247; New Roads and Street Work Act 1991, s. 86.

Highway Code. A standard of conduct for road users, issued by the Secretary of State for the Environment. Failure to observe the Code does not, in itself, render a person liable to criminal proceedings; it may, however, be taken into account in such proceedings (Road Traffic Act 1972, s. 37 (as substituted by Transport Act 1981, s. 60)). See Road Traffic Act 1988, s. 38.

highway, nuisance in relation to. "Any wrongful act or omission upon or near a highway, whereby the public are prevented from freely, safely and conveniently passing along the highway": *Jacobs* v *Lee* [1950] AC 361. See Highways Act 1980; *Haydon* v *Kent CC* [1978] QB 343.

highway, obstruction of. 1. If a person's land abuts on the highway he can maintain an action of trespass against a person who uses the highway in an unreasonable manner, e.g., by obstruction. See *Harrison* v *Duke of Rutland* [1893] 1 QB 142. 2. The wilful (i.e., intentional) obstruction of a highway is an offence. "An obstruction is something which permanently or temporarily removes the whole or part of the highway from public use": *per* Lord Evershed in *Trevett* v *Lee* [1955] 1 All ER 406. See Highways Act 1980, s. 137; Rights of Way Act 1990. *Cooper* v *MPC* (1986) 82 Cr App R 238; *Devon CC* v *Gateway Foodmarkets* [1990] COD 324.

hijacking. Unlawfully seizing by force or threats of any kind the control of an aircraft in flight: Aviation Security Act 1982, s. 1(1). For hijacking of a ship or fixed platform, see Aviation and Maritime Security Act 1990, ss. 9, 10.

hire. Payment for the temporary use of something, e.g., a good, or a person's labour power. In a contract of hire there is an implied warranty (q.v.) that the goods hired are as fit for the purpose of their hiring as skill and care can make them. Under C.C.A. 1974, a hirer is the bailee of goods under a consumer hire agreement (q.v.) or the person to whom the hirer's rights and duties under the agreement have passed by assignment (q.v.) or operation of law.

hire or reward, for. "The probable explanation of the composite phrase is that the words 'for hire' were used because they were the most familiar words to describe remuneration for carriage in some vehicles, and the words 'or reward' were added since 'reward' is a wider word and apt to cover some forms of remuneration or some arrangements for which the words 'for hire' might not be appropriate": *per* Lord Pearson in *Albert* v *Motor Insurers' Bureau* [1971] 2 All ER 1345.

hire purchase agreement. An agreement, other than a conditional sale agreement (q.v.) under which goods are bailed in return for periodical payments by the bailee and the property in the goods passes to the bailee if the terms of the agreement are not complied with and the bailee exercises his option to purchase or some other specified event occurs: C.C.A. 1974, s. 189(1). See I.C.T.A. 1988, s. 784(6).

historic buildings. *See* LISTED BUILDINGS.

HMSO. Her Majesty's Stationery Office, controlled by the Queen's Printer of Acts of Parliament and responsible for supplying official publications. Copyright of all government documents vests in the Controller of the Office.

holder. The holder of a bill is the payee or endorsee who is in possession of it,

or the bearer thereof: B.Ex.A. 1882, s. 2. *See* BILL OF EXCHANGE.

holder for value. Holder of a bill of exchange (q.v.) for which value has been given at some time (not necessarily by the holder himself).

holder in due course. A holder who has taken a bill which is regular and complete on the face of it under the following conditions: that he became the holder before it was overdue and without notice of its having been previously dishonoured (if that were so); that he took it in good faith and for value; that at the time the bill was negotiated he had no notice of defective title of the negotiator. See B.Ex.A. 1882, ss. 29(1), 30(2), 38(2). *See* BILL OF EXCHANGE.

holding charge. A minor charge made pending the investigation of a more serious charge. See, e.g., *Christie* v *Leachinsky* [1947] AC 573.

holding company. *See* SUBSIDIARY COMPANY.

holding out. A course of action which persuades others to believe in a party's possessing an authority which, in fact, does not exist. A person who acts in this way may be stopped from denying the truth of his representations if others have acted on them. "The holding out must be to the particular individual who says he relied on it, or under such circumstances of publicity as to justify the inference that he knew of it and acted upon it": *per* Lord Lindley in *Farquaharson Bros.* v *King & Co.* [1902] AC 325. See Partnership Act 1890, ss. 3, 14. *Hudgell Yeates & Co* v *Watson* [1978] 2 All ER 363.

holding over. The continuation in possession of land by a tenant (q.v.) after the expiration of the tenancy agreement. The tenant may become liable to an action for possession and double rent and damages.

holiday lettings. The letting of property for a holiday under terms allowing its recovery at the end of that period. Not a protected tenancy (q.v.): see Rent Act 1977, s. 9. ("Holiday" was considered in *Buchmann* v *May* [1978] 2 All ER 993, to be "a period of cessation from work or a period of recreation.")

holograph. A document, such as a will or deed, written entirely in the testator's or grantor's own hand. See *Re Ka-nani* (1978) 122 SJ 611.

homage. The ritual acknowledgement by a feudal vassal of the bond of tenure between himself and his lord. It included the act of kneeling (a symbolic surrender), the lord's clasping his hands (acceptance of surrender), and an oath of fealty. See FEUDAL SYSTEM.

home. One's dwelling place. See *Re Y.* [1985] Fam 136 – concept of "home" considered incapable of precise definition, but it should comprise an element of regular occupation (past, present or intended for the future) with a degree of permanency, based on some right of occupation; H.A. 1985, s. 81.

homelessness. "A person is homeless if he has no accommodation in England, Scotland or Wales": H.A. 1985, s. 58(1), and (2A)–(2B) (inserted by H. & P.A. 1986, s. 14). A person is treated as having no accommodation if, e.g., there is no accommodation which he, together with any person who normally resides with him as a member of the family or in circumstances in which it is reasonable for that person to reside with him, is entitled to occupy by virtue of an interest in it: s. 58(2). A person is threatened with homelessness if it is likely that he will become homeless within 28 days: s. 58(4). For "becoming homeless intentionally", see s. 60. A local housing authority (q.v.) must enquire into cases of possible or threatened homelessness and provide accommodation: ss. 62, 65. See, e.g., *R v Newham LBC, ex p Tower Hamlets BC* [1991] 1 WLR 1032. See ACCOMMODATION, PRIORITY NEED FOR.

home loss. Term used in Land Compensation Act 1973, as amended by Planning and Compensation Act 1991, s. 68, whereby compensation is made available for the loss of a house acquired by a local authority for demolition, and for injury sustained through the loss of a house.

home, mobile. A caravan (q.v.): Mobile Homes Act 1983, s. 5(1).

Home Secretary. The minister in charge of the Home Office, which deals, in general, with the domestic functions in England and Wales not specifically assigned to other departments of state.

He is generally responsible for the maintenance of law and order, and exercises some prerogative powers of the Crown, including the prerogative of mercy (q.v.). He is concerned, specifically, with the administration of justice, the prison service, treatment of offenders, community relations, immigration and naturalisation procedures, supervision of the control of firearms and dangerous drugs.

homeworker. Person who contracts with another for the execution of work to be done in a place not under the control or management of that other and who does not normally make use of the service of more than two persons in the carrying out of contracts for the execution of work with statutory minimum remuneration: Wages Act 1986, s. 26(1).

homicide. The killing of a human being by a human being. May be categorised as lawful (e.g., committed in the execution of justice) or unlawful, or as justifiable (q.v.) excusable, (q.v.) or criminal (i.e., a killing, neither justifiable nor excusable, such as murder, manslaughter, infanticide). See INFANTICIDE; MANSLAUGHTER; MURDER.

homosexual conduct. Sexual activity with a member of one's own sex. Buggery (q.v.) or gross indecency (q.v.) with another man is no longer an offence if both parties have attained the age of 21, if both have consented and the act is done in private: S.O.A. 1967. A consenting partner who is under 21 is guilty of an offence. Proceedings may require the consent of the DPP (q.v.). Lesbianism (q.v.) is not an offence. The promotion of homosexuality by teaching or by publishing material is prohibited under L.G.A. 1988, s. 28.

honeste vivere. Phrase used by the Roman jurist Ulpian and adopted in Justinian's *Institutes* (AD 533) in a summary of the basic precepts of the law, thus: *honeste vivere, alterum non laedere, suum cuique tribuere* (to live honestly, not to harm another and to give every man his due).

honorarium. A voluntary, or honorary, payment or reward, often given as compensation for services in circumstances in which payment cannot be enforced at law or in which custom and propriety might not allow a fee or fixed payment. *See* BARRISTER'S FEES.

honour clauses. Clauses in agreements intended as express declarations that transactions between the parties to which those agreements relate are not to be binding in law. The courts will generally give effect to such declarations. See, e.g., *Edwards* v *Skyways* [1964] 1 WLR 349.

hospital. A health service hospital within the meaning of the National Health Service Act 1977, or any accommodation provided by any person pursuant to arrangements made under the 1977 Act, s. 23(1), and used as a hospital: Disabled Persons (Services Consultation and Representation) Act 1986, s. 16.

hospital order. An order by the magistrates' court (q.v.) or Crown Court (q.v.) authorising an offender's admission to, and detention in a specified hospital. See M.H.A. 1983, s. 37; and Courts Act 1971, ss. 56, 62. Applications for discharge are heard by Area Mental Health Review Tribunals (q.v.). See *R* v *Castro* [1985] Crim LR 527.

hospital premises. Premises "used or to be used for the prevention, diagnosis or treatment of illness or for the reception of patients": Health Services Act 1976, s. 14(1).

hospital, special. *See* SPECIAL HOSPITAL.

hostage. 1. Person taken by a belligerent and held as security. 2. Person seized in the UK or elsewhere in order to compel a state, international governmental organisation or person to do or abstain from doing any act. One who threatens to kill, injure or continue to detain the hostage commits an offence under the Taking of Hostages Act 1982, s. 1(1). See Extradition Act 1989, s. 25.

hostel. A building in which is provided, for persons generally or for a class or classes of persons, residential accommodation (otherwise than in separate and self-contained sets of premises) and either board or facilities for the preparation of food adequate to the needs of those persons, or both: H.A. 1985, s. 622, as amended.

hostile witness. One who, in the opinion of the court, is hostile to the party calling him and is unwilling to

tell the truth. With leave of the court that party may cross-examine him. See Criminal Procedure Act 1865, s. 3; Civil Evidence Act 1968, s. 3(1) (*a*); *R* v *Pitt* [1983] QB 25; *R* v *Prefas* [1987] Crim LR 327. *See* WITNESS.

hostilities. Acts or operations, usually connected with war (q.v.), committed by belligerents: *Spinney's Ltd* v *Royal Insurance Co Ltd* [1980] 1 Lloyd's Rep. 406.

hotchpot. (*Hocher* = to shake together.) The bringing together of properties into a common lot so that equality of division may be assured. Thus, an advancement by a deceased person in his lifetime must be brought into account against the share which the child to whom the advancement has been made would receive under an intestacy (q.v.): see, e.g., *Taylor* v *Taylor* (1875) LR 20 Eq 155; and *Re Osoba* [1978] 1 WLR 791.

hotel. "An establishment held out by the proprietor as offering food, drink and, if required, sleeping accommodation, without special contract, to any traveller presenting himself who appears able and willing to pay a reasonable sum for the services and facilities provided and who is in a fit state to be received": Hotel Proprietors Act 1956, s. 1(3). See Capital Allowances Act 1990, s. 19. *See* INN.

hours of darkness. The time between half-an-hour after sunset and half-an-hour before sunrise: Highways Act 1980, s. 329(1).

house. Includes any part of a building occupied or intended to be occupied as a separate dwelling, and any yard, garden, outhouses and appurtenances belonging to the house or usually enjoyed with it: Housing Associations Act 1985, s. 106(1), as amended. See also Leasehold Reform Act 1967, s. 1; *Lake* v *Bennett* [1970] 1 QB 663; *Malpas* v *St Ermine's Property Co.* [1992] 17 EG 112 (maisonette may be a "house").

house bote. *See* ESTOVERS.

housebreaking. Breaking and entering (q.v.) a dwelling house or other building. *See* BURGLARY.

housebreaking implements, possession of. "A person shall be guilty of an offence if, when not at his place of abode, he has with him any article for use in the course of or in connection with any burglary, theft or cheat": Th.A. 1968, s. 25(1). See *R* v *Ellames* [1974] 3 All ER 130 (it was held that s. 25 was aimed at acts preparatory to a burglary, theft or cheat); *R* v *Bundy* [1977] 2 All ER 382. See BURGLARY.

household. The term has been held to have "an abstract meaning": *Santos* v *Santos* [1972] Fam 247. "A family unit or something akin to a family unit – a group of persons, held together by a particular kind of tie, who normally live together, even if individual members of the group may be temporarily separated from it": *per* Lord Emslie in *McGregor* v *Haswell* 1983, SLT 626.

house in multiple occupation. "A house which is occupied by persons who do not form a single household." See H.A. 1985, s. 365; L.G.H.A. 1989, s. 100(1). The Secretary of State may make provisions by regulations for ensuring that the person managing the house observes proper standards of management: s. 369.

housekeeping allowances, savings from. "If any question arises as to the right of a husband or wife to money derived from any allowance made by the husband for the expenses of the matrimonial home or for similar purposes, or to any property acquired out of such money, the money or property shall, in the absence of any agreement between them to the contrary, be treated as belonging to the husband and wife in equal shares": Married Women's Property Act 1964, s. 1.

House, Leader of the. Member of the House of Commons (and Minister of the Crown) who is responsible for the arrangement of government business in the House. The Leader of the Lords has similar functions. See Parliamentary and Other Pensions Act 1987, s. 5(1).

House of Commons. The Lower House of Parliament. A representative assembly elected by universal adult suffrage, consisting of 650 members (523 for England, 38 for Wales, 72 for Scotland, 17 for N Ireland). Its chief officer is the Speaker (q.v.). Persons disqualified for membership include: aliens; persons under 21; holders of certain judicial offices; civil servants; members of the police and regular armed forces; members of a legislature of a country outside the UK: House of Commons Disqualification Act 1975, s. 1(1). A quorum for voting purposes is 40 members. See PARLIAMENT.

House of Commons, Corporate Officer of. The Clerk of the House is empowered to acquire, hold and dispose of land and other property for any purpose of the House: Parliamentary Corporate Bodies Act 1992, s. 2. A similar officer is appointed for the Lords.

House of Lords. The Upper House of Parliament. It consists of the *Lords Temporal* (i.e., all hereditary peers and peeresses who have not disclaimed their peerages under the Peerage Act 1963, life peers and peeresses, Lords of Appeal in Ordinary) and the *Lords Spiritual* (Archbishops of Canterbury and York, Bishops of London, Winchester and Durham and 21 other senior bishops of the Church of England). The House (comprising 1186 members) is presided over by the Lord Chancellor. The Lords have a restricted right (see Parliament Acts 1911, 1949) to initiate, amend and reject Bills. See PARLIAMENT; PEER.

House of Lords, correction of its errors. "[Their Lordships] propose to modify their present practice and, while treating former decisions of this House as normally binding, to depart from a previous decision when it appears right to do so": *Practice Statement* [1966] 1 WLR 1234. See, e.g., *R* v *Shivpuri* [1987] AC 1. See PRECEDENT.

House of Lords, jurisdiction of. The right of a peer to be tried "by his peers" was abolished by the C.J.A. 1948. The House has full appellate jurisdiction. In civil cases it hears appeals from the Court of Appeal (q.v.) with leave of that court or the Appeals Committee of the House. In criminal cases it hears appeals from the Court of Appeal if that court certifies that a point of law of general public importance is involved and either the court or the House gives leave to appeal because the point is one which ought to be considered by the House. It may hear appeals from the High Court, the Court of Session, the Court of Appeal in N. Ireland, the Courts-Martial Appeals Court. The judges in the Lords are Lords of Appeal in Ordinary (q.v.)

and peers who have held, or hold, high judicial office (at least three designated Lords of Appeal must hear an appeal). Lay peers do not participate (see *O'Connell v R* (1844) 11 Cl & F 155). The Appellate Committee, presided over by the Lord Chancellor (q.v.) or the senior Lord of Appeal in Ordinary, reports its conclusions to the House. See A.J.A. 1960, s. 1; and Criminal Appeal Act 1968, s. 33.

House of Lords, petitions for appeal to. Petitions for leave to appeal are referred to the Appeal Committee (three Lords of Appeal) who will consider whether it appears competent to be received by the House and, if so, whether it should be referred for an oral hearing. See *House of Lords Directions as to Procedure* (1988) Cr App R 105.

housing accommodation, privately let. Local housing authorities may provide financial assistance for the purpose of acquisition, construction, conversion, improvement, maintenance of property intended to be privately let as housing accommodation: L.G.A. 1988, Part III.

housing action trust area. Area designated by order under H.A. 1988, s. 60, comprising two or more parcels of land, and involving the physical state, design, management of housing accommodation, social activities, etc. The trust may secure repair, improvement, proper management and use of that accommodation.

housing association. A society, body of trustees or company not trading for profit, established so as to construct, improve or manage houses: Housing Associations Act 1985, s. 1. For registration, see ss. 3–7, as amended by H.A. 1988, Sch. 18.

housing association tenancy. A tenancy arising where the interest of the landlord belongs to a housing association (q.v.) or housing trust (q.v.), or to the Housing Corporation (q.v.); Rent Act 1977, s. 86. For rent limits, see s. 88, as amended by H.A. 1988, Sch. 18. See also H.A. 1980, s. 56.

housing authority, local. A district council, London borough council, the Common Council of the City of London, the Council of the Isles of Scilly: H.A. 1985, s. 1. It is empowered to pro-

vide housing accommodation by erecting or acquiring houses or converting buildings into houses: s. 9. It may make such reasonable charges as it may determine for the tenancy or occupation of its houses: s. 24. For "public sector housing", see H.A. 1985, s. 429A (inserted by H. & P.A. 1986, s. 16).

housing benefit. Benefit under S.S. Contributions and Benefits Act 1992, s. 130; S.S. (Consequential Provisions) A. 1992, Sch. 2, amending Rent Act 1977, s. 72, paid to a claimant who is liable to make payments in respect of a house he occupies as his home and there is an appropriate maximum housing benefit in his case and he has no income or his income does not exceed the applicable amount.

Housing Corporation. An authority set up under H.A. 1964, s. 1, with extended powers and functions under H.A. 1974, s. 1 (both Acts now repealed and re-enacted), which is concerned with, e.g., promotion and assistance of development of registered housing associations and unregistered building societies. See Housing Associations Act 1985, Part III; T.C.G.A. 1992, s. 218.

housing subsidy. Subsidy payable to local authorities, new town corporations and Development Board for Rural Wales: H.A. 1985, s. 421. The subsidy to local authorities is calculated by adding the base amount (see s. 423) to the housing costs differential (see s. 424) and subtracting the local contribution differential (see s. 425): s. 422. For subsidy to other bodies, see s. 426. See L.G.H.A. 1989, Sch. 11.

housing trust. A corporation or body of persons which is required by the terms of its constituent instrument to devote its funds to the provision of houses, and other purposes incidental thereto, or is required to devote its funds to charitable purposes and in fact devotes them to the provision of houses: Housing Associations Act 1985, s. 2.

hue and cry. (*Huer* = to shout.) Ancient pursuit of a felon, with cries and shouts of alarm. The neighbours of the person wronged by the felon were under a duty to assist in the pursuit. *See* CLAMEUR DE HARO.

human habitation, unfitness for. A house will be regarded as unfit for human habitation if it is defective in one of the following matters so that it is not reasonably suitable for occupation in that condition: repair, stability, freedom from damp, lighting, ventilation, water supply, drainage and sanitary conveniences, cooking facilities. See H.A. 1985, s. 604, substituted by L.G.H.A. 1989, Sch. 11. *See* REPAIRING OBLIGATION.

Human Rights, European Convention on. Convention signed and ratified by members of the Council of Europe in November 1950 and in force since September 1953. Rights and freedoms it purports to protect include: right to life; freedom from torture and slavery; right to liberty and fair trial; freedom of thought and religion, etc. Under the Convention were created the Commission on Human Rights and the Court of Human Rights (q.v.). Not a part of English Law: *R* v *Secretary of State for Home Department, ex p Brind* [1991] 2 WLR 588. "The court can and should take the Convention into account. They should take it into account whenever interpreting a statute which affects the rights and liberties of the individual": *per* Lord Denning in *R* v *Secretary of State for the Home Department, ex p Bhajan Singh* [1975] 2 All ER 1081. See *Monnell and Morris* v *UK* [1988] 10 EHRR 205.

Human Rights, European Court of. *See* EUROPEAN COURT OF HUMAN RIGHTS.

Human Rights, Universal Declaration of. Adopted by the United Nations Commission on Human Rights and by the General Assembly in 1948. Relates to rights such as life, liberty, security of a person, freedom from arbitrary arrest, right to a fair hearing, freedom of thought and religion, right to social security and to work, right to education.

human tissue, removal of. Under Human Tissue Act 1961 (as amended by Corneal Tissue Act 1986), the removal of parts of the body of a deceased person by a medical practitioner for therapeutic purposes, medical education or research, is permitted if that person has so requested in writing, or orally during his last illness in the presence of two or more witnesses.

hundred. A territorial division, known in Anglo-Saxon society, consisting of a group of adjoining townships. It may have consisted of an area of one hundred households. Each hundred had its court, held once a month, presided over by the hundred *ealdor* (chief officer); its jurisdiction was based on custom.

hung jury. *See* JURY, HUNG.

husband and wife. At common law they were considered as "one person" so that, e.g., the husband was entitled on marriage to chattels and choses in possession (q.v.) belonging to his wife. Statutes have vitiated the significance of this concept. Thus, e.g., under Th.A. 1968, s. 30(1), husbands and wives are liable in respect of offences which they commit against one another's property as if they were not married; under Law Reform (Married Women and Tortfeasors) Act 1935, s. 1, a married woman is capable of acquiring, holding and alienating property as if a feme sole (q.v.). See also Law Reform (Husband and Wife) Act 1962; Matrimonial Proceedings and Property Act 1970; P. & C.E.A. 1984, s. 80; and O. 89.

husbandry. Generally, the business of a farmer. See I.C.T.A. 1988, s. 33; *Jones* v *Nuttall* (1926) 10 TC 346.

hybrid Bill. A parliamentary Bill which, though of general application, affects some local or private interests. A Bill of this nature is subject to special procedure; in general, it is treated like a private bill after its second reading.

hypothecation. The right of a ship's master, in case of necessity, to assign the ship or the ship and its cargo by bottomry bond undertaking to repay the principal and interest on the safe arrival of the ship. A *letter of hypothecation* is one addressed to a bank, giving details of a shipment of goods relating to a draft. In the event of dishonour of the draft, the bank is allowed to sell the goods. *See* BOTTOMRY.

hypothetical dispute. Issues based on mere supposition. In general, the courts will not adjudicate upon disputes of this kind: *Glasgow Navigation Co* v *Iron Ore Co* [1910] AC 293. Nor will the courts pronounce on abstract questions of law: *Ainsbury* v *Millington* [1987] 1 WLR 379.

I

id certum est quod certum reddi potest.
That is certain which can be made certain. See, e.g., *Plant* v *Bourne* [1897] 2 Ch 281.

identification parade. Procedure whereby persons, including an arrested suspect, are viewed by a witness for purposes of identification. See Code of Practice issued under P. & C.E.A. 1984; *R* v *McCay* [1990] 1 WLR 645; *R* v *Penny* (1991) The Times, 17 Oct.

identity, evidence of. 1. Primary evidence, e.g., obtained by an identification parade (q.v.) before trial. See also revised Code of Practice, under P. & C.E.A. 1984, Code D, allowing identification by video. For voice identification, see *R* v *Robb* (1991) The Times, 6 Feb. 2. Secondary evidence, e.g., by an identifying witness who swears that he identified the accused on a former occasion, and by another witness to say that he saw this. See *R* v *Christie* [1914] AC 545; *R* v *Turnbull* [1977] QB 224; *R* v *Fergus* (1991) The Times, 11 Nov. 3. Circumstantial evidence, e.g., the accused's fingerprints.

idle and disorderly person. One who was found guilty of a relatively trivial offence under the Vagrancy Act 1824, e.g., begging in a public place.

ignorantia juris neminem excusat. Ignorance of the law does not excuse. When mistake is pleaded as a defence, the mistake must be one of fact, not of law. "Every man of England is, in judgment of law, party to the making of an Act of Parliament, being present thereat by his representatives": Blackstone. "Every man must be taken to be cognisant of the law, otherwise there is no knowing of the extent to which the excuse of ignorance might be carried. It would be urged in almost every case": *R* v *Bailey* (1800) Russ & Ry 1. See *R* v *Esop* (1836) 7 C & P 456; *Shelley* v *Paddock* [1980] QB 348; *Secretary of State* v *Hart* [1982] 1 WLR 481.

illegal. In violation of a law or rule which has the force of law.

illegal contracts. Contracts which are forbidden by statute or are contrary to common law or public policy and are, therefore, generally void. Examples: a contract tending to injure the public service, e.g., by the attempted sale of a public office or a contract to procure a title of honour (see *Parkinson* v *College of Ambulance* [1925] 2 KB 1); a contract in restraint of trade (see *Nordenfelt* v *Maxim Nordenfelt Gun Co Ltd* [1894] AC 535); a contract to commit a criminal offence or civil wrong (see *Napier* v *National Business Agency* [1951] 2 All ER 263). See also *Howard* v *Shirlstar Container Transport Ltd* [1991] 1 WLR 1292. *See* CONTRACT.

illegal entrant. "A person unlawfully entering [the UK] or seeking to enter in breach of a deportation order or of the immigration laws and includes a person who has so entered": Immigration Act 1971, s. 33(1). His detention is lawful: Sch 2. See, e.g., *R* v *Secretary of State for the Home Department, ex p Chan* (1992) The Times, 1 Jan.; *R* v *Naille* (1992) The Times, 20 April (disembarkation is not entry).

illegal trust. One which offends against statute or morality or public policy. In the case of an intentional creation of a trust for an illegal purpose, a resulting trust (q.v.) may be implied in favour of the settlor if the illegal purpose has not been executed. See *Ayerst* v *Jenkins* (1873) LR 16 Eq 275. *See* TRUST.

illegitimate child. One born out of lawful wedlock. "References (however expressed) to any relationship between two persons shall, unless the contrary intention appears, be construed without regard to whether or not the father and mother of either of them, or the father and mother of any person through whom the relationship is deduced, have or had been married to each other": F.L.R.A. 1987, s. 1(1). For property rights, e.g., succession on intestacy, see 1987 Act, Part III. See also SI 1991/1980.

illusory appointment. An appointment (q.v.), under which a merely nominal share was appointed to an object, which could be set aside: *Wilson v Piggott* (1974) 2 Ves Jun 35. Under L.P.A. 1925, s. 158, no appointment is to be invalid merely on the ground that "an unsubstantial, illusory or nominal share only is appointed to or left unappointed to devolve upon any one or more of the objects of the power".

illusory trust. A conveyance by a debtor to trustees upon trust for creditors which can be revoked, in some circumstances, by the debtor, is an example. See *Johns v James* (1878) 8 Ch D 744. *See* TRUST.

immediate. "It does not mean instantaneous . . . it connotes proximity in time and proximity in causation": *R v Horseferry Rd Stipendiary Magistrate, ex p Siadatan* [1991] 1 All ER 324.

immigration. Entering a country for purposes of permanent residence there. See Immigration Act 1971, which confers the right of abode on, e.g., citizens of the UK and colonies who are connected with Britain by birth. Power to refuse leave to enter the UK rests initially with immigration officers. The Secretary of State has power to give leave to remain in the UK: s. 4. See also Immigration Act 1988.

immoral contracts. Agreements founded on an immoral consideration (q.v.). In general, they are void. See *Wilson v Carnley* [1908] 1 KB 729; *Fender v Mildmay* [1938] AC 11. *See* EX TURPI CAUSA NON ORITUR ACTIO.

immovables. Generally, land and property attached.

immunity. Freedom or exemption from some obligation, penalty, or power of another. Thus, e.g., a barrister (q.v.) has immunity from being sued in contract for professional negligence; no action lies against a judge in respect of words or actions arising in the exercise of his judicial office ("judicial immunity" (q.v.)); no action lies in respect of words spoken in the course of an action by, e.g., advocates or parties; no foreign sovereign may be impleaded in an action *in personam*, or *in*

rem (see *The Cristina* [1938] AC 485). For Crown immunity, see, e.g., Crown Proceedings Act 1947; *Pearce v Secretary of State for Defence* [1988] 2 WLR 1027.

immunity, diplomatic. Diplomatic privilege (q.v.).

immunity from jurisdiction, state. A state is immune from the jurisdiction of the courts of the UK and courts shall give effect to that immunity, even though the state does not appear in the proceedings in question: State Immunity Act 1978, s. 1. *See* IMMUNITY, RESTRICTIVE.

immunity, restrictive. Doctrine suggesting that, in the interests of justice, it may be necessary to allow individuals engaging in commercial transactions with states to bring such transactions before the courts. See *Trendtex Trading Corp v Central Bank of Nigeria* [1977] QB 529. The doctrine is accepted as part of the law of England: *I Congreso Del Partido* [1983] 1 AC 244.

immunity, vicarious. Principle that an agent performing a contract is entitled to any immunity conferred on his principal. It was enunciated in *Elder, Dempster & Co v Paterson, Zochonis & Co* [1929] AC 522, but rejected in *Scruttons Ltd v Midland Silicones Ltd* [1962] AC 446.

impeachable of waste. Liability of a person, e.g., tenant for life (q.v.), for waste. See, e.g., *Re Ridge* (1885) 31 Ch D 504. *See* WASTE.

impeachment. (Impeach = to challenge the credibility of; to accuse.) The prosecution of an offender by the House of Commons (q.v.) before the House of Lords (q.v.). The jurisdiction was last exercised in 1806 (in the case of Viscount Melville, First Lord of the Admiralty, for alleged malversation in office).

impeding apprehension or prosecution. "Where a person has committed an arrestable offence, any other person who, knowing or believing him to be guilty of the offence or of some other arrestable offence, does without lawful authority or reasonable excuse any act with intent to impede his apprehension or prosecution shall be guilty of an offence": C.L.A. 1967, s. 4. *See* ARRESTABLE OFFENCE.

imperative theory of law. Known also as the "command theory" (q.v.).

imperfect gift. *See* GIFT, IMPERFECT.

imperfect trust. An executory trust. *See* EXECUTORY.

imperitia culpae adnumeratur. Want of skill is considered a fault. See *Philips v William Whitely Ltd* [1938] 1 All ER 566; *Mutual Life and Citizens' Assurance Co Ltd v Evatt* [1971] AC 793.

impersonation. False personation (q.v.) for some improper motive.

implead. To sue or prosecute.

implied. Suggested or understood by implication or deduction from the circumstances.

implied condition. Where a buyer makes known to a seller, expressly or by implication, the purpose for which goods are required, in a manner showing that he relies on the seller's skill or judgment and the goods are of a description which it is in the course of the seller's business to supply, there is an implied condition that the goods are reasonably fit for the purpose: S.G.A. 1979, s. 14.

implied contract. A contract inferred from the conduct of parties or from some relationship existing between them. *See* CONTRACT; QUASI-CONTRACTS.

implied covenants. *See* COVENANTS, IMPLIED.

implied malice. 1. An intention (in a case of homicide) to do grievous bodily harm as compared with express malice, i.e., an intention to kill. 2. Malice inferred from all the circumstances. *See* MALICE.

implied tenancy. *See* TENANCY, IMPLIED.

implied term. A term which will be implied (e.g., from statute or custom) where it is necessary to carry out the presumed intention of the parties to a contract and is so obvious that the parties must have intended it to apply. Such a term will not override an express term (q.v.). See Supply of Goods (Implied Terms) Act 1973; Unfair Contract Terms Act 1977; *Liverpool CC v Irwin* [1977] AC 239; *Shell UK Ltd v Lostock Garage Ltd* [1977] 1 All ER 481.

implied trust. A trust which will be enforced by the court as a result of surrounding circumstances, or the language of the parties, so that effect is given to their implied, but unexpressed, intentions. Example: X purchases property in the name of Y; there is a presumption in equity that X

intended Y to hold that property in trust for him. See *Re Howes* (1905) 21 TLR 501. *See* TRUST.

importer. Includes any owner or other person for the time being possessed of or beneficially interested in goods coming from abroad (e.g., consignor, consignee, agent, broker).

importune. To make advances to another for an immoral purpose. It is an offence for a man persistently to solicit or importune in a public place for immoral purposes: S.O.A. 1956, s. 32. See *R v Ford* [1977] 1 WLR 1083; *R v Goddard* (1991) 92 Cr App R 185. It is an offence under S.O.A. 1985, s. 1, to "kerb-crawl", i.e., to solicit from a motor vehicle while it is in a street or public place. It is an offence for a common prostitute to loiter or solicit in a street or public place for the purpose of prostitution (q.v.): Street Offences Act 1959; s. 1; *Behrendt v Burridge* [1976] 3 All ER 285. See *R v Gray* (1982) 74 Cr App R 324; *Darroch v DPP* (1990) 91 Cr App R 378. *See* LOITER.

impossibility. That which is contrary to the law of nature, to some rule of law or to the very nature of some transaction.

impossibility of performance. Impossibility does not generally excuse from performance. Where, however, an event occurs which destroys the basis of the contract and which is not the fault of the parties, the contract is terminated. See *Taylor v Caldwell* (1863) 3 B & S 826. (For the validity of an "impossible term" in contract, see *Eurico v Philipp Bros* [1986] 2 Lloyd's Rep 387.) *See* FRUSTRATION OF CONTRACT.

impotence. The inability to have, or to permit, ordinary sexual intercourse. Impotence of either party to consummate a marriage is a ground for rendering the marriage voidable. See *S. v S.* [1956] P 1; *Wv W* [1967] 3 All ER 178.

imprisonment. The restraint of a person's liberty. A man is said to be a prisoner "so long as he hath not his liberty freely to go at all times to all places whither he will, without bail or mainprise or otherwise": *Termes de la Ley.*

imprisonment for life. *See* LIFE IMPRISONMENT.

imprisonment, imposing of. "Means to pass a sentence of imprisonment, or fix a term of imprisonment for failure to pay any sum of money, or for want of sufficient distress to satisfy any sum of money, or for failure to do or abstain from doing anything required to be done or left undone": M.C.A. 1980, s. 150(1).

improvement notice. Notice served on a person, e.g., under H.S.W.A. 1974, s. 21, by an inspector who is of the opinion that the person is contravening a provision in circumstances that make it likely that the contravention will continue or be repeated. The notice requires that the contravention shall be remedied. *See* PROHIBITION NOTICE.

improvement grants. Payments made by local housing authorities towards cost of works required for the improvement of dwellings, houses in multiple occupation: L.G.H.A. 1989, s. 101.

imputations. Statements ascribing misconduct or fault to some person. It was established in *Selvey* v *DPP* [1970] AC 304 that the Criminal Evidence Act 1898, s. 1(f)(ii), permits cross-examination (q.v.) of an accused person as to his character when imputations on the character of the prosecutor and witnesses are cast so as to show their unreliability as witnesses, independently of the evidence they have given, and when the casting of such imputations is essential to allow the accused to establish a defence.

imputed notice. *See* NOTICE.

inadvertence. Carelessness; lack of proper attention.

in aequali jure melior est conditio possidentis. Where the parties have equal rights, the claim of the actual possessor is the stronger. See *Bailey* v *Barnes* [1894] 1 Ch 25.

inalienability, rule against. Known also as the "rule against perpetual trusts". The general principle is that property must not be rendered inalienable. See, e.g., *Re Wightwick's WT* [1950] Ch 260.

inalienable. Incapable of being transferred.

in alieno solo. On another's land.

in bonis. In the goods of. Abbreviated to "*In b* Smith", and used in connection with litigation concerning the estate or goods of a deceased person.

in camera. In a [judge's] private room, i.e., private sittings. It refers to a case heard, not in open court, but in closed court or a judge's private room, e.g., where the case relates to aspects of the Official Secrets Act 1920, or involves hearing evidence relating to sexual capacity. See, e.g., M.C.A. 1980, s. 121(4); C.J.A. 1988, s. 159 (right of appeal against Crown Court orders restricting reports or excluding the public); *A.-G.* v *Leveller Magazine Ltd* [1979] AC 440; *Polly Peck plc* v *Nadir* (1991) The Times, 11 Nov. *See* OPEN JUSTICE.

incapable of self-support. "A person is incapable of self-support if, but only if, he is incapable of supporting himself by reason of physical or mental infirmity and is likely to remain so incapable for a prolonged period": S.S.A. 1975, Sch. 20.

incapable of work. One who cannot work "by reason of some specific disease or bodily or mental disablement, or deemed in accordance with regulations to be so incapable": S.S.A. 1973, s. 99(1). See S.S.A. 1986, Sch 11.

incapacitation and contract. *See* CONTRACT, INCAPACITATION AND.

incapacity. Lack of legal power, competence, because of, e.g., infancy.

in capite. In chief. A tenant *in capite* held, under the feudal system (q.v.), immediately from the King. Tenure *in capite* was abolished in 1660.

incendiarism. Arson (q.v.).

incest. Sexual intercourse between persons who are within certain degrees of consanguinity. It is an offence under S.O.A. 1956 for a man to have sexual intercourse with a woman whom he knows to be his granddaughter, daughter, sister or mother and for a woman of the age of 16 or over to permit a man whom she knows to be her grandfather, father, brother, or son to have intercourse with her by her consent: ss. 10, 11. See *R* v *Corless* (1989) 11 Cr App R (S.) 47; *A.-G.'s References (No. 1 of 1989)* [1989] 3 WLR 1117, and *(No. 4 of 1989)* (1989) The Times, 11 Nov.

incest, incitement to. It is an offence for a man to incite to have sexual intercourse with him a girl under the age of 16 whom he knows to be his granddaughter, daughter or sister: C.L.A. 1977, s. 54(1).

inchoate. Begun, or in an early stage, but not complete. Inchoate offences (e.g., incitement, attempt), are committed even though the substantive offences with which they are connected are not committed.

inchoate bill. A bill of exchange (q.v.) wanting in some material particular. The person in possession has prima facie authority to make good the omission as he thinks fit: B.Ex.A. 1882, s. 20. The bill must be completed within a reasonable time and in accordance with the authority given. See *Griffiths v Dalton* [1940] 2 KB 264.

incident. An accompanying condition, e.g., the incidents of tenure (such as homage) relating to the feudal system (q.v.).

incitement. The act of urging to a course of criminal action. It is a common law offence for one person to incite another to commit an offence. See Incitement to Mutiny Act 1797; Incitement to Disaffection Act 1934 (under which it is an offence, maliciously and advisedly to attempt to seduce a member of the armed forces from his duty or allegiance to the Crown); Official Secrets Act 1920, s. 7 (under which it is an offence for a person to incite another to commit an offence under the Act); *R v Higgins* (1801) 2 East 5; *R v Fitzmaurice* [1983] QB 1083 (incitement to do the impossible); *R v Sirat* (1986) 83 Cr App R 41.

inclosure. *See* ENCLOSURE.

inclusio unius est exclusio alterius. The inclusion of one is the exclusion of another.

income. The financial return from one's labour, business, land or capital. "The term 'income' means, as applied to a commercial business, the profits made in that business . . . the balance of gain over loss. It seems to me to be altogether straining the ordinary signification of the term 'income' to say that it means the volume of business. That is the 'turnover', not the 'income'": *Yates v Yates* (1913) 33 NZLR 281.

income-related benefits. Benefits under S.S. Contributions and Benefits Act 1992, Part VII, including income support (q.v.), family credit (q.v.) and housing benefit (q.v.).

income support. Benefit under S.S. Contributions and Benefits Act 1992, s. 124, paid to persons over 18 (or, in some cases, 16) who have no income

or whose income does not exceed the applicable amount, who are not engaged in remunerative work. The person must be available for employment and must not be receiving relevant education. See I.C.T.A. 1988, ss. 151, 617; *Chief Adjudication Officer v Foster* [1991] 3 All ER 846. For sums allowed for mortgage interest relief to be paid directly to the lender by the Secretary of State where a person is entitled to income support, see Social Security (Mortgage Interest Payments) Act 1992. For recovery of income support payments from a person who persistently refuses or neglects to maintain himself or any person he is liable to maintain, see S.S. Administration Act 1992, s. 105.

income tax. An annual tax charged on all income originating in the UK and on all income arising abroad of persons resident in the UK. It is imposed for the year of assessment beginning in April. The tax is based on the following schedules (see I.C.T.A. 1988, ss. 15–20): *A* (rents, rentcharges, other receipts from land ownership); *B* (occupation of commercial woodlands); *C* (profits from public revenue dividends); *D* (trade, professional profits or gains); *E* (salaries, wages, annuities, etc); *F* (company dividends, etc.). ("I regard it as fundamental and well-settled law that the Schedules to the Income Tax Act are mutually exclusive and that they afford a complete code for each class of income": *per* Viscount Simonds in *Mitchell v Ross* [1962] AC 813.) See the annual Finance Acts; Taxes Management Act 1970; and I.C.T.A. 1988. For "basic rate", see 1988 Act, s. 832(1).

income tax appeal tribunals. Bodies set up to hear disputes concerning the Inland Revenue relating to liability to tax, each consisting (in the case of General Commissioners of Income Tax) of local business and professional persons assisted by a qualified clerk, or (in the case of Special Commissioners) of barristers and members of the Inland Revenue Department. Appeal on a point of law lies to the High Court.

income tax, yearly assessment. "Every assessment and charge to income tax shall be made for a year commencing on April 6th and ending on the following April 5th": I.C.T.A. 1988, s. 2(2). For date of payment, see s. 5.

incommunicado. Isolated; without a way of communicating with others. By the *Code of Practice* issued under P. & C.E.A. 1984 (and revised in April 1991) a detainee has the right not to be held *incommunicado.* See *R* v *Quayson* [1989] Crim LR 218.

incompletely constituted trust. A trust which requires some further action by the settlor before it is perfectly created. See *Milroy* v *Lord* (1862) 4 De G & J 264; *Re Fry* [1946] 12 All ER 106. *See* TRUST.

inconsiderate driving. *See* DRIVING, CARELESS AND INCONSIDERATE.

in consimili casu, consimile debet esse remedium. In similar cases, the remedy should be similar. See the Statute of Westminster II 1285.

in contemplation of death. "It is sufficient that [the donor of a gift made in contemplation of death] is suffering at the relevant time from an illness which may prove mortal; in such circumstances the gift is taken to be made 'in contemplation of death' and the implication is that it is conditional on death": *Dufficy* v *Mollica* [1968] 3 NSWR 751. *See* DONATIO MORTIS CAUSA.

incorporate. 1. To combine into a whole, e.g., as where one document is taken to be part of another. 2. To admit to membership of a corporation. 3. To form into a corporation, e.g., by Act of Parliament. An "unincorporated body" has, in general, no independent legal personality, unlike the incorporated association; but see *Worthing RFC Trustees* v *IRC* [1987] 1 WLR 1057.

incorporation by reference. "If a testator, in a testamentary paper duly executed, refers to an existing unattested testamentary paper, the instrument so referred to becomes part of his will; in other words it is incorporated into it": *In b Smart* [1902] P 238. See *Re Tyler* [1967] 1 WLR 1269. *See* WILL.

incorporation, certificate of. Issued by the Registrar of Companies after inspection of a company's documents, e.g., memorandum and articles of association (q.v.), list of those who have consented to be directors. Issue incorporates members of the company into

a *persona* at law, and is conclusive evidence that the requirements of the Cos.A. relating to registration have been complied with. See Cos.A. 1985, ss. 13 (as amended), 117; Cos.A. 1989, s. 145, Sch. 19, para 14. *See* COMPANY.

incorporation, doctrine of. Doctrine that rules of international law are incorporated automatically into English law unless they are in conflict with an Act of Parliament, as contrasted with the doctrine of transformation (q.v.). The doctrine was accepted as correct in *Trendtex Trading Corporation* v *Central Bank of Nigeria* [1977] QB 529.

incorporeal hereditaments. Rights of property to which the law of real property applies, e.g., easements, profits. *See* HEREDITAMENTS.

incriminate. 1. To charge with a crime. 2. To involve in the possibility of a prosecution. A person cannot generally be compelled to answer a question the answer to which would incriminate him. See S.C.A. 1981, s. 72. *See* SELF-INCRIMINATION; SILENCE, RIGHT OF ACCUSED TO.

incumbrance. Encumbrance (q.v.).

indebitatus assumpsit. Being indebted he undertook. An action of *assumpsit* (q.v.) brought to recover a debt. The plaintiff alleged a debt, then a promise in consideration. Now obsolete. See *Slade's Case* (1602) 4 Co Rep 91a.

indecency. "Indecency is not confined to sexual indecency; indeed it is difficult to find any limit short of saying that it includes anything which an ordinary decent man or woman would find to be shocking, disgusting or revolting": *Knuller Ltd* v *DPP* [1972] 2 All ER 898. *See* OBSCENITY.

indecency, gross. *See* GROSS INDECENCY.

indecency with children. *See* GROSS INDECENCY.

indecent assault. An intentional assault capable of being considered by right-minded persons as indecent (or in relation to its accompanying circumstances). See S.O.A. 1956, ss. 14, 15; *R* v *Court* [1989] AC 28; *R* v *Culyer* (1992) The Times, 17 Apr. (The offence is one of basic intent.) "The offence is concerned with contravention of standards of decent behaviour in regard to sexual modesty or privacy": *R* v *Kowalski* (1988) 86 Cr App R 339 (indecent assault within marriage).

indecent assault on men. An offence under S.O.A. 1956, s. 14. A boy under 16, or a man who is a defective, cannot in law give any consent which would prevent an act being an assault for the purposes of s. 14. See *R* v *Sant* (1989) 11 Cr App R (S) 441 (indecent assault by woman on boy).

indecent assault on women. An offence under S.O.A. 1956, s. 14. A girl under 16, or a woman who is a defective, cannot in law give any consent which would prevent an act being an assault for the purposes of s. 14.

indecent display. If indecent matter is publicly displayed (i.e., displayed in or so as to be visible from any public place), the person making the display or causing or permitting the display is guilty of an offence: Indecent Displays (Control) Act 1981, s. 1(1), (2). "Public place" includes any place to which the public have access (whether on payment or otherwise); it does not include part of a shop which the public can enter only after passing an adequate warning notice: s. 1(3), (6). Certain specified matter is excluded from the Act, e.g., that included in a TV broadcast, the display of an art gallery: s. 1(4). See Cinemas Act 1985, Sch. 2.

indecent exposure. *See* EXPOSE.

indecent photographs. *See* CHILDREN, INDECENT PHOTOGRAPHS OF.

indefeasible. That cannot be annulled or made void.

indemnifying measure. *See* ACT OF INDEMNITY.

indemnity. 1. Exemption from incurred penalties. See, e.g., Indemnity Act 1920; and Charitable Trusts (Validation) Act 1954. 2. Compensation for injury or loss. See *W.H. Smith & Son* v *Clinton* (1908) 99 LT 840. 3. Indemnity insurance is based on the principle that the insured cannot recover more than his actual loss: *Darrell* v *Tibbitts* (1880) 5 QBD 560. 4. Contract of indemnity is exemplified thus: X and Y enter a shop and Y says to the shopkeeper, "Let X have these goods, I will see you are paid" (see *Birkmyr* v *Darnell* (1704) 1 Salk 27). Such a contract need not be in writing, unlike a contract of guarantee.

indemnity basis for costs. A standard applied to the consideration whether a sum incurred in litigation should be allowed to be paid by/to a party; under it the taxing officer will allow all costs except insofar as they are unreasonable in amount or have been unreasonably incurred, any doubts being resolved in favour of the receiving party (i.e., *for* allowance): O. 62, r. 12(2). See *Singh* v *Observer Ltd* [1989] 2 All ER 751. *See* COSTS, TAXATION OF.

indemnity clauses, unreasonable. "A person dealing as consumer cannot by reference to any contract term be made to indemnify another person (whether a party to the contract or not) in respect of liability that may be incurred by the other for negligence or breach of contract, except in so far as the contract term satisfies the requirement of reasonableness": Unfair Contract Terms Act 1977, s. 4(1).

indenture. A deed (q.v.) made on paper which was cut or indented, so that its two parts ("counterparts") could be fitted together. Although a deed which purports to be an indenture is not in fact indented, it may have the same effect: L.P.A. 1925, s. 56(2).

independent contractor. One who by contract agrees to perform a particular task for another and who, in the execution of his work, is not under the control of the person for whom it is performed, and who may use his discretion as to the general mode of execution. In general, an employer is not liable for the torts of an independent contractor unless he has authorised them explicitly or implicitly. (For an exception, i.e., liability where contractor has been employed to carry out an extra-hazardous task, see *Alcock* v *Wraith* (1991) The Times, 23 Dec.) See *Mersey Docks & Harbour Board* v *Coggins & Griffiths Ltd* [1947] AC 1; *D & F Estates* v *Church Commissioners* [1989] AC 177. See also I.C.T.A. 1988, s. 560.

independent trade union. *See* TRADE UNION, INDEPENDENT.

indexation. The linking of incomes, rents, pensions, benefits, etc, with changes in the index of retail prices. See, e.g., S.S.A. 1986, s. 63(1); *Wyndham Investments* v *Motorway Tyres* [1991] EGCS 9. For index-linked interest rates, see *Multi-Service Bookbinding* v *Marden* [1979] Ch 84. See T.C.G.A. 1992, s. 53 (indexation allowance).

index map. *See* PUBLIC INDEX MAP.

index section in statute. Recent innovation in Parliamentary Acts, listing expressions and relevant defining provisions. See, e.g., Human Fertilisation and Embryology Act 1990, s. 47.

indictable offence. An offence which, if committed by an adult, is triable on indictment (q.v.) whether it is exclusively so triable or triable either way: C.L.A. 1977, s. 64(1)(a). For procedure where trial on indictment appears more suitable, see M.C.A. 1980, s. 21; and S.C.A. 1981, s. 46. See also I.A. 1978, Sch 1. See OFFENCES TRIABLE EITHER WAY.

indictment. A written or printed accusation of a crime. "A plain, brief and certain narrative of an offence committed": 2 Hale PC 169. Its form is determined by the provisions of the Indictments Act 1915 and the Indictment Rules 1971. It consists of three parts: the commencement (name of case and defendant, court of trial, statement that named person is charged with offence(s) which follow(s)); the statement of offence(s); and the particulars (e.g., description of offence, date, place of offence, name of victim). See R v Tyler (1992) The Times, 7 Oct. See BILL OF INDICTMENT.

indictment, objection to. See OBJECTION TO INDICTMENT.

indictment, pleas to. See BAR, PLEAS IN; JURISDICTION, PLEA TO.

indirect evidence. See EVIDENCE, INDIRECT.

indivisible contract. See DIVISIBLE CONTRACT.

indorsement. Endorsement (q.v.).

inducement. 1. Persuasion by promise or threat to a course of action. 2. Introductory part of pleadings (q.v.). 3. Inducement or procuration leading to a breach of contract involves persuading an employee to break his contract. See Lumley v Gye (1853) 2 E & B 216 ("To draw a line between advice, persuasion, enticement and procurement is practically impossible in a court of justice").

industrial action. Concerted activities by employees in pursuance of a complaint and intended to affect the outcome of a dispute. See, e.g., T.U.L.R.(C.)A. 1992. Part V. Must be preceded by a ballot (q.v.) if organised by a union. Obligation to hold a ballot applies to employees and persons working under any contract under which one person personally does work or performs services for another: T.U.L.R.(C.)A. 1992, s. 233. The constituency for the ballot is a 'place of work'. See STRIKE.

industrial and provident society. A society registered under Industrial and Provident Societies Act 1965–78 which carried on an industry, business or trade specified in its rules, wholesale or retail, including dealings with land. See also I.C.T.A. 1988, s. 486.

industrial development certificate. Certificate issued by Secretary of State for the Environment, required before applying for planning permission to erect an industrial building or to alter the use of a building for industrial purposes.

industrial diseases benefits. Benefits payable to employees in respect of injuries and prescribed diseases arising from the nature of the employment. See, e.g., S.S.A. 1975, ss. 76–78.

industrial dispute. A dispute between workers and their employer or organisations of employers and one or more workers relating wholly or mainly to terms and conditions of work, engagement or non-engagement or suspension or termination of employment, allocation of work, etc. See T.U.L.R.(C.)A. 1992, s. 244.

industrial espionage. See ESPIONAGE, INDUSTRIAL.

industrial injuries benefits. Benefits provided under, e.g., S.S.A. 1975, ss. 50–75 (as amended by S.S.A. 1986, Sch. 3 and S.S. Contributions and Benefits Act 1992, Part V) to employed earners (q.v.) suffering personal injuries caused by accidents arising out of and in the course of their employment, and to the relatives and spouses of those killed in such accidents and to employed earners suffering prescribed diseases due to the nature of their employment. "Accidents" include mishaps arising where the employee is, at the time of the accident, in breach of orders or statutes or where the cause is misconduct or negligence on the part of some other person.

industrial premises. Premises used or designed or suitable for use for the carrying on of any such process or re-search (or ancillary premises used for those purposes) specified, e.g., in T.C.P.A. 1971, s. 66(1). For "industrial building or structure", see Capital Allowances Act 1990, s. 18.

industrial tribunals. First established under the Industrial Training Act 1964; developed, following other legislation (e.g., E.P.(C.)A. 1978, s. 128), into bodies hearing complaints relating to unfair dismissal, redundancy payments, terms of employment. Each tribunal consists of a legally qualified chairman (a barrister or solicitor who has been qualified for at least 7 years) appointed by the Lord Chancellor, and two other persons. The tribunals sit in over 50 centres in different parts of the country as and when required and may conduct proceedings in whatever manner is considered suitable. Appeal lies on points of law to the Employment Appeal Tribunal (q.v.); on other matters to QBD. For pre-hearing review of proceedings, at which a party may be required to pay a deposit if he wishes to continue to participate in the proceedings, see 1978 Act, Sch. 9, inserted by Employment Act 1989, s. 20. See SI 1985/16.

ineffective contract. Term applied to a case in which money has been paid by one party to another on the strength of a transaction which he believes is a contract, but which, in fact, is of no effect, as where there is a total failure of consideration. See, e.g., *Rowland* v *Divall* [1923] 2 KB 500.

in esse. State of actual existence, as compared with *in posse* (q.v.).

inevitable accident. An unlooked for mishap which could not have been avoided by the exercise of reasonable care or skill. See *Stanley* v *Powell* [1891] 1 QB 86; *Jones* v *LCC* (1932) 48 TLR 577.

in extenso. At length. Used with reference to the detailed, unabridged, reporting of a case, rather than a summary.

in extremis. In one's last extremity; final illness.

infamous conduct. "If a medical man in the pursuit of his profession has done something with regard to it which would be reasonably regarded as disgraceful or dishonourable to his pro-fessional brethren of good repute and competency, then it is open to the General Medical Council, if that be shown, to say that he has been guilty of infamous conduct in a professional respect": *Allinson* v *General Medical Council* [1894] 1 QB 750. See also Medical Act 1978; Dentists Act 1984.

infant. Under F.L.R.A. 1969. a person under the age of 18. Such a person may be described also as a "minor". For actions relating to a minor, see O. 80. See also Minors' Contracts Act 1987. *See* MINORS' CONTRACTS.

infanticide. The offence committed by a woman who by any wilful act or omission causes the death of her child, under the age of 12 months, when at the time of the act or omission the balance of her mind is disturbed by reason of her not having fully recovered from the effect of giving birth to the child or by reason of the effect of lactation consequent on the birth of the child. She is punished as if guilty of manslaughter (q.v.): Infanticide Act 1938, s. 1(1). See *R* v *Sainsbury* (1989) 11 Cr App R (S) 533; *R* v *Lewis* [1990] Crim LR 348.

inferential facts. *See* FACTS, INFERENTIAL.

inferior courts. Those courts, e.g., county courts, magistrates' courts, with a jurisdiction limited, geographically and in relation to the value of that which is in dispute and subject to the supervision of a superior court.

inferred agreement. An agreement in which the intention of the parties is a matter of inference from their conduct: see, e.g., *Wilkie* v *LPTB* [1947] 1 All ER 258.

inflicting bodily injury. *See* MALICIOUS WOUNDING.

influence, undue. *See* UNDUE INFLUENCE.

in forma pauperis. In the character of a pauper. Phrase formerly used to refer to a poor person who had permission to proceed in an action without liability for fees or costs. Cases of this nature are now dealt with under schemes for legal aid (q.v.).

information. Statement by which a magistrate is informed of the offence for which a summons or warrant is required. In general, any person may lay an information, unless there is a statutory rule to the contrary. An information will suffice if it merely describes the alleged offence in ordinary, non-technical language. It is usually in writing and may be substantiated on oath and includes the name of the party charged, the offence (when and where committed). See M.C.A. 1980, s. 1. *See* LAYING AN INFORMATION.

information   agreement. Agreement under Restrictive Trade Practices Act 1968, s. 5, for the furnishing of information relating to prices charged, costs, processes of manufacture, etc.

information, criminal. *See* CRIMINAL INFORMATION.

information, laying an. *See* LAYING AN INFORMATION.

information, disclosure of. See the Access to Personal Files Act 1987, imposing a duty on certain authorities to allow an individual access to "personal information" (q.v.) of which he is the subject. See also the Data Protection Act 1984.

informer. 1. One who brought an action, or informed, in a court so as to recover a penalty on a conviction. 2. One who informs the police of violations of the law. The police may not use informers in such a way that crimes result: *R* v *Birtles* [1969] 2 All ER 1131. See *R* v *Lowe* (1977) 66 Cr App R 122; *R* v *Agar* [1990] 2 All ER 442; *R* v *Ewitt* (1991) NLJ 160 (exclusionary rule protecting identity of police informers extends to location of police observation posts); *R* v *Vaillencourt* (1992) The Times, 12 June. 3. A "common informer" was one who sued for a penalty which went to the person informing of a breach. The procedure was abolished by the Common Informers Act 1951.

infringement. Violation of or trespass on some right.

in gross. *See* GROSS.

ingross. Engross (q.v.).

inhabitant. One who resides, actually and permanently, in some given place and has his domicile (q.v.) there. The word refers generally to something more permanent than mere residence (q.v.). See *IRC* v *Duchess of Portland* [1982] Ch 314.

inherent vice. A defect inherent in goods which causes damage to them, e.g., fruit rotting because of some latent defect (see *Bradley* v *Fed Steam Navigation Co* (1927) 137 LT 266);

couplings of a carriage breaking because of a defect in their construction (*Lister* v *Lancs and Yorks Rwy Co* [1903] 1 KB 878). A common carrier (q.v.) is not generally liable for damage resulting from inherent vice.

inheritance. That which descends to the heir (q.v.) on the death of the owner. The old canons of inheritance (largely abolished by A.E.A. 1925) were the rules concerning descent of land the owner of which died intestate.

inheritance tax. Formerly called capital gains tax (q.v.), the new scheme (see Finance Act 1986, ss. 100–107) differs mainly (see Inheritance Tax Act 1984, s. 101, Sch. 19) in excluding lifetime transfers from liability to the tax. See generally Inheritance Tax Act 1984 (originally passed as the Capital Transfer Tax Act 1984, a consolidating Act); Finance Act 1989, s. 171.

inhibition. An entry on the proprietorship register on application of any person interested, e.g., as where a proprietor's land certificate has been stolen. It prohibits the registration or entry of any dealing with registered land until the occurrence of an event named in the prohibition. See L.R.A. 1925, s. 57.

in invitum. Against a person's consent or will. Used with reference to the force of a law, or its impact, irrespective of one's assent.

injunction. An order of the court directing a person to refrain from doing or continuing to do an act complained of, or restraining him from continuing an omission. Non-compliance is a contempt of court (q.v.). Classified thus: (1) *prohibitory* (forbidding continuation or omission of a wrongful act); (2) *mandatory* (restraining continuation of omission by direct performance of a positive act); (3) *interlocutory* (q.v.) (temporary injunction, intended to maintain the *status quo* until trial); (4) *perpetual* (granted after the hearing of an action); (5) *ex parte* (q.v.): see O. 29; (6) *interim* (restraining the defendant until some specified date); (7) *quia timet* (q.v.). See S.C.A. 1981, s. 37; *Cambridge Nutrition Ltd* v *BBC* [1990] 3 All ER 523; *Wookey* v *Wookey* [1991] 3 WLR 135.

injunction, damages in lieu of. There is a discretionary power of the court to substitute damages for an injunction where, e.g., the injury to the plaintiff's right is slight and is capable of being estimated in, and compensated by, small monetary terms. Damages should be awarded, where, e.g., an injunction would effectively "stop a great enterprise and render it useless": *per* Lord Denning in *Allen* v *Gulf Oil Refining Ltd* [1980] QB 156. See Chancery Amendment Act 1858; S.C.A. 1981, s. 50; *Leeds Industrial Cooperative Society* v *Slack* [1924] AC 851.

injunction, interlocutory, grant of. Principles were clarified in *American Cyanamid Co* v *Ethicon Ltd* [1975] AC 396. There is no rule requiring the plaintiff to establish a prima facie case, The court must be satisfied that there is a serious, not frivolous, question for trial. Governing consideration is then the balance of convenience (although inadequacy of damages is of significance). Relative strength of the case of both parties is considered only as a last resort. See *Films Rover* v *Cannon Film Sales* [1986] 3 All ER 772.

injunction, Mareva. *See* MAREVA INJUNCTION.

injunctions, matrimonial. Injunctions available in the High Court (if ancillary to other matrimonial proceedings) and county court (q.v.) restraining the other party to a marriage from molesting the applicant or a child living with the applicant or excluding the other party from the matrimonial home (q.v.) or requiring the other party to permit the applicant to enter and remain in the matrimonial home. Available also in the case of a man and woman living in the same household as husband and wife: Domestic Violence and Matrimonial Proceedings Act 1976, s. 1. See *Carpenter* v *Carpenter* (1988) 18 Fam Law 56. A court has the power to attach a power of arrest to an injunction made in divorce proceedings or under the 1976 Act: *Lewis* v *Lewis* [1978] 1 All ER 729. See *Pidduck* v *Molloy* (1992) The Times, 9 Mar.; Law Commission Report No 207 (1992). *See* EXCLUSION ORDER.

injuria. A legal wrong.

injuria non excusat injuriam. An injury received does not justify doing an injury.

injuria sine damno. Wrong without damage. Phrase used in the law of torts to refer to the violation of an interest which may constitute an actionable tort (q.v.) without proof of damage (i.e., pecuniary loss).

injuries, personal, action for. "An action in which there is a claim for damages in respect of personal injuries to the plaintiff or any other person or in respect of a person's death; and 'personal injuries' includes any disease and any impairment of a person's physical or mental condition": O. 1, r. 4. See C.P.A. 1987, s. 45(1); I.C.T.A. 1988, s. 329; *H* v *Ministry of Defence* [1991] 2 WLR 192.

injurious affection. Land may be affected injuriously where part is taken from the owner by the state's exercise of compulsory purchasing powers and, in such a case, the owner may be entitled to compensation if, e.g., the value of the remaining land has fallen. See L.G.P.L.A. 1980, ss. 112, 113; Planning and Compensation Act 1991.

injurious falsehood. A tort (q.v.), resulting from written or oral falsehoods, maliciously published, calculated in the ordinary course of things to produce, and, in the event, producing, actual damage: *Ratcliffe* v *Evans* [1892] 2 QB 524. Known, at one time, as "slander of title" (q.v.) and "slander of goods" (q.v.). The Defamation Act 1952, s. 3(1), refers to "slander of title, slander of goods or other malicious falsehood". See *Fielding* v *Variety Incorporated* [1967] 2 All ER 497.

injury. 1. The violation of one's rights, or its results. 2. An actionable wrong. 3. "Any disease and any impairment of a person's physical or mental condition": Fatal Accidents Act 1967, s. 1(6).

injury benefit. Benefit payable under, e.g., S.S.A. 1975 in respect of an injury as a result of which an employee is incapable of work. See also S.S.A. 1986, Sch. 3.

injury, personal. Any disease and any impairment of a person's physical or mental condition: Lim.A. 1980, s. 38(1). See C.P.A. 1987, s. 45(1).

inland bill. A bill of exchange which is both drawn and payable within the British Isles or which is drawn within the British Isles upon some person resident therein. The term "foreign bill" is applied to any other bill. See B.Ex.A. 1882, s. 4. *See* BILL OF EXCHANGE.

Inland Revenue, Commissioners of. The government body which administers the laws relating to taxation and advises the Chancellor of the Exchequer on relevant matters.

inland waters. Waters [within Great Britain] which do not form part of the sea or of any creek, bay or estuary or of any river as far as the tide flows: T.C.P.A. 1990, s. 55(4A), inserted by Planning & Compensation Act 1991, s. 14. See also Water Resources Act 1991, s. 222; Transport and Works Act 1992, s. 67.

in lieu. In place of.

in limine. On the threshold; preliminary.

in loco parentis. In the place of a parent. Generally it refers to one who, although not the parent of a particular child, takes on himself parental offices and duties in relation to that child.

inn. At common law a house, the owner of which holds himself out as being willing to receive travellers who are willing to pay an appropriate price for accommodation. See Hotel Proprietors Act 1956; *Williams* v *Linnit* [1951] 1 KB 565. For limitation of an innkeeper's liability, see s. 2. *See* HOTEL.

Inner Temple. One of the Inns of Court (q.v.). It stands on land granted in perpetuity by James I in 1609.

inner urban area, assistance for. If the Secretary of State is satisfied that special social need exists in any inner urban area in Great Britain and that the causes could be alleviated by his exercising powers, he may by order specify a district including that area as a "designated district", empowered to make loans for the acquisition by any person of land within that district or the carrying out by any person of works on the land, intended to benefit the district. See Planning and Compensation Act 1991, Sch. 4.

innocence, presumption of. *See* PRESUMPTION OF INNOCENCE.

innocent misrepresentation. *See* MISREPRESENTATION.

innominate. Neither named nor classified. Innominate terms in a contract are also known as "intermediate terms" (q.v.): See *Hong Kong Fir Shipping Co* v *Kawasaki Ltd* [1962] 2 QB 26.

in nomine. In the name of.

Inns of Chancery. Former seminaries associated with the Inns of Court (q.v.),

which ceased to exist in the nineteenth century. They included Staple Inn, Lyon's Inn and Clement's Inn.

Inns of Court. Lincoln's Inn, Inner Temple, Middle Temple, and Gray's Inn (qq.v.), which have the exclusive right of call to the Bar (q.v.). Their members are benchers (q.v.), barristers (q.v.) and students.

innuendo. (*Innuere* = to hint.) A plea by the plaintiff in an action for defamation (q.v.) that, although the words are not defamatory in themselves, by reason of a conjuncton of the words and some extrinsic statement, they have, in effect, a secondary defamatory meaning. See, e.g., *Grappelli* v *Derek Block (Holdings)* [1981] 1 WLR 822; *Polly Peck (Holdings)* v *Trelford* [1986] QB 1000.

in pais. In the country (as contrasted with "in court"). Refers to that which has taken place without legal proceedings. *Trial per pais* referred to trial by jury (i.e., trial "by the country"). *See* ESTOPPEL.

in pari causa possessor potior haberi debet. Where both parties have an equally strong claim, he who is in possession is in the stronger position.

in pari delicto potior est conditio possidentis. Where both parties are equally in the wrong, the position of the possessor is the best.

in pari materia. In an analogous case. See, e.g., *Payne* v *Bradley* [1962] AC 343.

in personam. Against a person. Used to indicate, e.g., proceedings taken against some specific person (*actio in personam*). "Equity acts *in personam*" refers to the old procedure of the Court of Chancery which issued an order "upon a person" so that he was commanded to do or refrain from doing an act.

in posse. State of potential, not actual, existence (as compared with *in esse* (q.v.)).

inquest. *See* CORONER.

inquiry, preliminary. *See* PRELIMINARY INVESTIGATION.

inquiry, tribunals of. Bodies set up by Parliament to enquire into matters of urgent public importance. They may summon witnesses, take evidence on oath. Sittings are generally in public.

inquiry, writ of. Procedure, now abolished, by which, following a judgment in default, "twelve honest and lawful men" were asked on oath to estimate the damage sustained by the plaintiff.

inquisition. 1. Enquiry by a jury (q.v.). 2. Verdict of an inquest, consisting of three sections: caption (date, place of inquest, coroner, jury); verdict (finding of identity of deceased, time, place probable cause of death); attestation (signatures of coroner, concurring jurors). *See* CORONER.

inquisitorial procedure. System in force in some continental countries under which the judge searches for facts, listens to witnesses, examines documents and orders that evidence be taken, after which he makes further investigations if he considers them necessary. *See* ADVERSARIAL PROCEDURE.

in re. In the matter of; concerning.

in rem. Against a thing. An expression used to indicate, e.g., an action taken against no specific person, but rather "against the world", e.g., to assert a right of property against all persons (an action *in rem*, relating to *jura in rem*). A judgment *in rem* is the judgment of "a court of competent jurisdiction determining the status of a person or thing, or the disposition of a thing (as distinct from a particular interest in it of a party to the litigation)": *Lazarus-Barlow* v *Regent Estates* [1949] 2 KB 465.

insanity. Term used to refer to one whose state of mind prevents his knowing right from wrong so that he cannot be held responsible for his acts. See M.H.A. 1983. Every person is presumed sane until the contrary has been proved. The burden of proving insanity is generally on the accused: *Woolmington* v *DPP* [1935] AC 462. For sleepwalking and insanity see *R* v *Burgess* [1991] 2 WLR 1206. *See* M'NAGHTEN RULES.

insanity, not guilty by reason of. *See* SPECIAL VERDICT.

inscribed stock. Stock for which a certificate of ownership is not issued.

insider dealing. Dealing by "insiders" in current, listed securities of a company, using confidential information likely to affect their market value. Generally it is prohibited: see Company Securities (Insider Dealing) Act 1985; the F.S.A. 1986, Part VII; C.J.A. 1988, s. 48; Cos.A. 1989, s. 74; *A.-G's*

Reference (No. 1 of 1988) [1989] 2 WLR 729. "Insiders" include a person who, within the preceding six months has been knowingly connected with the company and has unpublished, price-sensitive information (q.v.) relating to the securities, and any person who has contemplated a take-over involving the company and is in possession of such information. s. 1. Under s. 2, specified individuals (e.g., some public servants) are prohibited from abusing information obtained in their official capacity: see F.S.A. 1986, s. 173(10). Prohibitions apply also to off-market deals (q.v.): ss. 4, 5.

in situ. In its original or natural position.

insolvency. Inability to pay one's debts, because of lack of sufficient property. See Insolvency Act 1986. Includes, in relation to a company, the approval of a voluntary arrangement, the making of an administrative order, the appointment of an administrative receiver: s. 247(1). See Insolvency Rules 1986 (S.I. 1986/1925); Cos.A. 1989, ss. 174, 183.

insolvency practitioner. A person acts as an insolvency practitioner in relation to a company by acting as its liquidator, provisional liquidator, administrator, administrative receiver or as supervisor of a voluntary arrangement; and, in relation to an individual, by acting as his trustee in bankruptcy, or receiver, or trustee under a deed of arrangement, or supervisor of a voluntary arrangement, or, in the case of a deceased person, as administrator of his estate: Ins.A. 1986, s. 388. See S.I. 1986/1995; *Re Adams* [1991] BCC 62.

insolvency practitioner, bars to acting as. An individual may not act as an insolvency practitioner (q.v.) unless he is authorised so to act by virtue of membership of a professional body, or holds an authorisation granted by a competent authority: Ins.A. 1986, ss. 390, 391, 393. He may not so act if he is an undischarged bankrupt or is disqualified under Company Directors Disqualification Act 1986, or is incapable because of mental disorder: s. 390(4). It is an offence (of strict liability) to act in this capacity when not qualified: s. 389(1).

insolvency, preferential debts in. In the case of a company or individual, these are (as listed in Ins.A. 1986 Sch. 6): money owed to Inland Revenue for income tax deducted at source; VAT, car tax, betting and gaming duties; social security and pension scheme contributions; remuneration of employees: s. 386(1). *See* BANKRUPTCY, PRIORITY OF DEBTS IN DISTRIBUTION.

Insolvency Services Account. Account kept by the Secretary of State with the Bank of England relating to sums standing to the credit of bankrupt estates or to liquidated companies: Ins.A. 1986, s. 403.

inspection and investigation of a company. Procedure whereby the Department of Trade is empowered to inspect a company's papers and books, to investigate a company's affairs, membership, director's interests in its shares or debentures. See, e.g., Cos.A. 1985. Part XIV. *See* COMPANY.

inspection by judge. Provision (see, e.g., O. 35) whereby a judge may inspect a place or thing with respect to which a question has arisen in a cause or other matter. "I think that a view is part of the evidence just as much as an exhibit. It is real evidence": *per* Denning LJ in *Goold* v *Evans & Co* [1951] 2 TLR 1189. See *Tito* v *Waddell* [1975] 3 All ER 997.

inspection of documents. *See* DISCOVERY AND INSPECTION OF DOCUMENTS.

inspection order, *ex parte*. Order *in personam* to permit inspection by the plaintiff, who fears that if notice is given to the defendant he may destroy relevant documents, or transfer them, thus preventing the effective discovery of documents (q.v.). See *Anton Piller KG* v *Manufacturing Processes Ltd* [1976] FSR 129. *See* ANTON PILLER ORDER.

instalment. Portions into which a sum of money, or a debt, may be divided for payment at fixed intervals.

instalment deliveries. Unless otherwise agreed, the buyer of goods is not bound to accept delivery of them by instalments: S.G.A. 1979, s. 31(1).

instance, court of first. A court in which proceedings are started; as contrasted with, e.g., the Court of Appeal (q.v.).

instant committal. Short committal. *See* COMMITTAL FOR TRIAL.

in statu quo. In the state or position in which something was or is.

instruct. To authorise an advocate to act, or to communicate information to him relating to proceedings.

instrument. A written document (such as a deed or will) executed formally, evidencing, e.g., rights, duties.

instrument, banking. *See* BANKING INSTRUMENT.

instrument, false. Phrase used in Forgery and Counterfeiting Act 1981 s. 1. An instrument is false if, e.g., it purports to have been made in the form in which it is made by a person who did not in fact make it in that form: s. 9(1). "Instrument" includes any document, formal or informal, stamp sold by the Post Office, Inland Revenue stamp, disc, tape. sound-track or similar device. See *R* v *Tobierre* [1986] 1 WLR 125; *R* v *Moore* [1986] Crim LR 552. *See* FORGERY.

insurable interest. An interest giving an insured person a right to enforce a contract of insurance. It exists if the insured person is liable to sustain some monetary loss, or if he may be claimed against following a loss to another. Examples: a father has not necessarily an insurable interest in his son's life (*Halford* v *Kymer* (1830) 10 B & C 724); a husband may insure his wife, and a wife her husband (*Griffiths* v *Fleming* [1909] 1 KB 805); a trustee may insure in respect of the interest of which he is trustee (*Tidswell* v *Ankerstein* (1792) Peake 151).

insurance. Generally a contract (q.v.) of indemnity against a contingency. The *insurer* assumes the risks of the contingency in consideration of payment of a *premium*, so that the *insured*, who suffers the damage, will be compensated from a common insurance fund. It is a contract *uberrimae fidei* (q.v.), necessitating full disclosure of *all* facts affecting the risk. "Insurance" is used with reference to events which *may* happen (e.g., fire on one's property); "assurance" (q.v.) is used to refer to events which *must* happen (e.g., death). A contract of insurance may be not only for the payment of money, but for a benefit corresponding to such payment: *Department of Trade and Industry* v *St Christopher's Motorists Association* [1974] 1 WLR 99. See Insurance Companies Act 1982; Policyholders Protection Act 1975; F.S.A. 1986, s. 133;

I.C.T.A. 1988, s. 431. For "insurance warranty", see *The Good Luck* (1990) 1 QB 818.

insurance business. Divided, under the Insurance Companies Act 1982, s. 1(1) into "long term business" (meaning insurance business of the classes specified in Sch. 1 – life and annuity, tontines (q.v.), pension fund managagement, etc) and "general business" (meaning insurance business of the classes specified in Sch. 2, Part I – accident, sickness, fire, damage to property, suretyship, etc). See 1982 Act, s. 95; F.S.A. 1986, ss. 22, 129–139; I.C.T.A. 1988, s. 431; Export and Investment Guarantees Act 1991 (insurance of overseas investments). For "financial year" in relation to insurance companies, see 1982 Act, s. 96.

insurance, double. Insurance by the insured of one risk on the same interest in the same property with more than one insurer. See *L.G.A.S. v Drake Insurance Co.* [1992] 1 All ER 283.

insurance, over-. Situation in which the aggregate of all the insurance exceeds the total value of the insured's interests.

intangible property. *See* TANGIBLE PROPERTY.

integration test. "One feature, which seems to run through the instances is that, under a contract of service (q.v.), a man is employed as part of the business, and his work is done as an integral part of the business; whereas, under a contract for services, his work, although done for the business, is not integrated into it, but is only necessary to it": *per* Denning LJ in *Stevenson, Jordan and Harrison v Macdonald & Evans* [1952] 1 TLR 101.

integrity, principle of legislative. Concept elaborated by the jurist, Dworkin, in *Law's Empire* (1986), suggesting that the legislature ought to strive to protect for all persons what it understands to be their moral and political rights, thereby maintaining public standards as an expression of a coherent scheme of justice and fairness.

intellectual property. A group of rights, e.g., patents, registered designs, copyright, trade marks, know-how (q.v.). See S.C.A. 1981, s. 72(5); Atomic Energy Authority Act 1986, s. 8(2); I.C.T.A. 1988, ss. 520–538. For attitude

of EEC, see *Deutsche Grammophon v Metro 78/70*; Treaty of Rome, art. 36.

intent, basic or general, crimes of. Offences in which either recklessness or intention will suffice as proof of the necessary *mens rea*. Examples: assault (common and indecent); rape (see *R v Eatch* [1980] Crim LR 650). See, e.g., *R v Hardie* [1984] 3 All ER 848; *R v Hutchins* [1988] Crim LR 379.

intention. "The most culpable form of blameworthiness." "A state of affairs which the party 'intending' does more than merely contemplate. It connotes a state of affairs which, on the contrary, he decides, so far as in him lies, to bring about, and which, in point of possibility, he has a reasonable prospect of being able to bring about by his own act of volition": *Cunliffe v Goodman* [1950] 2 KB 237. "The intention is the aim of the act, of which the motive is the spring": Austin. Intention may be inferred from foresight of consequences, but must not be equated with foresight: see *R v Moloney* [1985] 1 All ER 1025; *R v Hancock and Shankland* [1986] 1 All ER 641.

intention of a document. The sense of a document, derived from perusal and comprehension of its contents.

intention of Parliament. Phrase used in the interpretation of statutes (q.v.). "We do not sit here to pull the language of Parliament to pieces and make nonsense of it . . . We sit here to find out the intention of Parliament and of ministers and carry it out, and we do this better by filling in the gaps and making sense of the enactment than by opening it up to destructive analysis": *Magor and St Mellons RDC v Newport Corporation* [1950] 2 All ER 1226. This approach was rejected later by the House of Lords. See *Hadmor Productions v Hamilton* [1983] 1 AC 191. *See* HANSARD.

intent, specific or ulterior, crimes of. Offences in which the requirement of *mens rea* is satisfied only by proof beyond reasonable doubt that the defendant had the intention of committing the *actus reus*. Proof of negligence (q.v.) or recklessness (q.v.) will not suffice. Examples: murder; unlawful wounding; stealing.

intent, wounding with. *See* WOUNDING WITH INTENT.

inter alia. Among other things.

inter alios. Among other persons.

inter arma silent leges. In time of war the laws are silent. But see *Liversidge* v *Anderson* [1942] AC 206: "The laws may be changed, but they speak the same language in war as in peace": *per* Lord Atkin.

intercourse, sexual. *See* SEXUAL INTERCOURSE, PROOF OF.

interesse termini. Interest of a term. The legal, proprietary right, carrying with it a right of entry, which a lessee (q.v.) had before entering or taking possession of the land. Abolished under L.P.A. 1925, s. 149(1), (2). See *Lewis* v *Baker* [1905] 1 Ch 46.

interest. 1. A right, duty, claim, legal share in something. 2. A right in property. "It extendeth to estates, rights and titles that a man hath of, in, to, or out of lands": Coke. 3. The return on capital invested ("the price of money"). For "compound interest", see *The Maria* [1990] 1 All ER 78. 4. A share of control in, e.g., a company (q.v.). 5. Concern in the outcome of an event.

interest action. Action brought to settle the right of contending claimants to obtain a grant of administration (q.v.). It is brought in the Chancery Division and is commenced by a writ of summons issued out of Chancery Chambers; see O. 76.

interest, declaration against. *See* DECLARATION AGAINST INTEREST.

interest, disclosure of. The duty of, e.g., a member of a local authority to make known the fact that he has a direct or indirect pecuniary interest in a contract which is under discussion by the authority and to refrain from voting on it. See L.G.A. 1972, ss. 94–98; *Readman* v *DPP* (1991) The Times, 4 Mar.

interest, future. *See* FUTURE INTEREST.

interest in expectancy. A reversionary interest. *See* REVERSION.

interest in possession. An interest which confers a right to present enjoyment of property.

interest on debts and damages. The High Court and county courts (qq.v.) are empowered in proceedings for the recovery of a debt or damages to award simple interest at such rate as is thought fit: S.C.A. 1981, s. 35A (inserted by A.J.A. 1982, Sch. 1).

interest reipublicae ut sit finis litium. It concerns the State that litigation shall not be protracted. See *Ras Beharilal* v *King-Emperor* [1933] All ER 723. ("Finality is a good thing, but justice is a better": *per* Lord Atkin.)

interests, registrable. Those interests set out in L.R.A. 1925 as capable of substantive registration (i.e., in their own right under a specific title number). They comprise those estates capable of subsisting as legal estates. *See* LAND REGISTRATION.

interests, theory of. Theory, proposed by the American jurist, Pound (1870–1964), suggesting that the main problem for legislators is the balancing of individual, public and social interests. "Interests" were seen as demands, desires or expectations which human beings, individually or in groups, seek to satisfy.

interference with goods, wrongful. Conversion of goods (also called "trover" (q.v.)), trespass to goods, negligence so far as it results in damage to goods or to an interest in goods, any other tort so far as it results in damage to goods or to an interest in goods: Torts (Interference with Goods) Act 1977, s. 1. See also C.P.A. 1987, Sch. 4. Relief given may take form of: order for delivery of the goods and payment of consequential damages; or an order for delivery, but giving the defendant the alternative of paying damages by reference to the value of the goods, together in either alternative with payment of any consequential damages; or damages: s. 3(1), (2). See *Brandeis Goldschmidt Ltd* v *Weston Transport Ltd* [1981] QB 864.

interference with subsisting contract. Tort (q.v.) committed by X who, without lawful justification, intentionally interferes with a contract between Y and Z by persuading Y to break his contract with Z or by committing a tortious act which prevents Y's performing the contract. See *Torquay Hotel Ltd* v *Cousins* [1969] 2 Ch 106.

interference with vehicles. *See* VEHICLE INTERFERENCE.

interfering with witnesses. It is an offence at common law to attempt to dissuade or prevent a witness from appearing at a hearing or giving evidence. See, e.g., *Shaw* v *Shaw* (1861) 31 LJ PM & A 35.

interim dividend. A dividend declared at any time between two annual general meetings of a company (q.v.). It is not in the nature of a debt due from the company and cannot be sued for by a shareholder. See Table A, art. 103, and Cos.A. 1985, s. 272, as amended. *See* DIVIDEND.

interim order. An order issued pending further directions, e.g., one made pending appeal.

interim payment. A payment on account of any damages, debt or other sum (excluding any costs) which a party may be held liable to pay to or for the benefit of another party to proceedings if a final judgment or order of the court in the proceedings is given or made in favour of that other party: S.C.A. 1981, s. 32(5). See O. 29, rr. 9–17; *Schott Kem Ltd* v *Bentley* [1990] 3 All ER 850.

interim relief. Granting of an interlocutory injunction (q.v.). See S.C.A. 1981, s. 32 (interim payment of damages); O. 29; and *American Cyanamid Co* v *Ethicon* [1975] AC 396 ("balance of convenience" test for interlocutory injunctions).

interim rent. When a landlord (q.v.) has given notice to terminate a tenancy, or a tenant has requested a new one, the landlord can apply to the court to determine an interim rent to be paid until commencement of new tenancy. See Landlord and Tenant Act 1954, s. 24A; *Follett* v *Cabtell Investment Co* (1986) 280 EG 639.

interlineation. Writing between (or on) the lines of a document. Under the W.A. 1837. s. 21, no interlineation in a will made after execution will have effect except in so far as the words or effect of the will before interlineation shall not be apparent, unless it is executed as a will. See *In b Heath* [1892] P 253.

interlocutory. (*Interloqui* = to speak between.) Not final (i.e., during the course of an action). Examples: interlocutory injunction (q.v.) or interlocutory judgment or order (one which does not finally determine the rights of the parties).

interlocutory appeal. *See* APPEAL, INTERLOCUTORY.

interlocutory injunction. *See* INJUNCTION.

interlocutory proceedings. The preparatory stages of an action occurring between an originating summons or the issue of a writ and the trial of the resulting issues.

interlocutory relief, application for. Application is made: by motion (oral application to judge in open court); by summons (parties attending before a master or judge in chambers on the date specified in the summons – the "return day"); *ex parte* on affidavit.

intermediate term. Term (q.v.), the breach of which will not always entitle the innocent party to consider himself as discharged. See, e.g., *Hong Kong Fir Shipping Co* v *Kawasaki Kisen Kaishu* [1962] 2 QB 26; *Bunge Corporation* v *Tradax Export SA* [1981] 1 WLR 711; *The Aktion* [1981] 1 WLR 711. Known also as "innominate term".

intermixture. The commingling of substances so that the parts can no longer be distinguished. See *Smith* v *Torr* (1862) 7 F & F 505; *Sandeman & Sons* v *Tyzack* [1913] AC 680.

International Court of Justice. Principal judicial organ of the United Nations Organisation, which succeeded the Permanent Court of International Justice in 1946. Its seat is at The Hague and its function is to pass judgment on disputes between states. A state which has not accepted the court's jurisdiction cannot be sued without that state's consent. Disputes are decided in accordance with international law, customs and conventions, or (with agreement of parties) *ex aequo et bono*, i.e., on the foundation of a "fair solution".

international law. 1. The *corpus* of legal rules applying between sovereign states, known as *public international law*. 2. The body of rights and duties of citizens of different sovereign states towards one another, known as *private international law* (q.v.) or conflict of laws.

international supply contract. Phrase used in Unfair Contract Terms Act 1977, s. 26, to refer to a contract made by parties whose places of business (or, if they have none, habitual residences) are in the territories of different states, if the goods to which the contract relates are, at the time of its conclusion, in the course of carriage, or will be carried from the territory of one state to that of another, or the acts constituting the offer and acceptance have been done in the territories of different states, or the contract provides for the goods to be delivered to the territory of a state other than that within whose territory those acts were done.

internment. Detention within prescribed limits, generally without formal trial, e.g., as with enemy aliens in time of war.

inter partes. Between the parties.

interpleader summons. Procedure whereby a person who is sued, or expects to be sued, by rival claimants takes out a summons which is served on the claimants, calling on them to appear before a master so as to stake their claims. The court may then order that the issue between the claimants be tried and will direct who shall be the plaintiff and defendant. A *stakeholder's interpleader* relates to, e.g., a banker holding cash and faced with opposing claims. A *sheriff's interpleader* relates to goods seized under writ of *fi.fa* (q.v.) and a claim by a third person that they belong to him. See O. 17, O. 58, r. 7.

interpretation clause. Part of an Act which provides that certain words and phrases used in that Act shall have certain meanings. See, e.g., L.P.A. 1925, s. 205; C.C.A. 1974, ss. 184–189. "An interpretation clause of this kind is not meant to prevent the word receiving its ordinary, popular and natural sense whenever that would be properly applicable, but to enable the word as used in the Act, where there is nothing in the context or the subject-matter to the contrary, to be applied to some things to which it would not ordinarily be applicable": *per* Lord Selborne in *Robinson* v *Barton Eccles Local Board* (1883) 8 App Cas 198. See *Carter* v *Bradbeer* [1975] 3 All ER 158.

interpretation of statutes. Where a statute's words are not clear or not certain, the courts may be called upon to interpret them. In this they are guided by rules, such as: (1) Literal rule – words of a statute in their original sense will prevail unless they would produce unintended consequences: *Corocraft* v *Pan Am Airways* [1969] 1 All ER 82. (2) Golden rule (q.v.) – manifest absurdity resulting from interpretation to be avoided: *Becke* v *Smith*

(1836) 2 M & W. (3) Statute must be read as a whole. (4) There is a presumption against altering the law or ousting the courts' jurisdiction. (5) The court must adopt an interpretation which will correct the mischief which the statute was passed to remedy: *Heydon's Case* (1584) 3 Co Rep 7a. For conflicts between international obligations and specific statutory provisions see *Cheney* v *Conn* [1968] 1 All ER 779.

interpreter. One who translates the words of a witness. An accused who is unable to understand English properly is entitled to an interpreter's services: *R* v *Lee Kun* [1916] 1 KB 337. In civil proceedings the court has a discretion to allow the use of an interpreter: *Re Fuld* [1965] P 405. See *R* v *Attard* (1959) 43 Cr App R 90 (use of notes to refresh interpreter's memory); *R* v *Mayor of Tower Hamlets BC, ex p Begum* (1991) Imm AR 86 (competence of interpreter questioned).

interregnum. Period during which a throne is vacant, e.g., between the death of a monarch and accession of the successor.

interrogation. Questioning of suspects.

interrogatories. Written questions answerable on oath relating to any matter relevant to an action, which a party may administer, with leave, to an opponent. See O. 26. Their purpose is to obtain admissions and to limit the scope of an opponent's case. They must be answered within the time prescribed. "The allowance or disallowance of interrogatories is a matter for discretion, and they should be allowed or disallowed on the merits of the particular case": *Heaton* v *Goldney* [1910] 1 KB 758. Answers to interrogatories are binding. See *Riddick* v *Thames Board Mills* [1977] QB 88.

interrogatories, fishing. Questions posed which are not intended to further a genuine enquiry, but in order to elicit answers which may be used to support a case lacking in substance. See *Pankhurst* v *Hamilton* (1886) 2 TLR 682; *Re State of Norway's Application* [1987] QB 433.

in terrorem. By way of terror. Threat or intimidation, e.g., by way of a condition in a gift. Example: gift of personalty by X to Y, on condition that Y shall never marry Z. Conditions of this nature are usually void. See *Wilbeam v Ashton* (1807) 1 Camp 78 – penalty (q.v.) held over a party to a contract *in terrorem*; *Jenner v Turner* (1886) 16 Ch D 188.

interruption. The breaking of continuity, e.g., of enjoyment of some right. See, e.g., Prescription Act 1832, s. 4.

inter se. Between, or among, themselves.

intervener. One who intervenes in a suit (e.g., relating to divorce) in his own, or the public's interest. See QUEEN'S PROCTOR.

intervening cause. An independent cause coming between the original act or omission and an injury so that a result is produced which might not otherwise have occurred. "To break the chain of causation (q.v.) it must be shown that there is something which I will call ultroneous, something unwarrantable, a new cause which disturbs the sequence of events, something which can be described as either extraneous or extrinsic": *per* Lord Wright in *The Oropesa* [1943] P 32. See CAUSATION; NOVA CAUSA INTERVENIENS.

interview. A face-to-face discussion. It should not be given a restricted meaning for purposes of P. & C.E.A. 1984. A conversation may be an interview for related purposes: *R v Matthews* [1990] Crim LR 190. See *DPP v Rouse* [1991] Crim LR 911; *R v Pullen* [1991] Crim LR 911. *Code C*, revised in 1991, issued under the 1984 Act, restricts interviews outside police stations. For records of interviews, see *Code C*, para 11.5.

inter vivos. Between parties who are alive.

inter vivos, **gift.** See GIFT INTER VIVOS.

intestacy. State of dying intestate, i.e., without having made a valid will (q.v.). A partial intestacy results from a will which disposes of only part of deceased's property. For administration and devolution on intestacy see A.E.A. 1925; A.E.A. 1971; and Intestates' Estates Act 1952.

intimidation. The act of intentionally and unlawfully frightening or coercing another into a course of action. See S.O.A. 1956, s. 2 (offence of procuring a woman by threats or intimidation to have sexual intercourse); *A.-G. v Butterworth* [1963] 1 QB 696 (intimidation of

juror or witness, which is treated as a contempt (q.v.)). The tort of intimidation arises where A threatens B so that B acts, or refrains from acting, to B's and C's detriment. See *Rookes v Barnard* [1964] AC 1129; *Godwin v Uzoigwe* (1992) The Times, 18 June.

intoxicating liquor. Beer, cider, wine, spirits, etc. See the Licensing Acts 1964 and 1988; Licensing (Low Alcoholic Drinks) Act 1990. Under the 1990 Act, the level at which alcohol is classified as "intoxicating" is 0.5 per cent. For protection of persons under 18, see the 1988 Act, s. 16.

intoxication. Condition of stupefaction induced by alcohol or a narcotic. Self-intoxication is no defence to any crime, the definition of which does not require a specific intent. See *R v Lipman* [1970] 1 QB 152; *R v Caldwell* [1982] AC 341; *R v Fotheringham* (1989) 88 Cr App R 206. See ALCOHOLISM; DIMINISHED RESPONSIBILITY.

intoxication caused by inhalation. See SOLVENT ABUSE.

in transitu. During the passage. Right of stoppage *in transitu* is the right, under S.G.A. 1979, ss. 44–46, to stop goods in transit, to resume and to retain possession until the price is paid. The right is available when the buyer becomes insolvent.

intra vires. Within its powers.

intrinsic. Essential to, or inherent in, something.

intrinsic, evidence. See EVIDENCE, INTRINSIC.

inure. Enure (q.v.).

inventory. An itemised list or catalogue. Under A.E.A. 1925, s. 25(*a*), the personal representatives (q.v.) of a deceased person are under a duty to exhibit on oath a full inventory of the estate when required by court to do so.

in verbis non verba sed res et ratio quaerenda est. In interpreting words, one ought to look not only to the words but to the things and meaning behind them: Jenkins. ("Words, and particularly general words, cannot be read in isolation; their colour and content are derived from their context": *per* Viscount Simonds in *A.-G. v Prince Ernest Augustus of Hanover* [1957] AC 436.)

investigation of a company. See COMPANY, INVESTIGATION OF.

investigation, preliminary. *See* PRELIMINARY INVESTIGATION.

investitive facts. *See* FACTS, INVESTITIVE.

investment. "The verb 'to invest' when used in an investment clause may safely be said to include as one of its meanings 'to apply money in the purchase of some property from which interest or profit is expected and which property is purchased in order to be held for the sake of the income which it will yield'": *Re Wragg* [1919] 2 Ch 58. Generally, the term means the laying out of money with a view to earning an income from it, by way of interest, dividend, rent, etc. Under F.S.A. 1986, Sch 1, "investments" comprise assets, rights, interests (including shares, debentures, government and other public securities, long term insurance policies, etc): s. 1(1).

investment business. Includes dealing in, arranging deals in, managing and advising on, investments: F.S.A. 1986, s. 1, Sch. 1. The carrying on of such a business in the UK is restricted to authorised or exempted persons: ss. 3, 207, and Part I, Chap. III. For the conduct of such a business, see Part I, Chap. V (prohibiting, e.g., misleading statements inducing persons to enter investment agreements). For restrictions on advertising, see ss. 57, 58. For "investment trust", see I.C.T.A. 1988, s. 842; T.C.G.A. 1992, s. 99.

investment business, persons authorised to carry on. "The Secretary of State may issue statements of principle with respect to the conduct and financial standing expected of persons authorised to carry on investment business": F.S.A. 1986, s. 47A, inserted by Cos.A. 1989. This power has been delegated to the Securities and Investments Board.

investment company. Any company whose business consists wholly or mainly in the making of investments and the principal part of whose income is derived therefrom: I.C.T.A. 1988, s. 130.

investment, ethical, by charities. "If trustees are satisfied that investing in a company engaged in a particular type of business would conflict with the very objects their charity is seeking to achieve, they should not so invest": *per* Nicholls V.-C. in *Lord Bishop of Oxford v Church Commissioners* (1991) The Times, 30 Oct.

investment exchange. An organisation which offers to deal in securities with a subscriber whose identity is not revealed to other subscribers and which records and confirms acceptance of its offers: Company Securities (Insider Dealing) Act 1985, s. 13; F.S.A. 1986, s. 36, Sch. 4.

investment scheme, collective. An arrangement enabling participants to receive profits or income arising from investment, in which they have no day to day control over the management, and in which their contributions are pooled or the property is managed as a whole: F.S.A. 1986, s. 75. Promotion of such schemes is restricted: s. 76.

investment, trustees' powers of. In general, a trustee (q.v.) may not lawfully invest trust funds upon securities (q.v.) other than those authorised by the settlement or statute. Under the Trustee Investment Act 1961, trustees may invest in three types of investment: narrower-range type not requiring advice (e.g., National Savings Certificates); narrower-range type requiring advice (e.g., debentures); wider-range type (e.g., shares in designated building societies). Where trustees wish to invest in wider-range securities the trust fund must be divided into two parts: narrower-range part; wider-range part (of equal value at the time of the division): s. 2(1). See SI 1991/999; *Harries v Church Commissioners* (1991) The Times, 30 Oct. *See* INVESTMENT, ETHICAL, BY CHARITIES.

investors' compensation. *See* COMPENSATION SCHEME, INVESTORS'.

invitation to treat. An offer to receive an offer. "According to the ordinary law of contract the display of an article with a price on it in the shop window is merely an invitation to treat. It is in no sense an offer for sale, the acceptance of which constitutes a contract": *per* Lord Parker in *Fisher v Bell* [1961] 1 QB 394. See *Pharmaceutical Society of Great Britain v Boots* [1953] 1 All ER 482; *Gibson v Manchester CC* [1979] 1 WLR 294. *See* OFFER.

invitee. One who is present on property by the express or implied invitation of the owner or occupier, e.g., a person "invited to the premises by the owner or occupier for purposes of business or of material interest": *Fairman* v *Perpetual Investment Building Society* [1923] AC 74. See Occupiers' Liability Act 1957, s. 2; *Murphy* v *Bradford MC* (1991) The Times, 11 Feb. *See* OCCUPIERS' LIABILITY, PRINCIPLE OF.

in vitro. Refers to fertilisation of an egg outside the body. See *R* v *Ethical Committee of St Mary's Hospital, ex p Harriott* (1988) 18 Fam Law 165.

involuntary conduct. A person's action in circumstances in which his mind was not in control of his bodily movement. Generally a defence to a charge, except, e.g., where the accused has voluntarily consumed alcohol or drugs, or in the case of strict liability in criminal law (q.v.). "No act is punishable if it is done involuntarily": *Bratty* v *A.-G. for N Ireland* [1963] AC 386. *See* AUTOMATISM.

IOU. Abbreviation of phrase "I owe you", used as written acknowledgement of a debt. It is not generally a negotiable instrument, merely evidence of debt. See *Brooks* v *Elkins* (1836) 2 M & W 74.

ipse autem rex non debet esse sub homine sed sub Deo et sub lege, quia lex facit regem. The King himself should not be subject to any man, but he should be subject to God and the law, for the law makes him King: Bracton (*c.* 1250).

ipse dixit. He himself said it. Used in relation to an assertion based only on the authority of the speaker or writer, but not proved. See, e.g., *Creed* v *Scott* [1976] RTR 485.

ipso facto. By the fact itself.

irrationality. "It applies to a decision which is so outrageous in its defiance of logic or accepted moral standards that no sensible person who had applied his mind to the question to be decided could have arrived at it": *per* Lord Diplock in *CCSU* v *Minister for the Civil Service* [1985] AC 374. See *Hammersmith & Fulham LBC* v *Secretary of State for the Environment* [1990] 3 All ER 589.

irrebuttable presumptions. Those inferences which may not be rebutted because evidence will not be admitted to contradict them. Known also as "conclusive evidence". Example: the presumption that everyone knows the law. *See* PRESUMPTION.

irregularity, material. Some aspect of legal proceedings based upon a violation of, or failure to observe, rules and procedures. It is not synonymous with "illegality". See, e.g., *R* v *Pitman* [1991] 1 All ER 468.

irrelevant evidence. Facts not in issue or not tending to prove facts in issue, e.g., "similar fact evidence" (that a person has behaved in a certain way on other occasions). See, e.g., *Makin* v *A.-G. for NS Wales* [1894] AC 57; *Harris* v *DPP* [1952] AC 694. *See* EVIDENCE.

irresistible impulse, defence of. The defence of a man's having committed an offence under an uncontrollable impulse is not accepted. ". . . A fantastic theory . . . which if it were to become part of our criminal law, would be merely subversive": *R* v *Kopsch* (1925) 19 Cr App R 50.

irretrievable breakdown of marriage. *See* BREAKDOWN OF MARRIAGE.

irrevocable. Incapable of being revoked. Thus, a will (q.v.) is not irrevocable unless the testator (q.v.) ceases to be of sound mind, thus losing testamentary capacity. See *Vynior's Case* (1609) 8 Co Rep 81b; I.C.T.A. 1988, s. 665.

island company. An oversea company incorporated in the Channel Islands or the Isle of Man. See Cos.A. 1985, s. 699.

Isle of Man. A Crown dependency, not strictly a part of the UK, with its own legislative assembly, law and courts. See *Frankland* v *The Queen* [1987] AC 576 – appeal to JCPC from High Court of Justice of the Isle of Man. *See* TYNWALD, COURT OF.

issue. 1. Offspring. A person's issue comprises his children, grandchildren and other lineal descendants. See *Re Hammond* [1924] 2 Ch 276 (gift of personalty "to A and his issue"); *Re Manley's WT* [1976] 1 All ER 673; *Re Drummond* [1988] 1 WLR 234. 2. The outcome of, e.g., an action. 3. The matter in dispute. 4. A point in question. 5. Total amount of banknotes in circulation.

issued capital. That part of a company's nominal capital (q.v.) which has been issued to shareholders.

issue, dying without. *See* DYING WITHOUT ISSUE.

issue estoppel. "Issue estoppel can be said to exist when there is a judicial establishment of a proposition of law or fact between parties to earlier litigation and when the same question arises in later litigation between the same parties. In the latter litigation the established proposition is treated as conclusive between the same parties": *R* v *Hogan* [1974] 2 All ER 142. In *DPP* v *Humphrys* [1977] AC 1, the House of Lords held that issue estoppel was not part of the criminal law of England. See *Wall* v *Radford* [1991] 2 All ER 741; *Hines* v *Birkbeck College* [1991] 3 WLR 557.

itemised pay statement. *See* PAY STATE-MENT, ITEMISED.

J

J. Justice. (Title of High Court judge.)

JCPC. Judicial Committee of the Privy Council (q.v.).

jeopardy. 1. Vulnerability. 2. Risk of conviction and punishment.

jetsam. Equipment or cargo of a ship which is cast overboard and sinks.

jettison. To throw overboard a ship's cargo or tackle so as to lighten it in an emergency. (The first reported case is *Morse's Case* (1609) 12 Coke R 63.)

John Doe. *See* DOE, JOHN.

joinder of causes of action. The joining in one action of several causes of action against the same defendant. Joinder is not necessarily final and severance may be ordered. See O. 15, r. 1; *Bendir* v *Anson* [1936] 3 All ER 326.

joinder of charges. "Charges for any offences may be joined in the same indictment if those charges are founded on the same facts or form or are a part of a series of offences of the same or a similar character": Indictment Rules 1971, r. 9. See C.J.A. 1988, s. 40; *R* v *Marsh* (1986) 83 Cr App R 165; *R.* v *Simon* [1992] Crim LR 444.

joinder of documents. Phrase referring to the formation of, e.g., a memorandum by two or more documents read together.

joinder of offenders. The joint indictment (q.v.) of two or more persons alleged to have joined in the commission of an offence. See *R* v *Moghal* [1977] Crim LR 373; *Lui Mei Lin* v *R* [1989] 2 WLR 175.

joinder of parties. The joining together (as plaintiffs or defendants) of two or more persons in a single action, e.g., as where, if separate actions were brought by or against each of them, there would arise in all the actions some common question of fact or law. See O. 15, r. 4.

joint account clause. Statement inserted in a mortgage (q.v.) where two or more persons had lent money, declaring that on the death of one mortgagee, the survivor's receipt would suffice as a discharge for the money. See L.P.A. 1925, s. 111.

joint enterprise. 1. Commercial activity undertaken by a group of persons, e.g., partners. 2. Term used in criminal law to refer to the participation of two or more persons in a criminal activity. See, e.g., *R* v *Hyde* [1990] 3 All ER 892; *Hui Chi-ming* v *R* [1991] 3 All ER 897. *See* SECONDARY PARTY.

joint heir. Co-heir. *See* HEIR.

jointly and severally. Persons who are jointly and severally bound render themselves liable not only to a joint action against them, but also to separate actions against them individually.

joint mortgage. A mortgage made to persons jointly. The mortgage money is considered as having been lent on joint account so that a survivor may give a good receipt. See L.P.A. 1925, s. 111. *See* MORTGAGE.

joint obligation. A bond entered into jointly by two or more persons. All of those persons must sue, or be sued, upon the bond together. A release given to one will release all.

joint purchase. Where X and Y purchase property in Y's name there is generally a resulting trust (q.v.) in favour of X as a proportionate beneficiary (as to the money he advanced). See *Jones* v *Maynard* [1951] Ch 572.

joint stock company. "A company having a permanent paid-up or nominal share capital of fixed amount divided into shares, also of fixed amount, or held and transferable as stock, or dividend and held partly in one way and partly in the other, and formed on the principle of having for its members the holders of those shares or that stock, and no other persons": Cos.A. 1985, s. 683(1).

joint tenancy. Existed where land was held by two or more persons under a grant without words which indicated that they were to hold separate and distinct shares (e.g., "to X and Y in fee simple"). Each joint tenant was possessed of the property "by every part and by the whole". Joint tenants each enjoy *jus accrescendi* (q.v.). Possession was based on the "four unities" of possession, interest, time (of vesting) and title. Under the L.P.A. 1925, s. 36, joint tenants hold legal estate on trust for sale. Such a tenancy may be determined by: alienation to a stranger; acquisition by one tenant of a larger estate; agreed sale; partition; mutual agreement; any course of dealing suggesting that "the interests of all were mutually treated as constituting a tenancy in common": *Burgess* v *Rawnsley* [1975] Ch 429. *Hammersmith and Fulham LBC* v *Monk* [1991] 3 WLR 1144; *Hammond* v *Mitchell* [1991] 1 WLR 1127.

joint tortfeasors. Persons whose shares in the commission of a tort (q.v.) have resulted from concerted action in the furtherance of a common design. Examples: principal and agent; partners. Their liability is joint and several and the release under seal (or by way of accord and satisfaction (q.v.)) releases all (but this is not so in the case of concurrent tortfeasors (q.v.)). See *Ronex Properties Ltd* v *John Laing Ltd* [1983] QB 398. See also Civil Liability (Contribution) Act 1978 for the liability of tortfeasors *inter se*.

jointure. 1. A joint interest limited to husband and wife. 2. An estate (q.v.) settled on a wife, taken by her in place of dower (q.v.).

joint will. One document in which two or more persons incorporate their testamentary wishes. It takes effect as the separate wills of the persons who have made it. See *Re Duddell* [1932] 1 Ch 585. See WILL.

Journals. The authentic record of proceedings of the Lords and Commons, known as the *Journals of the House of Commons, and the Journals of the House of Lords*. They date from 1547 (Commons) and 1509 (Lords), and are published annually.

joy riding. Euphemism for a ride taken in a stolen vehicle. It is an offence to take a motor vehicle or other conveyance (q.v.) for one's own or another's use without the consent of the owner or other lawful authority, or knowing

that it has been taken without authority to drive it or to allow oneself to be carried in it: Th.A. 1968, s. 12(1). See VEHICLE-TAKING, AGGRAVATED.

J.P. Justice of the Peace. See MAGISTRATES.

judge. One with power to decide disputes and determine appropriate penalties, etc. In the UK, judges of the High Court, circuit judges and recorders (qq.v.) are recommended for appointment by the Lord Chancellor. Lords of Appeal in Ordinary, the Lord Chief Justice and the Master of the Rolls are recommended for appointment by the Prime Minister. See S.C.A. 1981, s. 10. For the precedence of judges of the Supreme Court, see s. 13. A judge is generally appointed from practising barristers (q.v.). Superior judges are subject to the power of removal only by the Queen on an address presented by both Houses of Parliament (which must originate in the Commons). (The last time a judge was removed in this way was in 1830 – Sir Jonah Barrington, a judge of the Irish Admiralty Court.) Their salaries and pensions are paid direct from the Consolidated Fund (q.v.). Retiring age is 75: S.C.A. 1981, s. 11(2). A judge is not liable in tort for any judicial act performed by him within his jurisdiction, or for acts, performed in good faith, in excess of that jurisdiction. See Courts Act 1971, ss. 17(4), 21(6).

judge advocate. A barrister (q.v.) appointed by the Office of the Judge Advocate-General (or, in the case of the Navy, a legally qualified serving officer appointed by the convening authority) to sit in a court-martial involving more serious cases. See *R* v *Aitken* (1992) The Times, 10 June.

Judge Advocate-General's Department. Advises the Secretary of State for Defence and the Defence Council on legal matters relating to the administration of military law, and reviews proceedings of courts-martial.

judges' clerks. Clerks attached to the Lord Chief Justice, Master of the Rolls, President of Family Division, Vice-Chancellor, Lords Justices of Appeal and puisne judges of the High Court. They are appointed by the Lord Chancellor. See S.C.A. 1981, s. 98; C.L.S.A. 1990, Sch. 10.

judges, district. Formerly "district registrars". Appointed by the Lord Chancellor for each county court district. See County C.A. 1984, ss. 6–9; C.L.S.A. 1990, s. 74. Their jurisdiction includes the determination of interlocutory applications, the conduct of pre-trial reviews, hearing claims where the amount involved is relatively small.

judge's oath. Oath taken by a judge on his appointment: "I do swear by Almighty God that . . . I will do right to all manner of people after the laws and usages of this Realm without fear or favour, affection or ill will." See Promissory Oaths Act 1868; S.C.A. 1981, s. 10(4); C.L.S.A. 1990, s. 76.

judge's order. An order made by a judge in chambers on a summons.

judges, presiding. See PRESIDING JUDGES.

Judges' Rules. Code of guidance for the police, last drawn up by the judges of the QBD in 1964, relating to questioning and charging. Superseded by the P. & C.E.A. 1984, Parts III–IV and Codes of Practice.

judge, undue intervention of. "The judge's part . . . is to hearken to the evidence, only himself asking questions of witnesses when it is necessary to clear up any point that has been overlooked or left obscure; to see that the advocates behave themselves and keep to the rules laid down by law; to exclude irrelevancies and discourage repetition; to make sure by wise intervention that he follows the points that the advocates are making and can assess their work; and at the end to make up his mind where the truth lies. If he goes beyond this, he drops the mantle of a judge and assumes the role of an advocate: and the change does not become him well": *per* Lord Denning in *Jones* v *NCB* [1957] 2 QB 55. See *R* v *Simbodyal* (1991) The Times, 10 Oct.

judgment. A formal decision made and pronounced by a court of law or other tribunal. It may include the reasoning leading to the decision. See C.J.J.A. 1982, s. 18(2).

judgment by consent. Voluntary settlement of an action (q.v.). *See* CONSENT JUDGMENT.

judgment creditor. *See* CREDITOR.

judgment debt. A sum payable under a judgment or order enforceable by a court (not being a magistrates' court (q.v.)); or order of a magistrates' court for payment of money recoverable summarily as a civil debt; or any order of any court which is enforceable as if it were for the payment of money so recoverable.

judgment debtor. One against whom judgment has been given for a sum of money, whose property may be taken in execution.

judgment, entering. Procedure whereby, after a judgment in an action has been given and drawn up, it is presented for entry and entered by an officer "in the book kept for the purpose": O. 42, r. 5(1). Party presenting judgment must produce an associate's certificate, pleadings, etc.

judgment in default. *See* DEFAULT.

judgment, mistakes in. *See* SLIP RULE.

judgment, reversal of. *See* REVERSAL OF JUDGMENT.

judgments, enforcement of. In the case of judgments for payment of money, they may be enforced: in the High Court (q.v.) under O. 45, r. 1, by writ of *fi. fa.* (q.v.), garnishee proceedings (q.v.), charging order, appointment of receiver, order of committal, writ of sequestration (q.v.); in the county court (q.v.) by judgment summons or order for attachment of earnings. In case of judgments for possession of land, enforcement may be by writ of possession. In case of judgments for delivery of goods, enforcement may be by writ of delivery. In case of judgments relating to performance of or abstention from some act, enforcement may be by order of committal or writ of sequestration. See also C.J.J.A. 1982, s. 4; C.L.S.A. 1990, s. 15.

judgment, summary. *See* SUMMARY JUDGMENT UNDER ORDER 14.

judgment summons. Procedure for enforcing judgments of the High Court and county court. See County C.A. 1984, s. 147(1).

judicial act. An act resulting from the exercise of judicial power, e.g., determination by the court of a question of rights. "No action lies for acts done or words spoken by a judge in the exercise of his judicial office, although his motive is malicious and the acts or words are not done or spoken in the honest exercise of his office": *Anderson* v *Gorrie.* [1895] 1 QB 668. *See.* JUDICIAL IMMUNITY.

Judicial Committee of the Privy Council. Created by the Judicial Committee Act 1833, amended by Appellate Jurisdiction Acts 1876–1947. Consists of the Lord Chancellor, Lord President of the Council, ex-Lord President and Lords of Appeal in Ordinary but can also include members of the Privy Council (q.v.) who have held high judicial office. Its jurisdiction includes: appeals from some Commonwealth courts outside the UK; appeals from ecclesiastical courts (q.v.); appeals from medical tribunals. It does not deliver a judgment, but tenders advice to the Sovereign, who acts on the report and approves an appropriate Order in Council. It is not bound by its own previous decisions (see, e.g., *Baker v R* [1975] AC 774). Dissenting opinions may be delivered in open court: Judicial Committee (Dissenting Opinions) Order in Council 1966. Decisions are not binding on English courts, but are treated by them as persuasive. See *Buxoo v R* [1988] 1 WLR 820.

judicial control of jury. *See* JURY, JUDICIAL CONTROL OF.

judicial creativity. Apparent power of the judges to modify the scope and pattern of existing offences and to create new offences, resulting in "judge-made law". See, e.g., *R v Soul* (1980) 70 App Cas 295. "The judges have no power to create new offences": *per* Viscount Dilhorne in *DPP v Withers* [1975] AC 842. "It may be that there is no authority to be found in the books, but, if this be so, all I can say is that the sooner we make one, the better": *per* Lord Denning in *A.-G. v Butterworth* [1963] 1 QB 696.

judicial decision, requisites of. A judicial decision presupposes an existing dispute between two or more parties and involves: presentation of case by parties to dispute; ascertainment of fact by means of evidence adduced by parties; submission of legal arguments; decision which disposes of the whole matter by a finding on disputed facts and an application of law of the land to facts so found, including, where necessary, ruling on any disputed question of law: Committee on Ministers' Powers 1932, Cmd 4060. See *R v*

Secretary of State for Employment, ex p Equal Opportunities Commission [1992] 1 All ER 545.

judicial decision, statement of reasons for. *See* COURTS' DECISIONS, STATEMENTS OF REASONS FOR.

judicial dicta. *See* OBITER DICTUM.

judicial discretion. *See* DISCRETION, JUDICIAL.

judicial evidence. *See* EVIDENCE, JUDICIAL.

judicial function, delegation of. In general, judicial functions may not be delegated: see *R v Gateshead Justices, ex p Tesco* [1981] QB 470.

judicial immunity. "Every judge of the courts of this land – from the highest to the lowest – should be protected to the same degree, and liable to the same degree. . . . Each should be protected from liability to damages when he is acting judicially. Each should be able to do his work in complete independence and free from fear. . . . Nothing will make him liable except it be shown that he was not acting judicially, knowing that he had no jurisdiction to do it": *Sirros v Moore* [1975] QB 118. *See* IMMUNITY; JUDICIAL ACT.

judicial independence. Practice in the UK whereby judges are freed from outside pressures. Secured by, e.g., the charging of judges' salaries on the Consolidated Fund (q.v.), separation of judiciary from Parliament, security of tenure of office, judicial immunity (q.v.).

judicial notice. Known also as "judicial cognisance". Means "those facts which a judge can be called upon to receive and to act upon either from his general knowledge of them, or from enquiries to be made by himself for his own information from sources to which it is proper for him to refer": *Commonwealth Shipping Representative v P & O Branch Services* [1923] AC 191. Examples of such facts are: territorial and geographical divisions; matters of common and certain knowledge; law and custom. The doctrine may extend also to juries in relation to matters within their everyday experience and knowledge. See I.A. 1978, s. 3; European Communities Act 1972, s. 3(2).

judicial precedent. *See* PRECEDENT.

judicial proceedings, reporting of. Publication of reports of proceedings, regulated by, e.g., the Judicial Proceedings (Regulation of Reports) Act 1926; and the Domestic and Appellate Proceedings Act 1968. Reports of nullity cases and cases concerning children usually carry only initials of parties. See also M.C.A. 1980, s. 69.

judicial review. Control exercised by courts over procedure of statutory authorities and other subordinate bodies which may result in grant of prerogative orders (q.v.), or declarations (q.v.) stating a person's rights. It is concerned not with the decision of which review is sought but with a review of the manner of the decision-making process: *R* v *Chief Constable of W Wales Police, ex p Evans* [1981] 1 WLR 1155; *R* v *Civil Service Appeal Board, ex p Cunningham* [1991] IRLR 297 (duty to give reasons for decision). For judicial review of criminal proceedings, see *R* v *Bolton Magistrates, ex p Scally* [1991] 2 WLR 239 (granting of certiorari (q.v.) to quash conviction). *See* ADMINISTRATIVE ACTIONS, REMEDIES FOR CONTROL OF.

judicial review, application for. "No application for review shall be made unless leave of the Court has been obtained . . . The Court shall not grant leave unless it considers that the applicant has sufficient interest in the matter to which the application relates": O. 53, r. 3(1), (5). See S.C.A. 1981, s. 31; *R* v *Secretary of State for the Environment, ex p Rose Theatre Trust* [1990] 2 WLR 186. "The application for judicial review . . . does not, indeed cannot, either extend or diminish the substantive law. Its function is limited to ensuring *ubi jus, ibi remedium* (q.v.)": *per* Lord Scarman. For "exclusivity principle" in relation to review, see *O'Reilly* v *Mackman* [1983] 2 AC 237; *R* v *FA, ex p Football League* [1992] COD 52.

judicial review, application for, time and. Application must be made promptly and in any event within three months from the date when grounds arose, unless the court considers there is a good reason for extending that period: O. 53, r. 4(1). But applicants are required to act with the utmost promptness, especially where third parties' rights might be affected: *R* v *Independent Television Commission, ex p TVNI Ltd* (1991) The Times, 30 Dec.

judicial review, discretionary nature of remedies. Relief may not be granted where: review would serve no useful purpose; an alternative appropriate remedy is available. See *R* v *IRC, ex p Preston* [1985] AC 835; *R* v *Football Association of Wales, ex p Flint Town FC* [1991] COD 44 (Football Association is not a public body amenable to public review); *R* v *Secretary of State for Home Department, ex p Ketowoglo* (1992) The Times, 6 Apr (duty on applicant not to mislead court).

judicial review of administrative action. Grounds of such a review were summarised by Lord Diplock as illegality, irrationality and procedural impropriety: *Council of Civil Service Unions* v *Minister for the Civil Service* [1985] AC 374. "In a system based on the rule of law, unfettered governmental discretion is a contradiction in terms": Wade (approved in *Tower Hamlets* v *Chetnik Developments* [1988] 1 AC 858). For restrictions on review, see, e.g., Interception of Communications Act 1985, s. 7(8); *R* v *Chief Constable of Merseyside, ex p Calveley* [1986] 2 QB 424.

judicial review, subject matter of. "The subject matter of every judicial review is a decision made by some person (or body of persons) whom I will call 'the decision maker' or else a refusal by him to make a decision. . . . The decision must have consequences which affect some person (or body of persons) other than the decision maker, although it may affect him too": *per* Lord Diplock in *CCSU* v *Minister for the Civil Service* [1985] AC 374.

judicial separation. Remedy based on a judicial decree under which it becomes no longer necessary for the petitioner to cohabit with the respondent. See Mat.C.A. 1973, s. 17. A petition may be presented by either party on grounds of, e.g., the respondent's adultery and the petitioner's finding it intolerable to live with the respondent, desertion for a period of two years by the respondent. There is no one-year time bar to presentation of the petition. Irretrievable breakdown of marriage need not be proved. For ancillary relief, see Mat.C.A. 1973, ss. 24, 24A. Grant of the decree is no bar to a subsequent divorce founded on the same facts: s. 4(1).

judicial trustee. "Any fit and proper person nominated for the purpose in the application [by a settlor, beneficiary or trustee (qq.v.)] may be appointed a judicial trustee, and, in the absence of such nomination, or if the court is not satisfied of the fitness of a person so nominated, an official of the court may be appointed": Judicial Trustees Act 1896, s. 1(3). See A.J.A. 1982, s. 57. He must audit accounts annually, on request of a beneficiary (q.v.) or trustee, and, on appointment, exercises all the powers of any other trustee. *See* TRUST.

judiciary. Term applied to the judges collectively.

judiciary, higher. Lords of Appeal in Ordinary, Judges of the Supreme Court of England and Wales, Judges of the Court of Session and Judges of the Supreme Court of N Ireland.

judicis est jus dicere, non dare. It is for the judge to administer, not to make, law. See, however, e.g., *R* v *Manley* [1933] 1 KB 529; *R* v *Soul* (1980) 70 Cr App R 295.

judicium Dei. Judgment of God. Principle at the basis of trial by ordeal (q.v.).

judicium parium. Judgment of one's peers: see Magna Carta (q.v.) 1215, cl. 39. (Holdsworth (*History of English Law*, 1903) denies that the phrase refers to trial by jury.)

junior barrister. 1. A barrister who is not a Queen's Counsel (q.v.). 2. The junior of two counsel appearing for a party.

jura in personam. Rights *in personam* (q.v.).

jura in rem. Rights *in rem* (q.v.)

jura in re propria. Rights over one's own property.

jural. Pertaining to rights, or the doctrines of rights.

jural correlatives. Concept used by the American jurist Hohfeld (1879–1917) to describe, e.g., a "claim" in X implying the presence of its correlative ("duty") in Y. A *jural opposite* describes a "claim" in X which implies the absence of a "no-claim" (a "liberty") in himself. A *jural contradictory* refers to a "claim" in X implying the absence of a "liberty" in Y.

jurat. *Jurare* = to swear. 1. Certificate which is part of an affidavit (q.v.) stating where, when, before whom it was made. See O. 41. 2. Magistrate in the Channel Islands.

juridical. Relating to, or acting in, the administration of justice.

jurimetrics. Term introduced by the American jurist, Loevinger: "Jurimetrics is concerned with such matters as the quantitative analysis of judical behaviour, the application of communication and information theory to legal expression, the use of mathematical logic in law, the retrieval of legal data by electronic and mechanical means, and the formulation of a calculus of legal predictability" (*Law and Contemporary Problems*).

jurisdiction. 1. Power of a court to hear and decide on a case. 2. Authority to legislate. 3. Territorial limits within which legal authority may be exercised. In the case of the English courts, held to comprise England, Wales, Berwick-on-Tweed and those parts of the sea claimed as territorial waters: *R* v *Kent Justices, ex p Lye* [1967] 2 QB 153. See *Union Transport plc* v *Continental Lines SA* [1992] 1 WLR 15. 4. The term "jurisdictional act" means a legislative, administrative or judicial measure of the Sovereign.

jurisdictional error. Error committed when, e.g., an administrative agency acts beyond the jurisdiction conferred on it. See *Pearlman* v *Keepers and Governors of Harrow School* [1979] 1 All ER 365; and *Re Racal Communications Ltd* [1980] 2 All ER 634.

jurisdiction, ouster of. *See* OUSTER OF JURISDICTION.

jurisdiction, plea to. Plea (now virtually obsolete) that the court lacks jurisdiction to try the defendant.

jurisdiction, service out of the. Serving of a writ based on leave granted under O. 11 (significantly revised in 1983 to allow a large number of cases to proceed without leave being required). Application is made *ex parte* to a master in chambers, based on an affidavit (q.v.) showing grounds upon which it is made. See *BP Exploration Co* v *Hunt* [1976] 3 All ER 879.

juris et de jure. Of law and from law. Term applied to irrebuttable presumptions (q.v.).

jurisprudence. The science or philosophy of law. "Recorded thinking about the source, nature, end and efficiency of law, substantive and adjective, and of legal institutions": Reuschlein (1951). "The lawyer's examination of the precepts, ideals, and techniques of the law in the light derived from present knowledge in disciplines other than the law": Stone (1964).

juristic act. *See* ACT, JURISTIC.

juristic person. *See* ARTIFICIAL PERSON.

juror. A member of a jury. See Juries Act 1974, Sch. 1; C.L.S.A. 1990, Sch. 18. *See* JURY.

juror's oath. "I swear by Almighty God that I will faithfully try the defendant and give a true verdict according to the evidence": *Practice Note* [1984] 3 All ER 528.

jury. A body of persons selected according to the law and sworn to give a verdict on some matter according to the evidence. See the S.C.A. 1981, s. 69; O. 33, r. 5; and the County C.A. 1984, s. 66. In general, the jury decides facts; the judge decides questions of law. Picked from those registered as electors, aged 18–70, who have been resident in the UK for at least five years since the age of 13: Juries Act 1974, s. 1, as amended. Those ineligible include barristers and solicitors, clergy, mentally ill, etc. Those disqualified include persons who, at any time in the last ten years have, in the UK, served any part of a sentence of imprisonment: Juries (Disqualification) Act 1984, s. 1(1). "Whenever a man is on trial for serious crime, or when in a civil case a man's honour or integrity is at stake, or when one or other party must be deliberately lying, then trial by jury has no equal": *Ward* v *James* [1966] 1 QB 273. See *R* v *Hornsey* [1990] Crim LR 731. For protection of juries, see *R* v *Ling* [1987] Crim LR 495. For coroner's inquest jury, see Coroners Act 1988, s. 9. *See* CHALLENGE TO JURY; VERDICT.

jury, challenge to. *See* CHALLENGE TO JURY.

jury, communication from. The judge must state in open court the nature and content of any note received from the jury, unless it raises a matter unconnected with the trial: *R* v *Gorman* [1987] 1 WLR 545. See *R* v *Woods* (1988) 87 Cr App R 60.

jury, direction to. A judge's instructions to a jury, relating to burden of proof, role of judge and jury, summary of issues of fact as to which a decision is required, summary of evidence, arguments, inferences to be drawn, etc. "[It] should be custom-built to make the jury understand their task in relation to a particular case": *per* Lord Hailsham in *R* v *Lawrence* [1982] AC 510. Where the evidence warrants it, a judge may instruct a jury to convict: *R* v *Ferguson* (1970) 54 Cr App R 410.

jury, foreman of. *See* FOREMAN OF JURY.

jury, grand. Originated in the Assize of Clarendon 1166. Comprised 12–23 persons before whom a bill of indictment had to be placed. Abolished under C.J.A. 1948.

jury, hung. Jury unable to agree on any verdict.

jury, judicial control of. Ways in which a judge exercises control over a jury, as where, e.g., he rules that there is no case to answer, or that there is insufficient evidence on an issue (so that the jury does not consider it), or by his summing up. See also Criminal Appeal Act 1968, s. 2(1); *R* v *McKenna* [1960] 1 QB 411 (implied threat by judge to jury).

jury, petty. Twelve "good and lawful men" called by a sheriff (q.v.) to try issues of fact in a criminal charge.

jury, retirement of. *See* RETIREMENT OF JURY.

jury's deliberations, confidentiality of. It is a contempt of court to obtain, disclose or solicit a jury's deliberations, arguments or votes cast: Contempt of Court Act 1981, s. 8.

jury, special. Jury formerly drawn from a panel of persons with property of a certain rateable value. Abolished under Courts Act 1971, s. 40(1).

jury trial in civil cases. Under S.C.A. 1981, s. 69, there is a qualified right to jury trial, e.g., where, in the case of an action to be tried in QBD, there is in issue a charge of fraud, or a claim relating to libel, slander, malicious prosecution, false imprisonment, and the trial will not require prolonged examination of documents. There is a discretion to order jury trial in other cases. See *Ward* v *James* [1966] 1 QB 273; *Rothermere* v *Times Newspapers* [1973] 1 WLR 448.

jury, vetting. The checking of potential jurors so as to exclude those who might be disqualified. Held to be not unlawful: see *R* v *Mason* [1981] QB 881. See *R* v *Sheffield Crown Court, ex p Brownlow* [1980] QB 530; and *A.-G.'s Guidelines* (1989) 88 Cr App R 124.

jus. A right, deriving from a rule of law – a concept of Roman law. 1. *Jus naturale*: "what nature has taught all living things" (an ideal to which the law should seek to conform). 2. *Jus gentium*: the law of peoples, i.e., law of universal application. 3. *Jus civile*: "the law each people has settled for itself". Used also to refer to the entire *corpus* of Roman Law.

jus accrescendi. Right of survivorship (q.v.).

jus accrescendi inter mercatores pro beneficio commercii locum non habet. For the benefit of commerce, the right of survivorship (q.v.) among merchants is not known.

jus cogens. Principle of general international law whereby a treaty would be invalidated if it departed from the body of principles or norms from which no derogation is generally permitted, e.g., *pacta sunt servanda* (q.v.). See Vienna Convention on Law of Treaties 1969, arts. 53, 64.

jus dicere. To say what the law is. "Judges ought to remember that their office is *jus dicere* and not *jus dare*, to interpret law, and not to make law, or give law": Bacon (*Of Judicature*). "Whoever hath an absolute authority to interpret any written or spoken laws, it is he who is truly the law-giver to all intents and purposes and not the person who first wrote or spoke them": Bishop Hoadly, in a sermon before George I in 1717.

jus disponendi. The right of disposition.

jus in re aliena. A right over the property of another (e.g., the right to enforce an encumbrance (q.v.)), as compared with *jus in re propria* (a right of the owner of a chattel).

jus mariti. A husband's right. The right to a wife's chattels acquired on marriage, prior to Married Women's Property Act 1882.

jus pascendi. The right of grazing.

jus quaesitum tertio. Right on account of third parties. Refers to a contract which purports to confer rights on a third party. "Our law knows nothing of a *jus quaesitum tertio* arising by way of contract. Such a right may be conferred by way of property, as, for example, under a trust, but it cannot be conferred on a stranger to a contract as a right to enforce the contract *in personam*": *Dunlop Pneumatic Tyre Co Ltd* v *Selfridge & Co Ltd* [1915] AC 847. See *Beswick* v *Beswick* [1968] AC 58. See CONTRACT.

jus soli. Law of the "place of one's birth". Principle that nationality by birth is determined by the country in which the birth takes place. It no longer applies in English law, following B.N.A. 1981: see s. 1.

jus spatiandi et manendi. The right to stray and remain. May form an easement (q.v.), as in the right to use a garden. See *Re Ellenborough Park* [1956] Ch 131.

jus tertii. Right of a third person. Defence set up by X who is apparently liable to Y and, on being sued by Y, asserts that the property or money claimed by Y belongs by paramount title to Z. In general, a wrongdoer may not set up *jus tertii* (but see Torts (Interference with Goods) Act 1977, s. 8(1)). See *Amory* v *Delamirie* (1721) 1 Stra 505 (in relation to conversion (q.v.)); *Asher* v *Whitlock* (1865) LR 1 QB 1 (in relation to ejectment (q.v.)).

just and equitable. Phrase used, e.g., in company law, relating to a petition to wind up a company when the court is of opinion that it is "just and equitable" that it should be wound up. Companies have been wound up under this head because of, e.g., deadlock among members, the company's insolvency; or the company has misapplied funds. See Cos.A. 1985, s. 517(1); *Re A & BC Chewing Gum Ltd* [1975] 1 WLR 579. *See* COMPANY.

justice. 1. The basic value underlying a system of law, or the objective which that system seeks to attain. 2. The virtue which results in each person receiving his due: Justinian. 3. The impartial resolution of disputes arising from conflicting claims. 4. "Justice is the correct application of a law, as opposed to arbitrariness": Ross.

justice, commutative, distributive and corrective. Jurisprudential concept derived from Aristotle. *Commutative jus-*

tice is rendering every person the exact measure of his dues. *Distributive justice* is concerned essentially with the allocation of rights, duties and burdens among the members of a community so that equilibrium is ensured. ("It orders the equal treatment of those equal before the law": Friedmann.) *Corrective* (or "remedial") *justice* corrects disequilibrium in a community. (It "is usually administered by a court or other organ invested with judicial or quasi-judicial powers": Bodenheimer.)

justice, natural. "Justice that is simple or elementary, as distinct from justice that is complex, sophisticated and technical": *John v Rees* [1970] Ch 345. "There must be due inquiry. The accused person must have notice of what he is accused. He must have an opportunity of being heard, and the decision must be honestly arrived at after he has had a full opportunity of being heard": *Leeson v General Medical Council* (1889) 43 Ch D 366. "It is to be implied, unless the contrary appears, that Parliament does not authorise by [an] Act the exercise of powers in breach of the principles of natural justice": *Fairmount Investments Ltd v Secretary of State for the Environment* [1976] 2 All ER 865. See, e.g., *R v Commissioner for Racial Equality, ex p Cottrell* [1980] 3 All ER 265.

justice, natural, requirements of. "The requirements must depend on the circumstances of the case, the nature of the inquiry, the rules under which the tribunal is acting, the subject matter that is being dealt with, and so forth": *per* Tucker LJ in *Russell v Duke of Norfolk* [1949] 1 All ER 109. See *R v Parole Board, ex p Wilson* (1992) The Times, 3 Feb.

justice, open. *See* OPEN JUSTICE.

justice, perverting the course of. *See* PERVERTING THE COURSE OF JUSTICE.

justice, retributive. Theory of punishment based on a supposed moral link between wrong-doing and justice. Offenders, it is claimed, ought to be punished under the law in proportion to their guilt and the injury inflicted on their victims.

justices' clerk. *See* MAGISTRATES' CLERK.

justices in eyre. Justices who travelled throughout the realm so as to try actions and investigate affairs in the counties. *See* EYRE.

justices of the peace. *See* MAGISTRATES; MAGISTRATES' COURTS.

justifiable homicide. The killing of one person by another where no blame attaches to the killer, e.g., as in the carrying out of an authorised death sentence. See *A.-G. for N Ireland's Reference (No 1 of 1975)* [1977] AC 105. *See* HOMICIDE.

justification. A defence which admits the plaintiff's allegations, but pleads that the events referred to were justifiable. Example: in libel (q.v.) the defendant admits that he published the words complained of, but pleads that they were true. The defendant must justify the precise imputation on which the plaintiff's allegation is founded. "Defendant has to prove not only that the facts are truly stated but also that any comments upon them are correct": *Cooper v Lawson* (1838) 8 A & E 746. See Defamation Act 1952, s. 5; O. 82; *Khashoggi v IPC Magazines* [1986] 1 WLR 1412; *Prager v Times Newspapers* [1988] 1 All ER 300.

justifying bail. Proof of sufficiency of bail or of sureties in relation to their ownership of property. *See* BAIL.

juvenile courts. Now renamed "youth courts" (C.J.A. 1991, s. 70). Magistrates' courts (q.v.) exercising jurisdiction over offences committed by, and other matters relating to, children and young persons. They consist of a chairman and other justices (see SI 1991/2099). At least one member of each court must be a woman. Proceedings are not generally open to the public, nor may the identity of the juvenile be published unless the court or Home Secretary so orders.

juvenile offenders. Known also as "young offenders" (C.J.A. 1991, Part III). Term usually applied to children (under 14) and young persons (14–16). For the right to trial by jury see *R v Islington Juvenile Court, ex p Daley* [1983] 1 AC 347 (House of Lords decision on when a juvenile becomes an adult, with reference to M.C.A. 1980, ss. 18(1), 24(1)).

K

kangaroo court. A parody of a hearing, in which elementary and generally accepted norms of justice are not observed. See *R* v *O'Dea* [1983] 72 FLR 436.

K.B. King's Bench. *See* COURT OF KING'S (QUEEN'S) BENCH.

K.C. King's Counsel.

keeping term. *See* TERM.

keeping the peace. In essence, being of good behaviour. A person can be bound over by a magistrate (q.v.) to keep the peace. See M.C.A. 1980, ss. 115, 116.

kerb-crawling. Importuning from a motor vehicle. See S.O.A. 1985; *Paul* v *DPP* (1990) 90 Cr App R 173. *See* IMPORTUNE.

kidnapping. The common law offence of stealing and carrying away, or secreting, of a person of any age, by force or fraud. See *R* v *Garwood* (1989) 11 Cr App R (S.) 141; *R* v *Mackay* (1990) 12 Cr App R (S.) 548. *See* ABDUCTION, CHILD.

kill. To cause the death of another by some act or omission. *See* HOMICIDE; MANSLAUGHTER; MURDER.

killing, acquisition of property by. A beneficiary (q.v.) who, by some criminal act kills the testator, or next of kin who kills an intestate, will not be allowed to benefit from his crime. See *Re Crippen* [1911] P 108; *Re Giles* [1972] Ch 544; Forfeiture Act 1982.

kin. Relationship by blood.

King. *See* MONARCHY; SOVEREIGN.

King can do no wrong. A rule of law, part of the so-called "prerogative of perfection", under which the Crown could not be sued at common law. The position was changed under Crown Proceedings Act 1947. Further modifications to the basic principle were contained in, e.g., National Health Service (Amendment) Act 1986 and Crown Proceedings (Armed Forces) Act 1987.

King's (Queen's) Bench, Court of. *See* COURT OF KING'S (QUEEN'S) BENCH.

Kings, Divine Right of. *See* DIVINE RIGHT OF KINGS.

King's (Queen's) Peace. *See* PEACE OF THE KING.

knight service. A feudal tenure, based on military service to the Sovereign in return for the grant of land. Its incidents included homage (q.v.), aids, reliefs, ransom and wardship. Abolished under Tenures Abolition Act 1660.

knock for knock. An agreement under which insurance agencies pay those they have insured, and do not insist on actions being brought by one party against the other. See *Hobbs* v *Marlowe* [1977] 2 All ER 241.

knock-out agreement. An agreement among bidders at an auction (q.v.) that some of them shall desist from bidding. Illegal when entered into by a dealer. See Auctions (Bidding Agreements) Acts 1927 and 1969; *Rawlings* v *General Trading Co* [1920] 3 KB 30.

know-how. Knowledge of how to accomplish something. Expert skill. "Any industrial information and techniques likely to assist in the manufacture or processing of goods or materials . . .": I.C.T.A. 1988, ss. 530, 531. "It indicates the way in which a skilled man does his job, and is an expression of his individual skill and experience": *Stevenson, Jordan and Harrison* v *Macdonald & Evans* [1952] 1 TLR 101. See also *Rolls-Royce* v *IRC* [1962] 1 WLR 425.

knowingly. With knowledge of the facts in question. "With a design": *R* v *Bannen* (1844) 1 Car & Kir 295.

knowledge. Awareness of, or acquaintance with, fact or truth. "The case of shutting the eyes is actual knowledge in the eyes of the law; . . . the legal conception of constructive knowledge (q.v.), generally speaking, has no place in the criminal law": *per* Devlin J in

Roper v *Taylor's Central Garage* [1951] 2 TLR 284. See *Warner* v *Metropolitan Police Commissioner* [1969] 2 AC 256; *Westminster CC* v *Croyalgrange Ltd* [1986] 1 WLR 674. *See* TURNING A BLIND EYE.

L

labour, manual. *See* MANUAL LABOUR.

laches. (*Lasche* = indolent.) Negligence and unreasonable delay in the assertion of a right will defeat equities. "A court of equity has always refused its aid to stale demands where a party has slept upon his rights and acquiesced for a great length of time. Nothing can call forth this court into activity but conscience, good faith and reasonable diligence": *Smith* v *Clay* (1767) Amb 645. See Lim. A. 1980, s. 36(2) *Wroth* v *Tyler* [1974] Ch 30.

lacuna. (Pl. *lacunae.*) Gap, omission, in a document.

laenland. Loanland. Anglo-Saxon land holding, specifically land which was leased without written charter, often involving incidents of tenure, e.g., military service.

land. 1. "Land in the legal signification comprehendeth any ground, soil or earth whatsoever, as meadows, pastures, woods, moor, waters, marshes, furzes and heath . . . It legally includeth also all castles, houses and other buildings": Coke. 2. " 'Land' includes land of any tenure, and mines and minerals, whether or not held apart from the surface, buildings or parts of buildings (whether the division is horizontal, vertical, or made in any other way) and other corporeal hereditaments; also a manor, an advowson, and a rent and other incorporeal hereditaments, and an easement, right, privilege, or benefit in, over, or derived from land . . .": L.P.A. 1925 s. 205(1) (x). See I.A 1978, Sch 1; Land Drainage Act 1991, s. 72 (1).

land, annual value of. Rent which might reasonably be expected to be obtained on a letting from year to year, with the tenant paying the usual rates and taxes and the landlord bearing costs of repairs, insurance and maintenance: I.C.T.A. 1988, s. 837(1).

land certificate. *See* CERTIFICATE, LAND.

land charges. Those rights and interests affecting land, e.g., estate contracts (q.v.), restrictive covenants (q.v.), general equitable charges and easements (q.v.). See L.C.A. 1972; *Phillips* v *Mobil Oil* [1989] 1 WLR 888.

land charges, local. *See* LOCAL LAND CHARGES.

land charges, register of. A register kept in the Land Charges Department of the Land Registry, recording six classes of charge: (1) *Class A.* Rent, or annuities, or principal money payable by instalments, not created by deed, but by charge on land created pursuant to some person's application under the provisions of statute; (2) *Class B.* Statutory land charges arising automatically; (3) *Class C.* Puisne mortgages, limited owner's charges, estate contracts, general equitable charges; (4) *Class D.* Charge for inheritance tax, restrictive covenants, equitable easements; (5) *Class E.* Annuities created before 1st January 1926 and not registered as annuities; (6) *Class F.* Those affecting land by virtue of Matrimonial Homes Acts 1967 and 1983 and Matrimonial Proceedings and Property Act 1970. See L.C.A. 1972; and Local Land Charges Act 1975. *See* LOCAL LAND CHARGES.

land, compulsory purchase of. The acquisition of land, freehold or leasehold by an authority under statute, commencing with a compulsory purchase order, followed, where necessary, by the hearing of objections. The expropriated owner must be compensated by the acquiring authority for the land taken, by way of purchase price, for any damage directly consequent on the taking and for depreciation of land he retains. Basis of compensation may be "market value", i.e., the amount which the land if sold in the open market by a willing seller might be expected to realise. See, e.g., Land Compensation Acts 1961 and 1973; Acquisition of Land Act 1981; Planning and Compensation Act 1991, Part III; *Procter and Gamble Ltd v Secretary of State for the Environment* [1991] EGCS 63. For ownership of land, in relation to planning permission, see T.C.P.A. 1990, s. 65(8), substituted by 1991 Act, s. 16 ("owner" is: fee simple owner; those entitled to tenancy in total exceeding 10 years of which at least 7 are unexpired; those entitled to an interest in a mineral prescribed by development order). *See* COMPULSORY PURCHASE ORDER.

land, contract for sale of. *See* CONTRACT FOR SALE OF LAND.

land, development. *See* DEVELOPMENT LAND.

landlord. The owner or holder of land (q.v.) leased to another. Includes under Rent Act 1977, s. 152(1), "any person from time to time deriving title under the original landlord." See e.g., H.A. 1988, s. 27(9)(c); Landlord and Tenant Act 1987, s. 2. For denial of landlord's title, see *W G Clarke Ltd v Dupre Properties* [1991] 3 WLR 579.

landlord's identity. In the case of tenancies and residential accommodation, but not including an assured tenancy (q.v.), the tenant may make a written request concerning disclosure of the landlord's identity: Landlord and Tenant Act 1985, s. 1. See *Morrow v Nadeem* [1986] 1 WLR 1381; Landlord and Tenant Act 1987, ss. 47, 51.

land planning control. System administered by a central authority (Department of Environment) and local planning authorities (i.e., county, district councils (qq.v.)). The county planning authority formulates policy and general proposals which it submits to the Secretary of State, who appoints persons to examine proposals publicly. Local plans are then published. See T.C.P.A. 1971, 1984; Inquiries Procedure Rules 1974; Planning and Compensation Act 1991.

land registration. System of registration of title, which now covers the entire country, based on Land Registration Acts and Rules. Title (normally legal freeholds and leases with more than 21 years to run: L.R.A. 1925, s. 123, amended by L.R.A. 1986, s. 2) is entered on a central register, the headings of which are "property", "proprietorship", "charges". In a sense, title is guaranteed by the state. The register may be rectified (see L.R.A. 1925, s. 82) when, e.g., there is fraud, or the court so orders, or where it is just. See *Hodgson v Marks* [1971] 1 Ch 892. See L.R.A. 1925–88; L.C.A. 1972, *See* MINOR INTERESTS; OVERRIDING INTERESTS; REGISTER AT LAND REGISTRY.

land registration, essence of. Principles have been described as "mirror" (register mirroring actual structure of rights in the land), "curtain" (overreaching (q.v.) of certain interests), and "guarantee" (state guarantee of title on register).

land registration, failure to effect. After two months from the date of grant or assignment, total failure to register renders the transfer void so far as regards the grant or conveyance of the legal estate: see L.R.A 1925, s. 123. The legal estate then revests in the transferor who will hold it on trust for the transferee.

Land Registry registers. Five registers are kept: pending actions; annuities; writs and orders affecting land; deeds of arrangement affecting land; land charges. See L.C.A 1972; and Local Land Charges Act 1975. *See* LAND CHARGES, REGISTER OF.

Lands Tribunal. Set up under Lands Tribunal Act 1949. Consists of a President, lawyers, surveyors and valuers who hear disputes relating, e.g., to compulsory purchase, assessment of compensation. Appeal lies to the Court of Appeal (q.v.) on a point of law by way of case stated.

lapse. Failure of a legacy (q.v.) or devise (q.v.) because of the death of the intended legatee or devisee before that of the testator. Doctrine of lapse does not apply: to beneficiaries under a secret trust (q.v.); in case of entailed interest if the devisee leaves descendants capable of inheriting who are living at the time of the testator's death (and this rule extends under L.P.A 1925, s. 130(1) to a similar bequest of personalty); in case of a legacy or devise to a child or other issue of the testator if the legatee or devisee leaves issue living at the time of the testator's death. See W.A. 1837, ss. 32, 33 (as substituted by A.J.A. 1982, s. 19); *Re Sinclair* [1984] 1 WLR 772.

lapse of offer. An offer is held to have lapsed: on the death either of the offeror or offeree before acceptance; where no time for acceptance is prescribed, by non-acceptance within a reasonable time; by non-acceptance within the time prescribed for acceptance by the offeror. *See* OFFER.

larceny. Theft, under the Larceny Act 1916, s. 1 (repealed by Th.A. 1968). *Petty larceny* referred to stolen property with a value not exceeding 12 pence; *grand larceny* referred to stolen property with a value exceeding 12 pence. *See* THEFT.

la reyne le veult; la reyne s'avisera. See ROYAL ASSENT.

last opportunity, rule of. Doctrine which allowed a plaintiff to recover, in spite of his own negligence, if the circumstances were such that defendant could have avoided the accident and plaintiff could not. The doctrine is now "gone forever": *per* Lord Denning in *Lloyds Bank v Budd* [1982] RTR 80.

latent ambiguity. *See* AMBIGUITY.

latent damage. *See* DAMAGE, LATENT.

latent defect. *See* DEFECT.

Latin jurisdiction, the. Name given in early times to the jurisdiction of the Court of Chancery based on petitions, where proceedings were recorded in Latin. (The Chancellor's equitable jurisdiction was known as "the English jurisdiction", because proceedings were recorded in English.)

laundering money. The processing through an apparently legal channel of money obtained illegally, so that its original sources cannot be traced. See, e.g., Drug Trafficking Offences Act 1986, s. 24.

law. 1. The written and unwritten body of rules largely derived from custom and formal enactment which are recognised as binding among those persons who constitute a community or state, so that they will be imposed upon and enforced among those persons by appropriate sanctions. "The body of rules and guidelines within which society requires its judges to administer justice": *per* Lord Scarman in *Duport Steels Ltd v Sirs* [1980] ICR 161. 2. One of the rules of law (i.e., "a law made by Parliament"). 3. Juris-

prudence (q.v.). 4. The general condition of a state in which laws are accepted and observed.

law and equity, conflict of. "Wherever there is any conflict or variance between the rules of equity and the rules of the common law . . . the rules of equity shall prevail": S.C.A. 1981, s. 49(1).

law and equity, fusion of. "The innate conservatism of English lawyers may have made them slow to recognise that by the Judicature Act 1873 the two systems of substantive and adjectival law formerly administered by courts of law and equity have surely mingled now": *per* Lord Diplock in *United Scientific Holdings Ltd v Burnley BC* [1978] AC 904.

law, classification of. Arbitrary division of law into categories, e.g.: (1) *Public law* – concerned with relationships of members of the community and the state, e.g., constitutional law, criminal law; (2) *Private law* – derived from relationships of members of the community *inter se*, e.g., contract, torts. Salmond classifies law by reference to sources: enacted law; case law; customary law; conventional law.

Law Commission. Permanent body established under the Law Commissions Act 1965, consisting of a chairman and four lawyers of high standing, whose duty it is to keep the law under review with a view to its systematic development and reform, including codification, elimination of anomalies, repeal of obsolete enactments, reduction in number of separate enactments. See C.L.S.A. 1990, Sch 10, para 25.

lawful. Warranted or authorised by, or not contrary to, nor forbidden by, the law. *See* LEGAL .

lawful homicide. Excusable or justifiable homicide (qq.v.).

law, functions of. Defined by Hoebel (1954) as: the purposive definition of personal relations within society; the allocation of authority and the determination of who may exercise physical coercion as a socially recognised privilege – right; the disposing of cases as they arise; the maintenance of adaptability through the redefinition of relations between individuals and groups.

law, inner morality of. Concept attributed to Fuller (1969) suggesting that a citizen's fidelity to the law depends on the presence of certain qualities in that law, e.g., it should be published, be comprehensible, free of retroactivity and contradiction, capable of being complied with, and longlasting.

Law Lords. Lord Chancellor, Lords of Appeal in Ordinary, ex-Lord Chancellors and other peers (21 in all) who have occupied high judicial office.

law merchant. That source of English law based on the settlement of disputes between merchants and their usages. "It is neither more nor less than the usages of merchants and traders in the different departments of trade, ratified by decisions of courts of law": *Goodwin* v *Robarts* (1875) LR 10 Ex 337. *See* USAGE.

law, natural. "It is possible to deduce from nature, that is to say from the nature of man, from the nature of society, and even from the nature of things, certain rules which provide an altogether adequate prescription for human behaviour, that by a careful examination of the facts of nature we can find the just solution of our social problems. Nature is conceived of as a legislator, the supreme legislator": Kelsen (1960). "It has operated as a literary, but not as a direct, source of law": Vinogradoff (1913).

law, natural, essence of. "This law of nature being coeval with mankind and dictated by God himself is of course superior in obligation to any other. It is binding over the whole globe, in all countries, and at all times. No human laws are of any validity if contrary to this, and such of them as are valid derive their force and all their authority, mediately or immediately from this original": Blackstone, *Commentaries.*

law, natural, minimum content of. Suggested by Hart (1961) as involving: restrictions on the use of violence; mutual forbearance and compromise; respect for property; creation and modification of obligations; sanctions if the law is broken.

law officers of the Crown. For England and Wales, the Attorney-General and Solicitor-General; for Scotland, the Lord Advocate and Solicitor-General for Scotland.

law, positive. The legal rules adopted and actually endorsed in formal fashion by the state. "Law established or '*positum*' in an independent political community by the express or tacit authority of its sovereign supreme government": Austin (1832).

law, private and public. *See* PRIVATE LAW; PUBLIC LAW.

law, pure theory of. Theory, promulgated in 1911 by Kelsen (1881–1973), explaining law in terms free from all extraneous, non-legal factors. Law is a coercive order of human behaviour and is built from "legal norms" which are valid only if authorised by legal norms of a higher rank. The norms rest ultimately upon the force of a "basic norm" (*Grundnorm*) e.g., that the British Parliament is sovereign. The basic norm is "a juristic presumption or postulate implicit in legal thinking"; it gives the quality of validity to a legal system.

Law Reform Committee. Consists of five judges, four practising barristers, two solicitors and three academic lawyers, appointed by the Lord Chancellor to consider changes which are desirable, having particular regard to judicial decisions.

Law Reports. Law reporting falls into three periods: (1) the Year Books (q.v.) *c.* 1270–1530; (2) the private reporters (Coke, Dyer, etc) *c.* 1535–1865; (3) the modern semi-official reports from 1865, undertaken by the Incorporated Council of Law Reporting for England and Wales (e.g., *Weekly Notes,* up to 1952, and *Weekly Law Reports,* from 1953) and the modern private reports, including, e.g., *All England Law Reports, Lloyd's Law Reports.* See *Roberts Petroleum Ltd* v *Bernard Kenny Ltd* [1983] 2 AC 192 (curbing the citation of unreported decisions). In the House of Lords and Court of Appeal, the rule is that, in general, the Law Reports published by the Incorporated Council should be cited in preference to other reports where there is some choice: see *Practice Direction* by the Master of the Rolls (1990) The Times, 7 Dec; *Bray* v *Best* [1989] 1 WLR 167.

law, rule of. 1. Government based on the general acceptance of the law. 2. A legal rule. 3. Concept outlined by Dicey (*Law of the Constitution,* 1881) –

the regular law of the land predominates over and excludes the arbitrary exercise of power by the government, all people are equally subject to the law administered by the ordinary courts and that law is derived from individuals' rights as declared by the courts.

law sittings. *See* SITTINGS.

Law Society. The body which controls solicitors, constituted under the Royal Charter of 1845. It is governed by an elected Council and its objects are "promoting professional improvement and facilitating the acquisition of legal knowledge". Under the Solicitors Act 1974 it may make regulations concerning legal education and training and examinations. See, e.g., C.L.S.A. 1990, s. 32 (rights of audience). In order to practise as a solicitor a person must have been admitted as a solicitor, must be enrolled on the Society's Roll and must have a current practising certificate: Solicitors Act 1974, s. 1. *See* SOLICITOR.

law, sources of EEC. *See* COMMUNITY LAW, SOURCES OF.

Law, sources of English. Generally held to include: common law; equity; legislation; custom; law merchant; canon law; EEC law.

law, substantive and adjective. *Substantive law* comprises those rules which guide the courts in arriving at decisions. *Adjective law* (or rules of procedure) comprises those rules which determine the course of an action, e.g., in which court a case is to be heard.

lawsuit. Contentious litigation.

law, wager of. *See* WAGER OF LAW.

lawyer. One who is a professional practitioner of the law. *See* LEGAL PROFESSION.

lay days. 1. Days during which a ship is delayed in port. 2. Days allowed by a charterparty (q.v.) for loading or unloading cargo. They begin to run against the charterer from the time he has notice that the vessel is ready to load: *Fairbridge* v *Pace* (1844) 1 C & K 317; *The Point Clear* [1975] 2 Lloyd's Rep 243.

laying an information. Procedure whereby a magistrate is informed, e.g., by a police officer, of a suspected offence. See the M.C.A. 1980, s. 1. "An information is . . . the statement by

which the magistrate is informed of the offence for which the summons or warrant is required": *R* v *Hughes* (1879) 4 QBD 614. "No objection shall be allowed to any information . . . for any defect in it in substance or in form, or for any variance between it and the evidence adduced on behalf of the prosecutor or complainant": M.C.A. 1980, s. 123. An information is laid when received by the office of the clerk to the justices: *R* v *Manchester Stipendiary Magistrate, ex p Hill* [1983] 1 AC 328. *See* INFORMATION.

laying documents before Parliament. Procedure whereby Parliamentary control is exercised over delegated legislation (e.g., SIs (q.v.)). If the "affirmative procedure" is followed, SIs or Orders in Council are subject to the requirement that their effect shall not continue unless one or both Houses approve the documents; the "negative procedure" arises from a provision in the parent Act that any instruments made thereunder are subjected to annulment following resolutions of either House. *See* DELEGATED LEGISLATION.

lay magistrates. Unpaid magistrates, as compared with stipendiaries. *See* MAGISTRATES.

L.C. Lord Chancellor (q.v.).

L.C.J. Lord Chief Justice (q.v.).

leader. Leading counsel in a case.

Leader of HM Opposition. *See* OPPOSITION, LEADER OF HM.

Leader of the House. *See* HOUSE, LEADER OF THE.

lead evidence, to. To call or adduce evidence (q.v.).

leading case. An important case, e.g., one which establishes principles so that it is often cited in court and text books.

leading questions. Questions put to a witness (q.v.) which suggest the desired answer or put the answer into his mouth or, in the case of a disputed matter, permit the reply, "Yes" or "No". Example: "Did you see X at noon in Trafalgar Square on Saturday, 18th October last?" Not generally allowed save, e.g., in examination-in-chief (q.v.), or where the matter is only introductory and not material, or in the case of matter already put in evidence by the other side, or in cross-examination.

" 'Leading' is a relative, not an absolute, term": Best. *See* EVIDENCE.

leapfrog procedure. Procedure introduced by A.J.A 1969, s. 12, whereby an appeal in civil proceedings can go directly from the High Court (q.v.) or a Divisional Court (q.v.) to the House of Lords (q.v.) without prior appeal to the Court of Appeal (q.v.). A certificate must be granted by the trial judge after agreement of all parties, and the Lords must grant leave: s. 13.

lease. A term of years (q.v.) (see *Re Land and Premises at Liss* [1971] Ch 986), or leasehold (q.v.) or the document used to bring into existence a term of years, i.e., an interest in land for a fixed period of a certain maximum duration. One of the two recognised legal estates (q.v.). Where L grants a lease to T, L is known as the *lessor*, or *landlord* (q.v.) and T is known as the *lessee*, or *tenant* (q.v.). Generally involves a grant of exclusive possession (q.v.) for a term at a rent. See *Street v Mountford* [1985] AC 809; *Prudential Assurance v LRB* (1992) The Times, 23 July; *Westminster CC v Clarke* [1992] 1 All ER 695. See T.C.G.A. 1992, Sch. 8, para 10.

lease and release. Procedure formerly employed at common law for conveyancing. Vendor (V) bargained and sold land for one year (i.e., as leasehold (q.v.)) to purchaser (P). V was then seised to P's use on the payment of the purchase price. P received legal estate, reversion (q.v.) remained in V. Then V extinguished his reversion on the next day by deed of release and, as a result, P's leasehold was transformed into fee simple (q.v.). Release was replaced by deed of grant under Real Property Act 1845.

lease, assignment of. Disposal by lessee (q.v.) of his estate in land. Assignment of a legal term must be by deed if it is to be effective at law; an assignment of an informal nature for value may be valid in equity. See L.P.A. 1925, ss. 52, 146(2); *Crago v Julian* [1992] 1 All ER 744. For unreasonable refusal by a landlord to consent to an assignment, see, e.g., *International Drilling Fluids Ltd v Louisville Investments Ltd* [1986] Ch 513. Under Landlord and Tenant Act 1988, s. 1, a landlord must give consent (unless he has a good reason for withholding it) within a reasonable period.

lease, concurrent. *See* CONCURRENT LEASE.

lease, contract to create. Doctrine of *Walsh v Lonsdale* (1882) 21 Ch D 9, converts the contract into a valid equitable lease. But the doctrine has limitations, e.g.: it does not create privity of estate (q.v.); the equitable tenant may be insecure against a third party who purchases the landlord's title, and he cannot claim the benefit of L.P.A. 1925, s. 62. See L.P. (Misc. Provs.) A. 1989.

lease, determination of. A lease may come to an end by: notice; expiry; surrender or merger; becoming a satisfied term (q.v.); forfeiture; enlargement; frustration.

lease, equitable. *See* EQUITABLE LEASE.

lease, forestry. A lease to the Minister of Agriculture for any purpose for which he is authorised to acquire land. Rent may be nominal for the first 10 years, or variable according to the annual value of timber cut. See also S.L.A. 1925, s. 48.

lease, future. *See* FUTURE LEASE.

leasehold. The interest, i.e., term of years, created by a lease (q.v.), or agreement for lease. If created by lease it is a *legal leasehold estate*; if created by agreement for lease, it is, in effect, an *equitable lease*. See *Walsh v Lonsdale* (1882) 21 Ch D 9. Leasehold estates recognised at law are: term of years; periodic tenancy; tenancy at will; tenancy at sufferance. *See* ESTATE; FREEHOLD; TERM OF YEARS; LEASE, CONTRACT TO CREATE; TENANCY.

leasehold, enfranchisement of. *See* ENFRANCHISEMENT OF TENANCY.

leasehold ownership. That which exists where the tenant (or lessee) is granted exclusive possession of land by the landlord (or lessor) with the intention that he should hold it as the tenant only for a fixed period of time less than that held by the landlord.

lease, legal. *See* LEGAL LEASE.

lease, parol. *See* PAROL LEASE.

lease, perpetually renewable. *See* PERPETUALLY RENEWABLE LEASE.

lease, renewal of. Grant of a further term of years in relation to an expiring lease. A contract for renewal of a lease or sub-lease for a term exceeding 60 years from the end of the lease or sub-lease is void: L.P.A. 1922, Sch. 15. See also L.P.A. 1925, s. 149.

leave to defend. At the hearing of a summons under O. 14, the master may give the defendant unconditional leave to defend, or conditional leave on such terms as to giving security or time or mode of trial or otherwise as is thought fit.

legacy. A gift of personal property by will (to a legatee). A legacy may be: (1) *specific* (gift of a specified thing, e.g., "my gold wedding ring"); (2) *demonstrative* (q.v.); (3) *general* (q.v.); (4) *pecuniary* (sum of money, but an annuity is also included under A.E.A. 1925, s. 55(1)); (5) *residuary* (i.e., residue of personal estate). A legacy may fail because of, e.g., disclaimer, lapse, ademption, uncertainty.

legacy, cumulative. Legacy additional to one previously given to the same legatee in the same or a subsequent instrument.

legacy, substitutional. Gift of personalty (q.v.) by a testator (q.v.) made in lieu of a previous gift where he indicates that he does not wish the legatee to take both gifts.

legal. 1. In accordance with forms of law. 2. According to common law (q.v.), but not equity (q.v.). See LAWFUL.

Legal Aid Board. Body established under the Legal Aid Act 1988, s.3, and Sch. 1, with overall responsibility for the Legal Aid Scheme. Its powers and duties are set out in ss. 4, 5. It comprises 11–17 members appointed by the Lord Chancellor.

legal aid, essence of. The provision of a framework for advice, assistance or representation for those who, on account of their means might otherwise be unable to obtain such help: see Legal Aid Act 1988, s. 1. "Representation" includes all such assistance as is usually given by a solicitor or counsel in proceedings: s. 1 (4). For civil legal aid, see 1988 Act, Part IV; for criminal legal aid, see Part V; for special cases, see Part VI.

legal aid scheme. Scheme providing free legal aid to meet the cost of work usually done by a lawyer. Expenses are paid out of a legal aid fund drawn from the Exchequer grant, costs and damages recovered in litigation, and contributions by assisted persons. Free aid is available to persons whose disposable income and capital do not exceed a certain sum. An applicant must show that he has reasonable grounds for asserting or disputing a claim. In criminal proceedings a legal aid order may be made by the court if it appears to be in the interests of justice and the defendant requires financial help to meet the costs of the proceedings. Legal advice and assistance, short of bringing actions, is also available. Known also as "Green Form Scheme". See Legal Aid Act 1988, s. 16 (6) allowing the Legal Aid Board a first charge (for the benefit of the Legal Aid Fund) on property recovered or preserved for an assisted party. For functions of Legal Aid Board, see 1988 Act, s. 3, Sch.1.

legal assignment. *See* ASSIGNMENT.

legal easement. An easement created by statute, deed or prescription for an interest equivalent to an estate in fee simple absolute in possession (q.v.) or a term of years absolute (q.v.). Enforceable against "all the world", unlike the equitable easement (q.v.) which cannot be enforced against the bona fide purchaser for value of the legal estate without notice. *See* EASEMENT.

legal estates. Estates (q.v.) capable of subsisting at law (q.v.). They involve rights *in rem* (q.v.) See L.P.A. 1925, s. 1 (1), restricting the number to two (fee simple, term of years absolute).

legal executives. Unadmitted staff employed by solicitors, e.g., managing clerks. The Institute of Legal Executives is responsible for regulations relating to qualifications, etc.

legal families, classification of. Theory of comparative law, dividing legal systems into groupings based on historical development, mode of legal thought, institutions, ideology, etc. Zweigert and Köst (1985) suggest the following groupings: Romanistic, Germanic, Nordic, Common Law, Socialist, Far Eastern, Islamic, Hindu.

legal fiction. *See* FICTION, LEGAL.

legal formalism. Pejorative term describing very strict adherence to the rigidities of external forms of rules.

legal interests and charges. Five categories capable of existence "at law", defined by L.P.A. 1925, s. 1(2) as: easements, rights and privileges; rentcharges; mortgages; miscellaneous charges; rights of entry.

legalism. Excessive reliance on the formal, literal interpretation, rather than the spirit, of the law.

legality, presumption of. See OMNIA PRAESUMUNTUR.

legality, principle of. See NULLUM CRIMEN SINE LEGE.

legal lease. A leasehold estate for a term of years created, in general, by deed. See L.P.A. 1925, ss. 1(1), 52(1), 54(2). See LEASE.

legal liability. See RESPONSIBILITY.

legal logic. 1. Process of legal reasoning. 2. Application of modes of formal logic to legal reasoning. "The life of the law has not been logic; it has been experience": Holmes, *The Common Law*, 1881. "Causes . . . are not to be decided by natural reason but by the artificial reason and judgment of law": Coke, *Prohibitions del Roy* (1607) 12 Co Rep 63. Note, however, commencement of the judgment delivered by Romer LJ in *Ex p Mwenya* [1960] 1 QB 241, utilising the manner of formal logic. ("The essential contention of the Crown . . . may be expressed syllogistically as follows . . . "). See LOGIC AND THE LAW.

legal memory. See TIME IMMEMORIAL.

legal mortgage. Mortgage created, in the case of freehold land by a demise for a term of years absolute with a provision for cesser on redemption, or by charge by deed expressed to be by way of legal mortgage; in the case of leasehold land, by sub-demise for a term of years absolute (q.v.) at least one day less than the mortgaged lease with a proviso for cesser on redemption, or by charge by deed expressed to be by way of legal mortgage. The legal mortgage operates so as to secure the repayment of a debt or the discharge of some other obligation. See L.P.A. 1925, s. 85. See EQUITY OF REDEMPTION; MORTGAGE.

legal personality. See PERSONALITY.

legal positivism. See POSITIVISM, LEGAL.

legal profession. Solicitors and barristers – a division dating from the fourteenth century, unique to parts of the British Commonwealth. See C.L.S.A. 1990. See BARRISTER; SOLICITOR.

legal professional privilege. See PRIVILEGE, LEGAL PROFESSIONAL.

legal relations intention to create. An essential element in the creation of a contract. Where the parties do not expressly deny the intention, it is a question of construction: *Balfour v Balfour* [1919] 2 KB 571. Where the parties expressly deny intention (as in the so-called gentlemen's agreement (q.v.)), the agreement will not generally be enforced: *Jones v Vernons Pools Ltd* [1938] 2 All ER 626. See also *Edwards v Skyways* [1964] 1 WLR 349. See CONTRACT.

legal rights. Rights *in rem* (q.v.), i.e., available "against the world at large", as compared with equitable rights (q.v.).

legal separation. See JUDICIAL SEPARATION.

Legal Services Ombudsman. See OMBUDSMAN, LEGAL SERVICES.

legal tender. Money that can be offered in the final discharge of a debt and cannot be refused by the creditor. Unlimited legal tender is money that can be tendered up to any amount (e.g., Bank of England notes).

legal year. The annual period of time constituted by the four sittings of the court (Michaelmas, Hilary, Easter, Trinity). See SITTINGS.

legatee. One to whom a legacy is left. See LEGACY.

leges posteriores priores contrarias abrogant. Later laws abrogate prior contrary laws. The basis of the doctrine of "repeal by implication", and a supporting concept of the doctrine that Parliament may never bind its successors. See, e.g., *Ellen Street Estates v Ministry of Health* [1934] KB 590.

legislation. 1. A body of statutes. 2. The making of laws by a competent authority. In the UK this takes three major forms: Acts of Parliament (q.v.); delegated legislation (q.v.); autonomic legislation, i.e., by bodies, such as the unions, making their internal rules and regulations.

legislation, proportionality of. Doctrine which examines whether the effect of a law exceeds what is necessary to be achieved, and whether it is in proportion to a specific objective. See, e.g., *Stoke on Trent CC v B&Q* [1990] 3 CMLR 867; *Brind v Secretary of State for Home Department* [1991] 2 WLR 588.

legislation, quasi-administrative. Administrative rules lacking direct legal force, e.g., codes of practice, guidelines and circulars. See, e.g., Codes of Practice issued under P. & C.E.A. 1984, ss. 66, 67.

legislation, subordinate. Delegated legislation (q.v.).

legislative history of an enactment. Term used in statutory interpretation to refer to the general background relating to the passing of a Bill, e.g., reports of committees, drafts of the Bill, parliamentary debates. The general rule is that no reference to these matters may be made where the meaning of the statute is plain without making recourse to it.

legislature. The Queen in Council in Parliament, i.e., Crown, Lords and Commons. The supreme authority in the realm. See PARLIAMENT.

legitimacy. Status of a child resulting from birth in lawful wedlock. See F.L.R.A. 1987. Under Family Law Act 1986; s. 56 (as substituted by F.L.R.A. 1987, s. 22), a person domiciled in England and Wales may apply to the court for a declaration that a person named in the application is or was his parent, or that he is the legitimate child of his parents.

legitimacy, presumption of. See PRESUMPTION OF LEGITIMACY.

legitimate expectation. See EXPECTATION, LEGITIMATE.

legitimation. Legitimation of a child by subsequent marriage of its parents (*per subsequens matrimonium*). See Legitimacy Acts 1926 (ss. 1, 8), 1976 (ss. 2, 3); Family Law Act 1986, s. 56 (as substituted by F.L.R.A. 1987, s. 22).

leonina societas. A partnership (q.v.) in which one partner takes all the profits (i.e., has "the lion's share") and another carries all the losses.

le roi le veult; le roi s'avisera. See ROYAL ASSENT.

lesbianism. Female homosexuality. Not a criminal offence. See *Kerr* v *Kennedy* [1942] 1 KB 409 (an imputation of lesbianism held to be an imputation of unchastity, in relation to an action for slander (q.v.)); *Gardner* v *Gardner* [1947] 1 All ER 630 (conduct of wife was ground for a divorce petition where the husband's health suffered, so that he could allege cruelty); *Harro-*

gate BC v *Simpson* (1985) 25 RVR 10; *B.* v *B.* [1991] 1 FLR 402.

lessee. One to whom a lease is made. Includes also those who derive title under him: L.P.A. 1925, s. 205(1) (xxiii). Known also as "tenant" (q.v.). See LEASE.

lessor. One who makes a lease to another. See *Adelphi Estates Ltd* v *Christie* (1983) 269 EG 221. See LEASE.

lethal. Causing or designed to cause death. See, e.g., Firearms Act 1968, s. 57(1). The test for a "lethal weapon" is that when misused it was capable of causing injury from which death might result: *R* v *Thorpe* [1987] 1 WLR 383.

letter before action. First letter by a prospective plaintiff's solicitor to prospective defendant, outlining claim to be made, general nature of allegation, summary of damage sustained.

letter of attorney. Power of attorney (q.v.).

letter of comfort. 1. Letter in which a person or body assumes a moral obligation to assist another person to meet liabilities. It has no contractual effect: *Kleinwort Benson Ltd* v *Malaysia Mining Corpn* [1989] 1 All ER 785; *Walford* v *Miles* [1992] 1 All ER 453. 2. Document issued by European Commission (q.v.) in the form of an opinion concerning a possible breach of Treaty of Rome, art. 85 (1) (relating to competition law). It does not have the legal status of a decision. See *Lancôme* v *ETOS* [1981] 2 CMLR 164.

letter of credit. Document provided, e.g., for the exporter by the importer, so that the exporter can draw his draft upon a bank. It usually states the period within which it can be drawn, the maximum amount, and refers to documents accompanying it. See *Power Curber Ltd* v *Nat Bank of Kuwait* [1981] 1 WLR 1233 (a letter of credit ranks as cash and must be honoured); *Forestal Mimosa Ltd* v *Oriental Credit Ltd* [1986] 1 WLR 631; *Bankers Trust Co* v *State of India* (1991) The Times, 25 June.

letter of hypothecation. See HYPOTHECATION.

letter of intent. Device whereby X indicates to Y that he (X) is very likely to enter into a contract with Y. May amount to a conditional contract. See *British Steel Corp* v *Cleveland Bridge Co Ltd* [1984] 1 All ER 504.

letter of request. Letter issued to a foreign court asking a judge to take the evidence of some person within that court's jurisdiction. See C.J.A. 1988, s. 29; Criminal Justice (International Co-operation) Act 1990, s. 3, O. 39, r. 2. Known also as a "rogatory letter". See *Re State of Norway's Application* [1987] QB 433; *Boeing Co.* v *PPG Industries* [1988] 3 All ER 839.

letters of administration. Document issued to an administrator (q.v.) granting his authority.

levant and couchant. (Rising and lying down.) 1. The number of cattle capable of being maintained on land to which a common of pasture was annexed. See now Commons Registration Act 1965. 2. Where cattle escape from X's land to Y's, because of Y's default, Y's landlord could not distrain them for rent until they had been on the land levant and couchant, i.e., at least one night.

levy. 1. Imposition of assessment or tax. 2. Body of men raised by order.

lex causae. The law relating to the legal system governing a matter. See, e.g., *Leroux* v *Brown* (1852) 12 CB 801.

lex domicilii. Law of the place of a person's domicile (q.v.).

lex et consuetudo parliamenti. The law and custom (or usage) of Parliament, i.e., the rules by which Parliament governs itself.

lex fori. Law of the place in which a case is heard.

lex loci actus. Law of the place where an act is carried out.

lex loci contractus. Law of the place where a contract is made. See *Bodley Head Ltd* v *Flegon* [1972] 1 WLR 680.

lex loci delicti commissi. Law of the place where a wrong was committed. See *Monro* v *American Cyanamid Corporation* [1944] 1 All ER 386. See also O. 11.

lex loci situs. Law of the place where the property in question is situated.

lex loci solutionis. Law of the place where the contract is to be performed, or payment made.

lex talionis. Law of retaliation. "An eye for an eye, a tooth for a tooth." See *Exodus*, xxi, 24.

liability. 1. Legal obligation or duty. 2. Amount owed.

liability, business. *See* BUSINESS LIABILITY.

liability, corporate. *See* CORPORATE LIABILITY.

liability for manufactured products. "A manufacturer of products which he sells in such a form as to show that he intends them to reach the ultimate consumer in the form in which they left him with no reasonable possibility of intermediate examination, and with the knowledge that the absence of reasonable care in the preparation or putting up of the products will result in an injury to the consumer's life or property, owes a duty to the consumer to take that reasonable care": *Donoghue* v *Stevenson* [1932] AC 562. See also C.P.A. 1987. *See* PRODUCT LIABILITY.

liability, legal. *See* RESPONSIBILITY.

liability, limited. *See* LIMITED LIABILITY.

liability, strict, in criminal law. *See* STRICT LIABILITY IN CRIMINAL LAW.

liability, vicarious. The liability which arises because of one person's relationship to another. Thus, in tort (q.v.) a master is generally liable for the acts of his servant performed in the course of his employment. See, e.g., *Harrison* v *Michelin Tyre Co* [1985] 1 All ER 918; *Heasmans* v *Clarity Cleaning Ltd* [1987] IRLR 321. In criminal law a master may sometimes be held liable for a servant's offences: see, e.g., Trade Descriptions Act 1968; *Ferguson* v *Weaving* [1951] 1 KB 814.

libel. The publication in permanent form of a statement which tends to expose a person to hatred, ridicule or contempt. The broadcasting of words by radio is treated as publication in permanent form; Defamation Act 1952, s. 1. Libel may be a crime as well as a tort if it is of a "serious kind", and is actionable *per se* without proof of special damage. See Law of Libel (Amendment) Act 1888; A.J.A. 1985, s. 57 (reducing the limitation period in libel cases); *Hulton* v *London Express Newspaper* [1940] 2 KB 507; *Sutcliffe* v *Pressdram Ltd* [1990] 1 All ER 269; *Keays* v *Murdoch Magazines* [1991] 1 WLR 1184; *Rechem International Ltd* v *Express Newspapers plc* (1992) The Times, 19 June. *See* DEFAMATION.

liberty. 1. Absence of restraint. "In accordance with British jurisprudence no member of the executive can interfere with the liberty or property of a British subject except on condition that he can support the legality of his action before a court of justice": *per*

Lord Atkin in *Eshugbayi Eleko* v *Government of Nigeria* [1931] AC 62. 2. The condition of government under the law. 3. A franchise (q.v.).

licence. 1. Necessary authority to act granted by a competent authority. 2. In land law, a licence is given by X to Y when X, the occupier of land, gives Y permission to perform an act which, in other circumstances, would be considered a trespass, e.g., where X allows Y to reside in X's house as a lodger. A *bare licence* is merely gratuitous permission. A licence may be coupled with an interest, as where X sells standing timber to Y on condition that Y is to sever the timber; in this case the sale implies the grant of a licence to Y to enter X's land. For *contractual licence* see *Horrocks* v *Forray* [1976] 1 WLR 230. See *Somma* v *Hazelhurst* [1978] 2 All ER 1011; *Street* v *Mountford* [1985] AC 809.

licence by estoppel. Where a licensee has been allowed by the licensor to act so that an estoppel emerges in his favour, the licensor is bound by it. See *Crabb* v *Aran DC* [1975] 3 All ER 865. *See* ESTOPPEL.

licence, release on. *See* PAROLE.

licence, vehicle driver's. It is an offence to drive a motor vehicle without a driver's licence: Road Traffic Act 1988, s. 87. See also Road Traffic (Driver Licensing & Info. Systems) Act 1989, s. 3. For tests of competence to drive, see 1988 Act, s. 89 as amended by 1989 Act, s. 4. For requirements of physical fitness of drivers, see 1988 Act, s. 92, as amended by Road Traffic Act 1991, s. 18. See also 1991 Act, s. 17.

licensed conveyancer. *See* CONVEYANCER, LICENSED.

licensee. 1. One who has permission, express or implied, to enter premises for his own purpose, but not for any business interest of the occupier. See H.A. 1980, s. 48. 2. One granted a licence, under Licensing Acts, 1964, 1988, for the sale of intoxicating liquor on the premises.

licensing of premises. The granting of justices' licences at the general annual licensing meeting, enabling intoxicating liquor to be sold on the premises. See Licensing Acts 1964 (as variously amended), 1988. *See* BREWSTER SESSIONS.

liege. One bound by allegiance and feudal service.

lie in grant. Phrase referring to property capable of passing by a deed of grant.

lie in livery. Phrase referring to property capable of passing by an act of physical delivery.

lien. *Ligare* = to bind. A right to hold and retain another's property until a claim is satisfied. 1. *Possessory lien.* Right to retain until a claim is met. Possession must be continuous, rightful and not for a particular purpose. It may be general or particular (qq.v.). 2. *Maritime lien.* Right specifically binding a ship or cargo for payment of claim arising under maritime law. It is not founded on possession. 3. *Equitable lien.* Charge on property conferred by law until claims have been satisfied. It is attached independently of possession and is binding on all who acquire the property with notice of the lien. 4. *Unpaid seller's lien.* Right of an unpaid seller of goods to retain possession of them until payment or tender of the price where, e.g., the buyer becomes insolvent: S.G.A. 1979, ss. 41–43.

lien, banker's. "I think we should discard the use of the word 'lien' in this context and speak simply of a banker's 'right to combine accounts' or a right to 'set off' one account against another": *per* Lord Denning in *Halesowen Presswork Ltd* v *Westminster Bank Ltd* [1971] 1 QB 1.

lien, vendor's. *See* VENDOR'S RIGHTS.

life annuity. Annual payment which continues during a life or lives. See I.C.T.A. 1988, s. 657(1). *See* ANNUITY.

life assurance. Contract (q.v.) based on agreement by the assurer to pay a given sum upon the happening of some event contingent upon the duration of life. A *whole life* policy secures a capital sum at death, whenever it may occur. An *endowment assurance policy* secures a capital sum on survival to a fixed date, or at an earlier death. A *last survivor assurance* secures a sum payable at the death of the last survivor of two or more lives. A *temporary assurance policy* secures a capital sum only if death takes place within a specified term. *See* ASSURANCE; INSURANCE.

life estate. An estate for the life of the tenant (e.g., by express limitation, such as a grant "to X for life") or by operation of law (as in curtesy) (q.v.) or *autre vie* (q.v.). *See* ESTATE.

life imprisonment. Fixed penalty for murder. See Murder (Abolition of Death Penalty) Act 1965. For some other offences, e.g., manslaughter, it is the maximum penalty. Where imposed for murder, the court is empowered to declare the minimum term which ought to be served before release on licence, but this does not bind the Home Secretary (who consults the Lord Chief Justice and trial judge before ordering such a release). Recommendation for a minimum term cannot be made except in the case of murder: *R* v *Flemming* [1973] 2 All ER 401. See *R* v *Secretary of State for Home Department, ex p Doody* (1992), The Times, 8 May.

life interest. An interest in property for one's life, or the life of another. Necessarily an equitable interest: see L.P.A. 1925, s. 1(3). *See* INTEREST.

life or lives in being. For purpose of the rule against perpetuities (q.v.), the common law rule was that the lives in being selected by the donor could be stated expressly or by implication and there is no restriction as to the number of lives selected: *Re Villar* [1928] Ch 471. All persons alive or conceived when the instrument creating interest becomes operative are eligible lives in being. Changes introduced by P. & A.A. 1964 relate to so-called "statutory lives" in being (q.v.).

life policy. Instrument by which a payment of money is assured on death (except death by accident only) or the happening of a contingency dependent on human life or an instrument evidencing a contract subject to the payment of premiums for a term dependent on human life: Insurance Companies Act 1982, s. 96(1). See I.C.T.A. 1988, s. 266.

life tenant. *See* TENANT FOR LIFE.

lifting the corporate veil. Phrase describing the process whereby the court and the public may look behind the "curtain of corporate secrecy". Thus, although the court is bound by the principle of a company's being a separate legal person distinct from its members, it will look at the underlying economic reality, e.g., where the company has been engaged in fraudulent

trading or where the company is a mere sham (q.v.). See Cos.A. 1985, ss. 117, 356; Ins.A. 1986, s. 213; *Creasey* v *Breachwood Motors Ltd* (1992) The Times, 29 July. *See* COMPANY.

light, easement of. The right that light flowing over adjoining land shall not be obstructed unreasonably. See *Colls* v *Home & Colonial Stores Ltd* [1904] AC 179; *Allen* v *Greenwood* [1980] Ch 119; *Dance* v *Triplow* (1991) The Times, 4 Dec. (burden of proving right to light). There is no natural right to light – the easement exists only in relation to a window or skylight. See Prescription Act 1832, s. 3; Local Land Charges Act 1975, s. 17. *See* EASEMENT.

limitation of actions. Provision whereby, after a certain period of time stated by statute, actions cannot be brought. Generally: in the case of land, 12 years from the date of accrual of action; in the case of tort and simple contract, six years from the date of accrual of action (for contract under seal, 12 years from the date of accrual). See Limitation Act 1980; Foreign Limitation Periods Act 1984; A.J.A. 1985; s. 57; Latent Damage Act 1986; C.P.A. 1987, Sch. 1. ("The English Limitation Acts bar the remedy and not the right": *per* Donaldson LJ in *Ronex Properties* v *John Laing Ltd* [1983] QB 398.) See *Stubbings* v *Webb* [1991] 3 WLR 383; *Howe* v *David Brown Tractors Ltd* [1991] 4 All ER 30; *Dale* v *BCC (No.1)* (1992) The Times, 25 June. *See* NULLUM TEMPUS OCCURRIT REGI.

limitation, words of. In land law, those words in an instrument which delimit the estate, i.e., which indicate the size of the interest given. Example: land given "to X and his heirs", the words of limitation are "and his heirs", indicating X's quantum of interest, but giving nothing to the heirs by direct gift (in this case X is the "purchaser" (q.v.)). Strict words of limitation must be used to create a fee tail (q.v.). See *Shelley's Case* (1581) 1 Co Rep 93b; and the L.P.A. 1925, s. 131. *See* PURCHASE, WORDS OF.

limited administration. Administration of the assets of a deceased person which is limited, e.g., in time (as where the person appointed sole executor is an infant (q.v.)), or pending legal proceedings or where the person nominated sole executor is of unsound mind. *See* ADMINISTRATION.

limited company. A public company (q.v.). It is considered to be a distinct being or *persona*: *Salomon* v *Salomon & Co Ltd* [1897] AC 22. Liability of each shareholder may be limited by shares of guarantee and the winding-up of the company, if insolvent, will not make members bankrupt (q.v.). Its powers are limited to those arising under the memorandum of association (q.v.). *See* COMPANY.

limited executor. One granted limited probate, e.g., where a testator (q.v.) limits his will to specific property. *See* EXECUTOR.

limited liability. Principle by which, in the case of a company limited by shares, no shareholder will be called upon to pay more than the amount remaining unpaid on his shares. See, e.g., the Cos.A. 1985, ss. 1(2)(*b*), 13, as amended.

limited owner. One who owns an interest in property which is less than the fee simple (q.v.).

limited owner's charge. An equitable charge acquired under statute by a tenant for life or a statutory owner. A Class C land charge (q.v.). *See* LAND CHARGES, REGISTER OF.

limited partnership. Consists of general partners (liable for the firm's debts and obligations) and limited partners (who, at the time of entry, contribute a sum as capital or property which is valued at a stated amount). It is not a legal entity distinct from the persons who compose the firm. See, e.g., Limited Partnerships Act 1907; the Cos.A. 1985, s. 716(2), (3); I.C.T.A. 1988, s. 117(2). *See* PARTNERSHIP.

Lincoln's Inn. One of the Inns of Court (q.v.). Its records commence in 1422, the Inn having been sited originally in Shoe Lane. Its name is derived from that of the Earl of Lincoln who, in the reign of Edward II, brought professors of law to teach there.

lineal consanguinity. Relationship between ascendants and descendants, e.g., grandfather and grandson.

lineal descent. Descent in direct line.

linked transaction. Term used in C.C.A. 1974, s. 19(1), to refer to the debtor's entry into one transaction linked with another (e.g., purchase of a deep freezer on credit and a later agreement to buy food for stocking purposes). Generally treated as a "regulated agreement" (q.v.).

liquidated damages. *See* DAMAGES.

liquidated demand. A demand in the nature of a debt, i.e., a specific sum of money due and payable under or by virtue of a contract. Its amount must either be already ascertained or capable of being ascertained as a mere matter of arithmetic: O. 6, r. 2(1).

liquidation. 1. Settling of an obligation. 2. The winding-up of the affairs of a business by identifying and converting assets into cash and paying off liabilities. See, generally, Ins.A. 1986, ss. 100, 101, 143–146.

liquidation, fraud relating to. Relevant offences include: falsification of a company's books; false representations to creditors; material omissions from statements relating to company affairs; transactions in fraud of creditors; fraud in anticipation of winding up: Ins.A. 1986, ss. 206–211.

liquidation, voluntary. *See* VOLUNTARY WINDING-UP.

liquidator, company. One who is appointed in the case of a company which is being wound up by the court, "to secure that the assets are got in, realised and distributed to creditors and, if there is a surplus, to those entitled to it": Ins.A. 1986, s. 143(1). He is empowered to summon a final meeting of creditors: s. 146. See, generally, ss. 163–174.

lis. Action; suit; dispute.

lis alibi pendens. Suit pending elsewhere. Such a situation may provide grounds for staying an action. See, e.g., *McHenry* v *Lewis* (1882) 22 Ch D 397.

lis mota. A lawsuit which is anticipated, or which is existing.

lis pendens. *See* PENDENS LIS.

listed buildings. Buildings of special architectural or historic interest listed by the Secretary of State: Planning (Listed Buildings and Conservation Areas) Act 1990, s. 1 (1). Their alteration, extension, demolition, require consent: ss. 7, 8, 17. For exceptions, see ss. 9, 60. See also T.C.P.A. 1990; Planning and Compensation Act 1991, s. 29.

listed securities. In relation to a company, means any securities of the company listed on a recognised stock exchange (q.v.): Company Securities (Insider Dealing) Act 1985, s. 12(*b*). See F.S.A. 1986, Part IV, Sch. 16, para. 28.

list of documents. *See* DOCUMENTS, LIST OF.

lite pendente. *See* PENDENTE LITE.

literal method. A method for the construction of a statute by the courts. Its basis is: that words are to be taken prima facie in their ordinary, literal or grammatical meaning; that they are to be taken to be used in the same sense they had when the statute was passed; that the same words carry the same meaning. But "the literal meaning of the words is never allowed to prevail where it would produce manifest absurdity or consequences which can never have been intended by the legislature": *Corocraft* v *Pan Am Airways* [1969] 1 QB 616. See *Duport Steels* v *Sirs* [1980] 1 WLR 142. See INTERPRETATION OF STATUTES.

literary work. "Any work, other than a dramatic or musical work, which is written, spoken or sung, and accordingly includes a table or compilation and a computer program": Copyright, Designs and Patents Act 1988, s. 3(1).

literary work, original. "The originality . . . relates to the expression of the thought": *per* Peterson J in *University of London Press* v *University Tutorial Press* [1916] 2 Ch 601. See Copyrights, Designs and Patents Act 1988, s. 3(1).

litigant. *See* LITIGATION.

litigant, assistance by adviser. A litigant appearing in person is entitled to have "quiet and unobtrusive advice" from another member of the public accompanying him as an assistant or adviser, but the court may refuse this right if it is deemed necessary to maintain order in the proceedings: *R* v *Leicester City Justices, ex p Barrow* [1991] 3 WLR 386.

litigant in person, costs of. Costs awarded to the litigant in person. He may recover for work reasonably done in his leisure time, and earnings lost through taking time off from work, to prepare or conduct the case. He may charge only for work which would have been done by a solicitor had he been legally represented.

litigation. The taking of legal action by a party, who is known as a "litigant".

litigator, authorised. Any person (in-

cluding a solicitor) who has a right to conduct litigation granted by an authorised body in accordance with provisions of C.L.S.A. 1990: C.L.S.A 1990, s. 119(1).

litter, offences in relation to. It is an offence to throw down, drop or otherwise deposit and leave litter in circumstances as to cause, or contribute to, or tend to lead to, the defacement by litter of any public open space and other places such as special roads. See En.P.A. 1990, s. 87. See also Litter Act 1983.

livery of seisin. Part of the early common law procedure of conveying a freehold (q.v.), known as *feoffment of fee with livery of seisin* (abolished under L.P.A 1925, s. 51). It consisted of *livery in law* (symbolic delivery of property within sight of the land to be conveyed) or *livery of deed* (grantor stood on land to be conveyed and invited grantee to enter).

lives in being, statutory. *See* STATUTORY LIVES IN BEING.

livestock. Any creature kept for the production of food, wool, skins or fur, or for the purpose of its use in the farming of land or the carrying on of any agricultural activity: Agricultural Holdings Act 1986, s. 96(1). "Cattle, horses, asses, mules, hinnies, sheep, pigs, goats and poultry, and also deer not in the wild state": Animals Act 1971, s. 11. The 1971 Act, s. 4, imposes liability on a person in possession of livestock which stray on to another's land and damage it or any property on it. Under s. 3, the keeper of a dog which causes damage by killing or injuring livestock is liable for the damage.

livestock, protection of. It is a defence to an action for injuring or killing a dog to prove that it was done by a person entitled so to act for the protection of livestock and that notice was given at a police station within 48 hours: Animals Act 1971, s. 9.

living apart. In relation to divorce proceedings, this does not mean mere physical separation, but it involves a spouse's ceasing to recognise the marriage as subsisting: *Santos* v *Santos* [1972] 2 All ER 246. By Mat.C.A. 1973, s. 2(6), husband and wife are treated as living apart unless they live in the same household with each other.

living expenses. The phrase is to be construed as meaning "expenses of living"; it is not limited to living expenses solely attributable to an individual person's expenditure. It includes expenses representing costs incurred for housing, food, clothing, necessary travelling and the like, and encompasses all the usual costs associated with any individual's particular life style: *Nutbrown* v *Rosier* (1982) The Times, 1 Mar.

living memory. "Time whereof the memory of man runneth not to the contrary."

living together. A man and his wife are not deemed to be living otherwise than together unless they are permanently living in separation either by agreement or under an order of the court, or one has deserted the other and the separation incident to the desertion has not come to an end. Under Mat.C.A. 1973, s. 2(6), a husband and wife are to be treated as living apart unless living with each other in the same household. See *Piper* v *Piper* (1978) 8 Fam Law 263. *See* CO-HABITATION.

L.J. Lord Justice of Appeal (q.v.).

Lloyd's. An insurance market place constituted by syndicates of London underwriters, incorporated by statute in 1871. Controlled by Lloyd's Act 1982 and the Insurance (Lloyd's) Regulations 1983, issued under the Insurance Companies Act 1982. The Society of Lloyd's and persons permitted by the Council of Lloyd's to act as underwriting agents at Lloyd's are exempted persons as respects investment business carried on in connection with or for the purpose of insurance business at Lloyd's: F.S.A. 1986, s. 42. For restriction of exemption, see s. 46. See *Touche Ross & Co and Others* v *Baker* (1992) The Times, 22 June (House of Lords decision on use of "discovery extension clauses", giving assured an option exercisable before the expiry of the policy to prolong cover for a further period on payment of additional premium, by a Lloyd's syndicate).

loan capital. *See* CAPITAL, LOAN.

loan, quasi-. *See* QUASI-LOAN.

local administration, commissions for. Bodies, for England and Wales, set up under L.G.A. 1974, s. 23(1), each including the Parliamentary Commissioner (q.v.), to investigate complaints of injustice in consequence of maladministration in local government. Each commission submits an annual report to its representative body, comprising representatives of authorities subject to the commissions' jurisdiction. *See also* OMBUDSMAN, LOCAL GOVERNMENT.

local authority. Body constituted for the administration of a local government unit. In relation to England and Wales, it means: a county council, district council, London Borough Council, a parish council, a community council, the Council of the Isles of Scilly, the Common Council of the City of London: L.G.A. 1988, s. 1(2). Defined under Finance Act 1974, s. 52(2), as "(*a*) any authority having power to make or determine a rate; (*b*) any authority having power to issue a precept, requisition or other demand for the payment of money to be raised out of a rate". A person is disqualified from membership of a local authority if he holds a "politically restricted" post, e.g., statutory chief officer: L.G.H.A. 1989, s. 1. *See* PRECEPT; RATES.

local authority, performance standards of. Under L.G.A. 1992, s. 1, the Audit Commission (q.v.) may direct the publication by relevant bodies of information concerning their activities in a financial year, facilitating the making of appropriate comparisons, by reference to criteria of costs, efficiency, etc., between standards of performance achieved by different relevant bodies.

local government. Government on a local basis by elected committees, forming part of the UK's administrative system, based on pattern of elected bodies for defined areas with responsibility for the provision of services within those areas. See L.G.A. 1972–92; *Hazell* v *Hammersmith and Fulham LBC* [1991] 2 WLR 372.

Local Government Commission for England. Body of 5–15 members established under L.G.A 1992, s. 12, to conduct a review of areas in England and recommend structural, boundary or electoral changes. See Sch. 2.

Local Government Ombudsman. *See* OMBUDSMAN, LOCAL GOVERNMENT.

local land charges. Any charge acquired by a local authority which is binding on successive owners of the land affected; any prohibition or restriction on the use of land imposed by a local authority or minister or government department which is binding on successive owners of the land affected; any positive obligation affecting land enforceable by a minister, government department or local authority binding on successive owners of the land affected: Local Land Charges Act 1975, s. 1. Registers of local land charges are kept in London by London boroughs and the City of London, and in other areas by district councils. See Local Land Charges Rules 1977, as amended; En.P.A. 1990, s. 143.

local land charges register. Consists of twelve parts: part 1 includes general financial charges; part 2 includes specific financial charges; part 3 includes planning charges; part 4 is reserved for charges not registrable in the other parts; part 5 includes fenland ways maintenance charges; part 6 relates to land compensation charges; part 7 refers to New Towns charges; part 8 includes civil aviation charges; part 9 refers to open-cast coal charges; part 10 is reserved for listed buildings charges; part 11 is for light obstruction notices; part 12 is for drainage scheme charges. Failure to register does not affect enforceability of the charge: Local Land Charges Act 1975, s. 10. See I.A. 1978, Sch. 1.

locatio conductio. A contract of bailment for hire, expressing letting and hiring.

locatio rei. The hiring of some thing. Bailment or letting of a thing to be used by the bailee for compensation to be paid by him.

loc. cit. *Loco citato* = in the place cited. At the passage [of a book] cited.

lock-out. The closing by an employer of a place of employment, or the suspension of work, or the refusal by an employer to continue to employ any number of persons employed by him, in consequence of a dispute. See, e.g., E.P.(C.)A. 1978, Sch. 13, para. 24; *Henthorn and Taylor v CEGB* [1980] IRLR 361.

lock-out agreement. Described in *Walford v Miles* [1992] 1 All ER 453, as an agreement for valuable consideration between a vendor of property (V) and a potential purchaser (P) that V will negotiate exclusively with P with a view to achieving at the end of the negotiation a binding contract for the sale of that property to P and will not deal with any other prospective purchaser. It is unenforceable as a contract because of lack of certainty.

loco parentis. See IN LOCO PARENTIS.

locum tenens. Holding an office. One who acts as a lawful substitute or deputy.

locus in quo. Place in which. Scene of the event. See *R v Hunter* [1985] 1 WLR 613.

locus poenitentiae. A "place for repentance". An opportunity of changing one's mind, e.g., by withdrawing from a planned criminal enterprise. See *R v Whitefield* [1984] Crim LR 97.

locus regit actum. The place governs the act, i.e., an act is governed by the law of the place where it is performed. See, e.g., *R v Bham* [1966] 1 QB 159.

locus sigilli. Place of the seal. "L.S." may be used in a document to show where the seal should be. See *First National Securities Ltd v Jones* [1978] 2 All ER 221. See SEALING.

locus standi. Place to stand. A right to be heard, a sufficient interest, or the legal capacity to challenge some decision. See, e.g., *R v Tower Hamlets LBC v Thrasyvalou* [1991] COD 123. See O. 53, r. 3(7). See AGGRIEVED PERSON.

lodger. One who occupies part of a house, but whose occupation is under control of a landlord or his representative who resides in or retains possession of or dominion over that house: *Thompson v Ward* [1906] 1 KB 60. ("The occupier is a lodger if the landlord provides attendance or services which require the landlord or his servants to exercise unrestricted access to and use of the premises. A lodger is entitled to live in the premises but cannot call the place his own": *per* Lord Templeman in *Street v Mountford* [1985] AC 809.) See *Brooker Settled Estates Ltd v Ayers* (1987) 19 LR 246.

lodging house, common. A house (other than a public assistance institution) provided for the purpose of accommodating by night poor persons, not being members of the same family, who resort to it and are allowed to occupy one common room for the purpose of sleeping or eating, and includes, where part only of a house is so used, the part so used: H.A. 1985, s. 401. Such houses must be registered: s. 402.

logical plenitude, theory of. Theory in jurisprudence (q.v.) stating that law is an organic *corpus* of principles with an inherent power of expansion and adaptation to new circumstances.

logic and the law. "The purpose and value of logic to the law is to ensure that persons whose relevant circumstances are similar receive similar treatment. It is in other words to promote equity: to use it to defeat equity is to misuse it": *per* Lord Simon in *Rugby Water Board* v *Shaw-Fox* [1973] AC 202. *See* LEGAL LOGIC.

logic, legal. *See* LEGAL LOGIC.

loiter. To act in a way which suggests that a person is idling in the street for an unlawful purpose. Loitering for purposes of prostitution is an offence: Street Offences Act 1959, s. 1. *See* IMPORTUNE.

London City of. *See* CITY OF LONDON.

London Gazette. An official journal of the Government, first published *c.* 1665. It contains, e.g., proclamations, notices of receiving orders.

long tenancy. "A tenancy granted for a term of years certain exceeding 21 years, whether or not subsequently extended by act of the parties or by any enactment, but excluding any tenancy which is, or may become, terminable before the end of the term by notice given to the tenant": L.G.H.A. 1989, Sch. 10. For security of tenure on ending of long residential tenancies, see s. 186.

long title. *See* TITLE, LONG.

long vacation. The former name for the period 1st August to 30th September during which the Supreme Court does not generally transact business except in urgent cases. See O. 64. The normal break has been reduced to the single month of August and this is subject to increasing exceptions.

looting. 1. Sacking; plundering; robbing. 2. Stealing from any person killed, injured or detained during military operations or taking otherwise than for the public service any vehicle, equipment or stores abandoned by the

enemy: Armed Forces Act 1971. See *R* v *Bailey* (1982) 4 Cr App R (S) 15.

lord. 1. Peer of the realm. 2. One of whom land is held by a tenant (q.v.).

Lord Advocate. The Crown's principal law officer in Scotland. He represents the Crown in legal proceedings and conducts Crown prosecutions.

Lord Chancellor. *See* CHANCELLOR.

Lord Chief Justice. Presides over the QBD and the Court of Appeal (Criminal Division) and ranks next to the Lord Chancellor in the legal hierarchy. Appointed by the Sovereign upon recommendation of the Prime Minister. See S.C.A. 1981, s. 10(2)(a).

Lord Lieutenant of the County. Office first created in the sixteenth century when the holder was commander of county militia and chief among county justices. Now appointed by the Crown on the advice of the Prime Minister. He recommends the appointment of magistrates.

Lord Privy Seal. Duties attaching to this office were abolished in 1884. The office remains and is filled by a member of the cabinet.

Lords, House of. *See* HOUSE OF LORDS.

Lords Justices of Appeal. Judges who sit in the Court of Appeal (q.v.), appointed by the Queen from High Court judges or persons with a 10-year High Court qualification (see C.L.S.A. 1990, s. 71): S.C.A. 1981, s. 10, as amended.

Lords of Appeal in Ordinary. Senior members of the judiciary, usually appointed from the Court of Appeal (q.v.), who hear appeals in the House of Lords (q.v.). They have held other high judicial office for two years, or have held a Supreme Court qualification, within the meaning of C.L.S.A. 1990, s. 71, for 15 years. See the Appellate Jurisdiction Acts 1876–1947; C.L.S.A. 1990, Sch. 10.

Lords Spiritual. *See* HOUSE OF LORDS.

Lords Temporal. *See* HOUSE OF LORDS.

loss leaders. Goods sold not primarily to make a profit but to attract customers so that they might also buy other goods, or to advertise the business: see Resale Prices Act 1976, s. 13(2); *JJB (Sports) Ltd* v *Milbro Sports Ltd* [1975] ICR 73.

loss, liability in marine insurance for. An insurer will be liable for losses proximately caused by a peril which has been insured against. A *partial loss* is a loss other than a total loss. A *total loss* may be *actual* or *constructive*; *actual total loss* is where the subject-matter insured is destroyed or so damaged that it has ceased to be a thing of the kind insured against; *constructive total loss* is where the subject-matter insured has been abandoned because its actual total loss seems unavoidable.

loss of consortium and services. *See* PER QUOD CONSORTIUM ET SERVITIUM AMISIT.

lost modern grant. Doctrine based on fiction (q.v.) whereby the court can presume from long user (i.e., 20 years) that a grant of easements and profits has been made at some time after 1189, but that it has now been lost. User as of right must be shown, right claimed must be capable of being acquired by grant. Claim may be made only where a presumption at common law is not possible in the circumstances: *Tehidy Minerals* v *Norman* [1971] 2 QB 528. See *Bridle* v *Ruby* [1988] 3 WLR 191 (presumption of lost modern grant was not rebutted by mistaken belief as to right of way); *Mills* v *Silver* [1991] 2 WLR 324.

lost years principle. Principle derived from *Oliver* v *Ashman* [1962] 2 QB 210 whereby courts were prevented from awarding to persons who had suffered injury or disease which shortened their lives damages for loss of what they might have earned during the "lost years". Overruled by the House of Lords in *Pickett* v *British Rail Engineering Ltd* [1979] 1 All ER 774. See also A.J.A 1982, s. 1.

lottery. A game of chance. Generally unlawful: Lotteries and Amusements Act 1976, s. 1. Exceptions: small lotteries incidental to "exempt entertainments" (e.g., bazaars, sales of work, dances); private lotteries (e.g., those in which the sale of tickets is restricted to members of one society); societies' lotteries (i.e., promoted on behalf of a society concerned with athletics, charitable purposes, etc.). A lottery ticket "includes any document evidencing the claim of a person to participate in the chances of the lottery": 1976 Act, s. 23(1). See *Imperial Tobacco Co.* v *A.-G.* [1981] AC 718.

loyalty. Faithfulness and allegiance (q.v.) to one's sovereign or government.

l.s. *Locus sigilli* (q.v.).

lucid interval. A temporary period of rational thought and behaviour between periods of insanity. A will (q.v.) made during such a period may be admitted to probate (q.v.). See *Chambers and Yatman* v *Queen's Proctor* (1840) 2 Curt 415, in which the deceased made a will during a lucid interval and killed himself, while insane, on the following day, and the will was admitted to probate.

lucri causa. For the purpose of gain.

lump sum award. A once-for-all award of damages, comprising pecuniary loss incurred up to the trial and a final estimate of future pecuniary and non-pecuniary loss. For lump sum order under Mat.C.A. 1973, see s. 24A.

lump sum contract. Contract (q.v.) by which it is intended that complete performance shall take place before payment may be demanded. Failure to complete performance prevents any payment being recovered. See *Sumpter* v *Hedges* [1898] 1 QB 673; *Hoenig* v *Isaacs* [1952] 1 All ER 176 (recovery of sum relating to faulty workmanship).

lump sum freight. *See* FREIGHT.

lunatic. An idiot or person of unsound mind: Lunacy Act 1890, s. 341. This term has now been replaced by "patient". See M.H.A. 1983, s. 145(1).

lunatic, criminal. *See* CRIMINAL LUNATIC.

M

machinery and plant. Expression relating to capital allowances, used in the Finance Acts in relation to a deduction against income tax, based on expenditure on machinery and plant purchased for the purpose of one's trade. See Capital Allowances Act 1990, Part II. *See* PLANT.

machinery, dangerous. *See* DANGEROUS MACHINERY.

magistrates. Honorary (or lay) magistrates (as contrasted with stipendiary magistrates (q.v.)) are part-time justices of the peace (q.v.) appointed by the Crown on the advice of the Lord Chancellor and Advisory Committees. The office of justice of the peace originated in the late twelfth century royal proclamation creating "knights of the peace" to aid the sheriff (q.v.) in the enforcement of the law. Known later as *custodes pacis* (keepers of the peace) and, from *c.* 1360, as "justices of the peace". See Justices of the Peace Act 1361, and (for the schemes for appointment, retirement, etc) Justices of the Peace Act 1979. They may be removed by the Lord Chancellor without showing cause. At the age of 70 they are placed on the supplemental list and cease to be entitled to exercise any judicial function (see A.J.A. 1973, s. 5; and Justices of the Peace Act 1979, s. 8). Functions include: committing offenders for trial by judge and jury; trying offences summarily; sitting with judges of the Crown Court to hear appeals from magistrates' courts; licensing of premises selling intoxicating liquor; etc. See M.C.A. 1980; S.C.A. 1980, ss. 8, 74, 75; Crown Court Rules 1982, rr. 3–5 (magistrates sitting in Crown Court); SI 1992/1856.

magistrates' clerk. A lawyer with possession of a 5-year magistrates' court qualification (see C.L.S.A. 1990, s. 71, Sch. 10), who advises magistrates at their request on law and procedure. Gener-

ally he should not go with magistrates when they retire to consider their verdict (see *R v E. Kerrier Justices, ex p Mundy* [1952] 2 QB 719); should they require his advice after they have retired they may send for him, but he should return to the court when his advice has been given. See Justices of the Peace Acts 1949, 1968 and 1979, ss. 25–30; M.C.A. 1980, s. 141; C.L.S.A. 1990, s. 117.

magistrates' courts. Some 400 courts, each constituted by any justice or justices of the peace acting under common law or any enactment or by virtue of a commission: M.C.A. 1980, s. 148. Consists generally of 2–7 part-time, unpaid JPs who hear complaints and try certain cases summarily. A single justice may conduct a preliminary investigation. See, e.g., M.C.A. 1980, s. 121(1). Jurisdiction, which is local, is civil and criminal, largely comprising matters relating to: summary offences; indictable offences triable summarily; indictable offences triable only on indictment; offences triable either way; some domestic proceedings. A stipendiary magistrate (q.v.) has, in effect, the powers of two lay justices. See C.L.A. 1977, ss. 28–32, 46; Justices of the Peace Act 1979, ss. 19–20; Magistrates' Courts Act 1980.

magistrates' courts, sittings of. A magistrates' court may sit on any day of the year, and (if the court thinks fit) on Christmas Day, Good Friday or any Sunday: M.C.A. 1980, s. 153.

magistrates, *ex-officio*. Those who became magistrates by virtue of holding another office, e.g., that of mayor. Generally abolished under Justices of the Peace Act 1968 and A.J.A. 1973, save for High Court judges and the Lord Mayor and some aldermen in the City of London.

magistrates, restrictions on imprisonment by. In general, a magistrates' court has no power to impose imprisonment for less than five days, or more than six months in respect of any one offence: M.C.A. 1980, ss. 31, 132. The aggregate of consecutive terms of imprisonment may not generally exceed six months: s. 133(1). (For exceptional cases involving twelve months, see s. 133(2).)

magistrates, stipendiary. *See* STIPENDIARY MAGISTRATES.

Magna Carta. The Great Charter (of Liberties), dated 15th June 1215. A statement in 37 chapters by King John of concessions to church and freemen, comprising a preamble and 63 clauses. It enunciated a number of fundamental principles, e.g., "to none will we sell, to none will we deny or delay right or justice". For recent reference to the Charter, see *A.-G.'s Reference No. 1 of 1990* (1992) NLJ 563.

mail, detaining or delaying. It is an offence for an officer of the Post Office wilfully to detain or delay contrary to his duty any postal packet or message (by telephone and telegraph) in the course of transmission by post. See Telegraph Act 1863, s. 45; Post Office Act 1953, s. 58, amended by Interception of Communications Act 1985, s. 11.

maim. To injure a person so that he is rendered less capable of defending himself.

main purpose rule. *See* REPUGNANCY.

main residence. A tenant who occupied more than one residence could exercise his rights under the Leasehold Reform Act 1967 only in relation to the house he occupied as his main residence: s. 1. Thus, one who owned a main residence abroad and the lease of a house in the UK would have no rights under the Act. Which of two houses is the main residence is a matter of fact and degree. See also Capital Gains Tax Act 1979, s. 101.

maintain, failure to. Either party to a marriage may apply to the court for an order that the other party has failed to provide reasonable maintenance for the applicant or for any child of the family: Mat.C.A. 1973, s. 27, as amended by D.P.A. 1978, s. 63.

maintain, liability to. A man is liable to maintain his wife and children, and a woman is liable to maintain her husband and children: see, e.g., S.S.A.

1975, s. 17. Each parent of a "qualifying child" is responsible for maintaining him: Child Support Act 1991, s. 1(1). A child is a "qualifying child" if one or both of his parents is, or are, not living in the same household with him, or he has his home with a person "with care" (e.g., one who usually provides day to day care for him): s. 3. For details of child support maintenance, see s. 4. For failure to maintain and income support (q.v.), see S.S. Administration Act 1992, s. 105.

maintenance. 1. Intermeddling in an action. "A taking in hand, bearing up or upholding of quarrels and sides, to the disturbance of the common right": Coke. Criminal and tortious liability for maintenance was abolished by C.L.A. 1967. 2. The supply of necessaries, e.g., food, clothing. Trustees (q.v.) may be empowered by provisions in a settlement or under Tr.A. 1925, to apply income of a trust fund towards the maintenance of a beneficiary (q.v.). See Tr.A. 1925, s. 31. 3. Financial arrangements embodied in a maintenance agreement (q.v.).

maintenance after termination of marriage. The court may make orders under Mat.C.A. 1973, ss. 23, 24, known as "financial provision orders" (for lump sums or secured or unsecured periodical payments) and "property adjustment orders" (for settlement or transfer of property, variation of ante- or post-nuptial settlements or reduction of interest in such settlements).

maintenance agreement. A written agreement made in respect of a child, between its father and mother and containing provision in respect of the making or securing of payments, or the disposition or use of any property, for the maintenance or education of the child: F.L.R.A. 1987, s. 15(1). See Ch. A. 1989, Sch. 1, paras 10, 11.

maintenance agreement by deceased person. Under Inheritance (Provision for Family and Dependants) Act 1975, s. 17(4), means: any agreement made, in writing or not, and whether before or after the commencement of the Act, by the deceased with any person with whom he entered into a marriage, being an agreement containing provisions governing rights and liabilities towards one another when living separately of the parties to that marriage (whether dissolved or annulled) in respect of the making or securing of payments or the disposition or use of any property, including any rights and liabilities with respect to maintenance or education of any child, whether or not a child of the deceased or a person treated by the deceased as a child of the family in relation to that marriage.

maintenance order. An order, which provides for the periodical payment of sums of money towards the maintenance of any person, being a person whom the person liable to make payments under the order is liable to maintain: Maintenance Orders (Reciprocal Enforcement) Act 1972, s. 21(1). See A.J.A. 1970, Sch. 8; D.P.A. 1978, s. 11, Sch. 2 (as amended); C.J.J.A. 1982, s. 37(1), Sch. 11; Maintenance Enforcement Act 1991, s. 1, empowering the High Court and county courts to order payment by standing order and to order a debtor who has unreasonably refused to open a banking account to open one for this purpose.

maintenance pending suit. Replaced "alimony (q.v.) pending suit". On petition for divorce, nullity or separation, the court may order either party to the marriage to make to the other periodical payments for his or her maintenance beginning not earlier than the date of the presentation of the petition and ending with the date of determination of the suit: Mat.C.A. 1973, s. 22.

majority. 1. Full age, 18, under F.L.R.A. 1969. 2. The greater number of those present, or voting, at an assembly or other meeting.

majority rule. 1. Basic principle of democratic organisation. 2. Principle whereby a company's shareholders exercise control of the company through the general meeting. Minority shareholders are protected by common law (see *Foss* v *Harbottle* (1843) 2 Hare 461) and the provisions of Cos.A. 1985.

majority verdict. *See* VERDICT, MAJORITY.

making off without payment. Offence under Th.A. 1978, s. 3, committed where a person who, knowing that payment on the spot for any goods supplied or service done is required or expected from him, dishonestly makes

off without having paid as required or expected and with intent to avoid payment of the amount. "Payment on the spot" includes payment at the time of collecting goods on which work has been done or in respect of which service has been provided. Does not apply where supply of goods or provision of service is contrary to law or where service done is such that payment is not legally enforceable. Any person may arrest without warrant anyone who is, or whom he, with reasonable cause, suspects to be, committing or attempting to commit this offence: s. 3(4). See *R* v *McDavitt* [1981] Crim LR 843 (upheld in *R* v *Brooks* (1983) 76 Cr App R 66); *R* v *Allen* [1985] AC 1029 (there must be an intent permanently to avoid payment).

maladministration. Insufficient, weak or dishonest administration. See, e.g., *R* v *Local Commissioner, ex p Bradford MCC* [1979] QB 287. There is no general right to damages for maladministration: *R* v *Knowsley MBC, ex p Maguire* (1992) The Times, 26 June. *See* OMBUDSMAN, LOCAL GOVERNMENT.

mala fides. Bad faith (q.v.).

mala in se. Acts wrong in themselves (e.g., murder).

mala praxis. A dereliction from professional duty resulting in injury, e.g., as where a physician injures a patient as a result of neglect. *See* PRACTICE, GENERAL AND APPROVED.

mala prohibita. Acts which are wrongs because they are prohibited by law, but which are not necessarily or obviously wrongs in themselves, e.g., failure to make tax returns. See, e.g., *R* v *McBride* (1980) 107 DLR (3d) 233.

male issue. Male descendants in the male line only (unlike "male descendants" which may refer to male descendants of the *propositus* (q.v.) through males or females). See *Re Du Cros' ST* [1961] 3 All ER 193.

malfeasance. The commission of an unlawful act. *See* MISFEASANCE.

malice. 1. Generally refers to an attitude inherent in "a wrongful act done intentionally without just cause or excuse": *Bromage* v *Prosser* (1825) 4 B & C 247. 2. In relation to *mens rea* (q.v.) of murder, categorised as: (1) *express* (an intention to kill); (2) *implied* (q.v.) (an intention to do only grievous bodily harm (q.v.)); (3) *universal* (e.g., where X fires a gun into a crowd, not caring who is killed, and killing Y); (4) *transferred* (as where X, intending to kill Y, shoots at him, but kills Z, who, unknown to X, was standing near Y, so that X's malice is considered as having been "transferred" to Z: *R* v *Salisbury* (1553) 1 Plowd 100; *R* v *Monger* [1973] Crim LR 301); (5) *constructive* (q.v.). See *R* v *Farrell* [1989] Crim LR 126. 3. A constituent of defamation (q.v.). The plaintiff must prove that words complained of were published maliciously, e.g., in abuse of fair comment. See the Defamation Act 1952, s. 4(6). *See* RECKLESSNESS, CATEGORIES OF.

malice aforethought. The mental element in the offence of murder (q.v.). The prosecution must prove malice aforethought solely by proof that defendant either intended to kill another person or that he intended to cause that person really serious harm. ("Foresight" is not to be equated with "intention".) See C.J.A. 1967, s. 8; *DPP* v *Smith* [1961] AC 290; *Hyam* v *DPP* [1975] AC 55; *R* v *Cunningham* [1982] AC 566; *R* v *Hancock and Shankland* [1986] AC 455; *Frankland* v *R* [1987] AC 576.

malice prepense. Malice aforethought (q.v.).

malicious arrest. *See* ARREST, MALICIOUS.

malicious communications. It is an offence, intending to cause distress, to send letters conveying threats, indecent or grossly offensive messages or information known to be false by the sender: Malicious Communications Act 1988, s. 1(1). For defences, see s. 1(2).

malicious damage. An offence involving damage to property caused by acts done unlawfully and maliciously under Malicious Damage Act 1861, repealed by Criminal Damage Act 1971. See *R* v *Gittins* [1982] RTR 363. *See* CRIMINAL DAMAGE.

malicious falsehood. A false and malicious statement concerning a person, made to someone other than that person, relating to his property or business interests which damages his general material interests. "Malicious" involves some dishonest or other improper motive (but not carelessness). Known also as "slander of title" (q.v.).

See Defamation Act 1952, s. 3(1); *Balden* v *Shorter* [1933] Ch 427; *Joyce* v *Sengupta* (1992) The Independent, 11 Aug.

malicious prosecution. A tort (q.v.) in which the plaintiff proves: that he has sustained damage; that the defendant prosecuted him; that the prosecution ended in the plaintiff's favour; that the prosecution lacked any reasonable and probable cause; that the defendant acted maliciously (i.e., with some other motive than desire to bring to justice a person whom the accuser believes to be guilty): *Brown* v *Hawkes* [1891] 2 QB 718.

malicious prosecution, reasonable and probable cause in relation to. Definition approved by the House of Lords in *Herniman* v *Smith* [1938] AC 305 is: "An honest belief in the guilt of accused based upon full conviction, founded upon reasonable grounds, of the existence of a state of circumstances, which, assuming them to be true, would reasonably lead any ordinarily prudent and cautious man, placed in the position of the accuser, to the conclusion that the person charged was probably guilty of the crime imputed."

malicious wounding. Offence committed under O.P.A. 1861, s. 20, by a person who unlawfully and maliciously wounds or inflicts any grievous bodily harm (q.v.) upon another either with or without any weapon or instrument. Known also as "unlawful wounding". *See* WOUNDING; WOUNDING WITH INTENT.

malicious wounding, proof of. The prosecution must prove either that defendant (D) intended or actually foresaw that his act would cause harm; it is not sufficient to show that D ought to have foreseen that his act would cause harm. It is unnecessary to show that D intended or foresaw the gravity of the harm that his acts would cause, as long as he foresaw some physical harm, even of a minor nature: *R* v *Savage* [1991] 4 All ER 698.

malingerer. One who falsely pretends to be suffering from sickness or disability; or who injures himself so as to render himself unfit for service, or causes himself to be injured by another with that intent, or who prolongs or aggravates any sickness or disability. See Army Act 1955, s. 42(1).

malitia supplet aetatem *See* DOLI CAPAX.

malversation. Misbehaviour or corruption in an office of public trust.

man. A male adult person. In the Sex Discrimination Act 1975, s. 82(1) it includes a male "of any age".

manager, appointment of. Equitable remedy allowing the court to appoint a manager who is empowered to continue a business. Often the same person is appointed as receiver and manager. "Nothing is better settled than that this court does not assume the management of a business or undertaking except with a view to the winding-up and sale of the business or undertaking": *Gardner* v *London Chatham and Dover Rwy* (1887) 2 Ch App 201.

manager, company. *See* COMPANY MANAGER.

manager, special. *See* SPECIAL MANAGER.

managing director. A director (q.v.) who has charge of the management of the company. See Table A, arts. 72, 84.

mandamus. We command. Originally a writ from the High Court (q.v.) ordering performance of a public duty. Replaced by an order, under A.J.A. 1938, s. 7. Used, e.g., to direct the holding of municipal elections (*Re Barnes Corporation* [1933] 1 KB 668); to compel hearing of an appeal by an inferior tribunal. See now S.C.A. 1981, ss. 29, 31.

mandate. 1. A direction from a superior to an inferior court. 2. A contract of agency to perform a task for another person. 3. An order or injunction. 4. A commission granted by the former League of Nations to a member state relating to the establishment of government over conquered territory, e.g., the former German territories in Africa after the First World War.

mandatory injunction. *See* INJUNCTION.

man of straw. 1. One who is used to shield another, e.g., in an action. 2. One of little means and, hence, not worth suing.

manor. A feudal unit, usually comprising the lord's manor house and the land he occupied and cultivated, together with land held by tenants and waste used for pasture. See L.P.A. 1925, s. 205(1) (ix).

manslaughter. Generally unlawful homicide which cannot be classified as murder (q.v.), e.g., as where X kills Y as a result of grossly negligent conduct. May be classified as (1) *voluntary*, i.e., as in the case of a killing which would have been murder, but is considered as manslaughter because the accused successfully pleads diminished responsibility (q.v.) or provocation; (2) *involuntary*, i.e., as where the *actus reus* (q.v.) of homicide is unaccompanied by malice aforethought, resulting from an act performed with criminal negligence. See *R* v *Bonnyman* (1942) 86 SJ 274; *R* v *Seymour* [1983] 2 AC 493; *R* v *Arobieke* [1988] Crim LR 314; *R* v *Coleman* (1991) The Times, 10 Dec. (sentencing guidelines for involuntary manslaughter); *R* v *Lebrun* [1991] 3 WLR 653 (problem of coincidence in time of *mens rea* and *actus reus*).

manslaughter, constructive. Type of manslaughter (q.v.) limited to death resulting from an offence likely to cause some harm. See *R* v *Dawson* (1985) 81 Cr App R 150 – the requisite "harm" was caused if the unlawful act so shocked the victim as to cause him physical injury. See *R* v *Watson* [1989] 1 WLR 684.

manslaughter, corporate body and. A corporate body is capable of being found guilty of manslaughter but only if the *mens rea* and the *actus reus* of the offence can be established against those that were identified as the embodiment of the corporate body: *R* v *HM Coroner for E. Kent, ex p Spooner* (1987) 3 BCC 638.

mansuetae naturae. Tame by nature. Term applied to animals, such as horses, dogs. *See* ANIMALS, CLASSIFICATION OF.

manual labour. Includes work done with the hands, even though it is highly skilled and technical: *Stone Lighting & Radio Ltd* v *Haygarth* [1968] AC 157.

Mareva injunction. Procedure based on an interlocutory prohibitory injunction, whereby the court comes to a creditor's aid when the debtor (resident or non-resident) has absconded or is overseas but has assets in this country. The assets required to satisfy a judgment or expected judgment are temporarily frozen. See *Mareva Compania Naviera SA* v *International Bulk-Carriers SA* [1975] 2 Lloyd's Rep 509. For guidelines on creditor's applications, see *Third Chandris Shipping Corp* v *Unimarine SA* [1979] QB 645. See S.C.A. 1981, s. 37; C.J.J.A. 1982, s. 25; *Capital Cameras* v *Harold Lines* [1991] 1 WLR 54; *Atlas Maritime Co.* v *Avalon Maritime (No. 3)* [1991] 1 WLR 917; *Lewis Peat Produce* v *Almatu Properties* (1992) The Times, 14 May.

marginal notes. Notes printed in margins of Acts of Parliament, explanatory of the clauses. They do not form part of an Act (except in the case of certain private Acts). They may be considered by the court in a case of ambiguity. See *Chandler* v *DPP* [1964] AC 763; *DPP* v *Schildkamp* [1971] AC 1.

marine adventure. The exposure of a ship, goods or other movables to maritime perils (i.e., perils consequent on, or incidental to, the navigation of the sea): Marine Insurance Act 1906, s. 3.

marine insurance contract. Contract (q.v.) whereby an insurer engages to indemnify the assured against those losses incident to a marine adventure (q.v.). See Marine Insurance Act 1906; *Rhesa Shipping* v *Edmunds* [1985] 1 WLR 948; *The Good Luck* [1991] 2 WLR 1279.

marine waters. Waters, other than inland waters (q.v.) within the seaward limits of the territorial sea adjacent to Great Britain: Diseases of Fish Act 1983, s. 7(8).

maritagium. 1. Right of a lord to give his infant ward in marriage. 2. An early mode of disposition of land, whereby a father, on the marriage of his daughter, conveyed land to her and the husband and the heirs of their bodies.

maritime lien. *See* LIEN.

maritime perils. Perils arising from navigation of the sea, e.g., fire, war, pirates, restraints of princes (q.v.), jettisons and other perils which may be designated by the insurance policy: see Marine Insurance Act 1906, s. 3. The term "perils of the seas" does not include the ordinary action of wind and waves: see *Samuel & Co* v *Dumas* (1922) 13 Ll L Rep 503. For "maritime claim", see C.J.J.A. 1982, Sch. 3.

market. 1. Trading area in which activities are held under common law by which "everyone was entitled to come into the market place to sell and buy

without let or hindrance, moving about or walking to and fro": *R* v *Barnsley Metropolitan BC, ex p Hook* [1976] 3 All ER 452. 2. "A place to which sellers who have not found buyers take their goods in the hope of finding buyers, and to which buyers resort in the hope of finding the goods they want": *Scottish CWS Ltd* v *Ulster Farmers' Mart Co Ltd* [1959] 2 All ER 486. See *Birmingham CC* v *Anvil Fairs* [1989] 1 WLR 312.

market, available. *See* AVAILABLE MARKET.

Market, Common. *See* COMMON MARKET.

market contract. Contract connected with a recognised investment exchange or recognised clearing house: Cos.A. 1989, s. 155(1).

market maker. A person (individual, partnership or company) who holds himself out in compliance with the rules of a recognised stock exchange as willing to buy and sell securities at prices specified by him, and is recognised as doing so by that exchange: Company Securities (Insider Dealing) Act 1985, s. 3(1) (inserted by F.S.A. 1986, s. 174(2)).

market overt. An "open public and legally constituted market". A market held on days prescribed by charter, custom or statute. It means, in the City of London (q.v.), every shop in which goods usually sold in that shop are exposed for sale. "The sale must not be in the night, but between the rising of the sun and the going down of the same": *Market Overt Case* (1596) 5 Co Rep 33b. Where goods are sold in market overt, the buyer obtains title provided they are bought in good faith and without notice of any defect or lack of title on part of the seller: S.G.A. 1979, s. 22(1). See *Bishopsgate Motor Finance Co* v *Transport Brakes Ltd* [1949] 1 KB 322; *R* v *Wheeler* (1991) 92 Cr App R 279.

market price. 1. "The value of marketable goods which a trader holds in stock either for sale or consumption in his business": *B.S.C. Footwear* v *Ridgway* [1971] 2 All ER 534. 2. Price at which buyers and sellers are ready and willing to buy and sell in the ordinary course of trade.

market value. 1. "The price of the commodity in the market as between the manufacturer and an ordinary purchaser": *Orchard* v *Simpson* (1857) 2 CBNS 299. See I.C.T.A. 1988, s. 146; T.C.G.A. 1992, s. 272. 2. In the case of compulsory purchase of land, the basis of compensation is the amount which the land if sold in the open market by a willing seller might be expected to realise. See the Land Compensation Act 1961, s. 5, Planning and Compensation Act 1991; *Palatine Graphic Art Co* v *Liverpool CC* [1986] QB 335. For the essence of "true market value", see *Singer and Friedlander* v *Wood* (1977) 243 EG 212.

marriage. The act or rite based on a consensual union creating the legal and social status of husband and wife. "The voluntary union for life of one man and one woman to the exclusion of all others": Mat.C.A. 1857. Minimum age of parties is 16: Marriage Act 1949, s. 2. (For parental consent, see Sch. 2 (modified by the F.L.R.A. 1987, s. 9).) Marriages in England must be registered. See, e.g., Marriage Acts 1949–1983; Marriage (Enabling) Act 1960; Marriage (Registrar General's Licence) Act 1970; Marriage (Prohibited Degrees of Relationship) Act 1986, Sch. 1; Foreign Marriage (Amendment) Act 1988.

marriage articles. Contract setting out terms upon which a marriage settlement (q.v.) is to be executed.

marriage, breakdown of. *See* BREAKDOWN OF MARRIAGE.

marriage ceremony, categories of. In English law, the principal categories are: civil marriage; marriage according to Anglican rites; marriage according to non- Anglican religious rites; Jewish and Quaker marriages.

marriage, Church of England. Under the Marriage Act 1949, s. 5, a Church of England marriage is solemnised only after publication of banns or by authority of a common or special licence or superintendent registrar's certificate. It must be celebrated by a clergyman in the presence of two or more witnesses: s. 47.

marriage, civil. Marriage which takes place in a register office in the presence of a registrar, and involving a secular ceremony. See Marriage Act 1949, ss. 45, 46.

marriage, common-law. *See* COMMON-LAW MARRIAGE.

marriage, common licence for. Licence, issued under the authority of the bishop of a diocese, enabling the parties to marry in the Church of England without waiting for the publication of banns (q.v.). See Marriage Act 1949.

marriage consideration. Marriage is "the most valuable consideration imaginable": *A.-G.* v *Jacobs-Smith* [1895] 2 QB 341. Persons within the consideration are husband, wife, issue of the marriage and grandchildren. See *Re Plumptre's Settlement* [1910] 1 Ch 609; *Re Cook's ST* [1965] Ch 902. *See* CONSIDERATION.

marriage, consummation of. *See* CONSUMMATION OF A MARRIAGE.

marriage, defects invalidating. Under the Marriage Act 1949, a marriage is void if the parties have knowingly and wilfully disregarded certain requirements, e.g., as in the case of a ceremony in the absence of a registrar, where that is required, or marriage by a person not in Holy Orders: see ss. 25, 49. Failure to obtain parental consent does not invalidate a marriage: s. 48(1).

marriage, mistake in. *See* MISTAKE AND MARRIAGE.

marriage, nullity of. *See* NULLITY OF MARRIAGE.

marriage of housebound and detained persons. Under the Marriage Act 1983, marriages may be solemnised at the place of residence if one of the parties is housebound, i.e, unable to leave the home because of illness or disability, or one of the parties is detained in prison, and notice has been given under the Marriage Act 1949, s. 27.

marriage, presumption of. *See* PRESUMPTION OF MARRIAGE VALIDITY.

marriage, proof of. Procedure whereby a valid marriage is proved by the production of the marriage certificate and proof of identity; by declaration of a deceased person against interest or in the course of duty; by records (see Civil Evidence Act 1968); by evidence of the ceremony given by one who was present; by presumption from cohabitation (see *Re Taylor* [1961] 1 WLR 9).

marriage, Registrar General's licence relating to. Under the Marriage (Registrar General's Licence) Act 1970, the Registrar General is empowered to license a marriage to be solemnised elsewhere than in a registered building or register office. Used where the Registrar General is satisfied that one of the persons to be married is not expected to recover from an illness and cannot be moved to a place where a normal marriage would be solemnised.

marriage, registration of. Procedure whereby the following particulars of a marriage are officially recorded: date; surname; residence of parties; surname and profession of male parents; church where marriage takes place (in the case of a Church of England marriage).

marriage settlement. Deed executed in consideration of a marriage which is to take place, relating to settlement of property between the intended husband and wife. It can be varied under, e.g., Mat.C.A. 1973, s. 24 or Inheritance (Provision for Family and Dependants) Act 1975, s. 2(1). See *Re Densham* [1975] 1 WLR 1519.

marriage, sham. See SHAM MARRIAGE.

marriage, special licence for. Special dispensation granted by the discretion of the Archbishop of Canterbury, enabling a marriage to be solemnised under Church of England rites at any convenient place and time. See Marriage Act 1949, s. 79(9).

marriage, Superintendent-Registrar's certificate relating to. Certificate issued by the Superintendent-Registrar of the district in which the parties have lived for the preceding seven days. Notice is issued in a document open to public inspection and displayed for 21 days. If no caveat is entered, the certificate is issued for production to the person before whom the marriage is solemnised. See Marriage Act 1949.

marriage, void and voidable. See NULLITY OF MARRIAGE.

marriage, will in contemplation of. In general, a will is revoked by a testator's marriage, but where it appears from the will that at the time it was made the testator was expecting to be married to a particular person and that he intended that the will should not be revoked by his marriage, the will is not revoked by his marriage to that person: W.A. 1837, s. 18(1), (3) (as substituted by A.J.A. 1982, s. 18(1)).

married couple. A man and woman who are married to each other and are members of the same household; S.S.A. 1986, s. 20(11). (An "unmarried couple" means a man and a woman who are not married to each other but are living together as husband and wife.)

marshalling. Equitable principle under which, where there are two creditors of one debtor, and one creditor is entitled to resort to one fund only for payment of the debt, while the other creditor is entitled to resort to two funds, the funds will be marshalled by the court so that both creditors may be satisfied, as far as possible. Example: X mortgages Blackacre and Whiteacre to Y. Later X mortgages Blackacre to Z. If Y takes out of Blackacre money owing to him which he could have taken out of Whiteacre, then, to that extent, equity will give Z a charge on Whiteacre. Doctrine applies only where the mortgagor of both properties is the same person. See *Trimmer* v *Bayne (No. 2)* (1803) 9 Ves 209.

martial law. Rule by military authorities during an emergency when the civil authority cannot function. See *Ex p Marais* [1902] AC 109.

master and servant. Relationship, known now as "employer and employee", subsisting between one person and another who controls his work. Distinguished from "independent contractor" (q.v.). "The ultimate question is . . . who is entitled to give the orders as to how the work shall be done": *Mersey Docks and Harbour Board* v *Coggins & Griffiths Ltd* [1947] 1 AC 1. Indicia of the relationship were held in *Short* v *Henderson Ltd* (1946) 62 TLR 427 to be: master's power of selection of his servant; payment of wages or other remuneration; master's right to control the method of doing the work; master's right of suspension or dismissal. In a relationship of this kind a master's implied duties are to retain the servant for an agreed period, to pay agreed remuneration and to take reasonable care for servant's safety. See, e.g., *Clifford* v *UDM* [1991] IRLR 518. See SERVANT.

Master of the Bench. Full title of a Bencher (q.v.).

Master of the Crown Office. Appointed under S.C.A. 1981, s. 89(2). He has custody of records relating to divisional court proceedings of Queen's Bench Division and is also registrar of criminal appeals. See O. 57.

Master of the Rolls. Formerly a keeper of the records of Chancery, and, later, a judge of the Court of Chancery. Now a member of the High Court (q.v.) and *ex-officio* member of the Court of Appeal (q.v.). Presides over the Civil Division of the Court of Appeal: see S.C.A. 1981, s. 10. For delegation of his functions, see C.L.S.A., s. 73.

master, practice. *See* PRACTICE MASTER.

Masters of the Supreme Court. Masters in the Chancery Division, Masters of the QBD and Masters who carry out taxation of costs and cases in the Chancery and QBD. A master has the general jurisdiction of a judge in chambers. See S.C.A. 1981, s. 89.

masters, taxing. *See* TAXING MASTERS.

material fact. "Every fact is material which would, if known, reasonably affect the minds of prudent, experienced insurers in deciding whether they will accept the risk": *Stroshein v Wawanesa Mutual Insurance Co* [1943] 3 WWR 509. See O. 18, r. 7; *Saker v Secretary of State for Social Services* (1988) The Times, 16 Jan.

material facts in pleadings. *See* PLEADINGS, MATERIAL FACTS IN.

maternity leave, right to return to work after. Right of an employee to return to work at any time before the end of 29 weeks which began with the week in which confinement began. Failure to permit return may be treated as dismissal, but not in the case of a firm employing no more than five workers, or where it is not reasonably practical for the employer to permit a return: E.P.(C.)A. 1978, s. 56 (as amended by E.P.A. 1980, s. 12). See *Institute of Motor Industry v Harvey* (1992) The Times, 16 Jan.

maternity pay, statutory. Introduced under S.S.A. 1986, Part V. A woman is entitled to maternity pay (for a period not exceeding 18 weeks) if she has been employed by the same employer for a continuous period of at least 26 weeks ending with the week prior to the fourteenth week before the expected week of confinement (q.v.). See S.S. Contributions and Benefits Act 1992, s. 35; Social Security Administration Act 1992, s. 15.

matrimonial cause. Action for divorce, nullity of marriage, judicial separation: Matrimonial and Family Proceedings Act 1984, s. 32. See Matrimonial Proceedings (Transfers) Act 1988.

matrimonial home. Place in which a husband and wife have resided together. The Matrimonial Homes Act 1983 gives a right not to be evicted or excluded from the dwelling house without the leave of the court, or, if out of occupation, a right to enter and occupy the dwelling house with leave of the court, where one spouse is entitled to occupy the house by virtue of a beneficial estate or interest or contract and the other is not so entitled: s. 1. These rights end on the granting of a decree absolute. The right is registrable as a Class F land charge in the register of land charges (q.v.). See also Domestic Violence and Matrimonial Proceedings Act 1976; Matrimonial Homes and Property Act 1981; Family Proceedings Rules 1991, r. 2.

matrimonial home, order restricting occupation of. Order available under the Matrimonial Homes Act 1983, s. 9, prohibiting, suspending or restricting the exercise by one spouse, or requiring one spouse to permit the exercise by the other, of the right, by virtue of a legal estate vested in them jointly, or by virtue of contract, to occupy a dwelling-house in which the spouses have had a matrimonial home. *See* OUSTER ORDER.

matrimonial injunctions. *See* INJUNCTIONS, MATRIMONIAL.

matrimonial offences. Basis of the pre-1971 law of divorce under which, subject to certain defences, divorce could be obtained upon proof of an "offence" such as adultery, desertion, insanity, cruelty, etc. See now, generally, Mat.C.A. 1973. *See* DIVORCE.

matrimonial order. Order for maintenance, etc (but no longer including any "separation" element), obtainable from magistrates under D.P.A. 1978.

maturity. Time at which a bill of exchange (q.v.) becomes due.

mayhem. Obsolete term for the injuring of a person so that his effective capacity for self-defence is impaired. *See* MAIM.

mayor. Chairman of a city council elected by councillors. See L.G.A. 1972, ss. 3–5, 245.

Mayor's and City of London Court. London court formally abolished under Courts Act 1971. The Act provides, however, that the county court for the City of London county court district is to be known as the Mayor's and City of London Court: s. 42.

measure. Legislation concerning matters relating to the Church of England, intended to have effect as statutes in accordance with the provisions of the Church of England (Assembly) Powers Act 1919, as amended by the Synodical Government Measure 1969. See, e.g., the Care of Cathedrals Measure 1990 (establishing the Cathedral Fabrics Commission).

measure of damages by reason of death. "The actual pecuniary loss of each individual entitled to sue can only be ascertained by balancing, on the one hand, the loss to him of the future pecuniary benefit, and on the other, any pecuniary advantage which from whatever source comes to him by reason of the death": *Davies* v *Powell Duffryn Associated Collieries Ltd* [1942] AC 601. The action is brought in the name of the executor or administrator of the deceased. It lies for the benefit of the wife, husband, children, grandchildren, father, mother, step-parents, grandparents, etc. See, e.g., *Taylor* v *O'Connor* [1971] AC 115. But see also A.J.A. 1982, s. 1.

measure of damages in contract. The principle upon which assessment of actual monetary compensation is to be paid for damage. In general, in the case of contract, there must be *restitutio in integrum* (q.v.), i.e., compensation in full must be paid for the damage suffered by the plaintiff. See *Hadley* v *Baxendale* (1854) 9 Exch 341; *Victoria Laundry Ltd* v *Newman Industries Ltd* [1949] 2 KB 528, "Where a party sustains a loss by reason of a breach of contract he is, as far as money can do it, to be placed in the same situation with respect to damages as if the contract had been performed": *per* Parke B in *Robinson* v *Harman* (1848) 1 Exch 850. *See* DAMAGES.

measure of damages in tort. "That sum of money which will put the party who has been injured, or who has suffered, in the same position as he would have been if he had not sustained the wrong for which he is now getting his compensation or reparation": *per* Lord Blackburn in *Livingstone* v *Rawyards Coal Co* (1880) 5 App Cas 25. See *Hicks* v *S. Yorks Police* [1992] 1 All ER 690.

mediation. The act of a third party relating to the settling of a dispute between two contending parties.

medical examination, remand for. Adjournment of a case for 3 or 4 weeks to enable a medical examination and report to be made concerning a person on trial by a magistrates' court for an offence punishable on summary conviction with imprisonment: M.C.A. 1980, s. 30.

medical practitioner. One who holds one or more primary UK qualifications and has passed a qualifying examination and satisfied the requirements of the Medical Act 1983, Part II, as to experience; or being a national of any member state of the Communities, holds one or more primary European qualifications: 1988 Act, s. 3. See also Medical Qualifications (Amendment) Act 1991.

medical treatment. Medical, surgical or rehabilitative treatment: S.S.A. 1975, s. 20. May include nursing: M.H.A. 1983, s. 145(1). See also S.S. Contributions and Benefits Act 1992, s. 122(1). For refusal of court to order a doctor to adopt a course of treatment, see *In re J.* (1992) The Times, 12 June.

medicine. "Everything which is to be applied for the purpose of healing, whether externally or internally": *per* Lush J in *Berry* v *Henderson* (1870) LR 5 QB 296.

mediums, fraudulent. *See* WITCHCRAFT.

meeting, board. *See* BOARD MEETING.

meetings, company. Meetings of a company (q.v.) attended by shareholders. (1) Annual general meetings (see Cos.A. 1985, s. 366) held each calendar year, with not more than 15 months between meetings. (2) Extraordinary general meetings, held whenever the directors wish (see Table A, art. 37) or on requisition by members holding at least one-tenth of the paid-up capital carrying right to vote. (3) Class meetings, called for a particular class of shareholder to discuss, e.g., variation of class rights. See Cos.A 1985, s. 371; *Cane* v *Jones* [1981] 1 All ER 533.

melior est conditio possidentis et rei quam actoris. The position of the possessor is the better, and that of defendant better than that of plaintiff.

Member of Parliament. One elected by a constituency to sit in the House of Commons (q.v.) Persons disqualified from membership of the Commons include, e.g., most peers, judges, mental patients, certain classes of prisoner. See House of Commons Disqualification Act 1975; and Representation of the People Acts 1983, 1985. *See* PARLIAMENT.

members of a company. Those who have subscribed to a company's memorandum of association (q.v.), or have agreed to become members by applying for an allotment of shares or by taking a transfer from an existing member. Persons cease to be members by, e.g., forfeiture, surrender, transfer, death. Capacity to become a member is that of the ordinary rules of contract. A company may not be "a member of itself": *Kirby* v *Wilkins* [1929] 2 Ch 444. See Cos.A. 1985, s. 22; Ins.A. 1986, s. 250. *See* COMPANY.

members, register of. *See* REGISTER OF MEMBERS.

memorandum. A note recording the particulars of an event, e.g., a commercial transaction.

memorandum of association. *See* ASSOCIATION, MEMORANDUM OF.

menaces, demand with. For the *actus reus* (q.v.) of blackmail see Th.A. 1968, s. 21. "If the circumstances of the case were such that an ordinary reasonable man would understand that a demand for money was being made upon him and that the demand was accompanied by menaces – not perhaps direct, but veiled menaces – so that his ordinary balance of mind was upset, then you would be justified in coming to the conclusion that a demand with menaces had been made": *R v Collister* (1955) 39 Cr App R 100; *R v Garwood* [1987] 1 WLR 319. *See* BLACKMAIL.

men, indecent assault on. *See* INDECENT ASSAULT ON MEN.

mens rea. Translated as "guilty mind" or "wicked mind". More accurately, "criminal intention, or an intention to do the act which is made penal by statute or by the common law": *Allard*

v *Selfridge Ltd* [1925] 1 KB 129. May include also recklessness relating to the circumstances and consequences of an act which comprise the *actus reus* (q.v.). See *R v Tolson* (1889) 23 QBD 168; *Sweet* v *Parsley* [1970] AC 132. *See* ACTUS NON FACIT REUM NISI MENS SIT REA.

mental disorder. "Mental illness, arrested or incomplete development of mind, psychopathic disorder, and any other disorder or disability of mind": M.H.A. 1983, s. 1(2). A person may not be classified as mentally disordered by reason only of "promiscuity or other immoral conduct, sexual deviancy (q.v.) or dependence on alcohol or drugs": M.H.A. 1983, s. 1(3). Categories include mental illness, severe mental impairment, mental impairment and psychopathic disorder (q.v.). "Severe mental impairment" is "a state of arrested or incomplete development of mind which includes severe impairment of intelligence and social functioning and is associated with abnormally aggressive or seriously irresponsible conduct": M.H.A. 1983, s. 1(2). ("Mental impairment" is defined similarly – see s. 1(2) – but includes "significant impairment of intelligence".) See M.H.A. 1983 Part I. For confessions by a mentally-handicapped person, see P. & C.E.A. 1984, s. 77.

mental distress. Generally involves worry, anxiety, grief, despair, etc. Should be differentiated from nervous shock (q.v.). Damages for mental distress are rarely awarded in an action for breach of contract (see *Addis* v *Gramophone Co* [1909] AC 488; *Jarvis* v *Swans Tours* [1973] QB 233); they may be awarded in tort where the cause is, e.g., nuisance or assault or battery (see *Bone* v *Seale* [1975] 1 WLR 797). For assessment of damages, see *Archer* v *Brown* [1984] 2 All ER 267.

Mental Health Commission. Authority set up under M.H.A. 1983, s. 121, with a general protective function over detained patients. May visit and interview patients and investigate complaints.

Mental Health Review Tribunals, Area. Bodies set up under the M.H.A. 1959, consisting of doctors, lawyers and others, to consider applications for the discharge of a mental patient (q.v.) made by the patient or, e.g., his nearest relative. See M.H.A. 1983, Part V; *Campbell* v *Secretary of State for Home Department* [1987] 3 WLR 522; *Pickering* v *Liverpool Daily Post plc* [1991] 1 All ER 622.

mental patient. One who is suffering, or appears to be suffering, from a mental disorder. See M.H.A. 1983, s. 145(1). For compulsory detention see M.H.A. 1983, Part III. See *Knight* v *Home Office* [1990] 3 All ER 237 (duty of care); *DPP* v *D'Souza* (1991) The Independent, 24 Sep. (powers of pursuit).

merchandise marks. Phrase used in relation to the marking of goods for sale. Merchandise Marks Acts 1887–1953 were repealed by Trade Descriptions Act 1968.

merchantable quality of goods. "Goods of any kind are of merchantable quality within the meaning of [this Act] if they are as fit for the purpose or purposes for which goods of that kind are commonly bought as it is reasonable to expect, having regard to any description applied to them, the price (if relevant) and all the other relevant circumstances": S.G.A. 1979, s. 14(6). See also ss. 14(2), 15(2)(c). See, e.g., *Rogers* v *Parish (Scarborough) Ltd* [1987] QB 933; *Bernstein* v *Pamson Motors* [1987] 2 All ER 220; *R & B Co. Ltd* v *United Dominions Trust* [1988] 1 All ER 847.

mercy killing. Offence, suggested by Criminal Law Revision Committee Report (August 1976) which would apply to one who, from compassion, (unlawfully) kills another who is believed by him to be (for example) permanently helpless or subject to rapid, incurable degeneration. It was rejected in the Committee's final report, 1980 (Cmnd 7844). See EUTHANASIA.

mercy, prerogative of. Power of the Crown, exercised through the Home Secretary, to commute, remit or suspend a sentence. See PARDON.

merger. 1. Acquisition of one firm by another, so that only one unit remains. Certain proposed mergers must be referred to the Monopolies Commission. See Fair Trading Act 1973, ss. 57–77; Cos.A. 1989, s. 146; *R* v *Monopolies and Mergers Commission, ex p S. Yorks Transport* [1992] 1 All ER 257. 2. Vesting of two estates or interests in property in one person by virtue of the same right. There is no merger by operation of law only of any estate the beneficial interest in which would not be deemed to be merged or extinguished in equity: L.P.A. 1925, s. 185. 3. No doctrine of merger (i.e., of attempt with the full offence) remains in criminal law since C.L.A. 1967: *Webley* v *Buxton* [1978] QB 481.

mesne. Middle; intermediate. A mesne lord was one who held land of a superior and of whom an inferior held.

mesne profits, action for. Action for trespass brought against an occupier of premises who remains in possession after the termination of his interest in those premises, to recover damages suffered by the plaintiff as the result of his having been out of possession. Damages are generally assessed on the basis of a rent representing fair value of premises during the relevant period of occupation. See O. 6, r. 2; *Associated Deliveries Ltd* v *Harrison* (1984) 272 EG 321.

messuage. A dwelling-house together with adjacent buildings, gardens, orchards.

metes and bounds. The boundaries of land related to natural or artificial features, e.g., streams, fences.

metropolitan stipendiary magistrates. Full-time, professional magistrates who sit as sole justices in Metropolitan Stipendiary Courts, i.e., petty sessional courts in London. See Justices of the Peace Act 1979, Part III. *See* STIPENDIARY MAGISTRATES.

Middle Temple. One of the Inns of Court (q.v.). It was granted its premises in perpetuity by James I in 1609.

military courts. Term applied to the old Court of Chivalry (q.v.) or courts-martial (q.v.).

military tenures. Tenures by knight service (q.v.), grand serjeanty (q.v.). Known also as "tenures in chivalry". Abolished (save for some honorary services of grand serjeanty) under Tenures Abolition Act 1660.

military testament. A privileged will (q.v.) made by a soldier on active service.

mine. "An excavation or system of excavations made for the purpose of, or in connection with, the getting, wholly or substantially by means involving the employment of persons below ground, of minerals . . . or products of minerals": Mines and Quarries Act 1954, s. 180(1).

minerals. "All substances in, on or under the land, obtainable by underground or surface working": S.L.A. 1925, s. 117(1)(xiv). See also I.C.T.A. 1988, s. 122(6); T.C.P.A. 1990, s. 336; Capital Allowances Act 1990, s. 161 (for "mineral deposits"); Planning and Compensation Act 1991, Sch. 1, para 7; T.C.G.A. 1992, s. 201 (mineral royalties).

minimum subscription. Minimum amount of capital, decided on by directors or promoters of a company (q.v.) which will allow them to provide for preliminary expenses, underwriting commissions, price of property to be paid from proceeds of issue, working capital. Must be stated in the prospectus (q.v.): Cos.A. 1985, s. 83.

minimum wages. See WAGES, MINIMUM.

mining lease. A tenant for life (q.v.) may lease the whole or part of the land for 100 years in the case of a mining lease: S.L.A. 1925, s. 41. If the tenant is impeachable for waste (q.v.) relating to minerals (q.v.), three-quarters of the rent becomes capital. For a definition of "mining operation", see T.C.P.A. 1990, s. 55. See the Mineral Workings Act 1985; I.C.T.A. 1988, s. 122(6); Capital Allowances Act 1990, s. 121.

ministerial responsibility. Doctrine (based on convention) that ministers of the government are responsible to Parliament (q.v.) for the exercise of the powers and duties of their departments, whether personally authorised by ministers or not. See COLLECTIVE RESPONSIBILITY.

Minister of the Crown. "The holder of any office in Her Majesty's Government in the UK, and includes the Treasury": Ministers of the Crown Act 1975, s. 8(1); Government Trading Act 1990, s. 1. Appointed by the Crown on the Prime Minister's advice. Ministers are ranked as: Cabinet Ministers, Ministers of State, Parliamentary Under-Secretaries of State, Parliamentary Secretaries, Parliamentary Private Secretaries.

Ministry. 1. The government, headed by the Prime Minister (q.v.). 2. A department of government.

minor. A person under the age of 18. See INFANT.

minor interests. Term used in land registration. "The interests not capable of being disposed of or created by registered dispositions and capable of being overridden (whether or not a purchaser has notice thereof) by the proprietors unless protected as provided by this Act, and all rights and interests which are not registered or protected on the register and are not overriding interests": L.R.A. 1925, s. 3(xv). They can be protected by a notice, inhibition (q.v.), restriction or caution (q.v.). See *Peffer* v *Rigg* [1977] 1 WLR 285; *Lyus* v *Prowsa Developments Ltd* [1982] 1 WLR 1044. See OVERRIDING INTERESTS.

minority. 1. The smaller group in number of those present at an assembly or other meeting. 2. Below 18 years of age: F.L.R.A. 1969.

minority, fraud on. See FRAUD ON MINORITY.

minority shareholders, oppression of. Conduct of a company (q.v.) unfairly prejudicial to the interests of some of its shareholders. See, e.g., *Foss* v *Harbottle* (1843) 2 Hare 461; *Re Sam Weller Ltd* [1990] BCLC 80 (test of oppression is objective). See Cos.A. 1985, s. 459, as amended by Cos.A. 1989, s. 145, Sch. 19, para 11. See SHAREHOLDERS, PROTECTION OF.

minors' contracts. A minor (q.v.) is bound by contracts: for the sale of necessary goods sold and actually delivered to him; for necessary services; for beneficial contracts of service, apprenticeship. See *Nash* v *Inman* [1908] 2 KB 1; *Doyle* v *White City Stadium* [1935] 1 KB 110. The Minors' Contracts Act 1987, s. 1, repealed the Infants Relief Act 1874 (which invalidated certain contracts made by minors and prohibited actions to enforce contracts ratified after majority) and the Betting and Loans (Infants) Act 1892 (invalidating contracts to repay loans advanced during minority). The 1987 Act gives the court a discretionary power to order restoration to a seller where a minor has acquired property on credit and fails to pay for it: s. 3. See NECESSARIES.

minutes. Notes providing a record of proceedings. A company must keep minutes of its meetings. See Cos.A. 1985, ss. 382, 722; Cos.A. 1989, s. 143. Minutes signed by a chairman are usually prima facie evidence of proceedings.

MIRAS. Mortgage interest relief at source. For details of the scheme, see I.C.T.A. 1988, ss. 369–377. See *R* v *HMI Taxes, ex p Kelly* [1991] BTC 387.

misadventure. An accident which is not the result of a criminal or negligent act. There is no valid distinction between a coroner's verdicts of "death by misadventure" and "accidental death": *R* v *Coroner for City of Portsmouth, ex p Anderson* [1987] 1 WLR 1640.

misappropriation. Dishonest appropriation of another's property. See Th.A. 1968, ss. 1, 3(1) (assumption of another's rights); *R* v *Gomez* [1991] 3 All ER 394.

miscarriage. 1. Failure in the administration of justice. For compensation, see C.J.A. 1988, s. 133. 2. Synonym for abortion (q.v.). 3. Term used in Statute of Frauds 1677, s. 4, relating to "that species of wrongful act for the consequences of which the law would make the party civilly responsible": *Kirkham* v *Marter* (1819) 2 B & Ald 613.

mischief. The "mischief of a statute" is the wrong for which it is intended to provide a remedy.

mischief rule. Method of construing a statute which necessitates asking: what was the common law before the statute; what was the mischief (q.v.) for which common law did not provide; what remedy has Parliament resolved so as to cure it; what is the true reason of that remedy? See *Heydon's Case* (1584) 3 Co Rep 7a. See *Maunsell* v *Olins* [1975] AC 373. *See* CONSTRUCTION.

misconduct. "It means no more than incorrect or erroneous conduct of any kind of a serious nature, and does not necessarily connote moral censure": *per* Webster J in *R* v *Pharmaceutical Society, ex p Sokoh* (1986) The Times, 4 Dec.

misconduct, professional. *See* PROFESSIONAL MISCONDUCT.

misconduct, wilful. *See* WILFUL MISCONDUCT.

misdemeanours. Offences not amounting to felonies (q.v.). Under C.L.A.

1967, s. 1, all distinctions between felony and misdemeanour are abolished.

misdescription. Usually refers to a description of the subject-matter of a contract which is false or misleading in some substantial way. In such a case the contract may be voidable at the option of the party who is misled.

misdescription of property. *See* PROPERTY, MISDESCRIPTION OF.

misdirection. Failure by the judge to direct the jury adequately as to the issues requiring a decision, or the law applicable, or the legal effect of evidence, or total failure to direct: *Hobbs* v *Tinling* [1929] 2 KB 1. A conviction may be quashed on this ground: see, e.g., *R* v *Trigg* [1963] 1 WLR 305. See O. 59, r. 11.

misfeasance. Improper performance of some essentially lawful act. See, e.g., Highways Act 1980, s. 58; *Griffiths* v *Liverpool Corporation* [1967] 1 QB 374; *Jones* v *Swansea CC* [1989] 3 All ER 162 (tort of misfeasance in public office). *See* MALFEASANCE.

misjoinder of parties. The wrongful joining of parties in an action. "No cause or matter shall be defeated by reason of the misjoinder or non-joinder of any party": O. 15, r. 6(1).

misleading price. *See* PRICE, MISLEADING.

misnomer. The giving of a wrong name to a person in pleadings. See O. 20.

mispleading. The omission in pleadings (q.v.) of that which is essential to the action.

misprision. (*Mesprendre* = to make a mistake.) Misprision of a felony was failure to report a felony (q.v.): *Sykes* v *DPP* [1962] AC 528. See C.L.A. 1967, s. 5(1) by which the offence no longer exists generally. Misprision of treason remains as a common-law offence committed when a person knows, or has reasonable cause to believe that another has committed treason and fails within a reasonable time to inform an appropriate authority. *See* TREASON.

misrepresentation. A false statement which misrepresents a material fact; which is made before the conclusion of a contract with a view to inducing another to enter that contract; which is made with the intention that the person to whom it is addressed shall act on it; which is acted on, having induced the contract. "In my opinion any behaviour, by words or conduct, is sufficient to be a misrepresentation if it is such as to mislead the other party. If it conveys a false impression, that is enough": *per* Denning LJ in *Curtis* v *Chemical Cleaning and Dyeing Co Ltd* [1951] 1 KB 805. See Misrepresentation Act 1967; *Hedley Byrne & Co* v *Heller & Partners* [1964] AC 465; *Royscott Trust Ltd* v *Rogerson* [1991] 3 WLR 57.

misrepresentation, fraudulent. A false representation made knowingly or without belief in its truth or recklessly, careless whether it be true or false: *Derry* v *Peek* (1889) 14 App Cas 337. See Misrepresentation Act 1967; *Doyle* v *Olby Ltd* [1969] 2 QB 158.

misrepresentation, innocent. A misrepresentation in which there is no element of fault, i.e., fraud or negligence. Remedies include avoidance and action for indemnity against any obligation created by the contract. See, e.g., *Lamare* v *Dixon* (1873) LR6 HL 414.

misrepresentation, negligent. A false statement made by a person who has no reasonable grounds for believing that statement to be true. Remedies include avoidance, damages and rescission (qq.v.). See *Box* v *Midland Bank* [1979] 2 Lloyd's Rep 391; *Hussey* v *Eels* [1990] 1 All ER 449.

mistake. *Common mistake* – both parties make the same error relating to a fundamental fact. *Mutual mistake* – both parties fail to understand each other. *Unilateral mistake* – only one party is mistaken. "If mistake operates at all, it operates so as to negative or in some cases to nullify consent": *Bell* v *Lever Bros Ltd* [1932] AC 161. Mistake is, generally, no defence to an intentional tort (q.v.). See Lim.A. 1980, s. 32 (as amended by Latent Damage Act 1986, s. 4); *Raffles* v *Wichelhaus* (1864) 2 H & C 906; *Foster* v *Mackinnon* (1869) LR 4 CP 704. For "mistake in equity", see *Laurence* v *Lexcourt Holdings* [1978] 2 All ER 810. For mistaken receipt of property, see Th.A. 1968, s. 5(4). See also S.G.A. 1979, s. 6.

mistake and marriage. A mistake is operative if it relates to the nature of the ceremony or the identity of the other party. See *Valier* v *Valier* (1925) 133 LT 830; *C.* v *C.* [1942] NZLR 356.

mistake of law. Error as to the law and its effects. Never a defence, since every person is presumed to know the law. *See* IGNORANTIA JURIS NEMINEM EXCUSAT.

mistake, operative. A mistake which operates so as to avoid a contract, e.g., mistake as to the identity or existence of the subject-matter, or as to the nature of the document signed. See *Hector* v *Lyons* (1989) 58 P & CR 156. See CONTRACT.

mistake, rectification in magistrates' court of. Power under statute enabling magistrates to vary or rescind a sentence or other defective order imposed by them in criminal proceedings: see M.C.A. 1980, s. 142; *R* v *West* [1964] 1 QB 15.

mistress. A woman who, without marriage, lives as a wife. See *Spindlow* v *Spindlow* [1979] 1 All ER 169; *Layton* v *Martin* (1986) 16 Fam Law 212.

mistrial. A false trial. "To constitute a mistrial the proceedings must have been abortive from beginning to end": *R* v *Middlesex Judges, ex p DPP* [1952] 2 QB 758.

mitigation. 1. Diminution, e.g., of some penalty. Plea in mitigation of sentence may be heard at the end of the trial. Nothing may be urged in mitigation which could have constituted a defence to the offence charged. 2. Mitigation of damages: it is the duty of the plaintiff to take all reasonable steps to mitigate the loss caused by a breach of contract (q.v.). See *R* v *Jones* [1980] Crim LR 58 (counsel's duty to make plea in mitigation). 3. Mitigation of tax involves taking advantage of the law so as to minimise the incidence of tax: see *Ensign Tankers Ltd* v *Stokes* (1992) The Times, 17 Mar.

mixed action. An action which in its nature relates to both real and personal actions (q.v.).

mixed fund. A fund comprising the proceeds of the sale of real and personal property.

mixed property. Property compounded of realty and personalty and having some of the legal attributes of both. For "mixed goods", see *Indian Oil Corporation* v *Greenstone Shipping Co* [1987] 3 WLR 869.

M'Naghten Rules. Answers of the House of Lords relating to questions arising from the verdict in *R* v *M'Naghten*

(1843) 10 C & F 200, where the accused, acting under insane delusion, killed the secretary of Sir Robert Peel and was found not guilty on the ground of insanity. The Rules remain legal criteria when insanity is pleaded as a defence. They state: (1) A person is presumed sane until the contrary is proved. (2) To establish a defence on the ground of insanity, it must be clearly proved that at the time of committing the offence, the accused was labouring under such a defect of reason, from disease of the mind (q.v.), as not to know the nature and quality of his act, or, if he did know it, that he did not know what he was doing was wrong. If the accused was conscious that the act was one he ought not to do and if that act was at the time contrary to law of the land, he is punishable. (3) Where a person under an insane delusion as to existing facts commits an offence in consequence thereof, and making the assumption that he labours under such partial delusion only, and is not in other respects insane, he is considered in the same situation as to responsibility as if the facts with respect to which the delusion exists were real. See *R v Codère* (1916) 12 Cr App R 21; *R v Windle* [1952] 2 QB 826; *R v Sullivan* [1983] 3 WLR 123.

mobilia sequuntur personam. Movable things follow the laws of the person (i.e., the owner). A person's powers of dealing with his personal estate and its devolution on his death are governed by the laws of his domicile. See *Freke v Carbery* (1873) LR 16, Eq 461.

mobility allowance. Non-contributory benefit payable under S.S.A. 1975 to a person suffering from a physical disablement such that he is either unable to walk or is virtually unable to do so. See also S.S.A. 1989, s. 8.

mock auction. Auction during which articles are given away or offered as gifts, or the right to bid is restricted to persons who have bought or agreed to buy an article, or any lot is sold to a bidder at a price lower than the amount of his highest bid for it, or part of the price is repaid or credited to him. An offence under the Mock Auctions Act 1961. A "lot" consists of or includes plate, linen, china, glass,

books, furniture, jewellery, etc. See *Allen v Simmons* [1978] 1 WLR 79. *See* AUCTION; DUTCH AUCTION.

modifications. "Includes additions, omissions and amendments": Disabled Persons (Services Consultation and Representation) Act 1986, s. 16. See C.P.A. 1987, s. 45(1).

moiety. One of two equal parts. See *Re Angus' WT* [1960] 1 WLR 1296.

molest. "A wide plain word which . . . if I had to find one synonym for it, I should select 'pester'": *per* Stephenson LJ in *Vaughan v Vaughan* [1973] 3 All ER 449.

molestation. 1. Acts, the tendency of which is, in general, to injure or annoy, which were intended to injure or annoy the complainant. See the Domestic Violence and Matrimonial Proceedings Act 1976, s. 1(1); and *Horner v Horner* [1982] Fam 90. 2. The following of a person in a persistent and disorderly manner, or by hiding his property, so as to compel him to do or abstain from doing an act.

molestation, non-, clause. *See* INJUNCTIONS, MATRIMONIAL.

monarchy. The institution of the Crown (q.v.). Dates of the reigns of England's monarchs are as shown in the following table:

House	Name	Year of accession
	William I	1066
	William II	1087
Normandy	Henry I	1100
	Stephen	1135
	Henry II	1154
	Richard I	1189
	John	1199
	Henry III	1216
Plantagenet	Edward I	1272
	Edward II	1307
	Edward III	1327
	Richard II	1377
	Henry IV	1399
Lancaster	Henry V	1413
	Henry VI	1422
	Edward IV	1461
York	Edward V	1483
	Richard III	1483
	Henry VII	1485
	Henry VIII	1509
	Edward VI	1547
Tudor	Jane	1553
	Mary	1553
	Elizabeth I	1558

251

House	Name	Year of accession
Stuart	James I	1603
	Charles I	1625
	{The Commonwealth	1649}
	{The Protectorate	1653}
Stuart	Charles II	1660
	James II	1685
	William & Mary	1689–94 }
	William III	1694–1702 }
	Anne	1702
Hanover	George I	1714
	George II	1727
	George III	1760
	George IV	1820
	William IV	1830
	Victoria	1837
Saxe-Coburg	Edward VII	1901
Windsor	George V	1910
	Edward VIII	1936
	George VI	1936
	Elizabeth II	1952

money. That which by common consent is used as a medium of exchange, measure and store of value and standard of deferred payment. "The word 'money' at the present time has a diversity of meanings, and when it is found in a will there is no presumption that it has one meaning rather than another": *Perrin* v *Morgan* [1943] AC 399. See Currency Act 1983, s. 1; *Re Gammon* [1986] CLY 3547.

money as property. "A man's money is property which is protected by law . . . If it is taken from the rightful owner . . . without his authority he can recover the money from any person into whose hands it can be traced": *per* Denning J in *Nelson* v *Larholt* [1948] 1 KB 339.

money Bill. A Bill (q.v.) usually introduced in the Commons which, in the opinion of the Speaker of the Commons, deals only with the imposition, repeal or alteration of taxation, the imposition of charges on the Consolidated Fund (q.v.), etc. If sent to the Lords at least one month before the end of the session and not passed by them, it is presented to the Crown and becomes an Act on the Royal Assent (q.v.) being signified: Parliament Act 1911. If the Speaker certifies a Bill to be a money Bill, this is recorded in the Journal; that certification is conclusive and may not be questioned in a court. *See* PARLIAMENT.

money had and received. Action, derived from a writ of account, by which the plaintiff claimed a sum of money as "had and received by defendant to his use", e.g., as where the defendant had received money on a consideration which had failed entirely.

money judgment, costs of enforcing. Where a person takes steps to enforce a judgment or order of the High Court or a county court for payment of a sum due, the costs of any previous attempt to enforce that judgment are recoverable to the same extent as if they had been incurred in the taking of those steps: S.C.A. 1981, s. 138, as inserted by C.L.S.A. 1990, s. 15(1). See *QBD Practice Direction*, No. 47, Nov. 1991.

moneylender. A person whose business is that of moneylending, or who advertises or announces himself or holds himself out in any way as carrying on that business. See Moneylenders Acts 1900 and 1927 (repealed by C.C.A. 1974). He must be licensed by the Director General of Fair Trading (q.v.) in his name at a registered address. See O. 83, r. 2 (action brought by moneylender or assignee); *Wills* v *Wood* (1984) 128 SJ 222.

money-lending company. A company, the ordinary business of which includes the making of loans or quasi-loans (q.v.) or the giving of guarantees in connection with them: Cos.A. 1985, s. 338(1). See also Cos.A. 1989, s. 138.

Monopolies and Mergers Commission. Appointed by the Secretary of State to investigate and report on any question referred to it under the Fair Trading Act 1973 with respect to: existence or possible existence of a monopoly situation (i.e., where at least one-quarter of the market is controlled by a single firm); the creation or possible creation of a merger situation (i.e., where two or more enterprises combine and the value of assets taken over exceeds a prescribed amount). See also Monopolies and Restrictive Practices (Inquiry and Control) Act 1948.

monopoly. 1. Market structure with only a single seller of a commodity or service. 2. Royal privilege for the buying, selling or making of a commodity, to be enjoyed by the grantee only. 3. Under the Fair Trading Act 1973, "control of one-quarter of the sales in a market". Under EEC legislation, state monopolies must not be allowed to obstruct free movement of goods and provision of services; their activities should be adjusted rather than prohibited: see Treaty of Rome 1957, art. 37. See *R v Monopolies and Mergers Commission, ex p S. Yorks Transport* [1922] 1 All ER 257.

month. There is a statutory presumption that in all deeds and other instruments coming into force on or after 1st January 1926, "month" means "calendar month" unless the context otherwise provides. See L.P.A. 1925, s. 61; O.3, r. 1; I.A. 1978, Sch. 1; and *Dodds v Walker* [1981] 2 All ER 609.

moot. An assembly of members of an Inn of Court (q.v.) at which points of law are argued.

moratorium. An authorised period of delay in the performing of an obligation, e.g., settling a debt.

moratorium for insolvent debtor. An interim order of the court issued under Ins.A. 1986, s. 252, where an individual debtor intends to make a voluntary arrangement or composition with his creditors. The order will not be made unless the court is satisfied that, e.g., no previous application has been made by the debtor for an interim order in the year ending with the present day of application: s. 255(1). *See* BANKRUPTCY.

mortgage. The disposition of an estate or interest in land or other property in order to secure the payment of a debt or the discharge of some other obligation. See *Santley v Wilde* [1989] 2 Ch 474. Example: A borrows money from B and later conveys property to B as security for repayment of the loan; A is the *mortgagor*, B is the *mortgagee*. A mortgage may be legal (q.v.) or equitable (q.v.). It may be discharged by foreclosure (q.v.), redemption (q.v.), exercise of mortgagee's power of sale, merger (q.v.) or under L.P.A. 1925, s. 115. For mortgage interest relief at source, see I.C.T.A. 1988, s. 369. See Law Comm. No. 204 (1991).

mortgage actions. Applications by mortgagees for possession of property or payment of principal, arrears, interest, etc. See O. 88; Lim.A. 1980, s. 29.

mortgage and consumer credit. A mortgage comes within C.C.A. 1974 if it is in effect a regulated agreement (q.v.),

i.e., a personal credit agreement under which the debtor is supplied by the creditor with a credit not above a statutorily-fixed amount (but loans made by a building society or local authority for house purchase are exempt). An improperly executed agreement can be enforced against a debtor by court order only. The court can open an agreement considered extortionate. The debtor may redeem prematurely at any time, on giving notice to the creditor: s. 94. A security cannot be enforced by reason of breach of the regulated agreement without notice served on the debtor: s. 87. See also ss. 113, 177(2).

mortgagee. *See* MORTGAGE.

mortgage, equitable. *See* EQUITABLE MORTGAGE.

mortgagee's rights. Generally: to take possession; to sell (in which case he has a duty to take reasonable precautions to obtain the true market value of the mortgaged property: *Cuckmere Brick Co. v Mutual Finance* [1971] Ch. 949); to foreclose; to lease; to hold title deeds; to appoint a receiver; to sue the mortgagor personally on covenants in the mortgage deed. See A.J.A. 1970, s. 36; *Western Bank v Schindler* [1977] Ch 1; *Tse Kwong Lam v Wong Chit Sen* [1983] 3 All ER 54; *Equity & Law Home Loans Ltd v Prestidge* [1992] 1 All ER 909.

mortgage, legal. *See* LEGAL MORTGAGE.

mortgage of registered land, protection of. *See* REGISTERED LAND, PROTECTION OF MORTGAGE OF.

mortgage, regulated. *See* REGULATED MORTGAGE.

mortgages, consolidation of. *See* CONSOLIDATION OF MORTGAGES.

mortgage, second. A mortgage generally subject to the prior claims of a first mortgage. It may be created: in the case of freeholds, by charge by deed expressed to be by way of legal mortgage, or by demise for a term of years absolute; in the case of leaseholds, by charge by deed, or by sub-demise for term of years absolute. A second mortgagee should register the mortgage as a Class C land charge (q.v.). *See* PRIORITIES, RULES CONCERNING MORTGAGES.

mortgages, local authority. A local authority may advance money to a person for the purpose of acquiring, constructing, altering, enlarging, repairing or improving a house or converting another building into a house, or for the purpose of facilitating the repayment of an amount outstanding on a previous loan made for any of these purposes: H.A. 1985, s. 435(1). The advance and interest on it must be secured by a mortgage of the land concerned: s. 436(1).

mortgages, priority of. See PRIORITIES, RULES CONCERNING MORTGAGES.

mortgage, standing. Procedure whereby the borrower pays interest regularly on the loan and repays the capital in a single lump sum.

mortgage, Welsh. See WELSH MORTGAGE.

mortgagor. See MORTGAGE.

mortgagor's rights. Generally he is entitled to possession of the property, to receive income and profits, to redeem. See *Britannia BS* v *Earl* [1990] 2 All ER 469 (right of possession and application for relief under A.J.A. 1970, s. 36). See EQUITY OF REDEMPTION.

mortmain. Dead hand. Phrase used to refer to land which was considered inalienable. Under statutes prohibiting alienation in mortmain, the devise of lands to a corporation was void, except for charitable uses. Law relating to mortmain was abolished under Charities Act 1960, s. 3.

mortuum vadium. Dead pledge. Early type of mortgage in which mortgagee took rents and profits in discharge of interest only.

mother. Female parent. See Human Fertilisation and Embryology Act 1990, s. 27; Ch. A. 1989, s. 4. *See* PARENTAL RESPONSIBILITY.

motion. 1. Formal proposal made at a meeting. 2. Oral application to a judge or court requesting an order directing performance of an action in the applicant's favour. See, e.g., O. 29; O. 53. For originating notices of motion see O. 8.

motive. That which incites to action. Not to be confused with *mens rea* (q.v.). Thus, X, in stealing Y's gloves may have as motive his desire for greater comfort, but this is not the *mens rea* required for the offence of stealing. The motive may be relevant as evidence or in deciding the punishment following conviction.

motor car. Mechanically-propelled vehicle, not being a motor cycle or invalid carriage, constructed to carry a load or passengers with an unladen weight not in excess of that stated in Road Traffic Act 1988, s. 185(1). See Capital Allowances Act 1990, s. 36. *Chief Constable of Avon* v *Fleming* [1987] 1 All ER 318.

motor cycle. Mechanically-propelled vehicle, not being an invalid carriage, with less than four wheels and an unladen weight not in excess of 410 kilograms: Road Traffic Act 1988, s. 185(1).

Motor Insurers' Bureau. Group of motor vehicle insurers which, by agreement with the Department of the Environment, undertakes to satisfy or cause to be satisfied, a judgment obtained against a motorist for a liability required to be covered by an insurance policy and which is not satisfied within seven days. The Bureau also makes payments relating to death or personal injury caused by a vehicle whose owner or driver cannot be traced. See Road Traffic Regulation Act 1984, s. 136.

motor vehicle, taking of. The unauthorised taking of a vehicle is an offence under Th.A. 1968, s. 12, as amended by Aggravated Vehicle Taking Act 1992, s. 1. See also P. & C.E.A. 1984, s. 1(8)(c). *See* CONVEYANCE; VEHICLE-TAKING, AGGRAVATED.

movables. Term generally applied to personal, as opposed to real (or "immovable"), property. See *R* v *Hoyles* [1911] 1 Ch 179.

M.P. Member of Parliament (q.v.).

M.R. Master of the Rolls (q.v.).

mugging. Colloquialism referring to robbery (q.v.) of an isolated pedestrian. See *R* v *Robinson* (1987) 9 Cr App R (S) 47.

multiple admissibility. Principle of evidence (q.v.) stating that if evidence is admissible for one purpose it may not be rejected solely because it is not admissible for some other purpose. See, e.g., *Morton* v *Morton* [1937] P 151.

multiple damages. An amount of damages (q.v.) calculated by multiplying the sum which might be truly compensatory. Under Protection of Trading Interests Act 1980, s. 6, there is a right of action for a UK citizen or a person carrying on business in the UK or a body corporate incorporated in the UK to recoup payment made on account of a foreign award of multiple damages. See also C.J.J.A. 1982, s. 38. *See* DOUBLE VALUE, ACTION FOR.

multiplicity of issues. Phrase relating to the exclusion of evidence (q.v.) which "raises side issues upon which the court cannot decide without injustice to other parties": *A.-G.* v *Nottingham Corporation* [1904] 1 Ch 673.

municipal law. The law of a nation or state, as distinguished from the law of nations (i.e., international law). May be divided into *public* and *private* law (qq.v.).

muniments. Title deeds and other evidence relating to title to land. *See* TITLE.

munitions. Explosives, explosive substances, firearms, ammunition, and anything used or capable of being used in their manufacture: N. Ireland (Emergency Provisions) Act 1991, s. 19(14).

murder. Unlawful homicide with malice aforethought (q.v.). Described by Coke as ". . . when any man of sound memory, and of the age of discretion, unlawfully killeth within any county of the realm any reasonable creature *in rerum natura* under the King's peace, with malice aforethought, either expressed by the party or implied by law, so as the party wounded, or hurt, etc., die of the wound or hurt, etc., within a year and a day (q.v.) after the same". See *DPP* v *Smith* [1961] AC 290; *Hyam* v *DPP* [1975] AC 55; *R* v *Moloney* [1985] AC 905; *R* v *Hancock and Shankland* [1986] AC 455. For conspiracy to murder, see *R* v *Basra* (1989) 11 Cr App R (S.) 327.

murder, attempted. The offence requires an intention to kill, not merely to cause grievous bodily harm: see *R* v *Whybrow* (1951) 36 Cr App R 141; *R* v *Jones* [1990] 1 WLR 1057; *R* v *Gotts* [1992] 2 WLR 284 (duress not a defence).

murder, body of victim. Where murder is charged, it is not necessary for a body to have been found. See *R* v *Onufrejczyk* 1955 1 QB 388: *Blanco* v *HM Advocate* (1991) The Times, 13 Dec.

murder, soliciting to. *See* SOLICITING TO MURDER.

murder, threats to. A person who without lawful excuse makes to another a threat, intending that that other would fear it would be carried out, to kill that other or a third person is guilty of an offence: O.P.A. 1861, s. 16. See *R* v *Cousins* [1982] QB 526; *R* v *Perry* (1986) 8 Cr App R(S) 132.

murdrum. (*Morth* = a secret killing.) A heavy fine imposed by the Normans on a hundred (q.v.) in which a Norman had been slain and the murderer remained at large. The term came to signify the actual killing. *See* PRESENTMENT OF ENGLISHRY.

mute. When asked to plead, an accused person may stand mute. If considered to be mute of malice (i.e., deliberately silent) a plea of not guilty is entered for him and the trial proceeds. If considered mute "by visitation of God" (i.e., deaf and dumb) an attempt is made to make him understand and answer the charge by some means and where this fails, a plea of not guilty is entered for him. Where there is doubt a jury will decide. See *R* v *Paling* (1978) 67 Cr App R 229; C.L.A. 1967, s. 6(1)(*c*).

mutiny. A combination between two or more persons subject to military law, or between persons, two at least of whom are subject to military law, to overthrow, or resist lawful authority in the Forces or any forces co-operating therewith, to disobey such authority so as to make the disobedience subversive of discipline, or to impede the performance of any duty or service in the Forces or in any forces co-operating therewith. "An offence of collective insubordination, collective defiance or disregard of authority or refusal to obey authority": *per* Lord Goddard in *R* v *Grant* [1957] 1 WLR 906. See, e.g., Army Act 1955, s. 31(3). *See* PRISON MUTINY.

mutual dealings. Where there have been mutual dealings between a debtor and one of his creditors, account must be taken of what is due from one to the other, and the balance of the account (but no more) shall be paid or claimed. See *Rolls Razor Ltd* v *Cox* [1967] 1 QB 552.

mutual desertion. Result of each spouse, independently and without just cause, leaving the other. See *Hosegood* v *Hose-*

good [1950] WN 218; *Price* v *Price* [1968] 3 All ER 543.

mutual wills. Wills made by two or more persons, conferring reciprocal benefits, and based on an agreement to make such wills and not to revoke them without consent of the other. See *Re Oldham* [1925] Ch 75; *Re Cleaver* [1981] 1 WLR 939. *See* WILL.

N

naked contract. *See* NUDUM PACTUM.

naked trust. Bare trust (q.v.).

name and arms clause. Clause in settlement (q.v.) or will (q.v.) directing forfeiture of a beneficiary's interests unless he takes and uses a stated surname on all occasions. See *Re Neeld* [1962] Ch 643.

name, change of. A surname may be changed by operation of law (as on marriage), by statutory declaration, by deed poll, by advertisement (in, e.g., a local newspaper). See *Dancer* v *Dancer* [1949] P 147 (change of name by repute). For change of a Christian name (i.e., that given at baptism) see *Re Parrott* [1946] Ch 183. For change of a child's name, see Ch.A. 1989, ss. 13, 33(7); for change of a child's name following a divorce, see M.C. Rules 1977, r. 92(8), and *W.* v *A.* [1981] Fam 14. *See* SURNAME.

name, family. *See* SURNAME.

National Audit Office. *See* COMPTROLLER.

National Health Service. *See* HEALTH SERVICE, NATIONAL.

National Health Service contracts. Arrangements under which one health services body (e.g., a Health Authority) plans for the provision to it by another health service body of goods or services which it reasonably requires for the purposes of its functions: NHS and Community Care Act 1990, s. 4.

National Health Service trusts. Bodies corporate appointed by the Secretary of State to assume responsibility for the ownership and management of hospitals previously managed by Health Authorities or to provide and manage hospitals or other establishments: NHS and Community Care Act 1990, s. 5.

national insurance. *See* SOCIAL SECURITY.

National Insurance Tribunals. *See* SOCIAL SECURITY TRIBUNALS.

nationalisation. The bringing of the ownership and management of firms or industries under state control. See, e.g., Coal Industry Nationalisation Act 1946 (as amended by Coal Industry Act 1987, Sch. 1).

nationality. The legal relationship attaching to membership of a nation resulting from, e.g., birth, naturalisation (q.v.), marriage. Generally implies duties of allegiance and protection by state. "'Nationality' in the sense of citizenship of a certain state must not be confused with nationality as meaning membership of a certain nation in the sense of race": *London Borough of Ealing* v *Race Relations Board* [1972] 1 All ER 104. "Dual nationality" refers to citizenship held simultaneously in two countries. See B.N.A. 1981; B.N. (Falkland Islands) A. 1983.

National Rivers Authority. Body corporate appointed by the Minister, with functions relating to water resources (Water Resources Act 1991, Part III), water pollution (1991 Act, Part III), flood defences (1991 Act, Part IV and Land Drainage Act 1991). etc: 1991 Act, ss. 1, 2.

national security. "Those who are responsible for the national security must be the sole judges of what the national security requires. It would be obviously undesirable that such matters should be made the subject of evidence in a court of law or otherwise discussed in public": *per* Lord Parker in *The Zamora* [1916] 2 AC 77. See *CCSU* v *Minister for the Civil Service* [1985] AC 374. *See* SECURITY SERVICE.

nations, law of. International law (q.v.).

natural allegiance. The allegiance (q.v.) owed to his country by a subject. See *Joyce* v *DPP* [1946] AC 347.

natural child. An illegitimate child (q.v.).

naturalisation. Process resulting in an alien's receiving the status pertaining to a native citizen. In the UK it follows the grant of a certificate and the taking of an oath of allegiance. The alien must show that he is of good character, has a sufficient knowledge of English, Welsh or Gaelic, that his principal home will be in the UK, that he was in the UK at the beginning of the period of five years ending with the date of his application and that he has not been absent in that period from the UK for more than 450 days and has not been in breach of immigration laws: B.N.A.1981, s. 6(1), Sch. 1.

natural justice. *See* JUSTICE, NATURAL.

natural law. *See* LAW, NATURAL.

natural person. A human being, as contrasted with an "artificial person" (q.v.), e.g., a corporation (q.v.).

natural rights. 1. Rights conferred upon man by the natural law (q.v.). 2. Those basic rights found commonly in the laws of civilised nations, e.g., freedom of speech. *See* RIGHT.

naval court. Summoned by the commander of one of HM ships on a foreign station to investigate a complaint, or loss of a ship in the area, and consisting of naval officers. Appeal lies to Divisional Court and Court of Appeal (q.v.).

navigation, right of. Right of the public to use a river as a highway for, e.g., shipping. Rights of Way Act 1932, s. 1(1), does not apply to waterways: *A.-G. ex rel Yorks Derwent Trust* v *Brotherton* [1991] 3 WLR 1126.

necessaries. 1. Goods suitable to the condition in life of an infant (q.v.) or minor or other person and to his actual requirements at the time of the sale and delivery. "A minor may bind himself to pay for his necessary meat, drink, apparel, necessary physic, and such other necessaries, and likewise for his good teaching and instruction, whereby he may profit himself afterwards": Co Litt 172a. See S.G.A. 1979, s. 3; *Nash* v *Inman* [1908] 2 KB 1. 2. In the case of husband and wife, "things that are really necessary and suitable to the style in which the husband chooses to live, in so far as the articles fall fairly within the domestic department which is ordinarily confided to the management of the wife": *Phillipson* v *Hayter* (1870) LR 6 CP 38. *See* MINORS' CONTRACTS.

necessaries, contracts made by wife for. A man is not generally liable on con-

tracts made by his wife for necessaries if: the trade has been expressly warned not to supply her with goods on credit; she has been forbidden to pledge her husband's credit; she was supplied with the means to purchase necessaries without pledging her husband's credit; the trader gave credit exclusively to her; the husband has a sufficient supply of the goods purchased. The common law rules concerning a wife's agency of necessity were abrogated by Matrimonial Proceedings and Property Act 1970, s. 41.

necessity. Circumstances compelling a course of action. As a defence, rejected in *R* v *Dudley and Stephens* (1884) 14 QBD 273 (ship-wrecked mariners killing and eating a boy so as to survive); *London Borough of Southwark* v *Williams* [1971] 2 All ER 175 (squatting by homeless persons). For recognition of defence in extreme circumstances, see *R* v *Martin* [1989] 1 All ER 652. In the case of tort (q.v.) the defence may succeed where the damage has been caused to prevent a greater evil and the act was reasonable: *Leigh* v *Gladstone* (1909) 26 TLR 139; *Rigby* v *CC of Northampton* [1985] 1 WLR 1242.

necessity, agent by. *See* AGENT.

neck verse. *See* BENEFIT OF CLERGY.

nec vi, nec clam, nec precario. Not by violence, stealth or entreaty. Phrase used in relation to, e.g., prescriptive acquisition as of right (i.e., the user must not be forcible, concealed in any way, or permissive, e.g., founded on a licence). See *A F Beckett* v *Lyons* [1967] Ch 449.

ne exeat regno. That he shall not leave the kingdom. Writ (q.v.) restraining a person's leaving the realm, used in the case of political offenders and, later, debtors where there was probable cause to believe that they were about to leave the country. See, for a review of the law, *Felton* v *Callis* [1969] 2 QB 200; *Allied Arab Bank* v *Hajjar* [1988] 2 WLR 942.

negative clearance. Procedure whereby parties to an agreement may seek a declaration that it does not come within the scope of, and therefore does not infringe, the Treaty of Rome 1957, art. 85 (prohibiting agreements which prevent, restrict or distort competition). See EEC Council Regulation No

17/62, art. 2; Commission Decision No 72/403/EEC [1973] CMLR 77; *Re London Grain Futures Market* [1986] 3 CMLR 709. *See* EEC.

negative pregnant. A literal answer to an allegation in pleadings (q.v.) which evades answering its substance. Example: it is alleged that X received £100 from Y; X merely denies the stated amount, whereas the essence of the allegation is X's receipt of money and not merely the amount. See O. 18, r. 13; *Tildesley* v *Harper* (1878) 17 Ch D 403.

neglect. Culpable omission to perform a duty. One who undertakes the care of another who, by reason of sickness or age, is incapable of providing necessaries for himself, is criminally responsible if his conscious neglect causes the death of that other. See *R* v *Instan* [1893] 1 QB 450; *R* v *Stone and Dobinson* [1977] QB 354 (in a case of manslaughter (q.v.) it is not necessary to prove that the defendant was reckless as to whether the victim might suffer serious bodily harm or death).

neglect, wilful. *See* WILFUL NEGLECT.

negligence. "Not a state of mind, but a falling short of an objective standard of conduct": Pollock. "In strict legal analysis, negligence means more than heedless or careless conduct, whether in omission or commission; it properly connotes the complex concept of duty, breach and damage thereby suffered by the person to whom the duty was owing": *per* Lord Wright in *Lochgelly Iron & Coal* v *M'Mullan* [1934] AC 1. "'Negligence' is not an affirmative word; it is a negative word; it is the absence of such care, skill and diligence as it was the duty of the person to bring to the performance of the work which he is said not to have performed": *per* Willes J in *Grill* v *General Iron Screw Co* (1860) 35 LJCP 330. Negligence and error are not the same: *per* Stoker LJ in *Flynn* v *Vange Scaffolding Ltd* (1987) The Times, 26 March. See also *Wilsher* v *Essex HA* [1988] 2 WLR 557; *Salih* v *Enfield HA* [1991] 3 All ER 400. In the Unfair Contract Terms Act 1977, s. 1(1), means the breach of any obligation arising from the express or implied terms of a contract, to take reasonable care or exercise reasonable skill in the performance of a contract, or the breach of any common-law duty to take reasonable care or exercise reasonable skill (but not any stricter duty), or the breach of the common duty of care imposed by Occupiers' Liability Act 1957. (See Occupiers' Liability Act 1984.) For professional negligence, see, e.g., *Swingcastle Ltd* v *Gibson* [1990] 3 All ER 463. *See* DUTY OF CARE; OCCUPIER'S LIABILITY TO NON-VISITORS.

negligence, advertent. Situation in which a tortfeasor (q.v.) displays "an attitude of mental indifference to obvious risks": *per* Eve J in *Hudston* v *Viney* [1921] 1 Ch 98. In *inadvertent negligence*, the tortfeasor has displayed mere carelessness.

negligence, contributory. *See* CONTRIBUTORY NEGLIGENCE.

negligence, criminal. *See* CRIMINAL NEGLIGENCE.

negligence, foreseeability and. "It is not necessary that the precise concatenation of circumstances should be envisaged. If the consequence was one within the general range which any reasonable person might foresee (and was not of an entirely different kind which no one would anticipate) then it is within the rule that a person who is guilty of negligence is liable for the consequences": *per* Lord Denning in *Stewart* v *W. African Air Terminals* (1964) 108 SJ 838.

negligence gross. *See* GROSS NEGLIGENCE.

negligence liability, avoidance of. By the Unfair Contract Terms Act 1977, s. 2(1), a person cannot by reference to any contract term or notice given to persons exclude or restrict his liability for death or personal injury resulting from negligence and, in the case of other loss or damage, he cannot so exclude or restrict his liability for negligence except in so far as the term or notice satisfies the requirement of reasonableness (which will be considered by reference to, e.g., strength of bargaining position of parties relative to each other, whether goods were manufactured to the customer's special order, whether the customer knew or ought reasonably to have known of existence and extent of the term: Sch. 2).

negligence, sport and. Participants in competitive sport owe a duty of care to one another to take all reasonable care, having regard to the particular circumstances in which they are placed: *Condon* v *Basi* [1985] 2 All ER 453.

negligence, tort of. The breach of a legal duty to take care, resulting in damage to the plaintiff which was not desired by the defendant. "The omission to do something which a reasonable man, guided upon those considerations which ordinarily regulate the conduct of human affairs, would do, or doing something which a prudent and reasonable man would not do": *Blyth* v *Birmingham Waterworks Co* (1856) 11 Ex 781. Burden of proof is generally on the plaintiff. See *Donoghue* v *Stevenson* [1932] AC 562. See DUTY OF CARE.

negligent misstatement. A statement carelessly made in circumstances where there is a duty to be honest and careful, resulting in loss to some person to whom that duty is owed and who has acted on the statement. Liability for such a statement may arise in tort (q.v.) and contract (q.v.). See *Hedley Byrne & Co Ltd* v *Heller and Partners* [1964] AC 793; *Esso Petroleum Co Ltd* v *Mardon* [1976] QB 801.

negotiable. In relation to an instrument, the quality of being transferable free from equities.

negotiable instrument. An instrument with the following characteristics: (1) title to it passes by delivery; (2) holder for the time being may sue in his own name; (3) notice of assignment need not be given to person liable thereon; (4) bona fide holder for value takes free from any defect in title of predecessors; (5) instrument is of a type recognised by law as negotiable. Examples: bills of exchange; promissory notes and cheques; dividend warrants; debentures payable to bearer (see *Bechuanaland Exploration Co* v *London Trading Bank Ltd* [1898] 2 QB 658). See B.Ex.A 1882, ss. 31, 32. *See* NOT NEGOTIABLE.

negotiable instruments, quasi-. Those choses in action (q.v.) which, although not completely negotiable, possess some of the characteristics of negotiable instruments. Examples: IOU; bill of lading.

negotiable instruments, renunciation of. When the holder of a bill, at or after its maturity, absolutely and uncondi-

tionally renounces his rights against the acceptor, the bill is discharged. The renunciation must be in writing, unless the bill is delivered up to the acceptor: see B. of Ex.A. 1882, s. 62(1).

negotiation of a bill. The transferring of a bill of exchange (q.v.) from one person to another so that the transferee becomes the holder of the bill: B.Ex.A. 1882, s. 31(1).

negotiorum gestio. The management of affairs. *Negotiorum gestior* is one who interferes in the affairs of another for that other's advantage, but without authority. Not generally recognised in English law; but see B.Ex.A. 1882, s. 65. See *Falcke* v *Scottish Insurance* (1887) 34 Ch D 249.

neighbour concept in law. *See* DUTY OF CARE.

nemine contradicente. Abbreviated to *nem con.* No one saying otherwise.

nemo dat quod non habet. No one can give that which he has not. See S.G.A. 1979, s. 21(1). Thus, a person cannot give better title than he has. In some cases, however, a buyer acquires a good title, notwithstanding a defect in the seller's title. Examples: sale in market overt (q.v.); sale under an order of the court; transfer of a negotiable instrument (q.v.) to a holder in due course; under the doctrine of estoppel (q.v.). See Factors Act 1889, s. 2; *Greenwood* v *Bennett* [1973] QB 195; *Shaw* v *Commissioner of Metropolitan Police* [1987] 1 WLR 1332.

nemo debet bis puniri pro uno delicto. No man ought to be punished twice for one offence. See *R* v *Statutory Ctee of Pharmaceutical Society of Great Britain* [1981] 1 WLR 886.

nemo debet bis vexari. No man ought to be twice vexed. No person should be again prosecuted upon the same facts if he has been tried by a competent court. *See* AUTREFOIS ACQUIT.

nemo debet esse judex in propria causa. No person should be a judge in his own cause. The rule applies also to any cause in which that person has an interest. See, e.g., *R* v *Barnsley Metropolitan BC, ex p Hook* [1976] 3 All ER 452. *See* BIAS, RULE AGAINST.

nemo est heres viventis. A living person has no heir (since not until that person's death can his heir be ascertained). *See* HEIR APPARENT.

nemo tenetur seipsum accusare. No person is bound to incriminate himself. See *Commissioners of Customs and Excise* v *Ingram* [1948] 1 All ER 927. *See* INCRIMINATE.

neonate. A newborn child. For medical duty in relation to handicapped neonates, see, e.g., *Re J.* [1990] 3 All ER 930.

nervous shock. Actual illness in the form of physical symptoms or psychiatric illness. Regarded as a personal, bodily hurt, constituting a tort (q.v.). "It is now well recognised that an action will lie for injury by shock sustained through the medium of the eye or ear without direct contact": *Bourhill* v *Young* [1943] AC 92. For manslaughter arising from shock, see *R* v *Dawson* (1985) 81 Cr App R 150.

nervous shock and liability. Liability for psychiatric illness depends on foreseeability and a relationship of proximity between claimant and defendant. It is not reasonable to regard viewing a television broadcast of a disaster as giving rise to shock, in the sense of a sudden assault on the nervous system. Psychiatric claims by plaintiffs in close family relationship with the victims are recognisable as based on the rebuttable presumption of love and affection normally associated with that relationship; but such claims are not to be confined to that relationship. See *Alcock and Others* v *CC of S. Yorks Police* [1991] 4 All ER 907; *Ravenscroft* v *Rederiaktiebologet Transatlantic* [1992] 2 All ER 470.

net estate. In relation to a deceased person, it includes: property which he had power to dispose of by will, less funeral, testamentary and administration expenses; property in respect of which he held a general power of appointment (q.v.) not exercised; sums which he nominated another to receive; *donationes mortis causa* (q.v.): Inheritance (Provision for Family and Dependants) Act 1975.

new. Recent, original. Whether an article is "new" is a question of fact or degree in every particular case: *Raynham Farm Co Ltd* v *Symbol Motor Corp Ltd* (1987) The Times, 27 Jan. See *R* v *Ford Motor Co Ltd* [1974] 1 WLR 1220.

next friend. An adult through whom an infant (q.v.) or patient (within the meaning of M.H.A. 1983) sues, e.g.,

the infant's father or person *in loco parentis*, patient's receiver, or Official Solicitor (qq.v.). His name must appear on the writ (q.v.) and he must undertake to be responsible for costs. In the High Court, the next friend may not appear in person; a solicitor must be retained. See O. 80, rr. 1–3.

next of kin. Generally, one's nearest blood relations. "Statutory next of kin" may be construed technically, to denote next of kin who, on a person's death intestate, would have taken his personalty (q.v.) under the Statute of Distributions. See *Re Sutcliffe* [1929] 1 Ch 123.

nexus. Connection or bond. For "familial nexus", see, e.g., *Dyson Holdings* v *Fox* [1976] QB 503.

night. The time from sunset to sunrise. See, e.g., SI 1991/2125.

nisi. Unless. Not final or absolute.

nisi per legale judicium parium suorum, vel per legem terrae. [No freeman is to be taken, imprisoned or exiled] unless by the lawful judgment of his peers or [and] by the law of the land. Provision of Magna Carta (q.v.).

nisi prius. Unless before. Trial at *nisi prius* followed after the sheriff (q.v.) was commanded to secure the attendance of a jury at Westminster "unless before" that day the county should be visited by a judge of assize (q.v.). The term was used in recent years to refer to commission to try causes conferred on judges of assize.

no case to answer. Submission by the defendant, at the close of the plaintiff's case, that a prima facie case has not been made out. The submission should be made in the absence of the jury: *R* v *Falconer-Atlee* (1973) 58 Cr App R 348. If the submission succeeds, judgment is entered for the defendant. It may be based on a point of law or absence of evidence relating to essential facts. See *R* v *Barker* (1975) 65 Cr App R 287; and *R* v *Galbraith* [1981] 1 WLR 1039.

noise. "Sound which is undesired by the recipient": *Wilson Report*, 1963. An action may lie in some circumstances for nuisance resulting from noise: see, e.g., *Lambert Flat Management Ltd* v *Lomas* [1981] 1 WLR 898. Includes vibration: see En.P.A. 1990, s. 79(g). See *Southwark LBC* v *Ince* (1989) 153 JP 597.

noise abatement zone. Zone so designated by order of a local authority, confirmed by the Secretary of State, in which noise levels exceeding those registered (in a noise level register) may be penalised under Control of Pollution Act 1974, s. 65, as amended. *R v Fenny Stratford Justices, ex p Watney Mann (Midlands) Ltd* [1976] 2 All ER 888.

nolens volens. Whether willingly or unwillingly.

nolle prosequi. Unwilling to prosecute. An undertaking by the plaintiff to discontinue an action. In a criminal case the entry of a *nolle prosequi*, which stays a prosecution on indictment (q.v.), is made by the Attorney-General (q.v.) before judgment. (The Crown Prosecution Service may discontinue a prosecution.) It is not an acquittal; fresh proceedings may be brought on the same charge at a later date.

nolo contendere. I do not wish to contend. Generally, an implied confession of guilt.

nominal capital. A company's authorised capital (q.v.). See Cos.A. 1985, s. 121.

nominal damages. *See* DAMAGES.

nominal partner. Known also as "ostensible partner". One who holds himself out as having an interest in a business.

nomination. 1. Designation or proposal by name for a vacant office. 2. A direction to a person who holds funds on behalf of another to pay them to a nominated person in the event of death. Nomination may be made by an adult or infant (q.v.) who has reached the age of 16. See *Baird v Baird* [1990] 2 All ER 301.

non assumpsit. He did not promise. Plea in action of *assumpsit* (q.v.), stating that the defendant made no promise.

non-commercial agreement. "A consumer credit agreement or a consumer hire agreement (qq.v.) not made by the creditor or owner in the course of a business carried on by him": C.C.A. 1974, s. 189(1). Example: agreement for a loan made between friends and not in the course of a business transaction.

non compos mentis. Not of sound mind.

non constat. It is not clear. It does not follow.

non-contentious business. Business not contained within the definition of contentious business (q.v.), e.g., drafting of a will, conveyancing. Mode and amount of remuneration are governed by orders under Solicitors Act 1974, s. 56. See S.C.A. 1981, s. 128.

non-delivery. Failure to deliver goods, which amounts to a breach of contract, may give rise to an action for damages. The principal rules of assessment of such damages are set out in S.G.A. 1979, s. 51. See, e.g., *Tai Hing Cotton Mill Ltd v Kamsing Knitting Factory* [1979] AC 91; *The Alecos M* [1991] 1 Lloyd's Rep 120.

non-direction. Failure of a trial judge to direct the jury on a necessary point of law.

non-disclosure. *See* DISCLOSURE, NON-.

non-discrimination notice. 1. Notice under Race Relations Act 1976, s. 58, after investigation by Commission for Racial Equality (q.v.) whereby a person who is committing or has committed an unlawful discriminatory act or an act contravening ss. 28–31, is required not to commit such acts. Appeal against notice may be made to an industrial tribunal (q.v.) or county court (q.v.). A register of such notices was established under s. 61. 2. Notice issued under Sex Discrimination Act 1975, s. 67, by Equal Opportunities Commission (q.v.) requiring a person not to commit an unlawful discriminatory act. There is a right of appeal under s. 68. See *R v Commission for Racial Equality, ex p Westminster CC* [1985] ICR 822.

non est factum. It is not [his] deed. Plea which denies that an instrument is that of the defendant, e.g., where there has been a mistake as to the nature of the transaction. See *Howatson v Webb* [1908] 1 Ch 1; *Chiswick Investments v Pevats* [1990] 1 NZLR 169; *Lloyds Bank v Waterhouse* [1991] 10 Tr LR 161. "A person who signs a document, and parts with it so that it may come into other hands, has a responsibility . . . to take care what he signs, which, if neglected, prevents him from denying his liability under the document": *United Dominions Trust Ltd v Western and Another* [1976] QB 513.

non est inventus. He has not been found. A return made by a sheriff (q.v.) to a writ of *capias* (q.v.) when the defendant cannot be found.

nonfeasance. Failure to perform an act which one is bound by law to do. "The distinction between misfeasance and nonfeasance is valid only in the case of highways repairable by the public at large. It does not apply to any other branch of law": *Pride of Derby Ltd v British Celanese Ltd* [1953] Ch 149. See also Highways Act 1980, s. 58. *See* MISFEASANCE.

non haec in foedera veni. It was not this that I promised to do. See *Davis Contractors Ltd v Fareham UDC* [1956] AC 696 (a "radical change in the obligation" is the appropriate test in considering whether a contract has been frustrated). See also *National Carriers v Panalpina* [1981] AC 675. *See* FRUSTRATION OF CONTRACT.

non-intervention principle. "Where a court is considering whether or not to make one or more orders under [Ch.A. 1989] with respect to a child, it shall not make the order, or any of the orders, unless it considers that doing so would be better for the child than making no order at all": Ch.A. 1989, s. 1(5).

non-joinder. A plea in abatement which alleged that the plaintiff has failed to join in the action all those who ought to have been parties. Under O. 15, r. 6, "no cause or matter shall be defeated by reason of misjoinder or nonjoinder of any party".

non-jury list. A list in the QBD of cases to be tried by a judge sitting alone, or with assessors (q.v.).

non-molestation clause. *See* INJUNCTIONS, MATRIMONIAL.

non obstante. Notwithstanding.

non obstante veredicto. Notwithstanding the verdict.

non placet. It does not please; it is not approved. Formula used by an assembly to record a negative vote.

non prosequitur. He does not follow up. Title of judgment for the defendant where the plaintiff did not take the proper steps within the prescribed period of time. See O. 19, r. 1.

non sequitur. It does not follow.

non-suit. The renouncing by the plaintiff of a suit before the verdict, e.g., on discovery of a defect. Refers also to the withdrawal by a judge of the case from the jury, and the direction of the verdict in the defendant's favour. Non-

suit in the High Court (q.v.) has been replaced by discontinuance (q.v.). See *Clack v Arthurs Engineering Ltd* [1959] 2 QB 211.

non-user. End of the exercise of rights. Thus, non-user may be evidence of abandonment of a private right of easement (q.v.). See *Swan v Sinclair* [1925] AC 227.

no-par-value shares. Because of the requirement that the nominal share capital of a company must be divided into shares of a fixed amount, shares of no-par-value cannot be issued. The *Jenkins Report 1962* recommended their issue.

norm. An authoritative standard or rule of behaviour. *See* LAW, PURE THEORY OF.

noscitur a sociis. Known from associates. A rule of interpretation whereby the meaning of a word may be ascertained by reference to its context. "English words derive colour from those which surround them": *Bourne v Norwich Crematorium Ltd* [1967] 2 All ER 576. See *Pengelly v Bell Punch Co Ltd* [1964] 2 All ER 945.

notary. Known also as "notary public". Rights and privileges arise from Public Notaries Acts 1801–43. Usually a solicitor who attests deeds, or one, who, in the case of a dishonoured bill, notes or protests it.

not guilty. 1. Plea to an indictment which is, in essence, a challenge to the prosecution to establish guilt. It may be changed once the trial has started. 2. Verdict following trial, which, in effect, is an acquittal. The accused may be found not guilty of offences specifically charged in the indictment, but guilty of another offence arising from allegations therein. Where the defendant pleads not guilty and the prosecution does not offer evidence, the judge may order the recording of a verdict of not guilty: C.J.A. 1967, s. 17. *See* GUILTY; VERDICT.

not guilty by reason of insanity. A special verdict (q.v.) which is, in form, an acquittal.

notice. Knowledge of some fact. May be (1) *actual*, as where, e.g., a purchaser is made aware during negotiations of the existence of a prior interest (see *Reeves v Pope* [1914] 2 KB 284); (2) *constructive* (q.v.); (3) *imputed*, as where, e.g., a purchaser employs a solicitor or other agent who obtains actual or constructive notice (see *Le Neve* v *Le Neve* (1747) 3 Atk 648).

notice, minimum periods of. Periods which an employer is required to give an employee if he wishes to terminate his contract – one week for each year of service up to maximum of 12 weeks after 12 years' service. See E.P.(C.)A. 1978, Part IV; *West* v *Kneels Ltd* [1987] ICR 146.

notice of abandonment. Written or oral notice indicating that the assured (under a policy of marine insurance) abandons the subject-matter insured unconditionally to the insured. If notice is not given, the loss is considered as partial. Notice must be given with reasonable diligence. *See* ABANDONMENT.

notice of dishonour. Notice that a bill of exchange (q.v.) is dishonoured must be given to the parties whom the holder is seeking to hold liable. See B.Ex.A. 1882, s. 49. *See* DISHONOUR OF BILL.

notice of title. Knowledge (actual, imputed, constructive) acquired by an intending purchaser that title is encumbered by rights or interests. *See* NOTICE; TITLE.

notice to admit. Notice calling on the party served to admit all or some specified part of another party's case or to admit to the authenticity of documents listed, but not to their truth. Failure to admit may result in the payment of costs of the proof of the issue(s) in question or of documents by the party served. See O. 27.

notice to produce. Notice by one party in an action to another to produce at the trial documents in his possession. In default of production, secondary evidence (q.v.) of documents may be given. See O. 24.

notice to quit. Notice required to be given by a landlord or tenant or their authorised agents prior to the determination of tenancy. No notice to quit premises let as a dwelling is valid unless in writing and contains information prescribed by the Secretary of State by statutory instrument, and is given not less than four weeks before the date on which it is to take effect: Protection from Eviction Act 1977, s. 5. See also L.P.A. 1925, s. 196; Rent Act

1977, ss. 103–106; *Rous* v *Mitchell* [1991] 1 WLR 469.

noting a bill. Process of attaching a memorandum to a bill of exchange by a notary (q.v.), giving the reason for its having been dishonoured, as the first step to a protest (q.v.). See B.Ex.A. 1882, s. 51. *See* BILL OF EXCHANGE.

not negotiable. Words marked on, e.g., a cheque or postal order, as a safeguard, so that the holder has no better right than the previous holder. See B.Ex.A. 1882, ss. 76, 81; *Redmond* v *Allied Irish Banks* [1987] FLR 307. *See* NEGOTIABLE INSTRUMENT.

notorious facts. Matters of common knowledge of which, generally, judicial notice (q.v.) will be taken, e.g., that human gestation cannot be completed within 14 days (see *R* v *Luffe* (1807) 8 East 193).

nova causa interveniens. New intervening cause. See, e.g., *Cummings* v *Sir William Arrol & Co Ltd* [1962] 1 All ER 623.

novation. Contract whereby a creditor at the request of a debtor agrees to take another person as debtor in place of the original debtor. The original debtor is thereby released from his obligations which fall on the new debtor. See *Scarfe* v *Jardine* (1882) 7 App Cas 345.

novel disseisin. An assize (q.v.) based on the complaint by P that D had, without judgment, unjustly disseised P of his freehold tenement. P requested that the King's court should give judgment to put him back into seisin (q.v.). Abolished by Real Property Limitation Act 1833, s. 36. *See* DISSEISIN.

novus actus interveniens. New act intervening. General defence in an action in tort (q.v.). When the act of a third person intervenes between the original act or omission and the damage, that act or omission is considered as the direct cause of the damage if the act of the third person could have been expected in the particular circumstances: *Scott* v *Shepherd* (1733) 2 Wm Bl 892. See *Knightley* v *Johns* [1982] 1 All ER 951; *R* v *Pagett* (1983) 76 Cr App R 279. *See* CAUSA REMOTA.

noxal. Referring to damage in ancient civil law caused by a slave or animal.

noxious. That which is offensive, or which causes or tends to cause injury to health. See O.P.A. 1861, ss. 23, 24; *R* v *Marcus* [1981] 1 WLR 774 (concept of a "noxious thing" depends not only on quality and nature of substance, but also the quantity administered); *R* v *Hill* (1986) 83 Cr App R 386.

nuclear installations, operation of. No person other than the UK Atomic Energy Authority may use any site for purposes of nuclear plant operation unless a licence has been granted by the minister. See, e.g., Nuclear Installations Acts 1965 and 1969; Nuclear Materials (Offences) Act 1983; Energy Act 1983; Atomic Energy Act 1989.

nudum pactum. A "nude" contract, i.e., "a bare promise of a thing without any consideration": Cowel. *See* CONSIDERATION; EX NUDO PACTO.

nugatory. Useless, invalid, ineffectual.

nuisance. In law of torts, an unlawful interference with another's use of, enjoyment of, or right over or in relation to, land, or damage resulting from such interference: *Read* v *Lyons & Co Ltd* [1945] KB 216. Nuisance may be *public* (in which case it is also a crime), e.g., obstruction of a highway, or *private*, e.g., causing unreasonable personal discomfort to another. Remedies include: abatement, action for damages, injunction (qq.v.). Defences include trivial injury only, result of lawful use of land (see *Bradford Corporation* v *Pickles* [1895] AC 587), prescriptive right. For "statutory nuisances" (i.e., nuisances which are inevitable and compulsory by statute) in relation to pollution, see En.P.A. 1990, s. 79. For exemplary damages, see *AB and Others* v *SW Water Services Ltd* (1992) NLJ 897. *See* PUBLIC NUISANCE; TORT.

nuisance, unreasonableness causing. "It may broadly be said that a useful test is perhaps what is reasonable according to the ordinary usages of mankind living in society"; *Sedleigh-Denfield* v *O'Callaghan* [1940] AC 880. "Those acts necessary for the common and ordinary use and occupation of land and houses may be done, if conveniently done, without subjecting those who do them to an action": *Bamford* v *Turnley* (1862) 3 B & S 66.

nulla bona. No goods. Statement by a sheriff (q.v.) in return to a writ of *fieri facias* (q.v.) when there are no goods to be seized.

null and void. Having no force; invalid.

nulla poena sine lege. No punishment without legal authority.

nulle terre sans seigneur. No land without a lord. Basis of the principle that all land in England was owned by the Crown, and that tenants held, ultimately from the Crown. *See* ALLODIAL LAND.

nullity decree, recognition of foreign. The decree is recognised if: granted by a court in the parties' common domicile; although granted elsewhere, it is recognised as effective by courts of common domicile; granted by a court of the parties' common residence or a court of the country in which a void marriage was celebrated; at the time of the decree either party had a substantial connection with the country granting the decree.

nullity of marriage. Marriages may be rendered *void* (because the parties are within prohibited degrees of relationship (q.v.), or either party is under 16, or either was lawfully married at the time of the ceremony) or *voidable* (because of, e.g., wilful refusal to consummate (q.v.), incapacity, pregnancy at time of marriage by some person other than the petitioner, lack of valid consent to the marriage). "A void marriage is one that will be regarded by every court in any case in which the existence of the marriage is in issue as never having taken place, and can be so treated by both parties to it without the necessity of any decree annulling it; a voidable marriage is one that will be regarded by every court as a valid and subsisting marriage until a decree annulling it has been pronounced": *De Reneville* v *De Reneville* [1948] P 100. See Mat.C.A. 1973, ss. 11, 12; Marriage Act 1983, s. 6; for time limits on bringing proceedings (and other bars to the decree) see Mat.C.A. 1973, s. 13 (as amended by Matrimonial and Family Proceedings Act 1984, s. 2).

nulli vendemus, nulli negabimus, aut differemus, rectum aut justitiam. To none will we sell, to none will we deny, to none will we delay either right or justice. Provision of Magna Carta (q.v.).

nullum crimen sine lege. No crime except in accordance with the law — an aspect of the so-called "principle of legality". "The great leading rule of criminal law is that nothing is a crime unless it is plainly forbidden by law. This rule is no doubt subject to exceptions but they are rare, narrow, and to be admitted with the greatest reluctance, and only upon the strongest reasons": *R* v *Price* (1884) 12 QBD 247.

nullum tempus occurrit regi. Time does not run against the Crown, i.e., there is no limitation period on prosecutions unless specifically provided by statute. See Lim A. 1980, s. 37; M.C.A. 1980, s. 127. See also *R* v *Lewis* [1979] 1 WLR 970.

nullus liber homo capiatur vel imprisonetur. No freeman shall be arrested or detained in prison [without a trial]. Provision of Magna Carta (q.v.).

nunc pro tunc. Now for then. Phrase relating to a judgment entered so that it takes effect as if entered at an earlier date. See O. 42, r. 3.

nuncupative will. (*Nuncupare* = to name, declare.) A verbal testament. Abolished under W.A. 1837, s. 9, except in the case of privileged wills (q.v.) made by those on active service.

O

oath. A solemn appeal (usually to God) to witness that some statement is true or that some promise is binding. In general all evidence (q.v.) must be on oath. A witness's oath is: "I swear by Almighty God that the evidence which I shall give shall be the truth, the whole truth and nothing but the truth". See Oaths Act 1978; C. & Y.P.A. 1963, s. 28; Ch.A. 1989, s. 96(1); *R v Bellamy* (1986) 82 Cr App R 222; *R v Kemble* [1990] 1 WLR 1111. See AFFIRM; PERJURY.

oath, judge's. *See* JUDGE'S OATH.

oath, juror's. *See* JUROR'S OATH.

oath of allegiance. Oath taken, e.g., by officers of the Crown on appointment. "I do swear that I will be faithful and bear true allegiance to Her Majesty Queen Elizabeth II, her heirs and successors, according to law." See Promissory Oaths Acts 1868 and 1971; C.L.S.A. 1990, s. 76. A somewhat similar oath is taken by an alien on obtaining a certificate of naturalisation.

Oaths, Commisioners for. *See* COMMISSIONERS FOR OATHS.

obedience to orders, defence of. In some circumstances obedience to a superior's orders may be relevant in negativing *mens rea* (q.v.). In the case of orders given by a military superior, a soldier acting under those orders "not being necessarily or manifestly illegal" would be justified by them: *Keighley v Bell* (1868) 4 F & F 773. See *R v James* (1837) 8 C & P 131.

obiter dictum. (*Pl*: *obiter dicta*.) Saying by the way. Refers to: a statement of the law based on facts which were not present, or not material, in a case (see, e.g., the judgment of Denning J in *Central London Property Trust Ltd v High Trees House Ltd* [1947] KB 30); a statement of law based on facts as found, but not forming the basis of the decision (e.g., a statement upon which a dissenting judgment is based). It will

be of persuasive authority only. See *West & Parners Ltd v Dick* [1969] 1 All ER 289. *See* RATIO DECIDENDI.

objection to indictment. Procedure whereby the accused attempts to show that the indictment (q.v.) is open to legal objection, e.g., because the court lacks jurisdiction to try that offence.

objects clause. Clause in the memorandum of association (q.v.) setting out the objects which a company (q.v.) has been formed to pursue. See Cos.A. 1985, s. 2(1)(c). A company may adopt a single object, namely to carry on any business or trade whatsoever: Cos.A. 1989, s. 110. Objects may be altered by special resolution: Cos.A. 1989, s. 110, amending Cos.A. 1985, s. 4. See *Brady v Brady* [1988] 3 CLC 2a.

objects of a power. Where an appointor is authorised to appoint an interest to the members of a generally restricted class (e.g., "amongst the children of X"), those whom he may select are known as the "objects of the power." *See* APPOINTMENT, POWER OF.

obligation. 1. A duty, usually legal or moral and of one's choosing, to undertake a course of action. "The word means, primarily, a tie. Legally it was in origin the binding tie established by what is called a 'bond' as between the obligor and the obligee": *per* Scott LJ in *Watkinson v Hollington* [1943] 2 All ER 573 "The positive legal norm which commands the behaviour of an individual by attaching a sanction to the opposite behaviour": Kelsen. 2. A bond (q.v.) with a condition annexed, usually involving a penalty for non-fulfilment. 3. A "planning obligation", under Planning and Compensation Act 1991, s. 12, restricts the development of land in a specified way.

obligee. *See* BOND.

obligor. *See* BOND.

obliteration. That which has been made impossible to decipher. In the case of a will (q.v.), no obliteration is valid except so far as the words of the will before the obliteration are not apparent, unless the obliteration has been properly signed and attested. A complete obliteration is usually valid, so that probate (q.v.) will be granted as though the will contained blanks. See *In b Horsford* (1872) LR 3 P & D 211.

obscenity. "An article shall be deemed to be obscene if its effect or (where the article comprises two or more distinct items) the effect of any one of its items is, if taken as a whole, such as to tend to deprave (q.v.) and corrupt persons who are likely, having regard to all relevant circumstances, to read, see or hear the matter contained or embodied in it": Obscene Publications Act 1959, s. 1(1). Obscenity is not confined to books, etc, dealing with sex: *Calder Publications Ltd v Powell* [1965] 1 QB 509. It is an offence to possess an obscene article for publication for gain (Obscene Publications Act 1964, s. 1(1)); to send by post a packet containing any indecent or obscene print or article (Post Office Act 1953, s. 11): see *R v Lee* (1988) 10 Cr App R (S.) 364. For obscene phone calls, constituting a public nuisance, see *R v Norbury* [1978] Crim LR 435. See Cable and Broadcasting Act 1984, s. 25; Broadcasting Act 1990, s. 162. See *R v Gibson* [1990] 3 WLR 595 (offence of outraging public decency at common law); *Darbo v DPP* [1992] Crim LR 56. *See* PUBLICATION.

obstruction of highway. *See* HIGHWAY, OBSTRUCTION OF.

obstruction of police. *See* POLICE, OBSTRUCTION OF.

obstruction of recovery of premises. *See* RECOVERY OF PREMISES, OBSTRUCTION OF.

obtaining credit, undischarged bankrupt. An offence if the bankrupt obtains credit to the extent of the prescribed amount or over without informing the intending creditor that he is an undischarged bankrupt, or without disclosing the name under which he was adjudged bankrupt. See Ins.A. 1986, s. 20.

obtaining pecuniary advantage. *See* DECEPTION, OBTAINING PROPERTY BY.

occupancy. The taking possession of, and acquiring title to, that which has no owner.

occupant. 1. One who takes by occupancy. 2. One who resides in a place.

occupation. 1. A person's trade, calling. 2. The taking and controlling of enemy territory by the armed forces of the Crown. 3. Control, actual physical possession of land, or its use. A person was held to be "in actual occupation" only if that occupation was recognisable as such and apparent to a purchaser: *Hodgson v Marks* [1970] 3 All ER 513. "Occupation is a matter of fact and only exists where there is sufficient measure of control to prevent strangers from interfering": *Newcastle CC v Royal Newcastle Hospital* [1959] 1 All ER 734.

occupational pension scheme. "Any scheme or arrangement which is comprised in one or more instruments or agreements and which has, or is capable of having, effect in relation to one or more descriptions or categories of employment so as to provide benefits, in the form of pensions or otherwise, payable on termination of service, or on death or retirement, to or in respect of earners with qualifying service in an employment of any such description or category": F.S.A. 1986, s. 207(1). See Sch. 1, para 11. For "contracting-out", see SI 1984/380. See S.S.A. 1990, Schs. 2, 4.

occupation road. *See* ROAD, OCCUPATION.

occupier. One who has possession as owner or tenant (q.v.) of land or a house and has the degree of control associated with his presence on the land or in the house. For "multiple occupancy", see, e.g., *Hadjiloucas v Crean* [1988] 1 WLR 1006.

occupier, residential. *See* RESIDENTIAL OCCUPIER.

occupiers' liability, principle of. An occupier has a common duty of care (q.v.) to all persons on his premises by his invitation or permission, express or implicit. "Wherever a person has a sufficient degree of control over premises to realise that any failure on his part to use care may result in injury to a person coming lawfully there, then he is an 'occupier'": *Wheat v Lacon & Co* [1966] AC 552. See Occupiers' Liability Acts 1957, 1984; Defective Premises Act 1972.

occupier's liability to non-visitors. An occupier of premises owes a duty to another (not being his visitor (q.v.)) if he is aware of any danger due to the state of the premises or has reasonable grounds to believe that the danger exists, and knows or has reasonable grounds to believe that the other is in the vicinity of the danger concerned and the risk is one against which, in all the circumstances, he may reasonably be expected to offer the other some protection: Occupiers' Liability Act 1984, s. 1. See *Smith* v *Littlewoods* [1987] AC 241.

occupying tenant. In relation to a dwelling, this means the person who is not an owner-occupier but who occupies or is entitled to occupy the dwelling as a lessee, or is a statutory tenant of the dwelling, or occupies the dwelling as a residence under a restricted contract (q.v.) or occupies or resides in the dwelling as part of his employment in agriculture: H.A. 1985, s. 236(2).

offence. Generally, that which is equivalent to a crime, i.e., an act or omission punishable under criminal law: *Derbyshire CC* v *Derby* [1896] 2 QB 57; *Horsfield* v *Brown* [1932] 1 KB 355. *See* OFFENDER.

offences, duplicated. *See* DUPLICATED OFFENCES.

offences, general classification of. Division of offences for purposes of criminal procedure into: indictable offences; summary offences; offences triable either way (qq.v.): C.L.A. 1977, s. 14 (now repealed without needing replacement).

offences triable either way. Offences which, if committed by an adult, are triable either on indictment (q.v.) or summarily (q.v.): C.L.A. 1977, s. 64(1)(c). See M.C.A. 1980, s. 17, Sch. 1; *Re Gillard* [1986] AC 442. For initial procedure on an information for offences triable either way see M.C.A. 1980, s. 18. Some offences triable either way may be tried summarily if the value involved is small: M.C.A. 1980, s. 22. See I.A. 1978, Sch. 1; *Practice Note* [1990] 3 All ER 979.

offence, weapon of. "An article made or adapted for use for causing injury to or incapacitating a person, or intended by the person having it with him for such use": T.L.A. 1968, s. 10(1)(a); C.L.A. 1977, s. 8(2). *See* OFFENSIVE WEAPON.

offender. One who is guilty of an offence (q.v.).

offender, fugitive. *See* FUGITIVE CRIMINAL

offensive trades. Trades so defined under Public Health Act 1936, s. 107, (e.g., glue-making) which may not be established without the consent of the local authority. See En.P.A. 1990, s. 84; *Epping Forest DC* v *Essex Rendering Ltd* [1983] 1 WLR 158.

offensive weapon. "Any article made or adapted for use for causing injury to the person, or intended by the person having it with him for such use by him": Prevention of Crime Act 1953, s. 1(4). It is an offence to have, without lawful authority, or reasonable excuse, such an article in any public place: s. 1(1). See P. & C.E.A. 1984, s. 1(9); C.J.A. 1988, ss. 139, 141; SI 1988/2019; *Houghton* v *Chief Constable of Manchester* (1987) 84 Cr App R 320; *Copus* v *DPP* [1989] Crim LR 577; *Godwin* v *DPP* (1992) The Times, 14 Aug (defence of "good reason").

offer. A proposal, written or oral, to give or do something e.g., to enter a legally binding contract. It may be *express* or *implied* from conduct. The person making the offer is the *offeror*; the person to whom it is made is the *offeree*. General rules are: (1) an offer may be made to a definite person, definite class of persons or the world at large; (2) an offer must be communicated to the offeree before acceptance; (3) it is only made when it reaches the offeree, not when it might have reached him in ordinary course of post. See, e.g., *Adams* v *Lindsell* (1818) 1 B & Ald 681; *Carlill* v *Carbolic Smoke Ball Co* [1893] 1 QB 256. *See* ACCEPTANCE; CONTRACT; LAPSE OF OFFER.

offer, counter-. Response of an offeree which, in effect, suggests an agreement on terms which differ from those of the original offer. Example: "You can have my car for £3,000." "I'll give you £2,800 for it." It amounts to a rejection of the original offer. See *Hyde* v *Wrench* (1840) 3 Beav 334; and *Butler Machine Tool Co* v *Ex-Cell-O Corp* [1979] 1 WLR 401.

offer for sale. Document offering shares to the public, issued by an issuing house which has bought the shares outright from a public company. See

Cos.A. 1985, s. 58 (now repealed: F.S.A. 1986, Parts IV, V).

offers, cross-. Offers which cross, e.g., in the post. Example: A and B discuss the sale and purchase of A's motor car; A then writes to B offering to sell the car for £2,000, and, simultaneously, B writes to A offering to buy it for £2,000. See *Tinn* v *Hoffman* (1873) 29 LT 271.

office of profit. A paid office under the Crown. Except as provided by House of Commons Disqualification Act 1975, a person shall not be disqualified from membership of the House by reason of his holding an office or place of profit under the Crown or any other office or place: 1975 Act, s. 1(4).

office premises. A building or part of a building, the sole or principal use of which is an office or for office purposes: Offices, Shops and Railway Premises Act 1963, s. 1. See also H.S.W.A. 1974.

officer. One holding a position of command, authority, trust. See *Moberley* v *Alsop* (1991) The Times, 13 Dec. (key to meaning of the word was in the designation of an employee to perform a particular duty).

Official Custodian for Charities. Created under the Charities Act 1960, s. 3. Charity property may be vested in him by a court order; he does not exercise powers of management, but has, in general, the same powers as a custodian trustee (q.v.). *See* CHARITY.

official receiver. Appointed by the Secretary of State for Trade in matters concerning bankruptcy (q.v.) and winding up (q.v.): Ins. A. 1986, s. 399. He is considered an officer of the court in relation to which he exercises the function: s. 400(2).

official referee. Judge appointed to consider, e.g., an arbitration agreement, trials involving substantial technical detail or documents or matters relating to accounts. See also Arbitration Act 1950, s. 11; C.L.S.A. 1990, s. 11. The office was abolished under the Courts Act 1971, s. 25, and jurisdiction conferred upon persons nominated by the Lord Chancellor to take "official referees' business". Appeal lies to the Court of Appeal. See S.C.A. 1981, s. 68 (as amended by A.J.A. 1982, s. 59); O.

36; *Tate and Lyle Ltd* v *Davy McKee Ltd* [1990] 1 All ER 157. *See* REFEREE.

official search. Search by the registrar, made on requisition (q.v.), so as to discover the existence of registrable incumbrances on land. The issue of an official certificate is conclusive in favour of a purchaser or intending purchaser, so that he is free from liability arising from rights which the official search failed to disclose.

official secrets. Matters concerning state security, covered under Official Secrets Acts 1911–1989. It is an offence for a person to approach or inspect a prohibited place for any purpose prejudicial to the safety or interests of the state, to use certain types of information for the benefit of a foreign power or in another manner prejudicial to state interests. Categories of official information, the unauthorised disclosure of which may be a crime, are set out in the 1989 Act; see also SI 1990/200. See the European Communities Act 1972, s. 11; *Chandler* v *DPP* [1962] 2 All ER 314; *R* v *Galvin* [1987] QB 862.

Official Solicitor. An official who acts for those involved in High Court (q.v.) proceedings who are under a disability. He will brief counsel to appear as "next friend" (q.v.) where there is no other person willing or competent to do so. He may also defend, e.g., a minor (q.v.) or patient as guardian *ad litem* (q.v.). He can be appointed as judicial trustee (q.v.) in proceedings relating to disputed trusts. See S.C.A. 1981, s. 90.

officina justitiae. See ORIGINAL WRIT.

off-market deals. Defined in Company Securities (Insider Dealing) Act 1985, s. 13 (as modified by F.S.A. 1986, s. 174), as dealings otherwise than on a recognised investment exchange (q.v.) in a company's advertised securities through an off-market dealer (i.e., one who is authorised under, e.g., Cos.A. 1985, s. 164). See Cos.A. 1985, s. 163 (as amended by F.S.A. 1986), Sch. 16 para. 17). *See* INSIDER DEALING.

Old Bailey. Central Criminal Court (q.v.).

Ombudsman. (*Swedish*: *representative.*) Parliamentary Commissioner for Administration (q.v.).

Ombudsman, Conveyancing. Appointed under C.L.S.A. 1990, s. 43, to consider and report on any breach of the regulations concerning the conduct of authorised conveyancing practitioners. See Sch. 7.

Ombudsman, Legal Services. Appointed under C.L.S.A. 1990, s. 21, by the Lord Chancellor to investigate the way in which a complaint has been handled by legal professional bodies. He is also empowered to investigate the original complaint: s. 22(2). He may recommend reconsideration of the complaint and payment of compensation for loss or distress suffered by the complainant: s. 23. For discharge of functions, see Sch. 3.

Ombudsman, Local Government. Commissioners appointed under the L.G.A. 1974, s. 23, with jurisdiction involving, e.g., the investigation of complaints against local councils, involving, e.g., maladministration (q.v.). See *Croydon LBC* v *Commissioner for Local Administration* (1988) The Times, 9 June.

Ombudsman, Pensions. Appointed under Social Security Pensions Act 1975, as amended by S.S.A. 1990, s. 12, Sch. 3, to investigate and determine written complaints in connection with any act or omission of the trustees or managers of an occupational or personal pension scheme. See OCCUPATIONAL PENSION SCHEME.

omission. A blank in a document. The general presumption (q.v.), where blanks are found to have been filled in a will by the testator, is that they were filled before the execution of the will. See *Birch* v *Birch* (1848) Not Cas 581; *Re Shearn* (1880) 50 LJP 15.

omission to act. Failure to execute a duty to act may constitute an element of an *actus reus* (q.v.). Examples include the duty to act imposed by: statute (see, e.g., Road Traffic Act 1988, s. 170); contract (see, e.g., *R* v *Pittwood* (1902) 19 TLR 37); relationship (see, e.g., *R* v *Smith* [1979] Crim LR 251); office (see *R* v *Dytham* [1979] QB 722).

omne quod solo inaedificatur solo cedit. All that which is built into the soil is merged therein.

omnia praesumuntur contra spoliatorem. All things are presumed against a wrongdoer. See, e.g., *Harwood* v *Goodwright* (1744) 1 Cowp 87. In criminal proceedings it becomes, in effect, a rebuttable presumption of fact: C.J.A. 1967, s. 8.

omnia praesumuntur rite et solemniter esse acta. All things are presumed to be done correctly and solemnly (i.e., until the contrary shall be proved). The so-called "presumption of legality". See, e.g., *Dillon* v *R* [1982] AC 484; *R* v *IRC, ex p Coombs* [1991] STC 97.

onerous. Unreasonably burdensome. For the power of a trustee in bankruptcy to disclaim onerous property (e.g., unprofitable contracts, unsaleable property), see the Ins.A. 1986, ss. 178(3), 315.

onus probandi. Burden of proof (q.v.). *See* PROOF.

open contract. In the case of a contract for sale of land it refers to one which merely contains, e.g., names of parties, price, description of property. Certain conditions are implied by law, e.g., that the vendor shall show good title. See *Bigg* v *Boyd Gibbins Ltd* [1971] 1 WLR 913. *See* FORMAL CONTRACT.

open court. Court to which public has access. See *Scott* v *Scott* [1913] AC 417; *R* v *Denbigh Justices* [1974] QB 759. *See* IN CAMERA.

opening speech. Speech made by prosecuting counsel comprising allegations against the defendant (in outline) and the evidence it is proposed to call. Defending counsel may make an opening speech where he is calling witnesses as to fact in addition to the defendant.

open justice. "It is not merely of some importance but is of fundamental importance that justice should not only be done, but should manifestly and undoubtedly be seen to be done": *per* Lord Hewart CJ in *R* v *Sussex Justices, ex p McCarthy* [1924] 1 KB 256. See Official Secrets Act 1920, s. 8; C.J.A. 1988, s. 159; *Re Crook* [1992] 2 All ER 687.

open space. Any land, enclosed or not, on which there are no buildings or of which not more than one-twentieth part is covered with buildings, and the whole or remainder of which is laid out as a garden or is used for recreational purposes, or lies waste and unoccupied: see Open Spaces Act 1906, s. 20. See also T.C.P.A. 1990, s. 336(1); *R* v *Plymouth CC, ex p Freeman* (1987) 19

HLR 328; *Ward* v *Secretary of State for the Environment* (1989) The Times, 5 Oct.

open verdict. Verdict of coroner's jury leaving open the question of how a person met his death.

operations in land development. Work which changes the physical characteristics of the land, or of what is below it, or of the air above it: *per* Lord Parker in *Cheshire CC* v *Woodward* [1962] 2 QB 126. *See* DEVELOPMENT.

operative part. That part of a deed (q.v.) in which the principal object is effected (e.g., actual conveyance of property) as contrasted with recitals (q.v.).

operative words. The precise words through which the purpose of some document is attained, e.g., the words which can create or transfer an estate (q.v.). *See* LIMITATION, WORDS OF.

opinion. Term applied to a judgment delivered by the Law Lords in the House of Lords (q.v.).

opinion, expert. *See* EXPERT OPINION.

opinions, EEC. *See* COMMUNITY LEGISLATION, FORMS OF.

opinions in evidence. Opinions of ordinary (non-expert) persons are generally irrelevant and inadmissible as evidence. Exceptions include: matters of identity; age; speed of a car; handwriting (where the witness has seen the accused person writing); proof that the witness understood a libel to refer to the plaintiff. Under Civil Evidence Act 1972, s. 3, in civil proceedings a non-expert witness may give his opinions on an ultimate issue in the form of a statement made as a way of conveying relevant facts personally perceived by him. *See* EXPERT OPINION.

Opposition, Leader of HM. "That member of the House [of Commons] who is for the time being the Leader in that House of the party in opposition to HM Government having the greatest numerical strength in the House of Commons": Ministerial and other Salaries Act 1975, s. 2(1).

oppression. "A disregard of the essentials of justice and the infliction of a penalty which is not properly related to the crime of which the party stands convicted, but is either to be regarded as merely vindictive or having proceeded upon some improper or irregular consideration": *Stewart* v *Cormack* 1941 SC(J) 73.

oppression leading to confession. "The exercise of authority or power in a burdensome, harsh or wrongful manner, unjust or cruel treatment of subjects, inferiors; the imposition of unreasonable or unjust burdens": O.E.D. definition adopted in *R* v *Fulling* [1987] QB 426. "'Oppression' includes torture, inhuman or degrading treatment, and the use or threat of violence (whether or not amounting to torture)": P. & C.E.A. 1984, s. 76(8). *See R* v *Ismail* [1990] Crim LR 109; *R* v *Beales* [1991] Crim LR 118. *See* CONFESSION; TORTURE.

option. A right which may be acquired by contract to accept or reject a present offer within a given period of time. Under S.L.A. 1925, s. 51, a tenant for life (q.v.) may grant an option to purchase or take a lease of the settled land within ten years. Provision that a mortgagee shall have an option to purchase the property is generally inconsistent with a mortgage and, therefore, void, but this may not be so if the option is part of an independent transaction: *Reeve* v *Lisle* [1902] AC 461. "Under an option, only one step is normally needed to accept a contract, namely the exercise of the option. Under a right of pre-emption two steps will usually be necessary, the making of the offer in accordance with the right of pre-emption, and the acceptance of that offer": *Brown* v *Gould* [1972] Ch 53. See *Pritchard* v *Briggs* [1980] Ch 338 (option to purchase may be an "estate contract" within L.C.A. 1972, s. 2(4)(iv)); *Spiro* v *Glencrown Properties* [1991] 2 WLR 931. For "share options" see *IRC* v *Burton Group plc* [1990] STC 242.

or. Used generally to connect words, phrases, clauses representing alternatives. For its interpretation as "and", see *Federal Steam Navigation Ltd* v *Department of Trade and Industry* [1974] 2 All ER 97. See also *R* v *Bingham* [1973] QB 870; *Ormerod* v *Blaslov* (1990) 52 SASR 263.

oral agreement, modification of contract by. Following a written contract, the parties are free, by a later oral agreement, to "either altogether waive, dissolve or annul the former agreement, or in any manner to add to, or subtract from, or vary or qualify the terms of it, and thus to make a new contract;

which is to be proved, partly by the subsequent verbal terms engrafted upon what will be thus left of the written agreement": *Goss* v *Nugent* (1833) 5 B & Ald 58. *See* CONTRACT.

oral evidence. *See* EVIDENCE, ORAL.

orality, principle of. The oral examination of witnesses, which is a fundamental feature of trial under English law. See, however, evidence given on affidavit (q.v.).

oral will. *See* NUNCUPATIVE WILL.

ordeal, trial by. Ancient procedure whereby an appeal was made to God to make manifest the guilt or innocence of the accused. It was considered as *judicium Dei* (q.v.). It could involve, e.g., ordeal *by fire* (in which guilt was established if the wounds of the accused sustained during the carrying of a heated iron for nine steps were not healed after three days), or *by water* (in which the accused was bound with a rope and let down into the water, innocence being established if he sank to a knot tied in the rope). Virtually abolished in 1215.

order, matrimonial. *See* MATRIMONIAL ORDER.

orders. 1. Directions of the court. 2. Constituents of the procedural codes of the Supreme Court and of the county courts.

Orders in Council. Orders made by the Sovereign and Privy Council (qq.v.) or by the government (which are sanctioned by the Privy Council). They may be used, e.g., to bring Acts into force. *See* DELEGATED LEGISLATION; STATUTORY INSTRUMENTS.

Orders of Council. Orders made by the Privy Council (q.v.) in the absence of the Sovereign.

ordinance. Decree promulgated by Parliament (q.v.) without the consent of a constituent element (e.g., Lords), or a declaration by the Sovereign made without Parliament's consent.

ordinarily resident. *See* RESIDENT IN UK.

ordinary meetings. *See* MEETINGS, COMPANY.

ordinary resolution. A resolution (q.v.) passed by a simple majority of those present at the general meeting of a company (q.v.). See, e.g., Cos. A. 1985, ss. 303, 386. *See* EXTRAORDINARY RESOLUTION.

ordinary shares. Those which carry the greatest risk and rank for repayment of capital and payment of dividends after debenture-holders and preference shareholders. Preferred ordinary shares are a type of participating preference shares (q.v.) without priority for repayment of capital. *See* SHARE.

organ, human. Any part of a human body consisting of a structured arrangement of tissues which, if wholly removed, cannot be replicated by the body: Human Organ Transplants Act 1989, s. 7(1). The Act prohibits any commercial dealing in human organs (s. 1) and restricts transplants between persons not genetically related (s. 2).

organisms, genetically modified. Organisms in which any of the genes or other genetic material have been modified by artificial techniques prescribed in authorised regulations, or are inherited from genes or other genetic material so modified: En.P.A. 1990, s. 106. For control, see 1990 Act, Part VI.

original writ. Ancient method of commencing a common-law action, by issue out of so-called *officina justitiae* (workshop of justice) controlled by the King's chancellor.

originating summons. "Every summons other than a summons in a pending cause or matter": O. 1, r. 4. Used to commence an action in Queen's Bench Division, e.g., to obtain a decision on a point of law. See also O. 7, r. 2.

orse. Otherwise.

ostensible authority. Apparent authority. See, e.g., *Freeman and Lockyer* v *Buckhurst Properties* [1964] 1 All ER 630; *The Ocean Frost* [1986] AC 717.

ostensible partner. Nominal partner (q.v.).

oust. To eject, dispossess, exclude, bar. See *Richards* v *Richards* [1984] AC 174.

ouster. An act which wrongfully deprives a person of his freehold (q.v.) or other inheritance.

ouster clause. A clause in a statute which excludes the jurisdiction of the courts (e.g., "This shall not be questioned in any legal proceedings whatsoever"). See, e.g., *Anisminic* v *Foreign Compensation Commission* [1969] 2 AC 147.

ouster le main. Out of the hand. 1. Judgment against the Crown on a *monstrans de droit.* 2. Ancient procedure whereby heirs or heiresses reaching the age of majority, had to "sue out their livery" by paying the lord (who had been entitled to wardship) half a year's profits so as to obtain delivery of their land.

ouster of jurisdiction. Removal from the court of its power to hear and determine an action. There is a presumption against a statute's ousting the jurisdiction of the courts: *Pyx Granite Co. Ltd* v *Minister of Housing* [1960] AC 260.

ouster order. Order under the Matrimonial Homes Act 1983, s. 1, prohibiting, suspending or restricting the exercise by a spouse of the right to occupy the matrimonial home. "A drastic order which should only be made in cases of real necessity": *Summers* v *Summers* (1987) The Times, 19 May. See also *Scott* v *Scott* [1991] FCR 879.

outer Bar. Known also as "utter Bar". Term used to refer to junior barristers who were said to plead "outside the bar" and were known as "utter barristers". *See* BARRISTER.

outlawry. Procedure whereby an offender was placed outside the protection of the law. His property was forfeited and he lost all civil rights, being stigmatised as "an animal to be hunted and struck down if encountered". Criminal outlawry was abolished in 1838; outlawry in civil proceedings, in 1879.

outstanding offences. Those offences which are outstanding may be taken into account when the court is considering sentence. They must not be dissimilar offences, or offences in respect of which the court has no jurisdiction.

outstanding term. A term of years (q.v.) which has not ended although the purpose for which it came into existence has been fulfilled. *See* SATISFIED TERM.

overcrowding. A dwelling is overcrowded when the number of persons sleeping there is such as to contravene the room standard (q.v.) or the space standard (q.v.): H.A. 1985, s. 324. A notice to abate overcrowding within 14 days of date of service may be issued by a local housing authority (q.v.) to the occupier: s. 338(1). For penalties for landlords causing or permitting over-

crowding, see s. 327, as amended by L.G.H.A. 1989, Sch. 11.

overdraft. Bank loan allowing a customer's current account to go into debit. See C.C.A. 1974, s. 74 (3), (3A) (inserted by Banking Act 1979), s. 38(1)). "A payment by a bank under an arrangement by which the customer may overdraw is a lending by the bank to the customer of the money"; *per* Harman J in *Re Hone* [1951] Ch 58.

overdue bill. A bill which remains in circulation after the due date. A bill payable on demand is deemed overdue, for purposes of negotiation, if it appears to have been in circulation for an unreasonable length of time. "Unreasonable" is a question of fact: B.Ex.A. 1882, s. 36(3). *See* BILL OF EXCHANGE.

overdue cheque. *See* CHEQUE, OVERDUE.

over-insurance. *See* INSURANCE, OVER-.

overreaching. "A conveyance to a purchaser of a legal estate in land shall overreach any equitable interest or power affecting that estate, whether or not he has notice thereof . . .": L.P.A. 1925, s. 2.

overreaching and land held on trust. Procedure whereby, e.g., land held on trust is sold to a purchaser free from the trust, even though he has notice of it. An equitable interest overreached is transferred from the land to money in the trustees' hands. Example: *ad hoc* trust for sale (q.v.). See, e.g., *Shiloh Spinners Ltd* v *Harding* [1973] AC 80; S.L.A. 1925, s. 72.

overriding interests. Those encumbrances, interests, rights and powers stated in L.R.A. 1925, s. 70(1), not entered on the register but subject to which registered dispositions of land take effect. Hence, a registered proprietor, or his alienee, is bound by such rights, irrespective of registration and notice. Examples: legal easements (q.v.), profits, local land charges, rights of persons in occupation (q.v.). An overridden interest cannot be enforced against anyone, whereas an overreached interest is transferred from land to money. See L.R.A. 1986, s. 4; *Williams & Glyn's Bank* v *Boland* [1981] AC 487; *City of London Building Society* v *Flegg* [1988] AC 54; *Abbey National BS* v *Cann* [1990] 2 WLR 832. Law Com Report (1987), No. 158. See L.R.A. 1925, s. 70. *See* LAND REGISTRATION; MINOR INTERESTS.

overriding interests, rights of people in occupation as. A claimant must prove that the right subsisted in reference to land, that the owner of the right was in actual occupation (or in receipt of rents or profits), and that no enquiry has been made of that person. "Actual occupation" is a question of fact. See L.R.A. 1925, s. 70(1)(g); *Strand Securities v Caswell* 1965 Ch 958; *Kingsnorth Finance Ltd v Tizard* [1986] 1 WLR 783.

overrule. To set aside. Thus, a decision may be overruled by statute, or a higher court. Overruling by the latter operates retrospectively; by the former, from the date on which the statute comes into operation. See, e.g., *Button v DPP* [1966] AC 591. Should be distinguished from reversal of judgment (q.v.).

oversea company. A company incorporated outside Britain which has established a place of business in Britain. See Cos.A. 1985, ss. 691, 694, 744; Banking Act 1987, s. 74(1). For "offshore funds", see I.C.T.A. 1988, s. 759. *See* COMPANY.

oversea company, name of. The Secretary of State may, if of the opinion that it is or would be undesirable for an oversea company to carry on the business in Great Britain under its corporate name, cause a notice to that effect to be served on the company by the registrar of companies: Cos. A. 1985, s. 694.

overseas branch register. A company having a share capital whose objects comprise the transaction of business in any of the countries or territories specified in Cos.A. 1985, Sch. 14, Part I, should keep in any such country or territory a branch register of members resident there: Cos.A. 1985, s. 362.

overt. Open, as in overt act, market overt (q.v.).

owner, in relation to premises. A person other than a mortgagee not in possession who is for the time being entitled to dispose of the fee simple (q.v.) in the premises, whether in possession or reversion, and a person holding or entitled to the rents and profits of the premises under a lease (q.v.) of which

the unexpired term exceeds three years: H.A. 1985, s. 56.

owner-occupier of a dwelling. "The person who, as owner or as lessee under a long tenancy, occupies or is entitled to occupy the dwelling": H.A. 1985, s. 237. "The person who occupies the whole or a substantial part of the hereditament in right of an owner's interest in it": T.C.P.A. 1990, s. 168(1).

ownership. Right to the exclusive enjoyment of some thing based on rightful title. "The entirety of the powers of use and disposal allowed by law": Pollock. "A right, indefinite in point of user, unrestricted in point of disposition, and unlimited in point of duration, over a determinate thing": Austin. It may be *absolute* or *restricted, corporeal* (relating to, e.g., a book, a car) or *incorporeal* (relating to, e.g., the right to recover a debt), *legal* (as where A has fee simple absolute in possession (q.v.)) or *equitable* (as where A has a life interest), *vested* or *contingent* In essence, it is based on a relationship *de jure* (q.v.), so that possession of the thing is not necessary. *See* POSSESSION.

ownership, acquisition of. Ownership may be acquired *originally* (e.g., by asserting ownership over something not previously owned by anyone), *derivatively* (e.g., by purchase), or by *succession* (e.g., by inheritance).

ownership, legal and equitable. Term used in land law to distinguish estates in land capable of being conveyed or created at law (fee simple absolute in possession (q.v.) in case of freeholds, and term of years absolute (q.v.) in case of leaseholds) and all other ownership interests. See L.P.A. 1925, s. 1.

ownership, proof of. Establishment of ownership of property by, e.g., production of authenticated documents of title; proof of possession; proof of ownership of connected property (in the case of land) showing the probability that its owner would also own the property in dispute.

oyer and terminer. To hear and determine. Commission issued to assize judges conferring criminal jurisdiction and directing them to hear and determine offences for which accused persons had been presented by grand juries. Effectively abolished under Courts Act 1971. *See* ASSIZE.

P

P. President of the Family Division (q.v.), as in, e.g., Sir Stephen Brown P. See S.C.A. 1981, s. 10.

pact. A contract, promise, covenant, treaty between states.

pacta sunt servanda. Contracts are to be kept.

pactum, nudum. See NUDUM PACTUM.

pais. Pays = country. *Trial per pais* is a trial "by the country", i.e., trial by jury.

palatine courts. Courts belonging to the counties palatine (*palatinus* = belonging to the palace), whose owners had sovereign rights, including the right to appoint judges, e.g., Durham, Lancaster, Chester. Abolished under Law Terms Act 1830 and Courts Act 1971.

palm prints. Impressions of the palm used for identification purposes. See *R v Tottenham Justices, ex p M.L.* (1986) 82 Cr App R 277. See FINGERPRINTS.

paramount. Superior. *Title paramount* is superior title. Example: where X held land in fee of Y, and Y held that land in fee of Z, so that Z was lord paramount. A *paramount clause* in a charter-party or bill of lading (qq.v.) is a clause incorporating all the Hague Rules: *Nea Agrex SA v Baltic Shipping Co Ltd* [1976] QB 933. For its use in relation to a child's welfare (q.v.), see Ch. A. 1989, s. 1; *Re K.D.* [1988] AC 806.

parcels. 1. Plots of land. 2. Term used in a conveyance (q.v.) to indicate the clause giving a physical description of property conveyed, e.g., "all that dwelling-house known as . . ." See *Scarfe v Adams* [1981] 1 All ER 843.

parceners. See COPARCENARY.

pardon. The excusing of an offence or remission of a punishment by the Sovereign (on the advice of the Home Secretary) or by Act of Parliament (q.v.). Some offences cannot be pardoned, e.g., committing a person to prison beyond the seas (see Habeas Corpus Act 1679). "A free pardon does not quash a conviction in the same way that the Court of Appeal can quash a conviction . . . it is, however, generally accepted that [it] has the effect of wiping out the conviction and all its consequences": Secretary of State for the Home Department (*Hansard*, 13 January 1977). *Ex gratia* payment may be offered by the Home Secretary. See C.J.A. 1988, s. 133. *See* MERCY, PREROGATIVE OF.

parens patriae. Parent of his country. Archaic term applied to, e.g., the Sovereign as guardian of those in need or under a legal disability. See *T. v T.* [1988] 2 WLR 189.

parent. Father or mother. Used, e.g., in the Child Benefit Act 1975, as including references to the natural parent or step-parent. *See* CHILD, PARENTAL RESPONSIBILITY FOR.

parentage, declaration of. *See* LEGITIMACY.

parental preferences concerning education. Local education authorities have duties to arrange for children's parents to express a preference for schools at which they wish their children to be educated: Education Act 1980, s. 6, as amended by Education Reform Act 1988, s. 30. See *R v Governors of Bishop Challoner RC School, ex p C.* (1991) The Times, 7 Nov.

parental responsibility. *See* CHILD, PARENTAL RESPONSIBILITY FOR.

parents' liability for children's torts. Parents are not generally liable for their child's torts, save, e.g., where the child is employed by a parent and commits a tort in the course of his employment and where torts are due to a parent's negligence, or if a parent had authorised the commission of the tort. See *Bebee v Sales* (1916) 32 TLR 413.

parish. Originally an ecclesiastical area (see Ecclesiastical Fees Measure 1986, s. 10); later a local government unit. Parish councils in England are constituted in a way similar to district and county councils (qq.v.). There must be a minimum of five members. Functions include responsibility for recreational facilities. In Wales, parishes are replaced by communities (q.v.). See L.G.A. 1972, Sch. 1.

Parks, National. Areas of natural beauty offering facilities for open air recreation, designated under the National Parks and Access to the Countryside Act 1949, Part II (e.g., the Peak District, Exmoor). See T.C.P.A. 1990, s. 4.

Parliament. The supreme legislature of the United Kingdom of Great Britain and Northern Ireland, consisting of the Queen, House of Lords and House of Commons. Its life is fixed for five years, divided into sessions (one or more each year). Its functions are: to pass laws; to vote taxes; to scrutinise government policy and admininistration; to debate current political issues of great importance. It can legislate as it pleases, since it is sovereign, for the whole of the UK or any constituent part. Legislation usually necessitates the concurrence of the Sovereign, Lords and Commons. See SOVEREIGNTY OF PARLIAMENT.

Parliamentary Commissioner for Administration. The "Ombudsman". Office created by the Parliamentary Commissioner Act 1967. The Commissioner, who is appointed by the Crown, investigates complaints by members of the public who believe they have suffered injustice as the result of maladministration arising from the functioning of government departments and public authorities. A written complaint is forwarded to a M.P. who sends it to the Commissioner. He then exercises his discretion whether or not to investigate. See Parliamentary and Health Service Commissioners Act 1987.

Parliamentary control. Control of government is based on power exercised by the House of Commons which is able to force its resignation or to reject votes of confidence. Other aspects of control include, e.g., question time, motions for adjournment.

Parliamentary counsel. Barristers (q.v.) who are civil servants engaged in drafting government Bills, amendments by the government to those Bills, etc.

Parliamentary Papers. 1. Command Papers published by the government for Parliament's consideration (in theory, presented by Her Majesty's Command; in practice, by a Minister). They may be: "*white papers*", i.e., statements of government policy or principles of a bill to be introduced (see *A.-G.'s Reference No 1 of 1988* (1989) 89 Cr App R 60 (reference to white paper for interpretation of criminal statute)); "*blue books*", i.e., reports of committees, commissions; "*green papers*", i.e., government plans intended for discussion. 2. Bills (q.v.). 3. House of Commons or House of Lords papers, published by order of the House, as reports of the Houses' own committees.

Parliamentary privilege. The aggregate of the particular rights and immunities enjoyed by each House of Parliament, designed to allow members to carry out their duties unhindered. They apply collectively and individually to every M.P. Questions of privilege may be referred to the Committee of Privileges. Privileges include: freedom of speech in debate (evidence of what is said and done in Parliament cannot be used in legal proceedings: *Church of Scientology* v *Johnson-Smith* [1972] 1 QB 522); the right to control proceedings; right to penalise those who commit breach of privilege; the right to expel members whom Parliament considers unfit to serve; freedom of access to the Sovereign; freedom from arrest or molestation. The absence of precedent does not prevent an act being considered a breach of privilege. See *Rost* v *Edwards* [1990] 2 WLR 1280.

Parliament, European. See EUROPEAN PARLIAMENT.

Parliament, intention of. See INTENTION OF PARLIAMENT.

Parliament, legislative supremacy of. Parliament alone can, by statute, make or unmake any law. "The very keystone of the constitution": Dicey. Parliament can pass Acts of indemnity (q.v.) and retrospective legislation. No other body in the state can declare any Act invalid: see, e.g., *Pitkin* v *British Rlwys Board* [1974] AC 765. It cannot, however, bind its successors. "A sovereign power cannot, while retaining its sovereign character, restrict its own powers by any parliamentary enactment": Dicey. See Treaty of Rome

1957, arts. 177, 189; European Communities Act 1972; *Manuel* v *A.-G.* [1983]; *R.v Secretary of State ex p Factortame Ltd* [1991] 3 All ER 1026. *See* SOVEREIGNTY OF PARLIAMENT.

Parliament, registration of Members' interests. Following a report of the Select Committee on Members' Interests (Declaration), endorsed by the Commons, June 1975, Members are required to register, e.g., remunerated directorships of companies, remunerated trades, professions, vocations, financial sponsorships, payments or material benefits received from or on behalf of foreign governments.

Parliament, summons and dissolution of. A new Parliament is summoned following a proclamation issued by the Queen on advice from the Privy Council (q.v.); that proclamation dissolves the old Parliament, commands the issue of writs by the Lord Chancellor, and states the date for the meeting of the new Parliament. Dissolution arises by proclamation or the passage of time (5 years under the the Parliament Act 1911, s. 7).

parol. Verbal, oral. Formerly applied to a contract not under seal; *Rann* v *Hughes* (1788) 7 TR 350.

parol contract. Simple contract (q.v.).

parole. Early release of prisoners by Parole Board: see C.J.A. 1991, s. 33.

parole for life prisoners. If recommended by the Parole Board, the Secretary of State may, after consultation with the Lord Chief Justice together with the trial judge, release a life prisoner who is not a "discretionary life prisoner": C.J.A. 1991, s. 35(1). A "discretionary life prisoner" (whose sentence was imposed for a violent or sexual offence) who has served the part of his sentence specified, may be released if the Parole Board is satisfied that it is no longer necessary for the protection of the public that he should be confined. See 1991 Act, ss. 34, 35.

parole for long-term and short-term prisoners. A long-term prisoner (one serving a sentence for 4 years or more) may be released if he has served two-thirds of his sentence, on licence. See C.J.A. 1991, ss. 33, 35. A short-term prisoner (one serving a sentence for a term of less than four years) may be released after serving one-half of his sentence. See C.J.A. 1991, s. 33.

parole on compassionate grounds. The Secretary of State may at any time release a prisoner on licence if satisfied that exceptional circumstances exist which justify his release on compassionate grounds. See C.J.A. 1991, s. 36(1).

parol evidence rule. Where the record of a transaction is embodied in a document, extrinsic evidence (q.v.) is not generally admissible to vary or interpret the document or as a substitute for it. See *Bank of Australasia* v *Palmer* [1898] AC 540. Abolition of the rule was recommended by *Law Commission Working Paper* 1976, No. 70. *See* EVIDENCE, PAROL.

parol lease. Lease (q.v.) taking effect in possession for a term not exceeding three years at the best rent which can be reasonably obtained without taking a fine; L.P.A. 1925, s. 54(2).

partial loss. *See* LOSS, LIABILITY IN MARINE INSURANCE FOR.

particular average. *See* AVERAGE.

particular estate. An estate less than a fee simple (q.v.), i.e., given for a particular period of time. Term used to refer to an estate granted out of a larger estate. *See* ESTATE.

particular lien. Right to retain goods until all charges incurred in respect of them have been paid. Example: lien in respect of goods carried by common carriers. See *Bowmaker* v *Wycombe Motors Ltd* [1946] KB 505. *See* LIEN.

particulars. Matters concerning pleadings in an action needed by the other party so that he shall understand the case to be made. They may be applied for by letter or by summons for an order for further and better particulars. See O. 18, r. 12. They will not be ordered in relation to a matter not pleaded specifically. "The object of particulars is to enable the party asking for them to know what case he has to meet at the trial and so to save unnecessary expense": *Spedding* v *Fitzpatrick* (1888) 38 Ch D 413. *See* PLEADINGS.

particular tenant. The owner of a particular estate (q.v.).

parties. 1. "They that make a deed and they to whom it is made are called parties to the deed": *Terms de la Ley.* 2. Those persons who sue or are sued.

Their names must be set out at the head of a writ (q.v.) and they form the title of the action. No one can appear on the record as both plaintiff and defendant: *Re Phillips* (1931) 101 LJ Ch 338.

partition. 1. Distribution, division. 2. Division of a governmental unit into two or more areas, each under a separate administration. 3. Term used in land law to refer to the disuniting of joint possession (q.v.) so that former co-tenants become separate owners. See *Biggs* v *Peacock* (1882) 22 Ch D 284. Now voluntary only, since compulsory partition was abolished by repeal of the Partition Acts in 1925. See L.P.A. 1925, s. 28(3).

partition of chattels. Where chattels belong to persons in undivided shares, the persons interested may apply to the court for an order for the division of all or any of them: L.P.A. 1925, s. 188.

partner, salaried. A partner "who receives a salary as remuneration, rather than a share of the profits, although he may, in addition to his salary, receive some bonus or other sum of money dependent on the profits": *per* Megarry J in *Stekel* v *Ellice* [1973] 1 All ER 463.

partners, duties of. To render true accounts and full information; to account for benefits derived from transactions concerning the partnership; to account for profits derived from a competing business; see Partnership Act 1890, ss. 28, 30. See *Law* v *Law* [1905] 1 Ch 40; *Pathirana* v *Pathirana* [1967] 1 AC 233.

partners, expulsion of. "No majority of the partners can expel any partner unless a power to do so has been conferred by express agreement between the partners": Partnership Act 1890, s. 25. See, e.g., *Hitchman* v *Crouch Butler Savage Associates* (1983) 127 SJ 441.

partnership. The relationship which subsists between persons carrying on a business in common with a view of profit: Partnership Act 1890, s. 1. See *Keith Spicer Ltd* v *Mansell* [1970] 1 All ER 462; *Strathearn Gordon Associates* v *Commissioner of Customs and Excise* (1985) VATTR 79. It cannot consist, in general, of more than 20 persons. See Cos.A. 1985, s. 716. (Exempt from this

limit are partnerships of solicitors, multi-national partnerships of lawyers (see SI 1991/2729), accountants, stockbrokers.) The liability of each partner in respect of the partnership's contracts is joint; in respect of the partnership's wrongs, the liability is joint and several. A partnership may be dissolved by order of court, by the parties themselves, or by death; see *Chandroutie* v *Gajadhar* [1987] AC 147. See Partnership Act 1890, s. 32; I.C.T.A. 1988, Ch. VII. For 'limited partner', see I.C.T.A. 1988, s. 117(2). See SI 1992/1028. *See* FIRM; LIMITED PARTNERSHIP.

partnership, agency and. "Every partner is an agent of the firm and his other partners for the purpose of the business of the partnership": Partnership Act 1890, s. 5. *See* AGENT.

partnership at will. A partnership determinable at will of either of the parties. See Partnership Act 1890, s. 26; *Abbott* v *Abbott* [1936] 3 All ER 823.

partnership books, inspection of. Right given by Partnership Act 1890, s. 24(9), to a partner to inspect and copy the partnership books. It can be exercised by an agent of the parties.

partnership by estoppel. Any person who by spoken or written words or conduct represents himself, or allows himself to be represented as a partner in a particular firm, is liable as a partner to anyone who has on the faith of any such representation given credit to that firm: Partnership Act 1890, s. 14(1). See *Tower Cabinet Co Ltd* v *Ingram* [1949] 2 KB 397.

partnership, dissolution of. A partnership may be dissolved by: expiration of the period for which it is to last, or notice of dissolution; illegality; order of the court or an arbitrator; death or bankruptcy of a partner; force of a clause giving right to claim dissolution on the occurrence of a specified event. See Partnership Act 1890, ss. 32–35.

partnership, limited. *See* LIMITED PARTNERSHIP.

part payment rule. Payment of a lesser sum on the due day cannot be satisfaction for the whole debt. See *Pinnel's Case* (1602) 5 Co Rep 117; *Foakes* v *Beer* (1884) 9 App Cas 605; Lim.A. 1980, s. 29.

part performance. Equitable doctrine, whereby defendant (q.v.) who had acquiesced in plaintiff's performance of a contract (q.v.) was barred from pleading absence of writing. See L.P. (Misc. Provs.) A. 1989 (doctrine no longer applies to contracts covered by s. 2).

party and party costs. A former mode of taxing costs, replaced in 1986.

party-wall. Generally, a wall of which the two adjoining owners were tenants in common. Under L.P.A. 1925, s. 38, a wall would be deemed to be severed vertically as between the respective owners, each of whom has a right to support and user. See *Watson v Gray* (1880) 14 Ch D 192; *Brace v SE Regional Housing Association* (1984) 270 EG 1286.

passenger. One who is carried in a conveyance for compensation.

passing off. A tort (q.v.) committed by one person who, in a manner calculated to deceive, and in the course of trade, passes off his goods or business as those of another, e.g., by imitating their appearance or selling them under a similar name or trade mark. Essence is deceit practised on the public: *Reckitt & Coleman Products v Borden* [1990] 1 All ER 873. The plaintiff's remedies include action for damages, injunction (qq.v.), account. See *Bollinger v Costa Brava Wine Co* [1960] Ch 262; *Associated Newspapers plc v Insert Media* [1991] 1 WLR 571.

passing of property in a sale of goods. Where there is a contract for the sale of specific or ascertained goods, the property in them is transferred to the buyer at such time as the parties intended. The intention of the parties is ascertained by reference to the terms of the contract, the parties' conduct and the circumstances of the case. See S.G.A. 1979, s. 17.

passive trust. A bare trust (q.v.).

passport. Document issued by the Foreign Office to citizens of the UK and British protected persons which is intended to ensure their safe passage from one country to another. In *Joyce v DPP* [1946] AC 347, it was held that the holder of a British passport owes allegiance to the Crown and that it is immaterial that he has no intention of availing himself of the Crown's protection. For visitor's passport, see *R v Secretary of State for Home Department, ex p Minta* (1992) The Times, 14 Apr.

past consideration. *See* CONSIDERATION, PAST.

pasture, common of. The right of feeding one's cattle on another's land. See *Tyrringham's Case* (1584) 4 Co Rep 36b. *See* PUR CAUSE DE VICINAGE.

patent. An exclusive right conferred on one who invents or discovers some process, machine, etc. to make, use, sell or assign it for a certain period of time (usually 20 years) which may be extended. See Patents Acts 1949–77; Copyright, Designs and Patents Act 1988; Treaty of Rome 1957, art. 85(1); *EEC Commission v UK* (Case C-30/90) (1992) The Times, 15 April.

patent agent. An individual registered as a patent agent in the register, a company lawfully practising as a patent agent in the UK or a person who satisfies the conditions in the Copyright, Designs and Patents Act 1988, ss. 274, 275. For "trade mark agents", see s. 282.

patent ambiguity. *See* AMBIGUITY.

patent defect. *See* DEFECT.

patentee. A person registered as grantee or proprietor of a patent (q.v.).

patent, grant of. A patent may be granted only for an invention in respect of which the following conditions are satisfied; it must be new; it must involve an inventive step; it must be capable of industrial application; it must not be an invention which will encourage offensive, immoral or anti-social action; it must not consist of a scientific theory, computer program, aesthetic creation, etc: Patents Act 1977, s. 1(1)–(3). It may be granted to the inventor, joint inventors, persons who by virtue of any enactment or treaty or agreement with the inventor were entitled to the whole of the property in it (other than equitable interests (q.v.)) in the UK, or successors in title of those persons: s. 7(2). The term of a patent is 20 years beginning with the date of filing of the application: s. 25.

patent, infringement of. A patent is infringed where a person does one of the following without the consent of the patent's proprietor: where the invention is a product and he makes, disposes of, offers to dispose of, uses or imports the product or keeps it for disposal or otherwise; where the invention is a process and he uses, or offers it for use in the UK when he knows this is an infringement; where the invention is a process and he disposes of, offers to dispose of, uses or imports any product obtained directly by means of the process or keeps it for disposal or otherwise: Patents Act 1977, s. 60(1).

patent, revocation of. The court may revoke a patent on any one of the following grounds: that it is not a patentable invention; that the patent was granted to a person who was not entitled to the grant; that the specification does not disclose the invention clearly and competently enough for it to be performed by a person skilled in the art; that the matter disclosed in the specification extends beyond that disclosed in the application for the patent; that the protection conferred by the patent has been extended by an amendment which should not have been allowed: Patents Act 1977, s. 72(1), as amended by Copyright, Design and Patents Act 1988, Sch. 5.

patent right. The right to do, or authorise the doing of, anything which, but for that right would be an infringement of a patent.

Patents Court. Constituted as part of the Chancery Division of the High Court (q.v.) "to take such proceedings relating to patents and other matters as may be prescribed by rules of court". Judges are puisne judges (q.v.) of the High Court nominated by the Lord Chancellor. Scientific advisers may be appointed to assist the Court: Patents Act 1977 s. 96(4). See S.C.A. 1981, ss. 6, 70. Patents county courts may be designated by the Lord Chancellor: Copyright, Design and Patents Act 1988, s. 277.

paternity, declaration of. Declaration that a stated person is the father of a stated child. See *Re J.S.* [1980] 1 All ER 1061. See Civil Evidence Act 1968, s. 12 (amended by F.L.R.A. 1987, s. 29, and Ch. A. 1989, Sch. 13). For paternity tests, see F.L.R.A. 1969 and Ch. A. 1989, s. 89.

patrial. The former name for a person who had a right of abode under Immigration Act 1971, s. 3. See B.N.A. 1981, s. 39.

patria potestas. Doctrine of Roman law, based on absolute power of the head of the family, who alone had full legal capacity.

patron. *See* ADVOWSON.

pawn. 1. An article subject to a pledge (q.v.): C.C.A. 1974, s. 189. 2. The delivery of a chattel (q.v.) by the pawnor to the pawnee as security for a loan. The chattel remains the property of the pawnor who has the right to redeem. See C.C.A. 1974, ss. 114–122. The pawnee may retain possession until the debt is paid and can sell the chattel if the debt is not paid on the date fixed: s. 121.

pawnbroker. One who is engaged in the business of taking goods and chattels in pawn. A licence is required from the Director General of Fair Trading (q.v.). See C.C.A. 1974, ss. 114–122.

pax regis. Peace of the King (q.v.).

payable at sight. *See* SIGHT, PAYABLE AT.

pay as you earn. System (known generally as PAYE) introduced in 1943, whereby wage and salary earners pay their income tax. Tax is deducted from earnings at source and accounted for to the Inland Revenue by the employer. See I.C.T.A. 1988, s. 203.

payee. One to whom a bill of exchange (q.v.) is made payable. The term "fictitious payee" is used where a cheque is drawn in favour of a fictitious, or non-existent payee. The cheque may then be treated as a bearer cheque: see B.Ex.A 1882, s. 7(3); *Clutton* v *Attenborough* [1897] AC 90.

pay, inability to. In relation to a bankruptcy petition, it is the debtor's apparent inability to pay a debt payable immediately, and either the petitioning creditor has served a statutory demand in prescribed form, and three weeks have elapsed and the debt has not been paid, or execution issued in respect of the debt has been returned unsatisfied: Ins.A. 1986, s. 268(1). A company's inability to pay its debts is shown by proof that the value of its assets is less than the amount of its liabilities, taking into account contingent and prospective liabilities: s. 123(2). See also s. 123(1). *See* BANKRUPTCY.

payment. The passing of money from payer to payee in satisfaction of some debt or obligation. For "payment under reserve", see *Banque de L'Indochine* v *JH Rayner Ltd* [1983] 1 All ER 1137.

payment in due course. Discharge of a bill of exchange (q.v.) by payment made at or after the maturity of bill by the acceptor to the holder thereof in good faith and without notice that his title is defective (if that is so): B.Ex.A. 1882, s. 59(1).

payment into court. Deposit of payment (through the Court Funds Office or the district registry) by the defendant (q.v.) in an action for debt or damages after acknowledging service of the writ and in attempted satisfaction of all or any of the plaintiff's claims. See O. 22; O. 59, r. 12A; O. 62, r. 9. An equivalent scheme operates in county courts: County Court Rules 1981, O. 11. See also A.J.A. 1982, ss. 38–47. The plaintiff must acknowledge receipt of the notice of payment within three days. Payment into court may not be disclosed during trial, except in an action to which a defence of tender before action is pleaded.

payment of money wages. For the purposes of the Wages Act 1986, means a payment in cash, by cheque, money or postal order, or by a payment (however effected) into any account kept with a bank or other institutions: s. 17(7). *See* WAGES.

payments, appropriation of. Where a debtor owes several debts to one creditor and payment is made, the debtor can appropriate the payment to a debt, expressly or by implication, at the time of payment. In absence of such appropriation, the creditor may appropriate at any time. See *Clayton's Case* (1816) 1 Mer 572; and *Siebe Gormand Co* v *Barclays Bank* [1979] 2 Lloyd's Rep 142. For appropriation of payments under a hire-purchase contract, see C.C.A. 1974, s. 81.

pay statement, itemised. Under E.P.(C)A. 1978, ss 8–9, at or before the time when the payment of wages or salary takes place, every employee is entitled to receive from his employer a statement showing: gross amount of wages or salary; net amount of wages or salary; amounts of fixed and variable deductions and purposes for which made. See *Coales* v *Wood & Co* [1986] ICR 71.

P.C. Privy Council (q.v.). Privy Councillor.

peace, breach of. *See* BREACH OF THE PEACE.

peace of the King. The security in his realm promised by the Sovereign to his subjects. Originally attached to the royal palace and "3,000 paces beyond the great road", so that breaches of the peace there were punished, and "royal justice supplanted private vengeance". On the occasion of a church festival it was extended throughout the realm.

peculiar. A parish (q.v.) exempt from the jurisdiction of the bishop.

pecuniary advantage. The cases in which a pecuniary advantage within the meaning of Th.A. 1968, s. 16 (obtaining pecuniary advantage by deception) arises are where: any debt or charge for which a person makes himself liable (including one not legally enforceable) is reduced or in whole or in part evaded or deferred; a person is allowed to borrow by way of overdraft or to take out any policy of insurance or annuity contract, or obtains an improvement of the terms on which he is allowed to do so; a person is given the opportunity to earn remuneration or greater remuneration in an office or employment, or to win money by betting. See, e.g., *R* v *Melwani* [1989] Crim LR 565; *R* v *Callender* (1992) NLJ 716. *See* DECEPTION, OBTAINING SERVICES BY.

pecuniary legacy. *See* LEGACY.

pedigree. A line of ancestors. Statements, oral or written, by deceased persons, related by marriage or blood made before litigation was in contemplation, are admissible to prove matters concerning pedigree. See *Berkeley Peerage Case* (1811) 4 Camp 401. *See* DECLARATION CONCERNING PEDIGREE.

pedlar. An itinerant person who sells wares carried from place to place and who regularly earns a part of his living from this activity. See Pedlars Act 1871; *Murphy* v *Duke* [1985] 2 All ER 274; *Watson* v *Malloy* [1988] 1 WLR 1026.

peer. The holder of a dignity entitling him to membership of the House of Lords (q.v.). A *peeress* is a woman who has the dignity of peerage as a result of marriage or in her own right. Grades, in ascending order, are baron, viscount, earl, marquess and duke.

Hereditary peers and peeresses may be created by the Crown, on advice of the Prime Minister, by issue of a writ of summons or by letters patent. The title can be disclaimed for life, within 12 months of succession (or one month in the case of members of, and candidates for, the Commons). See Peerage Act 1963. *Life peers and peeresses* are appointed by the Crown on advice of the Prime Minister, under the Life Peerages Act 1958.

peers, temporal. *See* HOUSE OF LORDS.

peers, trial by. Under Magna Carta (q.v.) a man was entitled to the judgment of his peers (i.e., those of the same rank). "Peer" was apparently misinterpreted as referring to the barons. A peer could be tried before the House of Lords (q.v.). (Thus, Lord De Clifford was tried and acquitted of manslaughter in 1935.) Trial by peers in cases of treason and felony was abolished under C.J.A. 1948, s. 30.

peine forte et dure. Strong and hard pain. A torture, consisting of piling weights on the body, administered so as to force the accused to accept jury trial. It may have originated in a misconstruing of the Statute of Westminster 1275, which ordered that such a person was to be "remanded to a hard and strong prison". The last fatal torture of this nature took place at Horsham Gaol in 1735. Abolished by Felony and Piracy Act 1772.

penal actions. *See* ACTIONS CIVIL AND PENAL.

penal servitude. Substitute for transportation introduced by the Penal Servitude Act 1853. It involved imprisonment with compulsory labour. Abolished by C.J.A. 1948.

penal statutes. 1. Statutes creating offences. 2. Statutes providing for the recovery of penalties in civil proceedings. There is a presumption in favour of the strict construction of a penal statute. See, e.g., *Salesmatic Ltd* v *Hinchcliffe* [1959] 3 All ER 401.

penalty. 1. A punishment. "Unless penalties are imposed in clear terms they are not enforceable": *A.-G.* v *Till* [1910] AC 50. 2. A threat, held over a party to a contract *in terrorem* (q.v.). The plaintiff who brings an action to enforce a penalty can generally recover only the damage suffered.

Whether a sum is or is not a penalty is to be decided "upon the terms and inherent circumstances of each particular contract, judged of as at the time of making the contract, not as at the time of the breach": *Dunlop Pneumatic Tyre Co Ltd* v *New Garage & Motor Co Ltd* [1915] AC 79. See also *ECGD* v *Universal Oil Products Co* [1983] 1 WLR 399.

penalty, fixed, notice. A constable may issue a driver with a fixed penalty notice on the spot, where the offence appears to the constable to be one listed under the Road Traffic Offenders Act 1988, Sch. 3, as amended by Road Traffic Act 1988, Sch. 8: 1988 Act, s. 51. For payment of penalty, see s. 69.

pendens lis. A pending action (q.v.).

pendente lite. While an action is pending.

pendente lite, **administration.** The court has power to appoint an administrator (q.v.) where there is a dispute as to the validity of a will (q.v.) or the right of administration. See S.C.A. 1981, s. 117. The appointment will be made only where it can be shown to be necessary. The administrator *pendente lite* is entitled to remuneration. *See* LIS PENDENS.

pending action. Actions or proceedings pending in court relating to land or any interest in or charge on land, which must be registered on the register of pending actions: L.C.A. 1972, s. 17(1). Actions of this type do not bind a purchaser without express notice of them, unless registered: s. 5(7). See *Arab Monetary Fund* v *Hashim* [1992] 1 All ER 645.

pension. Payments made periodically to a person on retirement from service. Generally taxable as earned income. Persons over 80, entitled to retirement pensions, are entitled to an "age addition": S.S. Contributions and Benefits Act 1992, s. 79. See e.g., Social Security Pensions Act 1975; S.S.A. 1986, Part I; *Barber* v *Guardian Assurance Group* [1990] 2 All ER 660 (pension schemes and EEC law). *See* OMBUDSMAN, PENSIONS.

pensionable age. *See* AGE, PENSIONABLE.

peppercorn rent. A nominal, usually insignificant, rent paid to keep alive a title. See L.P.A. 1925, s. 99; S.L.A. 1925, s. 44.

per annum. By the year; annually.

per autre vie. See AUTRE VIE; CESTUI QUE VIE.

per capita. By heads. Individually, as in distribution *per capita*, where property is divided among those entitled to it, each receiving a share.

per curiam. Abbreviated to *per cur.* By the court. Refers to a decision of the court as a whole, in contrast to the opinion of a single judge.

peremptory challenge. *See* CHALLENGE TO JURY.

peremptory pleas. Pleas in bar (q.v.).

perfect and imperfect rights. A *perfect* right is one recognised and enforced by a legal system; an *imperfect* right is one recognised, but not enforced directly, by the law. (Example: although a statute-barred debt cannot be recovered generally in a court, if the debtor pays, he cannot subsequently sue for recovery of the money as having been paid without consideration.) *See* RIGHT.

perfection of gift. *See* GIFT, IMPERFECT.

perfect trust. An executed trust (q.v.).

performance. 1. The completion of an act. 2. An act which, in precise and exact accordance with the terms of a contract, discharges it, e.g., by tender (q.v.), payment. For "partial performance", see S.G.A. 1979, s. 30(1).

performance bond. *See* BOND, PERFORMANCE.

performance, tender of. *See* TENDER OF PERFORMANCE.

perils, excepted. *See* EXCEPTED PERILS.

perils of the sea. An accident on the seas beyond the normal action of winds and waves. It includes damage caused by violent winds or storms, or striking a submerged rock. It does not include direct damage done to cargo by rats or bad stowage.

per incuriam. Through want of care; inadvertently. A mistaken decision of a court. It was held in *Young v Bristol Aeroplane Co Ltd* [1946] 1 All ER 98 that the Court of Appeal (q.v.) was not bound to follow one of its earlier decisions if satisfied that it was reached *per incuriam.* Application of the doctrine should be made only in the case of "decisions given in ignorance or forgetfulness of some inconsistent statutory provision or of some authority binding on the court concerned": *Morelle v Wakeling* [1955] 2 QB 379. See *Broome v Cassell* [1972] AC 1027; *Rakhit v Carty* [1990] 2 QB 315.

per infortunium. By mischance.

periodical payments. A court may order a husband to make regular payments e.g., to his wife for such a term as the court may direct (eg, until remarriage of the payee or death of either party). See Mat.C.A. 1973, s. 23(1). See also F.L.R.A. 1969, s. 6(3) (as modified by F.L.R.A. 1987, Sch. 1); D.P.A. 1978, Part I; Ch. A. 1989, s. 15, Sch. 1; *Twiname v Twiname* [1992] 1 FLR 29.

periodic tenancy. A tenancy (q.v.) which continues for an original period and then for subsequent similar periods until determined by notice given by either party, e.g., a tenancy from year to year. It may be created expressly or by implication. See *Centaploy Ltd v Matlodge Ltd.* [1974] Ch 1.

perished goods. In a contract for the sale of specific goods the contract is void if, unknown to the seller, the goods have perished at the time of the making of the contract: S.G.A. 1979, s. 6. See *Couturier v Hastie* (1856) 5 HL Cas 673; *Barrow, Lane Ltd v Phillips & Co* [1929] 1 KB 574.

perjury. Offence committed by a person lawfully sworn as a witness or interpreter in a judicial proceeding who wilfully makes a statement, material in that proceeding, which he knows to be false or does not believe to be true. See Perjury Act 1911; Prosecution of Offences Act 1985, s. 28; *R v Hall* (1982) 4 Cr App R (S.) 153; *R v Rider* (1986) 83 Cr App R 207; *R v Peach* [1990] 2 All ER 966.

perjury, subornation of. *See* SUBORNATION.

permanently depriving, intention of. Essential element in the *mens rea* of theft (q.v.), existing, e.g., where defendant intends to treat the property as his own to dispose of regardless of another's rights. See Th.A. 1968, s. 6; *R v Warner* (1970) 55 Cr App R 93; *R v Lloyd* [1985] QB 829; *R v Coffey* [1987] Crim LR 498.

per minas. By menaces.

permissive waste. That which arises from an omission by a tenant to do that which should be done, e.g., failing to repair a building. A tenant for life (q.v.) is not liable for permissible waste unless the agreement indicates otherwise: *Re Cartwright* (1889) 41 Ch D 532. *See* WASTE.

permit. "If a man permits a thing to be done, it means that he gives permission for it to be done, and if a man gives permission for a thing to be done, he knows what is to be done or is being done": *Lomas* v *Peek* [1947] 2 All ER 574.

per my et per tout. By the half and by all. Applied to a joint tenancy (q.v.) under which each joint tenant is possessed of the property *per my et per tout.* See L.P.A. 1925, s. 36.

per pais. *See* PAIS.

perpetual injunction. *See* INJUNCTION.

perpetually renewable lease. Lease (q.v.) the holder of which was entitled to enforce the perpetual renewal thereof. Abolished under L.P.A. 1922, as from 1926. Those existing on that date were converted into leases for 2,000 years from the date of commencement of the existing term. See *Marjorie Burnett Ltd* v *Barclay* (1981) 125 SJ 199.

perpetual trusts, rule against. *See* INALIENABILITY, RULE AGAINST.

perpetuating testimony. Procedure whereby evidence (q.v.) can be recorded where there is a danger of its loss and where it may be required for some future action. See O. 39, r. 15.

perpetuities, rule against. Where there is a possibility that a future interest (q.v.) in property might vest after expiration of the perpetuity period, such an interest is generally void. The common-law period is lives in being (q.v.) at the time the instrument creating the interest becomes effective, plus 21 years and any gestation period. Under P. & A.A. 1964, s. 1, the perpetuity period may be a fixed period of years not exceeding 80. See *Re Villar* [1928] Ch 471; *Re Green's Will Trusts* [1985] 3 All ER 455; *Re Drummond* [1988] 1 WLR 234. *See* WAIT AND SEE PRINCIPLE.

perpetuities rule, exceptions to. The rule does not apply to: interests following an entailed interest; a gift to charity followed by a gift over to another charity on a certain event; covenants for renewal contained in a lease; postponement of the mortgagor's right to redeem; the right of the lessor to enter on a breach of covenant.

per pro. (*Per procurationem* = by proxy.) Abbreviated to *p.p.* On behalf of. See *Charles* v *Blackwell* (1977) 2 CPD 151.

per quod. By reason of which.

per quod consortium et servitium amisit. By reason of which he lost her society and services. Action for damages brought by the husband against the person who had deprived him of his wife's society or services by some tortious act. Abolished by A.J.A. 1982, s. 2. *See* CONSORTIUM.

per se. By itself; taken on its own.

person. A *natural person* is a human being, capable of attracting rights and duties. An *artificial person* (known also as "juristic", "legal", "fictitious") is, e.g., a corporation to which the law attributes personality (q.v.). See I.A. 1978, Sch. 1. See also *Harford* v *Swiftrim* [1987] ICR 439 and *Worthing RFC Trustees* v *IRC* [1987] 1 WLR 1057.

personal action. *See* ACTIONS, REAL AND PERSONAL.

personal Bill. A private Bill concerning the property or status of an individual. *See* BILL.

personal chattel. *See* CHATTELS.

personal credit agreement. An agreement between a debtor and creditor by which the creditor provides the debtor with credit of any amount: C.C.A. 1974, s. 8(1).

personal information. "Information which relates to a living individual who can be identified from that information (or from that and other information in the possession of the authority keeping the record) including any expression of opinion about the individual but not any indication of the intentions of the authority with respect to that individual": Access to Personal Files Act 1987, s. 2(2). See also Access to Health Records Act 1989.

personal injuries. *See* INJURIES, PERSONAL, ACTION FOR.

personal injuries, provisional damages for. Provisional damages may be awarded if there is proved or admitted to be a chance that at some definite or indefinite time in the future the injured person will, as a result of the act or omission which gave rise to the cause of action, develop some serious deterioration in his physical or mental condition: S.C.A. 1981, s. 32A (inserted by A.J.A. 1982, s. 6(1)). "Chance" involves a possibility that had to be measurable rather than fanciful; "serious deterioration" means a clear risk of deterioration beyond the norm that could be expected: *Willson* v *Ministry of Defence* [1991] 1 All ER 638. For the procedural requirements see O. 38, rr. 7–10; these include a requirement that the claim be specifically pleaded (r. 8(1)(*a*)).

personality. *Legal personality* is the sum total of a person's legal rights and duties ("his advantages and disadvantages"). *Corporate personality* is the sum of rights and duties borne by a corporate body: see, e.g., the Cos.A. 1985, s. 13(3); *Salomon* v *Salomon* [1897] AC 22. *See* PERSON.

personal property. Property other than land, e.g., goods and chattels. Leasehold interests are classed as personal property. Divided into *choses in possession* and *choses in action* (q.v.). *See* PROPERTY.

personal representative. "The executor, original or by representation, or administrator for the time being of a deceased person": A.E.A. 1925, s. 55(1). See S.C.A. 1981, s. 114; I.C.T.A. 1988, s. 701(4). *See* ADMINISTRATOR; EXECUTOR.

personalty. Personal property (q.v.).

persona non grata. An "unacceptable person", e.g., a diplomatic official not acceptable to the government of the country to which he is accredited.

personation. Pretending to be another person for some improper motive. It is an offence, e.g., to personate a juryman (see *R* v *Clark* (1918) 82 JP 295); to personate a woman's husband so as to have sexual intercourse with her (S.O.A. 1956, s. 1); to vote as some other person in an election (Representation of the People Act 1983, s. 60(1)).

person in authority. For the purposes of a "confession" (q.v.), "persons in authority" have been held to include: prosecutor; prosecutor's spouse; police officer; magistrate; magistrate's clerk; but not a police officer's wife or a fellow prisoner or a prison chaplain. See P. & C.E.A. 1984, s. 82(1); *R* v *Platt* [1981] Crim LR 332.

person of unsound mind. One suffering from a mental disorder (q.v.).

per stirpes. According to stock. Refers to the distribution of property of an intestate divided among those entitled according to the stocks of descent.

persuasive authorities. Precedents (q.v.) which are not technically binding; decisions of inferior courts, decisions of Irish, Scottish, Commonwealth and foreign courts; some textbooks, e.g., Bracton.

perverse verdict. A verdict altogether against the evidence, or one given by a jury which refuses to follow a judge's direction relating to a matter of law. See, e.g., *R* v *Ponting* [1985] Crim LR 318. *See* VERDICT.

perverting the course of justice. Acting in a way which has a tendency and is intended to pervert the administration of public justice. See, e.g., *R* v *Bailey* [1956] NI 15 (false confession); *R* v *Murray* [1982] 1 WLR 475 (fabricating evidence); *R* v *Williams* (1991) 92 Cr App R 158 (attempting to pervert the course of justice is a substantive offence); *R* v *Firetto* [1991] Crim LR 208 (bogus sample of blood).

petition. A written application praying for relief or remedy, as in a petition for divorce, petition of right (q.v.). Available only where statute or Rules of the Supreme Court specifically prescribe it as a mode of procedure. See O. 9.

petition for winding up. Statement asking that a company (q.v.) be wound up by the court: See Ins.A. 1986, s. 122(1).

petition of right. 1. Declaration of the liberties of the people, made in 1628. 2. Procedure of obtaining restitution from the Crown or compensation in damages. See Crown Proceedings Act 1947; *Franklin* v *R* [1974] QB 202 (in which the form of the petition is set out).

petitions to Parliament. It is "the inherent right of every commoner in England to prepare and present petitions to the House of Commons in case of grievance, and the House of Commons to receive the same": Resolution of the Commons 1699. The petition should present a case in which the House has jurisdiction to interfere; it should be presented by an M.P.

petit treason. *See* HIGH TREASON.

petty jury. *See* JURY, PETTY.

petty larceny. *See* GRAND LARCENY.

petty serjeanty. *See* GRAND SERJEANTY.

petty sessions. Court of summary jurisdiction, based initially on a statute of

1946. Known as "magistrates' court" (q.v.). See M.C.A. 1980; Justices of the Peace Act 1979, s. 4; L.G.A. 1985, s. 12.

philanthropic purposes. Gifts for "philanthropic" or similar purposes have been held to be wider than gifts for "charitable purposes", so that they do not necessarily constitute a charity. "It seems to me that 'philanthropic' is wide enough to comprise purposes not technically charitable": *per* Stirling J in *Re Macduff* [1896] 2 Ch 451. *See* CHARITABLE TRUST.

phone tapping. *See* ELECTRONIC SURVEILLANCE.

photographs, right to take. "In my judgment no one possesses a right of preventing another person photographing him any more than he has a right of preventing another person giving a description of him, provided the description is not libellous or otherwise wrongful": *per* Horridge J in *Sports and General Press Agency* v *"Our Dogs" Publishing Co* [1916] 2 KB 880. For breach of copyright in photograph, see *Williams* v *Settle* [1960] 1 WLR 1072.

photographs, use of in identification. Photographs of suspects must not be shown to witnesses for the purpose of identification if circumstances allow of a personal identification. Photographs used must be available for production in court. See *R* v *Dwyer* [1925] 2 KB 799; *R* v *Cook* [1987] QB 417 (the rule against hearsay (q.v.) does not apply to photofit pictures).

picketing, criminal liability and. Pickets may commit the following offences in relation to their activities: obstruction of highway (Highways Act 1980, s. 137); public nuisance; criminal conspiracy; obstruction of constable (Police Act 1964, s. 51(3)); offences under Public Order Act 1986.

picketing, peaceful. It is lawful for a person, in contemplation or furtherance of a trade dispute, to attend at or near his own place of work, or, if he is a union official, at or near the place of work of a member of the union whom he is accompanying and whom he represents, for the purpose only of peacefully obtaining or communicating information, or peacefully persuading any person to work or abstain from working: T.U.L.R.(C.)A. 1992, s. 220. Those who picket another's place

of work lose their immunity in tort. See *Dupont Steels* v *Sirs* [1980] 1 WLR 142; *Rayware Ltd* v *TGWU* [1989] 1 WLR 675. See SI 1992/476 (*Code of Practice (Picketing)*). *See* SECONDARY ACTION; STRIKE.

pickpocket. One who steals money or property, usually secretly, from the person of another. See, e.g., *R* v *Daniel* (1988) 10 Cr App R (S.) 341.

pipe rolls. Rolls, so-called possibly because of their appearance when rolled up, which were originally the parchment Great Rolls of the Exchequer. Commenced *c.*1100 and continued until 1832. Contained information relating to Kings' debtors, administration, etc.

piracy. 1. Piracy *jure gentium* (piracy at common law) involves an act of armed violence committed upon the high seas within the jurisdiction of the Admiralty, and not being an act of war. The Piracy Act 1837 made piracy accompanied by dangerous violence or attempted murder a capital offence. (Term may include mutiny of passengers: *Naylor* v *Palmer* (1854) 10 Exch 382.) Piracy may also be committed against an aircraft: see Aviation Security Act 1982, s. 5. See *Athens Maritime Enterprises* v *Hellenic Mutual War Risks Assn.* [1982] Com LR 188. 2. Infringement of a copyright: see Copyrights, Designs and Patents Act 1988, s. 107; *R* v *Carter* (1992) The Times, 31 Jan. (distribution of pirated tapes akin to theft).

piscary, common of. Right to catch fish in waters belonging to another. See *Lovett* v *Fairclough* (1990) 61 P & CR 385. *See* FISHERY.

places open to public, removal of articles from. "Where the public have access to a building in order to view the building or part of it, or a collection or part of a collection housed in it, any person who without lawful authority removes from the building or its grounds the whole or any part of any article displayed or kept for display to the public in the building or that part of it or in its grounds shall be guilty of an offence": Th.A. 1968, s. 11(1). See *R* v *Durkin* [1973] 2 All ER 872.

placing of shares. *See* SHARES, PLACING OF.

plaint. 1. Cause on which a complaint is based. 2. Written statement of an action.

plaintiff. One who brings an action into the court.

planning control, breach of. Development of land (q.v.) without appropriate planning permission, or failure to comply with conditions attached to a permission. It can lead to a local planning authority serving an enforcement notice or stop notice (qq.v.) prohibiting specified operations on the land. See T.C.P.A. 1990, Part VII; Planning and Compensation Act 1991, ss. 2, 3. For limitation periods concerning enforcement, see 1991 Act, s. 4. For planning contravention order, see 1990 Act, s. 171C, inserted by 1991 Act, s. 1.

planning permission. Formal consent of a local planning authority which must be sought by one who wishes to develop land. For "planning authorities", see T.C.P.A. 1990, Part I. Permission may be granted unconditionally or subject to such conditions as the authority thinks fit, or may be refused. See generally, T.C.P.A. 1990; Planning and Compensation Act 1991, s. 10 (certificates of lawful use and development); *R* v *Exeter CC, ex p Thomas & Co.* [1990] 1 All ER 413. Planning inquiries should be held in public, subject to certain exemptions: see 1990 Act, ss. 320, 321, Sch. 8. For powers to revoke or modify planning permission, see 1990 Act, s. 97. For compensation, see ss. 120, 144; see also 1991 Act. *See* DEVELOPMENT.

planning zones, simplified. *See* ZONES, SIMPLIFIED PLANNING.

plant. "It includes whatever apparatus is used by a businessman for carrying on a business. Not his stock in trade which he buys or makes for sale, but all goods and chattels, fixed or movable, which he keeps for permanent employment in his business": *Yarmouth* v *France* (1887) 18 QBD 647. See Capital Allowances Act 1968; *IRC* v *Scottish & Newcastle Breweries Ltd* [1982] 1 WLR 322; *Carr* v *Sayer* (1992) The Times, 16 April. *See* MACHINERY AND PLANT.

plc. Abbreviation for "public limited company" (q.v.). *See* COMPANY NAME.

plea. An answer to the plaintiff's declaration in a common-law action; a defence; a pleading.

plea, ambiguous. A plea which, in response to an indictment, is equivocal or not clear. Example: "Guilty, but I wasn't sure that the goods did not belong to me." If a plea remains ambiguous, a plea of not guilty is entered on behalf of the accused: C.L.A. 1967, s. 6(1). See *R* v *Plymouth Justices, ex p Hart* [1986] QB 950.

plea bargaining. Informal procedure whereby the defendant may agree to plead guilty as an exchange for the prosecution's dropping other charges (or a sentence concession, i.e., "sentence bargaining"). In *R* v *Turner* [1970] 2 QB 321, Lord Parker suggested certain applicable principles: counsel must not persuade a client to plead guilty if he has not committed those acts constituting the crime with which he has been charged; the accused must be completely free to make a choice as to his plea; discussions between counsel for the defence and the judge should take place only in the presence of counsel for the prosecution; the judge should never indicate the sentence he has in mind to impose where there is any suggestion that it might be different if the accused pleads guilty or not guilty, as the case may be.

plea, change of. Change of plea by the accused at any stage of the trial. It must come from the accused personally. See *R* v *Drew* [1985] 1 WLR 914.

plead. To put forward a plea (q.v.); to allege in defence; to address the court.

pleading guilty by post. *See* POST, PLEA OF GUILTY BY.

pleadings. Formal written statements in a civil action, usually drafted by counsel, served by a party on his opponents, stating allegations of fact upon which the party pleading is claiming relief, but not the evidence by which the facts are to be proved. See O. 18. Must contain particulars of any claim on which party pleading relies. Usually consist of statement of claim (in summary form); defence; reply (qq.v.). See O. 18, r. 7(1). Intended to eradicate irrelevant matters, to state precisely issues in dispute and to allow the other party time to prepare reply.

pleadings, amendment of. Pleadings may be amended once without leave prior to the close of pleadings: O. 20, r. 3. An amended pleading must be served on the other party. After the close of pleadings, amendments may be made only with leave. See *Smith v Baron* (1991) The Times, 1 Feb.

pleadings, close of. Pleadings are deemed to be closed at the end of a period of 14 days after the service of reply or defence to counterclaim (qq.v.), or at the end of 14 days after the service of defence if neither reply nor defence to counterclaim has been served. See O. 18, r. 20.

pleadings, exchange of. Process of exchange between the plaintiff (q.v.) and defendant (q.v.) of the plaintiff's statement of claim, the defendant's defence and the plaintiff's reply. Further pleadings require leave (see O. 18, r. 4), e.g., the defendant's rejoinder, the plaintiff's surrejoinder, the defendant's rebutter, and the plaintiff's surrebutter (qq.v.).

pleadings, formal requirements. Requirements under O. 18, r. 6, whereby every pleading must bear on its face: letter, number of action and year of issue; title of action; Division of High Court (q.v.) to which the action is assigned and the name of judge(s) to whom assigned; description of pleading and the date on which served. Pleadings must be divided into consecutively numbered paragraphs. Dates and other numbers must be in figures.

pleadings, material facts in. Pleadings must contain only material facts. "The word 'material' means necessary for formulating a complete cause of action, and if any one 'material' fact is omitted, the statement of claim is bad": *Bruce v Odhams Press Ltd* [1936] 1 KB 712.

pleadings, striking out. Under O. 18, r. 19, the defendant can apply to have the plaintiff's statement of claim struck out because, e.g., it discloses no reasonable cause of action, or is frivolous, or may prejudice or delay the fair trial of action. Examples: action to recover payment apparently made by the plaintiff in contravention of statute (*Shaw v Shaw* [1965] 1 WLR 539); action against a M.P. for not presenting a petition to Parliament (*Chaffers v Goldsmid* [1894] 1 QB 186).

pleadings, subsequent. Pleadings subsequent to a reply or defence to counterclaim, served with leave of the court; the defendant's rejoinder; the plaintiff's surrejoinder; the defendant's rebutter, the plaintiff's surrebutter (qq.v.). See O. 18, r. 4.

pleadings, trial without. Procedure in any action commenced by a writ other than one based on a claim relating to libel, slander, malicious prosecution; false imprisonment or fraud, where the defendant has acknowledged service of the writ, where there is no substantial dispute, where parties agree on a statement of issues in dispute and where the court is satisfied that issues can be defined without pleadings. See O. 18, r. 21.

pleas in bar. Plea by the defendant in a trial on indictment, e.g., *autrefois acquit, autrefois convict* (qq.v.).

pleas of the Crown. Term formerly used to refer to criminal prosecutions, i.e., offences said to have been committed *contra pacem domini regis.* Formerly such pleas were triable in the King's Courts only.

pledge. 1. A surety. 2. Transfer of a chattel (q.v.) (or documents of title thereto) by the pledgor to the pledgee, as security for the payment of a debt incurred by the transferor, or performance of some engagement. See Factors Act 1889, ss. 1–5. 3. Pawnee's rights over an article taken in pawn: C.C.A. 1974, s. 189(1).

plene administravit. He has fully administered. Defence by an executor (q.v.) or administrator (q.v.) who is sued upon the testator's debts, claiming that he has administered the estate fully and has nothing left with which to satisfy the plaintiff's demands.

plenipotentiary. One invested with full powers, e.g., as the Sovereign's representative.

plough bote. Wood employed in the repair of instruments of husbandry. *See* BOTE.

plurality. The holding by one person of two or more benefices (q.v.). See Pluralities Acts 1838 and 1930 (as amended by Patronage (Benefices) Measure 1986, Schs. 4, 5).

poaching. Illegal taking of game or fish, and trespassing for that purpose. See Night Poaching Act 1828; Game Laws (Amendment) Act 1960; Th.A. 1968, Sch. 1; Wild Creatures and Forest Laws

Act 1971; the Deer Act 1991, s. 1(1); *R v King* (1991) The Times, 4 July.

poison. That which when administered is injurious to health or life. It is an offence under O.P.A. 1861, s. 23, unlawfully to administer to a person any poison so as to endanger life or inflict grievous bodily harm. See also O.P.A. 1861, s. 59 (procuring a poison: see *R v Mills* [1963] 1 QB 522); Poisons Act 1972, which regulates the sale of poisons. For sentencing principles, see *R v Jones* (1990) 12 Cr App R (S.) 323.

police authorities. Police committees controlling regular police forces. In England and Wales committees consist of local councillors and magistrates (q.v.). The police authority for the Metropolitan Police Force is the Home Secretary; for the City of London (q.v.), the Court of Common Council. It is the duty of an authority to provide an adequate police force for its area. See Police Act 1964. Income comes largely from central government and a local police rate.

police cadet. "Any person appointed to undergo training with a view to becoming a constable": Race Relations Act 1976, s. 16(5).

Police Complaints Authority. Body responsible for investigating complaints and matters of discipline concerning police forces in England and Wales: P. & C.E.A. 1984, Part IX. It consists of a chairman and not less than eight other members, and does not include any person who is or has been a constable: Sch. 4.

police court. Magistrates' court (q.v.).

police detention. *See* CUSTODY; DETENTION, POLICE.

police forces. There are 52 regular police forces in England, Scotland and Wales. Most counties have their own forces each under the direction and control of its Chief Constable: Police Act 1964, s. 5(1). The Metropolitan Police Force is responsible for the area within a radius of 24 km from Charing Cross; the City of London has its own force. Eventual control is with the Home Secretary, who is advised by HM Chief Inspector and five Inspectors of Constabulary. See also Ministry of Defence Police Act 1987; Atomic Weapons Establishment Act 1991, s. 4.

Police Negotiating Board. Board which

represents the interests of authorities who maintain police forces and members of those forces (and cadets); it is appointed to consider questions concerning leave, pay and allowances, pensions, hours of duty: Police Negotiating Board Act 1980, s. 1(1).

police, obstruction of. It is an offence under the Police Act 1964, s. 51, unlawfully to obstruct a constable in the execution of his duty, and this is not confined to physical obstruction but includes "anything making it more difficult for the police to carry out their duties": *Hinchcliffe v Sheldon* [1955] 1 WLR 1207. "What the prosecution have to prove is that there was an obstructing of a constable; that the constable was at the time acting in the execution of his duty and that the person obstructing did so wilfully": *Rice v Connolly* [1966] 2 QB 414. See *Green v DPP* [1991] Crim LR 782; *Plowden v DPP* [1991] Crim LR 850.

police officer. One who, belonging to a police force, exercises by virtue of his office, powers as a constable (q.v.). His responsibilities include: protection of people and property (see *R v Dytham* [1979] QB 722); investigation of offences; apprehension of offenders. See *Hill v Chief Constable of W Yorks* [1987] 2 WLR 1126. He is neither a servant, nor an agent, of the Crown. For police negligence, see *Ancell v McDermott* (1992) The Times, 17 Feb.

police right to question. *See* QUESTIONING BY POLICE.

policy of insurance. The instrument containing the contract made by the insurer with the insured. See Insurance Companies Act 1982, s. 96. *See* INSURANCE.

political asylum. Refuge and safety offered to one escaping from political oppression overseas. See Fugitive Offenders Act 1967; *R v Home Department, ex p Gunes* [1991] Imm AR 278.

political fund. That part of a union's total funds used exclusively in the furtherance of political objects (q.v.). See T.U.L.R.(C.)A. 1992, s. 71.

political objects. 1. In reference to a charity (q.v.): "Equity has always refused to recognise [political] objects as charitable": *Bowman v Secular Society Ltd* [1917] AC 406. These objects include, e.g., advancing the interests of a political party, opposing changes in the law, party political education. See *Webb* v *O'Doherty* (1991) The Times, 11 Feb. 2. For political objects on which trade unions may not expend money by using their political funds, see T.U.L.R.(C.)A. 1992, s. 72. *See* CHARITABLE TRUSTS.

political offence. Term used in relation to extradition (q.v.), which will not normally take place on the basis of a political offence. "In my opinion the idea that lies behind the phrase is that the fugitive is at odds with the state that applies for his extradition on some issue connected with the political control or government of the country": *per* Viscount Radcliffe in *Schtraks* v *Government of Israel* [1964] AC 556.

political offence, exclusion of cases from. Under the Suppression of Terrorism Act 1978, certain offences are not to be regarded as of a political character. They include: murder, manslaughter or culpable homicide, rape, kidnapping, false imprisonment, assault occasioning actual bodily harm or causing injury or wilful fire-raising; offences under O.P.A. 1861, ss. 18, 20–24, 28–30, 48, 55; offences under Explosive Substances Act 1883, ss. 2, 3; offences under Aviation Security Act 1982 and Aviation and Maritime Security Act 1990, s. 1; attempts to commit any of these offences. See 1978 Act, Sch. 1, as amended.

political office. The office of member of Parliament, member of the European Parliament, or member of a local authority, or any position within a political party: T.U.L.R.(C.)A. 1992, s. 72.

political uniforms. It is an offence to wear in any public place or public meeting a uniform "signifying association with any political organisation or the promotion of any political purpose": P.O.A. 1936, s. 1(1). See *O'Moran* v *DPP* [1975] QB 864.

poll. Procedure involved in taking, registering, counting votes and declaring the result in an election. See, e.g., Representation of the People Act 1983, Sch. 1; Cos. A. 1985, s. 373.

poll, deed. *See* DEED.

poll tax. Tax per person or head. *See* COMMUNITY CHARGE.

pollution. Action of rendering unclean. "Pollution of the environment"

means, under En.P.A. 1989, s. 1(1), pollution due to the release into any environmental medium, from any process of substances which are capable of causing harm to man or any other living organisms supported by the environment. "Harm" means harm to the health of living organisms or other interference with the ecological systems of which they form part, and, in the case of man, includes offence caused to any of his senses or harm to his property. See also Water Act 1989, Part III, Ch. 1.

polygamy. Practice under which a person has several spouses. See Matrimonial Proceedings (Polygamous Marriages) Act 1972; Mat.C.A. 1973, ss. 11, 47, Matrimonial Causes Rules 1977, r. 108. The Immigration Act 1988, s. 2, restricts the exercise of right of abode in the UK in cases of polygamy. See also S.S. Contributions and Benefits Act 1992, s. 133.

pornography. Obscene material (books, films, etc.). *See* OBSCENITY.

port. Includes harbours, rivers, estuaries, havens, docks, canals or other places where persons are empowered under statute to make charges in respect of ships entering and using the facilities: S.C.A. 1981, s. 22(2). See Ports Act 1991. *See* SAFE PORT.

portion. Gift of money or other property made to a child by a father or one *in loco parentis* (q.v.) so as to establish that child in life or to make a permanent provision for him. A "portion-debt" arises from a convenant to give a portion.

positive law. *See* LAW, POSITIVE.

positivism, legal. Doctrine in legal theory based on the examination of manmade law, which is set down (i.e., posited) by man for man. It is concerned, essentially, with law as it is, rather than as it ought to be. Hence propositions of law are "true" only when describing correctly the rules of law or the content of laws.

posse comitatus. Power of the county. Group of able-bodied men who could be called together by a sheriff (q.v.), e.g., to assist in keeping the peace, to pursue felons.

possession. Concept based on a degree of physical control and involving: *corpus* (that which is possessed) and *ani-*

mus possidendi (q.v.). May be prima facie evidence of ownership. Defined variously as, e.g., "physical detention coupled with intention to use the thing detained as one's own" (Maine); "continuing exercise of a claim to the exclusive use of some material object" (Salmond); "the present control of a thing, on one's own behalf and to the exclusion of all others": Taylor. See *Lockyer* v *Gibb* [1967] 2 QB 243 (possession without mental element in relation to crime). *See* OWNERSHIP.

possession action, fast. Provided by RSCO 113, or CCR, O. 44, allowing the court to make an order for possession by a landlord dispossessed by squatters or trespassers, five days after service of a summons. A master, rather than a judge, may hear proceedings in case of an emergency.

possession, exclusive. Concept of particular importance in relation to leases (q.v.) and licences (q.v.). A lease gives the grantee the right to exclusive possession of the demised premises, i.e., a degree of territorial control including the ability to keep out strangers (and the landlord, except, e.g., to view or repair). Not to be confused with "exclusive occupation". See *Street* v *Mountford* [1985] AC 809.

possession, interest in. *See* INTEREST IN POSSESSION.

possession, quiet. *See* QUIET POSSESSION.

possession, recent. *See* RECENT POSSESSION.

possession, unity of. *See* UNITY OF POSSESSION.

possession, unlawful, of drugs. It is an offence under the Misuse of Drugs Act 1971: to have a controlled drug in one's possession (s. 5(1)); to have a controlled drug in one's possession whether lawfully or not, with the intention to supply it to another in contravention of s. 4. "Possession" involves more than mere control; the person in control should know that the thing is in his control. See *Warner* v *Metropolitan Police Commissioner* [1969] AC 256; *R* v *Hunt* [1987] 1 All ER 1. *See* DRUGS, CONTROLLED; DRUGS, SUPPLY OF.

possession, writ of. Writ directing a sheriff (q.v.) to enter upon land so as to give vacant possession to the plaintiff. Used for direct enforcement of order or judgment for possession of land. See O. 45, r. 3; H.A. 1985, Sch. 2. For suspended possession order, see H.A. 1985, s. 84; *Thompson* v *Elmbridge BC* (1987) 19 HLR 526.

possessory lien. *See* LIEN.

possessory title. Title based on the possession of land where the applicant is, for the time being, unable to establish title in the usual way, e.g., by title deeds. First registration of such title has the effect of registering land with absolute title, but that title will not affect any rights or interests subsisting or capable of arising at the time of registration. See L.R.A. 1925, ss. 4, 6, 11; L.R.A. 1986, s. 1. Possessory title to leasehold land may be granted to an applicant in possession or in receipt of rents and profits. See *Jessamine Investment Co* v *Schwartz* [1976] 3 All ER 521. *See* TITLE.

possibility. Term used in land law (e.g., as in "double possibility" (q.v.)) to describe an interest in land which will arise on some uncertain event. "Bare possibility" described the expectation of an eldest son to succeed to his father's lands; "possibility coupled with an interest" refers to, e.g., a contingent remainder (q.v.).

post. After; following.

post, contracts by. Contracts made, e.g., by letter or telegram. In general, an offer by post must be accepted by post unless the offer has indicated anything to the contrary. Acceptance is complete as soon as the letter is properly addressed, prepaid and posted, whether it reaches the offeror or not. See *Adams* v *Lindsell* (1818) 1 B & Ald 681.

post-dated cheque. *See* CHEQUE, POST-DATED.

post diem. After the day.

posthumous child. A child born after the death of the father.

post litem motam. After the beginning of litigation.

post-mortem. After death. Term used to refer to the examination of a body after death so as to determine, e.g., the cause of death. Known also as an "autopsy". See Coroners Rules 1984; Coroners Act 1988, ss. 19–23; *R* v *Greater Manchester Coroner, ex p Worch* [1987] QB 627. *See* CORONER.

post, payment by. Generally not good payment where the letter is lost in post, unless the creditor requested payment by post. Such a request does not absolve the debtor from paying in a reasonable manner and in accordance with the accepted business practice. See *Pennington* v *Crossley & Son* (1897) 77 LT 43.

post, plea of guilty by. Procedure under M.C.A. 1980, s. 12, often used in motoring cases, and where the offence is summary and punishable by not more than three months' imprisonment. The prosecutor serves the summons and statement of facts to be placed before the court. The defendant must then inform the clerk that he wishes to plead guilty without appearance. (He may change his mind and appear.) The statement of facts read out in court must be exactly the same as that served on the defendant. The hearing is adjourned if the possibility of imprisonment or disqualification (motoring cases) arises.

post, service by. Where statute authorises or requires a document to be served by post, that service is deemed to be effected by properly addressing pre-paying and posting a letter containing the document: I.A. 1978, s. 7.

potior est conditio defendentis. The condition of a defendant is the better.

potior est conditio possidentis. The condition of a possessor is the better. See *E India Co* v *Tritton* (1824) 3 B & C 280.

poverty. "It is quite clearly established that poverty does not mean destitution; it is a word of wide and somewhat indefinite import; it may not unfairly be paraphrased as meaning persons who have to 'go short' in the ordinary acceptation of that term, due regard being had to their status in life, and so forth": *Re Coulthurst* [1951] Ch 661. See Charities Act 1985.

power. Authority vested in the donee (of the power) to modify a legal relationship, as where one disposes of property for his own or another's benefit. May be: simply collateral (q.v.) (where the donee has no interest in the property); in gross (q.v.); appendant or appurtenant (qq.v.). For "legal" and "equitable powers", see L.P.A. 1925, s. 205(1). *See* APPOINTMENT, POWER OF.

power, capricious. A power which is void because "it negatives a sensible consideration by the trustees of the exercise of the power": *Re Manisty's Settlement* [1974] Ch 17.

power coupled with interest. Power to perform some act, together with an interest (united in the same person) in the subject-matter of that act.

power of appointment. *See* APPOINTMENT, POWER OF.

power of attorney. Instrument authorising one person to act for another during the absence of that other. Under Tr.A. 1925, s. 25, as amended by Powers of Attorney Act 1971, a trustee (q.v.) has the power to delegate the exercise of his powers and discretions to an attorney. Under Enduring Powers of Attorney Act 1985, a person may appoint an attorney whose authority will not be revoked by that person's subsequent incapacity (defined in s. 13(1)). See *Re K.* [1988] 1 All ER 358; L.P. (Misc. Provs.) A. 1989, Sch. 1, 2.

power of sale. 1. Power of a tenant for life (q.v.) to sell settled land (q.v.) or any part thereof, or any easement, right or privilege over the land: S.L.A. 1925, s. 38. Sale must be made for the best consideration in money that can be obtained. 2. Power of trustee (q.v.), under the Tr.A. 1925, to sell or concur with any other person in selling all or part of the trust property. 3. Power of a mortgagee (q.v.), under L.P.A. 1925, s. 101(1), to sell when the legal date for redemption (q.v.) has passed.

power of search. *See* SEARCH, POWER OF.

p.p. *See* PER PRO.

practice. Formal procedures relating to proceedings in a court. Governed generally (in the Supreme Court) by Rules of the Supreme Court (q.v.).

Practice Directions. Directions and notes, generally published in the law reports, indicating the views of the judges of the Court of Appeal or the judges, masters, registrars of the High Court, relating to matters of practice and procedure of the courts. They do not have any statutory authority.

practice, general and approved. Practice taken into account in determining standard of care in actions for negligence. "A defendant . . . can clear [himself] if he shows that he acted in accordance with general and approved practice": *per* Lord Alness in *Vancouver*

General Hospital v *McDaniel* (1935) 152 LT 56. *See* MALA PRAXIS.

practice master. A master who controls the business of the Central Office of the Supreme Court (q.v.). See O. 63, r. 2.

practising certificate. Annual certificate issued to a solicitor (q.v.) by the Law Society, entitling him to practise. See Solicitors Act 1974, ss. 9–18; *Hudgell Yeates & Co* v *Weston* [1978] 2 All ER 363.

praecipe. Command. 1. Writ (q.v.) now abolished, ordering a person to perform some action, or to show the reason for non-performance. 2. Form used to secure the issue of various orders enforcing decisions of the High Court. See O. 45; O. 56.

praecipe, **tenant to the.** Procedure, now obsolete, whereby a tenant for life (q.v.) who was concurring in the barring of an entail (q.v.) conveyed the life estate to another so that a *praecipe* (q.v.) in recovery could be issued against that other, who was known as the *tenant to the praecipe.*

praemunire. *Praemoneri* = to be forewarned. Originally referred to an offence, punishable with life imprisonment and forfeiture of property, of asserting the supremacy of the Pope over the English Sovereign. It was later applied to offences relating to, e.g., the unlawful sending of a prisoner outside the realm to avoid the protection of Habeas Corpus Act (q.v.). See Statute of Praemunire 1392.

praemunire facias. Beginning of the writ of praemunire ("that you cause to be forewarned . . .").

praepositus. 1. One placed in authority. 2. One from whom descent might be traced.

preamble. Introduction to a statute or Bill, explaining the facts and assumptions behind it. Where an operative part of a statute is ambiguous, the preamble may be resorted to so as to show, e.g., the intention of the Act. "It is only when it conveys a clear and definite meaning in comparison with relatively obscure or indefinite enacting words that a preamble may legitimately prevail": *A.-G.* v *Prince Ernest Augustus of Hanover* [1957] 1 All ER 49. See also *The Norwhale* [1975] QB 589.

precarious possession. Possession simply at will. "What is 'precarious'? – that which depends not on right, but on the will of another person": *Burrows* v *Lang* [1901] 2 Ch 511.

precatory trust. Trust arising as a result of the use of precatory words (q.v.) and their construction. *See* TRUST.

precatory words. (*Precari* = to entreat.) Words of an entreaty, prayer, desire, etc, which, when they accompany a transfer or bequest of property, suggest that the transferor had in mind the creation of a trust (q.v.), e.g., "I most heartily beseech . . ."; "I will and desire that . . ." The court is guided by the intention of the testator (q.v.) apparent in the will (q.v.), and not by any particular words in which the wishes of the testator are expressed: *Re Williams* [1897] 2 Ch 12. See also *Re Adams and Kensington Vestry* (1884) 27 Ch D 394; *Re Diggles* (1888) 39 Ch D 253.

precedent. 1. Judgment or decision cited so as to justify a decision in a later, apparently similar, case. "The process by which forms of conduct are stamped in the judicial mint as law, and thereafter circulate freely as part of the coinage of the realm": Cardozo CJ. An *authoritative precedent* is generally binding and must be followed. A *persuasive precedent* (based, e.g., on *obiter dicta*) need not be followed. A *declaratory precedent* merely applies an existing rule of law. An *original precedent* creates and applies a new rule of law. Decisions on questions of fact must not be cited as precedents: *Qualcast Ltd* v *Haynes* [1959] AC 743. 2. Precedent as applied to the hierarchy of courts is as follows: *House of Lords* – generally bound by previous decisions (see *London Street Tramways Co* v *LCC* [1898] AC 375) but will depart from such decisions where it appears right to do so (see *R* v *Shivpuri* [1987] AC 1); *Court of Appeal (Civil Division)* – bound by previous decisions, except where given *per incuriam* (q.v.) or where inconsistent with a subsequent House of Lords decision; *Court of Appeal (Criminal Division)* – apparently bound by previous decisions; *High Court and Crown Court* – bound by decisions of superior courts; *county courts and magistrates' courts* – bound by decisions of superior courts. See *Young* v *Bristol Aeroplane Co Ltd* [1944] KB 718; *Davis* v *Johnson* [1978] 1 All ER 1132. See also S.S.A. 1990, Sch 6, para 7(2). *See* HOUSE OF LORDS, CORRECTION OF ITS ERRORS; STARE DECISIS.

precedent, condition. *See* CONDITION.

precedent, significance of. "Precedents should be stepping-stones and not halting-places": *per* Lord Macmillan in *Birch* v *Brown* [1931] AC 630. "The only proper use of precedents is to establish principles": Allen (1927).

precept. 1. Command. 2. Written order. 3. Order referring specifically to the payment of rates: L.G.A. 1972, s. 149. See L.G.A. 1988, Part IV. (For the limitation of precepting powers see, e.g., Local Government Finance Act 1992, Chap. V.)

predecessor. One (e.g., a settlor; testator (qq.v.)) from whom benefit is derived of succession to property. A "predecessor in title" is one through whom another is able to trace a title in property.

predictive theory of law. "The prophecies of what the courts will do, in fact, and nothing more pretentious, are what I mean by the law": Holmes (1841–1935).

pre-emption. Right to purchase before others. See L.P.A. 1925, s. 186; L.C.A. 1972, s. 2(4) (whereby it is registrable as an estate contract (q.v.)); *First National Securities* v *Chiltern DC* [1975] 2 All ER 786; *Pritchard* v *Briggs* [1980] 1 All ER 294; *Tuck* v *Baker* [1990] 32 EG 46. *See* OPTION.

preference, fraudulent. *See* FRAUDULENT PREFERENCE.

preference, right of. Right of a personal representative (q.v.) to pay one creditor in preference to another of the same class. Abolished in relation to deaths occurring after 1971: A.E.A. 1971, s. 10.

preference shares. Shares ranking for payment after debentures (q.v.) and before ordinary shares (q.v.). "Convertible preference shares" involve an option for holders to convert their shares into ordinary shares at a stated future date: see I.C.T.A. 1988, s. 832(1). For "fixed rate preference share capital", see 1988 Act, s. 312. *See* SHARE.

preferential debts. After payment of the costs of bankruptcy (q.v.), certain types of liabilities must be paid in priority to others. After preferential debts, ordinary liabilities of the bankrupt rank for dividend *pari passu inter se.*

preferment. 1. Advancement or promotion. See Bishops (Retirement) Measure 1986, r. 10(1). 2. Bringing or laying of a charge or bill of indictment (q.v.).

pregnancy. The processes involved in the female's carrying a developing child within her body. For purposes of Human Fertilisation and Embryology Act 1990, a woman is not to be treated as carrying a child until the embryo (q.v.) has been implanted: s. 2 (3). *See* ABORTION; FOETUS.

pregnancy, dismissal on grounds of. Dismissal from employment solely because of, or for any reason connected with, pregnancy. Treated as unfair dismissal: E.P.(C.).A. 1978, s. 60. See *Stockton BC* v *Brown* [1987] ICR 897; *Webb* v *Emo Air Cargo* [1992] IRLR 116. *See* MATERNITY LEAVE.

pregnancy per alium. Pregnancy by some other [person]. A marriage is voidable on the grounds that at the time of the marriage the respondent was pregnant by some person other than the petitioner. See Mat.C.A. 1973, s. 12 *See* NULLITY OF MARRIAGE.

pre-hearing assessment. Procedure concerning industrial tribunal (q.v.) whereby either party, or the tribunal, may ask for a pre-hearing. If it is then decided that the originating application is "unlikely to succeed or that the submission or arguments put by either party have no reasonable prospect of success" and the application is not withdrawn, costs may be awarded. See *Mulvaney* v *London Transport Executive* [1981] ICR 351.

pre-incorporation contract. A contract made between a person acting as agent (q.v.) or trustee (q.v.) for a company about to be formed and another party. Contracts intended to bind a company on incorporation, but entered into before registration, will be personally enforceable against those who purported to act for the company and enter the contract: Cos.A. 1985, s. 36(4); Cos.A. 1989, s. 130(4); *Rover International Ltd* v *Cannon Film Sales Ltd*

[1987] 1 WLR 1597; *Badgerhill Properties Ltd* v *Cottrell* [1991] BCLC 805.

prejudice. Preconceived judgment. "Without prejudice" is a term used so as to attempt to protect the writer of a document against the construing of its contents as an admission of liability and means, in effect, "without prejudice to rights of writer of the statement". See *Tomlin* v *Standard Telephones Ltd* [1969] 3 All ER 201; *Shropshire DC* v *Amos* [1987] 1 All ER 340; *McDowall* v *Hirschfield Lipson* (1992) The Times, 13 Feb.

preliminary investigation. Known also as "preliminary enquiry". Investigation by magistrates of a case which may go for trial to a higher court. The object is to establish whether the prosecution can show a prima facie case against the accused; if it can, the accused is committed for trial; if not, the defendant is discharged. See, e.g., M.C.A. 1980, ss. 4–7.

preliminary point of law. Point of law, e.g., whether or not certain facts constitute the offence charged, considered by the judge who hears the argument on it, following a plea of not guilty and before the jury (q.v.) is empanelled. See *R* v *Vickers* [1975] 2 All ER 945.

premises. 1. Those operative parts of a deed (q.v.) which precede the habendum (q.v.) and set out, e.g., the names of parties, property to be transferred. 2. Property, e.g., land, buildings. See, e.g., Building Act 1984, s. 126. 3. Propositions in an argument from which a conclusion is drawn.

premises, disposal of. *See* DISPOSAL OF PREMISES.

premises, domestic. *See* DOMESTIC PREMISES.

premises, industrial. *See* INDUSTRIAL PREMISES.

premium. 1. Periodical payment made for keeping up an insurance (q.v.). 2. Reward. 3. Sum paid over and above a fixed wage or price. 4. "Any fine or other like sum and any other pecuniary consideration in addition to rent and any sum paid by way of a deposit, other than one which does not exceed one-sixth of the annual rent and is reasonable in relation to the potential liability in respect of which it is paid": Rent Act 1977, s. 128 (as substituted by

H.A. 1980, s. 79). Premiums and loans (secured or unsecured) on a grant of protected tenancies (q.v.) were prohibited under the 1977 Act, s. 119. See H.A. 1988, s. 115.

premium, issue of shares at a. Issue of shares at a price above par or nominal value. Premium must be transferred to share premium account: Cos.A. 1985, s. 130.

preparatory hearings. *See* SERIOUS FRAUDS, PREPARATORY HEARINGS.

prerogative, judicial review of. "Whatever their source, powers which are defined, either by reference to their object or by reference to procedure for their exercise, or in some other way, and whether the definition is expressed or implied, are . . . normally subject to judicial control to ensure that they are not exceeded": *per* Lord Fraser in *CCSU* v *Minister for the Civil Service* [1985] AC 374. *See* JUDICIAL REVIEW; PREROGATIVE, ROYAL.

prerogative orders. Mandamus (q.v.); prohibition (q.v.); certiorari (q.v.).

prerogative, royal. "The residue of discretionary or arbitrary authority which at any given time is legally left in the hands of the Crown": Dicey. Examples: summoning and dissolving Parliament; appointing bishops and judges; exemption from most statutes. These are, today, nominal rather than substantial. See *A.-G.* v *De Keyser's Royal Hotel* [1920] AC 508; *Council for Civil Service Unions* v *Minister for the Civil Service* [1985] AC 374. *See* MERCY, PREROGATIVE OF; PREROGATIVE, JUDICIAL REVIEW OF.

prerogative writs. Prerogative orders (q.v.).

prescribe. 1. To claim by prescription (q.v.). 2. To set out under a regulation.

prescribed limits of alcohol in blood, etc. Proportions of alcohol in blood, etc, prescribed in relation to driving offences. They include: 35 microgrammes of alcohol in 100 millilitres of breath; 80 milligrammes in 100 millilitres of blood; 107 milligrammes in 100 millilitres of urine: Road Traffic Act 1988, s. 11(1).

prescription. Generally, acquisition or extinction of rights by lapse of time. Claim must be based on the actual and continuous user; enjoyment must be of right; the user must generally be by owner in fee simple (q.v.) against another owner in fee simple who has acquiesced in that user. Prescription at common law required proof of: user since time immemorial (q.v.); user *nec vi, nec clam, nec precario* (q.v.); continuous user. Under the Prescription Act 1832, in the case of easements (q.v.) other than light, the uninterrupted user for 60 years makes a claim to a *profit à prendre* indefeasible. See *Allen* v *Greenwood* [1980] Ch 119; *Jones* v *Price* (1992) The Independent, 16 Jan. See LOST MODERN GRANT.

prescription, custom and. "Prescription and custom are brothers, and ought to have the same age, and reason ought to be the father, and consequence the mother, and use the nurse, and time out of memory to fortify them both": *per* Coke CJ. in *Rowles* v *Mason* (1612) 2 B & G 192.

prescription, registered land and. "Easements, rights and privileges adversely affecting registered land may be acquired in equity by prescription in the same manner and to the same extent as if the land were not registered": L.R.R. 1925, r. 250(1).

present. To offer or tender.

presentment. 1. Presenting a bill of exchange (q.v.) to an acceptor for payment or to a drawee for acceptance. See B.Ex.A. 1882, s. 45. 2. Presentation to a benefice. See the Pastoral Measure 1968.

presentment of Englishry. In the immediate post-Norman Conquest era, fines were levied on a community in which a person who was apparently Norman had been slain, but not where it could be proved that the dead man was English. The presumption was that he was Norman unless presentment of Englishry, i.e., proof that he was English, was given. Abolished in 1340. See MURDRUM.

presents. As in the phrase "these presents". The phrase refers to the document itself in which the words are contained.

preservation order. Order issued under, e.g., T.C.P.A. 1990, in relation to work needed for the preservation of an unoccupied listed building (q.v.), or in relation to a non-listed building of special architectural or historic interest which is threatened with demolition or alteration, or in relation to trees: see

ss. 203, 211. "Preserving" can mean "not causing harm to" rather than "making a positive contribution to": *S. Lakeland DC* v *Secretary of State for the Environment* (1991) 2 PLR 97.

presiding judges. High Court judges assigned to circuits in England and Wales who have a general responsibility for a High Court and Crown Court centre.

presumption. 1. Assumption which must be made until the contrary is proved. 2. Conclusion that facts exist which must, or may, be drawn if other facts are proved or admitted.

presumption against a wrong-doer. See OMNIA PRAESUMUNTUR CONTRA SPOLIATOREM.

presumption concerning ouster of jurisdiction. See OUSTER OF JURISDICTION.

presumption concerning penal statutes. See PENAL STATUTES.

presumption concerning sexual incapacity. In criminal cases there is, effectively, a rule of law that a boy under 14 is not able to have sexual intercourse: see, e.g., *R* v *Waite* [1892] 2 QB 600. There is no such rule in paternity cases: *L.* v *K.* [1985] 1 All ER 961.

presumption concerning vested rights. See VESTED RIGHTS.

presumption of accuracy. Presumption that instruments (e.g., speedometers, watches) were in order on the occasion of the incident being investigated. See *Nicholas* v *Penny* [1950] 2 All ER 89.

presumption of advancement. See ADVANCEMENT.

presumption of continuance. Presumption of fact suggesting that any proved state of affairs can be presumed to have continued for some time. Thus, from the fact that a person was alive at one date it may be inferred that he was alive at some subsequent date. See *Re Forster's Settlement* [1942] Ch. 199.

presumption of death. "If a person has not been heard of for seven years, there is a presumption of law that he is dead": *Lal Chand Marwari* v *Mahant Ramrup Gir* (1925) 42 TLR 159. See O.P.A. 1861, s. 57; L.P.A. 1925, s. 184; *Chard* v *Chard* [1956] P 259. Under Mat. C.A. 1973, s. 19, a decree of presumption of death and dissolution of marriage is available. See DEATH, PROOF OF.

presumption of good faith and value. The holder of a bill is prima facie presumed to be a holder in due course (q.v.): B.Ex.A. 1882, s. 30(2).

presumption of innocence. An accused person is presumed innocent until the prosecution has proved the case against him beyond reasonable doubt. See *Woolmington* v *DPP* [1935] AC 462.

presumption of lawful origin. Persuasive presumption that he who possesses property is its owner.

presumption of legality. *See* OMNIA PRAESUMUNTUR RITE ET SOLEMNITER ESSE ACTA.

presumption of legitimacy. A child born during lawful wedlock is presumed to be legitimate: *Banbury Peerage Case* (1811) 1 Sim & St 153. The presumption may be rebutted only by strong preponderance of evidence (e.g., blood group evidence), but "even weak evidence against legitimacy must prevail if there is not other evidence to counterbalance it": *S.* v *McC.* [1972] AC 24. "Any presumption of law as to the legitimacy of any person may in civil proceedings be rebutted by evidence which shows that it is more probable than not that that person is illegitimate or legitimate, as the case may be, and it shall not be necessary to prove that fact beyond reasonable doubt in order to rebut the presumption": F.L.R.A. 1969, s. 26.

presumption of marriage validity. "Where there is evidence of a ceremony of marriage having been followed by cohabitation of the parties, the validity of the marriage will be presumed, in the absence of decisive evidence to the contrary": *Russell* v *A.-G.* [1949] P 391. There is a presumption also that the marriage is monogamous: *Cheni* v *Cheni* [1965] P 85.

presumption of negligence. *See* RES IPSA LOQUITUR.

presumption of sanity. A presumption that a person is sane until the contrary is proved. *See* M'NAGHTEN RULES.

presumption of survivorship. *See* COMMORIENTES.

presumptions, classifications of. 1. *Traditional classification:* (*a*) *Praesumptiones juris et de jure*, i.e., drawn by law and in an obligatory manner; inference of fact which cannot be con-

tradicted; (*b*) *Praesumptiones juris sed non jure*: inferences of fact which hold good only where there is no contradictory evidence; (*c*) *Praesumptiones facti*, i.e., inferences of fact which the court may, but need not, draw from the facts before it. 2. *Lord Denning's suggested classification* (see 61 LQR 379): (*a*) *Provisional*, i.e., presumptions of fact; (*b*) *Conclusive*, i.e., irrebuttable presumptions of law; (*c*) *Compelling*, i.e., conclusions which must be drawn when basic facts are proved "unless the other side proves the contrary or proves some other fact which the law recognises as sufficient to rebut the presumption" e.g., the presumption of legitimacy (q.v.).

presumptions, conflicting. Two presumptions having application to the same set of facts, thereby creating conflicting results. In such a case they are effectively cancelled out. See *R* v *Willshire* (1881) 6 QBD 366.

presumptions, irrebuttable. Known also as conclusive presumptions. In effect, rules of substantive law (q.v.). Evidence to contradict them cannot be called. Example: the presumption that a child under 10 cannot have a "guilty mind". See, e.g., Civil Evidence Act 1968, s. 13 (defamation); L.P. (Misc. Provs.) A. 1989, s. 1 (5) (conclusive presumption of authorisation to deliver an instrument as a deed).

presumptions, rebuttable. 1. *Of law*, which *must* be observed in the absence of evidence to the contrary, so that the burden of rebuttal is on opposing party. Example: L.P.A. 1925, s. 184, regarding commorientes (q.v.). 2. *Of fact*, which *may* be observed in the absence of evidence to the contrary. Example: omnia praesumuntur rite et solemniter esse acta (q.v.).

presumptions relating to construction of statutes. Presumptions laid down by the courts to assist in construing Acts of Parliament, i.e., legislative intent. They include: legislature does not make mistakes (see *Fisher* v *Bell* [1961] 1 QB 394); legislature does not intend what is unreasonable (see *Re A.B. & Co* [1900] 1 QB 541); words are presumed to be used in their popular sense in statutes (see *Re Hall's Settlement* [1954] 1 WLR 1185); the Crown is unaffected by a statute unless expressly named therein (see *Lord Advocate* v *Dumbarton DC* [1990] 1 All ER 1); presumptions against changes in the common law, against ousting the courts' jurisdiction, against interference with vested rights, against non-compliance with international law. *See* INTERPRETATION OF STATUTES.

presumptive heir. *See* HEIR PRESUMPTIVE.

presumptive title. Title arising only from occupancy (q.v.).

pretence, false. *See* FALSE PRETENCE.

pre-trial review. Procedure whereby in *civil actions* the registrar makes a preliminary consideration of an action to be heard in a county court. He gives all such directions as appear to him "necessary or desirable for securing the just, expeditious and economical disposal of the action" (see County Court Rules 1981, O, 17, r. 1). Evidence may be given by affidavit (q.v.). Failure of the defendant to appear combined with failure to deliver an admission or defence may result in the registrar's entering a judgment for the plaintiff. Comparable arrangements exist in the Crown Court and in some magistrates' courts with a view to simplifying (and therefore shortening) trials. For pre-trial review in *criminal cases*, see rules relating to such a type of hearing before the Central Criminal Court (q.v.): see R.C.C.P. App. 27. See also C.J.A. 1987; SI 1988/1691 (fraud cases).

previous consistent statements in criminal cases, proof of. Certain previous consistent statements in criminal cases may be proved, e.g., where they form part of the *res gestae* (q.v.); are complaints in charges of sexual offences; are made by the accused on arrest; are made at a date which tends to disprove the allegation that the witnesses' testimony had been recently concocted; are part of the identification of the accused by the prosecution witness. See *R* v *Roberts* [1942] 1 All ER 187. *See* EVIDENCE.

previous convictions, evidence of. Generally excluded as irrelevant, save where they form an essential ingredient of the offence, or where relevant to prove the offence itself, or in the course of cross-examination (q.v.) of the opposing witness as to credit, etc. See *Maxwell* v *DPP* [1935] AC 309; *R* v *Britzmann* [1983] 1 WLR 350. In civil proceedings a person's previous conviction may be relevant to prove that he committed the offence for which he was convicted: Civil Evidence Act 1968, s. 11. See Criminal Evidence Act 1898, s. 1 (*f*); Official Secrets Act 1911, s. 1(2); Th.A. 1968, s. 27(3); Rehabilitation of Offenders Act 1974 (relating to spent convictions (q.v.)); P. & C.E.A. 1984, s. 74. See, e.g., *R* v *Robertson* [1987] QB 920. For effect of previous convictions to prove guilty conduct and in sentencing, see *A.-G. of Hong Kong* v *Siu Yuk-shing* [1989] 1 WLR 236.

previous statements, inconsistent. "When a witness is shown to have made previous statements inconsistent with the evidence given by that witness at the trial the jury should not merely be directed that the evidence given at the trial should be regarded as unreliable; they should also be directed that the previous statements whether sworn or unsworn do not constitute evidence upon which they can act": *R* v *Golder, Jones and Porritt* [1960] 3 All ER 457. See also Civil Evidence Act 1968, s. 3(1) (*a*).

price. "In relation to any goods, services, accommodation or facilities, means the aggregate of the sums required to be paid by a consumer for or otherwise in respect of the supply (q.v.) of goods or the provision of services, or accommodation or facilitie": C.P.A. 1987, s. 20(6). See Price Indications Regulations 1991/199. *See* SALE.

price in contract of sale. May be fixed by the contract or left to be fixed in a manner therein agreed, or may be determined by a course of dealing between the parties: S.G.A. 1979, s. 8(1). Where the price is not determined in accordance with the foregoing provision, the buyer must pay a reasonable price: s. 8(2). See *Ingram* v *Little* [1961] 1 QB 31; *Baber* v *Kenwood* [1978] 1 Lloyd's Rep 175.

price, misleading. A misleading price, for the purposes of C.P.A. 1987, is one which indicates or suggests, e.g., that the price is less than in fact it is or that the price covers matters in respect of which an additional charge is in fact made, or that the applicability of the price does not depend on facts or circumstances on which its applicability does in fact depend: s. 21(1). It is an offence for a person, in the course of business to give such misleading indications: s. 20(1). For defences, see ss. 24, 39.

price-sensitive information. Phrase used in relation to insider dealing (q.v.) to refer to specific matters relating or of concern (directly or indirectly) to a company (i.e., information not of a general nature) and which is not generally known to those persons accustomed or likely to deal in the securities in question, but which, if it were known, would be likely materially to alter their market price: Company Securities (Insider Dealing) Act 1985, s. 10.

prima facie. Of first appearance; on the face of it. Based on a first impression. A prima facie case is one in which the evidence in favour of a party is sufficient to call for an answer from his opponent.

prima facie evidence. See EVIDENCE, PRIMA FACIE.

primary evidence. See EVIDENCE, PRIMARY.

primary facts. See FACTS, PRIMARY

Prime Minister. Conventional title of the Head of Her Majesty's Government, appointed by the Crown. Usually the leader of the party with a majority in the House of Commons (q.v.) and, by convention, always sits in the Commons. (By tradition he is also First Lord of the Treasury.) Duties include presiding over the Cabinet (q.v.) exercising general supervision over government departments and speaking for the government in the Commons.

primer seisin. Profits of lands which had to be paid to the King by the heir of a tenant who died, when the heir reached full age. See SEISIN.

primogeniture. System of inheritance whereby preference was given to the eldest son and his issue. Abolished under A.E.A. 1925, Part IV.

principal. 1. Sum of money invested. 2. One on whose behalf an agent (q.v.) works. 3. A principal in the *first degree* is the actual perpetrator of an offence; a principal in the *second degree* is one who, by being present, aids and abets.

principal clerks (in Chancery chambers). Officials who assist masters (q.v.), e.g., in the preparation of orders on an *ex parte* application relating to matters such as garnishee orders nisi. Without reference to a master they may sign certificates of attendance in chambers for the purpose of the taxation of costs (q.v.).

principal, undisclosed. Where an agent (q.v.) conceals the fact that he is merely a representative, and has authority at the time of the contract to act on behalf of another, either the agent or principal when discovered can be sued and can sue the other party to the contract. See *The Astyanax* [1985] 2 Lloyd's Rep 109.

priorities, rules concerning mortgages. The equitable rule by the application of which the rank of competing interests, e.g., successive mortgages (q.v.) of an equitable interest in property, will be determined. The fundamental rule is *qui prior est tempore potior est jure* (q.v.), i.e., priority is determined by the order of the creation of interests. The rule is qualified by the doctrine of purchaser without notice; fraud; negligence; estoppel (q.v.); registration of rights; overreaching of interests. See L.P.A. 1925, s. 97; L.R.A. 1925, s. 29 (mortgages of legal interests in registered land); *Dearle* v *Hall* (1828) 3 Russ 1; *Re Samuel Allen Ltd* [1907] 1 Ch 575; *Cheah Theam Swee* v *Equiticorp Finance* [1991] 4 All ER 989 (altering priority without mortgagor's consent).

priority notice. A person who is entitled to apply for registration as the first proprietor of land may reserve priority for that application by a priority notice. See L.R.A. 1925, s. 144; L.C.A. 1972, s. 11. See LAND REGISTRATION.

priority of debts of insolvent estate. The Lord Chancellor has power to direct that relevant provisions of Ins. A. 1986 should apply in relation to the administration of the estates of deceased persons which prove to be insolvent (see Ins. A. 1986, s. 421).

prison. Place of detention for those committed to custody under the law. Includes young offender institution or remand centre: C.J.A. 1991, s. 92(1). Prison policy is administered by the Prison Department of the Home Office through a prison service headed by a

Director-General. See Prison Act 1952; Prison Rules 1964; Prison Security Act 1992, s. 1(6). Reports on administration are made by boards of visitors (including magistrates) appointed by the Home Secretary.

prisoner. A person held in custody in a prison or kept in police detention after being charged with an offence, or who has been committed to detention in a police station under M.C.A. 1980, s. 128(7), or is in the custody of the court: C.J.A. 1991, s. 192(1). "Under English law, a convicted prisoner, in spite of his imprisonment retains all civil rights which are not taken away expressly or by implication": *per* Lord Wilberforce in *Raymond* v *Honey* [1983] AC 1. See *R* v *Secretary of State for Home Department, ex p Wynne* (1991) The Times, 27 Dec. (rights of prisoner to present his own case in court.

prisoners, early release of. *See* PAROLE.

prisoners, segregation of. "Where it appears desirable for the maintenance of good order or discipline or in his own interests, that a prisoner should not associate with other prisoners, either generally or for particular purposes, the prison governor may arrange for the prisoner's removal from association accordingly": Prison Rules 1964, r. 43(1). Removal of a prisoner under the rule is not to be used as a punishment: *Williams* v *Home Office (No. 2)* [1981] 1 All ER 121. See *H.* v *Secretary of State for Home Department* (1992) The Times, 7 May.

prison mutiny. An offence under Prison Security Act 1992, s. 1, committed where two or more prisoners, while on the premises of any prison, engage in conduct (including acts and omissions) which is intended to further a common purpose of overthrowing lawful authority in that prison. Where there is such a mutiny, a prisoner who has or who is given a reasonable opportunity of submitting to lawful authority fails, without reasonable excuse, to do so, shall be regarded as taking part in the mutiny: s. 1(4).

prison rules. See Prison Act 1952, s. 47; Prison Rules 1964. "The prison rules are regulatory in character, they provide a framework within which the prison regime operates, but they are not intended to protect prisoners

against loss, injury and damage, nor to give them a right of action in respect thereof": *per* Lord Jauncey in *Weldon* v *Home Office* [1991] 3 WLR 340. See *Hague* v *Deputy Governor of Parkhurst* [1991] 3 ELR 340.

privacy. Not defined by statute; seems to refer to an individual's personal seclusion. See the Calcutt Committee Report 1990 – right of the individual to be protected against intrusion into his personal life or affairs, or those of his family, by direct physical means or by publication of information. An unqualified right of personal privacy seems unknown in English law. "The eye cannot by the laws of England be guilty of a trespass": *per* Lord Camden in *Entick* v *Carrington* (1765) 19 St Tr 1029. See *Kaye* v *Robertson* 1991 FSR 62 (" . . . failure of both common law and statute to protect the personal privacy of indivduals": *per* Bingham LJ).

private Act of Parliament. An Act concerning private persons, or a local Act passed on behalf of a public company or municipal corporation. It must not impinge on an issue of public policy or be of general application.

private Bill. *See* BILL.

private company. A company which is not a public company: Cos.A. 1985, s. 1. It may be limited by shares or guarantee, or may be unlimited. It may be formed by one member: s. 1, SI 1992/1699. It may have an unlimited number of members. It may not offer its shares or debentures directly to the public: s. 81. There is no minimum nominal, issued or paid-up capital requirements, and it can convert to an unlimited company: s. 49.

private defence. Where a person commits a tort (q.v.) in defence of himself or his property, he is not necessarily liable if the act has been, in the circumstances, of a reasonable nature. See *Cockcroft* v *Smith* (1705) 2 Salk 642; *Barnard* v *Evans.* [1925] 1 KB 794.

private international law. That part of English law which deals with cases involving a foreign element and seeks to determine, e.g., whether English courts have jurisdiction over a case; if so, what system of law must be applied; circumstances in which English courts will recognise and enforce judgments of foreign courts. Known also as "conflict of laws".

private law. Those areas of the law concerned primarily with duties and rights of individuals with which the state is not immediately and directly concerned, e.g., the law of contract. For assertion of private law rights, see *Wandsworth LBC* v *Winder* [1985] AC 461. *See* PUBLIC LAW.

privately fostered children. Children under 16, cared for and provided with accommodation by, someone other than their parents or relatives: Ch.A. 1989, s. 66. Their welfare is a concern of the local authority: s. 67. For persons disqualified, see s. 68. For inspection of homes, see s.80. See SI 1991/910.

private members' Bills. Bills of a public nature introduced, not by the government, but by private members of either House of Parliament. See, e.g., Abortion Act 1967, sponsored by David Steel M.P.

private nuisance. *See* NUISANCE.

private persons' powers of arrest. *See* ARREST, POWERS OF PRIVATE PERSONS TO.

private prosecution. *See* PROSECUTION, PRIVATE.

privatisation. Policy of transferring enterprises from the state to the private sector. It generally involves a transfer of assets and undertakings of state or public corporations to public limited companies, with shares privately-owned. See, e.g., Public Utility Transfers and Water Charges Act 1988; Ports Act 1991.

privilege. A special right or immunity conferred on some person or body, e.g., members of Parliament; or a rule of evidence justifying a witness's refusal to produce a document or to answer a question. Some matters are protected from disclosure on the ground of privilege, e.g., affairs of state, professional confidences. *See* PARLIAMENTARY PRIVILEGE.

privilege, absolute. Protection attaching to certain statements, which would otherwise be defamatory, so that no action lies even though the statements might have been false and malicious. Example: statements made in the course of judicial proceedings or in Parliament.

privilege, claim of. Claim entitling a person to refuse, e.g., the production

of documents for inspection. See O. 24, r. 13(2). It may apply to communications between solicitors and clients; opinions of counsel; incriminating documents; state papers. *See* DISCOVERY AND INSPECTION OF DOCUMENTS.

privileged communication. A communication which, although containing defamatory material, is protected, or one which is generally protected from disclosure in evidence (q.v.). See, e.g., *D.* v *NSPCC* [1978] AC 171.

privileged nature of judicial statements. Judges may not be compelled to give evidence relating to the cases they have tried: *Buccleuch* v *Metropolitan Board of Works* (1872) LR 5 HL 418. See also Contempt of Court Act 1981, s. 8, protecting the confidentiality of a jury's deliberations.

privileged will. The right of a soldier being in actual military service, or a mariner or seaman being at sea to make a valid will without any formal requirements. The intention to make a will must be shown. See W.A. 1837, s. 11; Wills (Soldiers and Sailors) Act, 1918, s. 3(1); F.L.R.A. 1969, s. 3(1)(*b*); *Re Wingham* [1949] P 187; *Re Rapley* [1983] 1 WLR 1069. *See* WILL.

privilege, legal professional. Right whereby communications between the client and legal adviser may not generally be given in evidence without the client's consent if made in relation to contemplated or pending litigation, or made to enable the adviser to give, or the client to receive, legal advice. Such communications are defined under P. & C.E.A. 1984, s. 19(6) as "communications between a professional legal adviser and his client or any person representing his client made in connection with the giving of legal advice to the client . . . or in contemplation of legal proceedings." See *Alfred Crompton Amusement Machines.* v *Customs and Excise Commissioners* [1974] AC 405; *Ventouris* v *Mountain* [1991] 1 WLR 607.

privilege of witness. 1. Rule that a witness is not bound to answer certain types of question in legal proceedings. Examples: incriminating questions; questions relating to matters, publication of which might injure the state; questions relating to communications between counsel, solicitor and client on professional matters. 2. A witness is privileged (so that no action can be brought for defamation) to the extent of what he says during examination. "What he says before he enters or after he has left the witness box is not privileged": *Seaman* v *Netherclift* (1876) 2 CPD 56.

privilege, parliamentary. *See* PARLIAMENTARY PRIVILEGE.

privilege, public. Phrase used in a statement of principle excluding relevant evidence where disclosure could prejudice the public interest. Known also as "public interest immunity". See *Conway* v *Rimmer* [1968] AC 910; *Buttes Gas Co* v *Hammer* (*No. 3*) [1981] QB 223.

privilege, qualified. Protection afforded to the maker of a statement which may be defamatory, if made honestly, i.e., without malice. Includes: fair and accurate reports of parliamentary and judicial proceedings and reports of public meetings; statements made in pursuance of a legal, moral or social duty; statements made to procure redress of a public grievance. See Defamation Act 1952.

privity. Relationships arising from participation in or knowledge of some transaction or event. See *The Eurysthenes* [1976] 3 All ER 243.

privity of contract. Relationship subsisting between parties to a contract. "In the law of England certain principles are fundamental. One is that only a person who is a party to a contract may sue on it": *Dunlop Pneumatic Tyre Co Ltd* v *Selfridge Co Ltd* [1915] AC 47. See L.P.A. 1925, s. 56(1); *Beswick* v *Beswick* [1968] AC 58; *MacJordan Construction Ltd* v *Brookmount Ltd* (1991) The Times, 29 Oct. *See* CONTRACT.

privity of estate. Relationship of tenure existing between persons whose estates constitute one estate in law, i.e., all those who stand in position of landlord and tenant to one another, such as lessor and lessee, tenant and subtenant. See *Spencer's Case* (1583) 5 Co Rep 16a.

privy. Relating to participation in some act, or being in privity (q.v.) with another.

Privy Council. Until the eighteenth century, the chief source of executive power in the state. Now plays a much-diminished role, advising the Sovereign on Orders in Council (q.v.), issue of Royal proclamations, etc. Headed by the Lord President of the Council, it consists of Cabinet ministers, Archbishops, Lord Chief Justice, Master of the Rolls, Speaker of the Commons, etc. The whole Council (390 members in all) is called together on the death of the Sovereign. The Judicial Committee of the Privy Council (q.v.) has appellate jurisdiction.

prize competition. *See* COMPETITION FOR PRIZES.

prize courts. Courts specially set up to decide matters relating to the capture of ships in time of war. Appeal is to the Judicial Committee of the Privy Council (q.v.). See Naval Prize Acts 1864–1916; S.C.A. 1981, s. 16(2).

probate. Document issued under the seal of the court as official evidence of the authority of an executor (q.v.). If the validity of a will (q.v.) is contested, probate is granted only after the court has pronounced in favour (grant "in solemn form"). Probate "in common form" is granted where litigation is unnecessary. Documents required in order to obtain probate include: Inland Revenue account; executor's oath; any renunciations by executors; engrossments; affidavit of due execution.

probate action. "An action for the grant of probate of a will, or letters of administration of the estate, of a deceased person, or for the revocation of such a grant, or for a decree pronouncing for or against the validity of an alleged will, not being an action which is non-contentious or common form probate business": O. 76, r. 1(2).

probate, ancillary. Subsidiary grant of probate relating to a grant obtained outside the UK, giving powers of administration to a foreign executor over property in the UK.

Probate, Court of. *See* COURT OF PROBATE.

Probate, Divorce and Admiralty Division. Former division of the High Court (q.v.), renamed the Family Division by the A.J.A. 1970. Admiralty jurisdiction was assigned to the QBD, to be exercised by the Admiralty Court. Probate (other than non-contentious, common form probate business) was assigned to the Chancery Division. See S.C.A. 1981, s. 5(1)(c).

probate, resealed. Certificate of probate sealed for a second time, e.g., in order to give an executor (q.v.) powers of administration outside the UK.

probate rules. Rules of court made by the President of Family Division, concerned with regulating and prescribing the practice and procedure of the High Court with respect to non-contentious or common form probate business: S.C.A. 1981, s. 127.

probation. Process designed to assist in the rehabilitation of offenders aged 16 or over who are willing to be bound by a probation order requiring them to remain under the supervision of probation officers for 6 months–3 years and to be of good behaviour; or to assist in the protection of the public from harm from them, or preventing the commission by them of other offences. Failure to comply with the order may result in a sentence for the original offence. See the P.C.C.A. 1973, ss. 2–6, as amended by C.J.A. 1991, s. 8. For right of appeal from order see *R* v *Tucker* [1974] 1 WLR 615. See also C.L.A. 1977, s. 57(1), Sch. 9; C.J.A. 1982, s. 66; C.J.A. 1991, s. 11 (order combining probation and community service (q.v.)); *R* v *Heather* (1979) 1 Cr App R (S.) 189.

probation centres. Premises, approved by the Secretary of State, at which non-residential facilities are provided for use in connection with the rehabilitation of offenders and are suitable for persons subject to probation orders: see C.J.A. 1991, Sch. 1.

probationer. A person under supervision by virtue of a probation order.

probation officer. One appointed to supervise probationers and others placed under their supervision "and to advise, assist and befriend them": P.C.C.A. 1973, Sch. 3, Part I. For "inspectors of probation", see C.J.A. 1991, s. 73.

probative facts. *See* FACTS, INVESTITIVE.

procedendo. Prerogative writ issued when the judge of an inferior court (q.v.) delayed by refusing to give judgment.

procedure. Formal manner of conducting judicial proceedings. *See* RULES OF THE SUPREME COURT.

proceedings, interlocutory. *See* INTER-LOCUTORY PROCEEDINGS.

proceedings, legal. The systematic conducting of business before a court. See *Savings and Investment Bank Ltd* v *Gasco Investments (No. 2)* [1988] 1 All ER 975. "Any criminal or civil proceedings or inquiry in which evidence is or may be given": Bankers' Books Evidence Act 1879, s. 10.

proceedings, order of criminal. Generally: arraignment; empanelling and swearing of jury; opening speech by prosecution; prosecution case; defence submissions; defence opening speech; defence case; closing speeches; summing-up; verdict; plea in mitigation; sentencing.

proceedings, stay of. *See* STAY OF PRO-CEEDINGS.

proceeds. Money or other material returns derived from a transaction or other event. See Th.A. 1968, s. 5(4); *R* v *Davis* (1989) 88 Cr App R 347.

process. 1. Summons and warrant compelling the appearance of the defendant (q.v.). Before the issue of process, a magistrate (q.v.) must be satisfied that he has appropriate jurisdiction and that there is sufficient evidence against the person named to justify the issue. See M.C.A. 1980, s. 1; S.C.A. 1981, s. 80; Criminal Justice (International Co-operation) Act 1990, s. 1 (service of overseas process in UK). For the mode of commencing civil proceedings in the High Court see O. 5. 2. Mode of operation. Signifies "substantial uniformity or system of treatment": *Vibroplant* v *Holland* [1982] 1 All ER 792; See *Nurse* v *Morganite Crucible* [1989] 2 WLR 82.

process, abuse of. *See* ABUSE OF PROCESS.

procession. "A body of persons moving along a route": *Flockart* v *Robinson* [1950] 2 KB 498. *See* PUBLIC PROCESSION.

proclamation, royal. Formal public announcement by the Crown. No law can be made or unmade in this manner unless a proclamation is issued by the authority of an Act of Parliament (q.v.). See *Case of Proclamations* (1611) 12 Co Rep 74; *Re Grazebrook* (1865) 4 De G J & S 662.

procreation, words of. Words which limit persons mentioned in a grant to the issue of a particular individual, e.g., "To Z and the heirs of his body".

procurement. It is an offence for a person to procure a woman by threats, intimidation, false pretences or false representations to have unlawful sexual intercourse in any part of the world. S.O.A. 1956, s. 2.

procuring an offence. Bringing about, instigating, a crime, i.e., "setting out to see that it happens and taking the appropriate steps to produce that happening." It involves producing an offence "by some endeavour": *A.-G.'s Reference (No. 1 of 1975)* [1975] QB 773. The common law offence of procuring materials for crime was abolished under the Criminal Attempts Act 1981, s. 6(1). *See* AID OR ABET.

procuring breach of contract. *See* INDUCEMENT.

procuring execution of a valuable security. It is an offence when a person dishonestly, with a view to gain for himself or another or with intent to cause loss to another, by any deception procures the execution of a valuable security: Th.A. 1968, s. 20(2). For "execution", see *R* v *Kassim* [1991] 3 WLR 254. For "valuable security", see *R* v *Bolton* [1992] Crim LR 57.

producer. Means, in relation to a product, the manufacturer, the person who won or abstracted it, or the person who carried out the processes giving it its essential characteristics: see C.P.A. 1987, s. 1(2).

production appointment. Hearing, in relation to application for ancillary relief (q.v.), based on a party's application for a person to attend and produce documents which appear to the court "to be necessary for disposing fairly of the application for ancillary relief or for saving costs": Family Proceedings Rules 1991, r. 2. 62(7).

production of documents. Procedure ordered by court (see O. 24) by which documents and books must be produced for inspection. *See* DISCOVERY AND INSPECTION OF DOCUMENTS.

product liability. Generally, the liability of persons for damage caused by defective products. See: the "product liability directive" of EEC (85/374/EEC); C.P.A. 1987, Part I. *See* DEFECT IN A PRODUCT.

products, defective, liability for. Where damage is caused wholly or partly by a defect in a product, the following are liable: the producer of the product; any person who, by using a distinguishing mark or his own name on the product, has held himself out to be the producer (q.v.); any person who, in the course of business, has imported the product into a member state of EEC (q.v.) from outside EEC: C.P.A. 1987, s. 2(1), (2). "Damage" means death or personal injury or any loss or damage to property: s. 5(1). For defences, see s. 4. *See* DEFECT IN A PRODUCT.

profession. "A 'profession' in the present use of language involves the idea of an occupation requiring purely intellectual skill, or if any manual skill, as in painting and sculpture, or surgery, skill controlled by the intellectual skill of the operator": *per* Scrutton LJ in *IRC* v *Maxse* [1919] 1 KB 647. A "professional body" means a body which regulates the practice of a profession: F.S.A. 1986, s. 16(1).

professional misconduct. Behaviour considered by the governing body of a profession to be unworthy of a member of that profession. May lead to removal from a professional register. See, e.g., Medical Act 1983, Part V; Dentists Act 1984, s. 27; C.L.S.A. 1990, Sch. 10; *Doughty* v *General Dental Council* [1987] 3 WLR 769. *See* INFAMOUS CONDUCT; STRIKING OFF.

profit and loss account. Yearly account, which must be compiled up to a date not more than nine months before the date of a company's meeting, in accordance with the requirements of the Cos.A. 1985, Sch. 4, Part I. It must give a true and fair view of the company's profit and loss for the year: 1985 Act, s. 226(2). See I.C.T.A. 1988, chap. III. *See* COMPANY.

profits à prendre. Rights to enter another's land and take something off it (e.g., rights of common). May be created, e.g., by Act of Parliament or grant, and extinguished by statute, unity of seisin, release or alteration of dominant tenement (qq.v.). Cannot be claimed by custom (q.v.). See *White* v *Taylor* [1969] 1 Ch 160; *Lady Dunsany* v *Bedworth* (1979) 38 P & CR 546. *See* COMMON, RIGHT OF.

profits available for distribution. Under Cos.A. 1985, s. 263, a company may make a distribution only of profits available for that purpose, i.e., from accumulated realised profits less accumulated realised losses. A distribution must be justified by the accounts. A public company may make a distribution only if, at the time, its net assets are not less than the aggregate of called-up share capital plus non-distributable reserves, and if the distribution does not reduce those assets to less than that aggregate: s. 264(1). See also Cos.A. 1989, s. 4(1), Sch. 4, para. 91. *See* RESERVES, UNDISTRIBUTABLE.

profits, company's. "Profit for the year is regarded as any gains arising during the year which may be distributed while maintaining the amount of the shareholders' interest in the company at the beginning of the year, which is regarded as the company's capital": *Inflation Accounting 1975* (Cmnd 6225, para. 105). As to "where profits arise", see *CIR* v *Hang Seng Bank Ltd* [1990] 3 WLR 1120.

profits, with. *See* WITH PROFITS.

prohibited article. Under P. & C.E.A. 1984, s. 1(7), an offensive weapon (q.v.) which may be seized by the police if found in the course of a search. See Firearms Act 1968, s. 5(1)(b); *Brown* v *DPP* (1992) The Times, 27 Mar.

prohibited degrees of relationship. *See* RELATIONSHIPS, PROHIBITED DEGREES OF.

prohibited steps order. An order under Ch.A. 1989, Part II, that no step which could be taken by a parent in meeting his parental responsibility for a child, and which is of a kind specified in the order, should be taken by any person without the consent of the court: 1989 Act, s. 8(1).

prohibition. An order of the High Court (q.v.) preventing or prohibiting a body from acting, which will lie against an inferior tribunal or body in relation to decisions affecting an individual's rights. Issued, e.g., to prohibit an imposition of sentence on the accused if there has been no proper trial. See *Re Godden* [1971] 2 QB 662. For applications for an order see O. 53. See also S.C.A. 1981, s. 29.

prohibition notice. Notice served, e.g., by an inspector under H.S.W.A. 1974, s. 22. stating that the inspector is of the opinion that activities involve or will involve a risk of serious personal injury and directing that the activities

shall cease unless the matters specified are remedied. See also C.P.A. 1987, s. 13, Sch. 2; En.P.A. 1990, s. 14.

prohibitory injunction. *See* INJUNCTION.

prolixity. Term applied to pleadings (q.v.) which are superfluous or of unnecessary length. The offending party may be liable for the costs arising.

promise. An undertaking relating to some event. Of no legal effect generally unless in the form of a contract (q.v.) or covenant (q.v.). A promise is made by a *promisor* to a *promisee*.

promissory estoppel. *See* ESTOPPEL.

promissory note. "An unconditional promise in writing made by one person to another, signed by the maker, engaging to pay on demand or at a fixed or determinable future time, a sum certain in money to or to the order of a specified person, or to bearer": B.Ex.A. 1882, s. 83. The note is ineffective until delivered to the payee. See *Claydon* v *Bradley* [1987] 1 WLR 521; *Kwok* v *Commissioner of Estate Duty* [1988] 1 WLR 1035.

promoter. 1. One who begins the procedure for the passing of a local, personal, private Bill (q.v.). 2. "One who undertakes to form a company with reference to a given project, and to set it going, and who takes the necessary steps to accomplish that purpose": *Twycross* v *Grant* (1877) 36 LT 812. He is neither trustee (q.v.) nor agent (q.v.) for the company, but stands in a fiduciary relationship to it. Whether a person is or is not a promoter is a question of fact in every case: *Jubilee Cotton Mills* v *Lewis* [1924] AC 958. See Cos.A. 1985, s. 67(3) (now repealed, and term replaced by "issuer" (see F.S.A. 1986, ss. 142(7), 158(3)) and "person responsible for prospectus" (see ss. 152, 168)).

proof. Method by which the existence or non-existence of a fact is established to the satisfaction of the court. Means of proof include: evidence; presumptions; judicial notice (qq.v.). "Evidence becomes proof when the jury accept it as being sufficient for proof": Williams.

proof beyond reasonable doubt. "Proof beyond reasonable doubt does not mean proof beyond the shadow of a doubt . . . If the evidence is so strong against a man as to leave only a remote possibility in his favour, which can be dismissed with the sentence 'of course it is possible but not in the least probable' the case is proved beyond reasonable doubt, but nothing short of that will suffice": *Miller* v *Minister of Pensions* [1947] 2 All ER 372.

proof, burden of. *See* BURDEN OF PROOF.

proof, standards of. *See* STANDARDS OF PROOF.

proper law of a contract. Phrase used in private international law (q.v.) to denote the system of law which governs a contract. Defined by Dicey as "the law, or laws, by which the parties intended, or may be fairly presumed to have intended, the contract to be governed". "It is the law which the parties intended to apply. Their intention will be ascertained by the intention expressed in the contract, if any, which will be conclusive": *R* v *International Trustee* [1937] 2 All ER 164. *See* CONTRACT.

property. 1. That which can be owned. 2. Right to goods and land, etc. See S.G.A. 1979, s. 61. Must be "definable, identifiable by third parties, capable in its nature of assumption by third parties, and have some degree of permanence or stability": *National Provincial Bank* v *Ainsworth* [1965] AC 1175. "A foundation of expectation of deriving certain advantages from the thing said to be possessed": Bentham. 3. An aggregate of rights having money value. 4. "Includes money and all other property, real or personal, including things in action and other intangible property": Th.A. 1968, s. 4(1). Classified as *real property* (realty); *personal property* (personalty) (qq.v.). For "domestic property", see Local Government Finance Act 1988, s. 66. For "property development", see I.C.T.A. 1988, s. 298(5). *See* OWNERSHIP.

property adjustment order. Order made under the Mat.C.A. 1973, s. 21, relating to the transfer or settlement, of property or variation of settlement, on or after the grant of a decree of divorce (q.v.), nullity or judicial separation (q.v.). See *Potter* v *Potter* [1990] 2 FLR 27.

property in goods. May be: (1) *General*, i.e., title or ownership. ("Property means the general property in goods, and not merely a special property":

S.G.A. 1979, s. 62(1)); (2) *Special*, e.g., that which arises under a bailment (q.v.).

property, misdescription of. It is an offence to make false or misleading statements about any matter relating to land which is specified by an order made by the Secretary of State in the course of an estate agency business or a property development business: Property Misdescriptions Act 1991, s. 1. For defence of due diligence, see s.2.

property register. *See* REGISTER AT LAND REGISTRY.

property, right of. "That sole or despotic dominion which one man claims and exercises over the external things of the world, in total exclusion of the right of any other individual in the universe": Blackstone, *Commentaries*.

property, right to security of. "The great end for which men entered into society was to secure their property. That right is preserved sacred and is incommunicable in all instances where it has not been taken away or abridged by some public law for the good of the whole . . . No man can set his foot upon my ground without my licence but he is liable to an action: *per* Lord Camden in *Entick* v *Carrington* (1765) 19 St Tr 1029. *See* TRESPASS.

proponent. 1. The party who must raise an issue in the first instance (e.g.) the prosecutor, the plaintiff). 2. The party who bears the evidential burden of proof (q.v.) and, usually also, the legal burden.

proportionality. *See* LEGISLATION, PROPORTIONALITY OF.

propositus. 1. The person immediately concerned. 2. The person from whom descent is traced. 3. A testator (q.v.).

proprietary estoppel. *See* ESTOPPEL.

proprietary rights. Relating to private rights of ownership.

proprietor. One who has title to property.

proprietorship register. *See* REGISTER AT LAND REGISTRY.

propter defectum sanguinis. *See* ESCHEAT.

pro rata. Proportionately.

prorogation. The ending of a session of Parliament (q.v.) by exercise of the royal prerogative.

proscribed organisation. An organisation, association or combination of persons condemned or forbidden because its activities are harmful. See, Prevention of Terrorism (Temporary Provisions) Act 1989; Northern Ireland (Emergency Provisions) Act 1991, ss. 28, 29, Sch. 2 (enumerating nine proscribed organisations).

prosecution. The instituting of criminal proceedings in the courts.

prosecution, criteria for instituting proceedings. See *Code for Crown Prosecutors* issued under Prosecution of Offences Act 1985, s. 10. The Crown Prosecutor must be satisfied, e.g., that there is admissible, substantial and reliable evidence and a realistic prospect of conviction. He will consider also, likely penalty, offender's age, mental state, stress, attitude, etc.

prosecution, private. "[It] remains a valuable constitutional safeguard against inertia or partiality on the part of authority": *per* Lord Wilberforce in *Gouriet* v *UPW* [1978] AC 435. Legal aid is not available to a private prosecutor, but costs may be awarded out of central funds (see Prosecution of Offences Act 1985, s. 17) provided the case relates to an indictable offence. (For summary cases see s. 19.) See O.P.A. 1861, s. 42; Prosecution of Offences Act 1985, s. 6; *R* v *Lemon* [1979] AC 617 (which began as a private prosecution); *R.* v *Ealing Justices, ex p Dixon* [1989] 2 All ER 1050.

prosecutor. One who institutes criminal proceedings, usually in the name of the Crown. *See* DIRECTOR OF PUBLIC PROSECUTIONS.

prosecutor, non-appearance of. If the accused appears for the trial of an information (q.v.) and the prosecutor fails to appear, the court may dismiss the information or, if evidence has been received on a previous occasion, proceed in the absence of the prosecutor: M.C.A. 1980, s. 15. If both parties fail to appear, the court may dismiss the information or proceed in their absence: s. 16. *See* ACCUSED, NON-APPEARANCE OF.

prospectus. Any document containing information about securities: F.S.A. 1986, s. 159(1)(a).

prospectus, untrue statements in. If a person has acquired securities to which a prospectus relates and there is any untrue or misleading statement in the prospectus (or omission from it) which resulted in a loss to that person, the person responsible for the prospectus is liable to compensate for the loss: F.S.A. 1986, s. 166. For exemptions from liability see s. 167; for the definition of "person responsible" see s. 168. The general duty of disclosure in the prospectus is required by s. 163.

prostitution. "Prostitution is proved if it be shown that a woman offers her body for purposes amounting to common lewdness for payment in return": *R* v *Webb* [1964] 1 QB 357. It is not limited to cases involving sexual intercourse. It is not, in itself, an offence, but it is an offence to cause others to become prostitutes or to live on the earnings of prostitution: S.O.A. 1956. *R* v *Bell* [1978] Crim LR 233; *IRC* v *Aken* [1990] 1 WLR 1374 (taxation within Schedule D of earnings from prostitution); *R* v *Howard* (1992) 94 Cr App R 89.

prostitution, common. It is an offence to procure a woman for the purpose of common prostitution: S.O.A. 1956, s. 22(1). "Common" involves procuring a woman to act as a prostitute on more than one occasion: *R* v *Morris-Lowe* [1985] 1 WLR 29.

protected coin. A coin customarily used as money in any country or specified in an order made by the Treasury under Forgery and Counterfeiting Act 1981. See s. 27(1)(b). *See* COUNTERFEITING.

protected furnished tenancy. A protected tenancy (q.v.) under which the dwelling-house concerned is *bona fide* let at a rent which includes payments in respect of furniture, and in respect of which the amount of rent which is fairly attributable to the use of furniture, having regard to the value of that use to the tenant, forms a substantial part of the whole rent: Rent Act 1977, s. 152(1).

protected goods. Goods which, under C.C.A. 1974, s. 90, are the subject of a regulated hire purchase or credit sale agreement (qq.v.) and in relation to which the debtor has not terminated the agreement and has paid one-third or more of the total price in the goods. They cannot be recovered except by court order, or voluntary surrender by the debtor.

protected occupier. Phrase used in, e.g., Rent (Agriculture) Act 1976 referring to one whose occupation of a dwelling is protected by statute. *See* AGRICULTURAL OCCUPANCIES, ASSURED.

protected person. Head of State, member of body performing functions of Head of State, Head of Government or Minister of Foreign Affairs who is outside the territory of the state in which he holds office; persons who represent a state or international organisation of an inter-governmental character; person who is a member of the family of those mentioned above: Internationally Protected Persons Act 1978, s. 1(5). For offences relating to attacks and threats of attacks on them, see s. 1(1)–(4).

protected person, British. *See* BRITISH PROTECTED PERSON.

protected shorthold tenancy. Protected tenancy (q.v.) granted after the coming into force of the H.A. 1980, s. 52, for a term certain of 1–5 years; and which could not be terminated by the landlord before the expiry of the term (except in pursuance of provisions for re-entry, forfeiture for non-payment of rent, or breach of other obligation). Replaced under H.A. 1988, Part I, by assured shorthold tenancy (q.v.).

protected states. Member states of the Commonwealth (q.v.) over whose external affairs the UK exerts full control, but who have a considerable measure of control over internal affairs.

protected tenancy. A contractual tenancy concerning a dwelling-house let as a separate dwelling, formerly protected by the Rent Act 1977. For exclusions, see e.g., ss. 5–12. Replaced under H.A. 1988 by the "assured tenancy" (q.v.). No tenancy granted after Jan. 1989 can be "protected" unless entered into in pursuance of a pre-commencement contract: see 1988 Act, s. 34(1). See *Killick* v *Roberts* [1991] 4 All ER 289.

protection and indemnity associations. Known also as "P & I Clubs". Mutual insurance arrangement common in marine insurance, whereby shipowners contribute to the association on the basis of their tonnage, and the association agrees to meet the cost of certain liabilities not usually covered by marine hull insurance policies, e.g., quarantine expenses. See Third Parties (Rights Against Insurers) Act 1930; *Firma-C Trade SA* v *Newcastle P & I Association* [1990] 3 WLR 78.

Protection, Court of. *See* COURT OF PROTECTION.

protection order. 1. Court order, under C.C.A. 1974, s. 131, made on the application of creditor or owner under a regulated agreement (q.v.) to protect property from damage or depreciation pending the determination of proceedings under the Act. 2. Orders made under D.P.A. 1978, ss. 16–18, and injunctions under Domestic Violence and Matrimonial Proceedings Act 1976, s. 1, ordering respondent not to use or threaten to use violence against the applicant or a child of the family.

protective award. Award by an industrial tribunal (q.v.) for remuneration to a dismissed employee where an employer has failed to take appropriate steps relating to consultation with union representatives in the event of redundancy: see T.U.L.R.(C.)A. 1992, s. 188.

protective trust. A trust for life, or any lesser period, determinable on the occurrence of certain events, e.g., the beneficiary's bankruptcy, upon which the trust income will be applied at the absolute discretion of trustees for the support of the beneficiary and his family. Example: "Life interest to X until he shall become bankrupt." Can be created expressly or by implication. See Tr.A. 1925, s. 33; F.L.R.A. 1969, s. 15(3). *See* TRUST.

protectorates, British. *See* BRITISH PROTECTORATES.

Protectorate, the. Era (1653–8) during which Cromwell was Lord Protector of the Commonwealth of England, Scotland and Ireland. *See* COMMONWEALTH.

protector of settlement. One who could prevent a tenant in tail (q.v.) entitled only in remainder from disentailing. Today a tenant in tail in remainder can bar the entail (q.v.) by executing disentailing assurance with the protector's consent. Disentailment without the protector's consent will create a base fee (q.v.). See *Re Darnley's WT* [1970] 1 WLR 405. *See* SETTLEMENT.

protest. 1. Document under seal made by a notary (q.v.) attesting the dishonour of a bill of exchange (q.v.). Accepted as proof that bill has been dishonoured. 2. Payment under protest is made where the payer will not agree that money is due from him.

protest, right to. "Everyone has the right publicly to protest against anything which displeases him and publicly to proclaim his views, whatever they might be. It does not matter whether there is any reasonable basis for his protest or whether his views are sensible or silly": *per* Salmon LJ in *Morris v Crown Office* [1970] 1 All ER 1079.

protocol. 1. An original draft or preliminary memorandum. 2. Minutes of a meeting setting out matters of agreement. 3. Code of procedure. 4. An agreement between states which is less formal than a treaty or convention.

provident benefits. Includes any payment, expressly authorised by union rules, and made to a member during sickness, incapacity from personal injury or while unemployed, or by way of superannuation: Employment Act 1982, s. 17(3).

Provincial Courts. Ecclesiastical courts of the Archbishops of Canterbury and York, e.g., the Court of Arches.

proving a debt. Establishing a debt due from the estate of a bankrupt (q.v.). See S.I. 1986/1925, Part 4, Chap. 9, as amended.

proving a will. Obtaining probate (q.v.) of a will.

provisional bid. *See* BID.

provisional orders. Orders which normally do not take effect until confirmed by Parliament (q.v.), issued by government departments relating, e.g., to schemes of local authorities.

provision, financial. *See* FINANCIAL PROVISION, REASONABLE.

provision, transitional statutory. "Its operation is expected to be temporary, in that it becomes spent when all the past circumstances with which it is designed to deal have been dealt with, while the primary legislation continues to deal indefinitely with the new circumstances which arise after its passage": *per* Lord Keith in *R v Secretary of State for Social Security, ex p Britnell* [1991] 1 WLR 198.

proviso. 1. In a deed (q.v.), a condition upon which its general validity is based. May begin: ". . . provided always that . . .". 2. In a statute, a clause qualifying or exempting from the enactment something which, but for the proviso, would have been included. It is construed with the preceding part of the clause to which it is attached. It never enlarges an enactment unless that is unavoidable: *Ex p Partington* (1844) 6 QB 649.

proviso, applying the. Where the Court of Appeal or House of Lords is satisfied that the point raised in an appeal should be decided in favour of the appellant, they may, nevertheless, dismiss that appeal if they consider that no miscarriage of justice has actually occurred: Criminal Appeal Act 1968, proviso to s. 2(1). Exercise of this power is known as "applying the proviso".

provocation. May be pleaded only on a charge of murder so as to reduce the charge to manslaughter (q.v.). "Provocation is some act or series of acts done by the dead man to the accused, which would cause in any reasonable person and actually causes in the accused, a sudden and temporary loss of self-control, rendering accused so subject to passion as to make him for the moment not master of his mind": *R v Duffy* [1949] 1 All ER 932. "The question whether the provocation was enough to make a reasonable man do as [accused] did shall be left to be determined by the jury; and in determining that question the jury shall take into account everything both done and said according to the effect which, in their opinion, it would have on a reasonable man": Homicide Act 1957, s. 3. A jury should be told that a reasonable man must have the power of self-control to be expected of an ordinary person of the age and sex of the accused, but in other respects must share such of the characteristics of the accused as they think would affect the gravity of the provocation to him: *DPP v Camplin* [1978] AC 705. See *Mancini v DPP* [1942] AC 1; *R. v Johnson* [1989] 1 WLR 740 (self-induced provocation); *R. v Thornton* [1992] 1 All ER 306 (provocation in context of continuing domestic violence); *R. v Rossiter* (1992) NLJ 824.

provocation, question of time and. The issue is "whether there had been time for the blood to cool, and for reason to resume its seat . . . in which case the crime would amount to wilful murder": *per* Tindal CJ in *R* v *Hayward* (1833) 6 C & P 157. "The question is whether such a period of time had elapsed as would be sufficient to enable the mind to recover its balance": *per* Hannen J in *R.* v *Selten* (1871) 11 Cox C C 674.

proximate cause. *See* CAUSA PROXIMA ET NON REMOTA SPECTATUR.

proxy. 1. One appointed with authority or power to act for another in, e.g., attendance at meetings and elections. See Cos.A. 1985, s. 372; Representation of the People Act 1985, ss. 5, 6; Table A, arts. 59–63. 2. Document containing such an appointment.

psychopathic disorder. "A persistent disorder or disability of mind (whether or not including significant impairment of intelligence) which results in abnormally aggressive or seriously irresponsible conduct on the part of the person concerned": M.H.A. 1983, s. 1(2).

Public Accounts Commission. Comprises the Chairman of the House of Commons Committee of Public Accounts, Leader of the Commons, and seven other Members of Parliament (excluding Ministers). They examine the annual estimates of the National Audit Office (q.v.). See National Audit Act 1983, s. 2, Sch. 2.

public Act of Parliament. An Act (q.v.) which affects the public at large. Every Act passed after 1850 is a public Act unless it is expressly provided therein to the contrary: I.A. 1978, s. 3.

public assembly. An assembly of twenty or more persons in a public place which is wholly or partly open to the air: P.O.A. 1986, s. 16. For the imposition of conditions, see Part II.

publication. 1. Term applied in relation to defamation (q.v.) to refer to the communication of words complained of to at least one other person than the person defamed. See *Bata* v *Bata* [1948] WN 366. See also C.J.A. 1987, s. 11(15). 2. Term applied in relation to Obscene Publications Act 1959, whereby a person "publishes" an article who distributes, circulates, sells, lets on hire, gives, or lends it, or who offers it for sale or for letting on hire, or in the case of an article containing or embodying matter to be looked at, or a record, shows, plays or projects it. See 1959 Act, s. 1(3); *A.-G. 's Reference (No. 2 of 1975)* [1975] 2 All ER 753. 3. In relation to the Copyright, Designs and Patents Act 1988, means the issue of copies of a work to the public or making it available by electronic retrieval: s. 175.

public benefit. A valid charitable trust must promote some public benefit, i.e., "the benefit of the community or of an appreciably important class of the community": *Verge* v *Somerville* [1924] AC 496. A trust for the relief of poverty may be charitable, although not for the benefit of the public or even a "section" of it: *Re Coulthurst* [1951] 1 All ER 774. See *IRC* v *Educational Grants Association Ltd* [1967] Ch 123. *See* TRUST.

public Bill. *See* BILL.

public body. "A body . . . which has public or statutory duties to perform and which performs those duties and carries out its transactions for the benefit of the public and not for private profit": Halsbury, adopted in *DPP* v *Manners* [1978] AC 43.

public charitable collection. A charitable appeal which is made in any public place or by means of visits from house to house: Charities Act 1992, s. 65(1). For prohibitions on conducting unauthorised collections, see s. 66.

public company. Company (q.v.) either limited by shares or by guarantee with a minimum prescribed share capital, provided that its memorandum states that it is to be a public company and the statutory provisions concerning registration are complied with: Cos.A. 1985, s. 1(1). It must have at least two members (s. 1(1)), and at least two directors (s. 282). Its shares are, in general, freely transferable.

public corporation. A business organisation created by an Act, responsible for the day-to-day operation of public enterprises, e.g., the British Coal Corporation. Members are appointed by the relevant minister. Annual accounts must be placed before Parliament. Known also as a "statutory corporation". See, e.g., Finance Act 1987, Sch. 15, para. 7(1).

public decency. "I think that [the authorities] establish that it is an indictable offence to say or do or exhibit anything in public which outrages public decency, whether or not it also tends to corrupt and deprave those who see or hear it": *per* Lord Reid in *Shaw* v *DPP* [1961] 2 All ER 446. See also *Knuller Ltd* v *DPP* [1972] 2 All ER 898; *R* v *May* (1990) 91 Cr App R 157; *R* v *Rowley* [1991] 1 WLR 1020 (offence involves commission of an act which was, *per se,* lewd or obscene); *R* v *Lunberbech* [1991] Crim LR 784.

public document. "A document that is made for the purposes of the public making use of it, and being able to refer to it": *Sturla* v *Freccia* (1880) 5 App Cas 623. It is generally authenticated by a public officer. Examples: court records; public registers. Statements in a public document made by an officer in pursuance of a public duty are admissible evidence of the facts stated therein: Civil Evidence Act 1968, s. 9; Civil Evidence Act 1972.

public duties, time off for. An employer is under a duty, under the E.P.(C.)A. 1978, s. 29, as amended, to give time off to certain employees in relation to their duties, e.g., those who are magistrates, members of local authorities.

public good, defence of. Defence under Obscene Publications Act 1964, s. 4(1), whereby a person will not be convicted of an offence of possessing obscene articles for publication for gain if it is proved that publication was justified as being for the public good on the ground that it is in the interests of science, literature, art or learning, or of other objects of general concern. See *DPP* v *Jordan* [1976] 3 All ER 775. "Learning" means "a product of scholarship": *A.-G.'s Reference (No. 3 of 1977)* [1978] 1 WLR 1123.

public house. Premises licensed for the sale of intoxicating liquor for consumption on those premises where the sale of such liquor is, or is apart from any other trade or business ancillary or incidental to it, the only trade or business carried on there: L.G.A. 66, s. 17(2).

public index map. Index of separate parcels of registered land, kept at the Land Registry and open to inspection by any person: Land Registration Rules 1925, rr. 8, 12.

public interest immunity. *See* PRIVILEGE, PUBLIC.

public law. Those areas of the law concerned primarily with the duties and powers of the state itself, e.g., constitutional law. See *Roy* v *Kensington and Chelsea FPC* [1992] 1 All ER 705. *See* PRIVATE LAW.

public lending right. Right conferred on authors by the Public Lending Right Act 1979, s. 1(1), to receive out of a central fund payment in respect of books lent out to the public by libraries in the UK. See S.I. 1986/2106; S.I. 1989/2188.

public limited company. *See* PUBLIC COMPANY.

public meeting. Any meeting in a public place and any meeting which the public or any section thereof are permitted to attend, whether on payment or otherwise: P.O.A. 1936, s. 9 (as amended by C.J.A. 1972 and P.O.A. 1986, Sch. 3).

public mischief. Formerly an offence tending to the prejudice of the community: *R* v *Manley* [1933] 1 KB 529 (false statements causing the police to waste their time). In *DPP* v *Withers* [1974] 3 All ER 984, the House of Lords held that the law does not recognise a crime in an individual accused of conduct tending to cause a public mischief.

public morals, courts and. "In the sphere of criminal law I entertain no doubt that there remains in the courts of law a residual power to enforce the supreme and fundamental purpose of the law, to conserve not only the safety and order but also the moral welfare of the state . . . ": *per* Lord Simonds in *Shaw* v *DPP* [1961] 2 All ER 446.

public nuisance. "A nuisance which is so widespread in its range or so indiscriminate in its effects that it would not be reasonable to expect one person to take proceedings on his own responsibility to put a stop to it, but that it should be taken on the responsibility of the community at large": *per* Lord Denning in *A.-G.* v *PYA Quarries Ltd* [1957] 2 QB 169. See *AB* v *SW Water Services Ltd* (1992) The Times, 8 May (award of exemplary damages).

public office. Any office under the Crown, or under the charter of a city or borough, or under the Acts relating to local government or public health or public education: Representation of the People Act 1983, s. 185.

public officer. "An officer who discharges any duty in the discharge of which the public are interested, more clearly so if he is paid out of a fund provided by the public": *R* v *Whitaker* [1914] 2 KB 1283.

public or general rights, declaration concerning. *See* DECLARATION CONCERNING PUBLIC OR GENERAL RIGHTS.

public place. Any highway and any place to which at the material time the public or any section of the public has access, on payment or otherwise, as of right or by virtue of express, or implied permission: P.O.A. 1986, s. 16. See, e.g., *DPP* v *Vivier* [1991] 4 All ER 18.

public policy. "That principle of law which holds that no subject can lawfully do that which has a tendency to be injurious to the public, or against the public good": *Egerton* v *Brownlow* (1853) 4 HL Cas 1.

public privilege. *See* PRIVILEGE, PUBLIC.

public procession. A procession (q.v.) in a public place (q.v.): P.O.A. 1986, s. 16. For duties concerning the giving of advance notice, see Part II.

public prosecutor. Director of Public Prosecutions (q.v.).

public records, access to. Records in the Public Records Office are generally not available for public inspection until 30 years after the year next to that in which they were created, or other period as may be prescribed: see Public Records Acts 1958 and 1967. Longer periods have been prescribed for, e.g., exceptionally sensitive papers, documents containing information supplied in confidence, disclosure of which might constitute a breach of good faith.

public service, contracts tending to injure. Contracts (generally illegal), e.g., for the sale of public offices, for procurement of a title of honour for reward. See *Parkinson* v *College of Ambulance Ltd* [1925] 2 KB 1 (which led to the passing of Honours (Prevention of Abuses) Act 1925).

public trust. A trust which has as its object the promotion of the public welfare, as opposed to a private trust, which is for the benefit of an individual or class. *See* TRUST.

Public Trustee. Appointed under the Public Trustee Act 1906; he may act on the application of a beneficiary or trustee (qq.v.). He may be appointed as an ordinary trustee, or custodian trustee (q.v.), or personal representative (q.v.). He may decline to accept a trust, but not on the sole ground of its being of small value. Powers, duties and liabilities are those of an ordinary trustee. See Public Trustee and Administration of Funds Act 1986.

public utilities. Organisations supplying gas, water, electricity, etc. to the community. For standards of performance and service to customers, see Competition and Services (Utilities) Act 1992.

publish. *See* PUBLICATION.

puisne. (French: *puis* (after), *né* (born).) Junior, inferior. 1. A *puisne mortgage* is a legal mortgage (q.v.) not protected by the deposit of documents relating to the legal estate affected, and is a Class C charge under L.C.A. 1972. See L.P.A. 1969, s. 30(1). 2. High Court judges are styled *puisne judges* or "Justices of the High Court": S.C.A. 1981, s. 4(2).

punctual. On the day named for payment: *Leeds Theatre Co* v *Broadbent* [1898] 1 Ch 343.

punctuation. The division of words in a document by stops, commas, etc. "It is from the words and from the context, not from the punctuation, that the sense must be collected": *Sandford* v *Raikes* (1816) 1 Mer 646. See *DPP* v *Schildkamp* [1971] AC 1; *Hanlon* v *The Law Society* [1981] AC 124.

punishment. Penalty inflicted by a court on a convicted offender. The primary sanction of the criminal law. "A person is said to suffer punishment whenever he is legally deprived of the normal rights of a citizen on the ground that he has violated a rule of law, the violation having been established by trial according to due process of law, provided the deprivation has been carried out by the recognised legal authorities of the state, that the rule of law clearly specifies both the offence and the attached penalty, that the courts construe statutes strictly, and that the statute was on the books prior to the offence": Rawls (1969).

punishment, components of. "A social response which: occurs where there is a violation of a legal rule; is imposed and carried out by authorised persons on behalf of the legal order to which the violated rule belongs; involves suffering or at least other consequences normally considered unpleasant; expresses disapproval of the violator": Ross (1958).

punishment, corporal. Physical chastisement of a convicted offender (e.g., by flogging, whipping). See C.J.A. 1914, s. 36; C.J.A. 1948, s. 1 (abolishing the punishment). For corporal punishment in schools, see Education (No. 2) Act 1986, s. 47.

pur autre vie. See AUTRE VIE.

pur cause de vicinage. Because of vicinity. A right of pasturage arising where there is a custom allowing animals to stray and feed freely on the common of a neighbour.

purchaser. 1. One who acquires goods or land in exchange for money. 2. Under L.P.A. 1925, s. 205(1), a purchaser in good faith for valuable consideration, including a lessee and mortgagee. 3. Under L.C.A. 1972, s. 17(1) "any person (including a mortgagee or lessee) who, for valuable consideration, takes any interest in land or in a charge on land". 4. One to whom land is expressly transferred other than by descent, i.e., by the act of the parties by conveyance on sale, will, gift, etc. See *IRC* v *Gribble* [1913] 3 KB 212; *Powell* v *Cleland* [1948] 1 KB 262.

purchaser for value without notice. One who purchases property *bona fide* for valuable consideration without notice of any prior right or title. "Good faith" is a "separate test which may have to be passed even though absence of notice is proved": *per* Lord Wilberforce in *Midland Bank Trust Co* v *Green* [1981] AC 513. "Valuable consideration" means any consideration (q.v.) in money, money's worth or future marriage. He is generally bound only by equitable interests of which he did have notice. Mere equities, e.g., to re-open a foreclosure (q.v.), do not bind him: *Phillips* v *Phillips* (1862) 4 De G & J 208. See EQUITY'S DARLING.

purchase, words of. Words pointing out, by name or description, the transferee, i.e., the person, who is to acquire an interest in land, e.g., "to X and his heirs". (X is the "purchaser".) In effect, they are the words identifying the transferee or grantee.

pure theory of law. *See* LAW, PURE THEORY OF.

purpose. That which one seeks to accomplish. "I have no doubt that [the meaning] is subjective. A purpose must exist in the mind. It cannot exist anywhere else. The word can be used to designate either the main object which a man wants or hopes to achieve by the contemplated act, or it can be used to designate those objects which he knows will probably be achieved by the act, whether he wants them or not. I am satisfied that in the criminal law in general . . . its ordinary sense is the latter one": *per* Lord Devlin in *Chandler* v *DPP* [1962] 3 All ER 142.

purpose axiom. Concept in administrative law relating to the exercise of discretion (q.v.) by a public authority. "Parliament must have conferred the discretion with the intention that it should be used to promote the policy and objects of the Act; the policy and objects of the Act must be determined by construing the Act as a whole, and construction is always a matter of law for the court": *per* Lord Reid in *Padfield* v *Minister of Agriculture* [1968] AC 907.

purpose trust. *See* TRUST, PURPOSE.

putative father. The person alleged to be the father (q.v.) of an illegitimate child. See *Turner* v *Blunden* [1986] Fam 120; *In re L.* (1990) The Times, 22 Oct.

pyramid selling. Scheme whereby a distributor collects franchise payments from others who are subsequently introduced, qualifying for special benefits and terms according to the number of sub-agents introduced. Under the Fair Trading Act 1973, these schemes are controlled by, e.g., a cooling-off period for those who join schemes, and written contracts for participants.

Q

Q.B. Queen's Bench.

Q.B.D. Queen's Bench Division (q.v.).

Q.C. Queen's Counsel (q.v.).

qua. In the character of.

quaere. *See* SED QUAERE.

qualification shares. The number of shares or amount of stock which, under a company's articles (q.v.) must be held by a person acting as director.

qualified acceptance. Refers, e.g., to the conditional or partial acceptance of a bill of exchange (q.v.). See B.Ex.A. 1882, s. 19.

qualified privilege. *See* PRIVILEGE, QUALIFIED.

qualified property. Limited rights of property, e.g., chattel in possession of bailee.

qualified title. Title with which the applicant is registered under L.R.A. 1925, where the registrar is unable to grant absolute, good leasehold, or possessory title.

qualifying capital interest. *See* CAPITAL INTEREST, QUALIFYING.

quality. In relation to goods, includes their state or condition: S.GA 1979, s.61(1).

quamdiu se bene gesserit. For as long as he shall behave himself. Phrase used to indicate that an office (e.g., that of a judge) will be held during good behaviour and will not be lost, therefore, save for bad behaviour. See S.C.A. 1981, s. 11(3).

quangos. Quasi-autonomous, non-governmental organisations, generally carrying out regulatory and operational functions or commercial and semi-commercial activities, e.g., the British Council.

quantity, correct. A seller must deliver the correct quantity of goods: S.G.A. 1979, s. 30(1). Unless otherwise agreed, the buyer is not bound to accept delivery by instalments: s. 31(1). See *Duffus SA.* v *Berger & Co* [1984] AC 382.

quantum. How much. A quantity, amount.

quantum meruit. As much as he has earned. On breach of contract (q.v.) the party injured may be entitled to claim for work done and services performed. See *Planché* v *Colburn* (1831) 8 Bing 14; *British Steel Corporation* v *Cleveland Engineering Co* [1984] 1 All ER 504; *Crown House Engineering* v *AMEC Projects* (1990) Const LJ 141.

quantum valebat. As much as it was worth. Refers to an action for goods supplied, where no price had been agreed on.

quarantine. Period of time (originally 40 days) in which ships and persons coming from a country in which serious infectious disease has spread are isolated.

quare clausum fregit. *See* CLAUSUM FREGIT, QUARE.

quare ejecit infra terminum. Wherefore he ejected [him] within the term. Writ whereby a lessee (q.v.) could claim protection against the lessor (q.v.), his heirs and the assignees of the lessor in a case of ejectment (q.v.). Abolished under Real Property Limitation Act 1833.

quarter days. These are Lady Day (March 25), Midsummer Day (June 24), Michaelmas Day (September 29) and Christmas Day (December 25).

quash. To annul; to make void.

quasi. As if; apparent; having some resemblance to, but lacking some requisites.

quasi-arbitrator. "Where a matter is left by two parties to the judgment of a third who is to determine their rights, and the task is not merely one of arithmetic, but involving technical skill and knowledge, that person is in the position of a quasi-arbitrator": *Stevenson* v *Watson* (1879) 4 CPD 148. See *Palacath* v *Flanagan* [1985] 2 All ER 161.

quasi-contracts. Cases in which the law imposes on a person an obligation to make repayment on grounds of unjust benefit, e.g., when he has been enriched at the expense of another. See *Holt* v *Markham* [1923] 1 KB 504; *Shamia* v *Joory* [1958] 1 QB 448. *See* UNJUST ENRICHMENT.

quasi-easements. Where one person owns two or more adjoining and separate properties, rights which he may have been exercising over one or other of them are known as quasi- easements, since an owner cannot have an easement over his own land. See *Ward* v *Kirkland* [1967] Ch 194. *See* EASEMENT.

quasi-entail. An estate *pur autre vie* (q.v.), for the life of A granted "to B and the heirs of his body". See *Ex p Sterne* [1801] 6 Ves 156. *See* FEE TAIL.

quasi ex contractu. As if arising out of a contract.

quasi-indorser. One who signs a bill of exchange (q.v.) otherwise than as a drawer or acceptor, thereby incurring the liabilities of an indorser to a holder in due course (q.v.): see B.Ex.A 1882, s. 56.

quasi-judicial. Having a character which is partly-judicial, e.g., proceedings conducted by an arbitrator (q.v.).

quasi-loan. Used in Cos.A. 1985 to describe a transaction under which one party (the "creditor") agrees to pay, or pays otherwise than in pursuance of an agreement, a sum for another (the "borrower"), or agrees to reimburse, or reimburse otherwise than in pursuance of an agreement, expenditure incurred by another party for another (the "borrower"), on terms that the borrower (or a person on his behalf) will reimburse the creditor, or in circumstances giving rise to a liability on the borrower to reimburse the creditor: s. 331(3). In general, a non-private company may not make a quasi-loan to any of its directors: s. 332.

Queen's Bench, Court of. *See* COURT OF KING'S (QUEENS) BENCH.

Queen's Bench Division. Division of the High Court (q.v.), possessing civil, criminal, original, appellate and supervisory jurisdiction (including applications for *habeas corpus* (q.v.) and judicial review). It deals with, e.g., claims in tort and contract, and is presided over by the Lord Chief Justice (q.v.) with a staff of puisne judges (q.v.). It includes the Commercial Court and Admiralty Court (qq.v.). See S.C.A. 1981, ss. 5, 6, Sch 1. *See* DIVISIONAL COURTS.

Queen's Counsel (or King's). A senior barrister appointed on the recommendation of the Lord Chancellor. He wears a silk gown (hence the phrase "to take silk") and takes precedence over the other barristers in court. He may appear in any case for or against the Crown.

Queen's evidence. Evidence for the Crown given by one co-accused who "turns Queen's evidence", i.e., confesses guilt and acts as a competent witness against his associates. "It is the duty of the judge to warn the jury that, although they may convict upon his evidence, it is dangerous to do so unless it is corroborated": *Davis* v *DPP* [1965] AC 378.

Queen's Proctor. The solicitor (usually the Treasury Solicitor (q.v.)) representing the Crown who may intervene in the case of a petition for divorce. The court may direct papers to be sent to the Proctor who may instruct counsel to argue any question in relation to that case. Any person may, before the decree nisi (q.v.) is made absolute, give information to the Proctor on any matter relevant to the case, and the Proctor may then take such steps as are considered necessary. See Mat.C.A. 1973, s. 8; Matrimonial Causes Rules 1977, rr. 61–62; *Ebrahim* v *Ali* [1984] FLR 95. *See* DECREE.

Queen's Remembrancer. One who performed duties relating to debts due to the Crown. Now involved in, e.g., the selection of sheriffs. The office is held by a senior master of the Supreme Court. See Queen's Remembrancer Act 1859; and S.C.A. 1981, s. 89(4).

Queen, The. "Elizabeth the Second, by the Grace of God of the United Kingdom of Great Britain and Northern Ireland and of Her other Realms and Territories Queen, Head of the Commonwealth, Defender of the Faith": Royal Titles Act 1953. Nominally, the supreme executive power; supreme head of the church; head of defence forces. A *queen regent* or *regnant* holds the Crown in her own right; a *queen consort* is the king's wife; a *queen dowager* is the widow of a deceased king. *See* CROWN; MONARCHY; SOVEREIGN.

que estate, prescription in. Prescription (q.v.) in which the claimant pleaded user by himself and "those whose estate he had"—*ceux que estate il ad.* In effect, a right claimed by a prescription annexed to particular lands. See *Chesterfield* v *Harris* [1908] 2 Ch 397.

questioning by police. Following the *Codes of Practice* issued under the P. & C.E.A. 1984, a police officer may question any person from whom he thinks useful information can be obtained, subject to certain restrictions. The purpose of questioning is to obtain an explanation of facts, not necessarily an admission. For the questioning of juveniles by the police (in the presence of an "appropriate adult"), see *Code C.* Oppressive questioning is forbidden and an accurate record must be made of interviews with suspects. See OPPRESSION LEADING TO CONFESSION.

Question Time. An hour of Parliamentary time (usually on Mondays–Thursdays) in which ministers answer M.P.s' questions relating to their responsibilities. "Starred questions" require oral answers.

quia emptores. "Whereas purchasers [of lands and tenements] . . ." Title of statute enacted in 1290, taking its name from the beginning of the preamble. It allowed freemen to alienate land (except by will) and without consent of the lord. Alienees held not of the alienor, but of the lord from whom the alienor had held previously. In effect, it abolished subinfeudation (q.v.).

qui approbat non reprobat. He who accepts cannot reject. See ELECTION.

quia timet. Because he fears. Action for injunction (q.v.) relating to a virtually irreparable wrong merely feared or threatened, but not yet committed. The plaintiff must show a very strong probability of imminent grave damage accruing to him. The cost to the defendant must also be considered. "What is aimed at is justice between the parties, having regard to all the circumstances": *Hooper* v *Rogers* [1975] Ch 43.

quicquid plantatur solo, solo cedit. Whatever is affixed to the soil, belongs to the soil. See *Simmons* v *Midford* [1969] 2 Ch 415; and *Royco* v *Eatonwill Con-*struction [1979] Ch 276. See FIXTURES.

quid pro quo. Something for something. Applied, e.g., to the concept of consideration (q.v.) in contract.

quiet enjoyment. Implied obligations of a lessor that a lessee's peaceful enjoyment of the premises shall not be interfered with by the lessor or by any person who claims under him. "Quiet" is not restricted to an absence of noise; it has been interpreted as "uninterrupted". Tenant's remedies for breach are damages and injunction (qq.v.). See *Celsteel Ltd* v *Alton House Holdings (No 2)* [1987] 1 WLR 291; *Mira* v *Aylmer Square Investments* (1990) 22 HLR 182. See LEASE.

quiet possession. In a contract of sale there is an implied warranty (q.v.) that the buyer will enjoy quiet possession of the goods except so far as it may be disturbed by the owner or other person entitled to the benefit of any charge or encumbrance so disclosed or known: S.G.A. 1979, s. 12(2) (*b*). See *Microbeads AG* v *Vinhurst Road Markings Ltd* [1975] 1 WLR 218.

qui facit per alium facit per se. He who does a thing through another does it himself.

qui in utero est. He who is in the womb [is held as already born, whenever a question arises for his benefit]. See *B.* v *Islington HA* [1991] 2 WLR 501. See FOETUS.

qui prior est tempore potior est jure. He who is before in time is the better in right (i.e., priority in time gives preference in law). See L.P.A. 1925, s. 137; *Dearle* v *Hall* (1828) 3 Russ 1; *Barclays Bank* v *Bird* [1954] Ch 274.

qui sentit commodum sentire debet et onus; et e contra. He who enjoys the benefit should bear the burden; and vice versa.

quit, notice to. See NOTICE TO QUIT.

quit rent. Fixed rent paid by a copyholder to his lord in discharge of his obligation to perform agricultural services. See L.P.A. 1925, s. 121. See COPYHOLD.

quod permittat. Title of writs to abate the nuisance (q.v.) to a neighbour's land caused by those who had built, e.g., walls, houses. Abolished by Real Property Limitation Act 1833.

quo jure. By what right. Writ (q.v.) relating to the title of common pasture (q.v.).

quorum. Of whom. Referred formerly to the commission issued to justices of the peace (q.v.). Now used to indicate the specified number of members of a body, in the absence of which it cannot formally meet or act legally. See, e.g., Cos.A. 1985, s. 370(4), Table A, art. 40.

quotation. 1. Term used in C.C.A. 1974, ss. 152, 189(1), to refer to a document by which a person who carries on a consumer credit or hire business or business of credit brokerage or debt-adjusting gives prospective customers information about terms on which he is prepared to do business. 2. Amount of money suggested as a price. See *Scancarriers* v *Aotearoa International* (1985) NLJ 799 (difference between quotation and contractual offer).

quoted company. *See* COMPANY, QUOTED.

quo warranto. By what authority. Prerogative writ formerly issued by the King's Bench to enquire into the authority by which a public office was held or a franchise claimed. Replaced by information in nature of writ of *quo warranto* which was abolished by A.J. (Misc. Provs.) A. 1938, s. 9. See S.C.A. 1981, s. 30; O. 53, r. 1(1) (*b*).

R

R. Abbreviation for *Rex* (King) or *Regina* (Queen), as in *R* v *Smith.*

racial. "'Racial' is not a term of art, either legal or, I surmise, scientific. I apprehend that anthropologists would dispute how far the word 'race' is biologically at all relevant to the species amusingly called *homo sapiens*": *per* Lord Simon in *Ealing LBC* v *Race Relations Board* [1972] AC 342. "Within the human race there are very few, if any, distinctions which we scientifically recognise as racial": *per* Lord Fraser in *Mandla* v *Lee* [1983] 2 AC 548.

racial discrimination. *See* DISCRIMINATION, RACIAL.

Racial Equality, Commission for. Body of 8–15 individuals, set up under the Race Relations Act 1976, s. 43(1), to work towards the elimination of discrimination; to promote equality of opportunity and good relations between racial groups; to review the working of the 1976 Act. It is empowered to issue non-discrimination notices (q.v.) and apply for injunctions (q.v.) to restrain persistent discrimination.

racial group. "A group of persons defined by reference to colour, race, nationality or ethnic or national origins, and references to a person's racial group refer to any racial group within which he falls": Race Relations Act 1976, s. 3(1). See *Mandla* v *Lee* [1983] 2 AC 548; *Gwynned CC* v *Jones* [1986] ICR 833. *See* ETHNIC.

racial hatred. Hatred against a group of persons in Great Britain defined by reference to colour, race, nationality (including citizenship) or ethnic (q.v.) or national origins: P.O.A. 1986, s. 17.

racial hatred, offences relating to. Under P.O.A 1986, Part III, offences may be committed where a person intends to stir up racial hatred or, having regard to all the circumstances, racial hatred is likely to be stirred up. The offences include the use of words or behaviour or display of written material of a threatening, abusive or insulting nature (s. 18), publishing or distributing written material of this nature (s. 19), having in one's possession racially inflammatory material (s. 23).

racialist chanting. The repeated uttering of any words or sounds in concert with one or more others, consisting of or including matter which is threatening, abusive or insulting to a person by reason of his colour, race, nationality or ethnic or national origins. An offence under the Football (Offences) Act 1991, s. 3.

racial segregation. "Segregating a person from other persons on racial grounds is treating him less favourably than they are treated": Race Relations Act 1976, s. 1(2).

rack rent. 1. A rent (q.v.) which is not less than two-thirds of the rent at which the premises might reasonably be expected to be let from year to year, free from all usual tenant's rates and taxes and deducting therefrom the probable average annual cost of repairs, insurance and other expenses necessary to maintain the premises in a state to command such rent: Building Act 1984, s. 126. See *Newman* v *Dorrington Developments* [1975] 1 WLR 1642. 2. A rent raised to the highest level obtainable.

radar trap. Electronic devices used by the police to measure the speed of a motor vehicle. The devices must be of a type approved by the Secretary of State. See Road Traffic Offenders Act 1988, s. 20; Road Traffic Act 1991, s. 23; SI 1992/1209. *See* SPEEDING OFFENCE.

radioactive material. Any material having a specific activity in excess of 70 kilabecquerels per kilogram, or such lesser specific activity as may be specified by order of the Secretary of State:

Radioactive Material (Road Transport) Act 1991, s. 1(1).

railway. A system of transport employing parallel rails which provide support and guidance for vehicles carried on flanged wheels, and form a track which either is of a gauge of at least 350 millimetres or crosses a carriageway (whether or not on the same level), and is not a tramway: Transport and Works Act 1992, s. 67.

ransom. Price paid for release from captivity. See *R* v *Pitts* (1986) 8 Cr App R (S) 84. In feudal times it was an incident of knight service (q.v.).

rape. An offence under S.O.A. 1956, s. 1(1). Defined under common law as unlawful sexual intercourse with a woman without her consent, by force, fear, fraud. Defined by the S.O. (Amendment) A. 1976 s. 1(1) as unlawful sexual intercourse (q.v.) with a woman who at the time of the intercourse does not consent to it, where at that time [the accused] knows that she does not consent to the intercourse or he is reckless as to whether she consents to it. See *DPP* v *Morgan* [1975] 2 All ER 347; *Kaitamaki* v *R* [1985] AC 147; *R* v *Satnam and Kewal* (1984) 78 Cr App R 149; *R* v *Khan* [1990] 1 WLR 813 (intent in attempted rape). For sentencing guidelines, see *R* v *Billam* [1986] 1 WLR 349; *A.-G's References No 25 of 1990* [1991] Crim LR 924, *No 15 of 1991* [1992] Crim LR 454, *No 18 of 1991* [1992] Crim LR 455.

rape, anonymity in cases of. A complainant is given anonymity from the time of the complaint: C.J.A. 1988, s. 158(2). Under s. 158(5), anonymity given to defendant by S.O. (Amendment) A. 1976, s. 6, is removed.

rape, consent and. "Consent" in rape covers states of mind ranging from actual desire to reluctant acquiescence; it is no longer necessary in proving rape to establish that intercourse took place as a result of fear, fraud or force, but merely that it occurred without the woman's consent: *R* v *Olugboja* [1982] QB 320. See *R* v *Barton* [1987] Crim LR 399. For "assault with intent to rape" (which is no longer known to the law), see *R* v *P.* [1990] Crim LR 323. See *A.-G.'s Reference (No. 7 of 1989)* (1990) 12 Cr App R (S) 1.

rape offence. "Rape, attempted rape, aiding, abetting, counselling and procuring rape or attempted rape, and incitement to rape": S.O. (Amendment) A. 1976, s. 7(2). The Act imposes reporting restrictions in such cases: See *R* v *C* (1992) The Times, 11 Mar.

rape within marriage. "The supposed marital exemption in rape (see Hale 1 PC 627) forms no part of the law of England": *per* Lord Keith in *R* v *R* [1991] 3 WLR 767.

rashness. The mental state of one who "thinks of the probable mischief; but in consequence of a missupposition begotten by insufficient advertence, he assumes that a mischief will not ensue in the given instance": Austin.

rates. Local taxes paid by the occupiers of lands, houses, etc, so as to help to meet the cost of local services. Replaced by "community charge" (q.v.) under Local Government Finance Act 1988. *See* COUNCIL TAX.

ratification. Confirmation; approval. In the case of ratification of a contract made by an agent (q.v.), the contract must be made on behalf of the principal; the principal must be competent at the time of the contract; there should have been an act capable of ratification. See *Firth* v *Staines* [1897] 2 QB 70. *See* CONTRACT.

ratio decidendi. The reason for a judicial decision. Usually a statement of law applied to the problems of a particular case. In essence, the principle upon which a case is decided. (Goodhart suggests that this principle is to be found by taking account of the facts treated by the judge as material, and his decision as based on them: (1930) 40 Yale LJ 161.)

ratio decidendi, **descriptive and prescriptive.** Distinction drawn by J. Stone (see (1959) 22 MLR 597) between the process of reasoning by which a decision is reached (the *"descriptive"* ratio decidendi) and that which identifies and delimits the reasoning which a later court will be bound to follow (the *"prescriptive"* ratio decidendi).

ratio legis est anima legis. The reason for the law is the soul of the law (Jenk. Cent.45). *Ratio legis* was defined by Austin (1790–1859) as "the scope or determining cause of a statute law: that is to say, the end or purpose which determines the lawgiver to make it, as distinguished from the intent or purpose with which he actually makes it".

re. In the matter of.

readings. The stages through which a Bill (q.v.) must pass before it becomes law.

real. 1. Relating to things (*res*), as distinct from persons. 2. Relating to land, and, specifically, freehold interests, as in "real action".

real action. *See* ACTIONS, REAL AND PERSONAL.

real estate. "Chattels real, and land in possession, remainder, or reversion (qq.v.) and every interest in or over land to which a deceased person was entitled at the time of his death; and real estate held on trust (including settled land (q.v.)) or by way of mortgage or security, but not money to arise under a trust for sale of land, nor money secured or charged on land": A.E.A. 1925, s. 3(1).

real evidence. *See* EVIDENCE, REAL.

real property. Property which could be recovered in a real action, i.e., interests in land, more specifically, freehold interests.

real security. A security charged on land, See Tr.A. 1925, s. 5. *See* TRUST.

realty. Generally, freehold interest in land.

reasonable contemplation test. Principle relating to damages awarded for breach of contract (q.v.). "The damages . . . should be such as may fairly and reasonably be considered either arising naturally, i.e., according to the usual course of things, from such breach of contract itself, or such as may reasonably be supposed to have been in the contemplation of both parties at the time they made the contract as the probable result of the breach": *Hadley* v *Baxendale* (1854) 9 Exch 341. It is a test of remoteness, not of quantification: *Re National Coffee Palace Co* (1883) 24 Ch D 367.

reasonable doubt. "That degree of doubt which would prevent a reasonable and just man from coming to a conclusion": *Bater* v *Bater* [1951] P 35. "It is far better, instead of using the words 'reasonable doubt' and then trying to say what is a reasonable doubt, to say to a jury: 'You must not convict unless you are satisfied by the evidence given by the prosecution that

the offence has been committed' ": *R* v *Summers* [1952] 1 TLR 1164. "Jurymen themselves set the standard of what is reasonable in the circumstances . . . A reasonable doubt which a jury may entertain is not to be confined to a 'rational doubt' or a 'doubt founded on reason' ": *per* Barwick CJ in *Green* v *R* (1971) 126 CLR 28.

reasonable financial provision. *See* FINANCIAL PROVISION, REASONABLE.

reasonable force. The degree of force reasonably necessary, e.g., to effect an arrest, in all the circumstances. "A person may use such force as is reasonable in the circumstances in the prevention of crime, or in effecting or assisting in the lawful arrest of offenders or suspected offenders or of persons unlawfully at large": C.L.A. 1967, s. 3. See P. & C.E.A. 1984, s. 117; *R* v *Barrett* (1981) 72 Cr App R 212 (belief in right to use force); *R* v *Williams* [1987] 3 All ER 411.

reasonable man. "The fair and reasonable man who represents after all no more than the anthropomorphic conception of justice . . .": *Davis Contractors Ltd* v *Fareham UDC* [1956] AC 696. "It is left . . . to the judge to decide what, in the circumstances of the particular case, the reasonable man would have in contemplation, and what, accordingly, the party sought to be made liable ought to have foreseen . . . The standard of foresight of the reasonable man . . . eliminates the personal equation and is independent of the idiosyncrasies of the particular person whose conduct is in question": *Glasgow Corporation* v *Muir* [1943] AC 448.

reasonable man test in provocation. *See* PROVOCATION.

reasonable time. In relation to the delivery of goods, is a question of fact: S.G.A. 1979, s. 29(5). Where a contract does not refer specifically to time, there is an implication that the promised act will be carried out within a reasonable time: *Ford* v *Cotesworth* (1868) LR 4 QB 132. *See* TIME AS ESSENCE OF A CONTRACT.

rebate. Refund; credit; discount. See C.C.A. 1974 s. 94 (for an example of "statutory rebate").

rebellion. Organised resistance to the ruler or government with the intention of supplanting them or at least depriving them of authority over part of their territory: *Spinney's Ltd v Royal Insurance Co Ltd* [1980] 1 Lloyd's Rep 406.

rebus sic stantibus. In these circumstances. Doctrine of international law, which assumes as a condition of all treaties that they will cease to be obligatory if there is a substantial change of the facts on which they were founded.

rebut. To oppose; contradict; disprove.

rebutter. A term used in pleading to indicate the defendant's answer to the plaintiff's surrejoinder (q.v.). *See* PLEADINGS.

recall of witness. *See* WITNESS, RECALL OF.

recaption. The lawful retaking of one's chattels from another who has wrongfully taken and detained them. See, e.g., *Blades v Higgs* (1861) 10 CB NS 713.

receipt. Written acknowledgement of goods or money received.

receiver. 1. One appointed to enable a judgment creditor to obtain payment of a debt. May be known as "receiver by way of equitable execution". See L.P.A. 1925, s. 101(1) (appointment relating to mortgage money: see *Shamji v Johnson Matthey* [1991] BCLC 36); S.C.A. 1981, s. 37; A.J.A, 1977, s 7; O. 30; O. 51. *Bond Holdings Ltd v National Australia Bank Ltd* [1990] 1 ACSR 445. 2. One appointed to preserve property which is endangered, for the benefit of those entitled to it. 3. One who received stolen property. See now, Th.A 1968, s. 22.

receiver, administrative. A receiver or manager of a company's property appointed by or on behalf of holders of the company's debentures (q.v.) secured by a charge (q.v.) which, as created, was a floating charge, or by such a charge and one or more other securities: Ins.A. 1986, s. 29(2). For details of the statement of affairs to be submitted to him, see s. 47.

receiving. The former offence of receiving stolen goods knowing them to have been stolen: Larceny Act 1916, s. 33 (now repealed). Now part of the offence of "handling" (q.v.). See *R v Smythe* (1980) 72 Cr App R 8.

recent possession. "Convenient but grammatically incorrect expression to describe the possession by someone of things which had recently been stolen": *R v Hobbs and Geoffrey-Smith* (1982) 132 NLJ 435. It may raise a presumption of theft or handling (q.v.). See *R v Wanganeen* (1989) 50 SASR 433; *R v Powers* [1990] Cr LR 586; *R v Lloyd* [1992] Crim LR 361.

recidivist. A habitual criminal. See *R v Bailey* [1988] Crim LR 628.

reciprocity. Mutuality in relationships. Refers, in international law, to relationship between two states, each of which gives the other, and its inhabitants, similar privileges.

recitals. Part of a deed of conveyance of sale indicating the effect and purpose of that deed and stating the history of the property to be conveyed. They are not essential to the deed's validity. Recitals of particular facts may operate as an estoppel (q.v.): *Bensley v Burdon* (1830) 8 LJ Ch 85. See L.P.A. 1925, s. 45(6).

recklessness. The term is not defined by statute. The Law Commission (Report No. 89, 1978) suggested two standard tests of recklessness: as to *result* ("Did the person whose conduct is in issue foresee that his conduct might produce the result, and, if so, was it unreasonable for him to take the risk of producing it?"); as to *circumstances* ("Did the person whose conduct is in issue realise that the circumstances might exist and, if so, was it unreasonable for him to take the risk of their existence?").

recklessness, categories of. Two categories of recklessness in criminal law may be discerned. 1. "Cunningham-type" (*R v Cunningham* [1957] 2 QB 396): defendant knows the risk, is willing to take it and takes it deliberately. 2. "Caldwell-type" (*R v Caldwell* [1982] AC 341), which does not apply to any crimes of specific or ulterior intent: defendant performs an act which creates an obvious risk, and, when performing the act, he has either given no thought to the possibility of such a risk arising or he recognised that some risk existed, but went on to take it. (There is no such offence as "murder by recklessness": *Leung Kam Kwok v R* (1985) 81 Cr App R 83.) See, e.g., *Blakely v DPP* [1991] Crim LR 763.

recognisance. Formal undertaking to pay the Crown a specified sum if an accused person fails to surrender to custody. See R v *Reading Crown Court, ex p Bello* (1990) The Times, 10 Dec.

recognition, rule of. Jurisprudential concept, formulated by Hart (1961), stating the authoritative criteria allowing persons to identify primary rules of obligation. The criteria include reference to legislation, authoritative texts, customary practice, judicial decisions. *See* RULES, PRIMARY.

recommendations of EEC. *See* COMMUNITY LEGISLATION, FORMS OF.

reconciliation. The act of harmonising differences and settling disputes. Thus, under Mat.C.A. 1973, s. 6, provision is made by rules of court to require a solicitor acting for a petitioner for divorce to certify whether he has discussed with the petitioner the possibility of a reconciliation. Proceedings may be adjourned to enable attempts at reconciliation. A period of six months, or periods of up to a total of six months, during which spouses may resume cohabitation without loss of the chance of subsequent divorce, are known as "reconciliation periods". Provisions of s. 6 apply also to judicial separation. See also D.P.A. 1978, s. 26; Matrimonial Causes Rules 1977, r. 12(3). *See* DIVORCE.

reconstruction of company. The transference of a company's assets to a new company under an arrangement whereby the shareholders of the old company receive shares, or similar interests, in the new company. It can be effected by, e.g., a scheme of arrangement under Cos.A. 1985, ss. 425–7. See Ins.A. 1986, ss. 1–7. *See* COMPANY.

reconversion. Notional process whereby property which has been subject to notional conversion (q.v.) is treated as having been restored to its original state. Example: A devises land to B and C on trust to sell and pay the proceeds to D. D is then entitled (because of the doctrine of conversion) to the property in its converted form (i.e., as personalty (q.v.)) at A's death. If D elects to take it as land, reconversion has taken place. See *Re Cook* [1948] Ch 212.

reconveyance. Procedure whereby, before 1st January 1926, the mortgagee had to revest the legal estate in the mortgagor on redemption. A receipt on the mortgage deed now suffices to extinguish the mortgage. See L.P.A. 1925, s. 115. *See* MORTGAGE.

record. 1. To make a written account. 2. An authentic account of some event(s). 3. A memorial of an action heard in a court of record (q.v.) See P. & C.E.A. 1984, ss. 68–70; *H.* v *Schering Chemicals* [1983] 1 WLR 143. For computerised "records of opinion", see Civil Evidence Act 1968, s. 5. For "personal records" (i.e., documentary and other records concerning an individual, living or dead, who can be identified from them) see P. & C.E.A. 1984, s. 12.

record, contract of. *See* CONTRACT OF RECORD.

record, court of. *See* COURT OF RECORD.

Recorders. Appointed by the Queen on the recommendation of the Lord Chancellor to try criminal cases in the Crown Court (q.v.).

records admissible in civil cases. Records, i.e., documents (q.v.) containing information, admissible in evidence in civil proceedings. Under Civil Evidence Act 1968, ss. 4, 5, provision is made for the admissibility in evidence of documentary hearsay statements under certain conditions and of computerised records. See *Taylor* v *Taylor* [1970] 2 All ER 609. *See* EVIDENCE.

records admissible in criminal cases. Records in criminal proceedings which are admissible in evidence, i.e., when the record was compiled by a person acting under a duty from information supplied by a person (whether acting under a duty or not) who had, or might reasonably be supposed to have had, personal knowledge of the matters dealt with in that information and the supplier of information (*a*) is dead or is mentally or physically unfit to act as a witness; (*b*) is abroad and cannot reasonably be called as a witness; or (*c*) cannot reasonably be expected to have any active recollection of the matters in question. Further requirements include taking all reasonable steps to identify the supplier of information and to locate him. Comparable requirements apply to the use of computer records. See P. & C.E.A. 1984, ss. 68–70; *R* v *Canale* [1990] 2 All ER 187. *See also* EVIDENCE.

recovery. 1. An action for the recovery of land – "the modern equivalent of the old action of ejectment": *Bramwell v Bramwell* [1942] 1 KB 370. The action must be brought within 12 years of accrual of the cause of action: Lim. A. 1980, s. 15. 2. A collusive action, known as common recovery (q.v.).

recovery of costs. See COSTS, RECOVERY OF.

recovery of premises, obstruction of. Resistance to, or intentional obstruction of, court officers executing process for possession against unauthorised occupiers is an offence under C.L.A. 1977, s. 10(1). For defences, see s. 10(3).

recreational charity. A trust for the public benefit which provides facilities for recreation or other leisure time occupation in the interests of social welfare. See Recreational Charities Act 1958. *See* CHARITY; TRUST.

rectification. Where a written document does not accurately express an agreement between parties, as the result of some common mistake, equity has the power to rectify that mistake: *Craddock Bros* v *Hunt* [1923] 2 Ch 136. Rectification is not of the agreement itself, merely of the instrument recording the agreement. See *Freer* v *Unwins Ltd* [1976] Ch 288. For rectification of land register, see L.R.A. 1925, s. 82(1); *Norwich and Peterborough BS* v *Steed* (1992) The Independent, 10 Mar.

rectification of mistake in magistrates' court. *See* MISTAKE, RECTIFICATION IN MAGISTRATES' COURT OF.

rectification of will. If the court is satisfied that a will is so expressed that it fails to carry out the testator's intentions, in consequence of a clerical error or of a failure to understand his instructions, it may order rectification so as to carry out those intentions: A.J.A. 1982, s. 20(1). See, e.g., *Re Reynette-James* [1976] 1 WLR 116; *Wordingham* v *Royal Exchange Trust Ltd* [1992] 2 WLR 496.

reddendum. That which is to be paid. Clause in lease (q.v.) stating the amount of rent and when it is payable. See *King* v *King* (1980) 255 EG 1205.

redeemable preference shares. Preference shares (q.v.), first introduced by Cos.A 1929, that can be redeemed out of profits or out of a fresh issue of shares. See Table A, art. 3. Shares cannot be redeemed in this manner unless fully paid: Cos.A 1985, Part V, Chap. VII, ss. 159, 160; Cos.A 1989, s. 133.

redeem up, foreclose down. Rule relating to redemption of mortgage (q.v.). Example: M has mortgaged property to L1, L2, L3, L4, L5, in that order of priority. L4 wishes to redeem L2. L4 must redeem those mortgages between him and the prior mortgage he wishes to redeem and he must also foreclose any subsequent mortgagees and the mortgagor. L3, L5 and M must be made parties to the action. L3 must be redeemed. L5 and M must be foreclosed and allowed an opportunity to pay off the prior mortgage. *See* MORTGAGE.

redemption. The recovery (i.e., repossession) of mortgaged property on payment of the debt. The rights to redeem are: *legal* (right at law to redeem on the exact day fixed by the mortgage); *equitable* (right to redeem after that date has passed). See *Gomba Holdings* v *Minories Finance* (1992) Financial Times, 11 Feb. *See* EQUITY OF REDEMPTION; MORTGAGE.

redemption period for a pawn. The longest of the following periods: six months after the pawn was taken; any period fixed by the parties for duration of credit secured by the pledge (q.v.) or for duration of redemption period: C.C.A. 1974, s. 116. *See* PAWN.

redress. *See* RELIEF; REMEDY.

reduction into possession. Conversion of a chose in action (q.v.) into a chose in possession (q.v.). Example: a debt which is paid.

reduction of capital. A company limited by shares may, if its articles permit, reduce its capital by means of a special resolution (q.v.) to be confirmed by the court: Cos. A. 1985, s. 135. It may be effected for reasons such as: loss of capital by wastage of assets and the company wishes to write off the loss; share capital issued may not be fully paid and the company has the capital it needs. See Cos. A. 1985, Part V, Chap. IV, s. 171; *House of Fraser plc* v *ACGE Investments Ltd* [1987] 2 WLR 1083. *See* COMPANY.

redundancy. 1. Irrelevant matter in pleadings (q.v.). 2. Dismissal of an employee because his job has ceased to exist. See Redundancy Payments Act 1965; T.U.L.R.(C.)A. 1992, s. 195.

redundancy payments. Payments made to employees in the event of their dismissal by reason of redundancy, i.e., dismissal because of the actual or intended cessation of the business in which they are employed or the cessation of or decline for work of a particular kind. See Redundancy Payments Act 1965; E.P.(C.)A. 1978, Part VI; Employment Act 1989, s. 16 (abolishing the Redundancy Fund). "The purpose of redundancy pay is to compensate a worker for loss of job, irrespective of whether that loss leads to unemployment. It is to compensate him for loss of security, possible loss of earnings and fringe benefits, and the uncertainty and anxiety of change of job": *Wynes* v *Southrepps Broiler Farm Ltd* [1968] ITR 407. See, e.g., *British Coal Corporation* v *Cheesbrough* [1990] 1 All ER 641.

re-engagement order. Order under E.P. (C.) A. 1978, s. 69, whereby a former employee had to be re-engaged by the employer in employment comparable to that from which he was dismissed or other suitable employment. See *Lilley Ltd* v *Dunn* [1984] IRLR 483.

re-entry. Right of entry (q.v.).

re-examination. Examination of a witness (q.v.) by counsel or solicitor relating to matters arising out of his cross-examination (q.v.). In general, leading questions may not be asked, and questions on new matter may not be asked save by leave of the judge. See Civil Evidence Act 1968, s. 2; *Price* v *Samo* (1838) 7 LJ QB 123.

referee. 1. One to whom a dispute is referred for an opinion. In the case of statements by a referee: "If a man refers another upon any particular business to a third person, he is bound by what this third person says or does concerning it, as much as if that had been done or said by him": *Williams* v *Innes* (1804) 1 Camp 364. 2. One who provides a character reference for another.

referee, official. See OFFICIAL REFEREE.

reference. 1. Referring of a matter to an arbitrator (q.v.) for his decision. 2. Decision by an arbitrator or referee (q.v.). 3. An authority relied on in legal argument. 4. Declaration to a prospective employer concerning a person's character, work record, etc. See *Spring* v *Guardian Assurance plc* [1992] IRLR 173 (need for reasonable care in giving reference).

reference, incorporation by. See INCORPORATION BY REFERENCE.

referendum. The submission to popular vote of a question or a proposed legislative measure. See the (repealed) Referendum Act 1975 (relating to the UK's membership of the EEC (q.v.)).

referential bid. An arrangement to bid at an auction (q.v.) based on adjustment by reference to another bid. Example: "$10,000 in excess of any offer which you receive which is expressed as a fixed monetary amount and which is higher" (as in *Harvela Investments* v *Royal Trust of Canada* [1985] 2 All ER 966).

referential settlements. See SETTLEMENTS, REFERENTIAL.

refer to drawer. Phrase used by a bank in dishonouring a customer's cheque. Held, in *Jayson* v *Midland Bank* [1968] 1 Lloyd's Rep 409, to be libellous if used incorrectly. See (for interpretation of a similar phrase "present again") *Baker* v *Australia and New Zealand Bank* [1958] NZLR 907.

refreshing memory. Permission granted to a witness under examination to refer to a document so as to recall some matter. The document must generally have been made by the witness, or under his supervision, or checked by him, substantially at the time of occurrence of the event in question and must be handed to the opposite party for inspection, on request. A witness may refresh his memory from a note written by some other person, as long as he adopts it as his own, particularly if he does so by signing it: *Groves* v *Redbart* [1975] RTR 268. See also Civil Evidence Act 1968, s. 3(2); *Rv Da Silva* [1990] 1 WLR 31.

refugee. One who "owing to well-founded fear of being persecuted for reasons of race, religion, nationality, membership of a particular social group or political opinion, is outside the country of his nationality and is unable or, owing to such fear, is unwilling to avail himself of the protection of that country; or who, not having a nationality and being outside the country of his former habitual residence as a result of such events, is unable or, owing to such fear, is unwilling to return to it": Convention on the Status of Refugees, art 1. See *R* v *Home Secretary, ex p Sivakumaran* [1988] 2 WLR 92 (the test of a "well-founded fear" is objective); *R* v *Secretary of State for Home Department, ex p Yurekli* [1990] Imm AR 334 (harassment may not be sufficient to amount to persecution). See Immigration Rules 1990, r. 75.

refusal, wilful. *See* WILFUL REFUSAL.

regent. One appointed by Act of Parliament to fulfil royal functions if the Sovereign is under 18 on accession, or incapacitated. See Regency Acts 1937 and 1953.

regional development aid. Assistance, generally incompatible with EEC objectives, save where intended to promote economic development where there is serious regional unemployment: Treaty of Rome 1957, art. 92. See Industrial Development Act 1982, Part II. *See* EEC.

register at Land Registry. The register of title kept by the Land Registry, subdivided into *Property Register* (describing property and estate (q.v.) for which it is held); *Proprietorship Register* (stating class of title, e.g., absolute, qualified); *Charges Register* (containing notices of charges or incumbrances). See Land Registration Rules 1925, rr. 2–7. *See* LAND REGISTRATION.

registered land. Land, title to which is registered under L.R.A. 1925–86. *See* LAND REGISTRATION.

registered land, protection of mortgage of. "Unless and until the mortgage becomes a registered charge it shall take effect only in equity and it shall be capable of being overridden as a minor interest unless protected by a notice under s. 49 or a caution under s. 54": L.R.A. 1925, s. 106 (as substituted by A.J.A. 1977, s. 26). *See* CAUTION; MINOR INTERESTS; MORTGAGE.

registered office. A company's official address, which it must have at all times. It must be sent to the Registrar of Companies at the time the memorandum (q.v.) is submitted for registration: Cos.A. 1985, s. 10(6). The

Registrar must be notified of any change within 14 days: s. 287. See Cos.A. 1989, s. 136.

register of company charges. Every limited company must keep at its registered office a register of forms of security interest (fixed or floating) over property, other than an interest arising by operation of law: Cos.A. 1989, s. 93. For details of register and delivery of particulars for registration, see ss. 94–96. *See* CHARGE.

register of directors. *See* DIRECTORS, REGISTER OF.

register of interests. Register, kept under Cos.A. 1985, s. 325, in which directors notify the company of interests in voting share capital.

register of members. A register, required under Cos.A. 1985, s. 352, which must contain, e.g., names and addresses of members and shares held by them, together with the amount paid up on shares. This must be kept at the company's registered office and may be inspected by any member during business hours: ss. 353, 356.

registrar, county court. *See* JUDGES, DISTRICT.

registration of birth. *See* BIRTH, REGISTRATION OF.

registration of company. *See* COMPANY, REGISTRATION OF.

registration of death. *See* DEATH, REGISTRATION OF.

registration of land. *See* LAND REGISTRATION.

registration of marriage. *See* MARRIAGE, REGISTRATION OF.

registration of title. *See* LAND REGISTRATION.

registration, UK citizenship resulting from. *See* CITIZENSHIP, BRITISH, ACQUISITION BY REGISTRATION.

regularity, presumption of. *See* OMNIA PRAESUMUNTUR RITE ET SOLEMNITER ESSE ACTA.

regulated agreements. Agreements to which provisions of C.C.A. 1974 relate, i.e., consumer credit agreements; consumer hire agreements; credit token agreements (qq.v.). The agreements must be in writing, must contain all express terms in legible form, must comply with appropriate regulations and be signed by the debtor personally and by the other parties. Failure to comply renders agreements "improperly executed". See *Sovereign Leasing Ltd v Ali* [1992] CCLR 79.

regulated tenancy. A protected or statutory tenancy (qq.v.): Rent Act 1977, s. 18(1), amended by H.A. 1980, Sch. 26. No new regulated tenancies can be created as from Jan 1989 except by renewal or order of the court: H.A. 1988.

regulations of EEC. See COMMUNITY LEGISLATION, FORMS OF.

rehabilitation period. Periods of, e.g., 5–10 years, depending on the sentence, running from conviction, during which a person may be "rehabilitated" and his convictions considered as "spent" under the Rehabilitation of Offenders Act 1974. There is no rehabilitation under the Act where the sentence was, e.g., life imprisonment. See SPENT CONVICTIONS.

re-hearing. A second, or new, hearing of a case already adjudicated upon. Example: appeal to the Crown Court (q.v.) from conviction by a magistrates' court (q.v.), where there is a complete re-hearing and where fresh evidence may be introduced by either side without leave. See, e.g., *Griffith v Jenkins* [1992] 2 WLR 28. See O. 59, r. 3 for the civil procedure in the Court of Appeal.

reification. Philosophical term used in jurisprudential analysis to suggest the error of regarding a mental construction as a "thing" with an existence of its own.

reinstatement. 1. Restoring of an employee to the position he occupied prior to dismissal. An order for reinstatement, stating that an employer shall treat the former employee in all respects as if he had not been dismissed may be made after hearing a complaint against unfair dismissal (q.v.) under E.P.(C.)A. 1978, s. 69. 2. Replacement or repair of damaged property under insurance policy. See, e.g., Fires Prevention (Metropolis) Act 1774, s. 83; L.P.A. 1925, ss. 47, 108(2); Tr.A. 1925, s. 20(4).

reinsurance. Agreement between the re-insured (known as the "direct" or "primary" insurer) and the reinsurer whereby the reinsured undertakes to cede, and the reinsurer undertakes to accept, a fixed share of risk. It takes the form of "facultative reinsurance", i.e., re-insurance against liability on a stated policy, or "treaty reinsurance", i.e., reinsurance against liabilities on policies in general.

rejection of goods. Right of buyer, following breach of contract by seller, to repudiate contract of sale and refuse to accept the goods. See *Bernstein v Pamson Motors* [1987] 2 All ER 220; *Graanhandel v European Grain* [1989] 2 Lloyd's Rep 531. For loss of right, see S.G.A. 1987, s. 11(4).

rejection of offer. An offer (q.v.) is rejected: if the offeree communicates his rejection to the offeror; if the offeree accepts subject to conditions; if the offeree makes a counter-offer. See, e.g., *Jordan v Newton* (1838) 4 M & W 155.

rejoinder. The defendant's answer to a reply by the plaintiff (qq.v.). It cannot be served without leave of court. See O. 18.

related company. See COMPANY, RELATED.

relation back. Principle whereby an act is referred to a prior date, from which time it is construed as being effective. Example: the rule that probate when granted relates back to the time of the testator's death: *Whitehead v Taylor* (1839) 10 A & E 210.

relations. Generally, the next of kin (q.v.). Those who would take under the intestacy laws: *Re Bridgen* [1938] Ch 205.

relationships, prohibited degrees of. Relationships within which a marriage celebrated after July 1971 is void: Mat.C.A. 1973, s. 11(a)(i). They are: *for a man* – mother, daughter, grandmother, granddaughter, sister, aunt, niece, father's or son's or grandfather's or grandson's wife, wife's mother or daughter or grandmother or grand-daughter; *for a woman* – father, son, grandfather, grandson, brother, uncle, nephew, mother's or daughter's or grandmother's or grand-daughter's husband, husband's father or son or grandfather or grandson. The Marriage (Prohibited Degrees of Relationship) Act 1986 allows marriage between a man and a woman who is the daughter or granddaughter of a former spouse of his, if both parties are over 21 and the younger party has not, before attaining the age of 18, been a child of the family in relation to the other party.

relatives. Relations (q.v.). The term usually includes persons who are relatives by marriage or adoption and persons who would be relatives if some persons born illegitimate had been born legitimate: S.S.A. 1975, Sch. 20. See also Adoption Act 1976, s. 72(1); M.H.A. 1983, s. 26; I.C.T.A. 1988, s. 275. For "dependent relatives", see 1988 Act, s. 367.

relatives' identity, right to know. Adopted persons over 18 may be supplied by the Registrar General with names and addresses of relatives maintained on the Adopted Contact Register (which is not open to public inspection). "Relative" means any person other than an adopted relative who is related to the adopted person by blood (including half-blood) or marriage. See Adoption Act 1976, s. 51A, inserted by Ch.A. 1989, Sch. 10, para 21. See ADOPTION.

relator. A private person at whose suggestion an action is commenced by the Attorney-General (q.v.) (as in the case of a matter of public interest, such as a public nuisance). See *Gouriet* v *UPW* [1978] AC 435. For relator actions, see O. 15, r. 11. See ATTORNEY- GENERAL AND RELATOR ACTIONS.

release. 1. "The giving or discharge of the right or action which any hath or claimeth against another, or his land": *Termes de la Ley*. As a defence in an action, it must be specifically pleaded. See O. 18, r. 8(1). 2. A document which acts as discharge of a claim. 3. Discharge from custody.

release of prisoners, early. See PAROLE.

relevance. Known also as "relevancy", "logical relevancy". Term used in the law of evidence to refer to a connection or relationship between facts and events which ordinarily tends to render one probable from the very existence of the other. The general rule of relevance in evidence is that all facts which, though not in issue, may be given as evidence so that the court is enabled to reach a conclusion on facts in issue, are relevant. When one fact logically tends to prove a fact in issue it will be generally admissible unless excluded by some rule (exceptions include: hearsay (q.v.); opinion; reputation of the accused; conduct of the accused on other occasions). (Relev-

ance must be distinguished from "admissibility".) See ADMISSIBILITY OF EVIDENCE; EVIDENCE.

relevant evidence. Evidence relating to facts in issue. "Any two facts to which [the term 'relevant'] is applied are so related to each other that according to the common course of events one either taken by itself or in connection with other facts proves or renders probable the past, present, or future existence or non-existence of the other": Stephen. "Evidence is relevant if it is logically probative or disprobative of some matter which requires proof': *per* Lord Simon in *DPP* v *Kilbourne* [1973] AC 729. Relevant evidence may be excluded on the grounds of estoppel (q.v.), public policy (e.g., Crown privilege). See *R* v *Blastland* [1985] 2 All ER 1095. See EVIDENCE.

relevant facts. See FACTS, RELEVANT.

relief. 1. Payment by a feudal tenant who succeeded to land on the death of a former tenant. 2. Remedial action of a court. 2. Tax allowance. See, e.g., I.C.T.A. 1988. See REMEDY.

relief, financial. See FINANCIAL RELIEF.

relief, interim. See INTERIM RELIEF.

religion. "The Court of Chancery makes no distinction between one religion and another, unless the tenets of a particular sect inculcate doctrines adverse to the very foundations of all religions": *Thornton* v *Howe* (1862) 31 LJ Ch 767. "As between different religions the law stands neutral, but it seems that any religion is at least likely to be better than none": *Neville Estates Ltd* v *Madden* [1962] Ch 832. See *Re South Place Ethical Society* [1980] 1 WLR 1565; *Re Hetherington* [1989] 2 WLR 1094.

religion, advancement of. "To advance religion means to promote it, to spread its message ever wider among mankind; to take some positive steps to sustain and increase religious belief; and these things are done in a variety of ways which may be comprehensively described as pastoral and missionary": *United Grand Lodge* v *Holborn BC* [1957] 1 WLR 1080.

religion, freedom of. "The essence of the concept of freedom of religion is the right to entertain such religious beliefs as a person chooses, the right to declare religious beliefs openly and without fear of hindrance or reprisal, and the right to manifest belief by worship and practice, by teaching and dissemination": per Dickson CJC in *Big M Drug Mart Ltd* (1985) 18 DLR (4th) 321.

remainder. "A residue of an estate in land depending upon a particular estate and created together with the same at one time": Coke. Example: "to X for life, then to Y in fee simple" – X is entitled to actual possession (his estate is the *particular estate*), Y's estate is a *remainder*, and Y is the *remainderman*. A *vested remainder* is one ready to come into possession immediately the particular estate is determined, as contrasted with a *contingent remainder* (q.v.).

remainder, common law rules. A remainder was void: if limited after a fee simple (q.v.); if not preceded by a particular freehold estate created under the same instrument; if limited so that it took effect by defeating the particular estate; if limited so that there was abeyance of seisin (q.v.).

remainderman. See REMAINDER.

remand. To dispose of the person of an individual charged with a crime, e.g., on the adjournment of a hearing. Thus, magistrates may remand a defendant on bail (q.v.) or in custody when proceedings are adjourned. See, e.g., M.C.A. 1980, ss. 128–131 (as amended by P. & C.E.A. 1984, s. 48 and C.J.A. 1988); and Bail Act 1976. The period of remand may not generally exceed eight days without the release of the accused on bail; M.C.A. 1980, s. 128(6). See C.J.A. 1988, s. 155, allowing a new provision for remand for up to 28 days without consent of the accused, where he had been remanded in custody previously and a date had been set for the next part of the proceedings. In general a person may not be remanded in custody without being brought before the court: see, however, C.J.A. 1982, s. 59, Sch. 9, which introduced the now common practice of remanding a prisoner in his absence, provided he consents to the use of the procedure, for up to three successive hearings.

remand centres. Places for the detention of young persons who are re-

manded or committed in custody for trial or sentence: Prison Act 1952, s. 43(1) (*a*) (as substituted by C.J.A. 1982, s. 11).

remand for medical examination. See MEDICAL EXAMINATION, REMAND FOR.

remedial rights. See ANTECEDENT RIGHTS.

remedial statute. A statute intended to remedy an existing defect in the law.

remedy. 1. The means provided by the law to recover rights or to obtain redress or compensation for a wrong, e.g., action for damages. 2. The relief or redress given by a court.

remise. To release a claim; to surrender (by deed (q.v.)).

remission. 1. Pardoning of an offence. 2. Cancelling of the whole or part of some obligation. Remission of a prisoner's sentence is now abolished under C.J.A. 1991.

remoteness of damage. 1. In contract (q.v.), the general rule is that damages for breach will be too remote to be recovered unless such that the defendant, as a reasonable man, would have foreseen as likely to result: *Hadley* v *Baxendale* (1854) 9 Exch 341; *Parsons Ltd* v *Uttley Ingham & Co* [1978] 1 All ER 525. 2. In tort (q.v.), the general rule is that, once negligence (q.v.) is established, the defendant is liable for all the direct consequences, even though not foreseeable by an ordinary, reasonable man in similar circumstances: *Overseas Tankship (UK) Ltd* v *Morts Dock & Engineering Co Ltd* [1961] AC 388.

remoteness, rules against. General rules affecting the period of time for which control over property may be exercised by a person. They include rules against perpetuities, inalienability, accumulations.

removal of action. Transfer of proceedings, e.g., to the county court from the High Court (qq.v.) and vice versa. See, e.g., County C.A. 1984, s. 42.

remuneration. Consideration for services rendered, generally in the form of wages, salaries. Includes "any benefit, facility or advantage, whether in money or otherwise, provided by the employer": Remuneration, Charges and Grants Act 1975, s. 7. See *Perrott* v *Supplementary Benefits Commission* [1980] 3 All ER 110 (remuneration considered as arising from "work which is paid for, and not merely work resulting in a profit"). "Pay" under Treaty of Rome 1957, art. 119, means "the ordinary basic or minimum wage or salary or any other consideration whether in cash or kind received directly or indirectly by the worker in respect of his employment from his employer."

remuneration of directors. This must be stated in a company's balance sheet and prospectus: see Cos.A. 1985, Sch. 5, Part V; Table A, art. 82. Directors are not entitled to remuneration except by express agreement. Where the articles (q.v.) provide for remuneration there can be no change without a special resolution.

remuneration of trustees. Not usually permitted except where authorised under the trust instrument, or by order of the court, or under statute: see Tr.A. 1925, s. 42, and Judicial Tr.A. 1896, s. 1(5). See *Boardman v Phipps* [1966] 2 AC 46.

rendition. Doctrine in international law whereby an offender can be returned to a State to be tried there, under special arrangements or even in the absence of an extradition treaty. See *Barton v Commonwealth of Australia* (1974) 48 ALJR 161.

renewal areas. Where a local authority is satisfied that living conditions in an area within their district, consisting primarily of housing accommodation, are unsatisfactory, they may declare the area a "renewal area": Local Government and Housing Act 1989, s. 89. The authority is required to carry out appropriate works, including demolition, within that area: s. 93.

renewal of lease. *See* LEASE, RENEWAL OF.

renewal of writ. A writ (q.v.) is valid for 12 months from the date of issue. On application (e.g., where the defendant (q.v.) is untraceable) it may be renewed for a period of up to 12 months. See O. 6, r. 8: O. 46, r. 8.

renouncing probate. Refusal of executor (q.v.) to accept office. See the A.E.A. 1925, s. 5; *Re Russell* (1869) LR 1 P & D 634; *Re Biggs* [1966] P 118. *See* PROBATE.

rent. A periodic payment made by the tenant (q.v.) or other occupier of land to the owner for its possession and use. It is an acknowledgement of the landlord's reversionary title. Usually, but not always, it takes the form of money payment; services might be an alternative. See *Bostock v Bryant* (1991) 22 HLR 449.

rental period. "A period in respect of which a payment of rent falls to be made": H.A. 1985, s. 116. Rent is payable in arrear save where there is a contrary provision expressed clearly in the lease.

rent assessment committees. Committees, appointed by the Secretary of State, under the Rent Act 1977, s. 65 and Sch 10. See H.A. 1980, s. 142; Landlord and Tenant Act 1987, s. 31; H.A. 1988, s. 14; SI 1988/2199.

rent book. Document usually recording the terms of tenancy and rent payments. See Landlord and Tenant Act 1985, s. 4; SI 1988/2198.

rentcharge. "Any annual or other periodic sum charged on or issuing out of land except rent reserved by a lease or tenancy or any sum payable by way of interest": Rentcharges Act 1977, s. 1. The creation of rentcharges is now prohibited, under s. 2(1), save in the case of, e.g., the rentcharge having the effect of making land on which rent is charged settled land (q.v.) by virtue of S.L.A. 1925, s. 1(1) (v). Rentcharges are extinguished at the expiry of 60 years beginning with the passing of the 1977 Act or the date on which the rentcharge first became payable, whichever is the later. For apportionment, see s. 4. For release of charity rentcharges, see Charities Act 1992, s. 37.

rent chief. *See* CHIEF RENT.

rent, fair. *See* FAIR RENT.

rent, interim. *See* INTERIM RENT.

rent, non-payment, remedies. These include: distress (q.v.) on the tenant's goods; action for rent, based on express covenant in lease or agreement implied by law from parties' conduct; action for compensation for use and occupation; forfeiture of lease. See, e.g., L.P.A. 1925, s. 146; L.A. 1980, s. 19.

rent officers. Officers appointed under the Rent Act 1977, s. 63, as amended by H.A. 1988, s. 120, with powers to keep registers of rents, consider applications relating to fair rents (q.v.), etc. See SI 1989/580.

rent restrictions. Statutory limitations on the amount of rent payable by a tenant (q.v.). See, e.g., Rent Acts 1974 and 1977. Market rents must be paid in the case of assured, and assured shorthold, tenancies under H.A. 1988.

rent review clause. A clause in a lease (q.v.) allowing a rent to be increased at regular intervals to a "fair market value", based on a formula for rent reassessment. See, e.g., *Orchid Lodge Ltd* v *Extel Computing Ltd* [1991] 32 EG 57; *British Airways* v *Heathrow Airport* [1991] NPC 127.

rent seck. Dry rent (q.v.).

rent service. Periodic payment, or labour given, by a tenant (q.v.) to his landlord, deriving from tenure (q.v.), unlike a rentcharge (q.v.) which is not attributable to tenure.

rent tribunals. Appointed by the Secretary of State for the Environment, each consisting of a chairman and two other members, to consider references arising from rents under restricted contracts.

renunciation. Intentional abandonment of a right. A statement of, or action amounting to, disclaimer (q.v.). "There must be an absolute refusal [by one of the contracting parties] to perform his part of the contract": *per* Keating J in *Freeth* v *Burr* (1874) LR 208.

renunciation of negotiable instrument. *See* NEGOTIABLE INSTRUMENTS, RENUNCIATION OF.

renvoi. (*Renvoyer* = send back.) Doctrine in private international law (q.v.) involving the reference back of a question to English law. The concept of *partial renvoi* (where the court might make a reference to the whole of the foreign law and treat a remission to English law as a reference to English internal law) appears not to form a part of English law (but see *Re Johnson* [1903] 1 Ch 821). Where the court takes a reference to foreign law as meaning the law which the foreign court would in fact, apply to the question, this is known as "*total*" or "*double*" *renvoi*. See *Re Annesley* [1926] Ch 692.

repairing obligation. In a short lease, i.e., less than seven years, in this context (see Landlord and Tenant Act 1985, ss. 13, 14 as modified by L.G.H.A. 1989, Sch. 11), there is an implied covenant (q.v.) by the lessor to keep in repair the structure and exterior of the dwelling house, to keep in repair and proper working order water, gas, electricity and sanitation, space and water heating installations: s. 11(1). See H.A. 1988, s. 116. ("Lease" does not include a mortgage term: s. 16(*a*).) To "keep in repair" means to put and keep in repair: *Liverpool CC* v *Irwin* [1977] AC 239. Liability to repair arises only after notice has been given or there is actual knowledge of a defect: *O'Brien* v *Robinson* [1973] AC 912. See *Stent* v *Monmouth DC* (1987) 19 HLR 269; *King* v *S. Northants DC* [1992] 6 EG 152.

repair notice. Notice served on the person having control of a dwelling-house or house in multiple occupation by the local housing authority (q.v.) when they are satisfied that the house is unfit for human habitation, unless they are satisfied that service of the notice is the most satisfactory course of action: H.A. 1985, s. 189 as modified by L.G.H.A. 1989, Sch. 9. Appeal may be made to the county court within 21 days after service of the notice: s. 191(1). See also Planning (Listed Buildings etc.) Act 1990, s. 48.

repair, reasonable. In determining what is "reasonable repair" in relation to a dwelling or house, a local housing authority (q.v.) shall have regard to the age, character and locality of the dwelling or house and shall disregard the state of internal decorative repair: H.A. 1985, s. 519.

repairs. Work of maintenance, decoration or restoration. " 'Repair' always involves renewal; renewal of a part, of a subordinate part": *Lurcott* v *Wakely* [1911] 1 KB 905.

repatriation. 1. The resumption of one's former nationality by leaving one country and settling in another. 2. Sending back a person to his own country. See Repatriation of Prisoners Act 1984; Extradition Act 1989, s. 21.

repeal. To rescind or revoke. Refers, e.g., to the express or implied abrogation of one statute by a later Act. "The test of whether there has been a repeal by implication by subsequent legislation is this: are the provisions of a later Act so inconsistent with, or repugnant to, the provisions of an earlier Act that the two cannot stand together": *West Ham Church Wardens* v *Fourth City Montreal Building Society* [1892] 1 QB 654. See Statute Law (Repeals) Act 1986. Result of repealing a statute is that it is treated as though it had never been enacted, save for actions concluded prior to repeal: *Kay* v *Goodwin* (1836) 6 Bing 576. Where a person is charged under a repealed Act and convicted, the conviction will be quashed: *Stowers* v *Darnell* [1973] RTR 459. See also I.A. 1978, ss. 15, 16. For an example of a "self-repealing statute", see Road Traffic Act 1991, Sch. 8, repealing its own Sch. 4, para 79.

replevin. (*Replevire* = to give security.) Formerly a remedy of re-delivery for one whose chattels had been wrongfully seized by way of distress (q.v.); later used in cases involving wrongful detention of chattels. See Torts (Interference with Goods) Act 1977. See *Swaffer* v *Mulcahy* [1934] 1 KB 608.

reply. 1. Plaintiff's statement in pleadings (q.v.) replying to a defence or counterclaim (qq.v.). It must be served within 14 days after the defence has been served. See O. 18. 2. Counsel's speech for the plaintiff (q.v.) or for the prosecution answering the defendant's points.

reporting restrictions. Limitations placed on the media (press, TV, etc.) concerning the publication of information relating to court proceedings. See, e.g., C. & Y.P.A. 1933, s. 39; C.J.A. 1988, s. 158; *R* v *Crown Court, ex p Godwin* [1991] 3 All ER 818; *R* v *Dover Justices, ex p Dover DC* [1992] Crim LR 371.

repossession. Exercise of a mortgagee's right to take possession of the mortgaged property, which arises as soon as the mortgage is made, resulting in the entire estate vested in the mortgagor being conveyed to the mortgagee free from the mortgagor's equity of redemption (q.v.). See L.P.A. 1925, ss. 88, 89, 103, 104. The right may be exercised, e.g., where interest has fallen into arrear and is unpaid for at least two months. *See* MORTGAGE.

representation. 1. Taking the place of another, e.g., as in the relationship of principal and agent (qq.v.). 2. Being represented in a legislative body (e.g., the House of Commons (q.v.)). 3. A statement made by one party to another, relating to some past event or existing fact (but not as to law), which induces a course of action, e.g., signing of a contract. It may be inferred from conduct. Includes, under C.C.A. 1974, s. 189(1), any condition or warranty and any other statement or undertaking, whether oral or in writing. For representation in intestate succession, see the A.E.A. 1925, Part IV.

representation, chain of. *See* CHAIN OF REPRESENTATION.

representative. One who stands in the place of another, e.g., a personal representative (q.v.). See O. 6, r. 3.

representative action. Action brought by one or more of a number of persons having the same interest in proceedings. Judgment is binding on all those represented if (as plaintiffs) they have a common grievance and are able to benefit from the relief claimed. See O. 15, r. 12; *John* v *Rees* [1970] Ch 345; *Irish Shipping Ltd* v *Commercial Union* [1990] 2 WLR 117.

reprieve. Formal suspension of execution of a sentence.

republication of will. Where a testator (q.v.) desires that his unrevoked will should take effect as if written on a subsequent date, he may republish it with the formalities needed in the case of a will, by re-execution or by making a subsequent codicil (q.v.) showing the intention to republish. *See* WILL.

repudiation. Refusal to be bound by, e.g., a contract. It generally amounts to a breach of contract (q.v.), as where a party states that he will not carry out a promise (see *Heyman* v *Darwins Ltd* [1952] 1 All ER 337) or does some act which disables him from performing his promise (an implied repudiation). The test for implicit repudiation is whether the conduct "evinces an intention not to perform": *Freeth* v *Burr* (1874) LR 9 CP 208. See *Tai Hing Cotton Mill Ltd* v *Kamsing Knitting Factory* [1979] AC 91 – date for assessing damages for repudiation; *Photo Productions Ltd* v *Securicor Transport Ltd* [1980] AC 827; *Rigby* v *Ferodo* [1987] IRLR 516.

repugnancy. Inconsistency of two or more provisions in a deed (q.v.) or other document. The inconsistent provisions may be struck out by the court when no other method is possible to make effective the principal intention of the parties to the document (the so-called "main purpose" rule). If the court cannot say which of two provisions ought to be rejected, then the general rule is that, in the case of a will (q.v.) the later one remains, but in the case of a deed (q.v.), the earlier remains: *Gwynn* v *Neath Canal Co* (1865) LR 3 Ex 209. See *Evans & Son* v *Andrea Merzario* [1976] 1 WLR 1078.

reputation. The estimation in which a person is generally held. Disparagement of reputation may constitute defamation (q.v.). For the admissibility of evidence of reputation in civil proceedings, see, e.g., Civil Evidence Act 1968, s. 9(3), (4). *See* CHARACTER, EVIDENCE AS TO.

requesting court. Court or tribunal making application to a UK court for assistance in obtaining evidence for civil proceedings in that court: see, e.g., Evidence (Proceedings in Other Jurisdictions) Act 1975, s. 1.

request, letter of. *See* LETTER OF REQUEST.

Requests, Court of. *See* COURT OF REQUESTS.

requisition. 1. Demand by a purchaser for the official search relating to title (q.v.). See L.P.A. 1925, s. 45(1) (*b*). 2. Requests for supplies. 3. Compulsory taking of property, e.g., for military purposes.

re-registration. Procedure under Cos.A. 1985, ss. 43–55, whereby a private company is converted into a public company as from the date of its registration for all purposes, or a public company is converted into a private company, or an unlimited company becomes limited, or a limited company becomes unlimited.

res. A thing.

resale price maintenance. The imposition of conditions for the maintenance of minimum prices at which goods are to be resold. An agreement of this nature is generally void unless it can be shown, e.g., that the prices are such that, without them, the quality or variety of goods would be substantially reduced to the detriment of the public or that goods would be sold under conditions likely to cause danger to health. See Resale Prices Acts 1964 and 1976.

resale price maintenance, collective, prohibition of. Collective agreements by suppliers (carrying on the business of selling goods by wholesale or retail) based on the withholding of, or refusal to supply goods, save, e.g., on terms and conditions less favourable than those applicable in the case of others, which are unlawful under Resale Prices Act 1976, Part I. Goods may be exempted by the Restrictive Practices Court (q.v.) under s. 14.

resale price maintenance, exempted goods relating to. Goods exempted from provisions of Resale Prices Act 1976, following a successful application under the 1976 Act, s. 14 to the Restrictive Practices Court (q.v.). Grounds for exemption are, e.g., that the detriment to consumers would outweigh the detriment to them resulting from the maintenance of minimum resale prices, e.g., where the number of establishments in which the goods are sold by retail would be substantially reduced: s. 14.

resale price maintenance, individual, prohibition of. Terms or conditions of a contract for the sale of goods by the supplier to the dealer or agreements between them relating to such a sale which are void if they provide for the charging of minimum prices on the resale of goods in the UK: Resale Prices Act 1976, s. 9.

resale, right of. Right of the seller, under S.G.A. 1979, s. 48, to resell even though ownership has passed to the original buyer, if the goods are perishable or if he has given notice to the original buyer of his intention to resell and the original buyer does not make payment. See *Damon Cia Naviera* v *Hapag-Lloyd* [1985] 1 All ER 475.

rescission. Remedy for inducing a contract by innocent or fraudulent misrepresentation (q.v.), whereby the contract is abrogated. A party intending to rescind must notify the other party. A rescission *ab initio* results in the contract being treated as though it had never been. Right of rescission is lost: if *restitutio in integrum* (q.v.) is impossible; if the injured party takes a benefit under the contract with the knowledge of the misrepresentation; if a third party has acquired for value rights under the contract. See Misrepresentation Act 1967; *Lagunas Nitrate Co* v *Lagunas Syndicate* [1899] 2 Ch 392; *Peyman* v *Lanjani* [1985] Ch 457. *See* CONTRACT.

rescue cases. Cases in which the plaintiff is injured while intervening in a situation so as to save the life or property endangered by the defendant's negligence. Generally, if the plaintiff's intervention is reasonable in the circumstances, it does not constitute an assumption of risk, but if unreasonable, *volenti non fit injuria* (q.v.) applies. See *Haynes* v *Harwood* [1934] 2 KB 240; *Ogwo* v *Taylor* [1987] 3 All ER 961.

reservation. 1. Generally, a limiting condition. 2. Action by a vendor of land, selling part of it and wishing to reserve easements (q.v.) and profits. See L.P.A. 1925, s. 65; *Wiles* v *Banks* (1985) 50 P & C R 81.

reserve capital. That part of the uncalled capital which a limited company determines by special resoiution not to call up except when the company is being wound up: Cos.A. 1985, s. 124.

reserves, undistributable. Included are a company's share premium account, capital redemption reserve fund, accumulated unrealised profits less accumulated realised losses, other reserves which a company may not distribute: see Cos.A. 1985, s. 264 (3).

reserve, without. See WITHOUT RESERVE.

res extincta. The subject matter of an agreement which is, in fact, non-existent. In such a case no contract ensues. See, e.g., *Couturier* v *Hastie* (1856) 5 HL Cas 673.

res gestae. Things done; the events which happened. All the facts constituting, accompanying or explaining a fact in issue (the "transaction"). See *R* v *Christie* [1914] AC 545; *R* v *Andrews* [1987] AC 281. "As regards statements made after the event, it must be for the judge, by a preliminary ruling, to satisfy himself that the statement was so clearly made in circumstances of spontaneity or involvement in the event that the possibility of concoction can be disregarded . . . And the same must in principle be true of statements made before the event . . . The expression *res gestae* may conveniently sum up these criteria, but the reality of

them must always be kept in mind": *Ratten* v *R* [1972] AC 378.

residence. Place where a person abides, i.e., where he has his home. A "residence" in the sense of a "dwelling-house" can comprise several dwellings not physically joined: *Batey* v *Wakefield* [1982] 1 All ER 61. In the case of a corporation, the place where its management is carried on. See I.C.T.A. 1988, ss. 334–6; *Reed* v *Clark* [1986] Ch 1; for "residing with a tenant" (see Rent Act 1977, Sch. 1, Part 1, para. 1), see *Swanbrae Ltd* v *Elliott* (1987) 281 EG 916. "Habitual residence" was defined, in *R* v *Barnet LBC, ex p Shah* [1983] 2 WLR 16, as "voluntary residence with a degree of settled purpose". *See* ABODE; DOMICILE.

residence order. An order of the court settling the arrangements to be made as to the person with whom a child is to live: Ch.A. 1989, s. 8(1). For enforcement, see s. 14. See *In re G.* (1992), The Times, 9 Oct.

residential care homes. Term referring to houses for disabled, old persons and mentally disordered persons (not including hospitals, nursing or mental nursing homes). They must be registered. See Health and Social Services Adjudication Act 1983, Sch. 4; Registered Homes Act 1984, as amended by Registered Homes (Amendment) Act 1991; Community Care (Residential Accommodation) Act 1992.

residential occupier. A person occupying premises as a residence whether under a contract or by virtue of any enactment or rule of law giving him the right to remain in occupation or restricting the right of any other person to recover possession of the premises: Protection from Eviction Act 1977, s. 1(1). For "displaced residential occupier", see C.L.A. 1977, s. 12(3).

residential premises, adverse occupation of. *See* ADVERSE OCCUPATION OF RESIDENTIAL PREMISES.

residential property loan. Any loan secured on land in the UK made to an individual in respect of the acquisition of land which is for his residential use or the residential use of a dependant of his: C.L.S.A. 1990, s. 104(1). For the "tying-in" of such a loan to the provision of conveyancing services, see ss. 104, 105.

resident in UK. "Ordinarily resident" refers to a man's abode in a particular place which he has adopted voluntarily and for settled purposes as part of the regular order of his life for the time being, whether of short or long duration: *per* Lord Scarman in *Akbarali v Brent London BC* [1983] 2 AC 309. "Residence" implies lawful presence: see *R v Secretary of State ex p Marguerite* [1983] QB 180. A person who is resident in the UK for a period or periods totalling 183 days in any year is regarded as a resident in the UK for that year for tax purposes: I.C.T.A. 1988, s. 336. See *Levene v IRC* [1982] AC 217.

residual negative principle. Jurisprudential concept, suggesting that everything which is not legally prohibited is deemed to be legally permitted.

residuary body. Body corporate set up under L.G.A. 1985, Part VII, to deal with residual matters, e.g., the management of existing debt, custody of surplus property, preparation of final accounts, on the abolition of the Greater London Council and the metropolitan County Councils. See 1985 Act, Sch. 13.

residuary devise. *See* DEVISE.

residuary devisee. The devisee who takes the real property which remains after specific gifts of real property under a will (q.v.) have been satisfied. *See* DEVISE.

residuary estate. Testator's property not specifically bequeathed or devised. See A.E.A. 1925, s. 33.

residuary legacy. *See* LEGACY.

residue. That which remains of an estate after payment of debts, funeral expenses, testamentary expenses, legacies, annuities, costs of administration, etc. See I.C.T.A. 1988, s. 701 (6).

resignation. The deliberate relinquishing of some position or office. See, e.g., *Kwik-Fit Ltd v Lineham* (1991) The Times, 4 Dec (resignation and repudiation of contract).

resile. To withdraw from (e.g., an agreement).

res integra. A whole, "unopened", thing. A question on which there is no rule and no decision has been taken in a court of law and which must be resolved upon principle.

res inter alios acta alteri nocere non debet. A transaction between strangers should not prejudice another party. A special rule of evidence. Example: an admission generally binds only the person making it. See *Beswick v Beswick* [1968] AC 58; *Naumann v Ford* (1985) 275 EG 542.

res ipsa loquitur. The thing speaks for itself. A rule of evidence in actions for injury where the mere fact of an accident occurring raises the inference of the defendant's negligence, so that a prima facie case exists. "You may presume negligence from the mere fact that it happens": *Ballard v N British Rwy* (1923) SC 43. See *Byrne v Boadle* (1863) 2 H & C 722 (barrel falling from an upper floor); *Lloyde v W Midlands Gas Board* [1971] 1 WLR 749 (disintegration of a household gas system); *Ward v Tesco Ltd* [1976] 1 WLR 810 (slipping on a supermarket floor): *Waldie v Cook* (1988) 91 FLR 413 (no application in criminal law); *O'Reilly v Lavelle* [1990] 2 IR 372.

resisting arrest. *See* ARREST, RESISTING.

res judicata. A final judicial decision pronounced by a competent judicial tribunal. "It is a very substantial doctrine, and it is one of the most fundamental doctrines of all courts that there must be an end to all litigation, and that the parties have no right of their own accord, having tried a question between them, and obtained a decision of a court, to start that litigation over again on precisely the same question": *per* Brett MR in *Re May* (1885) 28 Ch D 516. See *Thomas v A.-G. of Trinidad and Tobago* (1990) The Times, 21 Nov.

res nova. A new matter.

res nullius. A thing belonging to no one. In international law, territory not under the sovereignty of any state.

resolution. A formal expression of opinion by an organised body, e.g., as in a meeting or assembly. In the case of companies, resolutions may be ordinary; extraordinary; special (qq.v.). See Cos.A. 1985, ss. 376–381; Table A, art. 53. *See* VOTING AT MEETINGS.

res perit domino. The loss falls on the owner. See S.G.A. 1979, ss. 7, 20, 32.

respondeat superior. Let the principal answer. In general, a master is responsible for the acts of his servant committed in the course of employment. *See* MASTER AND SERVANT.

respondent. One against whom a petition is presented or an appeal is brought.

respondentia. *See* BOTTOMRY.

responsibility. 1. Care and consideration for the outcome of one's actions. 2. Legal liability, i.e., accountability for some state of affairs to which one's conduct has contributed, together with an obligation to repair any injury caused.

responsibility, collective. *See* COLLECTIVE RESPONSIBILITY.

responsibility, ministerial. *See* MINISTERIAL RESPONSIBILITY.

res sua. One's own goods. Phrase used, e.g., where a person makes a contract (q.v.) to purchase that which, in fact, belongs to him. The contract is void. See *Bligh* v *Martin* [1968] 1 WLR 804.

restitutio in integrum. Restoration to the original position. Right to rescind a contract for misrepresentation is lost if *restitutio in integrum* is not possible. Rescission must put parties *in statu quo ante* and restore things "as between them to the position in which they stood before the contract was entered into": *Abram Steamship Co* v *Westville Shipping Co* [1923] AC 773. See *O'Sullivan* v *Management Agency* [1985] QB 428.

restitution. 1. Restoration to the rightful owner. Under Th.A. 1968, s. 28, the court may order anyone in possession or control of stolen goods to restore them to any person entitled to recover them from him. See also C.J.A. 1972, s. 6; C.J.A. 1988, Sch. 15. The equitable doctrine of restitution refers to the case, e.g., of an infant who, having fraudulently obtained goods, is ordered to restore his ill-gotten gains. See Minors' Contracts Act 1987, s. 3. 3. Writ (q.v.) restoring to a defendant (q.v.) who has appealed successfully against a judgment, that which he had lost following the execution of that judgment.

restitution of conjugal rights. *See* CONJUGAL RIGHTS, RESTITUTION OF.

restoration condition. Phrase used in relation to planning permission, referring to restoration of a site after working of minerals, by the use of subsoil, topsoil and soilmaking material: see T.C.P.A. 1971, s. 30A (inserted by T.C.P. (Minerals) A. 1981, s. 5). See T.C.P.A. 1990, Sch. 5. *See* AFTER CARE CONDITIONS.

restraint, bodily. Involves a total restraint of a person's liberty in every direction. See, e.g., *Bird* v *Jones* (1845) 7 QB 742. *See* FALSE IMPRISONMENT.

restraint of marriage. An attempt to prevent a person marrying, by a condition in a contract, is void as contrary to public policy if in general restraint, but not necessarily so if in partial restraint. A condition in restraint of a second marriage may be valid: *Allen* v *Jackson* (1875) 1 Ch D 399.

restraint of trade. "Any contract which interferes with the free exercise of [a person's] trade or business, by restricting him in the work he may do for others, or the arrangements which he may make with others, is a contract in restraint of trade. It is invalid unless it is reasonable as between the parties and not injurious to the public interest": *Petrofina* v *Martin* [1966] Ch 146. Question of reasonableness is for the court, not for the jury: *Dowden* v *Pook* [1904] 1 KB 48. See *Lobb Garages* v *Total Oil Ltd* [1985] 1 All ER 303; *Watson* v *Prager* [1991] 1 WLR 726.

restraint on alienation. *See* ALIENATION, RESTRAINT ON.

restraint on anticipation. *See* ANTICIPATION, RESTRAINT ON.

restraint, order. Order by the High Court, under C.J.A. 1988, s. 77, prohibiting a person from dealing with realisable property, so as to preserve it as the basis of a confiscation order under s. 71. See *Re M.* [1992] 1 All ER 537

restraints of princes. Phrase used in some insurance policies to indicate interference with or frustration of some commercial endeavour (in connection with, e.g., transport of goods by sea) as the result of activities of rulers of a country. See, e.g., *Rickards* v *Forestal Land Co* [1942] AC 50.

restricted-use credit agreement. A regulated consumer credit agreement (q.v.) to finance a transaction between a debtor and creditor, whether forming part of that agreement or not, or to finance a transaction between the debtor and a person other than the creditor, or to refinance any existing indebtedness of the debtor's whether to the creditor or another person: C.C.A. 1974, s. 11(1).

restriction order. An order based, e.g., on a hospital order (q.v.) subjecting the offender to special restrictions for a specified or unlimited time. See *R v Toland* (1974) 58 Cr App R 453; *R v Merseyside MH Review Tribunal, ex p K.* [1990] 1 All ER 694; M.H.A. 1983, s. 41.

restriction order, share. Where a company fails to disclose information concerning share acquisitions or disposals under Cos.A. 1985, s. 216, its shares are "frozen", i.e., they cannot be transferred and no voting rights may be exercised in respect of them. See *Re Lonrho* (1989) 5 BCC 776.

restrictive covenant. 1. A covenant by which use of the covenantor's land is restricted for the benefit of the covenantee's adjoining land. The burden of such a covenant may bind an assignee of the covenantor's tenement, i.e., it may be considered as a covenant running with the land (q.v.). See L.P.A. 1925, s. 56; L.C.A. 1972, s. 2(5). 2. Covenant restraining an employee from exercising his skills on the termination of his employment. See, e.g., *Kumar* v *Dunning* [1987] 3 WLR 1167; *Holdom* v *Kidd* [1991] 2 EG 163. *See* COVENANT.

restrictive covenants, discharge and modification of. Powers for discharge and modification of restrictive covenants concerning land are contained in L.P.A. 1925, s. 84 (as amended by the L.P.A. 1969, s. 28). Application is made to the Lands Tribunal (q.v.). "For an application to succeed on the ground of public interest is so important and immediate as to justify the serious interference with private rights and the sanctity of contract": *Re Collins'Applications* (1975) 30 P & CR 527.

restrictive indorsement. *See* ENDORSEMENT.

Restrictive Practices Court. A superior court of record (q.v.) created by Restrictive Trade Practices Act 1956, and now constituted under the Restrictive Practices Court Act 1976, presided over by a High Court judge. Cases are referred to it by the Director General of Fair Trading (q.v.) or parties to a restrictive agreement who have been ordered to give particulars to the court. Its task is to declare whether a restriction is contrary to public interest and,

if so, to declare it void. A restriction is deemed contrary to public interest unless shown to be, e.g., reasonably necessary to protect the public against injury or to counteract measures taken by some person not a party to the restrictive agreement. See, e.g., Restrictive Trade Practices Acts 1956–77; European Communities Act 1972, s. 10; Fair Trading Act 1973; Resale Prices Act 1976; Competition Act 1980, ss. 25–29.

restrictive trade practices. Practices which must be registered with the Director General of Fair Trading (q.v.) under Restrictive Trade Practices Acts 1956–77, based on certain agreements relating to goods (e.g., prices to be recommended, terms of supply, process of manufacture) or services. Agreements important to the national economy may be excepted: 1976 Act, s. 29. See Participation Agreements Act 1978; and *RICS* v *DG of Fair Trading* [1981] Com LR 112; F.S.A. 1986, Part I, Chap XIV.

resulting trust. A trust (q.v.) which arises in circumstances where the beneficial interest comes back ("results") to the person or his representatives who transferred the property to the trustee (q.v.) or who provided the means of obtaining the property. Example: X transfers funds to trustees to be held on the trusts of a marriage settlement; the marriage is later declared void *ab initio* (q.v.), so that the fund is held on a resulting trust for X. See L.P.A. 1925, s. 60; and *Universe Tankships, etc* v *ITWF* [1983] 1 AC 366; *Winkworth* v *Edward Baron Development Co.* [1986] 1 WLR 1512 (displacement of presumption of resulting trust); *Rowan* v *Dann* [1991] EGCS 19.

resulting use. An equitable interest arising where feoffment (q.v.) was made without declaring a use in favour of the feoffee (q.v.). See the L.P.A. 1925, s. 60(3). *See* USE.

retail transaction. "The sale or supply of goods, or the supply of services (including financial services)": Wages Act 1986, s. 2(2). See C.P.A. 1987, s. 10(5).

retainer, right of. Rights of a personal representative (q.v.) to retain debts due to him in preference to paying other creditors of the same degree. Abolished by A.E.A. 1971, s. 10.

retirement of jury. Period, following the summing-up (q.v.), in which the jury considers its verdict. No further evidence can be called once the jury has retired. "A jury shall deliberate in complete freedom, uninfluenced by any promise, unintimidated by any threat": *R* v *McKenna and Busby* (1960) 44 Cr App R 63.

retirement of trustees. A trustee (q.v.) can retire only under express power or statutory power conferred by the Tr.A. 1925, s. 39, or by the consent of all the beneficiaries, or by order of the court. *See* TRUSTEESHIP, TERMINATION OF.

retiring age, normal. The earliest age at which an employee could be required to retire; it is a matter of evidence, not depending exclusively on a contract of employment, although that provides the best evidence as to the normal retiring age: *Post Office* v *Wallser* [1981] 1 All ER 668. See E.P.(C.)A. 1978, s. 64(1)(b), as amended by Sex Discrimination Act 1986, s. 3(1); 1978 Act, s. 82(1); *Doughty* v *Rolls Royce* [1992] IRLR 126; S.S. Contributions and Benefits Act 1992, ss. 43–55.

retorsion. Also "retortion". Term used in international law for retaliation by one state against some inequitable, discourteous or objectionable act of another. It may take the form of an unfriendly, but legitimate, act within the competence of the affronted state, e.g., revocation of diplomatic privileges.

retour sans protêt. Return without protest. Request by the drawer of a bill that if it is dishonoured it can be returned without protest (q.v.). *See* BILL OF EXCHANGE.

retrial. *See* TRIAL, NEW.

retributive justice. *See* JUSTICE, RETRIBUTIVE.

retrospective legislation. Known also as "retroactive legislation". Laws which, expressly or by implication, operate so as to affect acts done prior to their having been passed. See, e.g., Validation of War-time Leases Act 1944; War Damage Act 1965; *Yew Bon Tew* v *Kanderaan Bas Mara* [1983] 1 AC 553. There is a presumption (q.v.) against the retrospective operation of a statute relating to substantive law (q.v.): *Re Athlumney* [1898] 2 QB 547. See *Arnold* v *C.E.G.B* [1988] AC 228. "The court

will not ascribe retrospective force to new laws affecting rights unless by express words or necessary implication it appears that such was the intention of the legislature": *per* Willes J in *Phillips* v *Eyre* (1870) LR 6QB 1. *See* EX POST FACTO.

return. 1. Formal statement or report, e.g., annual return (q.v.) required under the Cos.A. 1985, s. 363. 2. Election of a member to serve in Parliament (q.v.).

return day. *See* INTERLOCUTORY RELIEF, APPLICATION FOR.

returning officer. A person (e.g., sheriff, mayor (qq.v)) who is responsible for the conduct of a parliamentary election. See Representation of the People Act 1983, s. 27; *Greenway-Stanley* v *Paterson* [1977] 2 All ER 663.

return order. Court order for the return of goods to a creditor, under C.C.A. 1974, s. 133(1)(b)(i). It may be made, e.g., in an action brought by a creditor under a hire-purchase agreement to recover possession of the goods to which the agreement relates.

revenge. Retaliation, reprisal. "Revenge is a kind of wild justice, which the more man's nature runs to, the more ought law to weed it out . . . ": Bacon (1625). See *R* v *Watson* (1990) 12 Cr App R(S) (the court will not condone retaliatory violence).

revenue. Income; yield of taxes; return on investment.

revenue, cheating the. The common law offence does exist, but a conspiracy to cheat may be charged as a statutory offence under C.L.A. 1977, s. 1(1): *R* v *Mulligan* [1990] STC 220.

revenue statutes. Statutes concerned with, e.g., taxation. The general rule is that "the subject is not to be taxed except by plain words". Where clearly worded they must be applied no matter what their effect on persons, but "if [a provision] is capable of two alternative meanings, courts will prefer that meaning more favourable to the subject": *IRC* v *Ross and Coulter* [1948] 1 All ER 616.

reversal of judgment. The altering of a judgment on appeal. See O. 59. *See* OVERRULE.

reversion. Known also as "reverter". Where X, owner of fee simple in Blackacre, grants Blackacre to Y for life, X retains reversion, i.e., an interest which remains in him, since Blackacre will revert to him on Y's death. X is known as the "reversioner". A "reversionary interest" was defined in the Inheritance Tax Act 1984, s. 47, as "a future interest under a settlement, whether it is vested or contingent".

reversionary lease. A lease (q.v.) which is to become effective at some future time. Grant of such a lease is now void unless it takes effect within 21 years from the date of the instrument creating it: L.P.A. 1925, s. 149(3). See *Re Strand Properties* [1960] Ch 582 (option to renew contained in lease).

reverter, possibility of. Possibility of a grantor's having an estate at some future time. It was destroyed if the determining event could not occur. Example: land is given "to X and his heirs until Y marries", and Y dies unmarried. See Reverter of Sites Act 1987, s. 1, replacing the right of reverter in some cases by a trust for sale (q.v.).

revival of will. Where a testator (q.v.) has revoked his will and wishes later to restore it to effect, he may revive it by re-execution with appropriate formalities or by a subsequent codicil (q.v.), showing the intention to revive. The revived will takes effect as though written at the date of revival. See W.A. 1837, ss. 22, 34. *See* WILL.

revocation. An act by which one annuls something he has done.

revocation of offer. An offer may be revoked at any time before acceptance; after acceptance it is irrevocable. Revocation does not take effect until actually communicated to the offeree. See *Dickinson v Dodds* (1876) 2 Ch D 463; *Byrne v Van Tienhoven* (1880) 5 CPD 349. *See* OFFER.

revocation of probate. Revocation of a grant by the court when, e.g., one of the executors has become incapable of acting, or probate has been obtained by fraud, or the testator is found to be alive. See S.C.A. 1981, s. 121. *See* PROBATE.

revocation of will. A will can always be revoked by the testator before his death. Revocation may be effected by the destruction of the will, or by the execution of another will or codicil (q.v.), or as a result of marriage. See

W.A. 1837, ss. 18–20 (as amended by A.J.A. 1982, s. 18). (For revival of revoked will, see W.A. 1837, s. 22.) *Animus revocandi* (q.v.) at the time of the destruction of the will is essential. See *Gill v Gill* [1909] P 157; *Re Adams* [1990] 2 All ER 97; *Re Finnemore* [1991] 1 WLR 793. *See* MARRIAGE, WILL IN CONTEMPLATION OF; WILL.

rewards for return of goods. Where a public advertisement of a reward for the return of lost or stolen goods uses words to the effect that no questions will be asked or that the person producing the goods will be safe from apprehension, an offence is committed under Th.A. 1968, s. 23.

rex non potest peccare. The King can do no wrong (q.v.).

rex nunquam moritur. The King never dies. (In effect, there can be no interregnum.)

Richard Roe. *See* ROE, RICHARD.

rider. 1. Clause added to a Bill, or agenda. 2. Statement, e.g., a recommendation, appended to a jury's verdict.

right. 1. That to which a person has a just or lawful claim. 2. An interest which will be recognised and protected by a rule of law, respect for which is a legal duty, violation of which is a legal wrong: Salmond.

right *ex lege*. Right created directly by law without the consent of those bound consequently, e.g., right stemming from the law of torts.

right, new. "No new right in the law, fully-fledged with all the appropriate safeguards, can spring from the head of a judge deciding a particular case: only Parliament can create such a right . . . The wider and more indefinite the right claimed, the greater the undesirability of holding that such a right exists": *per* Sir Robert Megarry V.-C. in *Malone v MPC (No. 2)* [1979] Ch 344.

right of action. 1. The right to bring an action. 2. Chose in action (q.v.).

right of entry. Right of resuming possession of land by entering. Proviso for re-entry in a lease indicates that a lessor (q.v.) may re-enter on a breach of covenant by the lessor. Under L.P.A. 1925, s. 146, right of re-entry is not enforceable unless and until notice is served on the lessee and reasonable time is afforded to him to remedy the breach. See *Expert Clothing* v *Hillgate House* [1986] Ch 340. It is unlawful to enforce a right of re-entry except through court proceedings while the occupier is lawfully residing in the premises: Protection from Eviction Act 1977, s. 2. See T.C.P.A. 1990, s. 324.

right of resale. *See* RESALE, RIGHT OF.

right of retainer. *See* RETAINER, RIGHT OF.

right of support. The natural right to have one's soil supported by the soil of one's neighbour's land. The right to the support of buildings by adjoining buildings or land may be acquired as an easement (q.v.). See *Dalton* v *Angus & Co* (1881) 6 App Cas 740; *Midland Bank* v *Baragrove Properties* (1991) 24 Con LR 98.

right of way. The right to pass over another's land. A public right of way can be created by statute or by dedication and acceptance. For "prescriptive right of way", see *Ironside and Crabb* v *Cooke and Barefoot* (1981) 41 P & CR 326. See Highways Act 1980, Part IX, as amended by Rights of Way Act 1990, s. 1; T.C.P.A. 1990, s. 258; *Jones* v *Price* (1992) The Independent, 16 Jan. *See* DEDICATION OF WAY.

right, petition of. *See* PETITION OF RIGHT.

rights, antecedent. *See* ANTECEDENT RIGHTS.

rights as trumps. Metaphorical expression used in jurisprudence, suggesting, e.g., that individual rights may override some collective goal. See, e.g., Dworkin's *Taking Rights Seriously* (1978).

rights issue. Issues of shares whereby existing shareholders are given a prior right to take some part of the new issue at a price below the market value of the shares. See Cos.A. 1985, s. 89. *See* SHARE.

rights natural. *See* NATURAL RIGHTS.

rights offer. An offer of shares in a company made by "letter of rights" sent by the company to existing members in proportion to their existing holdings, e.g., two for one.

rights, perfect and imperfect. *See* PERFECT AND IMPERFECT RIGHTS.

rights, vested. *See* VESTED RIGHTS.

right to begin. Generally belongs to the party on whom the burden of proof (q.v.) rests. In criminal cases the prosecution begins. In civil cases the plaintiff (q.v.) begins where the onus of proving an issue is on him, and where he claims substantial and unliquidated damages. Where the onus of proving all issues is on a defendant (q.v.) he may generally begin. See O. 35, r. 7; *Mercer* v *Whall* (1845) 5 QBD 447.

right, writ of. Formerly used to claim right to lands in fee simple held unjustly by one other than the true owner. Abolished in 1833.

riot. Where twelve or more persons who are present together use or threaten unlawful violence for a common purpose and the conduct of them (taken together) is such as would cause a person of reasonable firmness present at the scene to fear for his personal safety, each of the persons using unlawful violence for the common purpose is guilty of riot: P.O.A. 1986, s. 1(1). A person is guilty only if he intends to use violence or is aware that his conduct may be violent: s. 6(1). See *R* v *Keys and Sween* [1987] Crim LR 207.

riparian. Relating to the bank of a river or stream. A riparian owner may, under common law, take and use water for ordinary purposes relating to tenement if the water is restored unaltered in character and substantially undiminished in value. See, e.g., *Embrey* v *Owen* (1851) 6 Exch 353.

risk, transfer of. Principle whereby, in performance of a contract for the sale of goods, risk generally passes with the property, unless the parties agree otherwise. See S.G.A. 1979, ss. 20, 33; *Pignataro* v *Gilroy* [1919] 1 KB 459; *Demby Hamilton* v *Barden* [1949] 1 All ER 435.

river. A natural stream of water flowing in a channel to the sea or another river, and including (see Salmon Act 1986, s. 40(1)) tributaries and any loch from or through which any river flows. See Water Resources Act 1991. For "main river", see 1991 Act, s. 113. *See* NATIONAL RIVERS AUTHORITY.

road. "Any highway or any other road to which the public has access, and includes bridges over which a road passes": Road Traffic Regulation Act 1984, s. 142. See also s. 60(4); *Laing* v *Hindhaugh* [1986] RTR 271. *See* ROAD CHECKS.

road checks. Police are empowered to block a road (see Road Traffic Act 1972, s. 159) under P. & C.E.A. 1984, s.

4, so as to stop a vehicle to ascertain whether it is carrying a person unlawfully at large (q.v.), or one who intends to commit, or has committed, a serious arrestable offence (q.v.) or a witness to such an offence.

road, Crown. See CROWN ROAD.

road, occupation. A road, the right to use which is confined to occupiers of land and premises which it serves. See Highways Act 1980, s. 31(3)(b); *Fitch v Rawling* (1795) 2 Hy Bl 393.

road-users, causing damage to. It is an offence for a person intentionally and without lawful authority or reasonable cause to cause anything to be on or over a road, or to interfere with a motor vehicle or traffic equipment in circumstances that it would be obvious to a reasonable person that to do so would be dangerous: Road Traffic Act 1988, s. 22A, inserted by Road Traffic Act 1991, s. 6.

robbery. Offence committed by one who steals and immediately before or at the time of doing so, and in order to do so, uses force on any person or puts or seeks to put any person in fear of being then and there subjected to force: Th.A. 1968, s. 8(1). See *R v Clouden* [1987] Crim LR 56; *R v Guy* (1991) 93 Cr App R 108 (robbery necessarily includes theft).

Roe, Richard. Name of a fictitious defendant (q.v.) used in an action of ejectment (q.v.).

rogatory letter. See LETTER OF REQUEST.

rogues and vagabonds. Persons who, under the Vagrancy Act 1824 as subsequently amended, are found in a building or an enclosed yard for any unlawful purpose, etc. See now C.J.A. 1982, s. 70.

rolled-up plea. Plea used in the defence of fair comment (q.v.) in an action for libel, which states that in so far as the words complained of consist of statements of fact, they are true in substance and in fact; in so far as they consist of expressions of opinion they are fair comment made in good faith and without malice relating to facts which are a matter of public interest. See *Lord v Sunday Telegraph* [1971] 1 QB 235; O. 82, r. 3(2).

Romalpa clause. Stipulation in a contract of sale that the property in goods shall not leave the seller until he has received full payment. Known also as "reserved title" or "retention of title" clause. See *Aluminium Industrie Vaassen BV v Romalpa Ltd* [1976] 2 All ER 552 (remedy of tracing allowed); *Armour v Thyssen AG* [1990] 3 All ER 481.

room standard. In relation to overcrowding (q.v.), the room standard is contravened when the number of persons sleeping in a dwelling and the number of rooms available as sleeping accommodation is such that two persons of opposite sexes who are not living together as husband or wife must sleep in the same room. (Children under 10 are left out of account; a room is considered to be available as sleeping accommodation if it is of a type used in the locality as a bedroom or living room.) See H.A. 1985, s. 325(1), (2).

root of contract. The fundamental, essential features of a particular contract. See, e.g., *Decro-Wall International SA v Practitioners in Marketing Ltd* [1971] 2 All ER 216.

root of title. Document which describes land to be sold so that it can be identified, which relates to the whole legal and equitable interest and which contains nothing to cast doubt on the title. See *Re Duce* [1937] Ch 642; and *Wimpey Ltd v Sohn* [1967] Ch 487. See TITLE.

Royal Assent. This transforms a Bill into an Act of Parliament (q.v.) and takes the following forms: for ordinary bills, *la reyne (le roi) le veult* (the Queen (King) desires this . . .); for private bills; *soit fait comme il est désiré* (let it be done as it is wished . . .); for money bills, *la reyne remercie ses bons sujets, accepte leur benevolence, et ainsi le veult* (the Queen thanks her subjects, accepts their kindness and agrees that it be done . . .). Refusal of the Assent (last exercised by Queen Anne in 1707) takes the form: *la Reyne s'avisera* (the Queen will take advice . . .). See Royal Assent Act 1967.

Royal prerogative. See PREROGATIVE, ROYAL.

royalties. Share of a product or profit paid to the owner of property from which it arises. Refers, in particular, to payments to an author by a publisher, usually based on a (fixed) percentage of the selling-price. See *Elton John v James* [1991] FSR 397.

Royal warrant. Authority issued to one who acts as a supplier of goods or services to a member of the Royal Family. See Trade Descriptions Act 1968, s. 2, which makes false representations as to Royal approval an offence.

R.S.C. Rules of the Supreme Court (q.v.).

rule. 1. A regulation, principle, direction. 2. A standard by which to judge an individual's conduct.

rule, main purpose. See REPUGNANCY.

rule of law. See LAW, RULE OF.

rules of court. Rules made by the authority having for the time being power to make rules or orders regulating the practice and procedure of a court: I.A. 1978, Sch 1.

Rules of the Supreme Court. Rules relating to practice and procedure in the Supreme Court made under S.C.A. 1981, s. 84, by a Rule Committee, consisting of the Lord Chancellor, Lord Chief Justice, Master of the Rolls, President of the Family Division, Vice-Chancellor, judges, barristers and solicitors (qq.v.). The rules are set out in the "White Book" (i.e., the *Supreme Court Practice*). Usually cited by Order and rule, e.g., "O 43, r. 1." See R.S.C. 1965 (as frequently amended).

rules, primary and secondary. Basis of jurisprudential theory of Hart (*The Concept of Law*, 1961), suggesting that a legal system involves a combination of *primary rules*, based on standards of behaviour and constituting rules of behaviour, and *secondary rules*, conferring public and private powers regulating the application of the primary rules. See RECOGNITION, RULE OF.

running account credit. See CREDIT.

running days. Phrase referring to a charterparty (q.v.) in which days run consecutively, as contrasted with "working days" (which exclude Sundays and public holidays).

running with the land. See COVENANT RUNNING WITH THE LAND.

S

s. Abbreviation for a "section" of an Act (q.v.), as in, e.g., L.P.A. 1925, s. 1.

sabotage. Malicious destruction of or damage to property, so as to injure, e.g., a business or the military potential of the state. "The saboteur just as much as the spy in the ordinary sense is contemplated as an offender under the Official Secrets Act": *Chandler* v *DPP* [1964] AC 763.

sacrilege. An offence consisting of breaking and entering and committing a felony in, or entering, committing a felony in and then breaking out of, any place of divine worship: Larceny Act 1916, s. 24 (repealed by Th.A. 1968). See now Th.A. 1968, s. 9. *See* BURGLARY.

safe goods. *See* GOODS, SAFE.

safe port. "A port to which a vessel can get laden as she is and at which she can lay and discharge, always afloat": *per* Sankey J in *Hall Bros* v *Paul Ltd* (1914) 111 LT 812. It must be a port from which the vessel can return safely: *Limerick SS Co.* v *Stott* [1921] 1 KB 568. See *Atkins International* v *Islamic Republic of Iran Shipping Lines* [1987] 1 FTLR 379.

safety at work. Under H.S.W.A. 1974, a general duty is placed on an employer to ensure the health and safety and welfare at work of his employees: s. 2. See *McDermid* v *Nash* [1986] 2 All ER 676 (employer's duty to provide safe place of work).

safety of goods. *See* CONSUMER SAFETY; GOODS, SAFE.

sale. 1. The act of selling. 2. A contract for the sale of goods whereby the seller transfers or agrees to transfer the property in goods to the buyer for a money consideration called the price: S.G.A. 1979, s. 2(1). It includes "bargain and sale" as well as "sale and delivery": s. 6(1). It does not include an agreement to sell (see s. 2(4)): *Shaw* v *CMP* [1987] 1 WLR 1332. *See* PRICE.

sale, bill of. *See* BILL OF SALE.

sale by description. *See* DESCRIPTION, SALE BY.

sale by the court. Sale of property following an order of the court, as in an action to enforce a mortgage.

sale of goods. *See* SALE.

sale of goods, passing of property in a. *See* PASSING OF PROPERTY IN A SALE OF GOODS.

sale or return. *See* APPROVAL, SALE ON.

sale, power of. *See* POWER OF SALE.

sale under voidable title. *See* VOIDABLE TITLE, SALE UNDER.

salus populi est suprema lex. The welfare of the people is the paramount law.

salvage. Reward to persons ("salvors") who save, or assist in saving, a ship, cargo or freight from shipwreck or similar jeopardy: *Wells* v *Owners of Whitton* [1897] AC 344. Amount payable usually assessed by the court and apportioned between owners, crew, officers and master of the salving vessel. It must be shown that any services rendered were voluntary, skilled and beneficial. It is restricted to operations in tidal waters (q.v.): *The Goring* [1988] 2 WLR 460. See *The Vatari* [1990] 1 Lloyd's Rep 336.

salvage of trust property. In a case of absolute necessity the court is able to sanction the mortgage or sale of part of an infant's beneficial interest for the benefit of property retained: *Re Jackson* (1882) 21 Ch D 786. *See* TRUST.

sample. Specimen presented for examination as evidence of the composition or quality of the whole. "The office of a sample is to present to the eye the real meaning and intention of the parties . . . The sample speaks for itself": *per* Lord Macnaghten in *Drummond* v *Van Ingen* (1887) 12 App Cas 297.

sample, intimate. There is a power, under P. & C.E.A. 1984, s. 62, to take from persons in police detention, with consent, samples of blood, semen, or other tissue fluid, urine, saliva, pubic hair or swabs from a body orifice. "Non-intimate sample" includes, e.g., foot-prints, samples of hair other than pubic.

sample, sale by. Under S.G.A. 1979, s. 15(2), it is implied in a contract of sale (q.v.) that the bulk shall correspond with the sample, that the buyer shall have a reasonable opportunity of com-paring bulk and sample and that goods shall be free from any defect rendering them unmerchantable which would not be apparent on rea-sonable examination of sample. See *Godley* v *Perry* [1960] 1 WLR 9.

sanction. 1. A solemn agreement. 2. That which authorises or confirms. 3. Measure used to punish some action. "The appointed consequences of dis-obedience": Pollock. See *R* v *Secretary of State for Department of Health, ex p Hickey* (1992) The Times, 25 June. 4. Measure adopted by nations to coerce into an acceptable course of action a state offending against international law.

sanctuary, right of. Right, formerly avail-able to an accused person, to seek re-fuge in a consecrated place. Largely abolished in 1623, and finally in 1723.

sanity, presumption of. *See* PRESUMPTION OF SANITY.

sans recours. Without recourse [to me]. Phrase used on a bill of exchange so that the endorser (e.g., the agent en-dorsing for the principal) is not per-sonally liable. See B.Ex.A. 1882, s. 16. *See* BILL OF EXCHANGE.

satisfaction. 1. Extinguishing of a claim, e.g., by performance. 2. Equitable doc-trine, i.e., "the donation of a thing with the intention that it is to be taken either wholly or in part in extinguish-ment of some prior claim of the donee": *Lord Chichester* v *Coventry* (1867) 36 LJ Ch 673. The general rule regarding satisfaction of debts by leg-acies (q.v.) is: "if one, being indebted to another in a sum of money, does by his will give him a sum of money as great as, or greater than, the debt, without taking any notice at all of the debt, this shall, nevertheless, be in satisfaction of the debt, so that he shall not have both the debt and the legacy": *Talbot* v *Duke of Shrewsbury* (1714) Prec Ch 394.

satisfied term. A term of years (q.v.) cre-ated for a purpose which is now ful-filled. See L.P.A. 1925, s. 5.

savings bank. A society formed in the UK for the purpose of accepting de-posits of money, accumulating the pro-duce of the deposits at compound interest and returning the deposits and produce to the depositors after deducting necessary expenses of man-agement but without deriving any benefit from the deposits or produce: Trustee Savings Bank Act 1981, s. 1(3) (since repealed). See the Trustee Sav-ings Bank Act 1985; Banking Act 1987; *Ross* v *Lord Advocate* [1986] 1 WLR 1077.

scandalous statement. Matter of an abu-sive or irrelevant nature introduced in pleadings (q.v.) and affidavits (q.v.) which can be struck out. See O. 18, r. 19(1) (*b*); O. 41, r. 6.

scandalum magnatum. Slander of mag-nates. Offence, abolished under Statute Law Revision Act 1888, com-mitted by a person who published scandalous statements resulting in dis-cord between the King and his sub-jects.

schedule. 1. A formal list. 2. An appen-dix to a Bill or Act. In the case of a contradiction between a schedule and a clause, the earlier enacted of the two prevails: *A.-G.* v *Lamplough* (1873) 3 Ex D 214. See *Buchanan & Co* v *Babco Ltd* [1978] AC 141.

scheme. 1. A scheme of arrangement is an agreement between a debtor and creditors allowing the debts to be paid under that agreement, rather than his being adjudged bankrupt. 2. An ar-rangement for the administration of a charitable trust (q.v.), e.g., so that it may be applied *cy-près* (q.v.). Whether it is ordered is in the discretion of the court: *Re Hanbey's WT* [1954] Ch 264.

school, maintained. Any county or vol-untary school; any maintained special school not established in a hospital; any grant-maintained school, except in relation to a local education authority: Education Reform Act 1988, s. 25(1). For prohibition of charges, see s. 106(1). For "school", see Further and Higher Education Act 1992, s. 14(5); for meaning of "pupil", see s. 14(6).

scienter rule. (*Sciens* = knowing.) Common law ruling that an animal must be kept securely by its owner from causing damage where he knows or is presumed to know of its mischievous disposition. See Animals Act 1971, s. 2(2); *Baker* v *Snell* [1908] 2 KB 825; *Hunt* v *Wallis* (1991) The Times, 13 May.

scilicet. Abbreviated to *scil.*, or *sc.* That is to say.

scintilla juris. A spark, or trace, of a right.

scire facias. That you cause him to know. Title or writ (q.v.), abolished in 1947, requiring a person to show a cause why someone should not have "advantage of the record".

scire feci. I have caused to be warned. Return by a sheriff (q.v.) to a writ of *scire facias* (q.v.)

screens in court. The trial judge may permit the use of a screen so that child witnesses cannot see the defendant when giving evidence: see *R* v *X* [1990] Crim LR 515; Home Office Circular 61/1990.

scrip. A certificate or memorandum of shares held in a company. Generally a negotiable instrument (q.v.).

scutage. *Scutagium* = shield money. A money payment, introduced *c.* 1166, levied, in commutation of providing the King's army with soldiers, on all tenants-in-chief, who collected it, in turn, from sub-tenants. Obsolete by the fourteenth century.

scuttling. The sinking of a ship, e.g., for the purpose of recovering insurance money. See *Probatina Shipping Co* v *Sun Insurance Office* [1974] QB 635.

seal. Wax impressed and attached to a document so as to authenticate it.

seal, contract under. *See* CONTRACT UNDER SEAL.

sealing. Process used in the execution of some documents, e.g., deeds (q.v.), based on signifying assent. "To constitute a sealing neither wax nor wafer nor a piece of paper, not even an impression is necessary": *Re Sandilands* (1871) LR 6 CP 411. The seal may be in the form of the word "seal" printed in a circle on the document. See L.P. (Misc. Provs.) A. 1989, s. 1(1) abolishing the requirement of sealing for the valid execution of an instrument as a deed by an individual. *See* LOCUS SIGILLI.

search and seizure cases. Cases in which police entering premises under a search warrant may seize goods which afford some evidence of a criminal offence (even though those goods are not of the description specified in that warrant). See also the *Anton Piller* orders (q.v.) See P. & C.E.A. 1984, s. 32; *R* v *Beckford* [1991] Crim LR 918.

searches. Investigations made, e.g., at the Land Charges Registry to check the existence of registrable encumbrances (q.v.).

search, intimate. A search of a detained person, which consists of the physical examination of the body's orifices, may be authorised by a police superintendent where there are reasonable grounds for believing that an object (which might be used to cause physical injury, or is a Class A drug) cannot be found without such a search: see P. & C.E.A. 1984, ss. 55(1), (2), 118(1). The court may draw such inferences "as appear proper" from a person's refusal to submit to such a search: s. 62(10). See *Brazil* v *Chief Constable of Surrey* [1983] 1 WLR 1155.

search, power of. Power to seek out, procure and preserve real evidence for the prosecution. There is no statutory power given to private individuals to search persons or property. Statutory power is given to, e.g., police officers, Department of Trade officials, customs officers. See, e.g., S.O.A. 1956, s. 42; Firearms Act 1968, s. 47; Th.A. 1968, s. 26; Criminal Damage Act 1971, s. 6; P. & C.E.A. 1984, ss. 1, 2, 17, and revised *Code B* (1991) (introducing a standard Notice of Powers and Rights to be given to the subjects of searches); Northern Ireland (Emergency Provs.) Act 1991, s. 19. The police may search private premises without a warrant when, e.g., they are given permission by the occupiers to do so, or in order to make an arrest. See Prevention of Terrorism (Temporary Provisions) Act 1989, s. 21. *See* ARREST, SEARCH UPON.

search upon arrest. *See* ARREST, SEARCH UPON.

search warrant. Warrant (q.v.) issued by magistrates, e.g., for the entry and search of premises for stolen goods, or drugs or firearms. See, e.g., Th.A. 1968, s. 26; Misuse of Drugs Act 1971, s. 23; P. & C.E.A. 1984, Part III.

seas, beyond the. See BEYOND THE SEAS.

sea, the. "Includes any area submerged at mean high water springs, and also includes, so far as the tide flows at mean high water springs, an estuary or an arm of the sea and the waters of any channel, creek, bay or river": Offshore Petroleum Development (Scotland) Act 1975, s. 20(2). See Territorial Sea Act 1987. See TERRITORIAL WATERS.

seaworthy. In the context of the Hague Rules means that the ship, with her master and crew, is fit to encounter the perils of the voyage and fit to carry her cargo safely on that voyage: *Actis Co* v *Stanko Steamship Co* [1982] 1 WLR 119. See *The Benlawers* [1989] 2 Lloyd's Rep 51.

seck rent. Dry rent (q.v.).

secondary action. Exists, in relation to a trade dispute (q.v.), only when a person induces another to break a contract of employment or interferes or induces another to interfere with its performance, or threatens that a contract of employment under which he or another is employed will be broken or its performance interfered with, or that he will induce another to break a contract of employment or to interfere with its performance, and the employer under the contract of employment is not the employer party to the dispute: T.U.L.R.(C.)A. 1992, s. 224.

secondary party. One, other than the principal offender, who participates in the commission of a crime. See *R* v *Dunnington* [1984] QB 472; *Chan Wing-sui* v *R* [1984] 3 All ER 877; *R* v *Hyde* [1990] 3 All ER 892.

secondary use. Shifting use (q.v.).

second marriage. Refers in O.P.A. 1861, s. 57, to the second marriage charged in the indictment: *R* v *Taylor* [1950] 2 KB 368. See *R* v *Sagoo* [1975] QB 885. See BIGAMY.

second mortgage. See MORTGAGE, SECOND.

secretary. See COMPANY SECRETARY.

Secretary of State. Member of the government in charge of a department. Appointed by the Crown and usually assisted by Parliamentary Under-Secretaries of State. See I.A. 1978, Sch. 1.

secret profits. Profits made by an agent acting in that capacity and not accounted for to his principal. See *Hippisley* v *Knee Bros* [1905] 1 KB 1;

Boardman v *Phipps* [1967] 2 AC 46. See, in relation to secret profit and theft, *A.-G's Reference (No. 1 of 1985)* [1986] QB 491. See AGENT.

secret reserves. Reserves not disclosed in the balance sheet or accounts.

secret trust. A trust which exists where a will (q.v.) or other instrument discloses neither the existence of the trust nor its terms. Example: X bequeaths a legacy to Y and, during his (X's) lifetime Y promises that he will hold the subject-matter of the legacy on trust for Z. See *Blackwell* v *Blackwell* [1929] AC 318; *Re Snowden* [1979] Ch 528. See TRUST.

sections of an Act. Distinct, numbered sub-divisions of an Act of Parliament. "Every section of an Act takes effect as a substantive enactment without introductory words": I.A. 1978, s. 1 (applying to Acts passed after the commencement of the 1978 Act and to existing Acts passed after 1850).

secundum legem. According to law.

secure accommodation. Accommodation for the restriction of liberty of children in care who have a history of absconding and are likely to suffer harm if they abscond: Ch.A. 1989, s. 25.

secured creditor. See CREDITOR.

secure tenancy. Applied to a dwelling house let as a separate dwelling where the landlord was a local authority, housing association etc, and the tenant was an individual, occupying the dwelling house as his only or principal home, or, in the case of a joint tenancy, each tenant was an individual, and at least one of them occupied the dwelling house as his only or principal home: see H.A. 1985, ss. 79–81. In general, a secure tenancy could not be brought to an end by the landlord except by obtaining an order for possession: s. 82. Following H.A. 1988, a tenancy entered into after commencement of the Act cannot be a secure tenancy unless entered into under a contract made before commencement of the Act, or the landlord's interest belongs to, e.g., a local authority, new town corporation: s. 35. See *S. Glamorgan CC* v *Griffiths* [1992] NPC 13. For succession to a deceased tenant, see H.A. 1985, s. 87; *Waltham Forest LBC* v *Thomas* (1992) The Times, 22 June. See ASSURED TENANCY.

securities. 1. Things deposited or pledged to ensure the fulfilling of an obligation. 2. Written evidence of ownership, e.g., certificates. 3. Under C.C.A. 1974, s. 189(1), in relation to an actual or prospective consumer credit or hire agreement, a security is a mortgage, charge, pledge, bond, debenture, indemnity, guarantee, bill, note or other right provided by the debtor or hirer to secure the carrying out of obligations under the agreement. See, e.g., Transport Act 1985, s. 137(1), under which "securities", in relation to a body corporate, means any shares, stock, debentures, debenture stock, and any other security of a similar nature, of that body; I.C.T.A. 1988, ss. 710, 729; T.C.G.A. 1992, Sch. 9 ("gilt-edged" securities (q.v.)).

Securities and Investments Board. Agency set up under F.S.A. 1986, Sch. 9, which authorises the carrying on of investment businesses. See *SIB* v *Pantell SA* (1992) The Times, 24 June.

securities, authorised. *See* AUTHORISED SECURITIES.

securities, listed. *See* LISTED SECURITIES.

securities, transfer of. The Secretary of State may make regulations for enabling title to securities to be evidenced and transferred without a written interest: Cos.A. 1989, s. 207(1). "Title" includes legal or equitable interest in securities.

security, national. *See* NATIONAL SECURITY.

security officers, court. Appointed under C.J.A. 1991, s. 76, to search persons entering the court-house, to exclude those who refuse to permit a search, or whose presence may interfere with the maintenance of order.

security of tenure. *See* TENURE, SECURITY OF.

Security Service. Operates under the authority of the Home Secretary. Its function is "the protection of national security and, in particular, its protection against threats from espionage, terrorism and sabotage, from the activities of agents of foreign powers and from actions intended to overthrow or undermine parliamentary democracy by political, industrial or violent means": Security Service Act 1989, s. 1. Its operations are controlled by a Director-General appointed by the Secretary of State: s. 2(1). A tribunal investigates complaints about the Service: s. 5(1), Schs. 1, 2. See also Official Secrets Act 1989, s. 1. *See* NATIONAL SECURITY.

security, valuable. Includes any document creating, transferring, surrendering or releasing a right in or over property, or authorising the payment of money or delivery of any property, or the satisfaction of any obligation: see Th.A. 1968, s. 20(3); *R* v *King* [1991] 3 WLR 246; *R* v *Kassim* [1991] 3 WLR 254.

security, valuable, execution of. *See* EXECUTION OF VALUABLE SECURITY.

secus. Otherwise.

se defendendo. In self-defence (q.v.).

sedition. The publication, orally or in writing, of words intended "to bring into hatred or contempt, or to excite disaffection against the person of Her Majesty, her heirs, or successors, or the government and constitution of the UK . . . or either House of Parliament . . . or to raise discontent or disaffection amongst Her Majesty's subjects, or to promote feelings of ill-will and hostility between different classes of such subjects": *R* v *Burns* (1886) 16 Cox CC 335.

seditious libel. Sedition (q.v.) in the form of printed words.

sed quaere. But question; enquire further.

seduction. Persuasion to disobedience, illicit sexual intercourse, desertion or other disloyalty. The common-law action for the seduction of a wife was abolished in 1857. The right of action by a parent for the seduction of a child on the grounds of deprivation of services was abolished by Law Reform (Misc. Provs.) Act 1970, s. 5. It is an offence under the Incitement to Disaffection Act 1934 to endeavour to seduce a member of the Forces from his duty and allegiance to the Crown. See *R* v *Arrowsmith* [1975] QB 678. *See* PER QUOD CONSORTIUM ET SERVITIUM AMISIT.

segregation. Isolation, or setting apart, of individuals or groups. *See* RACIAL SEGREGATION.

seignory. Powers, rights, authority of a feudal lord.

seised. Feudal term referring to one possessed of a freehold (q.v.). *See* SEISIN.

seisin. (*Saisir* = to seize.) Feudal concept based on the physical occupation of land, so that an estate in freehold involved a right to seisin. Proof of seisin was required in actions for recovery of land. *Seisin in law*: seisin possessed by an heir whose ancestor had died seised of the land. *Seisin in deed*: actual possession of the freehold.

seisin, abeyance of. Interruption of the tenancy of a freehold. Forbidden under early law, so that every transfer of land had to be open and necessitated public delivery of seisin.

seisina facit stipitem. Seisin makes the stock of descent. Prior to the Inheritance Act 1833, title by descent was to be traced, under this doctrine, from the person who had died last seised. *See* SEISIN.

seisin, livery of. *See* LIVERY OF SEISIN.

seisin, unity of. Situation whereby a person seised of land subject to an easement (q.v.) becomes seised of the land to which the easement is attached.

seizure. Taking possession by force. For powers of seizure exercisable by a constable, see P. & C.E.A. 1984, ss. 1(6), 19, 55(12). See also Th.A. 1968, s. 26(3).

select committee. *See* COMMITTEE, SELECT.

self-dealing. Transactions in which a trustee, acting for himself and in his capacity as trustee, is placed in a position wherein his obligations are opposed to his self-interest. See *Re Thompson's Settlement* [1985] 2 All ER 720.

self-defence. Acting so as to defend oneself, one's property or, possibly, some other person such as a parent, child, spouse, against violence or a reasonable apprehension of it. It may be an answer to a charge of, e.g., homicide (q.v.), where no more force is used than is necessary and there is an honest belief based on reasonable grounds that force is necessary. The plea is destroyed by a mistake of fact induced by voluntary intoxication: *R v O'Grady* [1987] 3 WLR 321. It is not the law that the accused should have retreated as far as possible before the attack: *R v McInnes* [1971] 3 All ER 295. See *R v Fisher* [1987] Crim LR 334.

self defence in crime prevention. *See* REASONABLE FORCE.

self-employed. A person who is gainfully employed in Great Britain otherwise than in employed earner's employment: see, e.g., S.S.A. 1975, s. 2(1) (*b*). See *Warner Holidays Ltd v Secretary of State for Social Services* [1983] ICR 440; *Hall v Lorimer* (1992) The Times, 4 June.

self-help. An extra-judicial remedy whereby, e.g., in the case of trespass to land, the person in possession may eject the trespasser, using such force as is reasonable in the circumstances. See *Perry v Fitzhowe* (1846) 8 QB 757; *Hemmings v Stoke Poges Golf Club* [1920] 1 KB 720.

self-incrimination. The giving by a person of evidence or replies to questions, the result of which might lead that person to be prosecuted. "When giving evidence, an accused person shall not be asked, and if asked shall not be required to answer, any question tending to show that he has committed or been convicted of or been charged with any offence other than that wherewith he is then charged or is of bad character", unless, e.g., he has given evidence against some other person charged with the same offence: Criminal Evidence Act 1898, s. 1(*f*) (as amended by Criminal Evidence Act 1979). See, Criminal Evidence Act 1968, s. 14(1); Criminal Damage Act 1971, s. 9; S.C.A. 1981, s. 72 (see *Istel Ltd v Tully* (1992) NLJ 88); *Bishopsgate Investment Management Ltd v Maxwell* (1992) The Times, 30 Jan; *In Re London United Investments plc* [1992] BCC 202; Cos.A. 1985, s. 434(5) as amended by Cos.A. 1989. *See* INCRIMINATE; SILENCE, RIGHT OF ACCUSED TO.

self-regulating organisation. A body, corporate or unincorporated, which regulates the carrying on of investment business of any kind by enforcing rules which are binding on persons carrying on business of that kind whether because they are members of that body or otherwise subject to its control: F.S.A. 1986, s. 8(1).

self-serving statement. Statement, cautioned or uncautioned, in which defendant denies an offence, or admits offence while offering an explanation. See *Leung Kam Kwok v R* (1985) 81 Cr App R 83.

sell, agreement to. Where under a contract of sale the transfer of the property in the goods is to take place at a future time or subject to some conditions later to be fulfilled, the contract is called an agreement to sell: S.G.A. 1979, s. 2(4). It confers no title under s. 21: *Shaw* v *CMP* [1987] 1 WLR 1332.

seller. Under S.G.A. 1979, s. 61(1), one who sells or agrees to sell goods. It may include a person who is in the position of a seller, e.g., as agent (q.v.).

seller, unpaid. *See* UNPAID SELLER.

semble. It seems. Word used to suggest that a particular point may be doubtful.

semper praesumitur pro negante. The presumption is always in favour of the negative, as where, on an equal division of votes in a committee or other body, the question is considered to be passed in the negative. *See Charter* v *Charter* (1874) LR 7 HL 364; *Paquin* v *Beauclerk* [1906] AC 148.

Senate of the Inns of Court and the Bar. Body formed in July 1974 to act as the governing body of the Bar (q.v.) consisting of 90 members (including the Attorney-General, Solicitor-General, Chairman of the Council of Legal Education, 24 Bench representatives, 12 Hall representatives, 39 Bar representatives and 12 additional persons). It regulates the admission of students and of the call to the Bar.

sentence. Punishment or penalty imposed on a person found guilty by the court. (It does not include committal in default of payment: M.C.A. 1980, s. 150(1).) Generally, save in case of murder or other offences for which penalty is fixed by law, the court has the discretion to select a sentence which it considers suitable in all the circumstances, e.g., the nature and gravity of offence, background and needs of the offender. Principles applied in sentencing were said, in *R* v *Sergeant* (1974) 118 SJ 753, to be retribution, deterrence, prevention and rehabilitation. See the comments of Hilbery J. on sentencing, in *R* v *Blake* (1961) 45 Cr App R 292; M.C.A. 1980, s. 108(3). For review of apparently unduly lenient sentences, see C.J.A. 1988, s. 36. See *Practice Statement* (C.J.A. 1991) (1992) The Times, 7 Oct.

sentence custodial. In relation to an offender of or over 21, a sentence of imprisonment and, to an offender under that age, a sentence of detention in a young offender institution or under C. & Y.P.A. 1933, s. 53, or a life sentence under C.J.A. 1982, s. 8(2): C.J.A. 1991, s. 31. Such a sentence may be passed only when the offence is of a violent or sexual nature and protection of the public is essential: 1991 Act, s. 1 (but the section does not apply to sentences fixed by law, e.g., for murder). The offence should be so serious that only such a sentence is justifiable s. 1(2). For length, see s. 2.

sentence, deferring of. *See* DEFERRING OF SENTENCE.

sentence, procedure on. The accused is asked if he has anything to say before sentence and pleas in mitigation are heard. Antecedents of the accused (character, etc) are given. The accused may be remanded for a medical or social enquiry report before sentence. He may ask for other offences to be taken into consideration. Sentence is then given orally by the trial judge.

sentence, suspended. *See* SUSPENDED SENTENCE.

separate trials. *See* JOINDER OF OFFENDERS.

separation as ground for divorce. There is evidence that a marriage has broken down irretrievably if: the parties to the marriage have lived apart for a continuous period of at least two years immediately preceding the presentation of the petition and the respondent consents to the granting of a decree; the parties have lived apart for a continuous period of at least five years immediately preceding the presentation of the petition (consent of respondent is not required). See Mat.C.A. 1973, s. 1. *See* BREAKDOWN OF MARRIAGE; DIVORCE; LIVING APART.

separation, judicial. *See* JUDICIAL SEPARATION.

separation of powers. The division of functions of government – legislative, executive, judicial – between independent, separate institutions (see Montesquieu's *L'Esprit des Lois* (1748)). "It cannot be too strongly emphasised that the British Constitution, though largely unwritten, is firmly based on the separation of powers": *per* Lord Diplock in *Duport Steels* v *Sirs* [1980] 1 All ER 529.

sequestration. Writ issued, e.g., where a person fails to perform an act or disobeys an injunction (q.v.), commanding persons ("sequestrators") to enter upon and take possession of his estate and keep it under sequestration (i.e., separated from the owner) until the judgment is complied with. See O. 45 r. 5. See *IRC* v *Hoogstraten* [1984] 3 All ER 245; *Richardson* v *Richardson* [1989] 3 WLR 865.

serf. An unfree person whose service was attached to the soil and who could be sold with it.

seriatim. In order; serially.

serious arrestable offence. See ARRESTABLE OFFENCE, SERIOUS.

Serious Fraud Office. Constituted under C.J.A 1987, s. 1(1), headed by a Director (appointed by the A.-G.) who may investigate "any suspected offence which appears to him on reasonable grounds to involve serious or complex fraud" (s. 1(3)). For procedure, see Sch. 1.

serious frauds, preparatory hearings. Where a Crown Court judge believes that evidence on indictment reveals a case of such seriousness and complexity that substantial benefits are likely to accrue from a hearing before the jury are sworn, he may order a preparatory hearing so as to identify material issues, expedite proceedings before the jury, and assist their comprehension of those issues: C.J.A. 1987, s. 7(1). See SI 1988/1699. Arraignment (q.v.) will take place at the start of the preparatory hearings: s. 8(2). See *R* v *Gunawardena* [1990] 2 All ER 477.

serjeants-at-law. Formerly senior advocates, who had a monopoly of audience at the Court of Common Pleas (q.v.) and from whom judges were chosen. The Order of the Coif (to which they belonged) died out after the abolition of the monopoly by J.A 1873, s. 8.

serjeanty. *See* GRAND SERJEANTY.

servant. One whose work is under the control of another. "Any person employed by another to do work for him on the terms that he, the servant, is to be subject to the control and direction of his employer in respect of the manner in which his work is to be done" (Salmond, approved in *Hewitt* v *Bonvin* [1940] 1 KB 188). Implied duties were: to attend the place of work; to obey lawful orders; to conduct oneself

properly; to exercise due care and skill; to observe good faith. See *Ready Mixed Concrete Ltd* v *Ministry of Pensions* [1968] 2 QB 497. *See* EMPLOYER; INDEPENDENT CONTRACTOR.

servant, Crown. *See* CROWN SERVANT.

servant's duty of care. *See* CARE, SERVANT'S CONTRACTUAL DUTY OF.

service. 1. Duty owned by a tenant to his lord, or servant to his master. 2. Delivery of writ or summons by personal service or service on the defendant's solicitor. There are extensive provisions allowing for postal service of many court processes, including writs and originating summonses. Service more than 12 months from date of issue is irregular: O. 6, r. 8(1). See O. 10; O. 11; O. 65; *Hastie* v *McMahon* [1991] 1 All ER 255 (service by fax acceptable under O. 65, r. 5 (1)). *See* DOCUMENT EXCHANGE; SUBSTITUTED SERVICE.

service, acknowledgement of. Procedure, replacing the entry of an appearance, introduced in 1979. The defendant must acknowledge service of writ within 14 days of service and must indicate whether he intends to contest proceedings, giving "notice of intention to defend": O. 12, r. 3. If he fails to return the acknowledgement within the prescribed time, or returns it without giving notice of intention to defend, the plaintiff can enter judgment immediately: O. 13.

service by post. *See* POST, SERVICE BY.

service charge. An amount payable by the tenant of a flat as part of or in addition to the rent, payable for services, repairs, maintenance or insurance or landlord's cost of management.

service, contract of. *See* CONTRACT OF SERVICE.

service, endorsement of. *See* ENDORSEMENT OF SERVICE.

service mark. "A mark (including a device, name, signature, word, letter, numeral, or any combination thereof) used or proposed to be used in relation to services for the purpose of indicating, or so as to indicate, that a particular person is connected, in the course of business, with the provision of those services, whether with or without any indication of the identity of the person": Patents, Designs and Marks Act 1986, s. 2(1).

service out of the jurisdiction. *See* JURIS-DICTION, SERVICE OUT OF THE.

services, loss of. *See* PER QUOD CONSOR-TIUM ET SERVITIUM AMISIT.

service, supply of a, contract for. "A contract under which a person agrees to carry out a service": Supply of Goods and Services Act 1982, s. 12(1). A contract of apprenticeship is excluded: s. 12(2). For implied terms concerning care and skill, see ss. 13–16. See, e.g., *Hanson v Rapid Civil Engineering Ltd* (1987) 38 Build LR 106.

servient tenement. Land over which a right *in alieno solo* is exercisable. *See* DOMINANT TENEMENT; EASEMENT.

servitudes. Rights over another's property, i.e., easements (q.v.) and *profits à prendre* (q.v.).

sessions. Sittings of Parliament or the courts, e.g., petty sessions (known also as "sessions of the peace").

set aside. To annul, make void, overrule.

set of bills. *See* BILLS IN A SET.

set-off. Pleading by way of defence to the whole or part of the plaintiff's claim. The defendant (q.v.) acknowledges the plaintiff's demand but sets up one which counterbalances it. Amount to be set off must have been due at the time of the issue of the writ: *Richards v James* (1848) 2 Exch 471. Nothing which is not a money claim may be set off. See O. 18, r. 17; Ins.A. 1986, s. 323; *Bhogal v Punjab National Bank* [1988] 1 FTLR 1; *Stewart Gill Ltd v Myer & Co.* [1992] 2 All ER 257.

setting aside. Cancelling; making void. Motion to the Court of Appeal (q.v.) to set aside a High Court judgment may be made by a party who alleges, e.g., that the judgment is wrong. See also O.13, r. 9, by which a judgment in default of acknowledgement may be set aside on such terms as the court thinks just.

setting down of action. Delivery to "the proper officer" (e.g., head clerk at the Crown Office) of a request that an action be set down for trial in that place stated in order for trial. An action in the QBD (q.v.) is set down in the jury list, non-jury list, short-cause list, or admiralty and commercial list. See O. 34.

settled. 1. With reference to an account, this means adjusted or paid. 2. With

reference to a dispute, it means adjusted or ended.

settled account. *See* ACCOUNT, SETTLED.

settled land. Land which is the subject of a settlement (q.v.): S.L.A. 1925, s. 2. See Law Comm Report (1989) No. 181.

Settled Land Act trustees. Those persons competent under S.L.A. 1925, s. 30, to act as trustees of the settlement, i.e., persons who under the settlement are trustees with the power of sale of the settled land; persons declared by settlement to be trustees; persons who under the settlement are trustees with the power of sale of any other land comprised in the settlement subject to the same limitations as the land being dealt with; persons who under the settlement are trustees with a future power of sale; persons appointed by deed by beneficiaries (who must be of full age and entitled to dispose of the entire settled estate).

settlement. 1. Limitation of property for persons usually by way of succession, e.g., "to X for life, remainder to Y in fee simple". The term includes "strict settlements" and "trusts for sale". For purposes of S.L.A. 1925, a settlement is created when land stands: limited in trust for any persons by way of succession; limited in trust for any person in possession (e.g., for a base or determinable fee (q.v.); limited in trust for any person for an estate in fee simple for a term of years absolute (q.v.) contingently on the happening of an event; charged for the benefit of persons. 2. The documents used to create a settlement. See I.C.T.A. 1988, s. 681; T.C.G.A. 1992, s. 68.

settlement, accumulation and maintenance. *See* ACCUMULATION AND MAINTENANCE SETTLEMENT.

settlement, compound. *See* COMPOUND SETTLEMENT.

settlement of action. Process whereby parties to an action come to terms voluntarily. Settlement may be made without the court's consent by notice of withdrawal before trial. Settlement of an action on behalf of a patient or infant (q.v.) requires the court's approval: O. 80, r. 11. See *Green v Rozen* [1955] 1 WLR 741.

settlements, *ad hoc*. Under S.L.A. 1925, s. 21, the owner of land can execute a vesting deed (q.v.) stating that the legal estate is vested in him on trust to give effect to those equitable interests affecting the estate. The deed must be executed by two or more trustees appointed by the court, or by a trust corporation (q.v.).

settlements, referential. Settlements (q.v.) which incorporate earlier settlements by reference: S.L.A. 1925, s. 32.

settlor. One who makes a settlement of his property. See T.C.G.A. 1992, Sch. 5, para 7.

several. Separate (in contrast to "joint").

several fishery. *See* FISHERY.

several tenancy. The separate holding of lands by a tenant (as contrasted with, e.g., joint tenancy (q.v.)).

severalty. Separate and exclusive possession. Property is said to belong to X, Y and Z in severalty when the share of each is sole and exclusive (as contrasted with concurrent or joint ownership (q.v.)).

severance. 1. The conversion of a joint tenancy (q.v.) into a tenancy in common, e.g., by alienation, contract to sever, acquisition of another interest in the land. See L.P.A. 1925, s. 36(2); *Harris* v *Goddard* [1983] 1WLR 1203. 2. Retention of the good points of a contract and rejection of the bad (e.g., as in a partly-illegal contract). The promises must be separate and independent. See *Attwood* v *Lamont* [1920] 3 KB 571; *Trigg* v *Staines UDC* [1969] 1 Ch 10. *See* BLUE PENCIL TEST.

severance pay. Payment to an employee whose contract of employment is terminated or whose contract of service has been cut short.

severance, words of. Words in a grant (q.v.) which served to show that tenants were to take a distinct share in the property, e.g., "in equal shares", or "to be divided between", or "equally", or "respectively".

sex, change of. ". . . The biological sexual constitution of an individual is fixed at birth (at the latest) and cannot be changed, either by medical or surgical means . . . The only cases where the term 'change of sex' is appropriate are those in which a mistake as to sex is made at birth and subsequently revealed by further medical examination": *Corbett* v *Corbett (orse Ash-*

ley) [1970] 2 All ER 33. See *White* v *British Sugar Corporation* [1977] IRLR 121; Mat.C.A. 1973, s. 11(*c*); *R* v *Tan* [1983] 2 All ER 12; *Rees* v *UK* (1987) 17 Fam Law 157; *Cossey* v *UK* [1991] 2 FLR 492.

sex discrimination. *See* DISCRIMINATION, SEX.

sex establishments. Sex cinemas (i.e., premises used to a significant degree for the exhibition of moving pictures concerned principally with the portrayal of, or intended to stimulate, sexual activity) and sex shops (i.e., premises used to a significant degree for the selling or hiring of sex articles): see Local Government (Misc. Provs.) Act 1982, Sch. 3, paras, 3, 4. For licensing requirements, see para 6.

sexual deviancy. The violation of conventional standards in the area of sexuality. "Sexual deviancy" in M.H.A 1983, s. 1(3), means indulgence in deviation and not a tendency to deviation: *R* v *Mental Health Review Tribunal, ex p Clatworthy* [1985] 3 All ER 699.

sexual harassment. *See* HARASSMENT, SEXUAL.

sexual immorality, contract for. An agreement to bring about, e.g., illicit intercourse: *Benyon* v *Nettlefield* (1850) 3 Mac & G 94. Generally it will be void, even if under seal.

sexual intercourse, proof of. "Intercourse shall be deemed complete upon proof of penetration only": S.O.A. 1956, s. 44. Proof of rupture of the hymen is not necessary. See *R* v *Russen* (1777) 1 East PC 438; *R* v *Lines* (1844) 1 C & K 393.

sexual intercourse, unlawful. Illicit intercourse. The use of the word "unlawful" in S.O. (Am.) A. 1976, s. 1(1) (definition of rape), adds nothing and should be treated as mere surplusage in the enactment: *per* Lord Keith in *R* v *R* [1991] 3 WLR 767.

sexual offences. Defined, for purposes of C.J.A. 1991, Part I, as including: an offence under S.O.A. 1956, Indecency with Children Act 1960, S.O.A. 1967, C.L.A. 1977, s. 54, or the Protection of Children Act 1978, other than an offence under S.O.A. 1956, ss. 12 or 13, which would not be an offence, but for S.O.A. 1967, s. 2, or an offence under the 1956 Act, ss. 30, 31, 33–36, or an offence under the 1967 Act, ss. 4, 5: C.J.A. 1991, s. 31(1). Anonymity is given to victims of certain sexual offences specified in S.O. (Amendment) A. 1992, s. 2.

sham. "Acts done or documents executed by the parties to the 'sham' which are intended by them to give to third parties or to the court the appearance of creating between the parties legal rights and obligations different from the actual legal rights and obligations (in any) which the parties intended to create": *per* Diplock LJ in *Snook* v *London & W. Riding Investments* [1967] 2 QB 786. See *Hilton* v *Plustitle* [1989] 1 WLR 149 – sham company let (q.v.).

sham marriage. Known also as "marriage of convenience". Ceremony of marriage intended primarily to achieve some motive such as avoidance of a country's immigration regulations. See, e.g., *Silver* v *Silver* [1955] 2 All ER 614; *R* v *Immigration Appeal Tribunal, ex p Ullah* (1983) The Times, 14 Jan – such marriages were held to be "not conducive to the public good".

sham pleas. *See* FALSE PLEA.

share. "The interest of a shareholder in the company measured by a sum of money for the purpose of liability in the first place and of dividend in the second, but also consisting of a series of mutual covenants entered into by all the shareholders *inter se* in accordance with [the Companies Act]. The contract contained in the Articles of Association is one of the original incidents of the share": *Borland's Trustee* v *Steel Bros & Co Ltd* [1901] 1 Ch 279. A portion of the capital of a company giving shareholders the right to receive, in general, a proportion of the company's profits. Shares are legal choses in action (*Humble* v *Mitchell* (1839) 11 Add El 205), and are classed as personal estate: Cos.A. 1985, s. 182(1). For the test in valuing shares, see *Holt* v *Holt* (1990) 134 SJ 1076. *See* COMPANY; SHARE, TYPES OF.

share acquisition, financial assistance for. It is illegal for a company to give direct or indirect financial assistance (e.g., by gift, loan, provision of guarantee) for this purpose: Cos.A. 1985, ss. 151, 152. For exceptions, see ss. 153–158. See *Belmont Finance* v *Williams Furniture* [1980] 1 All ER 393.

share and share alike. Phrase, often found in a will, creating a tenancy in common (q.v.); but where the context shows a joint tenancy (q.v.) to be intended, it is construed accordingly: *Armstrong* v *Eldridge* (1791) 3 Bro CC 215.

share capital. The total amount which a company's shareholders have contributed or are liable to contribute as payment for their shares. See Table A, art. 2. References on a company's stationery or order forms to its "share capital" must be to its paid-up share capital: Cos.A. 1985, s. 351(2) See I.C.T.A. 1988, s. 832(1); *Russell* v *Northern Bank Development Ltd* (1992) The Times, 19 June.

share capital, equity. The issued share capital of a company, excluding any part which, neither as respects dividend nor as respects capital, carries any right to participate beyond a specified amount in a distribution: Cos.A. 1985, s. 744.

share certificate. *See* CERTIFICATE OF SHARES.

share hawking. Also "share pushing". The personal offering of shares from house to house. Includes "cold calling" and any unsolicited personal call or oral communication without express invitation, and is prohibited by F.S.A. 1986, s. 56 (subject to exceptions under s. 57).

shareholder. One who owns shares as a member of a company (q.v.). See Cos.A. 1985, s. 22. For liability of subsequent holders of allotted shares, see Cos.A. 1985, s. 112. See also *Short* v *Treasury Commrs* [1948] 1 KB 116.

shareholders, protection of. The Cos.A. 1985, Part XVII, allows a member of a company to petition the court for an order on the ground of the company's affairs being, or having been, conducted in a way unfairly prejudicial to the interests of some part of the membership, including himself, or that an actual or proposed act of the company is or would be unfairly prejudicial. See *Eastmanco* v *GLC* [1982] 1 WLR 2.

share premium account. An account to which is transferred sums received from the issue of shares at a premium. The amount of the account appears in the balance sheet as part of the paid-up capital. See Cos.A. 1985, s. 130.

share restriction order. *See* RESTRICTION ORDER, SHARE.

shares, acquisition by a company of its own. In general, a company may not acquire its own shares, whether by purchase, subscription or otherwise: Cos.A. 1985, s. 143(1). For exceptions (e.g., in a reduction of capital duly made) see s. 143(3).

shares at a premium. See PREMIUM, ISSUES OF SHARES AT A.

shares, bearer. See BEARER SHARES.

shares, contracts for sale of. The contract need not be in any particular form. A "short sale" refers to shares which the seller does not yet own at the time of the contract. The seller's duty is to deliver the share certificate and an executed transfer to the buyer and to assist his registration as a company member.

shares, forfeiture of. See FORFEITURE OF SHARES.

shares, lien on. A lien or other charge of a public company (q.v.) on its own shares (whether taken expressly or otherwise) is generally void: Cos.A. 1985, s. 150(1). For the permitted charges, see s. 150(2), (3).

shares, mortgage of. In a *legal mortgage*, the legal title passes from mortgagor to mortgagee and the transfer is entered in the company register. In an *equitable mortgage*, the mortgagor retains the legal title to the shares and deposits his share certificate with the mortgagee. See *Cuckmere Brick Co Ltd* v *Mutual Finance Ltd* [1971] Ch 949.

shares, payment for. Shares allotted by a company may be paid for in money or money's worth (e.g., know-how, goodwill (qq.v.)): Cos.A. 1985, s. 99(1).

shares, placing of. Allocation of shares by a company to an issuing house which agrees to purchase and place them with clients.

shares, surrender of. See SURRENDER OF SHARES.

shares, transfer of. See TRANSFER OF SHARES.

shares, transmission of. See TRANS-MISSION OF SHARES.

share transfer. Document which must be prepared and furnished to a company when its shares are transferred, e.g., a stock transfer form, a brokers' transfer form. See, e.g., Stock Transfer Act 1963; Cos.A. 1985, s. 182. See TRANS-FER OF SHARES.

share, types of. Generally: ordinary (q.v.); preference (q.v.); deferred (q.v.).

share warrant. See WARRANT, SHARE.

sheriff. Originally the "shire-reeve". He exercised civil and criminal jurisdiction as a judge of the sheriff's county court and sheriff's tourn. Today, he is the Crown's appointee and chief officer in the county. He is in charge of, e.g., parliamentary elections, levying of forfeiture recognisances, and the execution of process issuing from criminal courts and the High Court (q.v.). See L.G.A. 1972, s. 219.

sheriff's interpleader. See INTERPLEADER SUMMONS.

shifting use. A use which cut short a preceding interest. Example: "To X and his heirs to the use of Y and his heirs, but to the use of Z and his heirs as soon as Z shall become a doctor of medicine." See L.P.A. 1925, ss. 1, 39; and S.L.A. 1925, s. 1 (ii). See USE.

ship. Any type of vessel used in navigation, propelled otherwise than by oars: Merchant Shipping Act 1894, s. 742. See C.P.A. 1987, s. 45(1); Capital Allowances Act 1990, s. 30. For "British ship", see Merchant Shipping Act 1988, s. 2. For qualifications for ownership, see s. 3. An owner is liable for the unsafe operation of his ship: 1988 Act, s. 31. See *The Derbyshire* [1987] 3 WLR 1181 (ship as "equipment").

ship, arrest of. See ARREST OF SHIP.

shipwreck. See WRECK.

shock, nervous. See NERVOUS SHOCK.

shop. Premises of which the sole and principal use is the carrying on there of retail trade or business; a building occupied by a wholesaler where goods are kept for sale, or part of a building so occupied; a building to which members of the public are invited to resort to deliver goods for repair or other treatment, or part of a building so used: Offices, Shops and Railway Premises Act 1963, s. 1(3) (*a*). See also Shops Act 1950, s 4; *Erewash BC* v *Ilkeston Co-op Society* (1989) 87 LGR 96.

shop-lifting. Stealing goods from a shop. See Th.A. 1968, ss. 1, 7. See THEFT.

shop steward. Elected, or appointed, union officer who represents members at a place of work.

shore. That ground between the ordinary high-water and low-water mark: Hale.

short cause list. List in the QBD of cases to be tried without jury and which are unlikely to last more than four hours because the defence is relatively simple and short. See O. 14, r. 6.

short committal. *See* COMMITTAL, SHORT.

shorthold tenancy. *See* PROTECTED SHORTHOLD TENANCY.

short title. *See* TITLE, SHORT.

S.I. Statutory instruments (q.v.).

sic. So; thus. Used so as to indicate that a word or statement is intended as written, in spite of an obvious error or absurdity.

sick pay, statutory. Scheme instituted by S.S. and Housing Benefits Act 1982 under which an employer becomes liable to pay to employees sick pay in a stated amount for a stipulated period of interruption of employment by reason of incapacity. See S.S.A. 1986, s. 67; Statutory Sick Pay Act 1991; S.S. Contributions and Benefits Act 1992, s. 31; Social Security Administration Act 1992, s. 14

sic utere tuo ut alienum non laedas. So use your own property as not to interfere with that of your neighbour. But, "a balance has to be maintained between the right of the occupier to do what he likes with his own, and the right of his neighbour not to be interfered with": *Sedleigh-Denfield* v *O'Callaghan* [1940] AC 880.

side by side rule. Rule, stated in *Sheers* v *Thimbleby & Sons* (1897) 76 LT 709, allowing documents signed by a defendant to be "read together" when placed side by side. See *Burgess* v *Cox* [1951] Ch 383, but note *Timmins* v *Moreland Street Property Co* [1958] Ch 110. *See* JOINDER OF DOCUMENTS.

side notes. Marginal notes (q.v.).

sight, payable at. In effect, a bill payable on demand. See B.Ex.A. 1882, s. 10 *See* BILL OF EXCHANGE.

signature. 1. A person's name written in his own hand. 2. Sign or other mark impressed on a document. "The signature of the party serves to identify the writing as the very writing by which the party is to be bound . . . signature does not necessarily mean writing a person's Christian name and surname, but any mark which identifies it as the act of the party": *per* Maule J in *Morton* v *Copeland* (1855) 139 ER 861.

signature of will. Under the W.A. 1837, s. 9 (as substituted by the A.J.A. 1982, s. 17), a will (q.v.) must be signed by the testator (or some person in his presence and at his direction) so that it appears that the testator intended by that signature to give effect to the will. The signature need not be written, so that a seal with the testator's initials affixed to the will has been held to suffice: *In b Emerson* (1882) 9 LR IR 443. See also *Re Adams* [1990] 2 All ER 97; *Wood* v *Smith* [1992] 3 All ER 556; A.J.A. 1982, ss. 17 *et seq* (making new provision for wills generally).

signing judgment. *See* JUDGMENT, ENTERING.

silence in relation to contract. Silence is not generally deemed consent: *Felthouse* v *Bindley* (1862) 11 CB NS 869. Mere silence is not generally misrepresentation, save in cases where it distorts a representation, or there is a fiduciary relationship between parties, or where contracts are *uberrimae fidei* (q.v.). See *Dimmock* v *Hallett* (1866) 2 Ch App 21; *Way and Waller Ltd* v *Ryde* [1944] 1 All ER 9. *See* CONTRACT.

silence, right of accused to. "Undoubtedly when persons are speaking on even terms, and a charge is made, and the person charged says nothing, and expresses no indignation, and does nothing to repel the charge, that is some evidence to show that he admits the charge to be true": *R* v *Mitchell* (1892) 17 Cox CC 503. Generally, a person commits no offence by refusing to answer questions put by one attempting to discover by whom an offence has been committed (but see, for exceptions, Official Secrets Act 1920, s. 6). Under the Criminal Evidence Act 1898, s. 1 (*b*), the prosecution must not comment on an accused person's failure to testify. See *R* v *Hubbard* (1991) The Times, 15 Jan; Report of Working Group on Right of Silence (Home Office, 1989); *In re Arrows* (1992) The Times, 1 May. "The legislature has not shrunk, where it has seemed appropriate, from interfering in a greater or lesser degree with the immunities grouped under the title of the right to silence": *per* Lord Mustill in *R* v *Director of Serious Fraud Office, ex p Smith* [1992] 1 All ER 730. *See* INCRIMINATE; SELF-INCRIMINATION.

silk, to take. *See* QUEEN'S COUNSEL.

similar fact evidence. *See* EVIDENCE, SIMILAR FACT.

similarity of facts. "[There are] two meanings of the term 'similarity'. First, in the wider sense and the popular sense, a fact is similar to another whenever the two possess a common characteristic; but that common characteristic may be insufficient to render the first fact relevant in the legal sense as proof of the other. Secondly, in the narrower sense, a fact is similar to another only when the common characteristic is the significant one for the purpose of the inquiry at hand": *per* Gummow J in *D F Lyons Pty Ltd v Commonwealth Bank of Australia* (1991) 100 ALR 468. *See* EVIDENCE, SIMILAR FACT.

similiter. In like manner.

simony. See *Acts* viii: 18. Corrupt purchase or sale of a church office. See Simony Act 1588 (amended by Patronage (Benefices) Measure 1986, Sch. 5); Simony Act 1913, repealed under the Statute Law (Repeals) Act 1971, Part II.

simple contract. Referred to also as "parol contract". Contract not under seal, and which requires consideration (q.v.) for its enforcement. May be oral or written. *See* CONTRACT.

simple trust. Bare trust (q.v.).

simplex commendatio non obligat. A mere recommendation [of goods by a seller] does not impose a liability upon him. See, e.g., *Scott* v *Hanson* (1829) 1 Russ & M 128.

simpliciter. Absolutely; without qualification; simply.

sine die. Without a day, i.e., indefinitely.

Single European Market. Concept of a united market involving complete freedom of movement of persons, goods, capital and services, which was to be achieved by the end of 1992. See Single European Act, signed in 1986 and incorporated into UK law by the European Communities (Amendment) Act 1986.

single woman. Generally, an unmarried woman. See, however, the extended meaning given in the (repealed) Affiliation Proceedings Act 1957, s. 1. "It seems to me that a woman whose husband has deserted her or cast her off can say to him, with as much force as

she can say it to anyone else, that he has reduced her to living as a single woman": *per* Devlin J in *Kruhlak* v *Kruhlak* [1958] 2 QB 32.

sit-in. Occupation of premises as an act of protest. Normally trespassory. See *Warwick University* v *De Graaf* [1975] 1 WLR 1126. See also C.L.A. 1977, s. 9.

sittings. Periods during which the Supreme Court sits: Hilary; Easter; Trinity; Michaelmas. See O. 64, r. 1. *See* VACATIONS.

sittings of magistrates' courts. *See* MAGISTRATES' COURTS, SITTINGS OF.

skeleton argument. A succinct outline of an argument to be presented, citing, e.g., principal authorities relied on. Submission is generally compulsory in appeals to the Court of Appeal (Civil Division): *Practice Direction* [1990] 1 WLR 794. See *R* v *Brent LBC, ex p King* (1991) The Times, 14 June.

slander. Spoken words (or gestures) which amount to the tort of defamation (q.v.). Words are defined by the Defamation Act 1952 to include pictures, visual images, broadcasting. It may be actionable *per se*, i.e., without proof of damage, in the case of, e.g., imputation of a crime, unfitness, incompetence.

slander of goods. Tort (q.v.) resulting from false and malicious comment on merchandise sold. See Defamation Act 1952, s. 3(1); *White* v *Mellin* [1895] AC 154.

slander of title. Tort (q.v.) resulting from attacking a person's title to property. See Defamation Act 1952, s. 3; Cable and Broadcasting Act 1984, s. 28; *Riding* v *Smith* (1876) Ex D 91.

slavery. Condition of unfree persons who have no rights and who are in the ownership of their masters. "The state of slavery is of such a nature . . . that nothing can be suffered to support it": *per* Lord Mansfield in *Sommersett's Case* (1772) 20 St Tr 1. "No one shall be held in slavery or servitude; slavery and the slave trade shall be prohibited in all their forms": Universal Declaration of Human Rights 1948, art. 4. See UN Convention on Law of the Sea 1982, art. 99.

sleeping partner. *See* DORMANT PARTNER.

sleeping rough. Colloquialism referring to the Vagrancy Act 1824 and C.J.A. 1982, s. 70. Includes "wandering abroad and lodging in any barn or out-house, or in any deserted or unoccu-pied building, or in the open air or under a tent . . . and not giving a good account of himself".

sleepwalking. Known also as "somnam-bulism". A neurotic reaction of a sleeper who leaves his bed and, while asleep, walks or performs other motor actions. For relation to McNaghten Rules, see *R* v *Burgess* [1991] 2 WLR 1206. "Can anyone doubt that a man, who, though he might be perfectly sane, committed what would otherwise be a crime in a state of somnambulism, would be entitled to be acquitted? And why is this? Simply because he would not know what he was doing": *R* v *Toulson* (1889) 23 QBD 187. See *R* v *Parks* (1990) 56 CCC (3d) 449. *See* AUTOMATISM.

slip. Cover note (q.v.) used, e.g., in a marine insurance contract containing the essential details of the risk in out-line form. See Marine Insurance Act 1906, ss. 21, 89.

slip rule. Rule whereby a clerical error in an order or judgment, or an error based on an omission or accidental slip, may be corrected by the court on application by a motion or summons without appeal. See L.R.R. 1925, r. 249; O. 20, r. 11; *R* v *Cripps, ex p Mul-doon* [1984] QB 686; *Craske* v *Norfolk CC* [1991] EGCS 10. The rule has no application to a mistake of the court "of its own in law or otherwise". See O. 20.

small agreements. Term used under C.C.A. 1974, s. 17(1), to refer to agree-ments where the credit limit or pay-ments under the agreement do not exceed a statutorily-fixed amount and are not regulated by the Act and do not constitute a hire purchase or con-ditional sale agreement (q.v.).

small claims. Claims usually involving consumers and based on some statu-torily-fixed amount, heard by county courts under a simple and informal a' bitration procedure. See County Cc ..rt Rules 1981, O. 19, rr. 1–6.

smuggling. Illegal export or import of merchandise, e.g., without payment of duties. See Customs and Excise Man-agement Act 1979, s. 50 (as amended by Forgery and Counterfeiting Act 1981, s. 23).

socage tenure. *Soc* = ploughshare. A re-sidual tenure, i.e., one which was neither military, spiritual nor servile. The name was derived from "soc-men", who sought the protection of a lord in return for fealty. The Tenures Abolition Act 1660 transformed almost all tenures into free and common soc-age.

Social Charter, EEC. Adopted by eleven governments (but not by the UK) in 1989. Its fundamental principles in-cluded, e.g., free movement of wor-kers, fair remuneration, freedom of association and collective bargaining, protection of children, the elderly and disabled.

social fund. 1. Fund operated by DSS, payments from which may be made to those on low incomes to meet, in pre-scribed circumstances, maternity and funeral expenses, cold weather pay-ments, community care grants, budget and crisis loans (qq.v.), and "other needs in accordance with directions given or guidance issued by the Secre-tary of State": S.S.A. 1986, Part III. See S.S. Contributions and Benefits Act 1992, Part VIII. 2. Fund established by the EEC Treaty, art. 123, intended to increase "the geographical and occu-pational mobility of workers within the community." See *R* v *Secretary of State for Social Services, ex p Stott* (1991) The Times, 31 Dec.

social inquiry report. Report based on the procedure under P.C.C.A. 1973, s. 45, whereby the court takes into ac-count any information relevant to a person's character, physical and men-tal condition, before sentencing him (if he has not previously served a prison sentence). See also C.J.A. 1982 ss. 2, 62; M.H.A. 1983, s. 14.

social policy rule. Interpretation of an Act (q.v.) by considering the social pol-icy which gave rise to it. The courts do not generally favour the rule and it has been described as "naked usurpation of the legislative function under the guise of interpretation": *Magor and St Mellors RDC* v *Newport Corporation* [1952] AC 189.

social security. Scheme, originally pro-vided for under the National Insur-ance Acts. See now: Social Security Contributions and Benefits Act 1992, Social Security Administration Act

1992, and Social Security (Consequential Provisions) Act 1992.

social security, categories of contributors. Classes of insured persons required to make contributions are: Class 1 – earnings related contributions paid by employed earners, employers and others; Class 2 – flat rate contributions payable weekly by self-employed earners; Class 3 – contributions paid voluntarily by earners, and others voluntarily; Class 4 – contributions payable in respect of profits, gains of a trade, profession or vocation, or in respect of equivalent earnings. See S.S. Contributions and Benefits Act 1992, s. 1; S.S. Administration Act 1992.

Social Security Commissioners. A Chief Commissioner and Commissioners hear appeals on points of law from Social Security Appeal Tribunals. There is a right of appeal to the Court of Appeal. See S.S. Administration Act 1992, ss. 22–24, 52.

Social Security Tribunals. Originally National Insurance Tribunals, they are the bodies which function under the S.S. Acts. See S.S. Administration Act 1992, s. 22. Local tribunals, each comprising a chairman and two panel members, hear appeals relating to, e.g., disablement benefit claims. Appeal lies to a Social Security Appeal Tribunal. See S.S.A. 1980, s. 14; S.S.A. 1986, s. 52; O. 59, r. 21; SI 1992/1121.

societas leonina. Leonine partnership. One in which a partner is liable for losses, but has no right to share in profits. Agreements to this end are usually void.

society, friendly. *See* FRIENDLY SOCIETY.

sodomy. Buggery (q.v.). See *Genesis* xiii: 13.

soit baillé aux seigneurs. Let it be handed to the Lords. Message used when a Bill (q.v.) is sent to the Lords from the Commons. When sent from the Lords to the Commons, it reads: *"Soit baillé aux communs".*

soit fait comme it est désiré. Let it be as it is desired. Form of Royal Assent (q.v.).

solatium. An additional allowance awarded for, e.g., injured feelings.

soldier's will. *See* PRIVILEGED WILL.

sole. Unmarried; single; separate.

sole, corporation. *See* CORPORATION.

solemn form. *See* PROBATE.

solicit. To importune (q.v.); to invite to a course of action.

soliciting to murder. It is an offence to "solicit, encourage, persuade or endeavour to persuade or . . . propose to any person, to murder any other person": O.P.A. 1861, s. 4 (as amended by C.L.A. 1977). See, e.g., *R v Most* (1881) 7 QBD 244; *R v Evans* [1986] Crim LR 470.

solicitor. A solicitor of the Supreme Court. One who may conduct legal proceedings or give advice on legal problems, having passed the examinations of The Law Society and possessing a certificate, which is in force, authorising him to practise. See C.L.S.A. 1990, s. 86. He may be liable for any loss resulting from his breach of duty or negligence: *Marsh v Joseph* [1897] 1 Ch 213. He has a duty of care to his client and an obligation to preserve confidence relating to communications with clients: *Minter v Priest* [1930] AC 558. He may employ a member of another profession, but may not form a partnership with him: Solicitors' Practice Rules 1990, r. 7(6). For conflict of duties, see *Re a Firm of Solicitors* (1991) NLJ 746. See also *Gran Gelato Ltd v Richcliff Ltd* [1992] 1 All ER 865; Solicitors' Accounts Rules 1991. See Solicitors Act 1974; A.J.A. 1985, Part I; *Ross v Caunters* [1980] Ch 297.

solicitor, access of detained person to. A person arrested and held in custody at a police station or other premises is entitled to consult a solicitor privately at any time; permission must be given within 36 hours: P. & C.E.A. 1984, s. 58(1), (5). In the case of a serious arrestable offence (q.v.), authorisation for delay may be given only by a police officer who believes that exercise of the right might, e.g., alert persons so that acts of terrorism become more difficult to prevent: s. 56(8), (13) (*c*). See *Code C* (revised, April 1991) para 3. 1. See *R v Deacon* [1987] Crim LR 404; *R v Samuel* [1988] QB 615.

solicitor and own client basis of costs. Basis of taxation of costs applicable between a party to an action and his solicitor. All costs incurred with the express or implied approval of the client are presumed to have been reasonably incurred and the amount to be reasonable if expressly or impliedly approved by the client; there are special provisions for unusual items. See now O. 62, r. 15. *See also* COSTS, TAXATION OF.

Solicitor-General. A law officer of the Crown, subordinate to the Attorney-General. He is usually a member of the House of Commons (q.v.) and holds office at the pleasure of the Crown.

Solicitors Disciplinary Tribunal. Formerly the Solicitors Disciplinary Committee. Composed of practising solicitors of not less than 10 years' standing and lay members appointed by the Master of the Rolls (q.v.) to hear and determine complaints. The Tribunal may strike the name of a solicitor off the Roll and restore to the Roll the name of one formerly struck off. Appeal lies to the Master of the Rolls or High Court. See Solicitors Act 1974, ss. 46–54, as amended by C.L.S.A. 1990, s. 92. For redress for inadequate professional services, see Solicitors Act 1974, s. 37A, inserted by C.L.S.A. 1990, s. 93.

solicitor's duty. *See* DUTY SOLICITORS.

solicitor's lien. Method by which a solicitor may protect his right to recover his costs from a client by: passive or retaining lien (i.e., holding papers, deeds and other personal chattels); common law lien on personal property of the client preserved or recovered by his efforts in litigation; statutory lien enforceable by charging order under Solicitors Act 1974, s. 73. *See* LIEN.

Solicitors' Practice Rules. Rules made by the Council of the Law Society under Solicitors Act 1974. The Council has power to waive in writing any of the provisions of the Rules.

solidary. As in "solidary obligation", i.e., a "joint and several" obligation, as where two or more creditors are entitled to the same obligation. See, e.g., *Ward* v *National Bank* (1883) 8 App Cas 755.

solitary confinement. Imprisonment during which a prisoner is not allowed to communicate with any other prisoner. See Prison Act 1952; s. 14; Prison Rules 1964, r. 43; and *Williams* v *Home Office (No. 2)* [1981] 1 All ER 1211.

solus agreement. (*Solus* = alone.) Agreement whereby a retailer binds himself to buy a product from one source only. Example: garage proprietor agreeing to buy all his petrol from one oil com-

pany. See *Esso Petroleum Co Ltd* v *Harper's Garage Ltd* [1968] AC 269; *Lobb Garages* v *Total Oil* [1983] 1 All ER 944. For the effect of the Treaty of Rome 1957, art. 85, on this type of agreement, see *Brasserie* v *de Haecht SA (No 1)* v *Wilkin* [1968] CMLR 26. *See* RESTRAINT OF TRADE.

solvency, declaration of. Where it is proposed to wind up a company voluntarily, the directors may make a statutory declaration that, after full enquiry, they believe the company will be able to pay its debts in full, plus interest, within a period not exceeding one year. See Ins.A. 1986, ss. 89, 251.

solvent. Able to pay all debts or claims.

solvent abuse. It is an offence to supply or offer to supply a substance other than a controlled drug to a person under 18 or to one who is acting on behalf of a person of that age if the supplier knows that the fumes are likely to be inhaled by the person under 18 for the purpose of causing intoxication: Intoxicating Substances (Supply) Act 1985, s. 1. Solvent sniffing is not drug abuse: *R* v *Southwark Coroner, ex p Kendall* (1988) The Times, 8 June.

solvitur ambulando. It is proved as one goes along. The problem may be resolved by action.

somnambulism. *See* SLEEPWALKING.

Sovereign. The supreme ruler of the state, e.g., King, Queen. "If a determinate human superior, not in a habit of obedience to a like superior, receive habitual obedience from the bulk of a given society, that determinate superior is sovereign in that society, and the society (including the superior) is a society political and independent": Austin. See I.A. 1978, s. 10. *See* MONARCHY.

sovereign authority. "The person (or body) to whose directions the law attributes legal force, the person in whom resides as of right the ultimate power either of laying down general rules or of issuing isolated rules or commands whose authority is that of the law itself": Bryce.

sovereignty. 1. Political and legal concept relating to ultimate authority in a state. 2. Freedom of a state from external control.

sovereignty of Parliament. Doctrine stating that Parliament is the supreme power in the state and possessed, therefore, of unlimited legal power. "What Parliament doth, no power on earth can undo": Blackstone. See *Macarthys Ltd* v *Smith* [1981] QB 180 (effect of EEC legislation). *See* PARLIAMENT.

space, outer. "Includes the moon and other celestial bodies": Outer Space Act 1986, s. 13(1). Activities to which the Act applies, and which must be licensed, comprise launching or procuring the launch of, or operating, a space object, and "any activity in outer space": s. 1. For "space objects", see s. 19(1).

space standard. In relation to overcrowding (q.v.), the space standard is contravened when the number of persons sleeping in a dwelling is in excess of the permitted number, having regard to the number and floor area of the rooms of the dwelling available as sleeping accommodation. (No account is taken of a child under the age of one.) A room is available as sleeping accommodation if it is of a type normally used in the locality as either a living room or a bedroom: see H.A. 1985, s. 327(1), (2). The "permitted numbers" are set out in s. 327(3).

Speaker of the House of Commons. Presiding officer of the Commons, elected by members of the House, subject to the Sovereign's approbation. The Speaker neither speaks nor votes save in an official capacity; is the channel through which the House communicates with the Crown; and gives a casting vote if the numbers in a division are equal. *See* PARLIAMENT.

Speaker of the House of Lords. The Lord Chancellor. *See* CHANCELLOR.

special acceptance. Acceptance of a bill of exchange (q.v.) as payable at a special place.

special administration. Limited administration (q.v.).

special agent. *See* AGENT, SPECIAL.

special business. Business of a company that is transacted at an extraordinary general meeting (with the exception of declaring a dividend, the consideration of accounts, and the reports of the directors and auditors, the election of the directors in the place of those retiring and the appointment of, and the fixing of the remuneration of, the auditors).

special case. Procedure (now commonly called "trial of a preliminary issue") whereby parties to an action, after the issue of a summons, agree on a statement of facts for submission to the court for an opinion on the law relating to those facts. See O. 33, r. 3. See also M.C.A. 1980, s. 111 (relating to the "case stated" procedure); *Berry* v *Berry* [1987] Fam 1.

special damages. *See* GENERAL AND SPECIAL DAMAGES.

special defence. A defence which was peculiar to one type of action and which had to be specifically pleaded. Example: defences of fair comment, justification, in an action for defamation (q.v.).

special hospital. Institution which receives dangerous, violent or criminal persons requiring special security, e.g., Broadmoor (q.v.) See M.H.A. 1983, Part III; *R* v *Macfarlane* (1975) 60 Cr App 320.

specialia generalibus derogant. Special words derogate from general words.

special jurisdiction, courts of. *See* COURTS OF SPECIAL JURISDICTION.

special jury. *See* JURY, SPECIAL.

special manager. Appointed by the court where a company has gone into liquidation. He prepares accounts and exercises other powers entrusted to him by the court: Ins.A. 1986, s. 177.

special plea. Plea in bar, e.g., plea of former acquittal. *See* AUTREFOIS ACQUIT.

special procedure for divorce. *See* DIVORCE AND JUDICIAL SEPARATION, SPECIAL PROCEDURE FOR.

special procedure material. Journalistic material, etc., other than items subject to legal privilege, and excluded material, held subject to some implied obligation to hold it in confidence: see P. & C.E.A. 1984, ss. 11–14. An application for search is needed: s. 9, Sch. 1. See *R* v *Inner London Crown Court, ex p Baines* [1988] 2 WLR 549.

special relationship. "It means no more than a relationship the nature of which is such that one party, for a variety of possible reasons, will be regarded by the law as under a duty of care to the other": *per* Ormrod J in *Esso Petroleum* v *Marden* [1976] QB 801.

special resolution. One passed by a majority of not less than three-quarters of those members who are entitled to, and do, vote in person, or where proxies are allowed, by proxy, at a general meeting of which at least 21 days' notice has been given. See Cos.A. 1985, s. 378. Necessary, e.g., for altering the name, objects or articles of a company. See Cos.A. 1985, ss. 4, 9, 135. *See* COMPANY.

specialty. A contract under seal (q.v.) ("specialty contract").

special verdict. A jury must not return a special verdict under the Trial of Lunatics Act 1883 (acquittal on ground of insanity) except on the written or oral evidence of two or more registered medical practitioners (at least one of whom is approved as having special experience in mental disorders): Criminal Procedure (Insanity and Unfitness to Plead) Act 1991, ss. 1, 6(1). See also M.H.A. 1983, ss. 37(2)(a), 54(2)(3). *See* UNFITNESS TO PLEAD.

specificatio. The making of a new article from the chattel of one person by the work of another.

specification. Form of information (relating to details of construction, operation, etc) required in the application for a patent (q.v.). See Patents Act 1977; Copyright, Designs and Patents Act 1988.

specific delivery, writ of. *See* DELIVERY, WRIT OF.

specific devise. *See* DEVISE.

specific goods. *See* GOODS.

specific issue order. One of a range of "section 8 orders", under Ch.A. 1989, whereby directions are given for the purpose of determining a specific question which has arisen, or may arise, in connection with any aspect of parental responsibility (q.v.) for a child: s. 8(1). These orders may be made upon application or upon the court's own motion: s. 10(1)(a)(b).

specific legacy. *See* LEGACY.

specific performance. Equitable, discretionary remedy *in personam* whereby a party to an agreement is ordered by the court to perform his obligations according to the terms of that agreement. Granted where the appropriate remedy at law is inadequate, and will not be granted if the court has no jurisdiction to do so: *Rushton* v *Smith* [1975] 2 All ER 905. Does not apply to

contracts made for no consideration, or involving continuous supervision, or for personal services, etc. See L.P.A. 1925, s. 49(2); S.G.A. 1979, s. 52; S.C.A. 1981, ss. 49, 50; O. 86; *Record* v *Bell* [1991] 1 WLR 853.

speeding offence. "A person who drives a motor vehicle on a road at a speed exceeding a limit imposed by or under any enactment to which this section applies shall be guilty of an offence": Road Traffic Regulation Act 1984, s. 89(1). See also s. 84, as amended by Road Traffic Act 1991, s. 45. The evidence of more than one witness is generally required to establish liability: s. 89(2). Fire brigade, ambulance and police vehicles may be exempted from observance of speed limits: s. 87. See, generally, 1984 Act, Part VI; Road Traffic Offenders Act 1988, s. 20, substituted by Road Traffic Act 1991, s. 23. *See* RADAR TRAP.

spent convictions. Convictions which, under Rehabilitation of Offenders Act 1974, need not be disclosed, after a rehabilitation period (q.v.), and which are not proper grounds for dismissal from office, profession, occupation or employment: s. 4. No one should refer in open court to a spent conviction without the judge's authority, which authority should not be given unless the interests of justice so require. See, e.g., F.S.A. 1986, s. 189; Banking Act 1987, s. 95.

spes successionis. Hope or expectation of succeeding to property, i.e., as next of kin. It is not a title to property. See *Re Simpson* [1904] 1 Ch 1.

split-trial procedure. In an action for personal injuries (q.v.) the court may, at any stage and of its own motion, order the issue of liability to be tried before any issue relating to the amount of damages to be awarded: O. 22, r. 33.

sporting events, offences relating to. It is an offence to breach an exclusion order made by the court following offences connected with violence or the threat of violence on a journey to or from a football match or, where specified, any other sporting event: P.O.A. 1986, Part IV. See also Sporting Events (Control of Alcohol, etc) Act 1985.

spot contract. *See* CONTRACT, SPOT.

spouse. Husband or wife. See *Fraser* v *Haight* (1987) 36 DLR 459.

spouses, evidence of. The spouse of the accused is competent to give evidence for the prosecution and generally compellable to give evidence on behalf of the accused: P. & C.E.A. 1984, s. 80. The spouse of the accused is competent to give evidence on behalf of the accused or any person charged jointly with the accused; s. 80(1) (*b*). Former spouses are competent and compellable to give evidence as if they had never been married to each other: s. 80(5). For evidence of communications made during the period of marriage, see s.80(9).

springing use. A use intended to come into existence *in futuro*. Example: "to X and his heirs to the use of Y when he shall marry". *See* USE.

spying. Secretly obtaining information for purposes hostile to the security of the state. See Official Secrets Act 1911, s. 1(1).

squatter. One who is wrongfully in occupation of land and claiming the right or title to it. See O. 113; *Swordheath Properties Ltd* v *Floydd* [1978] 1 All ER 721. *See* ADVERSE OCCUPATION OF RESIDENTIAL PREMISES.

S.R. & O. Statutory rules and orders. *See* STATUTORY INSTRUMENTS.

stag. Speculator who subscribes to an issue of shares with no intention of keeping those allotted to him, but in the hope that he can sell out at a profit. See *R* v *Greenstein* [1975] 1 WLR 1353 (process of "stagging").

stake. Sum of money risked for gain or loss on the outcome of some event attended by uncertainty.

stakeholder. One with whom a sum is deposited pending deciding of a wager or the outcome of some other event. See e.g., *Hastingwood Property* v *Saunders Bearman Anselm* [1990] 3 WLR 623.

stakeholder's interpleader. *See* INTERPLEADER SUMMONS.

stale. Ineffective, usually because of lapse of time. *See* LACHES.

stale cheque. *See* CHEQUE, STALE.

stamp duties. Taxes on certain types of instruments (rather than on the transactions represented), e.g., conveyances, first imposed by the Stamp Act 1765 (now repealed). The stamps may be *ad valorem*, i.e., proportionate to the value of the property on which the instrument is based, or fixed in amount.

standard basis for costs. A standard applied to the consideration whether a sum incurred in litigation should be allowed to be paid by/to a party; under it the taxing officer will allow a reasonable amount in respect of all costs reasonably incurred, any doubts being resolved in favour of the paying party (i.e., *against* allowance): O. 62, r. 12(1). In default of any other instruction, this is the basis used on taxations: O. 62, r. 12(3). See COSTS, TAXATION OF.

standard form contracts. Known also as "contracts of adhesion". Contracts (1) which set out terms on which mercantile transactions of common occurrence are to be carried out, e.g., charterparties; (2) which are exemplified by the "ticket cases" of the nineteenth century (see, e.g., *Parker* v *SE Rail Co* (1877) 2 CPD 416), the terms of which were not the subject of negotiations between the parties to them: *Schroeder Music Publishing Co* v *Macaulay* [1974] 1 WLR 1308. See Unfair Contract Terms Act 1977.

standards of proof. In *civil cases*, generally proof on a preponderance of probabilities. See, e.g., *Hornal* v *Neuberger Products Ltd* [1957] 1 QB 247. In *criminal cases*, where the burden of proof rests on the prosecution, proof beyond reasonable doubt (q.v.), but where the burden of proof is on the defence (see, e.g., *R* v *Podola* [1960] 1 QB 325) it is proof on a preponderance of probabilities. In *matrimonial cases*, it is, apparently, proof on a preponderance of probabilities (see *Blyth* v *Blyth* [1966] 1 All ER 524). If a crime is alleged in civil proceedings, the standard is the civil one. In the very unusual civil claim for damages for murder, it is the criminal standard: *Halford* v *Brookes and Another* (1991) The Times, 3 Oct. *See* PROOF; BALANCE OF PROBABILITIES.

standing by. Reference to the principle that where a person who knows what is happening is content to "stand by and see others fighting his battle", he ought to be bound by the result and should not be allowed to reopen the case. See *Nana Ofori Atta II* v *Nana Abu Bonsra II* [1958] AC 95.

standing civilian courts. Courts established under Armed Forces Act 1976, s. 6, for the trial outside the UK of civilians to whom Part II of Army Act 1955 or Part II of Air Force Act 1955 (as amended by Armed Forces Act 1986, s. 9), is applied by s. 209 of either Act. Trial is before a magistrate, appointed from assistants to the Judge Advocate-General, and assessors selected from a panel: s. 6(4)–(15). See 1976 Act, Sch. 3; C.J.A. 1982, Sch 8, as amended by C.J.A. 1988, s. 50.

standing committees. Committees appointed at the beginning of each parliamentary session by the Committee of Selection of the House of Commons (q.v.) to deal with public Bills at committee stage, or in the second reading and report stages. Chairmen are appointed from the Chairmen's Panel by the Speaker. There are standing committees on, e.g., matters relating to Scotland, Wales, Northern Ireland.

standing mute. See MUTE.

standing orders. Orders formulated by a body, e.g., the House of Commons (q.v.), for the conduct in formal manner of its proceedings.

stannaries. Districts in Cornwall and Devon in which tin was mined. Tinminers were exempted from any jurisdiction other than that of stannary courts, except in cases affecting "life, limb or land". The Stannaries Courts Abolition Act 1896 transferred the jurisdiction to the county courts (q.v.) of Cornwall. See *R v East Powder Justices, ex p Lampshire* [1979] QB 616.

staple. Town appointed by Edward I and II to be an exclusive market for certain staple products, e.g., wool and lead. Courts of the Staple were created in 1353 to settle disputes among merchants relating to debts, etc. See A.J.A. 1977, s. 23, Sch. 4, for restrictions on the business of such courts.

Star Chamber, Court of. Judicial body of the Tudor period. The name may be connected with *camera stellata* (room decorated with stars) in which it sat. It exercised criminal jurisdiction of the King in Council. Its procedure, was inquisitorial and torture may have been used during some trials. Abolished in 1641.

stare decisis. To stand by decided matters. (*Stare decisis et non quieta movere* =

to stand by precedent and not to disturb settled points.) Doctrine according to which previous judicial decisions must be followed. See PRECEDENT.

state. 1. A politically organised community under a sovereign government. 2. Social position. 3. Estate (q.v.).

statehood. The criteria, according to the Montevideo Convention 1933, are: permanent population; defined territory; government; capacity to enter into relations with other states.

state immunity. See IMMUNITY FROM JURISDICTION, STATE.

stateless person. One who has no nationality. For provisions for reducing statelessness under B.N.A. 1981, see s. 36, Sch. 2.

statement. Includes any representation of fact, whether made in words or otherwise: Civil Evidence Act 1968, s. 10(1).

statement of affairs. A statement required to be made by a bankrupt in certain cases, setting out details of his creditors, debts, liabilities, assets, etc, for the information of his official receiver: see the Ins.A. 1986, s. 288. See BANKRUPTCY.

statement of claim. Statement by the plaintiff (q.v.) of the material facts upon which he relies and the relief he seeks. Costs need not be claimed specifically: O. 18, r. 15(1). It must be signed by counsel, if settled by him and, if not, by the party's solicitor, or by the party if he sues or defends in person: O. 18, r. 6(5). The statement of claim can be indorsed on a writ: see O. 18, r. 1 and O. 62, r. 7. See PLEADINGS.

statement of defence. In civil procedure the defendant must usually serve a statement of defence on the plaintiff within 14 days of receiving the statement of claim, or of the expiration of the time limited for acknowledging service of the writ. Each allegation in the plaintiff's statement must be dealt with by, e.g., admission, traverse (q.v.), confession and avoidance (q.v.), objection in point of law.

statements, liability for careless. Liability resulting from the failure to observe a duty to avoid making careless statements resulting in harm to some person. See *Hedley Byrne & Co Ltd v*

Heller & Partners Ltd [1964] AC 465; *W.B. Anderson & Sons Ltd* v *Rhodes Ltd* [1967] 2 All ER 850.

statements, liability for false. *See* DECEIT.

state, minimal. Jurisprudential concept propounded by Nozick, in *Anarchy, State and Utopia* (1975). "A minimal state limited to the narrow functions of protection against force, theft, fraud, enforcement of contracts, and so on, is justified; the minimal state is inspiring as well as right."

state of emergency. *See* EMERGENCY POWERS.

status. "The condition of belonging to a class in society to which the law ascribes peculiar rights and duties, capacities and incapacities": *per* Lord Simon in *The Ampthill Peerage* [1977] AC 547. See, e.g., Family Law Act 1986, Part III.

status quo ante. The same state as before.

statute. An Act of Parliament (q.v.). "What the statute itself enacts cannot be unlawful, because what the statute says and provides is itself the law, and the highest form of law that is known to this country" *per* Ungoed-Thomas J in *Cheney* v *Conn* [1968] 1 All ER 779. For "acts done in pursuance of statute": see *Hampson* v *DES* [1990] 3 WLR 42.

statute-barred debt. Debts in respect of which a creditor may not bring proceedings because the periods of time stated in the Limitation Acts have passed. In the winding-up of a company (q.v.), the liquidator (q.v.) must not pay statute-barred debts if shareholders object: *Re Fleetwood Syndicate* [1915] 1 Ch 486.

statute book. Collective title of those Acts of Parliament which are in force.

statute, citation of. In early days statutes were cited by reference to the name of the place at which Parliament met, e.g., the Provisions of Oxford 1258. Later they were cited by reference to the regnal year and chapter; thus the Perjury Act 1911 was cited as 1 & 2 Geo. V, c. 6 (i.e., the sixth of the statutes passed in the parliamentary session of the first and second years of the reign of George V). Hence, the complete citation of a pre-1963 Act is, e.g., Homicide Act 1957 (5 & 6 Eliz. II, c. 11). Following the Acts of Parliament Numbering and Citation Act 1962, an Act passed after January 1963 is cited by reference to the calendar year in which it was passed, e.g., Criminal Damage Act 1971 (c. 48). See also I.A. 1978, s. 19.

statute, contempt of. *See* CONTEMPT OF STATUTE.

statute law. The body of law enacted by Parliament.

statutes, construction of. *See* INTERPRETATION OF STATUTES.

statutes, penal. *See* PENAL STATUTES

statutes, presumptions relating to construction of. *See* PRESUMPTIONS RELATING TO CONSTRUCTION OF STATUTES.

statutes, revenue. *See* REVENUE STATUTES.

statutorily protected tenancy. A protected tenancy (q.v.) within the meaning of the Rent Act 1977 or a tenancy to which Landlord and Tenant Act 1954, Part I, applied; a protected occupancy or statutory tenancy as defined in Rent (Agriculture) Act 1976; a tenancy to which Landlord and Tenant Act 1954, Part II, applied; a tenancy of an agricultural holding within Agricultural Holdings Act 1986; Protection from Eviction Act 1977, s. 8(1).

statutory authority, defence of. Defence in tort (q.v.), as where a statute authorises an action which interferes with some person's rights: see *Allen* v *Gulf Oil Refining Ltd* [1981] AC 1001.

statutory books. Registers and other documents which a company must keep, i.e: registers of members, directors and secretaries, directors' interests in debentures and shares, charges, interests in voting capital; minute books; directors' service contracts; records of receipts and expenditure; assets and liabilities, stock, sales and purchases. See, e.g., Cos.A. 1985, s. 221; Cos.A. 1989, s. 1.

statutory company. A company whose objects and powers are defined under a special private Act.

statutory corporation. Public corporation (q.v.).

statutory declaration. *See* DECLARATION.

statutory duty, breach of. Tort (q.v.) committed by one who injures another as the result of some breach of statute. The statutory duty must be owed to the plaintiff; the injury suffered must be of the nature which the statute was intended to prevent; the defendant must be guilty of a breach of his statutory obligation; the breach must have caused the damage. See *Wentworth v Wiltshire CC* (1992) 142 NLJ; *Murphy v Brentwood DC* [1990] 2 All ER 908.

statutory instruments. Documents by which power to make subordinate legislation has been exercised by the Queen in Council or a minister. Known formerly as "statutory rules and orders" and usually cited by calendar year, number and occasionally the title, e.g., Traffic Areas (Reorganisation) Order (No. 634) (SI 1991/634). (A "regulation" is a statutory instrument only where the parent Act declares the power to issue regulations is to be made by statutory instrument.) See Statutory Instruments Act 1946; Statutory Orders (Special Procedure) Acts 1945 and 1965. Their validity may be challenged in the courts on grounds of *ultra vires* or failure to follow correct procedures in making the instrument (see, e.g., *Raymond v Honey* [1983] AC 1). See DELEGATED LEGISLATION.

statutory instruments, committees concerning. The *SI Reference Committee* decides questions concerning classification and numbering. The *Joint Committee on SI*, consisting of 7 members of each House of Parliament, chaired by a Commons Member from the Opposition, considers SI laid before each House. It must consider, in particular, the possibility of, e.g., defective drafting, unauthorised retrospective effect, unjustifiable delay in publication, imposition of a charge on the public revenues. The *Commons Select Committee on SI* considers instruments directed by statute to be laid before the Commons.

statutory interpretation. See INTERPRETATION OF STATUTES.

statutory language, interpretation of. "Statutory language must always be given presumptively the most natural and ordinary meaning which is appropriate in the circumstances": *per* Lord Simon (dissenting judgment) in *Maunsell v Olins* [1975] AC 373.

statutory lives in being. Lives enumerated under P. & A.A. 1964, s. 3(5), for purposes of the perpetuities rule (q.v.) as: (1) the person who made the disposition; (2) the person to whom,

or in whose favour, the disposition was made; (3) parents and grandparents of the beneficiaries, in certain cases; (4) any person on the failure or determination of whose prior interest the disposition is limited to take effect. See *Re Thomas Meadows & Co Ltd* [1971] Ch 278.

statutory nuisance. See NUISANCE.

statutory owner. Term used in relation to a settlement to indicate those in whom, during a minority or where there is no tenant for life (q.v.), the legal estate is vested, i.e., persons of full age upon whom powers are conferred by the settlement and, in any other case, the trustees of the settlement: S.L.A. 1925, ss. 23, 117. They have the powers of a tenant for life. See SETTLEMENT.

statutory rules and orders. See STATUTORY INSTRUMENTS.

statutory tenancy. After the termination of a protected tenancy (q.v.) of a dwelling-house, the person who, immediately before that termination, was the protected tenant, shall, if and so long as he occupies the dwelling-house as his residence, be the statutory tenant of it and, when there is a statutory tenant of a dwelling-house that house is referred to as subject to a statutory tenancy: Rent Act 1977, s. 2(1)(*a*), (2). See H.A. 1988, s.39; *Killick v Roberts* [1991] 1 WLR 1146.

statutory tenant. One who holds under a statutory tenancy (q.v.). See TENANT BY SUCCESSION, STATUTORY.

statutory trusts. 1. Trusts created or implied by statute, e.g., under the L.P.A. 1925, ss. 34, 36 or A.E.A. 1925, s. 33. 2. Under A.E.A. 1925, s. 49 ("statutory trusts in favour of issue and other classes of relatives of an intestate"), part of the property is held by a personal representative (q.v.) to be divided equally among children who are alive at the death of the intestate as soon as they attain 18, or marry. See TRUST.

statutory undertakers. Persons authorised by any enactment to carry on transport, and other public undertakings. See, e.g., T.C.P.A. 1990, ss. 262, 271.

stay of execution. The suspending of operation of a judgment or order of the court. See O. 47; O. 59, r. 13. See JUDGMENTS, ENFORCEMENT OF.

stay of proceedings. The suspending of proceedings by the court, e.g., where proceedings are obviously frivolous. See O. 18, r. 19; *Edmeades* v *Thames Board Mills* [1969] 2 All ER 127 (in which it was held that the court had jurisdiction to stay an action while the plaintiff unreasonably refused to submit to a medical examination requested by the defendant); *A.-G's Reference (No. 1 of 1990)* (1992) The Times, 16 April.

stealing. Theft (q.v.).

stealing, going equipped for. See GOING EQUIPPED FOR STEALING.

sterilisation. Surgical removal of, or obstruction of the functions of, the reproductive organs so as to prevent reproduction. See *In Re B.* [1987] 2 WLR 1213 (House of Lords upheld order for sterilisation of a mentally-retarded 17-year old female ward. *Per* Lord Hailsham, LC: The basic human right of a woman to reproduce is only such where reproduction is the result of informed choice); *Re E.* (1991) The Times, 22 Feb.

still-born child. "A child which has issued forth from its mother after the 24th week of pregnancy and which did not at any time after being completely expelled from its mother breathe or show any other sign of life": Births and Deaths Registration Act 1953, s. 41, as amended by Still-Birth (Definition) Act 1992, s. 1.

stipendiary magistrates. Full-time, salaried magistrates who usually sit alone, who are appointed from lawyers of at least seven years' standing (see Justices of the Peace Act 1979, ss. 13, 31 and C.L.S.A. 1990, s. 71, Sch. 10), by the recommendation of the Lord Chancellor, in Inner London and in some large provincial centres (e.g., Leeds, Merseyside, Birmingham, Nottingham). A stipendiary magistrate generally has all the powers of two lay magistrates (q.v.): see Justices of the Peace Act 1979, ss. 13–16.

stipulation. Agreement; bond; undertaking.

stock. 1. Capital lent to the government or a local authority on which a fixed rate of interest is paid. 2. Fully-paid shares which have been converted and combined into one unit, so that a company's capital, consisting formerly of, e.g., 100,000 separate shares of £1 each becomes stock worth £100,000. See the Cos.A. 1985, s. 121(2); *Re Home and Foreign Investment Agency Ltd* [1912] 1 Ch 72. 3. Goods available for sale. 4. A family, or line of descent.

stock exchange. Recognised organisation of brokers and others who engage in the purchase and sale of stocks, shares and securities. See I.C.T.A. 1988, s. 841(1).

stock, inscribed. See INSCRIBED STOCK.

stock lending. Practice allowing dealers in securities to borrow them from appropriate institutions when they require them for delivery on sales. The dealer agrees to replace them at a later date with the same type and amount of securities. See Finance Act 1991, s. 57; SI 1992/572.

stop and search powers. Police powers, under the P. & C.E.A. 1984, Part I, to stop and search persons or vehicles in any place to which the public has access, for, e.g., stolen articles, offensive weapons. Reasonable force only may be used in exercise of the power: see s. 117. See *Revised Code A* (1991) issued under 1984 Act, s. 66.

stop list relating to planning control. Notice served by a local planning authority after the serving of an enforcement notice (q.v.) requiring a breach of the planning order to be remedied, where the authority considers it expedient to prevent some activity alleged by the notice to constitute a breach. It is an offence for a person to contravene the stop notice. See T.C.P.A. 1990, s. 183, amended by Planning and Compensation Act 1991, s. 9.

stop list, trade. A list, usually drawn up by a trade association, of persons with whom members of the association are forbidden to deal. See *Hardie and Lane Ltd* v *Chilton* [1928] 2 KB 306.

stop notice. A notice which can be served on, e.g., a company ordering it not to register a transfer of shares without serving notice on the judgment creditors (q.v.). Issued so as to prevent a disposition of securities, by a judgment debtor. See O. 50, relating to stop notices and orders prohibiting improper dealings with funds in the court, etc. For stop notices in relation to land planning, see T.C.P.A. 1990, ss.

183–7, amended by Planning and Compensation Act 1991.

stoppage in *transitu.* *See* IN TRANSITU.

storm. "Some sort of violent wind usually accompanied by rain or hail or snow. Storm does not mean persistent bad weather nor does it mean heavy rain or persistent rain by itself": *per* Veale J in *Oddy* v *Phoenix Assurance Co Ltd* [1966] 1 Lloyd's Rep 134.

stranger. One who is "not privy or party to an act": Cowel.

straw, man of. *See* MAN OF STRAW.

straying livestock. Where livestock belonging to any person strays on to land in the ownership or occupation of another and damages land or property thereon, or expenses are reasonably incurred by that other person in keeping the livestock (if, e.g., it cannot be restored at once to the owner), the person to whom the livestock belongs is liable for damage or expenses: Animals Act 1971, s. 11. See also the Highways Act 1980, s. 155.

street. Public or private roadway running in front of houses or other buildings in a continuous line. It includes any highway, road, lane, footpath, square, court, alley or passage, whether a thoroughfare or not: Highways Act 1980, s. 329(1). See New Roads and Street Works Act 1991, s. 48(1).

street offences. 1. Offences related to the obstruction of highways, disregard of police regulations. See, e.g., Metropolitan Police Act 1839, s, 54; *Grant* v *Taylor* [1986] Crim LR 252. 2. Importuning and loitering. *See* IMPORTUNE; LOITER.

street trading. The selling or exposing or offering for sale of any article (including a living thing) in a street: Local Government (Misc. Provs.) Act 1982, Sch. 4, para. 1.

stricti juris. According to strict right or law.

strict liability in criminal law. Term adopted in place of "absolute liability". "If a matter is made a criminal offence, it is essential that there should be something in the nature of *mens rea* . . . But there are exceptions to this rule . . . and the reason for this is, that the legislature has thought it so important to prevent the particular act from being committed that it absolutely forbids it to be done; and if it is

done the offender is liable to a penalty whether he has any *mens rea* or not, and whether or not he intended to commit a breach of the law": *Pearks, Gunston & Tee Ltd* v *Ward* [1902] 2 KB 1. See *Gammon* v *A.-G. of Hong Kong* [1985] AC 1; *Pharmaceutical Society* v *Storkwain Ltd* [1986] 1 WLR 903; *R* v *Bradish* [1990] 2 WLR 223 (Firearms Act 1968, s. 5, creating offence of strict liability). Where a statute is silent as to *mens rea,* the presumption that it is required may be rebutted, and in some cases (e.g., Food Safety Act 1990, ss. 20, 21) a statute imposing strict liability may also provide a defence.

strict liability in tort. *See* DANGEROUS THINGS, LIABILITY RELATING TO.

strict liability rule and contempt of court. *See* CONTEMPT OF COURT AND STRICT LIABILITY RULE.

strict settlement. Defined under S.L.A. 1925, s. 1, as amended. It arises from a deed, will, etc. under which land is limited in trust by way of succession; it excludes land held on trust for sale and involves the use of a trust instrument and a vesting deed. Example: a settlement which was usually made on marriage whereby the husband received a life interest, the children of the marriage received entailed interests and the wife received pin money (q.v.) during her husband's life and an annual sum during widowhood. See *Ungarian* v *Lesnoff* [1990] Ch. 206. *See* SETTLEMENT.

strike. The cessation of work by a body of persons employed acting in combination, or a concerted refusal, or a refusal under a common undertaking, of any number of persons employed to continue to work for an employer in consequence of a dispute, done as a means of compelling their employer or any person or body of persons employed, to accept terms or conditions of or affecting employment. See E.P.(C.)A. 1978, Sch. 13; T.U.L.R.(C.)A. 1992, s. 246. *See* BALLOT; INDUSTRIAL ACTION.

strike, official. A strike (q.v.) which is supported formally and financially by a recognised trade union (q.v.).

striking off. Removal from a register, e.g., for professional misconduct. Under the Medical Act 1983, Part V, the Professional Conduct Committee of the General Medical Council may erase from the register a person convicted in the UK of a criminal offence, or who has been judged by the Committee to have been guilty of serious professional misconduct (q.v.). Appeal is to JCPC (q.v.). For striking off a company, see *R* v *Registrar of Companies, ex p A.-G.* [1991] BCLC 746.

structure fixed to a building. In T.C.P.A. 1971, s. 54(9), means a structure which is ancillary and subordinate to the building itself and is either fixed to the main building or within its curtilage (q.v.): *Debenhams* v *Westminster CC* [1987] 1 All ER 51.

subinfeudation. A feudal tenure. King granted land to X, tenant in chief (q.v.), who created a subtenancy by transferring part of his holding to Y. Y created a further tenancy by transferring part of his holding to Z. In each case the transferee was a tenant of the transferor. *See* FEUDAL SYSTEM.

subject. Owing obedience to another (usually the Crown).

subject to contract. Generally, the use of this phrase prevents the document in which it is contained from being evidence of a concluded bargain. There may be a binding contract, however, if the court can conclude that all the terms of a bargain have been agreed and set down in writing and signed. See *Lyus* v *Prowsa Development* [1982] 1 WLR 1044; *Alpenstow Ltd* v *Regalian Properties* [1985] 1 WLR 721.

subject to survey. Use of the phrase in contract for the sale of property does not, apparently, prevent a binding contract from coming into existence. There is a duty on the purchaser, in such a case, to have a survey made. See *Ee* v *Kakar* (1980) 40 P & CR 223.

sub judice. Under judicial consideration; not yet decided.

sub judice **rule.** 1. Rule relating to contempt of court (q.v.) whereby the courts will act to prevent or punish the publishing of articles in the press which prejudice the fair trial of an action. See Contempt of Court Act 1981, s. 1. 2. Principle of parliamentary procedure whereby a matter awaiting judicial decision is not generally referred to in debate nor as the subject of a question to a minister.

sub-lease. A lease emerging from, and

shorter than, another leasehold interest. Known also as a "sub-tenancy" or "under-lease".

sub-letting. Leasing by a tenant (q.v.) of premises leased to him. An agreement not to sub-let is not broken by sub-leasing part of the premises: *Cook* v *Shoesmith* [1951] 1 KB 752. See also H.A. 1985, s. 94; Landlord and Tenant Act 1988; and *Scala House & District Property Co Ltd* v *Forbes* [1974] QB 575.

sub modo. Under some restriction, modification or qualification.

sub-mortgage. The mortgage of a mortgage, e.g., as where a mortgagee borrows money on the security of the mortgage. Under L.P.A. 1925, s. 86, where the mortgage has been created by a grant of a term of years a legal sub-mortgage can be made only by a grant of a sub-term or a legal charge. *See* MORTGAGE.

sub nom. *Sub nomine.* Under the name.

subordinate legislation. Delegated legislation (q.v.).

subornation. The procuring of a person to commit a criminal act. Thus, subornation of perjury is the offence of procuring another to commit perjury: Perjury Act 1911, s. 7(1). See *R* v *Ellahi* (1979) 1 Cr App R (S) 164.

subpoena. *Sub poena* = under a penalty. A writ (q.v.) which may take the form of *subpoena duces tecum*, or *subpoena ad testificandum*, directing a person to give evidence and bring relevant documents (see O. 38, r. 14). See S.C.A. 1981, ss. 36, 123; *Marcel* v *CPM* [1991] 2 WLR 1118.

subrogation. Substitution. Refers to, e.g., an insurer's right to enforce a remedy which the assured could have enforced against a third party. See *Phoenix Assurance Co* v *Spooner* [1905] 2 KB 753; *Orakpo* v *Manson Investments* [1978] AC 95.

sub rosa. Under the rose (a symbol that those present at a meeting are sworn to secrecy). Confidentially.

subscribing witness. One who signs a document as an attesting witness. *See* ATTESTATION.

subscription, minimum. *See* MINIMUM SUBSCRIPTION.

subsequent condition. *See* CONDITION.

subsequent pleadings. *See* PLEADINGS, SUBSEQUENT.

subsidence. The sinking of ground to a lower level, often resulting in damage to land and buildings in the immediate area. See, e.g., Coal Mining Subsidence Act 1991. For payments to houses rendered uninhabitable, see s. 22.

subsidiarity. Jurisprudential concept, concerned with the devolution of power, suggesting that the functions involved in the activities of a group, such as a society, should be carried out by the smallest group capable of so doing, in order that the autonomy of individuals within the group might be promoted. The concept has appeared in EEC administrative doctrine, referring to the principle of devolving decision-making and other activities as far down the power structure as is practicable and appropriate, e.g., at member state, rather than Commission, level.

subsidiary company. A company (S) is a subsidiary of another company (H) (its holding company) if H holds a majority of voting rights in S, or is a member of S and has the right to appoint or remove a majority of the board of directors of S, or is a member of S and controls alone, pursuant to an agreement with other shareholders or members, a majority of the voting rights in S, or if it is a subsidiary of a company which is itself a subsidiary of H: Cos.A. 1985, s. 736, substituted by Cos.A. 1989, s. 144.

subsidy. 1. Money formerly granted by Parliament to the Sovereign for extraordinary occasions. 2. Payment by the state to producers or distributors, intended to reduce prices paid by consumers.

sub silentio. Under silence; without notice having been given to some matter. For the use of the phrase, see *R* v *Gloucestershire CC* [1980] 2 All ER 746, referring to *Re DJMS* [1978] QB 120. For the rule that a precedent (q.v.) *sub silentio* is not authoritative, see, e.g., *Bradley-Hole* v *Cusen* [1953] 1 QB 305.

substantial damages. *See* DAMAGES.

substantive law. That part of the law concerned with the determination of rights, liabilities and duties, etc, as contrasted with adjective law (q.v.).

substantive offence. A definite, complete offence.

substituted service. Where the plaintiff (q.v.) cannot serve a writ on the defendant (q.v.) or his solicitor he may apply *ex parte* on affidavit to a master for an order for substituted service which, if made, states the form the service must take, e.g., by press advertisement. See O. 65, r. 4; *Paragon Group* v *Burnell* [1990] 3 All ER 923. *See* SERVICE.

substitutional legacy. *See* LEGACY, SUBSTITUTIONAL..

substitutionary gift. Gift, e.g., to children in equal shares which provides that the children of a deceased child will take the share of that child. (In such a case, those who are substituted take, in general, as joint tenants.) See *Re Bourke's WT* [1980] 1 All ER 219.

substitution, doctrine of. Principle that where there is limitation of property to persons in succession, ownership absolute and entire passes from beneficiary to beneficiary upon the prescribed event's occurrence.

substratum rule. Where the main object or substratum of a company fails, it must not continue to operate the business under an ancillary power. Shareholders may petition for winding-up where the entire substratum (i.e., the basis of the business) has gone. See Ins.A. 1986, s. 122(1)(*g*); *Re German Date Coffee Co* (1882) 20 Ch D 169.

sub-tenancy. Sub-lease (q.v.).

sub-tenant. An under-lease from the original tenant.

sub-tenant, unlawful. Person occupying under a lease or tenancy granted by the head tenant, in breach of some covenant or agreement against sub-letting, assigning or parting with possession. Recovery of possession may be sought under O. 133. See *Leith Properties* v *Byrne* [1983] QB 433.

sub tit. *Sub titulo* = under the title of.

sub-trust. Known also as a "derivate trust". Example: as where trustees A and B hold a fund in trust for C and D in equal shares, and C and D declare themselves trustees of their shares for their children. *See* TRUST.

sub voce. Under the title or heading.

succession. 1. The order in which persons succeed to property, or some title. 2. Term applied to the estate of a deceased person. 3. Process of becoming entitled to property of a deceased by operation of law or will. See A.E.A. 1925.

sue. 1. To seek justice by the process of law. 2. To bring an action against some person(s).

sufferance, tenancy at. Tenancy created where a tenant is in occupation "by lawful demise and after his estate endeth continueth in possession and wrongfully holdeth over": Coke. In effect, mere possession, created only by construction of law, arising where a valid tenancy terminates but the tenant is holding over (q.v.) without the landlord's permission. See *Remon* v *City of London Real Property Co.* [1921] 1 KB 49.

suffrage. Right or privilege to vote in an election.

suggestio falsi. Suggestion of falsehood; misrepresentation (q.v.).

suicide. The taking of one's own life intentionally and voluntarily. A crime until Suicide Act 1961. It is a crime, however, for a person to aid, abet, counsel or procure the suicide of another: s. 2(1). See *R* v *McShane* (1977) 66 Cr App R 97; *R* v *McGranaghan* (1988) 9 Cr App R (S) 447. Suicide must be strictly proved at a coroner's inquest; it is not a verdict which ought to be reached as being the most likely cause of death: *R* v *City of London Coroner* [1975] 1 WLR 1310; *Kirkham* v *Chief Constable of Greater Manchester Police* [1990] 3 All ER 246.

suicide pact. An agreement between two or more persons having for its object the death of all of them, whether or not each is to take his own life: Homicide Act 1957, s. 4(3). See also Suicide Act 1961, ss. 2, 3.

sui generis. Of its own right. Constituting a class of its own.

sui juris. Of one's own right. Having full legal capacity to act on one's own. *See* ALIENI JURIS.

suit. (*Suite* = act of following.) 1. Appeal to a superior (e.g., the King) for justice. 2. Action in court in pursuance of a right or claim. 3. Litigation in general.

suit of court. Feudal obligation on a tenant to attend his lord's court and assist in its deliberations.

suitor. One who is a party to a suit.

summary conviction. Conviction before magistrates.

summary dismissal. Dismissal of an employee without giving the notice to which the employee is entitled by virtue of the contract of employment. It is justified if the employee's conduct is such that it prevents "further satisfactory continuance of the relationship": *Sinclair* v *Neighbour* [1967] 2 QB 279. See E.P. (C.) A. 1978, s. 55(5).

summary judgment under Order 14. Procedure in an action begun by writ, except where it includes an allegation of fraud, libel, slander, malicious prosecution or false imprisonment. The plaintiff issues the summons having sworn to the belief that there is no defence to his claim. If the defendant contests the summons he must show that he has a triable defence. The master, at the hearing of the summons, may give judgment for the plaintiff unless the defendant shows that there is "an issue or question in dispute which ought to be tried or that there ought for some other reason to be a trial". He may give the defendant leave or unconditional leave to defend. See O. 14; O. 86 (relating to an analogous procedure for action for specific performance (q.v.) in the Chancery Division); see *European Asian Bank AG* v *Punjab and Sind Bank (No 2)* [1983] 1 WLR 642; *Putty* v *Hopkinson* [1990] 1 All ER 1057 (interest on judgment debt).

summary jurisdiction. Power of magistrates to try summary offences (q.v.). In general, the magistrates' court cannot try any information which was not laid within six months from the time of commission of the offence: M.C.A. 1980, s. 127.

summary jurisdiction, court of. *See* COURT OF SUMMARY JURISDICTION.

summary offence. An offence which, if committed by an adult, is triable only summarily: C.L.A. 1977, s. 64(1) (*b*). For general procedures see M.C.A. 1980, ss. 9–15. For procedure where summary trial of an offence triable either way appears more suitable, see M.C.A. 1980, s. 21. See also I.A. 1978, Sch. 1; C.J.A. 1988, ss. 37, 39, 40, 41.

summary trial. The trial of petty offences and other offences triable summarily by magistrates. See M.C.A. 1980, ss. 9–15.

summing-up. The judge's summary of a case made following the closing speeches. It usually includes a direction on points of law, a review of the evidence (including, e.g., onus of proof, effect of presumptions of law, etc). See *R* v *Briley* (1990) The Times, 13 Dec.

summons. 1. "A citation proceeding upon an information . . . laid before the magistrate who issues the summons, and conveying to the person cited the fact that the magistrate is satisfied that there is a prima facie case against him": *Dixon* v *Wells* (1890) 25 QBD 249. It must state the general matter of the information and the place and time the defendant is to appear and must be signed by the magistrate: *R* v *Brentford Justices, ex p Catlin* [1975] QB 455. See C.L.A. 1977, s. 39; and M.C.A. 1980, s. 1. 2. Application to a judge or master in chambers for a decision on the points of procedure before an action in court.

summons for directions. *See* DIRECTIONS, SUMMONS FOR.

summons, originating. *See* ORIGINATING SUMMONS.

summons, serving of. Procedure involving the delivery of a summons to the defendant or by leaving it with someone at his usual or last known place of abode, or by sending it by post to his usual or last known place of abode.

summons, writ of. The commencing stage of an action whereby the defendant is called on to acknowledge the claim being made by the plaintiff and to give notice of his intention to defend (if that be the case): see O.12. It (rather than an originating summons (q.v.)) must be used in the case of a claim relating to tort (other than trespass to land) or to an allegation of fraud or to damages in respect of death or personal injury. See O. 5; O. 6. It must be endorsed with a statement of claim (special endorsement) or a statement of the nature of the claim or relief or remedy required (general endorsement).

summum jus, summa injuria. Extreme law is the greatest injury.

Sunday trading prohibition. "Every shop shall, save as otherwise provided by . . . this Act, be closed for the serving of customers on Sunday": Shops Act 1950, s. 47. For exemptions see Fifth Schedule; for partial exemptions, see Sixth Schedule. See also L.G.A. 1972, s. 222; *Stoke-on-Trent CC* v

B&Q [1991] 2 WLR 42; *Kirklees BC* v *Wickes Building Supplies Ltd* (1992) The Times, 29 June.

super altum mare. Upon the high sea.

superannuation scheme. Payment of annuities or lump sums to persons on their retirement at a certain age, or earlier incapacitation, or to their personal representatives, widows, relatives or dependants.

superficies solo cedit. That which is attached to the land forms a part of it. See L.P.A. 1925, s. 62(1). *See* FIXTURES.

superior courts. Courts with a jurisdiction not limited, e.g., geographically or by value of the subject-matter of an action. They include, e.g., House of Lords, Court of Appeal, JCPC, High Court, Crown Court, Restrictive Practices Court. *See* INFERIOR COURTS.

superior orders, obedience to. *See* OBEDIENCE TO ORDERS, DEFENCE OF.

supersedeas. You shall desist. Writ (q.v.) staying or ending the exercise of jurisdiction.

superstitious uses. A trust (q.v.) for celebrating or teaching doctrines and practices of a religion not generally tolerated by law, and, therefore, generally void. See, e.g., *Bourne* v *Keane* [1919] AC 815; *Gilmour* v *Coats* [1949] AC 427.

supervening cause. *See* CAUSA REMOTA.

supervening event. That which takes place as something extraneous or additional.

supervision and treatment orders. Orders by the court requiring the supervision of a person by a social worker or probation officer, made under the Criminal Procedure (Insanity and Unfitness to Plead) Act 1991, s. 5, and Sch. 2, following evidence by two or more registered practitioners. For revocation of order, see Sch. 2, Part III. *See* UNFITNESS TO PLEAD.

supervision order. A "community order" (see C.J.A. 1991, s. 6(4)) to a supervised person to comply with instructions given by a supervisor, e.g., to live at a specified place for a specified period. See also P.C.C.A. 1973, s. 26 (for suspended sentence supervision orders).

supply. Includes: selling, hiring out, lending goods; entering a hire-purchase agreement to furnish the goods; the performance of any contract for work and materials to furnish the goods; providing the goods in exchange for any consideration (q.v.) other than money; providing the goods in connection with the performance of a statutory function; giving the goods as a prize or gift: C.P.A. 1987, s. 46(1).

supply estimates. Basis of Parliament's consideration of the sanctioning of expenditure by legislation. The estimates are: ordinary annual main estimates; votes on account; supplementary estimates excess votes. *See* WAYS AND MEANS.

support, right of. *See* RIGHT OF SUPPORT.

suppression of documents, dishonest. Offence committed by a person who "dishonestly with a view to gain for himself or another or with intent to cause loss to another, destroys, defaces or conceals any valuable security, any will or other testamentary document or any original document of or belonging to, or filed or deposited in, any court of justice or any government department . . .": Th.A. 1968, s. 20(1). See Finance Act 1989, s. 145 (falsification or destruction of documents relating to Inland Revenue).

suppressio veri, suggestio falsi. The suppression of truth is the suggestion of falsehood.

supra protest. *See* ACCEPTANCE OF A BILL.

Supreme Court. Consists of Court of Appeal, High Court of Justice, and Crown Court; the Lord Chancellor is President: S.C.A. 1981, s. 1.

Supreme Court, Masters of the. *See* MASTERS OF THE SUPREME COURT.

surcharge. The disallowing, following audits, of authorised expenditure. See *Lloyd* v *McMahon* [1987] AC 625.

surcharge and falsify. Term (virtually obsolete) referring to an account in which there is an omission of a sum which ought to have been credited and of which proof of a wrongly-inserted item can be given. See O. 43; *Williamson* v *Barbour* (1877) 9 Ch D 529.

surety. A person who gives security for another. The procedure whereby magistrates bind over (q.v.) a person may involve his being ordered to find sureties for his keeping the peace. See M.C.A. 1980, s. 115; Bail Act 1976; *R* v *Reading Crown Court, ex p Bello* (1991) 92 Cr App R 303 (principles to be applied to forfeiture of surety).

surname. Family, as distinct from Christian, name. A child's surname is that of his father, and a wife is incompetent to change her child's surname by deed poll or registration of birth without the husband's consent or a court order: *D.* v *B.* [1977] Fam 145. The name of a woman conferred by marriage is not lost upon her divorce: *Fendall* v *Goldsmid* (1877) 2 PD 263. See Mat. Causes Rules 1977, r. 92(8); *W.* v *A.* [1981] Fam. 14. *See* NAME, CHANGE OF.

surplusage. Unnecessary, irrelevant, excessive material in formal pleadings (q.v.).

surprise. Term applied, e.g., to an event which may be grounds for a new trial. Examples: where an action comes on unexpectedly while the applicant's witnesses are not available, or where the plaintiff introduces allegations which had not been pleaded: *Lloyde* v *W Midlands Gas Board* [1971] 1 WLR 749. See O. 59, r. 11.

surrebutter. Term used in pleadings (q.v.) to indicate the plaintiff's answer to a rebutter (q.v.).

surrejoinder. Answer by the plaintiff to a rejoinder by the defendant. *See* REJOINDER.

surrender and admittance. Formerly a mode of conveyance of copyhold (q.v.). The copyhold was "surrendered" but, until admittance, legal estate remained in transferor. Prior to 1926 a legal mortgage (q.v.) of copyhold could be made in this way, involving the mortgagor's convenanting to surrender the property to the mortgagee's use on the condition that surrender was void if money and interest were not paid on a fixed date; this covenant was followed by formal surrender and admittance.

surrender of shares. The yielding up, and acceptance by the directors of a company, of shares, for the purpose of being cancelled, etc. If it involves a reduction of capital it is unlawful, except when sanctioned by the court. See Cos.A. 1985, s. 146.

surrender of tenancy. A mode of determination of a tenancy (q.v.) whereby a tenant yields up his estate to the lessor. *Express surrender,* in the case of a lease exceeding 3 years, requires a deed: L.P.A. 1925, s. 52. *Implied surrender* occurs, e.g., if the tenant delivers possession to the lessor who accepts it.

surrender value. The amount an insurance company will repay to a policy holder who wishes to discontinue prior to the date of maturity.

surrogate. One appointed to act in place of another.

surrogate mother. A woman who carries a child in pursuance of an arrangement made before she began to carry the child, and made with a view to any child carried in pursuance of it being handed over to, and the parental rights being exercised by, another person or persons: Surrogacy Arrangements Act 1986, s. 1(1). The Act prohibits the negotiation of surrogacy arrangements on a commercial basis, and relevant advertisements: ss. 2, 3. See Human Fertilisation and Embryology Act 1990, s. 36; Human Fertilisation and Embryology (Disclosure of Information) Act 1992; *Re W.* [1991] 1 FLR 385.

survey. Skilled examination of land, dwellings, etc, in relation to apparent condition, generally undertaken in advance of the exchange of contracts. See *Bigg* v *Howard Son & Gooch* [1990] 12 EG 111 (measure of damages following negligent survey); *Swingcastle* v *Gibson* [1991] 2 WLR 1091.

survival of causes of action on death. *See* DEATH, SURVIVAL OF CAUSES OF ACTION ON.

survivors. "A word which has caused perhaps more difficulty in the interpretation of wills than any other in the language": *Re Pickworth* [1899] 1 Ch 642. When property is bequeathed to "the survivors" of individuals or members of a class, it is construed as meaning those who are living at the period of distribution: *Cripps* v *Wolcott* (1819) 4 Madd 11. See *Gilmour* v *MacPhillamy* [1930] 1 Ch 138.

survivorship, right of. The right of a survivor (e.g., of joint tenants (q.v.)) to the whole property. The death of a joint tenant vests the entire estate in the remaining joint tenants; his interest is extinguished. *See* JUS ACCRESCENDI (ETC).

suspend. 1. To debar temporarily from the exercise of an office or occupation. 2. To revoke a law temporarily. See the Bill of Rights 1688, which condemned the use of the power to suspend laws:

"The pretended power of dispensing with laws, or the execution of laws by regal authority . . . is illegal."

suspended sentence. Sentence ordered not to take effect immediately: P.C.C.A. 1973, s. 22, as amended by C.J.A. 1981, s. 5. The sentence must be for a term of not more than two years and suspension can be for a period of not less than one year or more than two years from the date of the order. See *R* v *Grant* (1989) 54 JPN 345; *R* v *Worsley* (1991) The Times, 3 Oct.

suspicion. An opinion or belief derived from circumstances or facts that do not constitute proof. "Suspicion in its ordinary meaning is a state of conjecture or surmise when proof is lacking": *per* Lord Devlin in *Hussein* v *Chong Fook Kam* [1970] AC 942.

sweepstake. A wager based on the outcome of some event, e.g., result of a race. Held, in *Ellesmere* v *Wallace* [1929] 2 Ch 1, to be illegal as a lottery "if the winner is determined by chance, but not if the winner is determined by skill". See Lotteries and Amusements Act 1976, s. 1; and *Imperial Tobacco* v *A.-G.* [1981] AC 781.

symbolic delivery. *See* DELIVERY.

synallagmatic contract. (*Synallagmatikos* = of a contract.) A reciprocal contract, i.e., one characterised by mutual duties and rights. "Every synallagmatic contract contains in it the seeds of the problem: in what event will a party be relieved of his undertaking to do that which he has agreed to do but has not yet done?": *per* Diplock LJ in *Hong Kong Fir Shipping Co* v *Kawasaki Kisen Kaisha* [1962] 2 QB 26. See *United Dominions Trust* v *Eagle Services Ltd* [1968] 1 All ER 104.

syndicate. Combination of firms or individuals for the promotion of a common interest, generally the spreading of risk in a commercial transaction. A member is liable *pro rata* for the amount he has underwritten. The syndicate does not have legal personality (q.v.).

system, evidence of. Evidence given to show a propensity to commit a given crime by use of a certain technique. See, e.g., *Thompson* v *R* [1918] AC 221; *R* v *Straffen* [1952] 2 QB 911.

T

Table A. Specimen set of regulations for management of a company limited by shares. See the Companies (Tables A to F) Regulations 1985 (S.I. 1985/805 as amended); Cos.A. 1985, s. 8. In so far as its contents are not excluded expressly, they are incorporated in the company's articles.

Table B. Form of memorandum of association (q.v.) for a private company limited by shares, set out in the 1985 Regulations.

Table C. Form of memorandum and articles of association (qq.v.) for a company limited by guarantee, and not having a share capital, set out in the 1985 Regulations.

Table D. Form of memorandum and articles of association (qq.v.) for a public company limited by guarantee, and having a share capital, set out in the 1985 Regulations.

Table E. Form of memorandum and articles of association (qq.v.) for an unlimited company having a share capital, set out in the 1985 Regulations.

Table F. Form of memorandum of association for a public company limited by shares, set out in the 1985 Regulations.

Table G. The Secretary of State may by regulations prescribe a Table G containing articles of association appropriate for a partnership company, that is, a company limited by shares whose shares are intended to be held to a substantial extent by or on behalf of its employees: Cos.A. 1985, Chapter I, inserted by Cos.A. 1989, s. 128.

tabula in naufragio. Plank in a shipwreck. Doctrine, abolished by L.P.A. 1925, s. 94, whereby if a legal mortgage to X was followed by an equitable mortgage to Y and then by an equitable mortgage to Z, then Z might obtain priority over Y by paying off X and acquiring the legal estate from him. The legal estate was considered as a "plank in the shipwreck" by the use of which one mortgagee saved himself "while the other was drowned". (This applied only where Z did not know of an earlier mortgage to Y when he made the loan.) *See* MORTGAGE.

tacking. Prior to L.P.A. 1925, a legal mortgagee who had made a further loan to the mortgagor could tack together both loans and recover them prior to the intervening mortgagee, if he had received no notice of the intervener. Under the 1925 Act s. 94, legal or equitable mortgagees may tack where intervening mortgagees concur, where further advance was made with no notice at the time of the intervening mortgage and where the mortgage involved an obligation to make a further advance. See *Burnes* v *Trade Credits Ltd* [1981] 1 WLR 805. *See* MORTGAGE.

tail. *See* FEE TAIL.

tail general. Widest form of entailed interest. Example: land limited "to X and the heirs of his body".

tail male general. Entailed interest which arises where land is limited "to X and the heirs male of his body begotten". Unlike the tail general (q.v.), only the *male heirs* of X may succeed. In case of *tail female general*, only *female heirs* take.

tail male special. Entailed interest arising by grant "to X and Y and the heirs male of their two bodies begotten". In case of *tail female special*, only *female heirs* take.

takeover offer. "An offer to acquire all the shares, or all the shares of any class or classes, in a company (other than shares which at the date of the offer are already held by the offeror), being an offer on terms which are the same in relation to all the shares to which the offer relates or, where those shares include shares of different classes, in relation to all the shares of each class": Cos.A. 1985, ss. 428–430 (as substituted by F.S.A. 1986, Sch. 12). See, e.g., *Lonrho* v *Fayed* (1988) The Independent, 19 July; *R* v *Spens* [1991] BCC 140.

talaq. Repudiation, in Islamic law of a wife by her husband by means of a formal, triple declaration. See *Fatima* v *Home Secretary* [1986] AC 527.

tales. From the phrase *tales de circumstantibus* = such (persons) of bystanders. Refers to the practice of making up the deficiency in the available number of jurors by commanding the sheriff (q.v.) to call others who can be found (known as *talesmen*). See now Juries Act 1974, ss. 6, 11.

tangible property. Corporeal property, e.g., goods, as compared with intangible property, e.g., choses in action (q.v.).

tape recorders in court. It is a contempt of court to use tape recorders in court, except by leave, or to publish a recording of legal proceedings made by means of such an instrument: Contempt of Court Act 1981, s. 9.

tape-recording. Record of sound imprinted on magnetic tape. Tape-recordings are treated as documents for the purposes of discovery and inspection of documents (q.v.): O. 24, r. 1; *Barker* v *Wilson* [1980] 1 WLR 884. See *Code E* (under which the police have a general discretion to tape record any interview) issued under P. & C.E.A. 1984; *R* v *Emmerson* (1991) 92 Cr App R 284; *R* v *Riaz* [1992] Crim LR 336; P. & C.E.A. 1984.

tariff. 1. A system of government-imposed duties on imports. 2. A scale of charges for a business or public utility.

tax. A compulsory contribution by individuals and companies to the State, levied on goods, services, income and wealth. See, e.g., I.C.T.A. 1988; T.C.G.A. 1992. Local taxation imposed by local authorities is known as "rates" (q.v.).

taxation of costs. *See* COSTS, TAXATION OF.

tax avoidance and evasion. Tax "avoidance" relates to the arrangement of one's affairs so that liability to tax is reduced or disappears. Tax "evasion" is the non-payment of taxes which one is under duty to pay, and is generally illegal. "The avoidance of tax may be lawful, but it is not yet a virtue": *Re Weston's Settlements* [1969] 1 Ch 223. See *Fitzwilliam (Countess)* v *IRC* (1992)

The Times, 27 Feb. See I.C.T.A. 1988, Part XVII. For "tax advantage", see s. 709. For repayment of tax unlawfully demanded, see *Woolwich BS* v *ICR* [1991] STC 364.

tax haven. Nation or locality levying relatively low taxes, or none at all, on foreigners. Examples (at one time or another): Channel Islands, Lichtenstein. See I.C.T.A. 1988, ss. 739–741.

taxing masters. Salaried officials of the Supreme Court Taxing Office who consider taxation of costs. See *R* v *Wilkinson* [1980] 1 All ER 597. They are appointed by the Lord Chancellor, with the agreement of the Treasury.

taxing officer. The person responsible for determining precisely what costs (q.v.) must be paid, after the judge has decided who is to pay and the basis for payment. His functions may be performed by a district judge in the county court, or in the High Court outside London, and a taxing master (q.v.).

taxing statutes. Acts imposing taxation. They are construed as other statutes, but the tax must be imposed by plain words before persons will be held liable. "The Crown does not tax by analogy but by statute": *Ormond Investment Co* v *Betts* [1928] AC 143. A construction which helps evasion will be avoided. See *IRC* v *Wolfson* [1949] 1 All ER 865.

tax month. "The period beginning with the 6th day of any calendar month and ending with the 5th day of the following calendar month": I.C.T.A. 1988, s. 825(8).

tax week. One of the successive periods in a tax year beginning with the first day of that year and every seventh day thereafter; the last day of a tax year (or, in the case of a tax year ending in a leap year, the last two days) to be treated accordingly as a separate tax week: S.S.A. 1975, Sch. 20.

tax year. *See* INCOME TAX, YEARLY ASSESSMENT.

telecommunication system, improper use of. The offence of sending a message or other matter that is grossly offensive, indecent, obscene or menacing by means of a public telecommunication system (defined in 1984 Act, ss. 4(1), 9(1)): Telecommunications Act 1984, s. 43.

telephone, exchange of contracts by. Exchange can be effected in any manner recognised by the law as amounting to an exchange, and this includes telephone conversations: *Domb* v *Isoz* [1980] 1 All ER 942. See The Law Society's General Conditions of Sale (1986).

telephone tapping. Form of electronic surveillance (q.v.) carried out by security services after authorisation by the Home Secretary. See *Malone* v *Commissioner for Metropolis* [1979] 2 All ER 620. *See* COMMUNICATIONS INTERCEPTION OF.

television links, evidence through. A person other than the accused may give evidence through a live television link in a trial on indictment or on appeal to the Court of Appeal (Criminal Division) or the hearing of a reference under the Criminal Appeal Act 1968, s. 17, if the witness is outside the UK or is under 14 and the offence charged is one stated in C.J.A. 1988, s. 32(2), but such evidence does require leave of the court: C.J.A. 1988, s. 32 (1). See *Garcin* v *Amerindo Investment Ltd* [1991] 1 WLR 1140.

telex. Instantaneous telex communication should follow the general rule that a contract is made when and where acceptance is received: *Brinkibon Ltd* v *Stahag Stahl* [1983] 2 AC 34.

temporary That which lasts, or is intended to last, for a limited period only. See *R* v *Social Security Commissioner, ex p Akbar* (1991) The Times, 6 Nov. (indefinite absence abroad may be construed as temporary).

tenancy. The relationship of a tenant (q.v.) to that land which he holds from another. See *Street* v *Mountford* [1985] 2 All ER 289; *Family Housing* v *Jones* [1990] 1 All ER 385. *See* LEASE.

tenancy, assured. *See* ASSURED TENANCY.

tenancy, at sufferance. *See* SUFFERANCE, TENANCY AT.

tenancy at will. *See* TENANT AT WILL.

tenancy by entireties. Where land was granted to a husband and wife so that, had they not been married, they would have taken as joint tenants, they were tenants by entireties; each was tenant of the whole land; when one died the land passed absolutely to the survivor. Abolished as a doctrine under L.P.A. 1925, s. 37. Tenancies by entireties existing at that date were converted into joint tenancies (q.v.).

tenancy by estoppel. Where, e.g., a mortgagor in possession grants a lease (q.v.) which does not satisfy the statutory provisions or the terms of the mortgage deed, the lease may bind the tenant and mortgagor (so that, e.g., he may sue for rent) under the doctrine of estoppel (q.v.). See *Trent* v *Hunt* (1853) 9 Exch 14. *See* MORTGAGE.

tenancy, enfranchisement of. *See* ENFRANCHISEMENT OF TENANCY.

tenancy, furnished, protected. *See* PROTECTED FURNISHED TENANCY.

tenancy, housing association. *See* HOUSING ASSOCIATION TENANCY.

tenancy, implied. Tenancy presumed from the payment and acceptance of a sum in the nature of rent. See *Longrigg Burrough* v *Smith* (1979) 251 EG 847.

tenancy in common. *See* COMMON, TENANCY IN.

tenancy, long. *See* LONG TENANCY.

tenancy, periodic. *See* PERIODIC TENANCY.

tenancy, protected. *See* PROTECTED TENANCY.

tenancy, protected shorthold. *See* PROTECTED SHORTHOLD TENANCY.

tenancy, regulated. *See* REGULATED TENANCY.

tenancy, secure. *See* SECURE TENANCY.

tenancy, statutory. *See* STATUTORY TENANCY.

tenancy, surrender of. *See* SURRENDER OF TENANCY.

tenancy, weekly. *See* WEEKLY TENANCY.

tenant. One who holds land of another. A lessee (q.v.). Includes, under Rent Act 1977, s. 152(1), "statutory tenant and also includes a sub-tenant and any person deriving title under the original tenant or sub-tenant". See H.A. 1985, s. 621(3).

tenantable repair. The quality of repair in a house rendering it fit for occupation by tenants. See, e.g., Landlord and Tenant Act 1985, s. 11.

tenant at sufferance. *See* SUFFERANCE, TENANCY AT.

tenant at will. One holding under a tenancy at will, which exists where the tenant (T) occupies L's land, with L's consent, on terms under which L or T may determine the tenancy at any time. "In this case the lessee is called tenant at will because he hath no certain or sure estate, for the lessor may put him out at what time it pleaseth him": Littleton. It may be created by express agreement or implication and may be ended by L or T if, e.g., either should assign land, or die. See, e.g., *Hagee Ltd v Erikson and Larson* [1976] QB 209; *Javad v Aquil* [1991] 1 All ER 243.

tenant by succession, statutory. After the termination of a protected tenancy (q.v.) of a dwelling- house, the person who, immediately before the termination, was the protected tenant of the dwelling-house is, so long as he occupied the house as his residence, the *statutory tenant* of it. One who, after the death of the statutory tenant, becomes the next statutory tenant is known as the "statutory tenant by succession". See Rent Act 1977, s. 2, Sch. 1; H.A. 1988, s. 39.

tenant by the curtesy. *See* CURTESY.

tenant for life. "The person of full age who is for the time being beneficially entitled under a settlement to possession of settled land for his life is for the purposes of this Act the tenant for life of that land and the tenant for life under that settlement": S.L.A. 1925, s. 19(1). Two or more persons of full age so entitled as joint tenants together constitute the tenant for life for purposes of the Act: s. 19(2). *See* SETTLEMENT.

tenant for life, powers of. These are conferred by S.L.A. 1925 and include power of sale and exchange, power to grant and accept leases, to borrow money and to apply capital money, to sell heirlooms and to compromise claims concerning settled land.

tenant for years. One who holds land for a term of years (q.v.).

tenant from year to year. One who holds a yearly tenancy, which may be created expressly ("to T from year to year") or by implication. It continues until ended by proper notice. See *Tickner v Buzzacott* [1965] Ch 426; *Prudential Assurance v LRB* (1992) The Times, 23 July.

tenant, harassment of. *See.* HARASSMENT OF OCCUPIER.

tenant-in-chief. *See* IN CAPITE.

tenant in tail. One who holds an estate in fee tail (q.v.).

tenant in tail after possibility. If a gift of land is made "to X and his heirs begotten by him on Y" and Y (X's wife) dies without leaving children, there exists no possibility of descendants of X and Y who could succeed. X (tenant in tail) is known as "tenant in tail after possibility of issue extinct" (or "tenant in tail after possibility"). X may not bar the entail in such a case, but he is given the statutory powers of a tenant for life (q.v.). See S.L.A. 1925, s. 20(1)(*i*). *See* FEE TAIL.

tenant, occupying. *See* OCCUPYING TENANT.

tenant *pur autre vie*. *See* AUTRE VIE.

tenant's fixtures. In general, a landlord is entitled to fixtures which have been attached to the land by his tenant. There may be exceptions in the case of ornamental, domestic, agricultural and trade fixtures. See, e.g., Agricultural Holdings Act 1986. s. 10. It is an offence under Th.A. 1968, s. 4(2), for a person who is in possession of land under a tenancy to appropriate the whole or part of any fixture let to be used with the land. *See* FIXTURES.

tenant, statutory. *See* TENANT BY SUCCESSION, STATUTORY.

tenant, sub-. *See* SUB-TENANT.

tenant to the *praecipe*. *See* PRAECIPE, TENANT TO THE.

tender. 1. To offer for sale. 2. To offer money, etc. in payment or satisfaction of a debt or other obligation. "Payment extinguishes the debt; tender does not." There must be actual production of the exact sum of money, or a dispensation of such production. See O. 22, r. 8. 3. An offer relating to the supply of goods. Thus, X requires 1,000 ingots and invites tenders. If he accepts Y's tender, there is a contract for the sale of 1,000 ingots by Y to X. See *Percival Ltd v LCC* (1918) 87 LJKB 672; *Marston Construction Ltd v Kigass Ltd* (1989) 15 Con LR 116. 4. Legal tender (q.v.).

tender before action, defence of. Plea by the defendant that he had offered to satisfy the plaintiff's claim before the issue of a writ, supported by payment into court of the amount alleged to have been tendered. See O. 18, r. 16.

tender of performance. Expressed readiness to perform an act in accordance with an obligation. May be equivalent to performance: *Startup v Macdonald* (1843) 6 Man & G 593. See *Farquharson v Pear Insurance Co Ltd* [1937] 3 All ER 124.

tenement. 1. Property held by tenure. 2. House in use as dwelling.

tenendum To be held. Clause in a conveyance (q.v.) formerly used to indicate the mode of tenure.

tenor. 1. The substance of some matter. 2. An exact copy of writing.

tenor, executor according to. *See* EXECUTOR.

tenure. A relationship of lord and tenant which determined the terms upon which land was held. The old feudal tenures (free, lay, spiritual, unfree) were generally abolished by the land legislation of the 1920s, so that today there is one principal tenure only, i.e., freehold, which is the name now used for free and common socage (q.v.). See Tenures Abolition Act 1660; L.P.A. 1922 and 1925.

tenure, free. Spiritual (frankalmoign) and lay tenure (i.e., by knight service, socage, sergeanty).

tenure, security of. Statutory protection, e.g., under Rent Act 1977, or Protection from Eviction Act 1977, afforded to tenants, concerning rents and the landlord's right to recover possession.

tenure, unfree. Copyhold tenure (known also as *villanagium* (q.v.)).

term. (*Terminus* = limit or boundary.) 1. A part of the year in which business could be transacted in the courts. Terms were abolished under J.A. 1875; the year now comprises sittings (q.v.) and vacations (q.v.). 2. To "keep term" is to dine in an Inn of Court (q.v.) on a specified number of formal occasions, as part of the qualification for the call to the Bar (q.v.). 3. A fixed period of time. 4. Period for which an estate is granted. 5. Condition, provision or limitation. 6. Substantive part of a contract, creating a contractual obligation for whose breach an action lies.

term, customary. Term in a contract implied by a trade usage or the custom of a locality. Should be certain, notorious, reasonable and not contrary to the intention of any statute. May be excluded expressly or impliedly. See, e.g., *Hutton* v *Warren* (1836) 1 M & W 466.

term, express. *See* EXPRESS TERM.

term, fixed. *See* FIXED TERM.

term for years. Term of years (q.v.).

term, implied. *See* IMPLIED TERM.

term, innominate. *See* INNOMINATE.

term, intermediate. *See* INTERMEDIATE TERM.

terminus ad quem. The limit to which. The point of ending.

terminus a quo. The limit from which. The point of commencement.

term of years. Known also as "term for years". A lease. In essence, an estate or interest in land limited to a certain fixed period, e.g., a lease for 21 years. (A lease for more than three years must be created by deed: see L.P. (Misc. Provs.) A. 1989 s.1); it must be based on a definite period (see *Swift* v *Macbean* [1942] 1 KB 375); it must confer on the lessee a right to exclusive possession (see *Crane* v *Morris* [1965] 1 WLR 1104). See *EWP Ltd* v *Moore* (1991) The Times, 10 Sep. *See* LEASE.

term of years absolute. A term that is to last for a certain fixed period, although it may be liable to end before the expiration of that period by notice, re-entry, operation of law, etc. Includes a term for less than a year, or for a year or years and a fraction of a year or from year to year: L.P.A. 1925, s. 205(1) (xxvii).

termor. One holding land for a term of years (q.v.).

territorial extent, rule relating to. "An Act of Parliament only applies to transactions within the UK and not to transactions outside": *C.E. Draper & Sons Ltd* v *Edward Turner & Sons Ltd* [1964] 3 All ER 148. See, however, *Pugh* v *Pugh* [1951] P 482.

territoriality, principle of. Concept in international law that a Sovereign ought not to engage in jurisdictional acts outside the limits of his territory. See *British Nylon Spinners* v *ICI Ltd* [1954] 3 All ER 88.

territorial waters. Sea area adjacent to a state's shores and subject to its exclusive jurisdiction. See, e.g., Territorial Waters Jurisdiction Act 1878; the Sea Fisheries Act 1968, s. 6; Territorial Sea Act 1987; I.C.T.A. 1988, s. 830; Water Resources Act 1991, s. 104(1).

terrorism. "The use of violence for political ends [including] any use of violence for the purpose of putting the public or any section of the public in fear": Prevention of Terrorism (Temporary Provisions) Act 1989, s. 20(1). See Suppression of Terrorism Act 1978; Aviation and Maritime Security

Act 1990; N. Ireland (Emergency Powers) Act 1991, Sch. 8; *R* v *Al-Mograbi* (1979) 70 Cr App R 24. See also P. & C.E.A. 1984, s. 116(5). *See* EXCLUSION ORDER.

terrorism, information concerning acts of. It is an offence for a person to fail, without reasonable excuse, to disclose to a constable as soon as reasonably practicable any information which he knows or believes might be of material assistance in preventing acts of terrorism or in securing the apprehension, prosecution or conviction of a person for an offence involving the commission, preparation or instigation of an act involving terrorism: Prevention of Terrorism (Temporary Provisions) Act 1989, s. 18.

terrorist. "A person who is or has been concerned in the commission, or attempted commission, of any act of terrorism or in directing, organising or training persons for the purpose of terrorism": N. Ireland (Emergency Powers) Act 1991, s. 66.

testable. 1. Legally capable of making a will (q.v.) or bearing witness. 2. Disposable under a will.

testament. A will. "The true declaration of our last will, of that we would be done after our death": *Termes de la Ley.* A distinction is sometimes drawn between a will (a disposition of *real property*) and a testament (relating to *personal property*). *See* WILL.

testamentary capacity. The ability in law to make a valid will, based on, e.g., the maker's being over 18, *animus testandi* (q.v.), and the ability to make a disposition of property "with understanding and reason". See *Re Simpson* (1977) 121 SJ 224. For delegation of testamentary power, see *Chichester Diocesan Fund* v *Simpson* [1944] 2 All ER 60; *Re Beatty's WT* [1990] 3 All ER 844.

testamentary expenses. Expenditure incurred in the proper performance of an executor's duties. See *Re Matthew's WT* [1961] 1 WLR 1415.

testamentary freedom. The right of a person to dispose of his property by will according to his wishes. Limited in practice by, e.g., Inheritance (Provision for Family and Dependants) Act 1975.

testamentary guardian. Guardian of an infant (q.v.) appointed by will.

testamentary intention. Known also as *animus testandi* (q.v.). Essential for the validity of a will. Thus, a will executed in jest, or brought about by force, fear, fraud or undue influence will be set aside. See *Boyce* v *Rossborough* (1856) 6 HL Cas 2; *Parfitt* v *Lawless* (1872) LR 2 P & D 462.

testamentary trust. An express trust intended to operate after death. It must be contained in an attested or duly executed will or codicil. *See* TRUST.

testate. Having made and left one's will. *See.* WILL.

testator. (*Fem: testatrix.*) A deceased person who has made a will (q.v.).

testator, presence of. Witnesses must attest and subscribe a will in the testator's presence: W.A. 1837, s. 9 (as substituted by A.J.A. 1982, s. 17). "Presence" means that testator must be able to see witnesses subscribe and know what they are doing. See *Wyatt* v *Berry* [1893] P 5; *Re Colling* [1972] 3 All ER 729. *See* WILL; ATTESTATION.

testatum. The beginning of the operative part of a deed (q.v.): "Now this deed witnesseth that . . .".

test case. An action determining the legal position of many persons who are not parties to the action, as contrasted with, e.g., a representative action (q.v.).

teste. (*Teste meipso* = witness myself.) The witnessing or concluding part of a writ (q.v.). See now O. 6, r. 1.

testimonial evidence. *See* EVIDENCE, TESTIMONIAL.

testimonium. That final part of a deed stating that the parties have signed the deed "in witness" of what it contains.

testimony. Statement of a witness in court, generally sworn, and offered as evidence of the truth of that which he asserts. The essence of judicial evidence (q.v.).

testimony, perpetuating. *See* PERPETUATING TESTIMONY.

textbooks, authority of. General rule is that books may be cited in court, if at all, by way of evidence as to the correct interpretation of the law, but not as independent sources from which the law can be derived. Exceptions are "books of authority", e.g., Coke, Blackstone. Some very few living writers are occasionally cited, but rarely referred to directly as authorities. Example of modern reliance on Coke: *Reid v Police Commissioner of the Metropolis* [1973] QB 551; example of adoption of contemporary writer's definition: *Re Ellenborough Park* [1956] Ch 131 ("easements", from Cheshire's *Modern Law of Real Property*).

theatre, obscenity in. It is an offence, under Theatres Act 1968, to present or direct an obscene performance unless the performance can be justified as being for the public good on grounds of literary or other artistic merit. For the stirring up of racial hatred in the theatre, see P.O.A. 1986, s. 20.

theft. A person is guilty of theft "if he dishonestly appropriates property belonging to another with the intention of permanently depriving the other of it; and 'thief' and 'steal' shall be construed accordingly": Th.A 1968, s. 1(1). *See* DISHONEST; PERMANENTLY DEPRIVING, INTENTION OF.

thing in action. Chose in action (q.v.).

thin skull principle. *See* EGG-SHELL SKULL PRINCIPLE.

third party. A person other than the principals in any proceedings. See O. 16. For "third party damages", see *Woodar Investment Ltd v Wimpey Ltd* [1980] 1 All ER 51.

third-party directions. Where a third party acknowledges service, the defendant who has issued a third-party notice must, by summons, apply to the court for directions: O. 16, r. 4(1).

third party, orders against. Orders issued under County C.A. 1984, ss. 52–54 (county courts) or S.C.A. 1981, ss. 33–35 (High Court), for the inspection, custody, etc, of property which is not the property of or in the possession of parties to the proceedings. Application for an order is by summons supported by affidavit (q.v.).

third-party proceedings. Proceedings brought by separate action for a remedy against a third party. Example: the plaintiff is the lessor, and the defendant is being sued for breach of covenant; the defendant could claim relief from a third party, such as a sub-lessee. The third party, can counterclaim against the defendant, not against the plaintiff. See O. 16; *Barclays Bank v Tom* [1923] 1 KB 221; *Harper v Gray and Walker* [1985] 1 WLR 1196.

third-party rights in land. Rights over another's land are binding on its successive owners, e.g., easements, restrictive covenants (qq.v.).

third-party risks, insurance against. It is an offence to use, to cause or permit any other person to use, a motor vehicle on a road unless there is in force in relation to the use of the vehicle by that person a policy of insurance or some security in respect of third-party risks (i.e., risks to persons not parties to the policy). See Road Traffic Acts 1988, Part VI, 1991, s. 20.

threat. The expression of an intention to inflict unlawful injury or damage of some kind "so as to intimidate or overcome the will of the person to whom it is addressed". "Threatening" is to be taken in its ordinary meaning: *Brutus v Cozens* [1973] AC 854. For a threat to kill, see *R v C.I. Williams* (1986) 84 Cr App R 299. For use of threatening words or behaviour, see P.O.A. 1986, s. 4; *DPP v Clarke* [1992] Crim. L.R. 60; *Winn v DPP* (1992) NLJ 527.

three-tier system of Crown Court. Locations for sittings of the Crown Court (q.v.). The major centres (first-tier) have criminal and civil jurisdiction and are served by High Court judges, circuit judges and recorders. Second-tier centres have criminal jurisdiction only and are served as are first-tier centres. Third-tier centres have only criminal jurisdiction and are served by circuit judges and recorders.

tidal waters. Those parts of the sea within territorial waters (q.v.) in which there is a real and perceptible ebb and flow of the tide.

tied cottage. Dwelling belonging to and maintained by an employer for occupancy by his employee. Common at one time among agricultural workers. A measure of security of tenure for agricultural workers housed by their employers and their successors was afforded under Rent (Agriculture) Act 1976, as amended by Rent Act 1977. See also Agricultural Holdings Act 1986; H.A. 1988, Sch. 4, Part II. *See* PROTECTED OCCUPIER.

tied house. A public house, the lessee of which has covenanted with the lessor to buy all his supplies of beer, etc. only from that lessor.

timber. "Oak, ash and elm are timber, provided they are of the age of 20 years and upwards, provided also they are not so old as not to have a reasonable quantity of usable wood in them, sufficient to make a good post. Timber, that is, the kind of tree which may be called timber, may be varied by local custom": *Honywood* v *Honywood* (1874) LR 18 Eq 306. See also *Dashwood* v *Magniac* [1891] 3 Ch 306.

time as essence of a contract. Phrase referring to the common law principle that in the absence of contrary intention, time is an essential condition in the performance of a contract if the nature of the subject matter of the contract or the surrounding circumstances indicate that it should be. Equitable doctrine was that time was not of the essence unless made so expressly or impliedly. Under L.P.A. 1925, s. 41: "Stipulations in a contract, as to time or otherwise, which according to rules of equity are not deemed to be or have become of the essence of the contract, are also construed and have effect at law in accordance with the same rules". See *Behzadi* v *Shaftesbury Hotels* [1991] 2 WLR 1251. See S.G.A. 1979, ss. 10, 59, relating to stipulations as to time of payment (which are not generally of the essence of the contract in the absence of contrary intention); *United Scientific Holdings* v *Burnley BC* [1978] AC 904.

time charter. A charterparty (q.v.) for a specified period (compared with one for a particular voyage).

time for performance of service contract. Where, under a contract for the supply of a service (q.v.) by a supplier acting in the course of a business, the time for the service to be carried out is not fixed by the contract, left to be fixed in a manner agreed by the contract or determined by the course of dealing between the parties, there is an implied term that the supplier will carry out the service within a reasonable time: Supply of Goods and Services Act 1982, s. 14(1). What is a "reasonable time" is a question of fact: s. 14(2).

time immemorial. Beyond legal memory, i.e., "time whereof the memory of man runneth not to the contrary". Fixed by the Statute of Westminster I 1275, as the first year of the reign of Richard I (1189). See *Bryant* v *Foot* (1868) LR 3 QB 497.

time order. Order made by court under C.C.A. 1974, s. 129, if it appears just to do so, allowing an extension of time on, e.g., an application for an enforcement order or an application made by a debtor or hirer after service on him of a default notice.

time out of mind. Time immemorial (q.v.).

time policy. Policy of marine insurance where the contract is to insure for a fixed period of time.

time, reasonable. *See* REASONABLE TIME.

timeshare accommodation. Any living accommodation in the UK or elsewhere, used or intended to be used, wholly or partly for leisure purposes by "timeshare users" all of whom have rights to use, or participate in arrangements under which they may use, that accommodation, or accommodation within a pool of accommodation to which that accommodation belongs, for intermittent periods of time: see Timeshare Act 1992, s.1. For rights to cancel timeshare agreements, see ss. 2, 3. See SI 1992/1943.

tithes. "The tenth part of all fruits, praedial, personal, and mixt which are due to God, and consequently to his churches' ministers for their maintenance": Cowel. (*Praedial* = arising from the ground; *personal* = profits from labour; *mixt* = arising from things nourished from the ground, e.g., eggs.) The Tithe Act 1936 replaced tithe rentcharges by redemption annuities. The Finance Act 1962 provided for compulsory redemption of such annuities on the sale of land. Their payment was ended under Finance Act 1977, s. 56.

title. 1. Appellation of office or distinction. 2. Right to land or goods, or evidence of such right. 3. "Good title" indicates that the evidence of claim of title is conclusive. For "defective title", see, e.g., *Rignall Developments* v *Halil* [1987] 3 WLR 394. 4. Title of an Act of Parliament (q.v.) is its heading. It is legitimate to use the title for the interpretation of the Act as a whole and to discover its scope: *Johnson.* v *Upham* (1859) 2 E & E 263.

title, abstract of. *See* ABSTRACT AND EPITOME OF TITLE.

title, chain of. *See* CHAIN OF TITLE.

title, conversion of. *See* CONVERSION OF TITLE.

title deeds. Those documents constituting evidence of legal ownership of land. See, e.g., L.P.A. 1925, s. 45(9); *Clayton* v *Clayton* [1930] 2 Ch 12.

title, long. Formal title of an Act of Parliament (q.v.), e.g., "An Act to consolidate the enactments relating to conveyancing and the law of property in England and Wales" (the long title of the Act, known generally by its short title of the Law of Property Act 1925). See *Ward* v *Holman* [1964] 2 QB 580.

title, paramount. *See* PARAMOUNT.

title, root of. *See* ROOT OF TITLE.

title, short. Title by which an Act is usually and conveniently cited. See Short Titles Act 1896. Usually stated towards the end of the statute in a separate section, e.g., Th.A. 1968, s. 36(1). It cannot be relied on for resolution of a doubt in construction. See *Re Boaler* [1915] 1 KB 21.

title to goods, documents of. *See* DOCUMENTS OF TITLE TO GOODS.

title to goods, transfer of. Where goods are sold by a person who is not their owner, and who does not sell them under the authority or with the consent of the owner, the buyer acquires no better title to the goods than the seller had, unless the owner of the goods is by his conduct precluded from denying the seller's authority to sell: S.G.A. 1979, s. 21(1).

title, voidable, sale under. *See* VOIDABLE TITLE, SALE UNDER.

tobacco, sales to children. It is an offence to sell any tobacco product to persons under 16: Protection of Children (Tobacco) Act 1986. See also C. & Y.P. (Protection from Tobacco) Act 1991; *St Helens MBC* v *Hill* (1992) The Times, 26 Mar (offence is one of strict liability). For "tobacco", see C. & Y.P.A. 1933, s.7.

toll. 1. Tax paid for some privilege. 2. Compensation for service provided. See New Roads and Street Works Act 1991, s. 6 (toll orders in relation to roads).

Tomlin Order. Order (drafted by Tomlin J) in which the court records the voluntary settlement of an action and stays all further proceedings except for the purpose of carrying the agreed terms into effect. See *Horton Technologies* v *Lucky Wealth Ltd* [1992] 1 WLR 24.

tonnage. 1. Tax formerly paid to the Crown on goods carried by ship. 2. A vessel's burden: Merchant Shipping Act 1965, s.1.

tontine. An insurance scheme whereby contributors pay into a fund which is divided, at the end of a specified period, among the survivors by way of payment of capital or an annuity.

tort. (*Tortus* = twisted, distorted.) A civil wrong independent of contract. Liability in tort arises from breach of a duty primarily fixed by law which is towards others generally, breach of which is redressable by an action for unliquidated damages (q.v.), affording some measure of compensation. *See* MEASURE OF DAMAGES IN TORT.

tortfeasor. One who commits a tort (q.v.).

tortious. Having the nature of a tort (q.v.).

tort, pure economic loss, and. No action in negligence can be brought by the owner or occupier of a defective building against persons involved in its construction save where the building has caused damage to property, or personal injury. Any pure economic loss sustained by the owner or occupier is irrecoverable: *Murphy* v *Brentwood DC* [1990] 2 All ER 908. See also *Department of the Environment* v *Thomas Bates* [1990] 2 All ER 943.

torts, classification of. 1. Wrongs to the person, e.g., assault. 2. Wrongs to reputation, e.g., defamation. 3. Wrongs to property, e.g., trespass. 4. Wrongs to persons or property, e.g., nuisance. 5. Wrongs of interference in contractual relations, e.g., inducing breach of contract. 6. Abuse of legal procedure, e.g., malicious prosecutions.

torture. An offence committed where a public official or person acting in an official capacity, intentionally inflicts severe pain or suffering on another in the performance of his official duties: C.J.A. 1988, s. 134(1). It is immaterial whether the pain or suffering is physical or mental or whether it is caused by an act or omission: s. 134(3).

tort, waiver of. *See* WAIVER OF TORT.

total loss. *See* LOSS, LIABILITY IN MARINE INSURANCE FOR.

totting up. Procedure of adding together penalty points based on convictions involving the endorsement of driving licences, and which may result in disqualification.

touching and concerning land. *See* COVENANT RUNNING WITH THE LAND.

town. At one time a group of dwellings that "hath, or in time past hath had, a church and celebration of divine service, sacraments and burials": Coke. Now refers to a group of houses, etc. bigger than a village. A parish or community can resolve to adopt the status of a town: L.G.A. 1972, s. 245.

town planning. Principles related to the improvement of land in the general interests of the community. See T.C.P.A. 1971, as variously amended; T.C.P.A. 1990; L.G.P.L.A. 1980, Part IX.

tracing trust property. Steps taken by beneficiaries to follow assets which have come into the hands of others. At common law the right to trace will be lost if the plaintiff's money has become mixed with another fund. In equity a charge can be imposed on the mixed fund to the full extent of the plaintiff's contribution. See *Re Hallett's Estate* (1879) 11 Ch D 772; *Re Diplock* [1948] Ch 495; *Re Registered Securities* [1991] 1 NZLR 545. For the right to trace where there is no trust, but some other fiduciary element, see *Aluminium Industrie Vaassen BV v Romalpa Aluminium Ltd* [1976] 2 All ER 552; *Agip (Africa) Ltd v Jackson* [1989] 3 WLR 1367.

trade. Business activity relating to the exchange of goods and services for money. "Includes every trade, manufacture, adventure or concern in the nature of trade": I.C.T.A. 1988, s. 832(1).

trade association. Phrase used, e.g., in Resale Prices Act 1976, s. 24(1), to mean "a body of persons (whether incorporated or not) which is formed for the purpose of furthering the trade interests of its members or the persons represented by its members".

trade description. Under the Trade Descriptions Act 1968, a description, direct or indirect, concerning goods, relating to: quantity, size, gauge; method of manufacture, production, etc; composition; fitness for purpose; other physical characteristics; testing and results; approval by any person: place or date of manufacture, production, etc.; person by whom manufactured or produced, etc.; other history. See *Denard v Smith* [1991] Crim LR 63; *May v Vincent* (1991) 10 TLR 1; *R v Bevlectric* (1992) NLJ 1342. *See* FALSE TRADE DESCRIPTION.

trade dispute. Under T.U.L.R.(C.)A. 1992, s. 218, a dispute between workers and their employers wholly or partly relating to: terms and conditions of employment, engagement or suspension of employment, allocation of work or other duties, discipline, union membership and non-membership, negotiating machinery and facilities for union officials. See S.S. Contributions and Benefits Act 1992, s. 27(3)(b).

trade dispute and tort. "An act done by a person in contemplation or furtherance of a trade dispute is not actionable in tort on the ground only that it induces another person to break a contract or interferes or induces another person to interfere with its performance, or that it consists in his threatening that a contract (whether one to which he is a party or not) will be broken or its performance interfered with, or that he will induce another person to break a contract or interfere with its performance": T.U.L.R.(C.)A. 1992, s. 219.

trade fixtures. A tenant may remove fixtures attached to the land for the purpose of conducting his trade. See *Smith v City Petroleum Co* [1940] 1 All ER 260. *See* FIXTURES.

trade mark. "A mark used or proposed to be used in relation to goods for the purpose of indicating or so as to indicate a connection in the course of trade between the goods and some person having the right either as proprietor or registered user to use the mark, whether with or without any indication of the identity of that person": Trade Marks Act 1938, s. 68(1) (as amended by Trade Marks (Amendment) Act 1984, Sch. 1; Patents, Designs and Marks Act 1986). "Mark" includes "a device, name, signature, word, letter, numeral, or any combination thereof". See Copyright, Designs and Patents Act 1988. *See* SERVICE MARK.

trade mark at common law. A mark used so widely in connection with a group or class of goods that the public recognise goods carrying that mark as associated with the owner of the mark. A dispute relating to such a mark may result in a passing-off action (q.v.).

trade, restraint of. *See* RESTRAINT OF TRADE.

trade secret. Some manufacturing or productive process, knowledge of which is generally confined to a firm and utilisation of which provides an advantage over competitors. Disclosure of such information, as the result of a breach of confidence or where it has resulted from employment under contract, can be prevented by injunction. See *Initial Service Ltd* v *Putterill* [1968] 1 QB 396; *Faccenda Chicken Ltd* v *Fowler* [1986] 1 All ER 617. *See* CONFIDENCE, BREACH OF; CONFIDENTIAL INFORMATION.

trade union. Under T.U.L.R.(C.)A. 1992, s. 1, an organisation (whether permanent or temporary) which consists wholly or mainly of workers and is an organisation whose principal purposes include the regulation of relations between workers and employers or employers' associations, or consists wholly or mainly of constituent or affiliated organisations which fulfil the above conditions, or of representatives of such constituent or affiliated organisations. The Certification Officer (q.v.) keeps a list of unions: 1992 Act, s. 2. They cannot be corporate bodies: 1992 Act, s. 10 (but a union's property is vested in trustees).

trade union duties and activities, time off for. An employer must permit an employee who is an official of an independent union recognised by the employer to take time off to carry out any duties of his, as such an official, concerned with negotiations with the employer that are related to or connected with matters within T.U.L.R.(C.)A. 1992, and in relation to which the union is recognised by the employer or any other duties concerned with the performance, on behalf of the employer's employees, of any functions related to matters falling within the 1992 Act, and that the employer has agreed may be so performed by the union.

trade union funds, use of. Use of funds for indemnifying unlawful conduct is illegal: T.U.L.R.(C.)A. 1992, s. 15.

trade union, independent. Under T.U.L.R.(C.)A. 1992, s. 5, a trade union which is not under the domination or control of an employer or group of employers or one or more employers' associations, and is not liable to interference by an employer or any such group or association (arising out of the provision of financial or material support or by any other means whatsoever) tending towards such control. Genuine and effective independence of employers must be demonstrated: *Blue Circle Staff Association* v *Certification Officer* [1977] 1 WLR 239.

trade union members, Commissioner for rights of. Appointed under T.U.L.R.(C.)A. 1992, s. 266, to provide assistance to union members who are considering, or bringing, proceedings against their unions under the 1992 Act, s. 109.

trade union official. "Any person who is an officer of the union or of a branch or section of the union or who is a person elected or appointed in accordance with the rules of the union to be a representative of its members or of some of them including any person so elected or appointed who is an employee of the same employer as the members or one or more of the members, whom he is to represent": T.U.L.R.(C.)A. 1992, s. 119. For responsibility of unions for acts of officials, see 1992 Act, ss. 20, 21.

trade union, resignation from. The contract of membership of a union contains an implied term allowing resignation on giving reasonable notice and complying with reasonable conditions: see T.U.L.R.(C.)A. 1992, s. 69.

trade unions, executive committee elections. The executive committee of a union must be elected, at intervals not exceeding five years, by ballot. For exemptions for certain unions, see T.U.L.R.(C.)A. 1992, s. 57.

trade unions, industrial action ballots. Under T.U.L.R.(C.)A. 1992, s. 226, immunity from legal action is removed where unions do not hold a ballot before authorising or endorsing a call for a strike (q.v.) or other form of industrial action which breaks a contract of employment of those called upon to participate in it. It must be held no later than four weeks before the action begins. For requirements to be satisfied, e.g., entitlement to vote, method of voting, conduct of ballot, see ss. 228–231.

trade union, unreasonable exclusion or expulsion from. Every person who is, or is seeking to be, in employment with an employer whose practice it is to employ union members, has the right not to have an application for membership of a union unreasonably refused and not to be unreasonably expelled from a union: T.U.L.R.(C.)A. 1992, s. 174. A complaint may be presented to an industrial tribunal (q.v.): s. 174(5). For right of member not to be unjustifiably disciplined, see s. 64.

trading business. "One which involves the purchase of goods and the selling of goods": *per* Lush J in *Higgins* v *Beauchamp* [1914] 3 KB 1192. For meaning of "trading" for tax purposes, see *Ensign Tankers Ltd* v *Stokes* [1992] STI 364.

trading certificate. Certificate to commence business issued by the registrar to a public company (q.v.) under Cos.A. 1985, s. 117, following a statutory declaration by the company, stating: that the nominal value of its allotted share capital is not less than the authorised minimum; amount of company's preliminary expenses and who paid them; amount paid up on company's allotted share capital, any amount paid or benefit given to a promoter and his consideration for it. (A private company (q.v.) can commence business on incorporation.)

trading, fraudulent. *See* FRAUDULENT TRADING.

trading interests, protection of. Under the Protection of Trading Interests Act 1980, the Secretary of State may make orders prohibiting persons who carry on a business in the UK from complying with requirements or prohibitions which might damage the UK's trading interests, or infringe the UK's jurisdiction, or are otherwise prejudicial to the UK's sovereignty.

trading stamps. Stamps exchanged by a retailer's customer for free gifts from a stamp company. Under Trading Stamps Act 1964, as amended, the stamp must be clearly marked with a monetary value and the name of the issuing organisation.

trading, wrongful. *See* WRONGFUL TRADING.

traditio brevi manu. A type of delivery, of a constructive nature, e.g., as where the transferee already held the thing but not as an owner. See, e.g., *Cain* v *Moon* [1896] 2 QB 283.

traffic calming works. Means, in relation to a highway, works affecting the movement of vehicular and other traffic for the purpose of promoting safety or preserving or improving the environment through which the highway runs: Highways Act 1980, s. 329, inserted by Traffic Calming Act 1992, s.1.

traffic sign. Any object or device fixed or portable, for conveying, to traffic on roads or any specified class of traffic, authorised warnings, information, requirements, restrictions or prohibitions: Road Traffic Regulation Act 1984, ss. 64, 74 (*g*). For duty to comply with traffic signs and directions, see Road Traffic Act 1988, ss. 35, 36.

traffic wardens. Persons appointed by police authorities to assist in control of road traffic. See Road Traffic Act 1972, Sch. 7, as amended.

transaction. An act, or series of acts, involving business negotiations, e.g., buying, selling, and resulting in a change of legal rights and duties of the participants. See, e.g., S.L.A. 1925, s. 64(2): "transaction" includes sale, exchange, grant, lease, surrender, reconveyance, etc. For "artificial transactions", see *Curtain Dream* v *Churchill Merchandising* (1990) 5 BCC 341. *See* DEALINGS, COMMERCIAL.

transcript. A copy, usually in longhand, of notes taken, e.g., in shorthand.

transfer. The conveyance of title or other interest in property from one person to another, e.g., by sale or gift. See S.G.A. 1979, Part III.

transferable. "The word 'transferable' is of the widest possible import, and includes every means by which property may be passed from one person to another": *Gathercole* v *Smith* (1875) 17 Ch D I.

transfer, blank. *See* BLANK TRANSFER.

transferee. "In relation to a contract for the transfer of goods means (depending on the context) a person to whom the property in the goods is transferred under the contract, or a person to whom the property is to be so transferred, or a person to whom the rights under the contract of either of those persons have passed": Supply of Goods and Services Act 1982, s. 18(1).

transfer of action. Removal of action (q.v.). See C.C.R. 1981, O. 16; R.S.C. O. 78 and O. 107; County C.A. 1984, ss. 40–45. Proceedings may be transferred between the Supreme Court and county courts for the purposes of enforcement: Act of 1984, ss. 105–106.

transfer of shares. Shares are transferable subject to any restrictions in a company's articles (q.v.), and as a consequence of orders imposing restrictions (e.g., for failure to disclose individual interests in shares under s. 210(5)): Cos.A. 1985, ss. 182(1), 454. A transfer cannot be registered unless a proper instrument of transfer, correctly stamped, has been delivered to the company, executed by or on behalf of the transferor: s. 183. See Stock Transfer Acts 1963 and 1982. *See* COMPANY; SHARE TRANSFER; SECURITIES, TRANSFER OF.

transferor. "In relation to a contract for the transfer of goods, means (depending on the context) a person who transfers the property in the goods under the contract, or a person who agrees to do so, or a person to whom the duties under the contract of either of those persons have passed": Supply of Goods and Services Act 1982, s. 18(1).

transfer order. Court order, under C.C.A. 1974, s. 133(1)(*b*)(ii), for the transfer to a debtor of a creditor's title to goods to which an agreement relates and the return to the creditor of the remainder of the goods.

transferred malice. *See* MALICE.

transformation, doctrine of. Doctrine that rules of international law are not to be considered a part of English law unless made a part of law by an Act of Parliament (q.v.), judges' decisions or long established customs, as contrasted with the doctrine of incorporation (q.v.). See *Chung Chi Cheung* v *The King* [1939] AC 160.

transit in rem judicatam. It passes into *res judicata* (q.v.). Refers to a cause of action disappearing as it is merged in a judgment.

transitu, **stoppage in.** *See* IN TRANSITU.

transmission of shares. The vesting of shares in another, not by virtue of transfer, but by the operation of law, e.g., on the death or bankruptcy (q.v.) of a shareholder. See the Cos.A. 1985, s. 182.

transplants. *See* ORGAN, HUMAN.

transposing of words. Changing position of words in a sentence contained in a document. "The law . . . doth often transpose words contrary to their order to bring them to the intent of the parties": *Parkhurst* v *Smith* (1742) Willes 327. See *Re Bacharach* [1959] Ch 245.

transsexual. *See* SEX, CHANGE OF.

travaux préparatoires. Phrase used in discussions of statutory interpretation to refer to the background of legislation, e.g., reports of Royal Commissions, debates in Parliament. The judicial consideration of such matter has been generally forbidden in English law. See *Davis* v *Johnson* [1978] 1 All ER 1132. May now be used, apparently, with caution, in the interpretation of statutes: *Fothergill* v *Monarch Air Lines* [1981] AC 251: *Gatoil International* v *Arkwright-Boston Insurance Co.* [1985] AC 255.

traverse. An express and specific denial of an allegation of fact made in a statement of claim. Example: "Plaintiff paid defendant £200"; traverse – "Plaintiff did not pay defendant £200 or any other sum". See O. 18, r. 13.

treachery. The offence under the Treachery Act 1940 (repealed in 1973), which related to the Second World War, by those who did, conspired or attempted to do, an act designed or likely to assist the military operations of the enemy or impede the operations of HM Forces.

treason. The capital offence under the Statute of Treasons 1351, which is, in essence, a breach of allegiance to the Crown. It comprises, e.g., the levying of war against the King in his realm, being adherent to the King's enemies in his realm, giving them aid and comfort in the realm or elsewhere. See, e.g., *R* v *Casement* [1917] 1 KB 98; *Joyce* v *DPP* [1946] AC 347.

treason felony. Offence under Treason Felony Act 1848, committed by one within or without the realm, who compasses, imagines, devises or intends, to deprive or depose the Queen from the style or royal name of the imperial crown, to levy war against the Queen in the UK, to stir any foreigner to invade the UK.

treason, misprision of. See MISPRISION.

treasure trove. "When any money, gold, silver, plate or bullion is found in any place and no man knoweth to whom the property is, then the property thereof belongeth to the King": *Termes de la Ley.* "It is the hiding, and not the abandonment of the property that entitles the King to it": *A.-G.* v *Trustees of British Museum* [1903] 2 Ch 598. See Th.A. 1968, s. 32(1)(a). The coroner (q.v.) is empowered to hold an inquest relating to treasure trove: *A.-G.* v *Moore* [1983] 1 Ch 676. See *A.-G. of Duchy of Lancaster.* v *Overton* [1982] Ch 277 (only gold and silver are treasure trove); *R* v *Hancock* [1990] 2 WLR 640; Coroners Act 1988, s. 30.

Treasury. The government department, headed by the Chancellor of the Exchequer, concerned with the finances and economic and monetary policy of the nation. The Prime Minister (q.v.) is the First Lord of the Treasury. It includes divisions concerned with domestic economy, overseas finance and public services.

Treasury Counsel. Barristers (q.v.) nominated by the A.-G. who receive briefs from the DPP relating to prosecutions at the Central Criminal Court (q.v.).

Treasury Solicitor. An official, who acts for the Treasury. See Treasury Solicitor Act 1876. The office was separated from that of the DPP (q.v.) in 1908. He instructs parliamentary counsel (q.v.) on Bills, advises on the interpretation of the law, may control the Statutory Publications Office and directs the work of the Queen's Proctor (q.v.).

treating. The offence of corruptly providing, before, during or after a parliamentary election, any meat, drink, entertainment or provision to or for any person for the purpose of corruptly influencing that person or any other person to vote or refrain from voting: Representation of the People Act 1983, s. 114. See CORRUPTION.

treat, invitation to. See INVITATION TO TREAT.

treaty. Written agreement, governed by international law, concluded between two or more states, or other subjects of international law, possessed of treaty-making capacity. In English law a treaty can be made only through the Crown. "Treaties and declarations do not become part of our law until they are made law by Parliament": *per* Lord Denning in *R.* v *Chief Immigration Officer, ex p Bibi* [1976] 1 WLR 979.

trespass. An unjustifiable interference with possession. A tort involving "direct and forcible injury". "Every invasion of private property, be it ever so minute, is a trespass": *Entick* v *Carrington* (1765) 19 St Tr 1029. See, e.g., Security Service Act 1990, s. 3, authorising entry on property by warrant. Known as "the fertile mother of actions", since from the writ of trespass (which appeared c. 1250) there developed a large number of personal actions. See PROPERTY, RIGHT TO SECURITY OF.

trespass by relation. The fiction (q.v.) whereby a person being entitled to immediate possession, and entering upon the land, is deemed to have been in possession from the time that his right accrued. See *Dunlop* v *Macedo* (1891) 8 TLR 43.

trespasser *ab initio*. See AB INITIO.

trespasser, occupier's duty to. In general, a trespasser must take the land as he finds it. But the occupier owes the trespasser a duty to take such steps as common humanity or common sense would dictate, so as to exclude, warn, reduce or avert a danger: *British Rlwys Board* v *Herrington* [1972] AC 877. See *Harris* v *Birkenhead Corporation and Another* [1975] 1 WLR 379; Occupiers' Liability Act 1984. See OCCUPIER'S LIABILITY TO NON-VISITORS.

trespassers, directions to leave land. The police are empowered to direct persons to leave land where they reasonably believe that two or more have entered as trespassers and are present there with the common purpose of residing there for any period, and that reasonable steps have been taken to ask them to leave, and that any of the persons has caused damage to property on the land or used threatening, abusive or insulting words and behaviour, or that they have brought 12 or more vehicles on the land: P.O.A. 1986, s. 39(1). See *Krumpa* v *DPP* [1989] Crim LR 295.

trespassing on premises of foreign missions. An offence under C.L.A. 1977, s. 9 (as amended by Diplomatic and Consular Premises Act 1987).

trespassing with weapon of offence. "A person who is on any premises as a trespasser, after having entered as such, is guilty of an offence if, without lawful authority or reasonable excuse, he has with him on the premises any weapon of offence": C.L.A. 1977, s. 8. *See* OFFENCE, WEAPON OF.

trespass on the case. Formerly, special writs of trespass based on indirect damage, e.g., trover and *assumpsit* (qq.v.).

trespass to goods. A wrongful, direct (and not consequential) or negligent interference with goods in plaintiff's possession at the time of the interference. Absence of intent is generally an excuse. See *Wilson* v *Lombank Ltd* [1963] 1 WLR 1294. See also Torts (Interference with Goods) Act 1977.

trespass to land. Unjustifiable, direct and immediate interference (of an intentional or negligent nature) with another's possession of land, e.g., by unauthorised walking on it, or improper use of a highway. It is actionable *per se*. See *Anchor Brewhouse Developments* v *Berkley House Development Ltd* [1987] 2 EGLR 173. For purposes of Th.A. 1968, s. 9(1)(*b*), a person is a trespasser if he enters the premises of another knowing that he is entering in excess of the permission given him or being reckless whether he is so doing: *R* v *Jones* [1976] 1 WLR 672. See C.L.A. 1977, s. 7; *R* v *Forest Justices, ex p Hartman* [1991] Crim LR 641 (failing as a trespasser to leave premises when required to do so).

trespass to the person. Wrong suffered by a person, in the nature of assault, battery, false imprisonment, etc. An intent to injure is not an essential ingredient of the tort: *Wilson* v *Pringle* [1987] QB 237. For defences, see *Barnes* v *Nayer* (1986) The Times, 19 Dec.

trial. The formal investigation and determination of matters in issue between parties before a court. See O. 33–

35. A trial starts at the time when a jury is sworn and the accused is put in their charge: *R* v *Tonner* [1985] 1 WLR 344.

trial by battle. *See* BATTLE, TRIAL BY.

trial, new. 1. In the case of a civil appeal, under O. 59, r. 11, the Court of Appeal (q.v.) may order a new trial (on appeal from judge and jury, or judge alone) on grounds including: the improper admission or rejection of evidence; a perverse jury verdict; the discovery of fresh evidence (see *Skone* v *Skone* [1971] 2 All ER 582); some irregularity at trial (see *Brassington* v *Brassington* [1962] P 276). 2. Under Criminal Appeal Act 1968, s. 7, a new trial may be ordered if the interests of justice so require. See S.C.A. 1981, s. 17; *R* v *Lee* [1984] 1 All ER 1080; *R* v *Ahluwalia* (1992) The Times, 8 Sep. *See* VENIRE DE NOVO.

trial of action, modes of. Types of mode of trial of an action set out in O. 33, r. 2, include trial before judge alone, or judge with jury, or judge with the assistance of assessors, or official referee with or without the assistance of assessors, or master, or special referee.

trial of action, place of. Place in which civil proceedings will commence as determined by an order made on a summons for directions, i.e., Royal Courts of Justice in London, or "one of the other places at which sittings of the High Court are authorised to be held for the trial of [those] proceedings or proceedings of the class to which they belong": O. 33, r. 1. For place of trial on indictment, see M.C.A. 1980, s. 7.

trial *per pais*. *See* IN PAIS.

trial, setting down for. *See* SETTING DOWN OF ACTION.

tribunals. Bodies outside the hierarchy of the courts with administrative or judicial functions. ("Administrative" tribunals are established by the state; "domestic tribunals" are set up by non-state bodies, e.g., professional associations.) Their members include lawyers and laymen with specialised knowledge. In some cases chairmen are selected from a panel and appointed by the Lord Chancellor. Appeal may lie (where statute provides) to the High Court or, in some cases to the JCPC. See Tribunals and Inquiries Act 1992.

tribunals, Council on. *See* COUNCIL ON TRIBUNALS.

trigger clause. Term in an agreement which, when broken, activates some other term. See, e.g., C.C.A. 1974, s. 88(3).

trover. An action on the case (q.v.) brought "to recover the value of personal chattels wrongly converted by another to his use": *Cooper* v *Chitty* (1756) 1 Burr. The term is also applied to an action for conversion. See Torts (Interference with Goods) Act 1977, s. 1. *See* CONVERSION, TORT OF.

truck system. Practice whereby wages were paid in goods or tokens, rather than money. Abolished by Truck Acts 1831–1940, which were repealed by Wages Act 1986, Sch. 5. Deductions may now be made if required or authorised by statute or a contractual provision, or if the worker has previously given written consent: s. 1(1). Complaints may be made to an industrial tribunal (q.v.) in respect of unauthorised deductions: s. 5. Methods of pay are now governed by the contract of employment.

trust. In essence, an equitable obligation which imposes on a person described as a trustee certain duties of dealing with property held and controlled by him for the benefit of the persons described as the beneficiaries, or, if there are not such persons, for some purpose recognised and enforceable at law. Example: A, the owner of Blackacre, conveys it to B in fee simple, directing B to hold it in trust for C; A is the *settlor*, B is the *trustee*, C is the *beneficiary* (or *cestui que trust* (q.v.)), Blackacre is the *trust property*. For the domicile of a trust, see C.J.J.A. 1982, s. 45. See Recognition of Trusts Act 1987, Schedule, embodying the Hague Conference Convention (1984), under which "the term 'trust' refers to the legal relationship created – inter vivos or on death – by a person, the settlor, when assets have been placed under the control of a trustee for the benefit of a beneficiary or for a specified purpose."

trust, breach of. *See* BREACH OF TRUST.

trust, characteristics of. For the purposes of the Hague Convention (1984): "(a) [The] assets constitute a separate fund and are not part of the trustee's own estate; (b) title to the trust assets stands in the name of the trustee or in the name of another person on behalf of the trustee; (c) the trustee has the power and the duty, in respect of which he is accountable, to manage, employ or dispose of the assets in accordance with the terms of the trust and the special duties imposed upon him by law. The reservation by the settlor of certain rights and powers, and the fact that the trustee may himself have rights as a beneficiary, are not necessarily inconsistent with the existence of a trust." (The Convention applies only to trusts created voluntarily and evidenced in writing.) See Recognition of Trusts Act 1987, Schedule.

trust, charitable. *See* CHARITABLE TRUST.

trust, completely constituted. *See* COMPLETELY CONSTITUTED TRUST.

trust, controlled. *See* CONTROLLED TRUST.

trust corporation. A corporation constituted under the law of the UK or any other member state of the EEC (q.v.), and empowered under its constitution to undertake trust business in England and Wales, having one or more places of business in the UK, being a registered company with a capital of not less than the prescribed amount (or its equivalent in the currency of the state wherein it is registered) of which not less than a prescribed amount, or the equivalent, is paid up in cash. The Treasury Solicitor, Official Solicitor and Public Trustee (qq.v.) are also included. See Tr.A. 1925, s. 68; S.L.A. 1925, s. 117(1); L.P. (Amendment) A. 1926, s. 3; and S.C.A. 1981, s. 115.

trust deed, debenture. Document securing debentures (q.v.) and debenture stock. The company offering debentures enters into a trust deed with trustees, e.g., a trust corporation; the trustees have a mortgage over the company's property so that those who subsequently make loans to the company do not gain priority over debenture holders or debenture stockholders.

trust, derivate. *See* SUB-TRUST.

trust documents. Documents in the possession of trustees *qua* trustees, containing trust information which beneficiaries are entitled to know, and in which they have a proprietary interest: see *Re Londonderry's ST* [1965] Ch 918.

trustee. One who holds property on trust for another, known as *cestui que trust* (q.v.) or beneficiary. Capacity to be a trustee exists where there is capacity to take or hold property. Trustees may be appointed by the settlor, under express power conferred by a trust instrument, by court, under Tr.A. 1925, s. 36.

trustee, acceptance of office by. Acceptance may be express or presumed. In general, in absence of evidence to the contrary, acceptance is presumed. Conduct may operate as acceptance. There can be no renunciation after acceptance. See *Re Sharman's WT* [1942] Ch. 311.

trustee *de son tort.* Where a person who is not a trustee and who has no authority from a trustee takes upon himself to intermeddle with trust matters or to carry out acts which are characteristic of the office of trustee, he makes himself a *trustee de son tort* ("of his own wrongdoing") and is held to be a constructive trustee. See *Re Barney* [1891] 2 Ch 265; and *Re Bell's Indenture* [1980] 3 All ER 425.

trustee, duties of. Generally: to become acquainted with the terms of the trust; to ensure that the trust property is vested; to act gratuitously and not to profit from the trust; not to delegate; to act impartially in the interests of all beneficiaries. See *Phipps* v *Boardman* [1967] 2 AC 44.

trustee, general liability of. A trustee is liable for any loss he has caused directly or indirectly to the trust estate: see, e.g., *Bartlett* v *Barclays Trust Co* [1980] Ch 515. See BREACH OF TRUST.

trustee in bankruptcy. See BANKRUPTCY, TRUSTEE IN.

trustee investments. See INVESTMENT, TRUSTEES' POWERS OF.

Trustee, Public. See PUBLIC TRUSTEE.

trustees' costs basis. A basis for taxation of costs whereby a party may recover his costs out of the fund of which he is trustee. The taxation is conducted on the same principles as for the indemnity basis for costs, but the costs are presumed to have been unreasonably incurred (and will therefore be disallowed) if they were incurred contrary to the duty of the trustee (or personal representative) as such: O. 62, r. 14(2). See COSTS, TAXATION OF.

trustee's discretion. Exercise of the discretion demands honesty and standard of diligence which ought to be shown by a businessman acting with prudence in the ordering of his own affairs. See *Learoyd* v *Whitely* (1887) 57 L J Ch 390; *Marley* v *Mutual Security Merchant Bank* [1991] 3 All ER 198.

trustees for sale, powers of. "Trustees for sale shall . . . have the powers of a tenant for life and the trustees of a settlement under S.L.A. 1925, including in relation to the land the powers of management conferred by that Act during a minority": L.P.A. 1925, s. 28(1). See also L.P.(Amendment)A. 1926, s. 7; *Re Wellsted's WT* [1949] Ch 296.

trusteeship, termination of. A trustee can retire under any express power, by statutory power conferred by Tr.A. 1925, s. 39, by the consent of all beneficiaries, or by order of the court. He can be removed from office under any express power, under statutory power (see Tr.A. 1925, ss. 36, 41), or by the court. Trusteeship terminates on death: where there are two or more trustees and one dies, the rule of survivorship applies, so that the office devolves on the surviving trustees. On the death of the sole surviving trustee, the estate devolves on his personal representatives.

trustees of the settlement. See SETTLED LAND ACT TRUSTEES.

trustees, protection of. The court may relieve a trustee either wholly or partly from personal liability for breach of trust if he has acted honestly and reasonably and ought fairly to be excused. The burden of establishing this is on the trustee. See Tr.A. 1925, s. 61; Lim.A. 1980, s. 21.

trustees, remuneration of. See REMUNERATION OF TRUSTEES.

trustees, Settled Land Act. See SETTLED LAND ACT TRUSTEES.

trust, executed. See EXECUTED.

trust, executory. See EXECUTORY.

trust, express. See EXPRESS TRUST.

trust for sale. Means, in relation to land, "an immediate binding trust for sale, whether or not exercisable at the request or with the consent of any person, and with or without a power at discretion to postpone the sale; 'trustees for sale' means the persons (including a personal representative) holding land on trust for sale; and 'power to postpone a sale' means power to postpone in the exercise of a discretion": L.P.A. 1925, s. 205(1)(xxix). See *Re Inns* [1947] Ch 576; *Miller* v *Lakefield Estates* [1989] 19 EG 67. It may arise expressly or by operation of statute (e.g., the A.E.A. 1925, s. 31(1), where an estate owner dies intestate and the personal representative holds property "as to the real estate upon trust to sell the same; and as to the personal estate upon trust to call in, sell and convert into money such part thereof as may not consist of money"). Trusts for sale, and strict settlements (q.v.), constitute "settlements". See L.R.A. 1925, ss. 8, 9. See CONVERSION.

trust, housing. See HOUSING TRUST.

trust instrument. The document used in the creation of a settlement (q.v.), which appoints trustees, contains the power to appoint new trustees and declares trusts affecting the settlement, etc. See S.L.A. 1925, ss. 4, 9, 117(1).

trust of land, creation of. "A declaration of trust respecting any land or any interest therein must be manifested and proved by some writing signed by some person who is able to declare such trust or by his will": L.P.A. 1925, s. 55(1)(b).

trust, power in nature of. Known also as "trust-power". Created where the donor has demonstrated a clear intention that property is to pass to the objects in any event. Whether it has been created or not is a matter of "intention or presumed intention to be derived from the language of the instrument": *Re Scarisbrick's WT* [1951] 1 All ER 822. See *Re Brierley* (1984) 39 SJ 647. See POWER.

trust property. In general, all property, real or personal, legal or equitable, may be made the object of a trust. See *Lord Strathcona SS Co* v *Dominion SS Co* [1926] AC 108.

trust, public. See PUBLIC TRUST.

trust, purpose. Term applied to a trust not in favour of ascertainable individuals, e.g., a charitable trust. See *Re Astor's ST* [1952] Ch 534 (trust "for the maintenance of good relations between nations"); *Re Grant's WT* [1979] 3 All ER 359.

trusts, classification of. 1. Imposed by statute. 2. Express. 3. Implied, or resulting and constructive. 4. Executed and executory. 5. Completely and incompletely constituted. 6. Private and public. 7. Simple and special. For an early classification by Lord Nottingham, see *Cook* v *Fountain* (1676) 3 Swan 585.

trust, sub-. See SUB-TRUST.

trusts, unenforceable. See UNENFORCEABLE TRUSTS.

trusts, unlawful. See UNLAWFUL TRUSTS.

trust, termination of by beneficiary. A beneficiary who is *sui juris* (q.v.) and absolutely entitled has the right to terminate a trust, irrespective of the wishes of the trustee or settlor. This applies also if there are several beneficiaries who are all *sui juris* and absolutely entitled: *Barton* v *Briscoe* (1822) Jac 603. Under these circumstances the trustees must convey trust property, thus bringing the trust to an end. See *IRC* v *Executors of Hamilton-Russell* [1943] 1 All ER 474.

trust territory. Non-self governing territory, a former mandate under the League of Nations, administered under the Trusteeship Council of the United Nations. See United Nations Charter (1945), arts. 76, 87.

trust, variation of. See VARIATION OF TRUST.

trust, void. A trust which, because it is illegal or contrary to public policy, will not be enforced. Example: a trust which is to take effect on the future separation of a husband and wife (see *Westmeath* v *Westmeath* (1831) 1 Dow & Cl 519).

trust, voidable. A trust which, having been created as a result of, e.g., fraud, mistake, duress, may be set aside or rectified in certain circumstances. Example: T, apparently about to die, executed a voluntary settlement which he did not understand, which was not read to him, and from which a power of revocation had been purposely omitted (see *Forshaw* v *Weisby* (1860) 30 Beav 243).

truth tests. Evidence produced by the administration of mechanical, hypnotic or chemical "truth tests" is not admissible: *Fennell* v *Jerome Property Maintenance* (1986) The Times, 26 November.

turbary, common of. Right to cut peat or turf on another's land, to be used as fuel.

turning a blind eye. "If a man, suspicious of the truth, turns a blind eye to it, and refrains from inquiry – so that he should not know it for certain – then he is to be regarded as knowing the truth. The 'turning a blind eye' is far more blameworthy than mere negligence. Negligence in not knowing the truth is not equivalent to knowledge of it": *per* Lord Denning in *The Eurysthenes* [1976] 2 Lloyd's Rep 171.

turning Queen's evidence. *See* QUEEN'S EVIDENCE..

turpis causa. Base cause. Consideration that is base (e.g., immoral) and that will not suffice to support a contractual obligation. *See* EX TURPI CAUSA NON ORITUR ACTIO.

two-counsel rule. Practice whereby the "freedom by a QC to supply his services without being accompanied by or assisted by a junior" was restricted. Abolished as from October 1977, following which a QC is entitled to accept instructions to appear alone in any particular case, but may refuse if by so doing he is unable to conduct the case in question (or any other cases) properly. See *Practice Direction* [1989] 1 WLR 618.

tying-in arrangements. The provision of residential property loans as part of a package including other services, such as conveyancing or removal services. Prohibited, under C.L.S.A. 1990, ss. 104–7, unless certain conditions are complied with.

Tynwald, Court of. Governor, Legislative Council and Assembly (House of Keys) of the Isle of Man. See, for proof of Acts of Tynwald, Isle of Man Act 1979, s. 12. *See* ISLE OF MAN.

U

uberrimae fidei. Of the utmost good faith. Applies to a contract (e.g., of insurance) in which the promisee must inform the promissor of all those facts and surrounding circumstances which could influence the promissor in deciding whether or not to enter the contract. See *Hair* v *Prudential Assurance Co* [1983] 2 Lloyds Rep 667; *Banque Financière* v *Westgate Insurance Co.* [1990] 3 WLR 364.

ubi jus ibi remedium. Where there is a right there is a remedy. See *Ashby* v *White* (1703) 2 Ld Raym 938.

ultra vires. Beyond the powers. Term relating generally to the excess of legal powers or authority; specifically, the exercise by a corporation of powers beyond those conferred on it explicitly or implicitly. See *Ashbury Rail Carriage Co* v *Riche* (1875) LR 7 HL 653 (subject-matter not included in the memorandum (q.v.) and on which the contract was based was held to be *ultra vires*); *Baroness Wenlock* v *River Dee Co* (1885) 10 App Cas 354; *Rolled Steel Products Ltd* v *British Steel Corp* [1986] Ch 246.

ultra vires rule and companies. The *ultra vires* doctrine (q.v.) was effectively abolished in relation to the company and a third person by Cos.A. 1989, s. 108, substituting a new s. 35 in Cos.A. 1985. The validity of an act done by a company shall not be called into question on the ground of lack of capacity by reason of anything in the company's memorandum (q.v.). S. 35(2)(a) preserves the individual shareholder's personal right to seek an injunction (q.v.) to prevent a proposed act contrary to the memorandum. Under Cos.A. 1985, s. 3A, inserted by Cos.A. 1989, s. 110, a company's memorandum may state a single object (e.g., to carry on business as a general commercial company, with the power to do all such things as are incidental or conducive to the carrying on of its business).

umpire. *See* ARBITRATION.

unascertained goods. Goods defined by description only, e.g., "1,000 tonnes of coal". Property in them does not pass until the goods are ascertained: S.G.A. 1979, s. 16. See *Pignatarou* v *Gilroy* [1919] 1 KB 459.

unborn person, duty of care to. A doctor is under no legal obligation to a foetus (q.v.) to terminate its life; a child's claim for damages, having "suffered entry into a life in which her injuries are highly debilitating", was considered contrary to public policy as being a violation of the sanctity of human life: *McKay* v *Essex Area Health Authority* [1982] QB 1166.

unborn persons, killing of. It is an offence to kill any child capable of being born alive (q.v.). See O.P.A. 1861, s. 58; Infant Life Preservation Act 1929, s. 1 (for the purposes of that Act evidence that a woman had been pregnant for 28 weeks was prima facie proof that she was pregnant of a child capable of being born alive); and Abortion Act 1967. *See* ABORTION; CHILD DESTRUCTION.

uncalled capital. The amount remaining unpaid on the nominal value of a share.

uncertainty, void for. Term applied to a document (e.g., a will) so ambiguous or obscure that it cannot be understood.

unchastity, imputation of. Actionable as slander (q.v.) without proof of special damage. See Slander of Women Act 1891; *Kerr* v *Kennedy* [1942] 1 KB 409.

uncollected goods, disposal of. *See* DISPOSAL OF UNCOLLECTED GOODS.

unconscionable transaction. One "such as no man in his senses and not under delusion could make on the one hand, and no honest and fair man would accept on the other; which are unequitable and unconscientious bargains": *Earl of Chesterfield* v *Jannsen* (1750) 2

Ves Sen 125. See *National Westminster Bank plc v Morgan* [1985] AC 686. "Was the bargain fair? . . . The test of fairness is, no doubt, whether the restrictions are both reasonably necessary for the protection of the legitimate interests of the promisee and commensurate with the benefits secured to the promisor under the contract. For the purposes of this test, all the provisions of the contract must be taken into consideration": *per* Lord Diplock. *See* CATCHING BARGAIN.

unconstitutional. Not in accordance with a constitution or rules of procedure. "It is often said that it would be unconstitutional for the United Kingdom Parliament to do certain things, meaning that moral, political and other reasons against doing them are so strong that most people would regard it as highly improper if Parliament did those things. But that does not mean that it is beyond the power of Parliament to do such things. If Parliament chose to do any of them the courts could not hold the Act of Parliament invalid": *per* Lord Reid in *Madzimbamuto v Lardner-Burke* [1969] 1 AC 645.

undefended cause. Cause in which the defendant fails to acknowledge service of the writ or other originating process or to give notice of his intention to defend the plaintiff's action, fails to put in statement of defence, or does not appear at the trial after having received notice. See O. 13, O. 19, O. 35.

undefended cause, in relation to matrimonial dispute. A case, under Mat.C.A. 1973, s. 3, in which the respondent has not given notice of the intention to defend within the time limit, or, in any case, a case in which no answer has been filed or any answer filed has been struck out or a case which is proceeding only on the respondent's answer and in which no reply or answer to the respondent's answer has been filed or any such reply or answer has been struck out: Matrimonial Causes Rules 1977, r. 2(2).

under-lease. A sub-lease (q.v.).

under protest. Acknowledgement of service of a writ while denying an obligation to participate in the case. Known also as "a conditional acknowledgement". See O. 12, rr. 7, 8.

understanding. An agreement or stipulation: *Hill v Fox* (1859) 4 H & N 364.

undertakers, statutory. *See* STATUTORY UNDERTAKERS.

undertaking. 1. Promise, usually resulting in an obligation. 2. A business or project. "A body corporate or partnership, or an incorporated association carrying on a trade or business, with or without a view to profit": Cos.A. 1989, s. 22. For "associated undertaking", see Cos.A. 1989, Sch. 2.

undervalue, transactions at an. A person enters into a transaction at an undervalue if he makes a gift on terms that provide for him to receive no consideration, or enters into a transaction in consideration of marriage, or enters into a transaction with another for a consideration the value of which is significantly less than the value of the consideration provided by that person: Ins.A. 1986, s. 339(3).

underwriter. One who subscribes his name to a policy of insurance against the sum for which he accepts liability. An underwriter of shares or debentures offers to take up shares and debentures not taken up by the public. A *sub-underwriting agreement* is a contract between an underwriter and another person which, in exchange for a commission, relieves the underwriter of liability. For the power of a company to pay underwriting commission, see Cos.A. 1985, s. 97. See I.C.T.A. 1988, s. 450.

underwriting contract. "An agreement entered into before shares are brought before the public that in the event of the public not taking up the whole of them, or the number mentioned in the agreement, the underwriter will, for an agreed commission, take an allotment of such part of the shares as the public has not applied for": *Re Licensed Victuallers' Association* (1889) 42 Ch D 1.

undisclosed principal. *See* PRINCIPAL, UNDISCLOSED.

undivided share. Term relating to property held jointly or in common. Cannot now be created in land, except as settled land or behind trust for sale (q.v.): L.P.A. 1925, s. 34; S.L.A. 1925, s. 36. *See* JOINT TENANCY.

undue influence. 1. Improper pressure on a person resulting in his being at a manifest disadvantage in relation to some transaction. Such a transaction may be set aside by the court. "The law requires that influence, however natural and however right, shall not be unduly exercised – that is, shall be exercised only in due proportion to the surrounding circumstances and the strength of the person submitting to it. The more powerful influence or the weaker patient alike evokes a stronger application of the safeguard": *Allcard* v *Skinner* (1887) 36 Ch D 145. See also *Re Craig* [1971] Ch 95. It must be shown that the transaction is to the manifest disadvantage of the person subjected to the dominating influence: *National Westminster Bank plc* v *Morgan* [1985] AC 686. See *Midland Bank plc* v *Shephard* [1988] 3 All ER 17; *Barclays Bank* v *Kennedy* (1989) 21 HLR 132. 2. A corrupt practice in relation to an election, under the Representation of the People Acts 1983–85.

unemployment benefit. Benefit paid in respect of any day of unemployment which forms part of a period of interruption of employment: S.S.A. 1975, s. 14(1)(*a*). See S.S.A. 1986, s. 44; S.S. Contributions and Benefit Act 1992, s. 25; *R* v *Secretary of State for Social Security, ex p Britnell* [1991] 1 WLR 198.

unenforceable contract. A contract (q.v.) which although valid cannot be enforced directly by action because of some technical defect, e.g., lapse of time.

unenforceable trusts. Trusts which cannot be enforced because, e.g., there is no *cestui que trust* to enforce them and they are not charitable. See *Pettingall* v *Pettingall* (1842) 11 LJCh 178; *Re Astor's ST* [1952] Ch 534. *See* TRUST.

unfair consumer practices. "Contraventions of one or more enactments which impose duties, prohibitions or restrictions enforceable by criminal proceedings, whether any such duty, prohibition or restriction is imposed in relation to consumers as such or not and whether the person carrying on the business has or has not been convicted of any offence in respect of such contravention . . . or things done or omitted to be done in the course of that business in breach of contract or in breach of duty . . .": Fair Trading Act 1973, s. 34.

unfair contract terms. Contractual terms, e.g., restricting or excluding liability for causing personal injury, or loss or damage resulting from negligence in manufacture of goods, and considered to be "unreasonable" in the circumstances which were or ought reasonably to have been known by, or in contemplation of, the parties when the contract was made. See Unfair Contract Terms Act 1977, Occupiers' Liability Act 1984; *Smith* v *Bush* [1990] 1 AC 831; *Tudor Grange Holdings Ltd* v *Citibank NA* [1991] 4 All ER 1.

unfair dismissal. *See* DISMISSAL, UNFAIR.

unfavourable witness. One who, called by a party to prove a fact in issue (q.v.) or relevant to the issue, fails to prove that fact or proves an opposite fact. *See* WITNESS.

unfitness or incompetence, imputation of. Actionable as slander (q.v.) without proof of special damage. See Defamation Act 1952, s.2.

unfitness to plead. A finding of unfitness to plead requires evidence from two or more registered medical practitioners, including one who is experienced in mental disorder: Criminal Procedure (Insanity) Act 1964, ss. 4, 4A, as substituted by Criminal Procedure (Insanity and Unfitness to Plead) Act 1991, s. 2. The issue may be raised by defence, prosecution or judge; it must be determined by a jury and, where the accused is found unfit, the trial shall not proceed or proceed further: s. 4A; nevertheless, on the basis of evidence adduced, a jury shall determine whether in respect of the counts charged, the accused was responsible for the offences: s. 4A(2).

unfitness to plead, Court of Appeal and. Where the Court of Appeal substitutes a finding of insanity or unfitness to plead on appeal against conviction, or affirms disability of the accused on appeal against a verdict of not guilty because of insanity (under the Criminal Appeal Act 1968, s. 12), the Court may make guardianship or supervision and treatment orders, etc.: see Criminal Appeal Act 1968, s. 6, substituted by Criminal Procedure (Insanity and Unfitness to Plead) Act 1991, s. 4. Where, having substituted a verdict of acquittal, but of the opinion (following the evidence of two or more medical practitioners) that the appellant should be admitted to a hospital for assessment, an appropriate admission order (see 1991 Act, Sch. 1) will be made.

unfitness to plead, powers concerning. Where a special verdict (q.v.) is returned or a jury finds that the accused is under a disability and that he did the act or made the omission charged, the court may make an admission order (q.v.) without a restriction direction, a supervision and treatment order (q.v.), or an order for absolute discharge: Criminal Procedure (Insanity) Act, 1964, s. 5, as substituted by Criminal Procedure (Insanity and Unfitness to Plead) Act 1991, s. 3. Where the sentence is fixed by law (as in murder), the court must make an admission order with a restriction direction unlimited in time.

uniform, wearing of. It is generally an offence to wear in a public place or public meeting a uniform signifying one's association with a political organisation: P.O.A. 1936, s. 1. See *O'Moran and Others* v *DPP* [1975] 1 All ER 473.

unilateral. One-sided.

unilateral contract. A contract (q.v.) arising where an offer is made in the form of a promise to pay in return for the performance of an act, so that the performance of the act is taken to imply assent. See, e.g., *Carlill* v *Carbolic Smoke Ball Co* [1893] 1 QB 256; *NZ Shipping Co* v *Satterthwaite & Co* [1975] AC 154.

unilateral discharge. In a contract, the terms of which are carried out by X, but not by Y (the other party), the release of Y from his obligations by X.

unilateral mistake. *See* MISTAKE.

unincorporated bodies. *See* INCORPORATE.

unintentional defamation. Plea entered under Defamation Act 1952, s. 4, whereby the defendant (q.v.) claims that he published the words innocently, that he did not intend to publish them and did not know of the circumstances by virtue of which the words might be understood to refer to the plaintiff (q.v.), or that the words were not defamatory on the face of them and that he did not know the circumstances by virtue of which they might be understood to be defamatory and that he exercised all reasonable care in relation to publication. He may then make an offer of amends. *See* DEFAMATION.

union, trade. *See* TRADE UNION.

United Kingdom. "The United Kingdom of Great Britain and Northern Ireland." It comprises England, Wales and Scotland (which make up Great Britain) plus Northern Ireland. See I.A. 1978, Sch. 1; and BNA 1981, s. 50(1).

United Nations. International organisation established on 24th October 1945, so as to maintain international peace and security, develop general welfare and relations among nations and encourage international co-operation in the solution of economic, social and humanitarian problems.

unities, four. *See* JOINT TENANCY.

unity of possession. Holding of one estate in undivided shares by two or more persons, or possession by one person of two or more rights based on separate titles.

unity of seisin. *See* SEISIN, UNITY OF.

universal agent. *See* AGENT, UNIVERSAL.

universal malice. *See* MALICE.

university. Includes a university college and any college, or institution in the nature of a college, in a university: Further and Higher Education Act 1992, s. 90(3). For power of institutions to award degrees, see 1992 Act, s. 76. For use of "university" in title of an institution, see s. 77.

unjust enrichment. The unjust obtaining of money benefits at the expense of another. See *Barclays Bank plc* v *Hammersmith and Fulham LBC* (1991) The Times, 27 Nov. For the principles of restitution, see *Boissevain* v *Weil* [1950] AC 327. *See* QUASI-CONTRACTS.

unlawful. Contrary to law. "In defining a criminal offence the word 'unlawful' is surely tautologous and can add nothing to its essential ingredients": *per* Hodgson J in *Albert* v *Lavin* [1981] 1 All ER 628.

unlawfully at large. Term applied to one who has escaped from lawful arrest, prison, detention centre, etc. See Prison Act 1952, s. 49(2) (as modified by C.J.A. 1982); M.H.A. 1983, s. 50(4); and P. & C.E.A. 1984, s. 17(1).

unlawful sexual intercourse. *See* SEXUAL INTERCOURSE, UNLAWFUL.

unlawful trusts. Trusts (q.v.) which are liable to be declared void, e.g., as offending the rule against perpetuities (q.v.) or as preventing the carrying out of parental duties (see *Re Sandbrook* [1912] 2 Ch 471) or in restraint of marriage (see *Leong* v *Chye* [1955] AC 648).

unlawful wounding. It is an offence to unlawfully and maliciously wound a person with intent to do grievous bodily harm: O.P.A. 1861, s. 18. See also s. 20. Provocation is no defence: *R* v *Cunningham* [1959] 1 QB 288. *See* WOUNDING; WOUNDING WITH INTENT.

unlimited company. Private company (q.v.) in which the liability of members is not limited. It need not have a share capital; it must have articles (q.v.). See Cos.A. 1985, ss. 1, 24(4). *See* LIMITED COMPANY.

unliquidated damages. *See* DAMAGES.

unnatural offence. Synonym for buggery (q.v.).

unopposed proceedings. Proceedings where a person who is entitled to oppose has been given the opportunity of doing so and has not done so.

unpaid seller. A seller in circumstances in which any portion of the price remains unpaid or where a negotiable instrument (q.v.) received as conditional payment has been dishonoured.

unpaid seller's rights. Even though the property in goods has passed to the buyer, the unpaid seller has a lien (q.v.) for the price, a right of stoppage *in transitu* (q.v.) if the buyer is insolvent and a right of resale (e.g., where the goods are of a perishable nature; S.G.A. 1979, s. 39). For loss of lien, see s. 43.

unread terms. In general, in the absence of fraud or misrepresentation (q.v.), a person who has not read the contents of a document or has chosen that they remain unread may be bound by his signature to that document. See, e.g., *L'Estrange* v *Graucob* [1934] 2 KB 394.

unreasonable "No one can properly be labelled as unreasonable unless he is not only wrong but unreasonably wrong, so wrong that no reasonable person could sensibly take that view": *per* Lord Denning in *Secretary of State for Education and Science* v *Tameside Metropolitan BC* [1976] 3 All ER 665.

unreasonable conduct. Under the Mat.C.A. 1973, s. 1(2)(*b*), conduct by respondent of such a type that the petitioner cannot reasonably be expected to live with respondent. Examples: physical violence, persistent drunkenness. It may justify the conclusion that the marriage has broken down irretrievably: *Stringfellow* v *Stringfellow* [1976] 1 WLR 645. See *Bergin* v *Bergin* [1983] 1 WLR 279. *See* BREAKDOWN OF MARRIAGE.

unregistered company. A company not registered under the provisions of Companies Acts. See Cos.A. 1985, s. 718 and Sch. 22 (provisions of the Act applying to unregistered companies).

unregistered land. Land, title to which has not been registered under L.R.A. 1925–86 and Land Registration Rules 1925.

unreported cases. Transcripts of cases that do not appear in the published law reports. Such transcripts relating to the Court of Appeal (Civil Division) may not be cited on appeal to the House of Lords except with its leave: *Roberts Petroleum Ltd* v *Bernard Kenny Ltd* [1983] 1 AC 192.

unrestricted-use credit. Any form of credit which is not restricted-use credit (q.v.): C.C.A. 1974, s. 11. Example: a bank overdraft.

unsecured creditor. *See* CREDITOR.

unsightly land. If it appears to the local planning authority that the amenity of a part of their area, or of an adjoining area, is adversely affected by the condition of land in their area, they may serve notice on the owner or occupier ordering steps to be taken for the remedying of that condition of land: T.C.P.A. 1990, s. 215.

unsolicited goods. Goods sent to persons who had not asked for them. Under the Unsolicited Goods and Services Act 1971, if such goods are sent or delivered for sale or hire, they become the property of the recipient as though they were an unconditional gift if the sender does not take them back within six months of their receipt, or earlier if the recipient gives notice to the sender. It is an offence to demand payment for unsolicited goods where the person making the demand has no cause to believe there is a right to payment. See also Unsolicited Goods and Services (Amendment) Act 1975.

unsound mind, persons of. Referred to, since M.H.A. 1959, as persons suffering from mental disorder (q.v.). "It is impossible to distinguish between unsoundness of mind and insanity": *per* Merriman P in *Smith* v *Smith* [1940] P 179.

unsworn evidence. See EVIDENCE, UNSWORN.

unsworn statement. Statement made by accused without being sworn. The right to make an unsworn statement was generally abolished (save for, e.g., a statement by the accused by way of mitigation) by C.J.A. 1982, s. 72.

unvalued policy. Policy of insurance (q.v.) where the value of the subject-matter is left to be ascertained later, subject to the limit of the amount insured.

urban development areas. Areas designated by the Secretary of State with the object of their regeneration through, e.g., bringing land and buildings into effective use, creating an attractive environment. See L.G.P.L.A. 1980, ss. 134–143. (The London Docklands and Merseyside have been designated.) See New Towns and Urban Development Corporations Act 1985; H. & P.A. 1986, Part III; T.C.P.A. 1990, s. 7.

urine test. A laboratory test carried out on the urine of a person arrested under Road Traffic Act 1972, ss. 5, 8. See Road Traffic Act 1972, ss. 6–12 (as substituted by Transport Act 1981, Sch. 8).

usage. A practice which has continued over a long period. " 'Usage' as a practice which the court will recognise is a mixed question of fact and law. For the practice to amount to such a recognised usage it must be certain, in the sense that the practice is clearly established; it must be notorious, in the sense that it is so well known in the market in which it is alleged to exist that those who conduct business in that market contract with usage as an implied term; and it must be reasonable. The burden lies on those alleging usage to establish it": *per* Ungoed-Thomas J in *Cunliffe-Owen* v *Teather* [1967] 3 All ER 561. "Usage is only admissible to explain what is doubtful, never to contradict what

is plain": *per* Lord Lyndhurst in *Blackett* v *Royal Exchange Assurance Corp* (1832) 3 C&J 244.

use. 1. Term which may have originated in *opus* (*X tenet ad opus Y*–X holds for the benefit of Y). Example: Tenant, A, transferred land by common-law conveyance to the transferee, B, who undertook to hold it "to the use of" (i.e., on behalf of) C. A was known as the *feoffor*, B was the *feoffee to uses* (i.e., party to whom feoffment of land had been made), C was *cestui que use* (shortened version of *cestui à que use le feoffment fuit fait* – to whom feoffment had been made). Before the Statute of Uses 1535 (repealed by the L.P.A. 1925, Sch. 7), B would have had the legal estate, C would have had the equitable estate. Following the Statute, C had the legal estate. 2. For the meaning of "to use", see *Hickman* v *Chichester DC* (1991) The Times, 25 Oct.

use and occupation. A claim which exists where one has used and occupied another's lands with his permission, but in the absence of a lease (q.v.) or agreement for a lease.

use classes. See DEVELOPMENT.

user. Use or enjoyment of property. See, e.g., Landlord and Tenant Act 1954, s. 53.

user as of right. See NEC VI, NEC CLAM, NEC PRECARIO.

user, continuous and apparent. Phrase used, in relation to implied grant of quasi-easements (q.v.), by Thesiger LJ in *Wheeldon* v *Burrows* (1879) 12 Ch D 31, to express a limiting condition of implication. "Continuous" has been held to refer to enjoyment of user over a considerable period of time; "apparent" refers to user which may be discovered "on careful inspection by a person ordinarily conversant with the subject": *Pyer* v *Carter* (1857) 1 H&N 916; *Hansford* v *Jago* [1921] 1 Ch 322.

user, evidence of. Evidence of the way in which parties to a document have acted before or after its execution. Will be received by the court: to show alterations by consent in a partnership deed; to remove uncertainty in a patent or latent ambiguity (q.v.); where there has been a change in the meaning of words used in an ancient document (see *NE Rlwy* v *Lord Hastings* [1900] AC 260). See EVIDENCE.

use upon a use. Conveyance "to X and his heirs to the use of Y and his heirs to the use of Z and his heirs". Void under *Tyrrel's Case* (1557) 2 Dy 115a, so that the entire legal and equitable interest was given to Y. Later, the second use was enforced in equity. See *Sambach* v *Dalston* (under *Morris* v *Darston* (1635) Nels 30). *See* USE.

usque ad medium filum aquae (viae). As far as the middle of the stream (or road). Refers to boundaries which are rivers or roads. In the absence of evidence to the contrary, each owner is presumed to own the river or road up to an imaginary line drawn through the centre of the river or road.

usucapion. Mode of acquiring title by uninterrupted possession. *See* PRESCRIPTION.

usufruct. Right of using and enjoying profits or fruits from something belonging to another.

usufructuary. One having a usufruct (q.v.) of property.

usurpation. Unauthorised or illegal assumption of rights, e.g., by dispossession.

usury. An exorbitant or illegal amount or rate of interest. Statutes relating to usury were largely repealed in 1854. See now C.C.A. 1974, ss. 137–140.

utilitarianism. Theory associated with Jeremy Bentham (1748–1832), according to which the ultimate end of legislation is "the greatest happiness of the greatest number". Such legislation should be aimed at the provision of subsistence, abundance and security, together with the lessening of inequalities.

utmost good faith. *See* UBERRIMAE FIDEI.

ut res magis valeat quam pereat. It is better for a thing to have effect than to be made void. See *Curtis* v *Stovin* (1889) 22 QBD 512.

utter bar. Outer bar (q.v.).

u.x.b. "Unexpected balance of established development value." Term used after 1955 to represent the limit up to which the Secretary of State would pay compensation for depreciation resulting from restrictions on a new development. See T.C.P.A. 1990, Sch. 12.

V

v. Versus (q.v.).

vacant possession. Term applied to premises sold or offered for sale and not subject to a lease. The vendor must give vacant possession on completion, subject to an agreement to the contrary. Means more than "empty and unoccupied; property conveyed must be capable of occupation by a purchaser": *Topfell* v *Galley Properties* [1979] 1 WLR 446.

vacation of register. The removal of an entry from, e.g., the registers in the Land Registry: see L.C.A. 1972, s. 1(6); *Calgary & Edmonton Land Co. Ltd* v *Dobinson* [1974] Ch 102. To "vacate" is to empty, cancel, remove. *See* LAND CHARGES, REGISTER OF.

vacations. Periods during which the Supreme Court (q.v.) does not sit for ordinary business, i.e., Long Vacation and Whitsun Vacation. See O. 64.

vacation sittings. Senior judges of each division will direct judges to hear such business during vacations "as requires to be immediately or promptly heard". See O. 64, r. 3.

vagabonds. *See* ROGUES AND VAGABONDS.

vagrant. One who, under the Vagrancy Act 1824, as amended, was found to be a rogue or vagabond, or an idle or disorderly person. See C.J.A. 1982, s. 70.

valuable consideration. *See* GOOD CONSIDERATION.

valuation. The act of ascertaining, or estimating, the value or price of some object. See S.G.A. 1979, s. 9 (sale of goods at a price to be fixed by valuation); *Swingcastle Ltd* v *Alastair Gibson* [1991] 2 WLR 1091 (damages for negligent valuation).

value. Generally, valuable consideration, as in "purchaser for value" (q.v.).

value-added tax. Tax introduced into the UK in 1973, under the Finance Act 1972. A broad, indirect tax falling on goods and services, with specified exemptions, levied at every stage of production and distribution on the value added at every point of sale. The rate is fixed in the annual Finance Acts. Local VAT tribunals hear disputes and appeal lies, on points of law only, to the High Court (q.v.). See Value Added Tax Act 1983; Finance Act 1987, Part I; Finance Acts 1988, Part II; 1989, Chap II; 1992, Chap II.

value received. Phrase referring to the acceptance for value of a bill of exchange (q.v.).

value-shifting. The transference of value from one class of shares in a company to another (so as to avoid stamp duty). See *Floor* v *Davis* [1980] AC 695; T.C.G.A. 1992, s. 29.

vandalism. Malicious, mindless injury to, or destruction of, property. See *Smith* v *Littlewoods Ltd* [1987] AC 241.

variance. Disagreement or difference between a statement in the writ (q.v.) and pleadings (q.v.), or between a statement in pleadings and supporting evidence given at a later stage.

variation of trust. Under Variation of Trusts Act 1958, the court may, if it thinks fit, approve any arrangement varying a trust, on behalf of persons unborn, persons having an interest in the trust but who are incapable of assenting, persons who may become entitled to an interest in the trust at some future date. "It is the agreement which has to be approved, not just the limited interest of the person on whose behalf the court's duty is to consider it". *Re Steed's WT* [1960] Ch 407. See Tr.A 1925, ss. 53, 57(1); S.L.A. 1925, s. 64(1); Charities Act 1985; *Trustees of the British Museum* v *A.-G.* [1984] 1 All ER 337; *Steel* v *Wellcome Custodian Trustees* [1988] 1 WLR 167. *See* TRUST.

vassal. (*Vassus* = servant.) Person under the protection of a feudal lord, holding lands from him and bound to render appropriate services. *See* FEUDAL SYSTEM.

V.A.T. Value-added tax (q.v.).

V.C. Vice-Chancellor (q.v.).

vehicle. That which can be, or is, used for the carriage of persons or things. For tests of vehicles, see Road Traffic Act 1988, ss. 45–47, 67.

vehicle, immobilisation of illegally parked. A constable may fix an immobilisation device to an illegally parked vehicle and affix a notice specifying the steps to be taken to secure its release: Road Traffic Regulation Act 1984, s. 104, amended by Road Traffic Act 1991, Sch. 4.

vehicle interference. Offence, under Criminal Attempts Act 1981, s. 9, of interfering with a motor vehicle or trailer or with anything carried therein with the intention of theft of the vehicle or trailer or part of it, or its contents or taking and driving away without the consent of the owner. A constable may arrest without warrant anyone who is or whom he with reasonable cause suspects to be guilty of an offence under s. 9: s. 9(4).

vehicle-taking, aggravated. It is an offence under Th.A. 1968, s. 12A, inserted by the Aggravated Vehicle-Taking Act 1992, s. 1, for a person to commit an offence under the 1968 Act, s. 12(1) and it is established that before recovery of the vehicle it was driven dangerously or was damaged or was driven in a way which led to personal injury or damage to other property. For defences, see 1968 Act, s. 12A (3). See DRIVING, DANGEROUS; JOY RIDING; MOTOR VEHICLE, TAKING OF.

veil, lifting the. See LIFTING THE CORPOR-ATE VEIL.

vendee. A buyer (of goods, or, more usually, land).

vendor. A seller (usually, of land).

vendor and purchaser summons. Procedure, introduced by Vendor and Purchaser Act 1874, now governed by L.P.A. 1925, s. 49(1), whereby parties to a contract for the sale of land who disagree on a matter which prevents completion of contract, e.g., construction of terms, may apply to a judge in chambers for an order. The court may grant an order and any consequential reliefs, e.g., the return of any deposit. See, e.g., *Faraqui* v *English Real Estate Ltd* [1979] 1 WLR 963.

vendor's lien. See VENDOR'S RIGHTS.

vendor's rights. Pending the completion of the sale of land, the vendor possesses an equitable lien (q.v.) on the property for the full amount of purchase money, and that lien arises at the date of the contract. He has a right to remain in possession until the purchase price is paid, and to rents and profits until the time fixed for completion. See *Re Birmingham* [1959] Ch 523; S.G.A. 1979, ss. 38–43; L.C.A. 1972, s. 2(4)(iii).

venereal disease. Disease (e.g., syphilis, gonorrhea) acquired as the result of sexual intercourse. It may be prima facie evidence of adultery (q.v.), the onus being on the respondent (q.v.) to rebut the presumption of its contraction as a result of intercourse with a person other than the petitioner: *Anthony* v *Anthony* (1919) 35 TLR 559. A marriage may be voidable on the grounds that at the time of the marriage the respondent was suffering from a venereal disease in a communicable form: Mat.C.A. 1973, s. 12(*e*). Treatment of these diseases other than by a qualified medical practitioner is illegal: Venereal Disease Act 1917, s. 1.

venia aetatis. Privilege of age. Privilege allowed an infant (q.v.) whereby he may act as though of full age.

venire de novo. Writ directing a new trial after a mistrial. The first trial is regarded as a nullity. See *R* v *Neal* [1949] 2 KB 590; and *R* v *Rose* [1982] AC 822. *See* TRIAL, NEW.

venire facias. That you cause to come. Title of a writ or summons to appear and be arraigned.

venue. Place where a case is to be tried. Originally it signified "a place next to that where any thing that comes to be tried is supposed to be done": *Termes de la Ley.* See O. 33, r. 4.

verba chartarum fortius accipiuntur contra proferentem. The words of deeds should be interpreted most strongly against the person who uses them [provided that this works no wrong]. See *GA Estates* v *Caviapen Trustees Ltd* (1991) The Times, 22 Oct.

verba ita sunt intelligenda ut res magis valeat quam pereat. Words are to be understood so that the object may be carried out and not fail. See, e.g., *Lloyd* v *Lloyd* (1837) 2 My & Cr 192.

verbatim. Word for word; exactly; precisely.

verdict. (*Vere dictum* = truly said.) Answer of a jury to a question committed to their examination and for their decision. Verdict is usually announced by the *foreman* (chosen by jury members to speak for them). The judge may not enquire into proceedings whereby the verdict was reached. Where the jury fail to agree they will be discharged and a new jury called to try the case. See *R v Watson* [1988] 1 All ER 897; *R v Buono* (1992) The Times, 20 May. If there is yet another disagreement it is usual for the prosecution not to offer evidence in a third trial and the accused is then acquitted. See C.J.A. 1967; Juries Act 1974, s. 17; *R v Andrews* (1986) 82 Cr App R 148; *R v McKechnie* (1991) The Times, 5 Aug. (appeal on inconsistency of verdict).

verdict, alternative. Verdict under C.L.A. 1967, s. 6(3), whereby a jury is enabled to return a verdict of not guilty of the offence specifically charged in the indictment, but guilty of another offence, provided that the allegations in the indictment amount to or include (expressly or by implication) an allegation of another offence. Where the defendant (q.v.) is convicted of an offence and the jury, on that same indictment, could have found him guilty of another offence, the court may substitute a verdict of guilty of that other offence and pass sentence for it: Criminal Appeal Act 1968, s. 3(1). See also Road Traffic Act 1991, s. 24. See, e.g., *R v Fairbanks* [1986] 1 WLR 1202; *R v Maxwell* [1990] 1 All ER 801.

verdict, finality of. A jury's verdict is considered complete as soon as it is announced. Evidence to show what has occurred in the jury room will not be considered by the Court of Appeal (q.v.); *R v Roads* [1967] 2 QB 108. See also Contempt of Court Act 1981, s. 8(1).

verdict, majority. Introduced under C.J.A. 1967. The verdict need not be unanimous if, in a case where there are not less than 11 jurors, 10 of them agree on the verdict, or in a case where there are 10 jurors, 9 of them agree on the verdict. A majority verdict is not accepted unless it appears to the court that the jury have had not less than two hours for deliberation (or longer where considered appropriate) and unless the foreman states the numbers agreeing and disagreeing with the verdict: Juries Act 1974, s. 17. In civil cases majority verdicts were introduced by the Courts Act 1971, s. 39 (now repealed and replaced by Juries Act 1974, s. 17). For the general directions required as to unanimity, before a majority verdict is contemplated, see *R v Watson* (1988) The Times, 10 March. See *R v Mendy* [1992] Crim LR 313.

verdict, open. *See* OPEN VERDICT.

verdict, perverse. *See* PERVERSE VERDICT.

verdict, special. *See* SPECIAL VERDICT.

versus. Against. Abbreviated to "v", as in *R v Jones.*

vessel. A ship or boat, rig, raft or floating platform, seaplane, hovercraft or any other amphibious vehicle: Dangerous Vessels Act 1985, s. 7. A "fishing vessel" is one which is used in connection with sea fishing other than a vessel used for fishing other than for profit: Merchant Shipping Act 1988, s. 12.

vest. 1. To put a person in possession of land. 2. To give legal rights to a person. See *Richardson. v Robertson* (1826) 6 LT 75.

vested in interest. Term indicating a present right to future enjoyment, e.g., "to X for life, remainder to Y for life, remainder to Z in fee simple should he survive Y". Y's interest is said to be "vested in interest". It is, in effect, a "vested remainder".

vested in possession. Term indicating an interest which gives a right of present enjoyment, e.g., "to X for life, remainder to Y for life . . ." X's interest is vested in possession.

vested remainder. *See* VESTED IN INTEREST.

vested rights. Rights secured to their possessor. "The well-established presumption is that the legislature does not intend to limit vested rights further than clearly appears from the enactment": *Metropolitan Film Studios v Twickenham Film Studios* [1962] 3 All ER 508.

vesting assent. An assent in writing, but not under seal, whereby a personal representative (q.v.) vests settled land in the person entitled as tenant for life (q.v.) or statutory owner. See S.L.A. 1925, ss. 8, 117(1) (xxx). *See* SETTLED LAND.

vesting, conditions of. A remainder (q.v.) is vested where the person entitled is ascertained and it is ready to take effect in possession at once. Where conditions are not satisfied the remainder is contingent only.

vesting declaration. Declaration under Tr.A. 1925 during the appointment of new trustees (q.v.), that the property is to vest in the trustees. In the case of an appointment of new trustees by deed executed after 1925, such a declaration is implied in the absence of a statement to the contrary. Trust property (q.v.) cannot be transferred by vesting declaration where, e.g., it consists of land held by trustees by way of a mortgage (q.v.) for securing trust property.

vesting deed. "Every settlement of a legal estate in land *inter vivos* shall, save as in this Act otherwise provided, be effected by two deeds, namely, a vesting deed and a trust instrument and if effected in any other way shall not operate to transfer or create a legal estate": S.L.A. 1925, s. 4(1). A vesting deed must contain, under s. 5(1): a description of settled land, the names of trustees of settlement, any additional powers conferred by the trust instrument, the name of any person entitled under trust instrument to appoint new trustees, and a statement that the settled land is vested in the person(s) to whom it is conveyed or in whom it is declared to be vested upon trusts from time to time affecting the settled land. It is known as the "principal vesting deed".

vesting deed, subsidiary. When other land is brought into a settlement (q.v.) which is in existence, a subsidiary vesting deed is needed, under S.L.A. 1925, s. 10. It contains: particulars of principal vesting instrument, names of trustees of settlement and of those entitled to appoint new trustees, and a statement that the land conveyed is to be held subject to the same trusts as the land comprised in the principal vesting instrument.

vesting order. A court order having the effect of vesting, conveying or creating a legal estate (q.v.) as if the legal estate

owner had executed a conveyance. See L.P.A. 1925, s. 9; Tr.A. 1925, ss. 44–56; S.L.A. 1925, ss. 12, 16; A.E.A. 1925, s. 38.

veto. 1. Power to prohibit or refuse. 2. Refusal to assent to a parliamentary Bill. 3. Power of any permanent members of the Security Council of the United Nations (q.v.) to refuse to agree to a proposed course of action.

vetting. Thorough, formal investigation of a person's activities and antecedents prior to grant of "security clearance" allowing employment in certain enterprises and government employment. See, e.g., Cmnd 8540 (May 1982) (criteria for clearance include references to "obvious indications of untrustworthiness", such as involvement with seditious activities; membership or sympathy with subversive organisations; character defects); *Vetting Guidelines* (HC Deb vol 177, 24 July 1990); Security Service Act 1989, s. 2(3); *R v Director of GCHQ, ex p Hodges* (1988) The Times, 26 July. See NATIONAL SECURITY.

vexatious action. An action which is brought (by a "vexatious litigant") merely to annoy an opponent, or which is frivolous. The court is empowered to stay such an action. See S.C.A. 1981, s. 42 (as amended by Prosecution of Offences Act 1985, s. 24); *Re Becker* [1975] 1 WLR 842; *R v Highbury Corner Magistrates, ex p Ewing* [1991] 3 All ER 192.

vicarious. Performed by one person as a substitute for, or for the benefit of, another.

vicarious immunity. See IMMUNITY, VICARIOUS.

vicarious liability. See LIABILITY, VICARIOUS.

vicarious performance of contract. Performance of a contract (q.v.) based on the delegation of work to a third person. Vicarious performance does not release the contracting party; obligations "cannot be shifted off the shoulders of a contractor or on to those of another without the consent of the contractee": *Tolhurst* v *Associated Portland Cement Manufacturers* [1902] 2 KB 660. Vicarious performance of a personal contract is generally no performance if personal performance is of the essence of the contract: *Davies* v *Collins* [1945] 1 All ER 247.

vicarious responsibility. *See* LIABILITY, VICARIOUS.

Vice-Chancellor. One of those first appointed in 1813 to assist the Lord Chancellor in the Court of Chancery (q.v.). They were transferred to the High Court in 1873 as judges of the Chancery Division. A Vice-Chancellor is appointed, with responsibility to the Lord Chancellor, for the organisation and management of Chancery Division business. See S.C.A. 1981, s. 10.

vice, inherent. *See* INHERENT VICE.

vicious propensity. Tendency of animals to act so as to endanger persons or property. See, e.g., Animals Act 1971, s. 2(2) *Wallace* v *Newton* [1982] 1 WLR 375.

video recording. Any disc or magnetic tape containing information by the use of which the whole or part of a video work (i.e., a series of visual images produced electronically and shown as a moving picture) may be produced: Video Recordings Act 1984, s. 1. It is an offence to supply a video recording of which no classification certificate has been issued unless the supply is exempted under the Act: s. 9. For video recordings as evidence, see *R* v *Z* [1990] 2 All ER 971; *Lam Chi-ming* v *R* [1991] 2 WLR 1082. See C.J.A. 1988, s. 162. For use of video recordings of testimony from child witnesses, see C.J.A. 1991, s. 54, amending C.J.A. 1988, s. 32.

viduity. Widowhood.

vi et armis. With force and arms. Words used to describe trespass resulting from the use of actual violence.

view. An inspection by a judge of some object or place outside the court where the characteristics of the object or place constitute facts from which facts in issue (q.v.) may be inferred. See O. 35. *See* INSPECTION BY JUDGE.

vigilantibus non dormientibus jura subveniunt. The laws give help to those who are watchful, not to those who sleep. Principle of the doctrine of laches (q.v.).

villanagium. Non-free tenure, later known as copyhold (q.v.).

villeinage. Villein tenure (q.v.).

villein tenure. (*Villa* = farm.) An unfree tenure in early days. *Privileged villein tenure* involved duties usually of an agricultural or domestic character, servile in nature and fixed in character

and time. *Pure villein tenure* involved services uncertain in character and time. A tenant in these conditions was known as a villein (or villain).

vinculo matrimonii. *See* A VINCULO MATRIMONII.

vinculum juris. A legal tie or bond.

vindictive damages. *See* DAMAGES.

violence. Defined, for the purposes of the P.O.A. 1986, as any violent conduct so that it includes violent conduct towards property as well as towards persons, and it is not restricted to conduct causing or intended to cause injury or damage, but includes any other violent conduct (e.g., throwing at or towards a person a missile of a kind capable of causing injury which does not hit or falls short): s. 8. See *Atkin.* v *DPP* [1989] Crim LR 581. For "act of violence" (which includes, e.g., murder, assault) see Aviation and Maritime Security Act 1990, s. 1(9). For "violent offence", see C.J.A. 1991, s. 31(1) ("an offence which leads, or is intended or likely to lead to a person's death or to physical injury to a person").

violence, domestic. *See* INJUNCTIONS, MATRIMONIAL.

violence for securing entry. *See* ENTRY, VIOLENCE FOR SECURING.

violent disorder. *See* DISORDER, VIOLENT.

virtute officii. By virtue of office.

visa. Endorsement on a passport indicating that it has been examined and found correct. Usually made by a foreign authority for the purpose of allowing entry to a country.

vis et metus. Force and fear.

visitor. 1. A person appointed to visit other persons and inspect institutions. See, e.g., Education Reform Act 1988, s. 206; *Pearce* v *University of Aston* [1991] 2 All ER 461. See also S.C.A. 1981, s. 44; M.H.A. 1983, s. 103. 2. In relation to premises, a visitor is one who would at common law have been treated as an invitee (q.v.) or licensee (q.v.): see Occupiers' Liability Acts 1957, 1984; *Greenhalgh* v *British Railways Board* [1969] 2 QB 286. *See* CARE, COMMON DUTY TOWARDS VISITORS.

vis major. Greater force; irresistible force, e.g., a storm which, because it cannot be prevented, may relieve parties to a contract from some obligations.

vitiate. To weaken, invalidate, make ineffective: e.g., a contract may be vitiated by fraud.

vivum vadium. Living pledge. The mortgagee could take possession of land, while rents and profits could be taken in discharge of principal and interest. *See* MORTGAGE.

vocation. One's regular occupation. "The way in which a person passes his life": *per* Denman J in *Partridge.* v *Mallandaine* (1886) 18 QBD 276. See also *Nagle.* v *Fielden* [1966] 2 QB 633.

void. Empty; without force; of no legal effect. "A void contract is a paradox; in truth there is no contract at all": *Fawcett* v *Star Car Sales Ltd* [1960] NZLR 406. For void and voidable orders made by a court, see *Isaacs* v *Robertson* [1985] AC 97.

voidable. Capable of being voided, i.e., set aside. A voidable contract has legal effect until avoided.

voidable marriage. *See* NULLITY OF MARRIAGE.

voidable title, sale under. When the seller of goods has a voidable title to them, but his title has not been avoided at the time of the sale, the buyer acquires a good title to the goods, provided he buys them in good faith and without notice of the seller's defect of title: S.G.A. 1979, s. 23.

voidable trust. *See* TRUST, VOIDABLE.

void marriage. *See* NULLITY OF MARRIAGE.

void trust. *See* TRUST, VOID.

voir dire. (Also *voire dire.*) *Vrai dire* = to speak the truth. Preliminary examination of a witness by the judge, e.g., to determine whether a confession was voluntary; i.e., the trial of incidental issues ("trial within a trial"). See *Wong Kam Ming* v *R* [1980] AC 247; P. & C.E.A. 1984, s. 76(5); *R.* v *Davis* [1990] Crim LR 860; *R* v *Cox* [1991] Crim LR 276.

volenti non fit injuria. That to which a person consents cannot be considered an injury. Term referring to the harm suffered with the plaintiff's freely-given assent and with his prior knowledge of the risk involved, and, hence, a general defence in tort. Knowledge is not assent, but merely evidence of assent: *Dann* v *Hamilton* [1939] 1 KB 509. A person does not necessarily assent to a situation because he has knowledge of its potential danger: *Baker* v *James*

[1921] 2 KB 674. "Knowledge of the risk of injury is not enough. Nor is a willingness to take the risk of injury. Nothing will suffice short of an agreement to waive any claim for negligence": *Nettleship* v *Weston* [1971] 3 All ER 581. See *Morris* v *Murray* [1990] 3 All ER 801.

voluntary. 1. Proceeding from some exercise of the will and involving an act of choice. 2. Without valuable consideration (q.v.).

voluntary bill procedure. *See* BILL PROCEDURE, VOLUNTARY.

voluntary conduct. Conduct resulting from the exercise of one's will. In general, a person will not be held liable for any harmful result produced by conduct which was not voluntary.

voluntary confession. *See* CONFESSION.

voluntary conveyance. *See* VOLUNTARY DISPOSITION.

voluntary disposition. A disposition of land not founded upon valuable consideration (q.v.). "Every voluntary disposition of land made with intent to defraud a subsequent purchaser is voidable at the instance of that purchaser": L.P.A. 1925, s. 173(1).

voluntary liquidation. *See* VOLUNTARY WINDING-UP.

voluntary settlement. A settlement (q.v.) made without valuable consideration.

voluntary waste. Waste (q.v.) arising from an injury to land actively caused by the tenant (q.v.), e.g., cutting timber. See *Honywood* v *Honywood* (1874) LR 18 Eq 306. A tenant for years, yearly tenant, tenant at sufferance, will be liable for voluntary waste.

voluntary winding-up. The winding-up of a company (q.v.) so that company and creditors may settle their affairs before coming to court. It may be carried out when: the period fixed for the duration of the company has ended; the company has passed a special resolution to wind up voluntarily; the company has passed an extraordinary resolution that it is expedient that the company be wound up. Voluntary winding-up dates from the passing of a resolution authorising it. The resolution must be advertised in the *London Gazette* within 14 days. See, e.g., Ins.A. 1986, s. 85.

volunteer. One who takes under a disposition for which neither he nor anyone on his behalf has given valuable consideration (q.v.). Equity will not aid a volunteer. See, e.g., *Plumptree's Marriage Settlement* [1910] 1 Ch 609.

vote. 1. To express one's opinion formally, as at an election: see Representation of the People Acts 1985, 1989. 2. That which is voted, e.g., a grant of money.

voting at meetings. Generally by show of hands. In the case of a registered company a resolution (q.v.) is decided on by show of hands, unless a poll (q.v.) is demanded. See Cos.A. 1985, s. 370; Table A, arts. 55–58.

voting shares, disclosure of interests in. Where a person, to his knowledge, acquires an interest in, or ceases to be interested in, a public company's relevant share capital, he must notify this to the company: Cos.A. 1985, s. 198(1). For "relevant share capital", see s. 198(2). See also Cos.A. 1989, s. 134(2).

vouch. 1. To summon. 2. To bear witness. 3. To answer for.

voucher. 1. Receipt. 2. Process of vouching to warranty, i.e., calling to court a person who has warranted land to another. A process used in the old common recovery (q.v.).

voyage, change of. *See* CHANGE OF VOYAGE.

voyage charter. A charterparty (q.v.) under which a ship is hired for one or more voyages (as compared with a time charter (q.v.)).

voyage policy. Term in marine insurance indicating a policy in which the subject-matter is insured for a particular voyage only.

vulnerable. Susceptible of injury. Less able to fend for oneself so that injury or detriment might result: *R. v Waveney DC, ex p Bowers* [1983] QB 238; *R v Lambeth LBC, ex p Carroll* (1987) The Times, 12 October.

W

wager. The risking of a sum of money on an uncertain, eventual outcome. See *Ellesmere* v *Wallace* [1929] 2 Ch 1. *See* BET.

wagering contract. "One by which two persons, professing to hold opposite views touching the issue of a future, uncertain even , mutually agree that, dependent upon the determination of that event, one shall win from the other, and the other shall pay or hand over to him, a sum of money or other stake; neither of the contracting parties having any other interest in that contract than the sum or stake he will so win or lose, there being no other real consideration for the making of such contract by either of the parties": *Carlill* v *Carbolic Smoke Ball Co* [1892] 2 QB 484. Null and void under, e.g., Gaming Act 1845, s. 18. See *Hill* v *William Hill Ltd* [1949] AC 530. *See* BET; GAMING.

wagering policy. A policy of assurance in the subject-matter of which the assured person does not have an interest, or for purposes of gambling. Example: insuring of a stranger's life.

wager of battle. *See* BATTLE, TRIAL BY.

wager of law. Procedure of compurgation (q.v.).

wages. Any sums payable to the worker (q.v.) by his employer in connection with his employment, including any fee, bonus, commission, holiday pay or other emolument referable to his employment, whether payable under his contract or otherwise: Wages Act 1986, s. 7(1). For the purposes of the subsection, the definition includes, e.g., maternity pay, statutory sick pay, etc. For deductions, see *York City Travel Ltd* v *Smith* [1990] IRLR 213. See *Delaney* v *Staples* [1992] 2 WLR 451 (payment in lieu of proper notice is not wages); *Kent Management Services Ltd* v *Butterfield* [1992] ICR 272.

wages councils. Bodies comprising representatives of employers and workers and independent persons appointed by the Secretary of State: Wages Act 1986, Sch. 2. No new councils may be established: s. 13(1). Workers under 21 are excluded from the councils' operations: s. 12(3). Councils are concerned solely with single minimum basic and overtime rates and accommodation charges: s. 14.

wages, minimum. Minimum wage levels which can be prescribed generally in industries which do not possess adequate bargaining machinery.

wait and see principle. Rule relating to perpetuities. Under common law there was no "wait and see", so that a limitation was void if it could *possibly* fail to vest during the perpetuity period. Under P. & A.A. 1964, s. 3, the principle applies to instruments which became effective after July 1964 in the following cases: an interest capable of vesting after the perpetuity period will not be treated as void under the perpetuity rule until it is established it will vest, if at all, after the end of the perpetuity period; in the case of a general power of appointment (q.v.) which could possibly be exercised after the end of the perpetuity period, the power will be treated as valid until such time (if any) as it becomes established that the power will not be exercised in the perpetuity period; in the case of a disposition consisting of the conferring of power, option or other right which might be exercised after the end of the perpetuity period, such disposition will be void only if, and so far as, the right is not fully exercised within that period. *See* PERPETUITIES, RULE AGAINST.

waiver. 1. Relinquishing of a claim freely. "The abandonment of a right in such a way that the other party is entitled to plead the abandonment by way of confession and avoidance if the right is thereafter asserted": *Banning* v *Wright* [1972] 2 All ER 987. "A waiver must be an intentional act with knowledge": *Darnley* v *London, Chatham and Dover Rwy* (1867) 16 LT 217. See *Chrisdell* v *Tickner* (1987) 19 HLR 406. 2. The instrument which declares an act of waiving. 3. Surrender by operation of law. 4. Variation of a contract (see *Hickman* v *Haynes* (1875) LR 10 CP 598).

waiver of tort. The foregoing by a person of a remedy in tort in favour of some other remedy (e.g., an action based on a quasi-contract). The waiver extinguishes the right of action in tort. See *Re Simmons* [1934] Ch 24. *See* TORT.

wall, party-. *See* PARTY-WALL.

war. Military operations and armed conflict between opposing forces of nations or states. In an insurance policy the word "war" includes "civil war" (see *Spinney's Ltd* v *Royal Insurance Co Ltd* [1980] 1 Lloyd's Rep 406) unless the context indicates different intentions: see *Pesquerias* v *Beer* (1949) 82 L1 LR 501. Whether a state of hostilities (q.v.) amounts to "war" is a question of fact in each case. *Kawasaki Kisen* v *Bantham Steamships (No. 2)* [1939] 2 KB 544. "With certain exceptions the outbreak of war prevents the further performance of contracts between persons in this country and persons in enemy territory": *per* Lord Reid in *Arab Bank Ltd* v *Barclays Bank* [1954] AC 495.

war crimes. Murder, manslaughter or culpable homicide committed by a person during 15 Sep 1939 – 5 June 1945 in a place which at the time was part of Germany or under German occupation and which constituted a violation of the laws and customs of war: see War Crimes Act 1991, s. 1(1). See also the Nuremberg Trial Indictment 1945.

ward. One under the protection or care of another. See Ch.A. 1989, s. 100, for restrictions on powers of the High Court, e.g., to make a child who is the subject of a care order a ward of court. See also *In re C.* (1991) The Times, 18 Nov.

wardship. 1. The exercise of care and protection of a ward (q.v.). "The golden thread running through the courts' jurisdiction is the child's welfare, considered first, last and all the time": *Re D.* [1977] Fam 158; Ch.A. 1989. 2. Right, exercised in feudal times, of the custody of a ward and the ward's property.

warning of caveat. Notice to one who has entered a caveat (q.v.) to appear so as to declare his interest.

warrant. 1. Document authorising some action, e.g., payment of money. 2. Document issued by a magistrate (q.v.) ordering that a person be arrested and brought before the court. The person must be mentioned by name, or described otherwise. It must contain a statement of the offence charged and it should be signed by the issuing magistrate. See C.L.A. 1977, s. 38; and M.C.A. 1980, s. 1.

warrant, arrest with and without. *See* ARREST AND WARRANT.

warrant backed for bail. *See* BACKED FOR BAIL.

warrant, entry without. Right, under common law or statute, of a constable to enter a dwelling-house or other premises without warrant. See P. & C.E.A. 1984, s. 17; Planning and Compensation Act 1991, s. 11; *Thomas* v *Sawkins* [1935] 2 KB 249; *McLorie* v *Oxford* [1982] QB 1290.

warrant, general. *See* GENERAL WARRANT.

warrant, Royal. *See* ROYAL WARRANT.

warrant, search. *See* SEARCH WARRANT.

warrant, share. Document under seal stating that the bearer is entitled to shares specified therein. A warrant is a negotiable instrument (q.v.). See Cos.A. 1985, s. 188, as amended by Cos.A. 1989, s. 130.

warranty. An agreement with reference to goods which are the subject of a contract of sale, but collateral to the main purpose of such contract, the breach of which gives rise to a claim for damages, but not to a right to reject the goods and treat the contract as repudiated: S.G.A. 1979, s. 61(1). It may be express or implied. See S.G.A. 1979, s. 11(1). For special meaning in contracts of marine insurance, see Marine Insurance Act 1906. *See* CONDITION.

waste. 1. Acts or omissions by a tenant which alter (often negatively) the nature of land or houses. They may be voluntary; permissive; ameliorating; equitable (qq.v.). See *Mancetter Developments Ltd* v *Garmanson Ltd* [1986] 1 All

ER 449. Remedies for waste include damages (i.e., loss of value to the reversion) and injunction. 2. Includes any substance which constitutes a scrap material or an effluent or other unwanted surplus substance arising from the application of any process and any substance or article which requires to be disposed of as being broken, worn out, contaminated or otherwise spoiled: En.P.A. 1990, s. 75.

waste, defences to action for. Proof that the damage resulted from the reasonable and ordinary use of premises or that it was caused by Act of God (q.v.) or that it resulted from the exercise of common law rights (e.g., to estovers (q.v.)). See, e.g., *Manchester Bonded Warehouse Co* v *Carr* (1880) 5 CPD 507.

waste land of a manor. "The open, uncultivated and unoccupied lands parcel of the manor, or open lands parcel of the manor other than the demesne lands of the manor": *A.-G.* v *Hammer* (1858) 27 LJ Ch 837, applied in *Re Britford Common* [1977] 1 WLR 39. See *Hampshire CC* v *Milburn* [1990] 2 WLR 1240.

waste, unlicensed disposal of. Except in prescribed cases, a person must not deposit on any land controlled waste (i.e., household, industrial and commercial waste): En.P.A. 1990, s. 33.

wasting assets. Assets or securities which are subject to depletion, or which have a terminating nature, e.g., leaseholds. See T.C.G.A. 1992, s. 44(1); *Lewis* v *Walters* [1992] STC 97. See CONVERT, DUTY TO.

watching and besetting. An offence which was committed by watching or besetting a house or other place where another resided or worked or carried on business or happened to be: Conspiracy and Protection of Property Act 1875, s. 7. See *Galt* v *Philp* [1984] IRLR 156; *DPP* v *Fidler* [1992] 1 WLR 91. See PICKETING, PEACEFUL.

water, classification of. At common law: tidal rivers and the sea; non-tidal (rivers, streams, lakes, ponds, water in art-ificial channels, etc.). See Water Resources Act 1991. For bulk supply of water, see 1991 Act, s. 40, substituted by Competition and Service (Utilities) Act 1992, s. 44.

watercourse. Includes all rivers, streams, ditches, drains, cuts, culverts, dykes,

sluices, sewers and passages through which water flows except mains and pipes used by the Water Authority or a water undertaker or any other person for the purpose of supplying water to premises: Water Act 1989, s. 189(1). See Land Drainage Act 1991, s. 72.

water ordeal. *See* ORDEAL, TRIAL BY.

waters, coastal. *See* COASTAL WATERS.

waters, inland. *See* INLAND WATERS.

waters, marine. *See* MARINE WATERS.

waters, territorial. *See* TERRITORIAL WATERS.

waters, tidal. *See* TIDAL WATERS.

way, right of. *See* RIGHT OF WAY.

ways and means. Parliamentary expression relating to the provision of revenue to meet national expenditure. Ways and means are taken to involve imposition of taxes, raising of loans, payments under the Consolidated Fund or the National Loans Fund. *See* SUPPLY ESTIMATES.

weapon, offensive. *See* OFFENSIVE WEAPON.

weapon of offence. *See* OFFENCE, WEAPON OF.

weapon, prohibited. *See* PROHIBITED ARTICLE.

wear and tear. Deterioration or depreciation of a thing resulting from its ordinary reasonable use. *See* FAIR WEAR AND TEAR.

Wednesbury principles. Stated by Lord Greene, in *Ass. Provincial Picture Houses* v *Wednesbury* [1948] 1 KB 123, relating to purported exercise by an executive authority of its discretion. "The exercise of such a discretion must be a *real* exercise of the discretion." Irrelevant collateral matters must be disregarded. The court will interfere only when the authority's conclusion is "so unreasonable that no reasonable authority could ever have come to it". See, e.g., *Notts CC* v *Secretary of State for the Environment* [1986] AC 240; *R* v *ITV Commission, ex p TSW Broadcasting* (1992) The Times, 30 Mar.

week. A period of seven days, beginning with midnight between Saturday and Sunday (except where otherwise defined): see, e.g., S.S.A. 1975, Sch. 20. See Wages Act 1986, s. 26(1).

weekly tenancy. A tenancy from week to week, which can be created similarly to a yearly tenancy, e.g., by express agreement, or by inference. *See* TENANCY.

weight, gross. *See* GROSS WEIGHT.

weights and measures. Units and standards of measurement referred to in the Weights and Measures Act 1985, Part I, under which, e.g., customers must be properly informed as to the weight and quantity of goods on sale.

welfare law. The area of law concerned with social security legislation, factory safety and welfare of workers, public health, housing, consumer protection, security of employment, preservation of amenities, legal aid, etc. For sentencing guidelines in welfare fraud cases, see *R v Stewart* [1987] 1 WLR 559.

welfare of a child. "Includes material welfare . . . More important are the stability and security, the loving and understanding care and guidance, the warm and compassionate relationship, that are essential for the full development of the child's own character, personality and talents": *per* Hardie Boyce J in *Walker v Harrison* (1981) NZLR. The paramount consideration for a court determining a question of a child's upbringing: Ch.A. 1989, s. 1(1). The court will have particular regard to, e.g., the child's wishes, his age, any harm he has suffered or is at risk of suffering, capability of each of his parents: s. 1(3). For welfare reports ordered by the court, see s. 7. See *In re P.* [1992] 1 FLR 316 (court's duty to listen to expression of child's wishes).

Welsh language, use in court proceedings of. Under the Welsh Language Act 1967, s. 1, the Welsh language may be used in any legal proceedings in Wales or Monmouthshire by any party desiring to use it. See *Collector of Taxes v Morgan* [1977] CLY 2537. See also Local Government Housing Act 1989, s. 160, Sch. 8 (use of Welsh language names for local authorities); SI 1992/1083.

Welsh mortgage. A mortgage (q.v.) in which there was no covenant for repayment of the loan and the mortgagee could not compel redemption or foreclosure (qq.v.). See now L.P.A. 1925, s. 85.

whip. 1. Government or Opposition official responsible for controlling the presence of MPs at debates and votes, arranging pairs, etc. 2. A command to an MP to attend a House of Commons (q.v.) vote. A "three-line whip" is an urgent command (underlined three times) to attend a vote. *See* PARLIAMENT.

White Book, The. *See* RULES OF THE SUPREME COURT.

white paper. *See* PARLIAMENTARY PAPERS.

whole blood. *See* BLOOD RELATIONSHIP.

widow's payment. Lump sum payment made if the widow's late husband had satisfied contribution payment requirements. It is not made if she and a man to whom she is not married are living together as husband and wife at the time of her husband's death: S.S.A. 1986, s. 36. See also S.S.A. 1989, s. 6 (widow's pension); S.S.A. 1990, s. 6; S.S. Contributions and Benefits Act 1992, s. 36.

wife, provision for. Under Inheritance (Provision for Family and Dependants) Act 1975, the wife or former wife of the deceased may apply for financial provision from the deceased's estate if the disposition of that estate effected by his will or the law relating to intestacy (q.v.) is not such as to make reasonable financial provision for the applicant: ss. 1, 2.

wife's equity, deserted. A deserted wife acquired at the date of desertion (q.v.) an equity against any third party to whom her husband had sold or mortgaged the home. Rejected in *National Provincial Bank v Ainsworth* [1965] AC 1175. The Matrimonial Homes Act 1983 confers statutory rights of occupation in the matrimonial home on defined categories of spouse. See Class F land charges (q.v.).

wife's services, loss of. *See* PER QUOD CONSORTIUM ET SERVITIUM AMISIT.

wild creatures, theft of. A person cannot steal a wild creature not tamed nor ordinarily kept in captivity unless it has been reduced into possession by or on behalf of another person and possession has not since been lost or abandoned: Th.A. 1968, s. 4(4). *See* ANIMAL, WILD.

wilful. Refers to the deliberate conduct of a person who is a free agent, knows what he is doing and intends to do what he is doing. "If a man permits a thing to be done, it means that he gives permission for it to be done, he knows what is to be done or is being done, and, if he knows that, it follows that it is wilful'': *Lomas* v *Peck* [1947] 2 All ER 574. Used synonymously with "intentional" in *Wheeler* v *New Merton Mills* [1933] 2 KB 669. "Wilfully" means "that the act is done deliberately and intentionally, not by accident or inadvertence, but so that the mind of the person who does the act goes with it'': *per* Lord Russell in *R* v *Senior* [1899] 1 QB 480. See *Dibble* v *Ingleton* [1972] 1 QB 480.

wilful default. "Either a consciousness of negligence or breach of duty, or a recklessness in the performance of a duty'': *Re City Equitable Fire Insurance Co* [1925] Ch 407.

wilful misconduct. "To be guilty of wilful misconduct the person concerned must appreciate that he is acting wrongfully, or is wrongfully omitting to act, and yet persists in so acting or omitting to act regardless of the consequences, or acts or omits to act with reckless indifference as to what the results may be'': *Horabin* v *BOAC* [1952] 2 All ER 1016.

wilful neglect. Intentional or purposeful omission to carry out some action.

wilful refusal. A refusal without adequate cause. For the imposition of imprisonment upon wilful refusal to pay a fine see M.C.A. 1980, ss. 76 *et seq.*

wilful refusal to consummate. "A wilful, determined and steadfast refusal to perform the obligations and to carry out the duties which the matrimonial contract involves'': *Dickinson* v *Dickinson* [1913] P 198. "A settled and definite decision come to without just excuse not to consummate'': *Horton* v *Horton* [1947] 2 All ER 871. See also *Jodla* v *Jodla* [1960] 1 All ER 625; Mat.C.A. 1973, s. 12. *See* CONSUMMATION OF A MARRIAGE.

will. A revocable declaration, made in the prescribed form, of the intentions of the maker concerning the disposition and devolution of his property, and other matters, which he desires should become effective on and after the event of his death. "The word 'will' shall extend to a testament, and to a codicil (q.v.), and to an appointment by will or by writing in the nature of a will in exercise of a power . . . and to any other testamentary disposition'': W.A. 1837, s. 1. See, e.g., *Re White* [1990] 3 WLR 187 (alteration of will).

will, conditional. *See* CONDITIONAL WILL.

will, forfeiture of benefit under. *See* FORFEITURE OF BENEFIT UNDER WILL.

will in contemplation of marriage. *See* MARRIAGE, WILL IN CONTEMPLATION OF.

will, international. Will made in accordance with Annex to Convention on International Wills as set out in A.J.A. 1982, Sch. 2. It is valid as regards form, irrespective particularly of the place where it is made, of the location of the assets and of the testator's nationality, domicile or residence.

will, nuncupative. *See* NUNCUPATIVE WILL.

will, partnership at. *See* PARTNERSHIP AT WILL.

will, privileged. *See* PRIVILEGED WILL.

will, rectification of. *See* RECTIFICATION OF WILL.

will, republication of. *See* REPUBLICATION OF WILL.

will, revival of. *See* REVIVAL OF WILL.

will, revocation of. *See* REVOCATION OF WILL.

wills, mutual. *See* MUTUAL WILLS.

will, tenant at. *See* TENANT AT WILL.

will, validity of. "No will shall be valid unless – (*a*) it is in writing, and signed by the testator, or by some other person in his presence and by his direction; and (*b*) it appears that the testator intended by his signature to give effect to the will; and (*c*) the signature is made or acknowledged by the testator in the presence of two or more witnesses present at the same time; and (*d*) each witness either (i) attests and signs the will; or (ii) acknowledges his signature, in the presence of the testator (but not necessarily in the presence of any other witness), but no form of attestation shall be necessry'': W.A. 1837, s. 9 (as substituted by A.J.A. 1982, s. 17). *See* SIGNATURE OF WILL.

windfalls. Trees and their fruit blown down by the wind. They belong, in general, to the owner of the inheritance; but dotards (q.v.) may be taken by the tenant (q.v.). See *Re Harrison's Trusts* (1885) 28 Ch D 220.

winding-up. Process whereby a company is brought to an end, e.g., following insolvency. It may be: compulsory winding-up by the court (q.v.); winding-up under the court's supervision; voluntary winding-up (q.v.). Thus, a company may be wound up: when the period fixed in the articles for the company's duration expires; if the company resolves by extraordinary resolution to wind up because of liabilities; for any cause if a sufficient number of members pass a special resolution to that end. See Ins.A. 1986, s. 84 (voluntary winding-up) and s. 122 (winding-up by the court); *Re McBacon Ltd (No. 2)* [1990] BCLC 607 (winding-up costs).

winding-up, compulsory. *See* COMPULSORY WINDING-UP BY THE COURT.

winding-up, voluntary. *See* VOLUNTARY WINDING-UP

witchcraft. Prior to Witchcraft Act 1735, a capital offence. The Fraudulent Mediums Act 1961 repealed the 1735 Act and provided that it is an offence for a person with intent to deceive and for reward to purport to act as a medium and in so purporting to act, to use a fraudulent device. See *R* v *Duncan and Others* [1944] KB 713.

with costs. Term referring to a successful party's entitlement to recover costs from the other party. *See* COSTS.

withdrawal of acknowledgement. Withdrawal of an acknowledgement, with leave of the court, by a party who has acknowledged service of a writ in an action. See O. 21, r. 1; and *Castanho v Brown and Root* [1981] 1 All ER 143.

withdrawal of defence. Procedure whereby the defendant serves notice on the plaintiff that he is not proceeding with his entire claim, or with some part of it. See O. 21, r. 2(2)(a). *See* DISCONTINUANCE, NOTICE OF.

withdrawal of issue from jury. Procedure whereby a judge, who is not satisfied that there is sufficient evidence in support of a proponent's contention, discharges the jury and enters judgment for the opponent, or directs the jury to return a verdict in the opponent's favour. See *Ryder v Wombwell* (1868) LR 4 Ex 32; *R v Abbott* [1955] 2 QB 497.

within. When used in the context of a period of time is capable of meaning "during" or "before or at the expiry of" that period: *Manorlike v Le Vitas Travel Agency* [1986] 1 All ER 573.

without prejudice. *See* PREJUDICE.

without recourse to me. *See* SANS RECOURS.

without reserve. Phrase used in a sale by auction (q.v.), showing that no price has been reserved.

with profits. Title of insurance policy under which bonuses from profits of the insurance company are used to increase value of the policy.

witness. 1. To give evidence or proof. 2. To attest by signature. 3. One who gives formal or sworn evidence at a hearing.

witnesses, adverse. *See* ADVERSE WITNESSES.

witnesses, children as. *See* CHILDREN'S EVIDENCE.

witnesses, compellable. Those who are obliged to give evidence. A witness is not generally compellable to answer a question which might expose him to a criminal charge: *R* v *Boyes* (1861) 30 LJQB 301. *See* SPOUSES, EVIDENCE OF.

witnesses, competence of. In general, all persons are competent to give evidence. Exceptions include, the Sovereign in his own cause, the mentally ill (unless the judge is sure that they understand the duty of telling the truth on oath), judges or jurors in a case they are hearing. An accused is not generally a competent witness for the prosecution. For witness statements, see C.L.S.A. 1990, s. 5. *See* SPOUSES, EVIDENCE OF.

witnesses, order of calling. Generally an advocate is entitled to call witnesses in order of his choice. ". . . [This is] solely a matter for counsel. It is a grave responsibility and it rests on him and him alone": *Briscoe v Briscoe* [1966] 1 All ER 465. See also *Barnes v BPC Ltd* [1975] 1 WLR 1565.

witnesses, securing attendance of. *See* WITNESS ORDER.

witness, eye. *See* EYE WITNESS.

witness, hostile. *See* HOSTILE WITNESS.

witness, interfering with. *See* INTERFERING WITH WITNESSES.

witness, intimidation of. *See* INTIMIDATION.

witness order. Procedure for the compelling of attendance by witnesses in criminal trials at the court, failure to comply with which is a contempt of court (q.v.): Criminal Procedure (Attendance of Witnesses) Act 1965. A "conditional witness order" requires him to attend only if given notice. See *R* v *Bradford Justices ex p Wilkinson* [1990] 2 All ER 833.

witness, privilege of. *See* PRIVILEGE OF WITNESS.

witness, recall of. The judge has a discretionary power to allow the recall of a witness after the close of a party's case to allow evidence in rebuttal. See, e.g., *R* v *Flynn* (1957) 42 Cr App R 15.

witness's notes. Notes used by a witness to refresh his memory. Cross-examining counsel is entitled to inspect them so as to check their content: *R* v *Britton* [1987] 1 WLR 539.

witness's oath. *See* OATH.

witness statements, exchange of. At any stage in any cause or matter the court may direct an exchange of written statements of oral evidence which a party intends to lead on issues of fact to be decided at the trial: see O. 38, r. 2A; *Mercer* v *Chief Constable of Lancs. Authority* [1991] 1 WLR 367.

witness, unfavourable. *See* UNFAVOURABLE WITNESS.

witness warrant. A notice ordering a witness who is required to attend before the Crown Court (q.v.) to attend forthwith or at a time specified in the future. See Criminal Procedure (Attendance of Witnesses) Act 1965; M.C.A. 1980, s. 97 (procuring attendance of witnesses at magistrates' courts).

witness, zealous. *See* ZEALOUS WITNESS.

woman. A female adult person. In Sex Discrimination Act 1975, s. 81(1), it is used to include a female "of any age".

women, abduction of. *See* ABDUCTION.

women, indecent assault on. *See* INDECENT ASSAULT ON WOMEN.

women, procurement of. *See* PROCUREMENT.

Woolsack. The seat of the Lord Chancellor in the House of Lords (q.v.). Technically, not within the House, so that when the Lord Chancellor wishes to address the House as a peer he must stand aside from it.

words of art. Words which have a particular, fixed legal meaning not generally modified by their context. See, e.g., *Barclays Bank* v *Cole* [1967] 2 QB 738 (meaning of "fraud").

words of limitation. *See* LIMITATION, WORDS OF.

words of procreation. *See* PROCREATION, WORDS OF.

words of purchase. *See* PURCHASE, WORDS OF.

words of severance. *See* SEVERANCE, WORDS OF.

words, operative. *See* OPERATIVE WORDS.

words, precatory. *See* PRECATORY WORDS.

words, primary and secondary meanings of. Phrase used in reference to the ordinary and extended meanings of words. "The first question to ask always is what is the ordinary meaning of [a] word or phrase in its context in the statute. It is only when that meaning leads to some result which cannot reasonably be supposed to have been the intention of the legislature that it is proper to look for some other permissible meaning of the word or phrase": *Pinner* v *Everett* [1962] 3 All ER 257 ("There is no word the primary meaning of which may not be modified by the context": *per* Griffith CJ in *Nicol* v *Chant* (1909) 7 CLR 69.) See also *IRC* v *Hinchy* [1960] AC 748; *Wiltshire* v *Barrett* [1966] 1 QB 312. "We have been warned time and again not to substitute other words for the words of a statute. And there is very good reason for that. Few words have exact synonyms. The overtones are almost always different": *per* Denning LJ in *British Launderers' Association* v *Borough of Hendon* [1949] 1 KB 462.

work. "Either the labour which a man bestows upon a thing, or the thing upon which the labour is bestowed": *Atkinson* v *Lumb* [1903] 1 KB 861. "An employee is 'at work' throughout the time when he is in the course of his employment but not otherwise; and the self-employed person is at work throughout such time as he devotes to work as a self-employed person": H.S.W.A. 1974, s. 52. See *Clear* v *Smith* [1981] 1 WLR 399. "Working place" means every place at which men are working or may be expected to work: *Hammond* v *NCB* [1984] 1 WLR 1218.

work done and materials supplied, contracts for. Contracts in which there is an implied condition that work is to be properly done in the manner contemplated and that materials supplied are to be reasonably fit for the purpose contemplated. Example: it was an implied condition that dentures would fit the person for whom they were made (*Samuels* v *Davis* [1943] 1 KB 526).

worker. An individual who has entered into or works (or has worked) under a contract of service, or apprenticeship and any other contract whereby the individual undertakes to do or perform personally any work or services for another party to the contract whose status is not by virtue of the contract that of a client or customer of any profession or business carried on by the individual: Wages Act 1986, s. 8. See also E.P.(C.)A. 1978, s. 153(1).

worker, piece and time. A piece worker is one whose contract provides for the remuneration payable to him in respect of work executed by him to be calculated only by reference to piece rates; a time worker is "a worker other than a piece worker (whether the worker's remuneration is determined by reference to the actual number of hours worked by him or not)": Wages Act 1986, s. 26(1).

workers, freedom of movement for. Under the Treaty of Rome 1957, art. 48, there is a right to work freely within the territory of member states and this involves "the abolition of any discrimination based on nationality between the workers of member states [of the EEC] as regards employment, remuneration and other conditions of work and employment". This does not apply to employment in the public service. See *R* v *Pieck* [1981] QB 571. For definition of "worker" under EEC legislation, see Regulation 1408/71.

work-in. A type of industrial action, in which employees occupy their place of work and continue production. Normally trespassory. Injunctions (q.v.) to restrain this type of action can be given.

working class. Those persons within a community who exchange their labour power for a wage. The concept is not obsolete even though Parliament has given up its use for the purpose of the Housing Acts: *Westminster CC* v *Duke of Westminster* (1990) 23 HLR 174. See *Belcher* v *Reading* [1950] Ch. 380.

working day. Any day other than: Saturday or Sunday; Good Friday or Easter Monday; last Monday in May and August; Christmas Day; 26 December (if it is not a Sunday); or 27 December in a year in which either 25 or 26 December is a Sunday. See Banking and Financial Dealings Act 1971.

working life. The period between (inclusive) the year in which a person attained the age of 16 and (exclusive)

the year in which he attained pensionable age or died under that age: S.S.A. 1975, s. 27(2).

work in progress. Any services performed in the ordinary course of a trade, the performance of which was partly completed at a material time and for which it would be reasonable to expect that a charge will subsequently be made, and any article produced, and any such material as is used, in the performance of any such services: Finance Act 1981, Sch. 9, Part V.

work, system of. "It is the distinction between what is permanent or continuous on the one hand, and what is merely casual . . . It may include the physical lay-out of the job . . . the sequence in which the work is to be carried out . . . and the issue of special instructions": *per* Lord Greene in *Speed* v *Thomas Swift & Co Ltd* [1943] KB 557.

work to rule. A type of industrial action in which employees work in literal compliance with the terms of their contracts, so that the pace of work is slowed down or brought to a halt. See *Henthorn* v *CEGB* [1980] IRLR 36.

World Court. International Court of Justice (q.v.).

worship. "Worship I take to be something which must have some, at least, of the following characteristics: submission to the object worshipped, veneration of that object, praise, thanksgiving, prayer or intercession": *per* Buckley LJ in *R* v *Registrar General, ex p Segerdal* [1970] 3 All ER 886. For "collective worship" in relation to educational institutions, see Further and Higher Education Act 1992, s. 44.

wounding. The infliction of an injury which breaks the continuity of the skin, internal or external. A scratch or burn is not a wound. See *R* v *Wood* (1830) 4 C & P 381; *C.* v *Eisenhower* (1984) 78 Cr App R 48.

wounding, malicious. *See* MALICIOUS WOUNDING.

wounding with intent. It is an offence under O.P.A. 1861, s. 18, as amended by C.L.A. 1967, Sch. 3, Part III, unlawfully and maliciously by any means whatsoever to wound or cause any grievous bodily harm to any person, with intent to do some grievous bodily harm to any person, or with intent to resist or prevent the lawful apprehension or detainer of any person. See *R* v *Belfon* [1976] 1 WLR 741; *R* v *Pearman* [1985] RTR 39; *A.-G.'s Reference (No. 23 of 1990)* (1990) 12 Cr App R(S) 575. *See* MALICIOUS WOUNDING.

wreck. 1. The damage of a ship so that she ceases to be of service. 2. Goods which, after shipwreck, are cast on land.

writ. 1. Instrument under seal issued in the name of the Sovereign, declaring some command. 2. Order in the name of the Sovereign or court, ordering some action or forbearance from some action. 3. A *judicial writ* is issued by a court to originate some actions. See O. 5, r. 2. Writs originated in the granting by the King to a suitor of a right to petition where justice had been denied in the local courts. A Register of Writs was created and writs enforceable in the King's courts were increased in number.

writ, amendment of. Under O. 20 the plaintiff may amend a writ once without leave prior to the close of pleadings (q.v.) and the amended version must be served on the defendant.

writ, concurrent. *See* CONCURRENT WRITS.

writ, endorsement of. *See* ENDORSEMENT OF WRIT, FORMAL.

writing. Term includes printing, lithography, photography and other modes of representation or reproduction of words in a variable form: I.A. 1978, Sch. 1. "Includes any form of notation or code, whether by hand or otherwise and regardless of the method by which, or medium in which, it is recorded": Copyright, Designs and Patents Act 1988, s. 178.

writ, issuing of. Procedure following the preparation and endorsement of a writ, so that it becomes an official document emanating from the court. The writ must be in the prescribed form: O. 6, r. 1. Leave to issue is necessary, e.g., if the defendant is beyond the jurisdiction. The plaintiff sends two copies to the Central Office or a District Registry, where one copy is stamped and the other returned to him. See O. 6, r. 7: Civil Jurisdiction and Judgments Act 1982.

writ of right. *See* RIGHT, WRIT OF.

writ of summons. *See* SUMMONS, WRIT OF.

writ of summons, leave to issue. Permission required, e.g., if the defendant is outside the jurisdiction, or if the plaintiff is designated by the High Court as a vexatious litigant. *See* VEXATIOUS ACTION.

writ, service of. *See* SERVICE.

wrong. 1. An act contrary to the rules of natural or legal justice. "Every wrong is an act which is malicious in the eye of the law – an act to which the law attributes harmful consequences": Salmond. 2. A tort (q.v.) involving the infringement of a right. 3. In the M'Naghten Rules (q.v.) "wrong means contrary to law and not 'wrong' according to the opinion of one man or of a number of people on the question whether a particular act might or might not be justified": *R* v *Windle* [1952] 2 QB 826.

wrongful dismissal. Dismissal of an employee without justification, which is, in effect, a repudiation of the contract. *See* DISMISSAL, UNFAIR.

wrongful interference with goods. *See* INTERFERENCE WITH GOODS, WRONGFUL.

wrongful trading. Under Ins. A. 1986, s. 214, a director may be made personally liable by court order for a company's debts if he allows the company to continue trading when he knew or should have known that there was no reasonable prospect of the company being able to avoid liquidation. See *Re Produce Marketing Consortium Ltd* (1989) 5 BCC 569.

X

xc. Stock Exchange abbreviation for ex capitalisation.

xd. Stock Exchange abbreviation for *ex dividend. See* EX DIV.

xr. Stock Exchange abbreviation for ex rights (q.v.).

Y

year. A period of 12 calendar months calculated either from 1st January or some other stated day and consisting of 365 days (or 366 in a leap year). See *Gibson v Barton* (1875) LR 10 QB 329. *IRC v Hobhouse* [1956] 1 WLR 1393; L.G.P.L.A. 1980, s. 68(1).

year and day rule. Common law rule that no person may be convicted of murder or manslaughter "where the death does not occur within a year and a day after the injury was inflicted, for in that event it must be attributed to some other cause": *per* Lord Alverstone in *R v Dyson* [1908] 2 KB 454. See *Criminal Law (1980) Revision Committee Report, No. 14*, recommending retention of rule.

year and thereafter. The expression "to T for a year and thereafter from year to year" confers a minimum tenancy of two years upon T, i.e., an express term of one year plus a yearly tenancy which may be terminated not earlier than the end of the second year. See *Re Searle* [1912] 1 Ch 610.

Year Books. A series of reports, authors unknown, running from 1282–1536, spanning the reigns of Edward I and Henry VIII. The title is derived from their being grouped under the regnal years of the Sovereigns in whose reigns the cases reported were decided.

year, day and waste. A royal prerogative, now abolished, allowing the monarch to take the profits for one year and one day of persons convicted of felony or petty treason (qq.v.) and to commit waste (q.v.) on that person's lands.

year, executor's. *See* EXECUTOR'S YEAR.

year, financial. *See* FINANCIAL YEAR.

year, legal. *See* LEGAL YEAR.

yearly tenancy. *See* TENANT FROM YEAR TO YEAR.

years, estate for. An estate (q.v.) granted for a term of years (q.v.).

year to year. *See* TENANT FROM YEAR TO YEAR.

York–Antwerp rules. Shipping code, formulated in 1877, referring to rules of general average (q.v.) etc, which is usually incorporated in contracts of affreightment (q.v.).

young adult offenders. Offenders generally aged 17–20. There are special types of custodial treatment ("community sentence orders") for this group, e.g., attendance centres (q.v.). See C.J.A. 1991, ss. 6(4)(f), 63; A.J.A. 1982, Part I.

young offenders, detention of. Where an offender under 21, but not less than 15, is convicted of an offence which is punishable with imprisonment in the case of a person aged 21 or over, and the court is satisfied that he qualifies for a custodial sentence, e.g., because of his previous failure to respond to non-custodial penalties, he should be detained in a young offender institute: C.J.A. 1988, s. 123, as amended by C.J.A. 1991, s. 63. For supervision after release, see 1991 Act, s. 65. See *Rv Danga* [1992] 2 WLR 277.

young offenders, fining of. Pecuniary penalties imposed on young offenders under, e.g., M.C.A. 1980, s. 36. *See* FINE.

young person. Generally one who has reached 14 and is under 17: C. & Y.P.A. 1933, s. 107(1). Under Factories Act 1961, one over compulsory school age, but not yet 18. See C.J.A. 1991, s. 68

youth courts. *See* JUVENILE COURTS.

Z

zealous witness. A witness who attempts to give evidence in a manner which makes it as favourable as possible for a party to the proceedings. *See* WITNESS.

zebra crossing. A road crossing, the presence and limits of which are indicated in accordance with the provisions of S.I. 1971/1524, Sch. 2, as amended. An "uncontrolled zebra crossing" is a zebra crossing at which traffic is not for the time being controlled by a police constable in uniform or by a traffic warden. See *Connor v Paterson* [1977] 1 All ER 516.

zero rating. Term used in the administration of value-added tax (q.v.) to indicate that no tax is levied on certain goods sold to final customers and that any tax charged on an input used to produce those goods can be recovered. Principal zero-rated categories include exports, books and newspapers. See Value Added Tax Act 1983; *EC Commissioner* v *UK* (1988) The Times, 22 June.

zones, simplified planning. Introduced under H. & P.A. 1986, Part III and Sch. 6. Local planning authorities may grant general planning permission for a SPZ, and developers may then undertake development up to the parameters of the scheme without need for further planning permission. See T.C.P.A. 1990, s. 82; Planning and Compensation Act 1991, Sch. 5. Land in a National Park (q.v.) or conservation area may not be included in a SPZ: 1990 Act, s. 87.

zoo. An establishment where wild animals are kept for exhibition to the public otherwise than for purposes of a circus and otherwise than in a pet shop: Zoo Licensing Act 1981, s. 1(2).